PRINCIPLES OF MANAGEMENT

An analysis of managerial functions

McGRAW-HILL SERIES IN MANAGEMENT

Keith Davis, *Consulting Editor*

PRINCIPLES
OF MANAGEMENT *fourth edition*

An analysis of managerial functions

HAROLD KOONTZ
Graduate School of Business Administration
University of California, Los Angeles

CYRIL O'DONNELL
Graduate School of Business Administration
University of California, Los Angeles

McGRAW-HILL BOOK COMPANY
New York   St. Louis   San Francisco   Toronto   London   Sydney

PREFACE

It is the purpose of this book to provide a conceptual framework for the orderly presentation of fundamental knowledge in management. The authors have attempted to do so in an operational way by relating this knowledge to the functions of planning, organizing, staffing, directing, and controlling, and by following in other ways concepts and approaches meaningful for perceptive management practice. Even though attempting to make this book operational in every respect, they recognize that the best underpinning to practice is a sound basic theoretical framework in which significant knowledge about managing may be organized. In the view of the authors, this is an essential step in developing a science and in making this science useful for those who must apply it, as practitioners, to reality.

Some distillation of this knowledge has been accomplished through the device of formulating major principles that have been found in the process of managing. In undertaking this task, the authors have drawn freely upon the discoveries, formulations, and researches of many managers and scholars who have studied various aspects of the problem. While they have attempted formulation of many principles from their long managerial experience, observation, and research, the authors readily acknowledge a heavy debt to the many who have made contributions to this important field.

At the outset, the authors would like again, as they have done in previous editions, to make certain aspects of their position clear. While they recognize that managers seldom, if ever, spend all their time and talents in managing, it is their conviction that the functions of a manager, as manager, are essentially the same whether he is a first-line supervisor or the top executive of an enterprise; the reader will find, therefore, no basic distinction made among managers, executives, administrators, or supervisors. To be sure, the environment of each may differ, the scope of authority held may vary, the types of problems dealt with may be considerably different, and a person in a managerial role may also be a salesman, engineer, or financier. But the fact remains that, *as managers,* all who obtain results by establishing an environment for effective and efficient performance of individuals operating in groups undertake the same basic functions.

Moreover, the principles related to the task of managing apply to any kind of enterprise. The purposes of different enterprises may vary, but all which are organized do rely on effective group operation for efficient attainment of whatever their goals are. It is true that many of the case examples and techniques used in this book are drawn from business enterprises. In doing so, however, the authors have no intention of overlooking the fact that the same fundamental truths are applicable elsewhere.

Principles are used here in the sense of fundamental truths applicable to a given set of circumstances and having value in predicting results. An attempt has been made in this revision to recast most of these fundamental truths in the form of propositions with independent and dependent variables. In a few cases, principles are very little more than concepts. In other instances, concepts and basic truths are introduced without elevating them to the status of major principles. In either event, however, an attempt has been made to recognize the indisputable fact that clear concepts are the initial requirement of science and understanding. The major principles emphasized, to the extent that they reflect fundamentals in a given area, may be referred to as theory—a body of related principles dealing systematically with a subject. Even though principles and theory are referred to throughout the book, the reader must not gain the impression that they are impractical. If accurately formulated and properly used, principles and theory should be eminently practical. The real test of their validity is in the crucible of practice.

There are those who object to using the term "principles" for fundamental truths not supported by elaborate and complete verification of their validity. Such persons would prefer to see these principles characterized as hypotheses. Perhaps, strictly speaking, many are. However, even far more statistically verified principles in the so-called exact sciences are virtually always regarded as subjects for further verification. Moreover, the authors are completely aware that the formulation of many principles made here represents essentially a preliminary attempt to codify a number of basic truths and, by placing them in a framework believed to be logical, an attempt to move toward a theory of management. Being preliminary, these summaries are not intended as a final scheme of a theory of management. But they are believed to be a convenient and useful way of packaging some of the major truths that experience and research have found to have a high degree of credibility and predictability.

In this edition, as in those preceding it, the authors have attempted to respond to two major influences. One is the continuing help from a comprehensive survey of teachers and scholars who have honored us by using the past editions of this book at various levels of academic and practical management education in a wide variety of universities and operating enterprises. Another is the burgeoning volume of research, new ideas, and advanced techniques, particularly those being applied to management from the behavioral and physical sciences. From the first source, the authors have been led to sharpen concepts, rearrange certain material, and expand the coverage of this book. From the second, they have added much new material and given more emphasis to those findings, while still placing them within the framework of the managerial functions.

In this particular edition, one of the main concerns has been to improve the presentation of concepts and techniques which have given rise to the appreciated acceptance of the previous editions. But more has been done. In the first place most major principles are restated in a propositional form. Yet, in doing so, the authors have been aware that principles will actually be applied in a normative way, and the measure of surplus of results in attaining objectives over costs and other inputs has been suggested as a norm. In the second place, the chapters in the parts on "Staffing" and "Directing" have been completely rewritten to incorporate the most applicable of the latest behavioral research. A third change has been to emphasize, even more than heretofore, the systems elements in managing and to incorporate more thoroughly, without the complication of many mathematical formulas, the newer techniques of the physical sciences.

A major change in this revision has been to add an additional part on "Managers and the Changing Environment." This is in response to the belief expressed by many users of the book that the external environment was not given adequate attention in previous editions. It is true that the primary focus of this book has always been on the principles and techniques underlying development of an internal enterprise environment conducive to the effective and efficient operation of individuals so that they may contribute to enterprise objectives. At many points throughout this and earlier editions, the authors nevertheless have emphasized that the external environment cannot be overlooked. This is true in every aspect of the tasks of the manager since external environmental factors greatly influence what the manager, who is really responsive to his external environment, does.

It did seem wise to emphasize this point more than has been done in prior editions. As a consequence, there is included in this edition a new part with chapters on "The Enterprise Manager in His Social Setting," "Comparative Management," and "Management and the Future." The first of these emphasizes the social and ethical responsibility of managers. The second deals with the problem of analyzing and comparing management in varying cultures. In the third the authors have undertaken to summarize a number of major factors that are changing the role of the typical manager and to outline areas believed to be of great importance for managers of tomorrow if they are to handle their jobs effectively. Also, this final chapter serves to underscore the fact that managing is an intellectually challenging occupation which can demand the highest talent and imagination if its socially important role of optimizing the use of human and material resources toward desired goals is to be attained.

As might be expected in a book of this kind which now enters its fourth edition, the authors are indebted to so many persons that a complete acknowledgment would be encyclopedic. Some managers and scholars are acknowledged through footnotes and other references to their contributions. Many managers with whom the authors have served in business, government, education, and other enterprises have contributed by word and precept. Thousands of managers in all levels and kinds of enterprise have honored the authors over the years by allowing them to test their ideas in executive training classes and lectures. To the executives of the various companies with which they have been privileged to work as directors or consultants, the authors are grateful for the opportunity to continue the clinical practice of management.

In previous editions, special appreciation has been expressed to a number of individuals who have contributed materially to the writing of the book. While they are not again named here, their contributions, by shaping many parts of earlier editions, have also been important to this one. In particular, however, the authors would like to express appreciation for the thoughtful, helpful, and sometimes brutal criticisms offered in comprehensive reviews made by Professor Henry G. Baker of the University of Cincinnati, Professors Robert D. Henderson and J. A. Nordstrom of Bowling Green State University, Professor John Wallis Johnston of Georgetown University, Professor Louis Kaufman of California State Polytechnic College, Professor B. K. Marks of Sam Houston State College, and Professor Robert M. Rompf of Michigan State University. Appreciation is also due Professor A. John Lindemann of the University of Wisconsin for many helpful criticisms of the third edition. Likewise, the authors would like to express their appreciation to Mr. W. Sidney Taylor of the U. S. Department of Defense for his intelligent emphasis on the desirability of creating simplicity in a world of complexity. The authors also wish to acknowledge the able and cheerful assistance of Miss Judy Finer, who assumed the wearisome task of preparing the manuscript of this edition for publication.

Harold Koontz
Cyril O'Donnell

CONTENTS

part one

THE BASIS OF MANAGEMENT

This book undertakes the study of management by utilizing analysis of the basic managerial functions as a framework for organizing knowledge and techniques in the field. Managing is defined here as the design or creation and maintenance of an internal environment in an enterprise where individuals, working together in groups, can perform efficiently and effectively toward the attainment of group goals. Essentially, managing is the art of doing and management is the body of organized knowledge which underlies the art.

Each of the managerial functions (planning, organizing, staffing, directing, and controlling) is analyzed and described in a systematic way. As this is done, both the distilled experience of practical managers and the findings of scholars are presented. This is approached in such a way that the reader may grasp the relationships between each of the functions, obtain a clear view of the major principles underlying them, and be given means of organizing the existing knowledge in the field.

Part 1 is an introduction to the basis of management through a study of the nature and operation of management principles (Chapter 1), a description of the various schools and approaches of management theory (Chapter 2), the functions of the manager (Chapter 3), and a brief analytical inquiry into a major foundation of management—authority and responsibility (Chapter 4). Each succeeding part of the book takes up one of the five managerial functions: planning, organizing, staffing, direction, control. If the reader keeps in mind the fact that all managerial knowledge can be organized under these five categories, he will provide himself with a useful tool which will help him in his understanding of a complex subject.

The first chapter of this part discusses the role of management principles. These are defined as fundamental truths of general validity which have value in predicting the results of managerial action. These principles aid in furnishing the groundwork for a science of management. A management principle distills and organizes knowledge that has been built up through experience and analysis. While the authors agree that a science of management is only now developing and is still very inexact, they nonetheless believe that understanding and applying such principles can materially improve the quality of management practice. Although management, like all life sciences, has far to go to become an exact science, it is hoped that research and reflection will continue to improve it. If the reader understands at the outset that this book is not a description of an exact science but rather an endeavor to codify, as accurately as possible, an inexact body of knowledge, his task will be lighter. Even the physical sciences which we now regard as mature and "exact" went through a long period of inexact experimentation and probing after principles. These principles eventually led to the discovery of scientific laws. Managing, like engineering and the practice of medicine, will probably never be wholly scientific. Rather, it will remain largely an art in which the practitioner uses whatever scientific knowledge is available but must supplement it with a great deal of personal judgment. To many, this very reliance on personal ability makes managing a very rewarding career.

Chapter 2 of this part describes the various schools or approaches to management theory. There is a danger that the reader will become puzzled about the orientation of the authors. There is a mathematical school, a social system school, a behavioristic approach, and many others. What then is the school of the authors? This book adheres to the "management process" or "operational" school. It looks at managing as a series of actions which are taken to achieve a goal determined in advance. In other words, managing is an intelligent, purposeful activity—a process, not a series of unrelated actions which occur as a result of accident or sociological or psychological pressures. This approach has the advantage of being realistic and therefore "operational" in that it deals with the whole subject of management in the language and from the point of view of the practicing manager. Yet the authors are aware that others approach the study of management differently. In fact, these differing approaches have resulted in different meanings for a number of words used very frequently in management literature. Chapter 2 seeks to give the reader a clear picture of the various schools of management. If the reader grasps the differing orientations of the schools, the manner in which they use the language of management will become clear.

Chapter 3 very briefly defines and describes the five basic functions of the manager—planning, organizing, staffing, direction, and control—and serves primarily as an orientation to the remaining five parts of the book. The authors believe that these five functions are the same for every manager in all kinds of enterprise and at all levels. The president of a large American corporation is a manager. His Holiness the Pope also manages. Both men must plan the results to be obtained and lay out the means, organize accordingly, staff their organizations by choosing and developing adequate subordinates, direct them in the accomplishment of work, and control (check on performance and correct deficiencies). Thus, the process itself is a system, a complex of interrelated and interacting elements and activities. The same could be said of a military leader and many of his subordinates. Although the functions of managers are the same, the specific *content* of the work is not. For instance, a general plans but he usually does so in state of comparative calm (peace) for a sudden, rather short period of activity to begin in the future (war). The business manager is most often forced to plan continuously amid a continuous flux of daily work. The other functions vary too according to the specific nature of the job. This superficial difference has helped to obscure the universality of the five management functions and has delayed the development of sound management principles.

Underlying the managerial task is the concept of organizational authority and responsibility dealt with in the fourth and last chapter of this part of the book. The authors see authority as the power to direct and control the actions of others. But it is equally the power to exercise discretion, be creative, design, and maintain an environment conducive to individual performance. Responsibility is the obligation to use this power in a way and for the purposes desired by those who bestow it. Authority does not necessarily imply arbitrary or dictatorial use of it but it does imply that final responsibility for accomplishment rests with the manager. A clear understanding of the authority-responsibility concept is the most important thing to be gained from this chapter.

managing and management principles

Perhaps there is no more important area of human activity than managing, for it is the task of the manager to establish and maintain an internal environment in which people working together in groups can perform effectively and efficiently toward the attainment of group goals. In other words, it is the manager who is charged with the responsibility of undertaking those actions calculated to make it possible for individuals to make their best contributions toward group objectives. While the emphasis is on the internal environment of the enterprise or a department of it, clearly no manager can perform this task well unless he has an understanding of and is responsive to the many elements of the ethical, social, economic, political, and technical environment which affect his area of operations.

How the manager does his task and what basic science underlies it is the focus of this book. As many managers in all types of enterprises and many scholars in the field have found, this analysis is approached most meaningfully by breaking down the total managerial task into its primary functions and organizing the principles, techniques, and knowledge of managing around these functions. That is what this book attempts to do.

In undertaking this task, the authors have utilized the functions of the manager—planning, organizing, staffing, directing, and controlling—as a logical framework within which to classify the basic practice and knowledge of management. It is recognized that there are other classifications of managerial functions which differ slightly, and with most of these the authors have no quarrel. It does seem, however, that the classification used here has the advantages of being comprehensive, of being divisible into enough parts to permit logical analysis, and of being operational in the sense that it portrays functions as managers themselves see them. Moreover, these functions sharply distinguish the task of the manager from the non-managerial activities of the specialist or technician.

WHY GROUP ACTIVITY?

Our modern civilization has increasingly become one of cooperative endeavor. Whether in business, government, the church, philanthropic institutions, or other forms of enterprise, the effectiveness with which people work together toward the attainment of enterprise goals is largely determined by the ability of those who hold managerial positions. It is to little avail to have scientific knowledge, engineering skills, technical abilities, or vast material resources unless the quality of managing in organized groups permits effective coordination of human resources.

But in looking to the reason why group activity exists at all, it is easy to see that man has found it necessary to cooperate with others. Because of his own physical, biological, and psychic limitations, he must do so in order to attain most of his personal goals. Also, any individual wishes to obtain the maximum possible of personal goal satisfaction with the least expenditure of time, money, unpleasantness, or other unsought consequences. This desire to accomplish goals through cooperation, and to do so efficiently, applies whether group action involves business, military, religious, charitable, social, or other objectives.

WHY MANAGEMENT?

Not all groups believe that they need managing. As a matter of fact, certain critics of modern management feel that people would work together better and with more personal satisfaction if there were no managers. They prefer to refer to the ideal group operation as a "team" effort. They apparently do not realize that in the most rudimentary form of team play, individuals playing the game have clear group goals as well as personal ones, are assigned to positions, follow play patterns, allow someone to call the plays, and follow certain rules and guidelines. Indeed, it is a characteristic of every effective group effort designed to attain group goals at the least cost of time, money, material, or discomfort, that it reflects the basic process and principles of management.

Managing is essential in all organized cooperation, as well as at all levels of organization in an enterprise. It is the function not only of the corporation president and the army general, but also of the shop foreman and the company commander. In working with many enterprises and organizations, the authors have heard repeatedly that the "trouble" with the enterprise is "the management," meaning persons at a higher level in the organization. There have been instances where even vice-presidents of a company have made this observation. While weaknesses and difficulties may appear at any level of management, effective and perceptive management demands that all those responsible for the work of others, at all levels and in any type of enterprise, regard themselves as managers. It is in this sense that this term is used in this book.

Thus, the reader will find no basic distinction between managers and executives, or administrators, or supervisors. To be sure, a given environment may differ considerably between various levels in an organization or various types of enterprise, the scope of authority held may vary, the types of problems dealt with may be considerably different, and a person in a managerial role may also be a salesman, engineer, or financier; but the fact remains that, *as managers*, all who obtain results by establishing an environment for effective group endeavor undertake the same functions.

Even so, there is seldom anyone in a managerial role who spends all his time and talents in managing, and the organization roles which individuals fill almost invariably involve nonmanagerial duties. One has only to look at the duties and performance of perhaps the most complex managerial role in our society—that of the President of the United States—to realize that much of his work is nonmanagerial. Even in a business corporation, a company president finds himself doing a considerable amount of nonmanagerial work. And, as one goes down the organization ladder, the number of nonmanagerial duties tends to increase. Nevertheless, this fact of life should not detract in any way from the key significance of managing.

THE GOAL OF ALL MANAGERS

It is sometimes said by nonbusiness executives that the top business manager has it easy. They say that he has profit as his goal. As will be elaborated in later discussions, profit is only a measure of the surplus of business results over costs. In a very real sense the goal of every manager must be surplus. His task must be so to establish the environment for group effort that individuals will contribute to group objectives with the least costs—whether money, time, effort, discomfort, or materials. By the very definition of his task, this becomes his goal. But if he is ever to know whether the efforts of those for whom he is responsible are effective—attaining goals and efficiently attaining them with least costs—he obviously must know them. Not only must these be known, preferably to all those for whom he is responsible as well as to himself, but they should be known in a verifiable way. Otherwise, he cannot ever measure his and his group's effectiveness or efficiency.

Thus, the goal of managers, as managers, is fundamentally the same in business and nonbusiness enterprises. It is also the same at every level. The corporation president, the city administrator, the hospital department head, the government first-line supervisor, the Boy Scout leader, the bishop, the baseball manager, the university president or dean, all, as managers, have the same goals. The purposes of their enterprise or their department of it may vary, and these purposes may be more difficult to define in one situation than in another, but their basic managerial goal does not vary.

IS MANAGING A SCIENCE OR AN ART?

The question is often raised whether managing is a science or an art. Actually, the practice of managing, like all other arts—whether medicine, music composition, engineering, baseball, or accountancy—makes use of underlying organized knowledge—science—and applies it in the light of realities to gain a desired, practical result. In doing so, practice must design a solution which will work, that is, get the results desired. Art, then, is the "know-how" to accomplish a desired concrete result. It is what Chester I. Barnard has called "behavioral knowledge."[1] Those who diagnose "by the book" or design wholly by formula or attempt to manage by memorization of principles are almost certain to overlook practical realities. As such it can be seen that, with the possible exception of formulating science itself, art is the most creative of all human pursuits. When it is appreciated how important effective and efficient group cooperation is in any society, it is not difficult to argue that managing is the most important of all arts.

The most productive art is always based on an understanding of the science underlying it. Thus, science and art are not mutually exclusive but are complementary. As science improves, so should art, as has happened in the physical and biological sciences. The physician without a knowledge of science becomes a witch doctor; with science, an artful surgeon. The executive attempting to manage without a theory and knowledge structured by it must trust to luck, intuition, or what he did in the past; with organized knowledge he has a far better opportunity to design a workable and sound solution to a managerial problem. However, mere knowledge of principles or theory will not assure successful practice because one must know how to use them. Also, since there is no science in which everything is known and all relationships proved, science cannot be a comprehensive tool of the artist. This is true in diagnosing illness, designing bridges, or managing a company.

One of the common errors in utilizing theory and science is overlooking the necessity of compromising, or blending, in order to achieve a total desired result. An airplane designer must make a compromise between weight and strength on the one hand and cost on the other. A manager may wisely give an employee more than one superior—breaking the principle of unity of command—if he is certain that *total* results attained will be better that way. But in disregarding principles and the other elements of science, one must calculate the cost and weigh it against the total result. The ability to compromise with the least of undesired consequences is the essence of art.

Another problem often results from the attempt to solve a practical

---

[1] As Barnard says in *The Functions of the Executive* (Cambridge, Mass.: Harvard University Press, 1938), pp. 290–291: "It is the function of the arts to accomplish concrete ends, effect results, produce situations, that would not come about without the deliberate efforts to secure them. These arts must be mastered and applied by those who deal in the concrete and for the future. The function of the sciences, on the other hand, is to explain the phenomena, the events, the situations, of the past. Their aim is not to produce specific events, effects, or situations, but explanations which we call knowledge. It has not been the aim of science to be a system of technology, and it could not be such a system. There is required in order to manipulate the concrete a vast amount of knowledge of a temporary, local, specific character, of no general value or interest, that it is not the function of a science to have or to present and only to explain to the extent that it is generally significant."

situation by applying a principle not designed to cover it. One would not apply a theory of metal stresses to an engineering problem where stresses were unimportant and the cost of material was. Nor would one be likely to apply a principle of management to a problem of medical diagnosis. But one of the difficulties of many management scholars and practitioners is that they may try to force a principle into a situation which it was not designed to explain.

SCIENCE AND MANAGEMENT

Although the organization of human beings for the attainment of common objectives is ages old, a science of management is just now developing. Since World War II there has been an increasing awareness that the quality of managing is important to modern life, resulting in extensive analysis and study of the management process, its environment, and its technique.

The culture of present-day society is characterized by revolutionary improvements in the physical and biological sciences, while the social sciences have lagged far behind. Yet, unless man can learn to harness human resources and coordinate the activities of people, inefficiency and waste in applying technical discoveries will continue. One has only to look at the incredible waste of human and material resources, in the light of unfulfilled social objectives, to realize that the social sciences are far from doing their job of guiding social policy and action.

Certain of the social sciences have progressed further than others. With all its deficiencies, economics, for example, has progressed far in explaining what courses of action will yield optimum output at the least expenditure of labor and capital. But economic principles assume that economic objectives can be attained through the coordination of human activity and that the enterprise, as well as groups of enterprises, will be well managed. Other social sciences, such as sociology and anthropology, have gone far in explaining man's cultural environment. Even though the foundations of these sciences suffer from incompleteness and inexactness, the theories have helped social scientists to understand our society.

The study and analysis of management have lagged behind other sciences until recent years. Yet, as in other fields, the development of an underlying science must precede an improved practice.

Science and the Scientific Method Science explains phenomena. It is based on a belief in the rationality of nature, on the idea that relationships can be found between two or more sets of events. The essential feature of science is that knowledge has been systematized through the application of scientific method to a given area. Thus, we speak of a science of astronomy or chemistry to indicate accumulated knowledge formulated with reference to the discovery of general truths in these areas. Science is systematized in the sense that relationships between variables and limits have been ascertained and underlying principles discovered.

Scientific method involves determination of facts through observation of events or things and verifying the accuracy of these facts through continued observations. After classification and analysis of the facts, the scientist looks for and finds some causal relationships which he believes to be true. Such generalizations, called hypotheses, are then tested for verification of their accuracy. When hypotheses are found to be true and to reflect or explain reality and therefore to have value in predicting what will happen in similar circumstances, they are called principles.

Application of scientific method to the development of principles does not totally eliminate doubt. Every generalization, however proved, may be subject to further research and analysis. Even so long-standing a generalization as Newton's law of gravitation might be modified with new knowledge and phenomena. But, without new facts, induction from them of significant relationships, testing of hypotheses, and development of principles, man would never understand his universe.

Principles and Causal Relationships   As has been properly pointed out by a student of management theory, if principles are to explain management behavior, they should be formulated to predict results.[2] In connection with many of the principles stated in this book, it is not explicitly stated that a certain course of action will bring "good" results. This is implied. Since principles are designed to predict results in given circumstances, the reader must be aware of what the authors regard as "good." The standard used in this book—one with which managers would certainly agree—is the efficient and effective attainment of enterprise or departmental objectives, whether economic, political, educational, social, or religious.

This includes the objective of maintaining the organized enterprises as an effective joint effort over time, that is, of providing for the survival of the group until basic goals are reached. For most enterprises, these goals are so continuing, of so long a duration, that this means indefinite survival. Thus, a business enterprise—unless set up for a specific short-term purpose, such as building a bridge—has a continuing goal of making profits and justifying the confidence of investors, just as an educational or religious enterprise pursues continuing goals of educating or furthering spiritual life.

Even though the principles as stated in this book may not always be established as complete causal propositions, the reader should interpret them as such. They can always be read in the sense that if this or that is done, the result will be more efficient and effective attainment of objectives.

Management as an Inexact Science   It is often pointed out that the social sciences are "inexact" sciences, as compared to the "exact" physical sciences. It is also sometimes indicated that management is perhaps the most inexact of the social sciences. It is true that the social sciences, and management in

---

[2] John F. Halff, "Applying Scientific Method to the Study of Management," *Journal of the Academy of Management*, vol. 3, no. 3, pp. 193–196 (December, 1960). The authors are indebted to Mr. Halff for his insistence on clarifying this point.

particular, deal with complex phenomena about which too little is known. It is true, likewise, that the structure and behavior of the atom are far less complex than the structure and behavior of groups of people.

But we should not forget that even in the most exact of the "exact" sciences—physics—there are areas where scientific knowledge must be replaced with speculation and hypothesis. As much as is known of bridge mechanics, there are still cases where bridges fail through such causes as vibrations set up from wind currents. And as we move from the longer-known areas of physics into the biological sciences, we find that areas of exactness tend to diminish.

Since virtually all areas of knowledge have tremendous expanses of the unknown, people working in the social sciences should not be defeatist. A scientific approach to management cannot wait until an exact science of management can be developed. Had the physical and biological sciences thus waited, man might have still been living in caves.

Certainly, the observations of perceptive managers must substitute for the desirable laboratory-proved facts of the management scientist, at least until such facts can be determined. Statistical proof of principles of management are desirable, but there is no use waiting for such proof before giving credence to principles derived from experience. After all, no one has been able to give statistical proof of the validity of the Golden Rule, but people of many religions have accepted this fundamental precept as a guide to behavior for centuries, and there are few who would doubt that its observance improves human conduct.

In looking at general management from an intellectual and scientific point of view, the earliest contributions came from such experienced business managers as Fayol, Mooney, Alvin Brown, Sheldon, Barnard, and Urwick. Many of the propositions offered in this book are based on the distilled experience of these and other practitioners. Admittedly, much of the research has been done without questionnaires, controlled interviews, laboratory experiments, or mathematics, but it can hardly be regarded as "armchair" or lacking in experienced observation. To be sure, management is an inexact science. But the questions one must ask are these: Does the use of such theory as is available or postulated help us understand management and aid in improving management practice now? Are we better off using such theory now—for guidelines in research and practice—or waiting until that perhaps distant future when the science can be "proved"? Does such theory help in substituting rationality for confusion? Does it increase objectivity in the understanding and practice of management?

PRINCIPLES AND THEORY

Principles are thus fundamental truths, or what are believed to be truths at a given time, explaining relationships between two or more sets of variables. In its purest form, a principle embodies an independent and a dependent variable. Thus, in physics, as Galileo discovered, if gravity is the only force acting on a falling body, it will fall at a uniformly accelerated speed (at 32.16 feet per second at the latitude of New York City). Or take the much less physical example of Parkinson's law that work tends to expand to fill the time available; thus work depends on time available.

March and Simon point out that propositions explaining relationships may be of various forms.[3] One type comprises propositions that state the dependence of one variable on one or more other independent variables. Another kind are propositions embodying a qualitative, descriptive generalization about a subject. They use an example of this as: "One of the important activities that goes on in an organization is the development of programs for new activities that need to be routinized for day-to-day performance."[4] As can be seen, this is little more than the concept type of proposition. A third type of proposition mentioned by these authors is one where a particular phenomenon performs a particular function, such as: "Rigidity of behavior increases the defensibility of individual action."[5] Although all three types of the March and Simon propositions might be used to indicate principles, the most meaningful type of principle is one which involves causal relationships with dependent and independent variables.

Theory is a systematic grouping of interrelated principles. Its task is to tie together, to give a framework to, significant knowledge. Scattered data, such as the miscellaneous numbers or diagrams typically found on a blackboard after a group of engineers has been discussing a problem, are not information unless the observer has a knowledge of the theory which explains their relationships. With this knowledge he can tie them together and probably comprehend what they mean. Theory is, as Homans has said, "in its lowest form a classification, a set of pigeon holes, a filing cabinet in which fact can accumulate. Nothing is more lost than a loose fact."[6]

The importance of theory to the development of organized knowledge has been dramatically indicated by the various essays of Talcott Parsons. In one, he says:[7]

> It is scarcely too much to say that the most important index of the state of maturity of a science is the state of its systematic theory. This includes the character of the general conceptual scheme in use in the field, the kinds and degrees of logical integration of the different elements which make it up, and the ways in which it is actually used in empirical research.

Any system of principles or theory requires clarity of concepts—mental images of a thing formed by generalization from particulars. Obviously, a

---

[3] J. G. March and H. A. Simon, *Organizations* (New York: John Wiley & Sons, Inc., 1958), pp. 7–9.

[4] *Ibid.*, p. 8.

[5] *Ibid.*

[6] G. C. Homans, *The Human Group* (New York: Harcourt, Brace & World, Inc., 1950), p. 5.

[7] *Essays in Sociological Theory, Pure and Applied* (New York: The Free Press of Glencoe, 1949), p. 17.

clear definition of a word is an elemental type of concept. Concepts are the building blocks of theory and principles. Unless concepts are clear, meaningful to those who use them, and used consistently, what may be said by one person who attempts to explain knowledge will not transfer to another in the same way. Indeed, this is one of the major difficulties with management as a science. As will be noted in the next chapter, the same word or term does not imply the same phenomena between various persons. One need only to reflect on the term "organization" to see how true this is.

Principles are often referred to as being "descriptive," "prescriptive," or "normative." As might be drawn from these terms, a principle is descriptive if it merely describes a relationship between variables. It is referred to as being prescriptive, or normative, if it is stated in such a way as to indicate what a person *should* do. Obviously, the principle of falling bodies, referred to above, is purely descriptive. It has no implication as to whether a person *ought* to jump off a high building, but is only an indication that, so far as gravity is concerned, if he does, he will fall at a certain speed. On the other hand, when principles are applied against some scale of values, they may be referred to as prescribing action or as being "prescriptive," or "normative." If the reader agrees with the thesis of the authors that it is the goal of all managers so to operate as to gain organization purpose effectively and efficiently, he has a value against which to apply management principles. It is consequently easy to make management principles "normative" as well as "descriptive." Indeed, with the standard of effectiveness and efficiency in mind, we have difficulty in not doing this.

THE NEED FOR PRINCIPLES OF MANAGEMENT

Obviously, principles of management can have a tremendous impact upon the practice of management, simplifying and improving it. Since in all fields of human cooperation, efficiency of group effort lags far behind that of machines, application of principles of management will further human progress.

The need for a clear concept of management and for a framework of related principles has been recognized for many years by such practical scholars of management as Henri Fayol, Chester Barnard, and Alvin Brown.[8]

To Increase Efficiency When management principles can be developed, proved, and used, managerial efficiency will inevitably improve. Then the

---

[8] In *General and Industrial Management* (New York: Pitman Publishing Corporation, 1949), pp. 14–15, Fayol bemoaned the lack of management teaching in vocational schools, but ascribed it to a lack of theory, since, as he said, "without theory no teaching is possible." Likewise, Barnard (*op. cit.*, p. 289) deplored the lack of literature and instruction for executives and, above all, the lack of "an accepted conceptual scheme with which to exchange their thought." Alvin Brown, in *Organization of Industry* (Englewood Cliffs, N.J.: Prentice-Hall, Inc., 1947), p. vi, held that the understanding and development of the art of management must be a study "grounded in principle."

conscientious manager can become more effective by using established guidelines to help solve his problems, without engaging in original laborious research or risky trial and error.[9]

It is not always appreciated that what can be learned from experience and transferred to new situations are only the fundamentals involved. The kind of experience, on which many managers rely too heavily, is only a hodgepodge of problems and solutions existing in the past and never exactly duplicated. Two management situations are seldom alike in all respects, and a manager cannot assume that exact techniques applicable in one situation will necessarily work in another. However, if a manager can *distill* experience, seek out and recognize the *fundamental* causal relationships in different circumstances, he can apply this knowledge to the solution of new problems. In other words, solutions become simplified if dealt with in terms of principles. The value in understanding management as a conceptual scheme of principles is that it lets one see and understand what would otherwise remain unseen. Theory can solve future problems arising in an ever-changing environment.

To Crystallize the Nature of Management   Lack of understanding of the principles of management makes it difficult to analyze the management job and to train managers. Principles act as a check list of the elements of management. Without principles, the training of managers depends upon haphazard trial and error. To some extent, this will be the case until an adequate science of management has been developed. Meanwhile in business, government, and other enterprise a considerable body of management principles does already exist and serves increasingly to crystallize the nature of management and to simplify manager training.

To Improve Research   As pointed out above, all hypotheses can be used to further research. And if research is undertaken to build further theory or otherwise to expand the horizons of knowledge, establishment of a structural framework of knowledge would appear to be useful for productive research.

In view of the rush of interest in management in the past two decades and the tremendous amount of study by students and managers, better channeling of continued research is bound to be productive. Since management deals in part with people, and groups of people are unpredictable and complex, effective research is difficult. Management also deals with the planning of action, the devising of controls, and the grouping of activities, in all of which progress in research is slow and costly. The need for tested knowledge of organized enterprise is great, and anything which makes management research more pointed will help improve management practice.

To Attain Social Goals   In a broad sense, management coordinates the efforts of people so that individual objectives become translated into social attain-

---

[9] As Urwick has aptly said: "And we should not forget that in the field of management our errors are other people's trials."

ments. Development of management principles, by increasing efficiency in the use of human as well as material resources, would unquestionably have a revolutionary impact on the cultural level of society. To illustrate this point, nations with a high material standard of living tend to have a high level of intelligence and skill in their management of business. Although ample raw materials and favorable political climate have been important in accounting for the economic productivity of the United States, equally significant, particularly in the twentieth century, has been the relatively high quality of management in American business.

Reasons for Delay in Development   Considering the pressing need for principles of management, it seems surprising that the development of a theory of management has been confined to the past few decades and that businessmen and others generally have been awakening to the need only since World War II.

In pointing to some of the reasons for this delay, one cannot overlook those centuries in which business was held in low esteem. Although business institutions of insurance, credit, and marketing developed in the Middle Ages and although these and still others were well formed by the time of the industrial revolution, business itself was regarded as a degrading occupation. Aristotle's characterization of buying and selling as "unnatural" money-making,[10] Adam Smith's disparaging remarks concerning businessmen,[11] and Napoleon's castigation of England as a "nation of shopkeepers" are evidences of this fact. Even in the past century, business was often regarded by the educated as a somewhat inglorious occupation. Indeed, one can say that only in the past half century has the businessman begun to hold a place of respect.

Another reason for the delay has been the preoccupation of economists with political economy and the nonmanagerial aspects of business. In their analysis of business enterprise and the development of philosophical precepts concerning business, the early economists generally followed the lead of Adam Smith, whose concern was for measures to increase the wealth of a nation; of Ricardo, whose emphasis was upon the distribution of wealth to the factors of production; and of Alfred Marshall and others, who refined some of the marginal analyses in competitive and monopolistic marketing. The modern treatment of the economics of the individual firm is largely a development of the past three decades. Even the work of Chamberlin and Robinson, which has so changed the course of economic theory since 1933,

[10] In *Politics and Ethics*, Aristotle wrote: "Of the two sorts of money-making, one is a part of household management, the other is retail trade; the former necessary and honorable, the latter a kind of exchange which is justly censured, for it is unnatural, and a mode by which men gain from one another."

[11] In *Wealth of Nations* (New York: Modern Library, Inc., 1917), p. 250, Adam Smith said of certain businessmen that they are "an order of men, whose interest is never the same with that of the public, who have generally an interest to deceive and even to oppress the public, and who accordingly have, upon many occasions, both deceived and oppressed it."

assumes the existence of an effective business management. These preoccupations kept economists from examining the theoretical implications of the significant job of business management until recent years.

One might expect that political science would have been the father of a theory of management, since the administration of policies is one of the major tasks of government, and government itself is the oldest and most comprehensive form of social organization. Yet, despite its obvious importance, early political theorists were slow to turn their atttention to the problem of administration. They, like the early economists, were too preoccupied with policy making on a national and international level; therefore, they largely overlooked the executive process, at least until recent years. Some of the early contributions to the theory of management, nevertheless, have come from scholars in the field of public administration, and important contributions have continued to come from this source at an accelerated pace.

To some extent the delay has also been due to the tendency to compartmentize the disciplines within the broad field of social science, as in the failure to apply the research of sociologists to the area of business management. The theories of sociology concerning formal and informal organizations have only recently been applied to the functions of the business manager. Likewise, research of psychologists in the fields of individual motivation, reactions to authority, and the meaning and measurement of leadership has extended to the area of management only in the past few years.

In addition to these reasons, there has been a widespread belief among managers in business, government, and other organizations that management is not susceptible to principles—that management is an art, not a science.

Moreover, businessmen themselves have in the past discouraged the development of a theory of management. Too often their emphasis has been on technology, price, and the balance sheet—an orientation hardly conducive to the understanding of, and inquiry into, the job of the manager.

It is interesting to note that the opening wedge to the present study of management as a science was driven by the so-called scientific management school of Frederick W. Taylor.

Recent Impetus   Impetus to the development of a theory of business management has come in the past three decades as the result of the recognition that one missing link in the attainment of an effective enterprise system is human relations. The Great Depression following 1929 brought forth such symptoms of human unrest as the New Deal and national unionism and emphasized to alert businessmen that, among the deficiencies of American industrial development, perhaps the greatest was the concentration on the mere manipulation of resources. It is probably not too much to say that the upheaval of the 1930s and the attack by government and other social groups upon the institution of free private enterprise were instrumental in forcing business managers to examine the nature of their job.

World War II and the subsequent defense programs were of even greater importance in the development of a theory of business management. The emphasis upon production with the least cost in materials and manpower focused attention on the job of the manager—at every level in an organization—as the strategic factor in accomplishing the objective. The importance of the manager has increased in the postwar years. For one thing, the siphoning off of some of the best young men into military programs during the war left a shortage of promotable manpower after the war. For another thing, the technical advances which accompanied the war exaggerated the lag between managerial knowledge and technical knowledge.

Also, the decade of feverish productive activity set off by military preparation accelerated the movement toward larger and more complex business enterprises. The challenge to effective management increases as business size increases. Thus, as business methods and products become more complex and relationships with other businesses, consumers, workers, and the government become more intricate, the need for skilled management, even in the small firm, expands materially.

In more recent years, tremendous impetus to the development of management theory and to the search for scientific underpinnings to improve practice has come from the world-wide rivalry for markets, power, and progress. This might be called the era of supercompetition. Increasingly severe competition has come from such factors as (1) dissemination of technical knowledge, which has allowed an increasing number of firms and nations to compete for world markets; (2) the freeing of trade; (3) the change from sellers' to buyers' markets; (4) the increase of capital investment and capacity and the rise of break-even points;[12] and (5) the rapid rate of technological change, which can make a product obsolete or lower its costs virtually overnight.

In addition to the growth of competition from these factors, both within the United States and on an increasing world front, businessmen have been faced with cost-price squeezes. The pressure for wage and fringe increases has raised costs to a point where businesses which fail to use modern techniques of management are at the mercy of those which do. With the tendency of wages to rise faster than labor productivity, the firm which would continue to enjoy profit dares not be content to be mediocre, but must aggressively attempt to be more efficient than its competitors.

This intense rivalry applies not only to business firms. In government, universities, churches, and other enterprises, one sees forces at work which indicate that group effectiveness may be a key to continued survival. In government, the demand for public services tends to outstrip the tax resources available to support them, and the same atmosphere of pressure exists in other nonbusiness enterprises.

These forces, always important but now of such magnitude as to affect survival, have placed heavy emphasis on management effectiveness. It may

---

[12] For discussion of break-even points, see chap. 28.

be that technical know-how will become less important to the maintenance of high living standards in the United States and elsewhere than the continued improvement of management. The present enthusiasm for developing management principles reflects this possibility.

EARLY CONTRIBUTIONS TO MANAGEMENT PRINCIPLES

Management naturally has been of some concern to organized society throughout civilized history. Most of the earlier so-called contributions came, of course, from practitioners, not theorists. Since early in the century, particularly through the contributions of Taylor and Fayol, there have been scattered but significant contributions to management theory. But the epoch of upsurge in management inquiry and research, in which academicians have participated with practitioners, is largely a development of recent years.

Management in Antiquity   Interpretations of early Egyptian papyri, extending as far back as 1300 B.C., indicate the recognition of the importance of organization and administration in the bureaucratic states of antiquity.[13] Similar records exist for ancient China. Confucius's parables include practical suggestions for proper public administration, and admonitions to choose honest, unselfish, and capable public officers.[14]

Although the records of early Greece do not give much insight into the principles of management, the very existence of the Athenian commonwealth, with its councils, popular courts, administrative officials, and board of generals indicates an appreciation of the managerial function. Socrates's definition of management as a skill separate from technical knowledge and experience is remarkably close to current understanding of the function.[15]

The records of management in ancient Rome are incomplete, although

---

[13] See A. Lepawsky, *Administration* (New York: Alfred A. Knopf, Inc., 1949), pp. 78–81, and numerous original and secondary sources there quoted.

[14] L. S. Hsu, *The Political Philosophy of Confucianism* (New York: E. P. Dutton & Co., Inc., 1932), p. 124. For excerpts from this study as well as other sources of early Chinese works on administration, see Lepawsky, *op. cit.*, pp. 82–84.

[15] In his discourse with Nicomachides (*Plato and Xenophon: Socratic Discourses,* book III, chap. 4, New York: E. P. Dutton & Co., Inc., 1910), Socrates is reported to have made the following observations on management: " I say that over whatever a man may preside, he will, if he knows what he needs, and is able to provide it, be a good president, whether he have the direction of a chorus, a family, a city, or an army. . . . Is it not also the duty . . . to appoint fitting persons to fulfill the various duties . . . ? To punish the bad, and to honour the good. . . . Do not, therefore, Nicomachides, despise men skillful in managing a household; for the conduct of private affairs differs from that of public concerns only in magnitude; in other respects they are similar, but what is most to be observed is, that neither of them are managed without men; and that private matters are not managed by one species of men, and public matters by another; for those who conduct public business make use of men not at all differing in nature from those whom the managers of private affairs employ; and those who know how to employ them, conduct either private or public affairs judiciously, while those who do not know, will err in the management of both."

it is well known that the complexity of the administrative job evoked considerable development of management techniques. The existence of the Roman magistrates, with their functional areas of authority and degrees of importance, indicates a scalar relationship characteristic of organization. Indeed, it is thought that the real genius of the Romans and the secret of success of the Roman Empire lay in their ability to organize. Through the use of the scalar principle and the delegation of authority, the city of Rome was expanded to an empire with an efficiency of organization never before observed.[16]

The Roman Catholic Church　If one is to judge by age, the most efficient formal organization in the history of Western civilization has been the Roman Catholic Church. Its long organizational life has been due not only to the appeal of its objectives but also to the effectiveness of its organization and management techniques. The development of the hierarchy of authority with its scalar territorial organization, the specialization of activities along functional lines, and the early use of the staff device are striking examples of these techniques. It is remarkable that, for centuries, their successful employment by the Church had virtually no influence on other organizations. In his study of this, Mooney expresses the belief that "nothing but the general neglect of the study of organization" can explain why the staff principle, so important to the organization of the Catholic Church, did not take root in other organizations until fairly recently.

Military Organizations　As might be expected, some of the more important principles and practices of modern business management may be traced to military organizations. Except for the Church, no other form of organization in the history of Western civilization has been forced, by the problems of managing large groups, to develop organization principles. Yet despite the need military organizations failed to put theory to use before the past two centuries.

Although military organizations remained fairly simple until recent times, being limited largely to refinements of authority relationships, they have, over the centuries, gradually improved techniques of direction. Early armies, even those comprised of mercenaries, were often characterized by adequate morale and the complementary relationship of individual and group objectives. History is replete with examples of military leaders who communicated their plans and objectives to their followers, thereby developing what Mooney calls a "unity of doctrine" in the organization. Even as autocratic a commander as Napoleon supplemented his power to command with a careful explanation of the purpose of his orders.

More recently, however, military organizations have applied other man-

[16] For an excellent analysis of the Roman genius for organization, see J. D. Mooney, *The Principles of Organization*, rev. ed. (New York: Harper & Row, Publishers, Incorporated, 1947), pp. 62–72.

agement principles. Among the most important of these has been the staff principle. Although the term "general staff" is found in the French army of 1790 and certain staff functions have characterized military organizations for many centuries, the modern concept of general staff can be traced to the Prussian armies of the nineteenth century. This group, organized under a chief of staff, furnished specialized advice and information and supplied auxiliary services which have come to be essential features of military and business enterprises.

The Cameralists The cameralists were a group of German and Austrian public administrators and intellectuals who generally held, from the six-teenth to the eighteenth century, the same tenets as the British mercantilist and the French physiocratic schools of political economy. They all believed that, to enhance the position of a state, it was necessary to maximize ma-terial wealth. But the cameralist school alone emphasized systematic admin-istration as a source of strength and was one of the earliest groups to do so.[17]

The cameralists believed as well in the universality of management techniques, noting that the same qualities which increased an individual's wealth were called for in the proper administration of the state and its departments. In developing management principles, they emphasized spe-cialization of function, care in selection and training of subordinates for administrative positions, establishment of the office of comptroller in the government, expedition of legal processes, and simplification of adminis-trative procedures.

Taylor's Principles of Management Although Frederick W. Taylor is properly called the founder of modern scientific management, the roots of his prin-ciples of management are found in earlier writings. As in other fields of knowledge, the principles of scientific management were discovered as the occasion for their use arose, necessity being the mother of invention. The rise of large industry and the factory system and the introduction of expen-sive machinery occasioned the new interest in problems of management.

Although Taylor's principles were intended for broad application, his emphasis was not on general management but on management at the shop level. He was concerned mainly with the efficiency of workers and managers in actual production. This preoccupation screened out the need to discover and use management principles at all levels and in all functions of business.

Taylor's famous work, *The Principles of Scientific Management,* was published in 1911. Despite his apparent intent to provide principles ap-plicable to management, his main concern was with achieving efficiency of human beings and machines through time and motion study, which has been referred to as the "cornerstone of scientific management."[18]

---

[17] For one of the most scholarly analyses of cameralism, see A. Small, *The Cam-eralists* (Chicago: The University of Chicago Press, 1909).

[18] R. F. Hoxie, "Scientific Management and Labor Welfare," *Journal of Political Economy,* vol. 24, p. 838 (November, 1916).

Perhaps Taylor's principal contribution to management theory is his insistence upon the application of scientific method. Thus, Taylor held that *The Principles of Scientific Management* had been written:[19]

> First: To point out, through a series of simple illustrations, the great loss which the whole country is suffering through inefficiency in almost all of our daily acts.
> Second: To try to convince the reader that the remedy for this inefficiency lies in systematic management, rather than in searching for some unusual or extraordinary man.
> Third: To prove that the best management is a true science, resting upon clearly defined laws, rules, and principles, as a foundation. And further to show that the fundamental principles of scientific management are applicable to all kinds of human activities, from our simplest individual acts to the work of our great corporations, which call for the most elaborate co-operation. And, briefly, through a series of illustrations, to convince the reader that whenever these principles are correctly applied, results must follow which are truly astounding.

In developing his theory, Taylor pointed out that a new philosophy of management was involved, a philosophy under which management would take more responsibility for planning and supervision and for reducing the knowledge of labor and machine techniques to rules, laws, and formulas, thereby "immensely" helping employees to work at lower cost to the employer and with higher returns to themselves.

Taylor saw several new functions for managers: (1) replacing rule-of-thumb methods with scientific determination of each element of a man's job; (2) scientific selection and training of workmen; (3) cooperation of management and labor to accomplish work in accordance with scientific method; and (4) a more equal division of responsibility between managers and workers, with managers planning and organizing the work.[20]

Taylor's contributions, however, were not an unmixed blessing. Through his stress on efficiency at the shop level and economies gained through time and motion study, he caused attention to be drawn so completely to the shop that for a time the study of management became in effect the study of shop management, while the more general aspects were overlooked, particularly in the United States and Great Britain. As discussed below, had the work of Henri Fayol not been overshadowed by enthusiasm for Taylorism, the history of management theory might well have been different and the principles of general management advanced much earlier.

Fayol's Theory   Perhaps the real father of modern management theory is the French industrialist, Henri Fayol. Although there is little evidence that management scholars, either in England or in the United States, paid much heed

---

[19] Frederick W. Taylor, *The Principles of Scientific Management* (New York: Harper & Brothers, 1911), p. 7.
[20] *Ibid.*, pp. 36–38.

to, or knew much about, Fayol's work until the 1920s or even later, his acute observations on the principles of general management first appeared in 1916 in French, under the title of *Administration Industrielle et Générale*. This monograph, reprinted in French several times, was not translated into English until 1929; even then it was printed by the International Institute of Management at Geneva, and only a few copies were made available for sale outside Great Britain. No English translation was published in the United States until 1949, although the work of Fayol was brought to the attention of American management scholars by Sarah Greer's translation in 1923 of one of Fayol's papers, later incorporated in a collection of papers by Gulick and Urwick.[21] In this same collection, the more general aspects of Fayol's works were referred to in a paper by the British management consultant and scholar, Lyndall Urwick.[22]

Thus, even though Fayol's monograph did not appear in the United States in a form for general reading until 1949,[23] and despite the fact that few in this country knew of Fayol's work until 1937—more than two decades after its original publication and more than a decade after the author's death —a study of Fayol's monograph, with its practical and clear approach to the job of the manager and its perception of the universality of management principles, discloses an extraordinary insight into the basic problems of modern business management. Indeed, even though the thinking of certain students of management was clearly affected by Fayol long before his work was brought to the attention of the general public, one regrets that few serious students of business management had the advantage of Fayol's analysis. Most of those who have contributed to the principles of business management—such as Sheldon, Dennison, Mooney, and Barnard—show little evidence of having been familiar with the work of Fayol.

Fayol wrote as the practical man of business reflecting on his long managerial career and setting down the principles he had observed. In doing so, he made no attempt to develop a logical theory or a self-contained philosophy of management. His observations, however, fit amazingly well into the currently developing mold of management theory.

Fayol found that all activities of industrial undertaking could be divided into six groups: (1) technical (production); (2) commercial (buying, selling, and exchange); (3) financial (search for, and optimum use of, capital); (4) security (protection of property and persons); (5) accounting (including statistics); and (6) managerial (planning, organization, command, coordination, and control).[24] Pointing out that these activities exist in businesses of

[21] L. Gulick and L. Urwick (eds.), *Papers on the Science of Administration* (New York: Institute of Public Administration, 1937). Fayol's paper was translated by Miss Greer as "The Administrative Theory of the State."

[22] "The Function of Administration," in *ibid.*

[23] H. Fayol, *General and Industrial Administration* (London: Sir Isaac Pitman & Sons, Ltd., 1949). Most of the biographical material used here has been drawn from Urwick's interesting introduction in this edition.

[24] *Ibid.*, p. 3.

every size, Fayol observed that the first five were well known and consequently devoted most of his book to an analysis of the sixth.

Because there will be many occasions to refer to Fayol in succeeding pages, it will be helpful at this point to outline briefly the contents of his remarkable monograph. The book may be divided into observations on managerial qualities and training, general principles of management, and elements of management. Fayol distinguished between principles and elements by reserving the former term for rules or guides and the latter for functions.

Managerial qualities and training   Fayol considered the qualities required by managers to be physical ("health, vigor, address"), mental ("ability to understand and learn, judgment, mental vigor, and adaptability"), moral ("energy, firmness, willingness to accept responsibility, initiative, loyalty, tact, dignity"), educational ("general acquaintance with matters not belonging exclusively to the function performed"), technical ("peculiar to the function"), and experience ("arising from the work proper").[25] He also identified abilities requisite for the six principal activities of business, classifying them as managerial, technical, commercial, financial, security, and accounting abilities.

With insight, confirmed in more recent studies, Fayol observed that, while the most important ability for a worker is technical ability, the relative importance of managerial ability increases as one goes up the scalar chain, becoming the most important ability for top-level executives. On the basis of this conclusion, Fayol recognized a widespread need for principles of management and for management teaching, and decried the lack of management teaching in the technical schools of his time. He held that managerial ability should be acquired as technical ability is, first in school and later in the workshop. In the absence of a well-developed and accepted theory of management, he set himself early in the twentieth century to fill this need in a manner which, if followed more assiduously by succeeding scholars of management, would probably have gone far toward closing a gap which still exists today.

General principles of management   Noting that principles of management are flexible, not absolute, and must be usable regardless of changing and special conditions, Fayol listed fourteen principles of management growing out of his experience and summarized as follows:

1. Division of work. This is the specialization which economists consider necessary to efficiency in the use of labor. Fayol applies the principle to all kinds of work, managerial as well as technical.
2. Authority and responsibility. Here Fayol finds authority and responsibility to be related, with the latter the corollary of the former and arising from the former. He sees authority as a combination of

official—deriving from the manager's position—and personal—"compounded of intelligence, experience, moral worth, past services, etc."

3. Discipline. Seeing discipline as "respect for agreements which are directed at achieving obedience, application, energy, and the outward marks of respect," Fayol declares that discipline requires good superiors at all levels.

4. Unity of command. This means that employees should receive orders from one superior only.

5. Unity of direction. According to this, each group of activities having the same objective must have one head and one plan. As distinguished from No. 4, it relates to the "body corporate," rather than to personnel.

6. Subordination of individual to general interest. This is self-explanatory; when the two are found to differ, management must reconcile them.

7. Remuneration. Remuneration and methods of payment should be fair and afford the maximum possible satisfaction to employees and employer.

8. Centralization. Without using the term "centralization of authority," Fayol refers to the extent to which authority is concentrated or dispersed. Individual circumstances will determine the degree that will "give the best over-all yield."

9. Scalar chain. Fayol thinks of this as a "chain of superiors" from the highest to the lowest ranks, which, while not to be departed from needlessly, should be short-circuited when scrupulous following of it would be detrimental.

10. Order. Breaking this into "material" and "social" order, Fayol follows the simple adage of "a place for everything (everyone), and everything (everyone) in its (his) place." This is essentially a principle of organization in the arrangement of things and people.

11. Equity. Loyalty and devotion should be elicited from personnel by a combination of kindliness and justice in managers dealing with subordinates.

12. Stability of tenure. Finding unnecessary turnover to be both the cause and the effect of bad management, Fayol points out its dangers and costs.

13. Initiative. Initiative is conceived of as the thinking out and execution of a plan. Since it is one of the "keenest satisfactions for an intelligent man to experience," Fayol exhorts managers to "sacrifice personal vanity" in order to permit subordinates to exercise it.

14. *Esprit de corps*. This is the principle that in "union there is strength," as well as an extension of the principle of unity of command, emphasizing the need for teamwork and the importance of communication in obtaining it.

In concluding his discussion of these principles, Fayol observed that he had made no attempt to be exhaustive but had tried only to describe those he had had the most occasion to use, because some kind of codification of principles appeared to be indispensable in every undertaking.

Elements of management As stated above, Fayol regarded the elements of management as its functions—planning, organizing, commanding, coordinating, and controlling.[26] A large part of his treatise is given to an examination of these functions, and his observations are, on the whole, still valid, after more than five decades of study and experience of others in the field. Throughout Fayol's treatise, there exists an understanding of the universality of principles. Again and again, he points out that these apply not only to business but also to political, religious, philanthropic, military, or other undertakings. Since all enterprise requires management, the formulation of a theory of management is necessary to provide effective teaching of management.

THE EMERGENCE OF MODERN THOUGHT

Since the time of Fayol and Taylor, a universally applicable theory of management has been developing at an increasing rate. Although long neglected in favor of research into the more technical and functional aspects of behavior, the realization of the peculiar role of the manager and the desire to improve his effectiveness through selection and training and, gradually, through self-appraisal, have resulted in slowly increasing research. Although it is impossible to recount here all the significant contributions to a theory of management, some of the most important ones can be noted.

Contributions of Public Administrators Coincident with the scientific-management movement and encouraged by it, a number of scholars attempted to bring about increased efficiency in government by improved personnel practices and better management. One of the leading apostles of this movement was Woodrow Wilson, who, as early as 1885 and on many occasions later, sounded the call for efficient government.[27] In a quest for economy and efficiency, those interested in public administration have naturally stressed organization, personnel practices, budgetary controls, and planning; to these fields many public administrators and political scientists have made major contributions. Among these are such scholars as Luther Gulick, with his observations on government organization and his long research in the applica-

---

[26] *Ibid.*, chap. 5.

[27] See, for example, Wilson's *Congressional Government* (Boston: Houghton Mifflin Company, 1885) and "The Study of Administration," *Political Science Quarterly*, vol. 2, pp. 197–222 (June, 1887). Note also, with regard to developments in Great Britain, D. B. Eaton, *Civil Service in Great Britain* (New York: Harper & Brothers, 1880).

tion of scientific methodology to public administration,[28] and such other pioneers as White,[29] Gaus,[30] Friedrich,[31] Stene,[32] Dimock,[33] Simon,[34] and Merriam,[35] who have approached the field not only as practical public administrators but as university scholars.

Contributions of Business Managers   The most significant contributions to the field of management theory have been made by businessmen, including Taylor and Fayol. One of these early writers was Russell Robb, who in 1910, at the Graduate School of Business Administration at Harvard, gave a special group of three lectures on organization.[36] Drawing from his business experience, Robb saw organization as a tool for the efficient utilization of manpower and materials, a tool which had to be suited to the circumstances of each enterprise but which could also be overused. Robb was one of the first to warn of overorganization.[37] Emphasizing the importance of definite authority, harmony, and "team play," Robb warned that too much functional specialization would result in problems of coordination.

Of the comprehensive works on management, perhaps one of the most significant is *The Philosophy of Management*,[38] written in 1923 by the

---

[28] See "Notes on the Theory of Organization" and "Science, Values, and Public Administration," in L. Gulick and L. Urwick (eds.), *Papers on the Science of Administration* (New York: Institute of Public Administration, 1937).

[29] L. D. White, *Introduction to the Study of Public Administration* (New York: The Macmillan Company, 1939).

[30] J. M. Gaus, "The Responsibility of Public Administration," in J. M. Gaus, L. D. White, and M. E. Dimock (eds.), *The Frontiers of Public Administration* (Chicago: The University of Chicago Press, 1936), pp. 26–44; also (with L. O. Wolcott), *Public Administration and the U.S. Dept. of Agriculture* (Chicago: Public Administration Service, 1941).

[31] C. J. Friedrich, *Constitutional Government and Politics* (New York: Harper & Brothers, 1937); also, *Responsible Bureaucracy* (Cambridge, Mass.: Harvard University Press, 1932); and "Public Policy and the Nature of Administrative Responsibility," in *Public Policy* (Cambridge, Mass.: Harvard University Press, 1940).

[32] E. O. Stene, "An Approach to a Science of Administration," *American Political Science Review*, vol. 34, pp. 1124–1137 (December, 1940).

[33] M. E. Dimock, "The Criteria and Objectives of Public Administration," in Gaus, White, and Dimock, *op. cit.*, pp. 116–133.

[34] H. A. Simon, *Administrative Behavior* (New York: The Macmillan Company, 1950); also, *Determining Work Loads for Professional Staff in a Public Welfare Agency* (Berkeley, Calif.: University of California Bureau of Public Administration, 1941); and *Public Administration* (New York: Alfred A. Knopf, Inc., 1950).

[35] C. E. Merriam, *Political Power, Its Composition and Incidence* (New York: McGraw-Hill Book Company, 1934); also, *The New Democracy and the New Despotism* (New York: McGraw-Hill Book Company, 1939).

[36] *Lectures on Organization* (privately printed, 1910); incorporated in Catheryn Seckler-Hudson (ed.), *Processes of Organization and Management* (Washington, D.C.: Public Affairs Press, 1948), pp. 99–124, 269–281.

[37] In speaking of organization to control costs, Robb sagely remarks: "While it pays to know costs, it also pays to find out how much it costs to know costs." *Ibid.*, p. 45.

[38] O. Sheldon, *The Philosophy of Management* (London: Sir Isaac Pitman & Sons, Ltd., 1923).

scholarly British industrial consultant, Oliver Sheldon. Like Fayol, Sheldon sought to formulate a theory of "management as a whole," through defining its purpose, tracing its line of growth, and spelling out the principles governing its practice. Sheldon thought of management in broad terms, as including the determination of policy and coordination of functions (administration), the execution of policy and employment of organization (management proper), and the combination of the work of individuals or groups "with the faculties necessary for its execution" (organization).[39] Although Sheldon stressed such matters as the social responsibilities of management and examined functional fields of management, such as personnel ("labour management") and production management, many of his principles are similar to those of Fayol. One receives the impression from Sheldon's work, however, that he did not have Fayol's breadth of understanding and that, except for organization, he did not see the functions of managers as having universal application. For example, his discussion of planning revolves primarily around factory planning.[40]

Another important contribution by a businessman to the development of management theory is that of Henry Dennison, a Massachusetts industrialist whose advanced management techniques in the Dennison Manufacturing Company permitted him to explore the principles of management. In a book published in 1931,[41] Dennison set out to study the scientific aspects of management, particularly organization, and ascertain whether the methods of the engineer might not be applicable. In doing so, Dennison developed concepts of motivation, leadership, and teamwork and analyzed the structural factors of organization in their effects on personalities. Although Dennison did not develop a theory of management, his emphasis upon human engineering and the role of leadership made his contribution significant.

Perhaps the most illuminating attempt by businessmen to develop a logical framework for the theory of organization is in the work of Mooney and Reiley.[42] Drawing upon lessons from history, particularly that of the church and military organizations, these authors undertook to combine the elements of organization into a logical pattern of principle, process, and effect. Starting with the principle of coordination, they moved into the concepts of scalar organization and functionalism, arriving at a total of nine principles of organization. While the work of Mooney and Reiley has been

---

[39] *Ibid.*, p. 32. It is interesting that Sheldon drew these concepts of the function of management from an American, J. N. Shultze, in a paper read before the Taylor Society in 1919.

[40] Note that Sheldon defines planning as "the business of directing and controlling the processes of production to a given end." *Ibid.*, p. 218.

[41] H. S. Dennison, *Organization Engineering* (New York: McGraw-Hill Book Company, 1931).

[42] First published as J. D. Mooney and A. C. Reiley, *Onward Industry* (New York: Harper & Brothers, 1931), this work later appeared with slight modifications as *The Principles of Organization* (New York: Harper & Brothers, 1939). A later edition, in 1947, appeared with only the name of Mooney as author.

criticized as being too doctrinaire,[43] it represents a logical approach for relating fundamental principles of organization to one another.

One of the most influential and comprehensive treatises in this field is Chester I. Barnard's *The Functions of the Executive*, published in 1938.[44] During his long career as a business executive, Barnard was impressed with the need for some universal fundamentals to explain the executive's job and help him to improve his ability as a manager. Drawing heavily upon the research of sociologists and, to some extent, of psychologists, Barnard produced an extraordinarily provocative work. His treatise is, as he points out in the introduction, really two short treatises, one dealing with the theory of organization, the other with the functions of executives. His theory of organization, heavily sociological in approach, moves from the principles of group cooperation to those of formal organization. His principles of executive functions lean on this theory and consequently place great stress on leadership and the importance of communication. His examination of decision making, with particular attention to the search for strategic factors, is also penetrating. Barnard's work is so comprehensive that it cannot well be summarized. However, his contribution is as much a matter of provocation as it is of content, for he opens many vistas into further pursuit of management principles.

Another contribution by a practicing business executive is Alvin Brown's *Organization of Industry*, published in 1947.[45] This treatise is essentially an analysis of the delegation of authority, with an attempt to construct a theory of organization and a division of the managerial functions into the "phases of administration" of planning, doing, and seeing. Although Brown often refers to "responsibility" when he means authority or authority plus an assigned activity, his work is outstanding as a thorough analysis of authority delegation and an attempt to codify a number of principles of management.

Among other contributions by business and professional management people, one should not overlook the crisp reasoning and syntheses of Lyndall Urwick,[46] the papers of Mary Parker Follett,[47] and the pioneering work of Ordway Tead[48] and Paul Holden,[49] to mention only a few. Nor should one overlook the tremendous force which has been exerted by the Society for the Advancement of Management and the American Management Association. The latter organization, particularly, has its roots in the top managerial group in this country, its members being drawn mostly from among the alert

---

[43] Lepawsky, *op. cit.*, p. 253.

[44] (Cambridge, Mass.: Harvard University Press, 1938.)

[45] (Englewood Cliffs, N.J.: Prentice-Hall, Inc., 1947.)

[46] See especially *The Elements of Administration* (New York: Harper & Row, Publishers, Incorporated, 1943) and *Management of Tomorrow* (New York: Harper & Row, Publishers, Incorporated, 1933).

[47] H. C. Metcalf and L. Urwick (eds.), *Dynamic Administration: The Collected Papers of Mary Parker Follett* (New York: Harper & Row, Publishers, Incorporated, 1941).

[48] *The Art of Leadership* (New York: McGraw-Hill Book Company, 1935).

[49] With L. S. Fish and H. L. Smith, *Top-management Organization and Control* (New York: McGraw-Hill Book Company, 1951).

business managers who sincerely seek a scientific foundation for their jobs. The Society for the Advancement of Management, an equally important group, is an outgrowth of the Taylor Society, and much of its early emphasis was upon the production management aspects of general management.

The fact that the major contributions to management theory to date have come from persons to whom the practice of management has been a real and challenging task speaks well for the importance of the field and the realism with which it is being approached.

Contributions of the Behavioralists Spurred on by the Hawthorne experiments of 1927–1932 and the awakened interest in human relations in the 1930s and 1940s, there has been a tremendous influx of behavioral scientists into the study of management in recent years. The Hawthorne experiments, undertaken by Mayo and Roethlisberger of the Harvard Business School, disclosed that attitudes toward people—people being regarded as people— are more important to efficiency and productivity than are such material factors as rest periods, illumination, and even money.[50] This disclosure, as well as the more basic work done by psychologists and sociologists in prior years, resulted in a considerable volume of academic writing by the behavioral scientists.

Much of the focus of the behavioral scientists was stimulated by the belief that every management theorist had assumed that people were an "inert" instrument and the human organism a "simple machine." One finds this accusation at the base of many of the behavioral studies on management. Perhaps it is true that practicing followers of the early management writers did overemphasize the mechanistic aspects of so-called classical theory. But careful review of these "classicists" will show that the leaders did not do so. Even in the writings of Frederick Taylor, the importance of the human element was recognized.[51] And Fayol,[52] Henry Gantt,[53] Mary Parker Follett,[54] and Urwick,[55] to mention only a few, took positions nearly

[50] For a complete account of the studies, see F. J. Roethlisberger and W. J. Dickson, *Management and the Worker: An Account of a Research Program Conducted by the Western Electric Company, Hawthorne Works, Chicago* (Cambridge, Mass.: Harvard University Press, 1939).

[51] See, for example, *Principles of Scientific Management* (New York: Harper & Brothers, 1911), p. 29.

[52] For example, *General and Industrial Management* (New York: Pitman Publishing Corporation, 1949), p. 40.

[53] See A. W. Rathe (ed.), *Gantt on Management* (New York: American Management Association, 1961), pp. 60–66, 211–236.

[54] *Freedom and Coordination* (London: Management Publications Trust, Ltd., 1949), pp. 47–76. These two papers on "The Essentials of Leadership" and "Coordination" were actually given in 1933. It is interesting that in Miss Follett's paper on coordination, she emphasized that, "The fair test of business administration, of industrial organization, is whether you have a business with all its parts so coordinated, so moving together in their closely knit and adjusting activities, so linking, interlocking, inter-relating, that they make a working unit, not a congeries of separate pieces." (At p. 61.)

[55] *The Elements of Administration* (New York: Harper & Row, Publishers, Incorporated, 1944), pp. 32–33, 49–51, 89–94.

four decades ago which support points emphasized by behavioralists in recent years with understandably greater sophistication and insight. And one of the leading "classicists," Lillian M. Gilbreth, wrote one of the earliest treatises on industrial psychology.[56]

Although one cannot say that prior to the 1940s sociologists, anthropologists, psychologists, and social psychologists were particularly interested in the problems of management, by now their contributions to management theory have been considerable. While those in all areas of behavioral science who have made significant contributions to management are too numerous to detail,[57] a few can be named.

Sociologists have contributed much to understanding the anatomy of organizations through their work on groups, cultural patterns, group cohesiveness, and cooperation. Among the sociologists who might be mentioned are Weber,[58] Bakke,[59] Selznick,[60] Homans,[61] Dubin,[62] and Dalton.[63]

Psychologists have likewise contributed to management understanding through their illumination of the aspects of rational behavior and influence, the sources of motivation, and the nature of leadership. Among the many in the area of individual and social psychology who have contributed materially to management are McGregor,[64] Likert,[65] Argyris,[66] March and Simon,[67] Leavitt,[68] Blake,[69] Sayles,[70] Tannenbaum and his associates,[71] and Bennis.[72]

---

[56] *The Psychology of Management* (New York: The Macmillan Company, 1914).

[57] For an inventory of scientific findings in the behavioral sciences, but with particular reference to contributions of psychologists, see B. Berelson and G. A. Steiner, *Human Behavior* (New York: Harcourt, Brace & World, Inc., 1964).

[58] *The Theory of Social and Economic Organization* (Fair Lawn, N.J.: Oxford University Press, 1947).

[59] See, for example, *Bonds of Organization* (New York: Harper & Row, Publishers, Incorporated, 1950).

[60] See, for example, "Foundations of the Theory of Organization," *American Sociological Review*, vol. 13, pp. 25–35 (February, 1948).

[61] *The Human Group* (New York: Harcourt, Brace & World, Inc., 1950).

[62] For example, *The World of Work: Industrial Society and Human Relations* (Englewood Cliffs, N.J.: Prentice-Hall, Inc., 1958).

[63] *Men Who Manage* (New York: John Wiley & Sons, Inc., 1959).

[64] *The Human Side of Enterprise* (New York: McGraw-Hill Book Company, 1960).

[65] *New Patterns of Management* (New York: McGraw-Hill Book Company, 1961).

[66] For example, *Integrating the Individual and the Organization* (New York: John Wiley & Sons, Inc., 1964).

[67] *Organizations* (New York: John Wiley & Sons, Inc., 1958).

[68] *Managerial Psychology* (Chicago: The University of Chicago Press, 1958 and 1964).

[69] R. B. Blake and J. S. Mouton, *The Managerial Grid* (Houston, Texas: Gulf Publishing Company, 1964).

[70] *Managerial Behavior* (New York: McGraw-Hill Book Company, 1964).

[71] See, for example, R. Tannenbaum, I. R. Weschler, and F. Massarik, *Leadership and Organization: A Behavioral Science Approach* (New York: McGraw-Hill Book Company, 1961).

[72] *Changing Organizations* (New York: McGraw-Hill Book Company, 1966).

These scholars and others have shown how the human being brings to his task aspects of behavior which the effective manager should profitably understand. After all, it is individuals and groups with which a manager is concerned and, while organizational roles are designed to accomplish group purposes, these roles must be filled by people. Likewise, as will be pointed out later, the most effective manager is a leader, and understanding how leadership emerges is a key to understanding management itself.

Contributions of the Systems Scientists A major contribution has been made to management in recent years by the introduction into its concepts, theory, and practice of the systems approach, which has been so basic and fruitful in the physical sciences. A system, as defined in the *Oxford English Dictionary*, is simply "a set or assemblage of things connected, or interdependent, so as to form a complex unity; a whole composed of parts in orderly arrangement according to some scheme or plan." To see any system is to see phenomena as an interrelated set of interacting components.

Thus, a business, government, or other type of enterprise, or a department within it, is a system, and managing any one of these represents a subsystem of them. Also, management plans are systems involving such components as people, authority, information flow, materials, and facilities. The advantage of approaching any area of inquiry as a system is to see the critical variables and constraints and their interactions. This is obviously of great importance in management.

It is true that Barnard saw the executive as a component of a system of formal organization, and the latter as a part of an entire cooperative system involving biological, physical, social, and psychological elements. It is likewise true that those who have approached managing as a process have long seen it as an interlocking, interacting system. But perhaps the major contribution of systems approach to the field of management came with the introduction of operations research[73] into the areas of management planning and control. This was certainly one of the first attempts to bring into management planning and control problems the rigorous treatment required by clear-cut goals, measures of effectiveness, mathematical models, and the attempt to develop quantified answers.

This introduction of the systems approach after World War II has blossomed into many other devices and techniques to give structure and rigor to management thinking and practice. It has also made a major contribution by forcing scholars and practitioners in the field to be constantly aware that one single element, phenomenon, or problem should not be treated without regard for its interacting consequences with other elements.

These varied contributions indicate that management is not the exclusive bailiwick of the business executive or the public administrator. As will be shown in the following chapters, the theory of management necessarily draws upon all disciplines seeking to understand individual and group ac-

[73] See below, chap. 8.

tion. In fact, the noteworthy absence of writing and research in the formative period of modern management theory is more than made up for, in recent years, by a deluge of research and writing from the academic halls. What is interesting, and perhaps nothing more than a sign of the unsophisticated adolescence of management theory, is how the current flood has brought with it a wave of different approaches to management analysis. The following chapter identifies the main "schools" of management and explains some of the differences leading to confusion in this field.

FOR DISCUSSION

1. How would you expect a theory of management to differ from a theory of mechanics? To what extent would a profession of management have elements similar to the professions of medicine, law, or engineering?

2. Must a principle be valid in all circumstances to which it is designed to apply in order to be a true principle?

3. Look up the terms "theory" and "principle" in an acceptable dictionary and determine how they are used.

4. It is sometimes said that a manager must believe in theory since he has nowhere else to turn. Do you agree?

5. Theory and principles are sometimes referred to as descriptive or normative. How would you classify management theory or principles?

SELECTED REFERENCES

Albers, H. H.: *Organized Executive Action*, 2d ed., chaps. 1–2, New York: John Wiley & Sons, Inc., 1965.

Barnard, C. I.: *The Functions of the Executive*, Cambridge, Mass.: Harvard University Press, 1938.

Berelson, B., and G. A. Steiner: *Human Behavior*, New York: Harcourt, Brace & World, Inc., 1964.

Bergmann, Gustav: *The Philosophy of Science*, Madison, Wis.: University of Wisconsin Press, 1957.

Boddewyn, J.: "Management: The Trees, the Forest and the Landscape," *International Management Review*, vol. 7, nos. 2–3, pp. 131–136 (1967).

Campbell, Norman: *What Is Science?* New York: Dover Publications, Inc., 1921.

Dale, Ernest: *The Great Organizers*, New York: McGraw-Hill Book Company, 1960.

Davis, R. C.: *The Fundamentals of Top Management*, chap. 1, New York: Harper & Row, Publishers, Incorporated, 1951.

Dubin, Robert: *Human Relations in Administration*, 2d ed., Englewood Cliffs, N.J.: Prentice-Hall, Inc., 1961.

Fayol, Henri: *General and Industrial Management*, chaps. 1–3, New York: Pitman Publishing Corporation, 1949.

Halff, J. F.: "Applying Scientific Management to the Study of Management," *Journal of the Academy of Management*, vol. 3, no. 3, pp. 193–196 (December, 1960).

Helmer, O., and N. Rescher: *On the Epistemology of the Inexact Sciences,* p. 1513, Santa Monica, Calif.: The Rand Corporation, 1958.

Mayo, Elton: *The Social Problems of an Industrial Civilization,* part I, chaps. 1–2, Boston: Division of Research, Harvard Business School, 1945.

Mee, J. F.: *Management Thought in a Dynamic Economy,* New York: New York University Press, 1963.

Suojanen, W. W.: *The Dynamics of Management,* New York: Holt, Rinehart and Winston, Inc., 1966.

Urwick, L.: *Notes on the Theory of Organization,* part 1, New York: American Management Association, 1952.

————: *The Elements of Administration,* chap. 1, New York: Harper & Row, Publishers, Incorporated, 1944.

CHAPTER TWO

patterns of management analysis

Because of the extraordinary interest in management in recent years, there have developed a number of approaches to its study. Their variety and the large number of persons, particularly from universities, who espouse them, have resulted in much confusion as to what management is, what management theory is, and how management should be studied. One of the authors has called the present situation "the management theory jungle."[1]

THE SCHOOLS OF MANAGEMENT

It is perhaps more important that there be one approach to management than that there be a single approach to psychology or trout fishing. What is important is for students and managers to be able to classify and recognize the various patterns of management analysis. Management is a difficult enough field without those in it being forced to face confusion and apparent contradiction. This approach might best be referred to as the operational school since it attempts to analyze management in terms of what managers actually do.[2]

This book considers management to be a process of designing and maintaining the internal environment for organized effort to accomplish group goals. In this context, the authors believe that they analyze management in a way most useful to the manager, reflecting the way he sees his job. The

---

[1] See Harold Koontz, "The Management Theory Jungle," *Journal of the Academy of Management*, vol. 4, no. 3, pp. 174–188. See also Harold Koontz, "Making Sense of Management Theory," *Harvard Business Review*, vol. 40, no. 4, pp. 24ff. (July–August, 1962). Much of the material in these chapters has been drawn from these articles.

[2] For a discussion of the operational approach to concepts and analysis, see P. W. Bridgman, *The Logic of Modern Physics* (New York: The Macmillan Company, 1938), pp. 2–32.

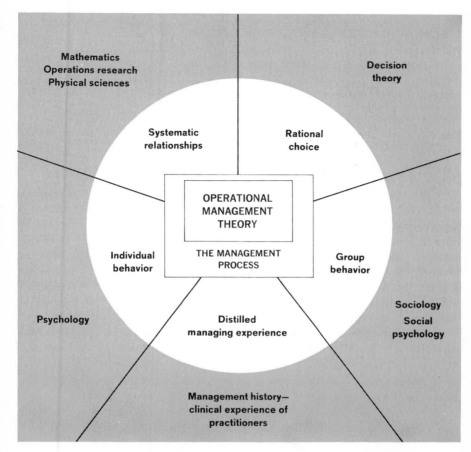

Fig. 2.1 Management Theory as a System Drawing on Other Areas of Organized Knowledge . . . *The "operational" or "management process" school of management represents an organized body of knowledge and theory, but it also draws techniques and theoretical knowledge from other disciplines. This diagram shows the major areas which make contributions. The area of management theory not only includes the central discipline, but also is eclectic in that it draws on other disciplines. The area of the diagram shown in white is the area of management theory.*

authors nevertheless recognize that other analyses of management are useful and important and that contributions made by proponents of other approaches have been significant.

The various schools of management are here grouped into the following categories: (1) the operational (management process) school, (2) the empirical or case school, (3) the human behavior school, (4) the social system school, (5) the decision theory school, and (6) the mathematical school.

In the following summary, the authors do not attempt to deal with all the nuances of the different patterns of analysis or do more than sketch the theory of each.

The Operational School   This school analyzes the management process, establishes a conceptual framework for it, identifies its principles, and builds a theory of management from them. It regards management as a universal process, regardless of the type or level of enterprise, although recognizing that obviously the environment of managing differs widely between enterprises and levels. It looks upon management theory as a way of organizing experience so that practice can be improved through research, empirical testing of principles, and proper teaching of fundamentals.[3]

Often referred to, especially by its critics, as "traditional" or "universalist," this school was fathered by Henri Fayol, although many of his offspring did not know of their parent, since Fayol's work was eclipsed by the bright light of his contemporary, Frederick Taylor, and clouded by the lack of a widely available English translation until 1949. Other than Fayol, most of the early contributors to this school dealt only with the organization function of management, largely because of their greater experience with this function and the simple fact that planning, control, and staffing were given little attention by managers before 1940.

This school bases its analysis of management on the fundamental beliefs that:

1. Managing is an operational process best dissected intellectually by analyzing managerial functions.
2. Long experience with managing in a variety of enterprise situations can be grounds for distillation of basic truths or principles having a clarifying and predictive value in the understanding and improvement of managing.
3. These principles can become focal points for useful research both to ascertain their validity and to improve their applicability.
4. Such principles can furnish elements, at least until disproved and certainly until sharpened, of a useful theory of management.
5. Managing is an art that, like medicine or engineering, should rely on thorough grounding in principles.
6. Management principles, like those of logical and physical sciences, are nonetheless true even if a practitioner in a given situation

---

[3] It is interesting that one of the scholars strongly oriented to the human relations and behavioral approaches to management has recently noted that "theory can be viewed as a way of organizing experience" and that "once initial sense is made out of experienced environment, the way is cleared for an even more adequate organization of this experience." See Robert Dubin in "Psyche, Sensitivity, and Social Structure," critical comment in Robert Tannenbaum, I. R. Weschler, and Fred Massarik, *Leadership and Organization: A Behavioral Science Approach* (New York: McGraw-Hill Book Company, 1961), p. 401.

chooses to ignore them and the costs involved in so doing, or attempts to accomplish some other benefit that offsets the costs incurred.

7. While the total culture and the physical and biological universe variously affect the manager's environment, as they do every field of science and art, management theory need not encompass all knowledge in order for it to serve as a scientific foundation of management principles.

The basic approach of this school, then, is first to identify the functions of managers and then to distill within them the fundamental principles of the complicated practice of management. The authors have found it useful to classify their analysis of these functions around the following essential questions: (1) What is the nature of the function? (2) What is the purpose of the function? (3) What explains the structure of the function? (4) What explains the process of the function? Perhaps there are more useful approaches, but the authors have found that they can place everything pertaining to management (even some rather remote research and concepts) in this framework.

Also, to make the area of management theory intellectually manageable, subscribers to this school do not include in their theory entire areas of sociology, economics, biology, psychology, physics, chemistry, or other sciences, not because these have no bearing on management, but because all progress in science has entailed partitioning of knowledge. Yet it would be foolish not to realize that an activity dealing with people's production and marketing of anything from bread and money to religion and education cannot be completely independent of their physical, biological, and cultural universe.

The Empirical School   The empirical school analyzes management by a study of experience, sometimes with intent to draw generalizations, but usually merely as a means of transferring experience to the student. Typical of this school are those who teach management of "policy" by the study and analysis of cases and by Ernest Dale's "comparative approach."[4] In a real sense, this school also uses an operational approach.

This approach is based upon the premise that through study of the successes and mistakes made by managers in individual cases, and of attempts to solve specific problems, students and practitioners will somehow come to understand and learn to apply effective techniques in comparable situations. No one can deny the importance of analyzing past experience or the "how-it-was-done" of management. But management, unlike law, is not a science based on precedent, and future situations exactly resembling those of the past are unlikely to occur. Indeed, there is a positive danger in relying too much on past experience and on undistilled history of managerial problem solving, for the simple reason that a technique found "right" in the past may be far from an exact fit for a somewhat similar situation of the future.

---

[4] *The Great Organizers* (New York: McGraw-Hill Book Company, 1960), pp. 11–28.

The empiricists are likely to say that in analyzing cases or history they draw from them certain generalizations to be applied as useful guides for future thought or action. As a matter of fact, Ernest Dale, after claiming to find "so little practical value" in the principles enunciated by the operationalists, drew such generalizations or criteria from his valuable study of a number of great managers.[5] Although Dale does not profess to have found universal truths, there is some question as to whether his comparative approach does not really tend toward the operational approach he decries.

By the emphasis of the empirical school on study of experience, it appears that the research and thought so engendered may hasten a verification of principles. It is also possible that the empiricists may come up with a more useful framework of principles than that of the operational or process school. But, to the extent that the empirical school draws generalizations from research into past cases and that it seems necessary to do this to avoid exchanging meaningless and structureless experience, it tends to be and do the same as the management process or operational school.

The Human Behavior School   This analysis is based on the thesis that, since managing involves getting things done with and through people, its study should be centered on interpersonal relations. Variously called the "human relations," "leadership," or "behavioral sciences" approach, this school brings to bear "existing and newly-developed theories, methods, and techniques of the relevant social sciences upon the study of inter- and intrapersonal phenomena, ranging fully from the personality dynamics of individuals at one extreme to the relations of cultures at the other."[6] In other words, this school concentrates on the human aspect of management and the principle that, when people work together to accomplish group objectives, "people should understand people."

The scholars in this school are heavily oriented to individual and social psychology. Their focus is the individual and his motivations as a sociopsychological being. Their emphasis varies from those who see psychology as a necessary part of the manager's job—a tool to help understand and get the best from people by responding to their needs and motivation—to those who use the psychological behavior of individuals and groups as the core of management.

In this school are those who emphasize human relations as an art that the manager should understand and practice. There are those who focus attention on the manager as a leader and sometimes equate managership with leadership, thus, in effect, treating all "led" activities as "managed" situations. There are those who see the study of group dynamics and interpersonal relationships as simply a study of sociopsychological relationships and seem, therefore, merely to be attaching this term "management" to the field of social psychology.

[5] *Ibid.*, pp. 11, 26–28, 62–68.
[6] Tannenbaum, Weschler, and Massarik, *op. cit.*, p. 9.

That managing involves human behavior can hardly be denied. That the study of human interactions, whether in the context of management or otherwise, is important and useful cannot be disputed. And it would be a serious mistake to regard good leadership as unimportant in good managership. But to assert that the field of human behavior is equivalent to the field of management is quite another thing.

The Social System School   This school is closely related to the human behavior school and often confused or intertwined with it. It includes those who look upon management as a social system, that is, a system of cultural interrelationships. Sometimes, as in the case of J. G. March and H. A. Simon,[7] system is limited to formal organizations, the term "organization" being equivalent to enterprise, rather than used in the authority-activity sense employed most often in management. In other cases, formal organization is not distinguished and any kind of system of human relationships is encompassed. Strongly sociological in flavor, this pattern of analysis does essentially what any study of sociology does: It describes the cultural relationships of various social groups and attempts to integrate them into a system.

Perhaps the spiritual father of this school of theorists is Chester I. Barnard.[8] In seeking fundamental explanations of the management process, this thoughtful executive developed a theory of cooperation grounded in the need of the individual to offset, through cooperation, the biological, physical, and social limitations affecting him and his environment. Barnard's idea of formal organization, quite unlike that usually held by management practitioners, is defined as any cooperative system in which people are able to communicate with each other and are willing to contribute action toward a conscious common purpose.

The Barnard concept of cooperation pervades the work of many contributors to the social system school of management. For example, Herbert Simon[9] at one time defined human organizations as "systems of interdependent activity, encompassing at least several primary groups, and usually characterized, at the level of consciousness of participants, by a high degree of rational direction of behavior toward ends that are objects of common knowledge." Simon and others have subsequently seemed to expand this concept to include any cooperative and purposeful group interrelationship or behavior.

This school has made many noteworthy contributions to management. The recognition of organized enterprise as a social organism, subject to all the pressures and conflicts of the cultural environment, has been helpful to both theorist and practicing manager. Among the helpful aspects are the awareness of the institutional foundations of organization authority, the in-

[7] *Organizations* (New York: John Wiley & Sons, Inc., 1958).

[8] *The Functions of the Executive* (Cambridge, Mass.: Harvard University Press, 1938).

[9] "Comments on the Theory of Organizations," *American Political Science Review,* vol. 46, no. 4, p. 1130 (December, 1952).

fluence of informal organization,[10] and such social factors as those Wight Bakke has called the "bonds of organization."[11] Likewise, many of Barnard's helpful insights, such as that into the economy of incentives and his theory of opportunism, have brought the power of sociological understanding into the realm of management practice.

Basic sociology—analysis of social behavior and study of group behavior in the social systems—does have great value in the field of management. But one may ask whether this *is* management. Is the field of management coterminous with the field of sociology? Or is sociology an important underpinning, like language or psychology?

The Decision Theory School This school concentrates on rational decision—the selection, from among possible alternatives, of a course of action. Decision theorists may deal with the decision itself, with the persons or organized group making the decision, or with an analysis of the decision process. Some limit themselves essentially to the economic rationale of the decision; others regard anything that happens in an enterprise as a subject for analysis; and still others expand decision theory to cover the psychological and sociological aspects and environment of decisions and decision makers.

The decision theory school is apparently an outgrowth of the theory of consumer's choice with which economists have long been concerned. It has arisen out of such economic considerations as utility maximization, indifference curves, marginal utility, and economic behavior under risks and uncertainties. It is, therefore, no surprise that most of the members of this school are economic theorists. It is likewise no surprise to find the content of this theory oriented to model construction and mathematics.

The decision theory school has expanded its horizon considerably beyond the process of evaluating alternatives. That has become for many only a springboard for examination of the entire sphere of enterprise activity, including the nature of organization structure, the psychological and social reactions of individuals and groups, development of basic information for decisions, and analysis of values—particularly, value considerations with respect to goals. As one would expect, when the decision theorists start with study of the small, but central, area of decision *making*, they are led by this keyhole look at management to consider the entire field of enterprise operation and its environment. The result is that decision theory is no longer a neat and narrow concentration on decision but becomes a broad view of the enterprise as a social system.

There are those who believe that, since management is characterized

[10] For a discussion of the nature of informal organization, see pp. 422–423.

[11] *Bonds of Organization* (New York: Harper & Row, Publishers, Incorporated, 1950). These "bonds" or devices of organization are identified by Bakke as (1) the functional specifications system (a system of teamwork arising from job specifications and arrangements for association); (2) the status system (a vertical hierarchy of authority); (3) the communications system; (4) the reward and penalty system; and (5) the organization charter (ideas and means which give character and individuality to the organization).

by decision making, the future development of management theory will use the decision as its central focus and that the rest of management theory will be hung on this structural center. This may occur, and certainly the study of the decision, the decision process, and the decision maker can be much extended. Nevertheless, one wonders whether this focus could not also be used to build around it the entire area of human knowledge. For, as most decision theorists recognize, the problem of choice is individual as well as organizational, and most of pure decision theory could be applied to the existence and thinking of a Robinson Crusoe as well as the United States Steel Corporation.

The Mathematical School   Although mathematical methods can be used by any school of management theory, we refer here to those theorists who see management as a system of mathematical models and processes. Perhaps the most widely known of these are the operations researchers or operations analysts, who sometimes call themselves "management scientists." The belief of this group is that, if management or organization or planning or decision making is a logical process, it can be expressed in mathematical symbols and relationships. The focus of this school is the model, for through this device the problem is expressed in its basic relationships and in terms of selected goals.

There can be no doubt of the great usefulness of the mathematical approach to any field of inquiry. It forces upon the researcher the definition of a problem or problem area; it conveniently allows the insertion of symbols for unknown data; and its logical methodology, developed over years of scientific application and abstraction, furnishes a powerful tool for solving or simplifying complex phenomena.

But it is hard to see mathematics as a truly separate school of management theory, any more than it is a separate school in physics, chemistry, engineering, or medicine. It is dealt with here as such only because there has developed around mathematical analysts a kind of cult which has, at times, appeared to believe that this encompasses the whole area of management.

In pointing out that mathematics is a tool, rather than a school, there is no intention of underestimating the impact of mathematics on the science and practice of management. By bringing to the important and complex field of management the techniques of the physical sciences, mathematicians have already made an immense contribution to orderly thinking. They have forced on people in management the means and desirability of seeing many problems more clearly; they have pressed on both students and managers the need for establishing goals and ways of measuring effectiveness; they have been extremely helpful in promoting the concept of management as a logical system of relationships; and they have caused people in management to review and occasionally reorganize information sources and systems so that mathematics can be given sensible quantitative meaning. But even with this contribution and the greater sharpness and sophistication of planning which are resulting, it is difficult to see that mathematics is management theory any more than it is astronomy.

FACTORS CONTRIBUTING TO DIFFERENCES

Like the widely differing and often contentious denominations of the Christian religion, the various schools or patterns of management analysis all have essentially the same goals and deal with essentially the same world. Two of the main differences in approach are semantics and varying definitions.

Semantics   As is so often true when intelligent men differ in their interpretations of problems, some of the trouble lies in key words. In the field of management, there are even differences in application of the word *management*. Most people would agree that it means getting things done through and with people. In this book, the reference is to establishing an effective environment for people operating in formal organizational groups; in other studies, the reference is expanded to apply to people in any kind of group. And there are even treatises purporting to deal with management which cover all kinds of interpersonal relations.

Perhaps a major point of confusion lies in the word *organization*. Most members of the operational school apply it to the intentional structure of roles. In this case, organization represents the formal framework for the role environment in which people perform within an enterprise. Certainly, in the experience and observation of the authors, most managers believe they are organizing when they establish such a framework. Yet, many organization theorists conceive of organization as the sum total of human relationships, thus making it equivalent to social structure. And some use organization to mean enterprise.

Other semantic differences might be mentioned. By some theorists, decision making is regarded, as it is in this book, as the act of choosing a course of action from among alternatives; others include in decision making the total managerial task and its environment. Leadership is differentiated from managership in this book; others often make them synonymous. Communications may mean anything from written or oral reports to a vast network of formal and informal relationships.

Differing Definitions of Management   While it is generally agreed that management involves getting things done through and with people, does it deal with all human relationships? Is a street peddler a manager? Is a leader of a disorganized mob a manager? Is a parent a manager? Does the field of management equal the fields of sociology and social psychology combined?

Certainly if a field of knowledge is not to become bogged down in a quagmire of misunderstandings, the first need is for definition of the field, not in sharp, detailed, and inflexible terms, but rather along lines which will give it fairly specific content. The authors suggest that the field of management be defined in the light of the able and discerning manager's frame of reference, because theoretical science unrelated to the practical art it is designed to serve is unlikely to be productive.

In defining the field of management, care must be taken to distinguish between tools and content. Thus, mathematics, operations research, accounting, economic theory, sociometry, and psychometrics, to mention a few, are *tools* of management but are not, in themselves, a part of its *content*. This is not to say that these fields are unimportant to the study and practice of management, as important contributions have been made from them. Nor does it mean that they may not further push back the frontiers of knowledge of management. But they should not be confused with the basic content of the management field.

In defining the field, too, it seems imperative to draw some limits for purposes of analysis and research. If one is to call the entire cultural, biological, and physical universe the field of management, he can make no more progress than could have been made if chemistry or geology had undertaken to cover such a field rather than to carve out a specific area for inquiry. In general, one might say that the field of management should deal with an area of knowledge and inquiry that is manageable. No great advances in scientific knowledge were made as long as man contemplated the whole universe. In other words, knowledge of the field of management must be recognized as a part of a larger universe of knowledge but need not encompass that universe.

MANAGEMENT AS A SYSTEM

It is sometimes forgotten that management, even as defined here, is a system just as a space satellite is a system, or an automobile, a thermostat, an assembly line, or a company. To analyze management and its various parts as systems enables the student of management to apply the essentials of systems theory, so profitably applied in engineering, to the appreciation and practice of management.

As pointed out earlier, a system may be defined as an assemblage of objects or functions united by some interaction or interdependence. It is, then, two or more factors which stand in some definite relationship to each other and among which the action of one causes a reaction in another. Thus, in an automobile, the starter is a complete system in which the input of electrical energy plus the closing of a switch causes a motor to start and the starter gear to engage with the automobile engine, thus turning the engine; as a system, it does not stop there, for when the engine starts, the starter disengages.

Systems may be open loop or closed loop. The open-loop system is characterized by a one-way cause-and-effect relationship, while the closed-loop system is characterized by a feedback of information to correct errors which might go unnoticed in the open loop. Closed loop can be illustrated by the system of controls on a diesel locomotive. Because there is danger of burning out generators or motors by applying too high an amperage of electricity, most locomotives are equipped with an automatic cutout which will keep the amperage at tolerable levels despite what the engineer does. Again, when a company has a set of quality-control specifications for a product and the inspector is instructed simply to reject products which do not meet the specifications, a straight cause-and-effect relationship or open-loop system exists. But if, as *should* be the case, the observance of variances from standard is accompanied by some information feedback which assures that action is taken to correct the cause of production below standard, then it is a closed-loop system.

Management is a system of interrelated variables, constraints, and parameters. If control is effective, the system is of the closed-loop variety. For example, if a manager lays out a program for developing a new product and passes it on to his research and engineering department and then does nothing to see that his program is carried out, one would refer to this series of interrelated circumstances as an open-loop system. However, if, through reports or other means, the manager follows the program to see that it is working as he intended, and takes action, he has closed the loop.

Systems have certain characteristics. In the first place, every system is part of a still larger system, or it encompasses many subsystems. A company is a system, but it is a part of an industrial system, a social system, a system of government, and, ultimately, of the systematized universe. Likewise, within the company, the marketing department is a system and within it the sales department, and so on. In the second place, every system—whether physical, biological, or social—has a specific purpose to which all its parts are designed to contribute. Without such a common purpose, the interrelationships would be meaningless. The third essential characteristic of a system is that it is complex, in the sense that a change in one variable will effect change in others.

Norbert Weiner, who has made considerable contribution to systems theory, has given us certain systems principles which are as applicable to management as to any mechanical or biological system.[12] He notes that all systems tend to lose energy at an increased rate, particularly as systems become more complex. This energy loss is due primarily to the frictional effects of communication (or energy transfer) between the various components of a system. As a result, the designed structure of a machine or organization is an index of the performance which may be expected from it. In a machine this performance might depend upon the design of gears, the kinds of lubricants, the strength of metals, the tolerances of moving parts, and similar factors. In an organization structure, performance might depend upon the clarity of goals and authority delegations, the way activities are grouped, and other variables that affect the means by which inputs are translated into desirable outputs.

The systems approach to management, then, simply recognizes that a management system—a formal, systematically organized complex of relationships between people—has, as a system, characteristics similar to those physical and biological systems. It recognizes that there are total systems and subsystems; that a system is characterized by an arrangement of variables and constants; that there are interactions and communications problems; that there are inputs and outputs; that a closed loop is the best assurance of getting desired results; and that, above all, the effective manager must, in a very real sense, be a scientific and creative designer of workable systems.

FOR DISCUSSION

1. Taking any four articles or books on management you like, determine how the authors are defining "management," "organization," "leadership," and "decision making." Why is semantics a problem in management theory?

2. Are there really various "schools" of management, are these simply ways of approaching the subject, or do they merely represent an intellectual division of labor?

3. Taking each approach to, or "school" of, management, discuss how the major concerns and findings of each can be integrated into the area outlined by the operational school.

4. By reference to a company or department with which you are familiar, sketch some of the major system and subsystem relationships and determine whether they involve open loops or closed loops.

SELECTED REFERENCES

Operational School

Albers, H. H.: *Principles of Organization and Management*, 2d ed., New York: John Wiley & Sons, Inc., 1961.

Davis, R. C.: *The Fundamentals of Top Management*, New York: Harper & Row, Publishers, Incorporated, 1951.

Fayol, H.: *General and Industrial Management*, New York: Pitman Publishing Corporation, 1949.

McFarland, D. E.: *Management Principles and Practices*, New York: The Macmillan Company, 1958.

Moore, F. G.: *Management Organization and Practice*, New York: Harper & Row, Publishers, Incorporated, 1964.

Newman, W. H., and C. E. Summer, Jr.: *The Process of Management*, Englewood Cliffs, N.J.: Prentice-Hall, Inc., 1961.

Urwick, L.: *The Elements of Administration*, New York: Harper & Row, Publishers, Incorporated, 1944.

Empirical School

Dale, Ernest: *The Great Organizers*, New York: McGraw-Hill Book Company, 1961.

Learned, E. P., C. R. Christensen, K. R. Andrews, and W. D. Guth: *Business Policy*, Homewood, Ill.: Richard D. Irwin, Inc., 1965.

Human Behavior School

Argyris, C.: *Integrating the Individual and the Organization*, New York: John Wiley & Sons, Inc., 1964.

Bennis, W. G.: *Changing Organizations*, New York: McGraw-Hill Book Company, 1966.

Likert, R.: *New Patterns of Management*, New York: McGraw-Hill Book Company, 1961.

Litterer, J. A.: *The Analysis of Organizations,* New York: John Wiley & Sons, Inc., 1965.

Sayles, L.: *Managerial Behavior,* New York: McGraw-Hill Book Company, 1964.

Tannenbaum, R., I. R. Weschler, and F. Massarik: *Leadership and Organization: A Behavioral Science Approach,* New York: McGraw-Hill Book Company, 1961.

Social System School

Bakke, E. W.: *Bonds of Organization,* New York: Harper & Row, Publishers, Incorporated, 1950.

Barnard, C. I.: *The Functions of the Executive,* Cambridge, Mass.: Harvard University Press, 1938.

Blau, P. M., and W. R. Scott: *Formal Organizations,* San Francisco: Chandler Publishing Co., 1962.

March, J. G., and H. A. Simon: *Organizations,* New York: John Wiley & Sons, Inc., 1958.

Thompson, J. D.: *Organizations in Action,* New York: McGraw-Hill Book Company, 1967.

Decision Theory School

Jones, M. H.: *Executive Decision Making,* Homewood, Ill.: Richard D. Irwin, Inc., 1957.

Kepner, C. H., and B. B. Tregoe: *The Rational Manager,* New York: McGraw-Hill Book Company, 1965.

Luce, R. D., and H. Raifa: *Games and Decisions,* New York: John Wiley & Sons, Inc., 1957.

Marschak, J.: "Efficient and Viable Organization Forms," in M. Haire (ed.), *Modern Organization Theory,* New York: John Wiley & Sons, Inc., 1959.

Miller, D. W., and M. K. Starr: *Executive Decisions and Operations Research,* Englewood Cliffs, N.J.: Prentice-Hall, Inc., 1960.

Mathematical School

Carr, C. R., and C. W. Howe: *Quantitative Decision Procedures in Management and Economics,* New York: McGraw-Hill Book Company, 1964.

Churchman, C. W., R. L. Ackoff, and E. L. Arnoff: *Introduction to Operations Research,* New York: John Wiley & Sons, Inc., 1957.

Kaufman, A.: *Methods and Models of Operations Research,* Englewood Cliffs, N.J.: Prentice-Hall, Inc., 1963.

Levin, R. I., and C. A. Kirkpatrick: *Quantitative Approaches to Management,* New York: McGraw-Hill Book Company, 1965.

McCloskey, J. F., and F. N. Trefethen: *Operations Research for Management,* Baltimore: The Johns Hopkins Press, 1954.

Morris, W. T.: *Management Science in Action,* Homewood, Ill.: Richard D. Irwin, Inc., 1963.

Management as a System

Beer, S.: *Cybernetics and Management,* London: The English Universities Press, Ltd., 1959.

————: *Decision and Control,* New York: John Wiley & Sons, Inc., 1966.

Johnson, R. A., F. E. Kast, and J. E. Rosenzweig: *The Theory and Management of Systems,* 2d ed., New York: McGraw-Hill Book Company, 1967.

the functions of the manager

The over-all job of a manager is to create within the enterprise the environment which will facilitate the accomplishment of its objective. He will, of course, be also vitally affected by the external environment in which the firm must operate, but he will have little, if any, power to influence government policy, economic conditions, and international relations. Within the firm, however, the manager is responsible for the environment in which his subordinates work. In cooperative enterprises—whether these be government bureaus, universities, churches, hospitals, or business firms—the able manager creates conditions conducive to effective work. In doing this, the manager plans the operations of his subordinates, selects them and trains them, organizes task relationships, directs their work, and measures actual results.

CLASSIFICATION OF FUNCTIONS

In classifying the functions of management, one must distinguish clearly those of operation, such as selling, manufacturing, accounting, engineering, and purchasing. These differ from one enterprise to another but the functions of the manager are common to all.

Although the development of a theory and science of management suffers from disagreement among scholars and managers as to the classification of managerial functions, a general pattern of practice and terminology has emerged. Adopted here and used by managers in many fields, this pattern avoids artificial terminology, so that students and businessmen need not learn new definitions—rather, they may be forced to use terms with greater precision. It is also hoped that managers, using common terms with ordinary meanings, will be encouraged to adopt an increasingly scientific approach to their important task.

The most useful method of classifying managerial functions is to group them around the activities of planning, organizing, staffing, directing, and control. It is not always possible in practice to slice all managerial functions neatly into these categories, since the functions tend to coalesce; however, this classification is a helpful and realistic tool for analysis and understanding.

Some authorities suggest representation as a distinct management function. They have in mind the manager who represents his firm in trade association and government relationships with a view to modifying the external environment or committing the firm to a contractual obligation, or the manager who represents his division or department in committee meetings which may affect the internal environment. There is also the larger problem of the "corporate image," which is influenced by the behavior of all employees, whether managerial or not. The authors have excluded representation as a separate function, because it appears to be a complex made up partly of communication and of the exercise of authority (included in direction and organization, respectively) and partly because of the influence of nonmanagers on the corporate image.

Occasionally, scholars concern themselves about the order in which the functions should be undertaken. Theoretically, planning comes first, and organizing, staffing, directing, and control follow. But according to this logic, an enterprise carries out only one all-encompassing master plan. In practice, managers find themselves performing all their functions at once. Plans beget subordinate plans, old plans require modifications, and new plans develop while old ones are in effect. Thus it is impractical to insist on a special time sequence for the various functions.

Planning Planning involves selecting the objectives and the policies, programs, and procedures for achieving them—either for the entire enterprise or for any organized part thereof. Planning is, of course, decision making, since it involves selecting among alternatives. There are, for example, policies relating to authority, prices, and competition; programs of production, management succession, and internal audit; and procedures requiring a specific method of handling paper, products, and people.

Considerable confusion has arisen about who should plan and when. Ever since the work of F. W. Taylor, executives have toyed with separating planning from performance,[1] a practice that may be unworkable when two managers command the same subordinates. If, however, the planning is undertaken as an advisory service to the manager in charge of performance, the separation is often highly productive. But planning and responsibility for planning cannot be completely separated from managerial performance because all managers have responsibility for planning, whether they are at the top, middle, or bottom of the organization structure.

---

[1] P. E. Holden, L. S. Fish, and H. L. Smith, *Top-management Organization and Control* (New York: McGraw-Hill Book Company, 1951), part B, sec. 3.

Organizing | Organizing involves the establishment of an intentional structure of roles through determination and enumeration of the activities required to achieve the goals of the enterprise and each part of it, the grouping of these activities, the assignment of such groups of activities to a manager, the delegation of authority to carry them out, and provision for coordination of authority relationships horizontally and vertically in the organization structure. Sometimes all these factors are included in the term "organization structure"; sometimes they are referred to as "managerial authority relationships." In any case, it is the totality of such activities and authority relationships that comprises the organization function.

There are several implications of this concept of organization. In the first place, the one-man business cannot possibly be organized. Since the owner or operator himself performs the only managerial functions, he delegates no authority. Let him, however, split off the buying activities, assign them to a subordinate, and provide coordination of activity between the buyer and himself, and the enterprise will have become organized. Thus, an organized enterprise requires at least two managers, either on the same level or in a superior-subordinate relationship.

A second implication is that all managers, when they decide to organize an enterprise or a department, proceed in the same way. Whether he be president, sales manager, controller, or office manager, he will reflect the goals toward which he is striving by grouping the activities for which he is responsible, assigning some of them to subordinates, delegating the requisite authority to accomplish results, and providing for the coordination of these authorities.

The organization structure is, of course, not an end in itself but a tool for accomplishing enterprise objectives. Efficient organization will contribute to the success of the enterprise, and for this reason the application of organization principles is very important. But striving for a "pretty" structure, without regard for its precise use, is futile. The organization must fit the task—not vice versa—and must reflect any compromises and limitations imposed on the manager by people, since organizational roles must be manned.

Staffing Staffing involves manning, and keeping manned, the positions provided for by the organization structure. It thus necessitates defining manpower requirements for the job to be done, and includes inventorying, appraising, and selecting candidates for positions; compensating; and training or otherwise developing both candidates and incumbents to accomplish their tasks effectively. Since this book is devoted to managers, the staffing function will be dealt with as it concerns managers rather than nonmanagers, but the needs and principles involved apply in most instances to both groups.

Directing Directing involves guiding and supervising subordinates. Although this concept is very simple, the methods of directing may be of extraordinary complexity. The superior manager must inculcate in his subordinates a keen appreciation of enterprise traditions, history, objectives, and policies. Subordinates must learn the organization structure and the inter-departmental relationships of activities and personalities, their duties and authority. Once subordinates are oriented, the superior has a continuing responsibility for clarifying their assignments, guiding them toward im-proved performance, and motivating them to work with zeal and confidence.

The methods a superior will employ are, of course, various. The success-ful direction of subordinates results in knowledgeable, well-trained people who work efficiently toward the enterprise objectives.

Controlling Control seeks to compel events to conform to plans. Thus it measures performance, corrects negative deviations, and assures the accom-plishment of plans. Although planning must precede control, plans are not self-achieving. Carrying them out means prescribing the activities of em-ployees at designated times. The plan guides the manager in the timely use of resources to accomplish specific goals. Then activities are monitored to determine whether they conform to planned action.

In the past, control activities generally related to the measurement of objective achievement. Such control devices as the budget for controllable expense, inspection records, and the record of man-hours lost are generally familiar. Each has the characteristic of objective counting; each shows whether plans are working out. If abnormal deviations persist, correction is indicated. But what is corrected? Activities. But this is done through per-sons. Nothing can be done about reducing scrap, buying according to speci-fications, or sales returns until the personal responsibility for deviations has been determined. Compelling events to conform to plans means locating the persons responsible for negative deviations from planned action and taking the necessary steps to improve performance. Thus, things are controlled by controlling what people do.

COORDINATION, THE ESSENCE OF MANAGERSHIP

Many authorities consider coordination as a separate function of the man-ager. It seems more accurate, however, to regard it as the essence of man-agership, for the achievement of harmony of individual effort toward the accomplishment of group goals is the purpose of management. Each of the managerial functions is an exercise in coordination.

Need for Coordination The necessity for synchronizing individual action arises out of differences in opinion as to how group goals can be reached or how individual and group objectives can be harmonized. Even in the case of a church or a fraternal organization, individuals often interpret similar interests in different ways, and their efforts toward mutual goals do not automatically mesh with the efforts of others. It thus becomes the central task of the manager to reconcile differences in approach, timing, effort, or interest and to harmonize cooperative and individual goals.

The best coordination occurs when individuals see how their jobs contribute to the dominant goals of the enterprise. This implies knowledge and understanding of enterprise objectives, not just on the part of a few at the top but by everyone throughout the enterprise. If, for example, managers are not sure whether the basic goal of their firm is profit, quality, advanced techniques, or customer service, they cannot coordinate their efforts to achieve the true objective. Each would be guided by his own ideas of what is in the interest of the firm or, without any such conviction, would work for self-aggrandizement. To avoid such splintering efforts, the dominant goal of the enterprise should be clearly defined and communicated to everyone concerned. And, naturally, goals of subordinate departments must be designed to contribute to enterprise goals.

Principles of Coordination Perhaps the most original and constructive thought on the concept of coordination has been that of Mary Parker Follett,[2] who has sifted principles from techniques and clarified the conditions for creating synchronized effort.

The principle of direct contact states that coordination must be achieved through interpersonal, vertical, and horizontal relationships of people in an enterprise. People exchange ideas, ideals, prejudices, and purposes through direct personal communication much more efficiently than by any other method, and, with the understanding gained in this way, they find means to achieve both common and personal goals. This recognized identity of ultimate interests then tends to bring agreement on methods and actions. For instance, rivalry and consequent criticism, which all too frequently mar the relationships of employees in sales and manufacturing departments, are evidences of poor coordination. Salespersons are understandably interested in offering products that will suit the customer. On the other hand, production personnel think in terms of permissible tolerances, straight-line manufacturing, and the minimum in variety and design. Unless the personnel of these departments exchange ideas and reach an understanding, there can be little coordination between them. No *order* to coordinate can achieve coordination.

A second principle stresses the importance of achieving coordination in the early stages of planning and policy making. It is clear that *after* departmental plans are put into operation it becomes more difficult to unify and time them properly. There is the treasurer, for example, who suddenly tightens up credit without first clearing with the sales department; or the engineer who specifies tighter tolerances without consulting the production department or waiting until the proper equipment, men, and training can be provided. The cry, "Why doesn't someone tell me about this?" thus becomes a common refrain.

The third principle states that all factors in a situation are reciprocally

[2] H. C. Metcalf and L. Urwick (eds.), *Dynamic Administration: The Collected Papers of Mary Parker Follett* (New York: Harper & Row, Publishers, Incorporated, 1941), pp. 297ff.

related. When A works with B, for instance, each influences the other, and both are influenced by all persons in the total situation. The people in the marketing research department are influenced by others in the sales department or by the attitude of those in production or finance. A department that has not entrenched itself is highly sensitive to the criticism of other units, and its planning and practices will be trimmed accordingly.

These principles indicate, finally, that the method of achieving coordination is largely horizontal rather than vertical. People cooperate as a result of understanding one another's tasks, and the line officer's dictum, "Coordinate!" is both unrealistic and unenforceable.

The need for continuous interchange of information can hardly be overemphasized. Enterprise never stays put. It is continually being modified by alterations in the external environment and by internal actions and decisions. The achievement of coordination itself modifies the strength of contending forces, often creating new ones and not infrequently deflating the old. Issues crumble before the adjustments of interested personnel; compromises are reached by the interchange of information or the modification of details. When these adjustments are made, problems disappear. New strengths and weaknesses may be uncovered and, in time, may build up again to the stature of a problem—a critical relationship of numerous complex forces. Good coordination will attack the problems as they arise; excellent coordination will anticipate them and prevent their occurrence.

Techniques of Coordination   The oldest as well as the most important device for achieving coordination is the supervisor. His chief duty to his own superior is to see that his subordinates are achieving a high quality of coordinated effort among themselves and in their relationships with other groups. This does not mean that supervisors directly coordinate the work of their subordinates. It does mean that they employ directional devices, teach principles of coordination, illustrate their application, and apply tests to determine the quality of synchronized effort.

Because the span of management limits the number of subordinates that a supervisor can properly direct[3] and because enterprises may be of a size which requires the services of many supervisors, organization is a very important device for achieving coordination. Careful attention to its principles will produce a structure in which the authority and functions of the several divisions will be clearly defined and whose framework will facilitate the interaction essential to the correlation of activity.

Although personal contact is by all odds the most effective means of achieving such coordination, many supplementary devices are also utilized. These include all types of written communications, such as procedures, letters, and bulletins, as well as modern mechanical devices for the transmission of ideas. Since skill in the use of such timesavers varies, employees need instruction in expressing ideas in the absence of personal contact. They

[3] For discussion of this point, see chap. 12.

must learn what information it is essential to pass on to their superiors without loss of time.

Group meetings are effective for achieving a high quality of coordination. They represent a deliberate effort on the part of the superior to bring into personal contact the people especially concerned with a subject. Their purpose is not to "tell" the members something—since coordination cannot be imposed from the top—but to encourage members to integrate their own efforts.

Finally, there is the not unusual device of using liaison men to facilitate coordination. Indeed, there were few firms during World War II that did not have their expediters, and expediting continues as an important activity in many firms. However, this device on any but a temporary basis is usually evidence of a poor organization structure.

Managerial Functions and Coordination   What the manager does to accomplish synchronized effort of subordinates is to carry out managerial functions, that is, to plan, organize, staff, direct, and control. It is the manager's responsibility, then, to achieve coordination. He achieves it in two ways. First, he assures that the environment facilitates coordination by creating an appropriate organization structure, selecting skillful subordinates and training and supervising them effectively, providing and explaining the integrated plans and programs that subordinates will carry out, and establishing means to determine whether plans are being carried out properly and programs are on schedule. Second, he makes certain that his subordinates understand the principles of coordination and the importance of acting upon them.

THE NATURE OF MANAGING

At least three groups have an interest in understanding the nature of managing. Those who occupy managerial positions obviously need a clear understanding of their duties: a blurred concept frequently results in time lost in nonmanagerial activities, to the neglect of executive duties. A second group is that of employed persons who do not manage—laborers, clerks, union representatives, and others. Because their goals derive from the firm, they want to feel confident that their managers know how to manage, and their favorable evaluation is an important source of support for any superior. If, on the other hand, workers commonly believe that managers "do nothing," it reflects a failure to understand that executives get things done by working through others. The third interested group includes students, teachers, and scholars in this field.

Writers describing the nature of managing and the separate activities of managers and nonmanagers have adopted the technique of observation and comparison—that of eliminating activities common to both and classifying the remainder. Similar results can be obtained by deductive reasoning.

Managers may sometimes engage in activities that are not managerial, that is, functions performed by nonmanagers. For example, a manager may type his own letters, try his hand at writing advertising copy, sell a house account, write a book, act as staff expert to his superior, or run a drill press at one time or another. But these activities are not managerial, since they are not characteristic of executives. Differentiating between managers and nonmanagers involves the recognition of their characteristic functions. Although executives may, at their discretion or whim, engage in nonmanagerial activities, those who are not managers do not undertake executive functions.

Universality of Managerial Functions   As was pointed out in the opening chapter, managers perform the same functions regardless of their place in the organization structure or the type of enterprise in which they are engaged. Acting in their managerial capacity, presidents, department heads, foremen, supervisors, college deans, bishops, and heads of governmental agencies all do the same thing. As managers, they are all engaged in part in getting things done with and through people. As a manager, each must, at one time or another, carry out all the duties characteristic of managers. This is the principle of the universality of managerial functions.

The implications of this principle are several. In the first place, it means that anything significant that is said about the functions of one manager applies to all managers. As a consequence, it is now possible to develop a theory of management applicable to all executives in all occupations.[4] This is a significant forward step, for if the principle failed to hold, writers could report only fragmentarily on managerial activities.

In the second place, the principle implies that managerial knowledge and experience are transferable from department to department and from enterprise to enterprise: merchandising executives may be shifted to manufacturing; the military commander to peaceful pursuits; foreman from flour milling to warehousing; and production managers to sales. To the extent that their tasks are managerial rather than technical, and with the proper motivation and orientation to the environment of managing, executives may employ their skill as well in one occupation as in another.

Functions versus Techniques   It is useful to distinguish between functions and techniques, because of the tendency to classify techniques along with functions in describing what managers do. Functions are the characteristic duties of the manager, while techniques refer to the way these functions are carried out. Thus a manager may be engaged in the function of directing but he may use the technique of command or persuasion. His function of controlling a subordinate's activities may be exercised through the technique of a budget; or he may organize his department with the help of the technique of written job descriptions or charts showing lines of authority.

---

[4] Compare Urwick's remark in H. R. Light, *The Nature of Management* (London: Sir Isaac Pitman & Sons, Ltd., 1950), p. 10: "Knowledge of a particular branch of business was, and still is in many instances, the sole criterion of competence. It has only recently been recognized that there is a general ability to manage which can be made the subject of a recognized 'discipline' based upon objective research."

Functions versus Nonmanagerial Skills   The failure to distinguish executive functions from nonmanagerial technical skills is another source of confusion. Technical skills, acquired through study and practice, are attributes of such experts as the chemist, the statistician, the physicist, the accountant, and the engineer. These people are, of course, vitally important to the success of their enterprises, a fact recognized in the often-heard statement that the day of the unspecialized worker is over. The technician applies his skill to any problem assigned to him in his field. A lawyer is employed to draw up sales contracts; a physicist, to undertake research in natural science; an accountant, to keep records; an engineer, to design an electronic tube. Their skills are by no means managerial in nature. Rather, the manager employs these men, because they can contribute to the achievement of the enterprise objective.

The manager himself, on the other hand, may or may not possess such technical skills. In his managerial capacity he certainly is not utilizing such operating expertness. Nevertheless, in the course of his past experience he normally will have acquired a degree of facility in one or more specialized activities. A district sales manager, for instance, troubled by the inability of his office to recruit good salesmen, may spend enough time studying this problem, becoming acquainted with the current literature, and applying various techniques of selection, that eventually he may become a recognized expert. Should he later be appointed general sales manager, he might no longer use this experience but would be said to possess an unused skill. Middle- and large-scale enterprises employ men with varying skills. Since no one lives long enough to acquire many skills, the manager cannot have the skills of all those he is directing. But if he can rely upon and successfully use the technical skills of others, he need not possess a nonmanagerial skill at all.

Can the possession of technical operating skills be a handicap to managers? Evidence points in both directions. Most businessmen can list accountants, lawyers, engineers, or other technical experts who are now corporation presidents, but always the sample is too small to indicate reliably whether they make better or worse presidents than men with a broad production or sales background. In American business history there has been a tendency for corporations seeking presidents to name production men when their problems were those of production, sales managers when their problems were of distribution, and engineers when their problems concerned research and development. This practice has generally escaped criticism, either because it was not known what the managers were supposed to do or because those selected either were already qualified as managers as well as technical specialists or they developed into good managers after their appointment.

The primary problem of the technically skilled manager involves time spent in acquiring and practicing his specialty. Continued application of a skill for ten or twenty years may narrow one's outlook. The specialist may either neglect to keep up in his own field or lose sight of the relation of his activities to those of the department or enterprise. What is more, in his capacity as an expert he is given no opportunity to practice *managing*. As managers, such men are poor risks, becoming too often, in F. C. Hooper's characterization, "one-eyed specialists in life-long grooves and niches."[5]

There are, however, two things a manager must know about technical skills. In the first place, he must know which skills should be employed in his particular enterprise and be familiar enough with their potentiality to ask discerning questions of his technical advisers. For instance, the president of a firm that manufactures a hair restorer may well read about the research on this subject being carried on at Johns Hopkins University. His technical advisers may not know about this or, as is frequently the case, may not be able to see its commercial application. This independent source of information, however, will enable the president to counsel with his advisers and broaden their activities.

In the second place, a manager must understand both the role of each skill employed and the interrelationships between skills. The physicist, the chemist, the engineer, and the lawyer may delve into the same problem from different points of view. The manager then must know what to assign to and expect of each and whether all phases of the issue are being studied. He must also determine the relationship of the work of each technician to that of the others and to all other phases of the enterprise process and must decide such questions as those concerning the number of specialists in each activity, the ratio of their progress to budget, and their individual and group effect upon the product, its quality, price, and market.

Because of this necessity for familiarity with the possibilities of each pertinent skill, new general managers are not expected to make important decisions from the moment they are appointed. Instead, they are expected to spend considerable time in the study of the enterprise purpose, its policies and practices, its position in the industry, and its strong and weak points— all of which involve a broad acquaintance with the relevant technical skills.

In addition, most managers, particularly at lower levels in the typical organization, have technical as well as managerial functions. The director of purchasing is likely to be also the president's chief adviser on procurement policy. The head of the market research department will probably serve as the company's principal technical expert in this area. But in all such cases, the distinction must be drawn between that portion of the job which is managerial and that which is technical. Only the latter part depends upon competence as a technical expert.

Material Resources versus Human Resources   Another source of confusion for some writers and students of management theory has been the attempt to utilize the economists' classification of productive factors as a basis for de-

---

[5] F. C. Hooper, *Management Survey* (London: Sir Isaac Pitman & Sons, Ltd., 1948), p. 150.

scribing the functions of managers.[6] Such a procedure inevitably leads to a discussion of the management of material as well as human resources.

The extent of the error involved in such an analysis may be appreciated by pointing out that managers achieve enterprise objectives through the execution of management functions as they relate to the efficient and effective use of the factors of production. A manager who develops a plan to achieve a production target is constrained by a budget that permits his use of a certain number of square feet of floor space, certain machines and other equipment in a given state of repair, the services of other groups such as those in procurement and industrial relations, and a given number of people with specific types of skills. The manager must organize his productive resources in terms of the layout of work place and equipment, and the activities of his employees in terms of groups, functions, and authority relationships. Since his budget provides for a given number of people, he must recruit these in terms of their required skills, provide training as necessary, and evaluate their performance. As a going concern the manager must direct his people so that they understand their functions, communicate effectively both internally and externally, and provide the quality of leadership that results in their working with zeal and confidence. Finally, the manager controls the total operation by comparing actual performance of his productive factors with the planned performance.

Thus it is that the manager establishes the internal environment wherein the available productive factors can best be combined to achieve his objective(s). The execution of his managerial functions is the *means* by which land, labor, and capital are made productive. The execution of the managerial functions and the application of resources have no meaning except in terms of achieving an anticipated objective. The manager gets things done through people all right, but in order to improve their productive power he provides them with capital and land or space. A manager must take responsibility for the purchase, lease, and use of the inanimate factors as he does for the employment of labor. In managing it is men who are important, for they include the manager himself and the people he employs to buy or lease and use the inanimate factors so that goods and services may be produced and sold at a price. One does not manage capital and land: he uses them. But managers deal with people.

FOR DISCUSSION

1. Do you see any advantage in attempts to classify the functions of managers? Is there any advantage in the use of the same classifications by scholars and managers?

[6] See W. H. Newman, *Business Policies and Management*, 2d ed. (Cincinnati: South-Western Publishing Company, 1949), part IV; and R. T. Livingston, *The Engineering of Organization and Management* (New York: McGraw-Hill Book Company, 1949), chap. 2.

2. Propose a scheme of classification which appeals to you and explain your preference.

3. Why should the functions of integrating, motivating, and coordinating not be included in the functions of managers?

4. Can you see how the five functions of managers are really an integrated social sytem?

SELECTED REFERENCES

Barnard, C. I.: *The Functions of the Executive*, chaps. 15–17, Cambridge, Mass.: Harvard University Press, 1938.

Beishline, J. R.: *Military Management for National Defense*, chap. 3, Englewood Cliffs, N.J.: Prentice-Hall, Inc., 1950.

Fayol, H.: *General and Industrial Management*, chap. 5, New York: Pitman Publishing Corporation, 1949.

Goetz, B. E.: *Management Planning and Control*, chap. 2, New York: McGraw-Hill Book Company, 1949.

Holden, P. E., L. S. Fish, and H. L. Smith: *Top-management Organization and Control*, part A, New York: McGraw-Hill Book Company, 1951.

Hooper, F. C.: *Management Survey*, chap. 1, London: Sir Isaac Pitman & Sons, Ltd., 1948.

Huddle, F. P.: "Coordination," *California Management Review*, vol. 9, no. 2, pp. 9–16 (Winter, 1966).

Mee, J. F.: *Management Thought in a Dynamic Economy*, chap. 2, New York: New York University Press, 1963.

authority and responsibility

Although the term "authority" is used in various ways by management experts, the standard definition is "legal or rightful power, a right to command or to act." Applied to the managerial job, authority is the power to command others, to act or not to act in a manner deemed by the possessor of the authority to further enterprise or departmental purpose.

As will be seen later in the discussion of organization, authority is the basis for responsibility and the binding force in organization. The process of organizing encompasses grouping of activities for purposes of management and specification of authority relationships between superiors and subordinates and horizontally between managers. Consequently, there are authority and responsibility relationships in all undertaking where the superior-subordinate link exists.

As Mooney[1] has stated, "Coordination is the all-inclusive principle of organization" and finds its foundation in authority, "the supreme coordinating power." According to Mooney, this power must lie somewhere in organization if consistency in internal objectives is to be realized.

Authority is the key to the management job. Since managers must work through people to get things done, management theory is necessarily concerned with a complex of superior-subordinate relationships and is therefore founded on the concept of authority. In the manager of a company, division, department, branch, or section is vested power sufficient to force compliance, whether through persuasion, coercion, economic or social sanctions, or other means.

But the power connotations of authority are at times exaggerated. Actually authority vested in a managerial position is the power to use dis-

---

[1] J. D. Mooney, *The Principles of Organization,* rev. ed. (New York: Harper & Row, Publishers, Incorporated, 1947), pp. 6–7.

cretion, the power to create and maintain an environment for the performance of individuals working together in groups. The true implication of this ability to create is then not autocratic use of power. It is, perhaps, no accident that "authority" derives from the same Latin root word that "author" does.

Despite the importance of authority, managers tend to avoid using the word, perhaps because of its connotation of power. Thus, subordinates are spoken of as having responsibility delegated to them, even though it is authority, rather than responsibility, that is delegated. For, as will be seen later, the essence of responsibility is obligation—the obligation to one's superior to perform assigned duties. Similarly, one hears of managers being assigned responsibilities, when what is meant is that they are assigned duties or activities. This misused terminology may be corrected by noting that managers have authority (power or the right to command) *delegated* to them, responsibility *exacted* from them, and duties *assigned* to them.

SOURCE OF AUTHORITY

Some disagreement has developed in the field of management as to the source of authority, experts being mainly divided between those who subscribe to the formal authority theory and those who subscribe to the acceptance theory.

The Formal Authority Theory Until recent years, it rarely occurred to writers on management that there could be any argument about the source of a manager's authority. One had only to trace authority delegations upward from any managerial position. Thus, the supervisor of cash control obtained his authority from the assistant treasurer, who obtained his from the treasurer, who in turn got his from the president of the company, whose authority was delegated by the board of directors, who obtained theirs from the stockholders, who held theirs by virtue of the institution of private property as modified by incorporation and other laws. Thus, in a business firm, the ultimate source of authority lies principally in the institution of private property—a complex of rights, laws, mores, and folkways vesting in a person power over material resources. Naturally, this authority arises also from other social institutions. The manager, as well as the stockholder, finds himself limited by laws, by political and ethical considerations, and by such economic institutions as competition, banking, and labor unions. Governmental controls—whether in the form of direct regulations or such indirect controls as fiscal policies—constitute an institutional framework that gives added meaning and substance to the authority of corporate executives. Social institutions—whether political, economic, religious, or educational—define the bounds and content of private property and, in so doing, define the authority of the person who has the property rights. Moreover, in political or religious organizations, the authority of managers (whether governors or bishops) originates from such social institutions as representative government, the federal system of government, or the various elements of church doctrine and organization.

The origin of authority, then—whether in economic institutions or in social institutions where private property is nonexistent—may be traced to the elements of basic group behavior. As these elements change, the institution must change. One has only to look at the recently changing nature of private property to see how an institution responds to the desires, objectives, and practices of the group.

The concept of authority as being power transmitted from basic social institutions to individual managers has been called formal authority.[2] For example, in the case of private business, this authority is hierarchical, originating from the top in the institution of private property and being delegated through owners to their representatives, the managers, and through them to their subordinates.

Most formal authority theorists emphasize the legal aspects of private property as the source of authority, though good sociological analysis would broaden the source to include all related social institutions.[3]

Under our democratic form of government the right upon which managerial authority is based appears to have its primary source in the Constitution of the United States. Since the Constitution is the creature of the people, subject to amendment and modification by the will of the people, it follows that the total society, through government, is the source from which authority flows to ownership and thence to management. Indeed, the entire social institution of private property is molded not only by the Constitution, but by many federal and state legislative and administrative regulations, and by the mores of the entire American society.

The Acceptance Theory The notion that the real source of managerial authority is acceptance by subordinates of the power the manager holds over them can be traced directly from the syndicalists through Laski to the American business executive, Chester I. Barnard, and is perhaps best expressed by Barnard's definition of authority:[4]

> . . . the character of a communication (order) in a formal organization by virtue of which it is accepted by a contributor to or "member" of the organization as governing the action he contributes; that is, as governing or determining what he does or is not to do so far as the organization is concerned. According to this definition, authority involves two aspects: first, the subjective, the personal, the accepting of a communication as authoritative . . . ; and, second, the objective aspect—the character in the communication by virtue of which it is accepted.

[2] C. I. Barnard, *The Functions of the Executive* (Cambridge, Mass.: Harvard University Press, 1938), pp. 162ff.

[3] Note that "institutions," as here used in the sociological sense, means a complex of laws, codes, mores, and folkways by which a social group attains and enforces group purpose.

[4] Barnard, *op. cit.*, p. 163.

Barnard argues that ". . . the necessity of the assent of the individual to establish authority *for him* is inescapable."[5] Barnard's position is that a subordinate will "accept" the authority of a command if he understands it, if he believes it consistent with organization purpose and compatible with his own interests, and if he is mentally and physically able to comply with it. A subordinate must, then, determine if these conditions exist before obeying. But even Barnard thinks this improbable, for he carefully explains that, in enduring organizations, orders usually conform to the above conditions; within an "indifference zone" in each individual, orders are acceptable without question, and group pressure is on the side of accepting orders. Thus, instead of the subordinate making a complex decision to obey or disobey, as required by the bald statement of the acceptance theory, Barnard makes it easy for him by saying that most orders are automatically acceptable, the subordinate doesn't care really, and group pressure will make him comply anyway. Moreover, Barnard dilutes his own theory somewhat by admitting that a "fiction"—which is nonetheless real—of superior authority exists and is necessary; he also admits that "authority in the aggregate arises from *all* contributors to a cooperative system."[6]

It is difficult to adopt the acceptance theorists' hedonistic formula for the source of managerial authority.[7] The very fact that some of the most important advantages of accepting and disadvantages of not accepting authority arise from the manager's power to grant or withhold rewards or to dismiss the subordinate makes the theory unreal. The soldier's obedience of commands—because the alternative is the guardhouse or the firing squad— is hardly genuine acceptance, nor is acceptance more genuine where a civilian's alternative is to quit his job or be fired.

Moreover, the implications of the theory are serious for the continuation of order in organization. If acceptance were the source of authority, the manager would, strictly speaking, be in the position of not knowing from one command to another whether he would be obeyed, for until he was obeyed, he would have no authority to command. Furthermore, if subordinates confer managerial power, they must also confer power to levy sanctions.

The basic error of the acceptance theorists consists not only in conceiving authority without sanctions but also in overlooking the powerful effect of social institutions, which confer powers that supersede individual desires. The authority of ownership involved in the institution of private property, for example, carries with it the right to contract for services or to grant or withhold remuneration, except, of course, as the right has been circumscribed by such other institutional developments as labor unions and labor legislation.

Order in organized behavior cannot be achieved without authority, since this force unifies the social group. The alternative, as Malinowski has

---

[5] *Ibid.*, p. 167.

[6] *Ibid.*, pp. 170 and 168n.

[7] For an extended analysis of this problem, see Cyril O'Donnell, "The Source of Managerial Authority," *Political Science Quarterly*, vol. 47, pp. 583–588 (December, 1952).

pointed out,[8] is chaos: "Submission to laws as well as the power to enforce laws and rules are indispensable to human behavior." In a free society, the person who contracts to work for another agrees, *at that time,* to obey the proper orders of superiors while in their employ. Also, in a free society, the employee may resign if he no longer wishes to obey. But, during the period of employment, he has no power to confer authority on his superior. In unfree societies, the subordinate has no choice but to obey if he wishes to escape jail or execution.

It appears, then, that the acceptance theorists are not discussing authority at all, but leadership—the ability to persuade others to work well to accomplish a group goal. Leadership, as well as authority, is essential to managers.

But the use of authority is much more comprehensive than merely to secure the compliance of subordinates. Managers use authority to contract with labor unions concerning working conditions and practices, with financial firms for raising capital, and with vendors for the acquisition of land and capital. The acceptance theory fails entirely to explain the source of authority to accomplish these ends.

The Competence Theory   In addition to the formal and acceptance theories of the source of authority, although perhaps more closely related to the latter, is the belief that authority is generated by personal qualities of technical competence.[9] Under this heading is the individual who has made, in effect, subordinates of others through sheer force of personality and the engineer or economist who exerts influence by furnishing answers or sound advice. These may have no actual authority, yet their advice may be so eagerly sought and so unerringly followed that it appears to carry the weight of an order.

But, above all, one cannot discount the importance of formal authority with its institutional foundations. Buttressed by the qualities of leadership implicit in the acceptance theory, formal authority is basic to the managerial job. Once possessed, it may be delegated or withheld, used or misused, and can be as effective in capable hands as it is ineffective in inept hands.

LIMITS OF AUTHORITY

The generality of the right to command decreases as it proceeds from the highest to the lowest echelon of an organization structure, as illustrated in Figure 4.1. One may visualize this characteristic of authority as an inverted

[8] Bronislaw Malinowski, *Freedom and Civilization* (New York: Roy Publishers, 1944), p. 27. Ranyard West, in speaking of primitive organizations, has observed that "the prime requisite and firm creator of any community life is a law of order maintained by force." See his *Conscience and Society* (London: Methuen & Co., Ltd., 1942).

[9] L. F. Urwick, *The Elements of Administration* (New York: Harper & Row, Publishers, Incorporated, 1944). In a discussion on p. 47, Urwick speaks of "formal" authority as being "conferred by organization," of "technical" authority as being "implicit in special knowledge or skill," and of "personal" authority as being "conferred by seniority or popularity."

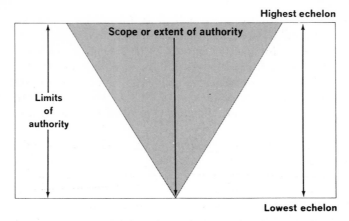

Fig. 4.1 Limits of Authority of Various Echelons of an Organization Structure

pyramid, with the front-line manager at its bottom point. His right to command is severely restricted in every direction. But as one follows the chain of command to the top of the organization structure, the area of authority of the executives at each level gradually expands.

However, the institutional foundation of authority implies that this power is never absolute but that it, like private property, changes with shifts in group behavior. Within an enterprise, the exerciser of authority must remember that his power is limited by the mores of his subordinates. A minority racial group, for example, or a small-town group will each react to authority in its own individual way, while the managerial subordinates and the nonmanagerial employees of a highly organized company may react differently from a group of stockholding subordinates. These, then, are examples of social limitations on the exercise of authority.

There are also biological limitations placed on authority by the fact that human beings do not have the capacity to do certain things; one can hardly, for instance, order a person to walk up the side of a building. Other limitations are physical—climate, geography, physical laws, and chemical elements; an order to make gold from copper would be futile. In addition, there are technological constraints; a factory would not be ordered on the moon—at least not until technology had made this possible. There are also economic limitations on managerial authority: competitor prices and service levels determined by the market, and ownership by a rival of an advantageous resource or location, for example.

There are other diverse and complex limitations upon executive authority. The power to change enterprise objectives and methods is frequently hedged about in partnership agreements and in articles of incorporation. The statutes reserve to stockholders certain broad powers; bylaws frequently delimit authority, as when the power to employ an auditor is reserved to the board of directors; and policies, procedures, and programs further guide action. Obviously, every manager, whether of high or low degree, must respect such restrictions, which affect all managers alike; neither the president nor a superior is ever free to ignore a procedure, violate a policy, or modify a program. Changes can be made, of course, but not at the whim of any individual.

Each manager, in addition, is subject to specific limitations, ordinarily found in the delegation of authority and assignment of duties. A sales manager may, for instance, find his capital expenditures limited to $1,000, his power to adjust wages and salaries limited to a total of $1,000 per month, and his power to discharge an employee nonexistent.

The advertising manager, his subordinate, may be restricted to capital expenditures of $200 and power to adjust employees' salaries to a total of $750 per month. The incidence of restriction thus grows more narrow with each degree of managerial subordination.

RESPONSIBILITY

Responsibility is one of the most misunderstood terms in the literature of management. It is common to hear and read about "delegating responsibilities," "holding a person responsible," "discharging responsibility," and "carrying out a responsibility." Responsibility is variously used to mean duty, activity, or, as has already been noted, authority.

Viewed internally with respect to the enterprise, responsibility may be defined as the obligation of a subordinate, to whom a duty has been assigned, to perform the duty. The essence of responsibility is, then, *obligation.* Responsibility has no meaning except as applied to a person; a building, a machine, or an animal cannot be held responsible.

Responsibility arises from the superior-subordinate relationship, from the fact that someone (in this case, a manager) has the authority to require specified services from another person. This authority in business normally results from a contractual arrangement by which the subordinate agrees to perform such services—perhaps using delegated authority—in return for monetary and other rewards. Thus, authority flows from the superior to the subordinate manager when duties are assigned; and responsibility is the obligation simultaneously exacted from the subordinate for the accomplishment of these duties.

Responsibility may be a continuing obligation, or it may be discharged by a single action and not arise again. The relationship between a president and his sales manager is typical of a continuing obligation; on the other hand, the president may hire, for an organization study, a consulting management engineer whose obligation will cease when the assignment is completed.

A problem in responsibility sometimes arises when informal leadership appears. For example, a sales manager may have as subordinates an advertising manager, a sales promotion manager, and three district sales managers. For many reasons—among them, perhaps, the powerful position of the production manager—some of the sales manager's subordinates may look to the production manager for guidance. This informal relationship may have the effect of reducing the influence and power of the sales manager over his subordinates. Unless this shift is made with the approval of the president or the sales manager—thus constituting a change in the organization structure itself—the basic responsibility relationships would not be changed. The president would still hold the sales manager responsible for the department's performance, and the subordinates would still be responsible to the sales manager.

Responsibility and Delegation Responsibility cannot be delegated. While a manager may delegate to a subordinate authority to accomplish a service and the subordinate, in turn, may delegate a portion of the authority received, neither delegates any of his responsibility. Responsibility, being an obligation to perform, is owed to one's superior, and no subordinate reduces his responsibility by delegating to another the authority to perform a duty.

No manager, then, can shift responsibility to his subordinates. The president employed by the board of directors cannot avoid total responsibility for the conduct of the enterprise. If employees are derelict in their duties, enrage customers, or carry on warfare with a trade union, the president must answer to the board for these things and all other actions of any employee. He cannot claim to have "delegated the responsibility" to a manager, who may, indeed, have caused the trouble.

This inability to delegate responsibility is illustrated by an incident at a company developing a careful financial plan, where a simple arithmetic error made by a clerk affected the projection of cash needs so much that, when discovered, it caused considerable embarrassment. The error was disclosed at the meeting between the board finance committee and bankers arranging the loan. The finance vice-president who had presented the forecast could hardly waive responsibility by explaining that a clerk in a unit of the planning section of the assistant treasurer's office in the treasurer's department had made the error. The finance vice-president was responsible to the board for the mistake, the treasurer was responsible to the vice-president, the assistant treasurer to the treasurer, the planning section chief to the assistant treasurer, the forecast unit head to the planning chief, and the clerk to the forecast unit head. Although authority had been delegated and duties assigned at each level, no one was relieved of his responsibility.

Accountability A few writers in the field of management use the term "accountability" to indicate liability for the proper discharge of duties by the subordinate.[10] The concept of accountability is also widely used in military organizations to indicate the duty of an officer to keep accurate records and

---

[10] R. C. Davis, *The Fundamentals of Top Management* (New York: Harper & Row, Publishers, Incorporated, 1951), pp. 120ff.; E. Petersen and E. G. Plowman, *Business Organization and Management*, 4th ed. (Homewood, Ill.: Richard D. Irwin, Inc., 1958), pp. 72–74; and J. R. Beishline, *Military Management and National Defense* (Englewood Cliffs, N.J.: Prentice-Hall, Inc., 1950), pp. 135–136.

to safeguard public property and funds. Although it may be useful in military organizations, it clearly has strong overtones of a control technique, and, as such, will be covered in the later discussion of this subject.

In this usage accountability means responsibility; and since the latter term has much wider currency in the literature of management, it will be employed here exclusively.

DELEGATION OF AUTHORITY

Just as authority is the key to the manager's job, delegation of authority is the key to organization. The grouping of duties into subdivisions of the enterprise involves delegating authority to perform these duties. Delegation is the process and authority the cement of organization.

The primary purpose of delegation is to make organization possible. Just as no one person in an enterprise can do all the tasks necessary for accomplishment of group purpose, so is it impossible, as an enterprise grows, for one person to exercise all the authority for making decisions. As is shown in Chapter 12, there is a limit to the number of persons a manager can effectively supervise and for whom he can make decisions. Once this limit is passed, authority must be delegated to subordinates who will make decisions within the area of their assigned duties.

Delegation as an Art   Delegation of authority is an elementary art of management.[11] Yet, observation and study of organizations and managerial situations lead to the conclusion that it is not generally well practiced. Many studies of management indicate that a principal reason for the failure of managers lies in their inability to delegate authority.[12]

Like other arts, delegation of authority has certain working rules, or fundamentals, useful in making good delegations. But the mere understanding of principles and techniques will not assure good delegation because the art consists of knowing how and when to use them.

How Authority Is Delegated   Authority is delegated when organization power is vested in a subordinate by a superior. Clearly, no superior can delegate authority he does not have, whether he is a board member, the president, a vice-president, or a foreman. Equally clear, a superior cannot delegate all his authority without, in effect, passing on his position to his subordinate.

The entire process of delegation involves the *assignment* of tasks, the *delegation* of authority for accomplishing these tasks, and the *exaction* of responsibility for their accomplishment. In practice, it is impossible to split

---

[11] For one of the best and most detailed treatises on the process of delegation, see Alvin Brown, *Organization of Industry* (Englewood Cliffs, N.J.: Prentice-Hall, Inc., 1947), chaps. 2–12.

[12] See, for example, the study made by F. J. Gaudet of managerial failures in 200 companies, in which one of the three principal deficiencies was found to be inability to delegate authority. "The Mystery of Executive Talent," *Business Week*, pp. 43–46 (May 21, 1955).

this process, since an assignment of a task without the authority to accomplish it is meaningless, as is the delegation of authority without a definition of the area over which the power is to be used. Moreover, since responsibility cannot be delegated, the delegant has no practical alternative but to exact responsibility from his subordinate for completing the assignment.

Clarity of Delegation   Delegations of authority may be specific or general, written or unwritten, but they must be accompanied by some kind of assignment of duties. If the delegation is unclear, a manager may not understand the nature of his duties. The job assignment of a company treasurer, for example, may specify such functions as accounting, credit control, cash control, financing, export-license handling, and preparation of financial statistics, and these broad functions may even be broken down into more definite duties. Or, a treasurer may be told merely that he is expected to do what treasurers generally do.

Specific written delegations of authority are extremely helpful both to the manager who receives them and to the delegant, who will thereby more easily see conflicts or overlaps with other positions. He will also be able better to isolate those things for which he can and should hold a subordinate responsible.

One top executive claims he never delegates authority but merely tells his subordinate managers to take charge of a department or plant and then holds them responsible for doing so. This particular executive is actually making an extremely broad delegation of authority—that of full power to operate as the subordinates see fit. However, in too many cases where such nonspecific delegations are made, the subordinate is forced to feel his way and—by testing through practice what the superior will stand—define his authority delegation by trial and error. Unless he is very familiar with top company policies and traditions, knows the personality of his boss, and exercises sound judgment, he may be placed at a disadvantage. An executive will do well to balance the costs of uncertainty against the effort to make the delegation specific.

On the other hand, there are those who argue that, especially in the upper levels of management, it is too difficult to make authority delegations specific and that the subordinate, robbed of flexibility, will be unable to develop in the best way. Sometimes, particularly for new top jobs, delegations cannot be very specific, at least at the outset. If a large company establishes for the first time a traffic manager to coordinate transportation activities at its various plants, the president may be unclear about the amount of authority called for. But this situation should be remedied as soon as possible. One of the first duties of the new appointee should be a description of the job and clearance of the description with his superior and, ideally, with those other managers on the same level whose cooperation is necessary. Otherwise, organizational frictions, unnecessary meetings and negotiations, jealousies, and numerous other disadvantages result from vague authority relationships. Too many top executives believe they have a happy team of subordinates who do not need specific authority delegations, when, in fact, they have a dissident group of frustrated managers.

The fear that specific delegations will result in inflexibility is best met by developing a tradition of flexibility. It is true that, if authority delegations are specific, a manager may regard his job as a staked claim with a high fence around it. But this attitude can be eliminated by making necessary changes in organization structure an accepted and expected thing. Much of the inflexibility of definite delegations comes from managerial laziness and failure to reorganize often enough for the smooth accomplishment of objectives.

Splintered Authority   Splintered authority exists wherever a problem cannot be solved or a decision made without pooling the authority delegations of two or more managers. Thus, when the superintendent of plant A sees an opportunity to reduce his costs through a minor modification in procedures in plant B, his authority cannot encompass the change. But if the superintendents of the two plants can agree upon the change and if it affects no other equal or superior manager, all they need do is pool their authority and make the decision. Individually, their authority is said to be "splintered." In day-to-day operations of any company, there are many cases of splintered authority, and probably most managerial conferences are held because of the necessity of pooling authority to make a decision.

As can readily be seen, such problems can be handled by merely referring the decision upward until one person can make it. In the case of the two plant superintendents, it would lie within the authority of the vice-president in charge of manufacturing. However, in many cases, the splinters of authority, although far down in the organization, exist in departments that have their common superior only in the office of the president. For example, one of the authors observed the solution of a problem involving a Western railroad with headquarters in Chicago. The problem was relatively minor, but a decision on it in Los Angeles required the consolidated authority of the traffic department, the operating department, and the public relations department. It could have been referred up the line by each of the managers to the president's office, where sufficient authority for making the decision was concentrated. But if such decisions were always to be handled by upward reference, the president's office would be swamped. In this case, the managers of the three departments in the Los Angeles office met briefly, pooled their delegated authority, and quickly made the decision.

Splintered authority cannot be avoided, especially in making decisions. However, recurring decisions on the same matters may be evidence that authority delegations have not been properly made and that some reorganization is required.

Recovery of Delegated Authority   All delegations of authority are subject to recovery by the grantor. It is a characteristic of authority that the original possessor does not permanently dispossess himself of this power by delegating it. To do so would be to change the basic nature of authority. Just as, in the political area, the right of Americans to change or revoke the Constitution and thus redistribute power is unchallenged, so, in the area of enterprise operation, the right of the manager to recover authority is unquestioned. Delegated authority is frequently recovered when the need arises to modify enterprise objectives, policies, and programs and organization structure, department objectives, and the assignments of personnel.

Reorganization inevitably involves recovery and redelegation of authority. A shuffle in organization means that power is recovered by the responsible head of the firm or a department and then redelegated to managers of new or modified departments, so that the head of a new department may receive the authority formerly held by managers now shorn of many of their powers. For example, when a reorganization takes quality control away from the works manager and assigns it to a new manager of quality control reporting to the vice-president in charge of manufacturing, the vice-president has recovered some of the authority formerly delegated to the works manager and has redelegated it to the new executive. The superior manager also may recover all the formerly delegated authority and then redelegate only part of it, or he may delegate more power to the new man than was exercised by his predecessor.

Centralization and Decentralization Authority delegations may be extensive or very limited. Much authority delegated through the echelons of an organization is referred to as decentralization of authority, while authority is said to be centralized wherever a manager delegates little of it.

A president who delegates little or no authority not only limits the number of managers in his organization but also severely limits its size, since departmentation requires authority delegations and since an executive cannot manage too large an area. On the other hand, extensive delegation of authority makes possible expansion of the enterprise to an appropriate size. The number of subordinates reporting to an executive is then within manageable proportions, permitting the creation of useful positions that do not require too much ability. In other words, authority is limited to that for which an individual may properly be held responsible.

Personal Attitudes toward Delegation Although charting an organization and outlining managerial duties will help in making delegations and knowledge of the principles of delegation will furnish a basis for it, certain personal attitudes lie back of making real delegations.

Receptiveness An underlying attribute of the manager who would delegate authority is a willingness to give other people's ideas a chance. Decision making always involves some discretion, and this means that a subordinate's decision is not likely to be *exactly* that which his superior would have made. The manager who knows how to delegate, as John

Corson[13] has pointed out, must have a minimum of NIH ("not invented here") factor and "must be able not only to welcome the ideas of others but to plant his own ideas in the minds of others and to compliment them on their ingenuity."

Willingness to let go   The manager who would effectively delegate authority must be willing to release decision-making power to his subordinates. A great fault of managers who move up the executive ladder—or of the pioneer who has built a large business from the small beginnings of, say, a garage machine shop—is that they want to continue to make decisions for the positions they have left. The authors have seen corporate presidents and vice-presidents insist upon confirming the appointment of every workman or secretary, not, perhaps, realizing that doing so took time and attention from far more important decisions.

Where size or complexity forces delegation of authority, managers must realize—even if their superiors must go out of their way to teach them—that there is a kind of law of comparative managerial advantage, somewhat like the law of comparative economic advantage that applies to nations. Well known to economists and logically indisputable, the law of comparative economic advantage states that a country's wealth will be enhanced if it exports what it produces most efficiently and imports what it produces less efficiently, even though it could produce such imports more cheaply than any other nation. Likewise, a manager will enhance his contribution to the firm if he concentrates on tasks that contribute most to the firm's objectives and assigns to subordinates other tasks, even though he could accomplish the latter better himself. This is hard to practice, but failure to do so defeats the very purpose of delegation.

Willingness to let others make mistakes   Although no responsible manager would sit idly by and let a subordinate make a mistake that might endanger the company or the subordinate's position in the company, continual checking on the subordinate to assure that no mistakes are ever made will make true delegation impossible. As everyone makes mistakes, a subordinate must be allowed to make them, and their cost must be charged to investment in his development.

Serious or repeated mistakes can be largely avoided without negating delegation or hindering the development of the subordinate. Patient counseling, asking leading or discerning questions, and careful explanation of objectives and policies are among the tools available to the manager who would delegate well. None of these involve discouraging the subordinate by intimidating criticism, harping on shortcomings, or hovering over him.

Willingness to trust subordinates   Closely allied to willingness to let others make mistakes is willingness to trust subordinates. Superiors have no

[13] "How to Delegate Responsibility," *Nation's Business,* p. 86 (May, 1956).

alternative for trusting their subordinates, for delegation implies a trustful attitude between the two. This is sometimes hard to come by. The superior may put off delegation with the thought that the subordinate is not well enough seasoned, that he cannot handle men, that he has not yet developed judgment, or that he does not appreciate all the facts bearing on a situation. Sometimes these thoughts are true, but then the superior should either train subordinates or else select others who are prepared to assume the responsibility. Too often, however, the boss distrusts his subordinates because he does not wish to let go, does not delegate wisely, or does not know how to set up controls to assure proper use of the authority.

Willingness to establish and use broad controls   Since a superior cannot delegate his responsibility for performance, he should not delegate authority unless he is willing to find means ("feedback") of assuring himself that the authority is being used to support enterprise or department goals and plans. As will be noted in later chapters, the establishing of effective controls is one of the more difficult arts of management. Obviously, controls cannot be established and exercised unless goals, policies, and plans are used as basic standards for judging the activities of subordinates. More often than not, reluctance to delegate and to trust subordinates lies in the planning deficiencies of the superior.

Guides for Overcoming Weak Delegation   Fuzzy delegations, partial delegations, pseudo delegations, delegations inconsistent with the results expected, and the hovering of superiors who refuse to allow subordinates to use their authority are among the many widely found weaknesses of delegation of authority.

Combine with these weaknesses untrained, inept, or weak subordinates who go to their bosses for decisions, and subordinates who won't accept responsibility, plus lack of plans, planning information, and incentives, and the failure of delegation is partly explained. But most of the responsibility for weak delegation lies with superiors and, primarily, with top managers, who should furnish an environment of decision for subordinates and select and train them for delegating and being delegated. In overcoming the errors of weak delegation—and emphasizing the principles outlined below—the five following guides are practical in making delegation real:

1. *Define assignments and delegate authority in the light of results expected.* Or, to put it another way, grant authority to make possible the accomplishment of assignments.
2. *Select the man in the light of the job to be done.* This is the purpose of the managerial function of staffing and must be borne in mind, since the qualifications of the man must influence the nature of the delegation of authority. Although the good organizer will approach delegation primarily from the standpoint of the task to be accomplished, he cannot, in the final analysis, ignore the staffing angle.

3. *Maintain open lines of communication.* Since the superior does not delegate all authority, or abdicate his responsibility, and since, therefore, managerial autonomy does not exist, decentralization should not lead to insulation. Because plans change and decisions must be made in the light of changing conditions, delegations tend to be fluid and to be given meaning in the light of such changes. This means that there should be a free flow of information between superior and subordinate, furnishing the subordinate information with which to make decisions and to interpret properly the authority delegated to him.

4. *Establish proper controls.* Because no manager can relinquish his responsibility, delegations should be accompanied by techniques to make sure the authority is properly used. But if controls are not to interfere with delegation, they must be relatively broad and designed to show deviations from plans rather than detailed actions of subordinates.

5. *Reward effective delegation and successful assumption of authority.* It is seldom sufficient to suggest that authority be delegated, or even to order that this be done. Managers should ever be watchful for means of rewarding both effective delegation and effective assumption of authority. Although many of these rewards will be pecuniary, the granting of greater authority and prestige—both in a given position and in promotion to a higher position—is often even more welcome.

PRINCIPLES OF DELEGATION

The following principles are guides to delegation of authority. Unless carefully recognized in practice, delegation may be ineffective, organization may fail, and the managerial process may be seriously impeded.

Principle of functional definition To develop departmentation, activities must be grouped to facilitate the accomplishment of goals; and the manager of each subdivision must have authority to coordinate its activities with the organization as a whole. This gives rise to the principle of functional definition: the more a position or a department has clear definitions of results expected, activities to be undertaken, organization authority delegated, and authority and informational relationships with other positions, the more adequately individuals responsible can contribute toward accomplishing enterprise objectives. To do otherwise is to risk confusion as to what is expected of whom. This principle—which is both a principle of delegation and of departmentation—although simple in concept, is often difficult to apply. To define a job and delegate authority to do it requires, in most cases, patience, intelligence, and clarity of objectives and plans. It is obviously difficult to define a job if the superior himself does not know what he wants done.

Scalar principle The scalar principle refers to the chain of direct authority relationships from superior to subordinate throughout the organization. Ultimate authority must always rest somewhere. The more clear the line of authority from the ultimate authority for management in an enterprise to every subordinate position, the more effective will be the responsible decision making and organization communication. The scale is described by Fayol[14] as

> . . . the chain of superiors ranging from the ultimate authority to the lowest ranks. The line of authority is the route followed—via every link in the chain—by all communications which start from or go to the ultimate authority. This path is dictated both by the need for some transmission and by the principle of unity of command, but it is not always the swiftest. It is even at times disastrously lengthy in large concerns, notably in governmental ones.

A clear understanding of the scalar principle is necessary for proper organization functioning. Every subordinate must know who delegates authority to him, and to whom matters beyond his own authority must be referred. Although the chain of command may be safely departed from for purposes of information, departure for purposes of decision making destroys authority and undermines managership itself.

Authority-level principle Functional definition plus the scalar principle gives rise to the authority-level principle. This principle implies that, at some organization level, authority exists for making any decision within the competence of the enterprise, and that only decisions that cannot be made at a given level should be referred upward. In other words, each manager at each level should make whatever decisions he can in the light of his authority, and only matters that authority limitations keep him from deciding should be referred to his superior.

It is obvious from the authority-level principle that, if a manager wishes to make effective authority delegations and thereby to be relieved from some of the burden of decision making, he must make sure that delegations are clear and that the subordinate understands them. Moreover, he will do well to avoid the temptation to make decisions for subordinates. The superior often delegates decision-making power in matters concerning which he once made the decisions. Having been accustomed to making these decisions, he is strongly tempted to continue to do so. In this way, well-meant authority delegations are often canceled.

Principle of unity of command A basic management principle, often disregarded for what are believed to be compelling circumstances,[15] is that of unity of command. It may be stated: The more completely an individual has a reporting relationship to a single superior, the less the problem of

[14] Henri Fayol, *General and Industrial Administration* (New York: Pitman Publishing Corporation, 1949), p. 14.

[15] Note in chap. 15 the case of functional authority.

conflict in instructions and the greater the feeling of personal responsibility for results. In discussing delegation of authority, it has been assumed that—except for the inevitable instances of splintered authority (see above, page 69)—power over a particular activity will flow from a single superior to a subordinate. Although it is possible for a subordinate to receive authority from two or more superiors and logically possible for him to be held responsible by them, the practical difficulties of serving two or more masters are obvious. An obligation is essentially personal, and authority delegation by more than one person is likely to result in conflicts in both authority and responsibility. Moreover, unless a manager has total authority to hold his subordinate responsible, his position becomes undermined.

The principle of unity of command is useful in the clarification of authority-responsibility relationships. A president, for example, does not normally divide sales activities among sales, manufacturing, public relations, finance, accounting, and personnel, with no single person responsible for them. Instead, since sales is a cohesive activity, he assigns it to the sales manager. Unity of command would not exist if, instead of a single sales manager, the president appointed an executive committee to run the department. To force every major subordinate in the sales department to owe his full obligation to each committee member rather than to one manager would produce confusion, buck passing, and general inefficiency. Similarly, it is undesirable to have several managers assign duties to one employee, who would then be obligated to each of the several managers.

Principle of delegation by results expected   Since authority is intended to furnish managers with a tool for so managing as to gain contributions to enterprise objectives, authority delegated to an individual manager should be adequate to assure his ability to accomplish the results expected of him.[16] Too many managers try to partition and define authority on the basis of the amount of power to be delegated, or withheld, rather than looking first at the job to be done and then determining how much authority is necessary to do it. In no other way can a manager delegate authority in accordance with the responsibility exacted. Often a superior has some idea, vague or fixed, as to what he wants done, but does not trouble to determine whether the subordinate has the authority to do it. Sometimes the superior does not want to admit how much power it takes to do the job, and, reluctant to delegate the needed power, he is likewise reluctant to define the results expected. Perhaps it is no wonder that it has become common in enterprises to speak erroneously of delegating "responsibilities."

Delegation by results expected implies that goals have been set and plans made, that these are communicated and understood, and that jobs have been set up to fit in with them. It also demonstrates that planning is a prerequisite to all the tasks of management, and that the managerial functions in practice coalesce into a single job.

---

[16] On this subject see the excellent work of Edward C. Schleh, *Successful Executive Action* (Englewood Cliffs, N.J.: Prentice-Hall, Inc., 1955), chaps. 21 and 23.

Principle of absoluteness of responsibility As discussed above, since responsibility cannot be delegated, no superior can escape, through delegation, responsibility for the activities of subordinates, for it is he who has delegated authority and assigned duties. Likewise, the responsibility of the subordinate to his superior is absolute once he has accepted an assignment and the power to carry it out.

Principle of parity of authority and responsibility Since authority is the power to carry out assignments and responsibility is the obligation to accomplish them, it logically follows that the authority needed to do this should correspond to the responsibility. This parity is not mathematical but, rather, coextensive, because both relate to the same assignments. The president of a firm may, for example, assign duties, such as buying raw materials and machine tools and hiring subordinates, to his manufacturing vice-president. The vice-president would be unable to perform these duties without being given enough authority to meet his responsibility. Nor should he, on the other hand, have more authority than his responsibilities call for. Managers often try to hold subordinates responsible for duties for which they do not have the requisite authority. This is, of course, unfair. Sometimes sufficient authority is delegated, but the delegant is not held responsible for its proper use. This is, obviously, a case of poor managerial direction and control and has no bearing upon the principle of parity.[17]

Managers are sometimes said to be given authority to do that for which they cannot be held responsible; thus, a sales manager is given authority to sell, but he cannot be responsible for making people buy. The answer to this is that the sales manager has the authority to use certain material and human resources to obtain sales wherever possible. Obviously, no one can hold him responsible for compelling people to buy. Here, parity consists of his responsibility as an executive for managing the sales force in the best possible way, equated with his authority to sell.

AUTHORITY, THE MANAGER, AND LEADERSHIP

As the key to the managerial job, authority clothes the manager with the recognized right to direct subordinates to carry out activities consistent with achieving enterprise objectives. Centralization of direction avoids the chaotic condition that would permit subordinates to act as they please or to give orders helter-skelter to one another. Furthermore, without the right to direct, there would be no managing and the job of manager would disappear.

In pointing out the central role of authority in making organization and managership possible and recognizing authority as a right to command or

---

[17] For a discussion of this point, see L. Urwick, *Notes on the Theory of Organization* (New York: American Management Association, 1952). Urwick quotes C. I. Barnard as one of those who challenge the principle of parity of authority and responsibility on the ground that individuals are often placed in a position where they have responsibility but cannot have authority.

act, it must be emphasized that the existence of authority does not imply authoritarian use of it. A manager may literally order his subordinates, or he may ask, suggest, persuade, or cajole them; he may also use such techniques of direction as counseling, teaching, suggesting, or allowing a decision to arise naturally from a discussion. But regardless of how the authority is applied, the manager must have it, and its dispersal in the organization must be coordinated. Managers, to be effective, cannot and should not shy away from the fact of their having authority. Managers who find authority distasteful and pose as operating "democratically" seldom deceive subordinates, who readily understand that their chief has, and must have, certain powers of decision that can affect their jobs.

The manager exercises his authority as he carries out his functions. He requires subordinates to carry out plans and measures their achievements; he decides upon the organizational structure and places men in charge of grouped activities. He cannot be a manager without subordinates.

Subordinates respond to direction in all organized activities. They respond because, on balance, they stand to gain net advantages in meeting their physical, social, and psychic needs. Disregard of authority tends to exclude them from the enterprise. In a democratic society, they may be free to join another cooperative group, but here also they would be required to deal with superiors. Even with numbers large enough to revolt successfully, a new cooperative arrangement would develop, requiring response to superiors who would ultimately obtain authority from a majority of the members of the society.

Moreover, it is sometimes overlooked that the most essential use of managerial authority is to give the manager the means by which he can create and maintain an environment for performance. By having the power either to specify or to work out meaningful goals with subordinates, to give them the power in turn to accomplish these goals and the means and assistance to do so, to give them training and understanding of their role in the enterprise and of their relationships to others, and to reward them through promotion, pay increases, and improved status, the manager is truly using authority in a creative way.

Authority is not a social invention to give people power for prestige or authoritarian conduct, but an instrument to place in an organizational role the means of doing something creative. It behooves the intelligent manager never to forget this simple fact.

It was pointed out earlier, in discussing the acceptance theory, that managers must have leadership ability. A manager's real success depends on his ability to influence his subordinates, thereby getting things done through people. In other words, able managing usually gives rise to a situation in which subordinates find that their best interests lie in following superiors they can respect.

However, the purpose of authority is to make sure that plans will be coordinated and tasks assigned to persons able to do them. Good employees respond best to leaders who plan soundly; organize clearly; select, train, and direct subordinates well; and bring plans to fruition. Undue emphasis on human relations often befogs the fact that the best human relations grow out of successful group accomplishment. This is not to regard interpersonal relations and the human element as other than extremely important aspects of the managerial job. But managerial leadership requires much more than smooth interpersonal relationships.

Most of the aspects and techniques of leadership are encompassed in the managerial function of direction, which will be discussed in later chapters.

FOR DISCUSSION

1. When you are accepted for a position, what authority are you agreeing to obey? Can you later take back your agreement to abide by this authority?

2. Cite several ways in which the word "responsibility" is used in practice.

3. It has been said that a person is responsible for "things," not "people." Do you agree?

4. What use do you think the word "accountability" serves?

5. How can authority be used creatively?

SELECTED REFERENCES

Allen, L. A.: *Management and Organization,* chaps. 6–7, New York: McGraw-Hill Book Company, 1958.

Barnard, C. I.: *The Functions of the Executive,* chap. 12, Cambridge, Mass.: Harvard University Press, 1938.

Benne, K. D.: *A Conception of Authority,* Contributions to Education No. 895, New York: Bureau of Publications, Teachers College, Columbia University, 1943.

Brown, W.: "What Is Work?" *Harvard Business Review,* vol. 40, no. 5, pp. 121–129 (September–October, 1962).

Dale, E.: "Management Must Be Made Accountable," *Harvard Business Review,* vol. 38, no. 2 (March–April, 1960).

Friedrich, C. J.: *Authority,* Cambridge, Mass.: Harvard University Press, 1958.

Laird, D. A., and E. C. Laird: *The Techniques of Delegating,* New York: McGraw-Hill Book Company, 1957.

Newman, W. H.: "Overcoming Obstacles to Effective Delegation," *Management Review,* vol. 45, no. 1, pp. 36–41 (January, 1956).

———— and C. E. Summer, Jr.: *The Process of Management,* chap. 4, Englewood Cliffs, N.J.: Prentice-Hall, Inc., 1961.

O'Donnell, C.: "The Source of Managerial Authority," *Political Science Quarterly,* vol. 67, no. 4 (December, 1952).

Petersen, E., and E. G. Plowman: *Business Organization and Management,* 4th ed., chap. 3, Homewood, Ill.: Richard D. Irwin, Inc., 1958.

Pfiffner, J. M., and F. P. Sherwood: *Administrative Organization,* chap. 11, Englewood Cliffs, N.J.: Prentice-Hall, Inc., 1960.

Schleh, E. C.: *Management by Results,* chap. 2, New York: McGraw-Hill Book Company, 1961.

————: *Successful Executive Action,* chap. 2, Englewood Cliffs, N.J.: Prentice-Hall, Inc., 1955.

part two

PLANNING

The reader is now familiar with the development of basic management theory and is oriented to the five managerial functions: planning, organizing, staffing, directing, and controlling. The six chapters on planning which follow form Part 2 of the book.

Planning is the most basic of all management functions since it involves selection from among alternative courses of action for the enterprise as a whole and for every department and person in it. Not only is planning a basic function for *all* managers at *all* levels in the enterprise, but the four other functions of the manager must reflect it. Thus a manager organizes, staffs, directs, and controls to assure the attainment of goals according to plans.

Planning involves selection of enterprise and departmental objectives and goals as well as determination of the means of reaching them. It is thus the provision of a rational approach to preselected objectives and goals. Since this approach does not take place in a vacuum, good planning must consider the nature of the future in which planning decisions and actions are intended to operate.

In the first chapter of this part, the reasons for planning and the general kinds of plans are explained. The logical process of planning is discussed and attention is given to such practical matters as the length of time into the future for which a manager should plan.

This is followed by a chapter on objectives—the end points of planning, the determination of which decides the basic nature of total planned action and, through a hierarchy of derivative goals, determines a host of supporting plans which are developed by the component units of the organization.

Plans are made to operate in the future. Therefore, a key part of planning is the establishment of clear planning premises. To assure coordination among all managers who make plans in a given organization, these premises should be used by all concerned. Premises guide planning. They spell out the "stage" of the expected future events which is believed will exist when plans operate. They are the expected environment of plans. Chapter 7 gives the reader a clear view of "premising" in management, including methods of making these important planning determinants clear to enterprise planners.

The next chapter of this part analyzes the decision-making process, which is an essential part of planning. Of course, every manager must make decisions throughout his working life. But decisions are at the core of planning since they represent that part of the process where a selection is made of a course of future action. Therefore, decision making is treated in the planning section of this book rather than elsewhere. As will be seen, one of the major developments in decision making is the increasing use of the research methodology of the physical sciences and a greater reliance on mathematics.

Policy formulation is the subject of Chapter 9. Policies, written or unwritten, may be thought of quite simply as guides to thinking in decision making. They act as guidelines so that all managers in an organization make consistent decisions that contribute to the achievement of goals in an orderly and accurate way. Unfortunately, there is often confusion about policy. Some believe policy should never be broken even for very good reasons unless the policy is revised first. Others feel that policy can be written so that it allows for logical exceptions. This conflict often leads to confusion in management. Therefore, considerable attention is paid to the development of clear company policies and to practical methods of making them effective.

The last chapter of this part deals with some of the major considerations involved in putting plans into action, such as coordination of plans, communication for planning, the importance of getting participation in making plans, and the use of financial forecasts as tools to summarize and view plans. The problems of limitations in plans and the difficulties encountered in making plans operate effectively are analyzed and suggestions are offered as to the major elements necessary for an effective planning environment.

the nature and purpose of planning

The most basic of management functions is planning, the selection from among alternatives of future courses of action for the enterprise as a whole and each department within it. Every manager plans and his other functions depend upon his planning. Plans involve selecting enterprise objectives and departmental goals and programs and determining ways of reaching them. Plans thus provide a rational approach to preselected objectives.

As Billy E. Goetz[1] has said, planning is "fundamentally choosing" and "a planning problem arises only when an alternative course of action is discovered." In this range, it is essentially decision making, although, as will be seen, it is also more than this. Indeed, actual and final choosing between alternatives may be the easiest part of planning. Planning depends on the existence of alternatives, and there are few business decisions for which some kind of alternative does not exist—even when it comes to meeting legal or other requirements imposed by forces beyond the manager's control.

Planning is deciding in advance what to do, how to do it, when to do it, and who is to do it. Planning bridges the gap from where we are to where we want to go. It makes it possible for things to occur which would not otherwise happen. Although the exact future can seldom be predicted and factors beyond control may interfere with the best-laid plans, without planning events are left to chance. Planning is an intellectual process, the conscious determination of courses of action, the basing of decisions on purpose, facts, and considered estimates.

A strong aspect of the managerial revolution of the past two decades has been a tremendous interest in planning by all forms of enterprise—business, government, education, and others. Note that this strong interest in

[1] Billy E. Goetz, *Management Planning and Control* (New York: McGraw-Hill Book Company, 1949), p. 2.

planning is primarily a phenomenon of the past two decades, although in areas such as factory operations production planning has been stressed for a half century. Production managers found early that, without planning, their mistakes showed up within days as production lines came to a halt through a misfit part or the absence of a needed component. Also, well-managed companies have long planned to meet cash needs before their checks bounced. But, generally speaking, planning as a widely recognized and actively pursued managerial function is a recent development.

Now, nearly everyone plans. Enterprises of all kinds plan further into the future, plan more aspects of their operations, plan less by intuition or hunch, and lean more heavily on forecasts and studies. In fact, a few years ago, an economic consulting firm advising a large company board stated that the development of business planning has been as revolutionary a movement as the technological revolution or the revolution in expansion of income.

We are in an economic, technological, social, and political era in which planning, like the other functions of managers, has become requisite for enterprise survival. Change and economic growth bring opportunities, but they also bring risk, particularly in an era of world-wide rivalry for markets, resources, and influence. It is exactly the task of planning to minimize risk while taking advantage of opportunities.

With all the interest in planning and all the sense of urgency brought about by modern supercompetition, there is danger that planning could become merely a costly fad, not very useful, and even disillusioning. To plan well, to make plans that will succeed, planning—again, like the other managerial functions—must take place in a context of fundamental principles.

THE NATURE OF PLANNING

The essential nature of planning can be understood through four basic planning principles: contribution to objectives, primacy of planning, pervasiveness of planning, and efficiency of plans.

Contribution to Objectives The purpose of every plan and all derivative plans is to contribute positively toward the accomplishment of enterprise objectives. This principle derives from the nature of organized enterprise, which exists for the accomplishment of group purpose through deliberate cooperation. This principle was emphasized by Goetz when he said:[2]

> Plans alone cannot make an enterprise successful. Action is required; the enterprise must operate. Plans can, however, focus action on purposes. They can forecast which actions will tend toward the ultimate objective . . . , which tend away, which will likely offset one another, and which are merely irrelevant. Managerial planning seeks to achieve a consistent, co-ordinated structure of operations focused on desired ends. Without plans, action must become merely random activity, producing nothing but chaos.

[2] *Ibid.,* p. 63.

Primacy of Planning Since managerial operations in organizing, staffing, directing, and controlling are designed to support the accomplishment of enterprise objectives, planning is the primary requisite of these functions. Although all the functions intermesh, planning is unique in that it establishes the objectives necessary for all group effort. Besides, plans must be made to accomplish these objectives before the manager knows what kind of organization relationships and personal qualifications are needed, along which course subordinates are to be directed, and what kind of control is to be applied. And, of course, each of the other managerial functions must be planned if they are to be effective.

Planning and control are inseparable—the Siamese twins of management. Unplanned action cannot be controlled, for control involves keeping subordinates on course by correcting deviations from plans. Any attempt to control without plans would be meaningless, since there is no way anyone can tell whether he is going where he wants to go—the task of control—unless first he knows where he wants to go—the task of planning. Plans thus furnish the standards of control.

Pervasiveness of Planning Although, by definition, all managerial functions pervade all managerial jobs, and therefore this is not a principle peculiar to planning, pervasiveness of planning needs especially to be emphasized. Planning is a function of every manager, although the character and breadth of planning will vary with his authority and the nature of policies and plans outlined by his superior. It is virtually impossible so to circumscribe his area of choice that he can exercise no discretion, and unless he has some planning responsibility, it is doubtful that he is truly a manager.

Recognition of the pervasiveness of planning goes far in clarifying the attempt on the part of some students of management to distinguish between policy making (the setting of guides for thinking in decision making) and administration, or between the "manager" and the "administrator" or "supervisor." One manager, because of his authority delegation or position in the organization, may do more planning or more important planning than another, or the planning of one may be more basic and applicable to a larger portion of the enterprise than that of another. However, all managers—from presidents to foremen—plan. The foreman of a road gang or a factory crew plans in a limited area under fairly strict orders and procedures. Interestingly, in studies of work satisfactions, a principal factor found to account for the success of supervisors at the lowest organization level has been their ability to plan.[3]

Efficiency of Plans The efficiency of a plan is measured by the amount it contributes to objectives as offset by the costs and other unsought conse-

[3] D. Katz et al., *Productivity, Supervision and Morale among Railroad Workers* (Ann Arbor, Mich.: Survey Research Center, Institute for Social Research, University of Michigan, 1951).

quences required to formulate and operate it.[4] A plan can contribute to the attainment of objectives, but at too high or unnecessarily high costs. This concept of efficiency implies the normal ratio of input to output, but goes beyond the usual understanding of inputs and outputs in terms of dollars, man-hours, or units of production to include such values as individual and group satisfactions.

Many managers have followed plans, such as in the acquisition of certain aircraft by airlines, where costs were greater than the revenues obtainable. Companies have inefficiently attempted to attain objectives in the face of the unsought consequence of market unacceptability, as happened when a motorcar manufacturer tried to capture a postwar market by emphasizing engineering without competitive advances in style. Plans may also become inefficient in the attainment of objectives by jeopardizing group satisfactions. The new president of a company that was losing money attempted quickly to reorganize and cut expenses by wholesale and unplanned layoffs of key personnel. The result in fear, resentment, and loss of morale led to so much lower productivity as to defeat his laudable objective of eliminating losses and making profits. And many attempts to install management appraisal and development programs have failed because of group resentment of the methods used, regardless of whether these methods, if accepted, would have developed a better management.

TYPES OF PLANS

Identifying the types of plans in the typical enterprise illustrates the breadth of planning. They may be classified as objectives, policies, procedures, rules, programs, budgets, grand strategies, and competitive strategies.

Objectives Objectives, or goals, are the ends toward which activity is aimed. They represent not only the end point of planning, but, as has been noted, the end toward which organizing, staffing, directing, and controlling are aimed. While enterprise objectives constitute the basic plan of the firm, a department may also have objectives or goals. The goals of a department naturally contribute to the attainment of enterprise objectives, but the two sets of goals may be entirely different. Thus, if the objective of a business is to make a profit in electronics, the goal of the manufacturing department might be to produce the required number of television sets of a given design and quality at the lowest possible cost. These objectives are consistent, but they differ in that the manufacturing department alone cannot assure a profit.

The nature of objectives and their relationship to planning are discussed

---

[4] The authors are indebted to Chester I. Barnard for having so clearly pointed out the applicability of concepts of effectiveness and efficiency to systems of human cooperation. See *The Functions of the Executive* (Cambridge, Mass.: Harvard University Press, 1938), pp. 19–20.

in the following chapter. It is enough to emphasize here that objectives, or goals, are plans, that they involve the same planning process as any other type of planning, even though they are at the same time end points of planning. A profit goal, for example, cannot be guessed at or wished but needs to be determined in the light of purpose and circumstances. Likewise, a plan to accomplish a certain profit goal will have within it, or as derivatives of it, project or departmental goals.

Policies   Policies, also, may be thought of as plans. Policies are general statements or understandings which guide or channel thinking in decision making of subordinates. One can hardly refer to all policies as "statements," since they are often merely implied from the actions of managers. Although many policies are stated verbally, others simply grow, like Topsy. The president of a company, for example, may strictly follow—perhaps for convenience rather than as policy—the practice of promoting from within; the practice may then be interpreted as policy and rigorously followed by his subordinates. In fact, one of the problems of the manager is to make sure that subordinates do not interpret as policy minor decisions which he makes without intending them to serve as precedents.

Policies delimit an area within which a decision is to be made and assure that the decision will be consistent with and contributive to objectives. Policies tend to predecide issues, avoid repeated analysis and consideration of general courses of action, and give a unified structure to other types of plans, thus permitting managers to delegate authority while maintaining control. For example, a certain railroad has the policy of acquiring industrial land to replace all acreage sold along its right of way. This permits the manager of the land department to develop his acquisition plans without continual reference to top management, which is nevertheless furnished with a standard of control.

Both policies and objectives guide thinking and action, but with a difference. Objectives are end points of planning, while policies channel decisions along the way to these ends; or, to put it another way, policies lead to objectives, the way a series of alternate highway routes lead to a city.

Policies ordinarily have at least as many levels as organization, ranging from major company policies through major departmental policies to minor or derivative policies applicable to the smallest segment of the organization. They may also be related to functions—such as sales and finance—or merely to a project—such as that of designing a new product with materials to meet a specified competition.

The varieties of policies are legion. Examples are company policies to promote from within, to conform strictly to a high standard of business ethics, to compete on a price basis, to insist on fixed rather than cost-plus pricing, to forsake civilian business for military, or to shun publicity; department policies to hire only university-trained engineers, to require adherence to lunch-hour schedules, or to encourage employee suggestions for improved cooperation.

Being guides to thinking in decision making, it follows that true policies must allow for some discretion. Otherwise, they would be rules. Too often policies are established as a kind of Ten Commandments which leave no room for discretion. Although the discretion area, in some instances, is quite broad, it can be exceedingly narrow. For example, a policy to buy from the lowest of three qualified bidders leaves for discretion only the question of which bidders are qualified; a policy to buy from a certain company, regardless of price or service, becomes a rule.

Because policies are so often misunderstood, the authors have selected examples from a company's policy manual. It will be noted in each case that there is an area for a person in a decision-making capacity to use discretion. The following are interesting examples.

1. Gifts from suppliers. Except for token gifts of purely nominal or advertising value, no employee shall accept any gift or gratuity from any supplier at any time.
2. Entertainment. No officer or employee shall accept favors or entertainment from an outside organization or agency which are substantial enough to cause undue influence in his selection of goods or services for the company.
3. Outside employment. It is improper for any employee to work for any company customers, or for any competitors, or for any vendors or suppliers of goods or services to the company; outside employment is further prohibited if it: (a) results in a division of loyalty to the company or a conflict of interests, or (b) interferes with or adversely affects the employee's work or opportunity for advancement in the company.
4. Pricing. Each territorial division manager may establish such prices for the products under his control as he deems in the division's interest so long as (a) these prices result in gross profit margins for any line of products which are consistent with his approved profit plan; (b) price reductions will not result in detrimental effects on prices of similar products of another company division in another state or country; and (c) prices meet the legal requirements of the state or country in which the prices are effective.

As will be noted, the area of discretion in most of these policies is fairly general. However, in the pricing policy shown, the discretion area is fairly specifically defined. Likewise, in the outside employment policy, that portion dealing with employment with any vendors or suppliers leaves no discretion and is, consequently, a rule.

Subordinates should interpret policy through the exercise of initiative as well as discretion. The amount of freedom possible will naturally depend upon the policy, which in turn reflects position and authority in the organization. The president of a company with a policy of aggressive price competition has a broad area of discretion and initiative in which to interpret

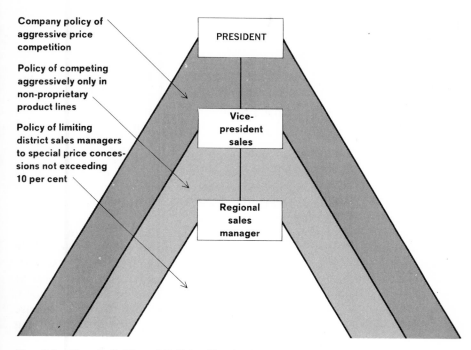

Company policy of aggressive price competition

Policy of competing aggressively only in non-proprietary product lines

Policy of limiting district sales managers to special price concessions not exceeding 10 per cent

PRESIDENT

Vice-president sales

Regional sales manager

Fig. 5.1   How Definition of Policies May Be Successively Limiting

and apply this policy. The district sales manager abides by the same basic policy, but the interpretations made by the president, the vice-president for sales, and the regional sales manager become derivative policies which narrow his scope to where, for example, he may be permitted only to approve a special sale price to meet competition not exceeding a 10 per cent reduction.

Making policies consistent and integrated enough to facilitate the realization of enterprise objectives is difficult for many reasons. First, policies are too seldom written and their exact interpretations too little known. Second, the very delegation of authority that policies are intended to implement leads, through its decentralizing influence, to widespread participation in policy making and interpretation, with almost certain variations among individuals. Third, it is not always easy to control policy, in the sense of comparing actual policy with intended policy, because actual policy may be difficult to ascertain and intended policy not always clear.

Procedures   Procedures are plans in that they establish a customary method of handling future activities. They are truly guides to action rather than to thinking, and they detail the exact manner in which a certain activity must be accomplished. Their essence is chronological sequence of required actions.

Their pervasiveness in the organization is readily apparent. The board of directors follows many procedures quite different from those of the foremen; the expense account of the vice-president goes through quite different approval procedures from that of the salesman; the procedures for carrying out vacation and sick-leave provisions may vary considerably at various levels of organization. But the important fact is that procedures exist throughout an organization, even though, as one might expect, they become more exacting and numerous in the lower levels, largely because of the necessity for more careful control, the economic advantages of spelling out actions in detail, the reduced need for discretion, and the fact that routine jobs lend themselves to obtaining greater efficiency through prescription of the one best way.

As in other types of plans, procedures have a hierarchy of importance. Thus, in a typical corporation, one may find a manual of "Corporation Standard Practice," outlining procedures for the corporation as a whole, a manual of "Division Standard Practice," and special sets of procedures for a department, a branch, a section, or a unit.

Procedures often cut across department lines. For example, in a manufacturing company, the procedure for handling orders will almost certainly encompass the sales department (for the original order), the finance department (for acknowledgment of receipt of funds and for customer credit determination), the accounting department (for recording the transaction), the production department (for order to produce or authority to release from stock), and the traffic department (for determination of the shipping means and route).

The relationship between procedures and policies may best be indicated by a few examples. Company policy may grant employees two-week annual vacations; procedures established to implement this policy will schedule vacations to avoid disruption of work, set methods and rates of vacation pay, maintain records to assure each employee a vacation, and provide means of applying for the vacation. A company may have a policy of shipping orders quickly; particularly in a large company, careful procedures will be necessary to assure that the orders are handled expeditiously. Company policy may require clearance by the public relations department of public utterances by its employees; to implement this policy, procedures must be established to obtain clearance with a minimum of inconvenience and delay.[5]

Rules Rules are plans in that they are a course of required actions which, like other plans, are chosen from among alternatives. They are usually the simplest type of plan.

Rules are frequently confused with policies or procedures, although they are entirely distinct. A rule requires that a specific and definite action be taken or not taken with respect to a situation. It is thus related to a procedure, in that it guides action, but it specifies no time sequence. A rule may or may not be part of a procedure. For example, "no smoking" is a rule

---

[5] For an excellent study of procedures, see Richard F. Neuschel, *Management by System* (New York: McGraw-Hill Book Company, 1960).

quite unrelated to any procedure; but a procedure governing the handling of orders may incorporate the rule that all orders must be confirmed the day they are received. This rule allows no deviation from a stated course of action and in no way interferes with the procedure for handling orders. It is comparable to a rule that all fractions over half an ounce are to be counted a full ounce or that receiving inspection must count or weigh all materials against the purchase order. The essence of a rule is that it reflects a managerial decision that certain action be taken—or not be taken.

Rules should also be distinguished from policies. The purpose of policies is to guide thinking in decision making by marking off areas of discretion. Although rules also serve as guides, they may be distinguished from policies in that they allow no discretion in their application.

Programs Programs are a complex of policies, procedures, rules, task assignments, and other elements necessary to carry out a given course of action; they are ordinarily supported by necessary capital and operating budgets. Programs may be as major as that of an airline to acquire a 200-million-dollar fleet of jets, or the five-year program embarked upon by the Ford Motor Company several years ago to improve the status and quality of its thousands of foremen. Or they may be as minor as a program formulated by a single foreman in a parts manufacturing department of a farm machinery company to improve the morale of his workers.

A primary program may call for many derivative programs. For example, an airline program to invest in new jets, costing many millions of dollars for the aircraft and the necessary spare parts, requires many derivative programs if the investment is to be properly used. A program for providing the maintenance and operating bases with spare components and parts must be developed in detail. Special maintenance facilities must be prepared and maintenance personnel trained. Pilots and flight engineers must also be trained, and, if the new jets mean a net addition to flying hours, flight personnel recruited. Flight schedules must be revised and ground-station personnel trained to handle the new airplanes and their schedules as service is expanded to new cities in the airline's system. Advertising programs must give adequate publicity to the new service. Plans to finance the aircraft and provide for insurance coverage must be developed.

These and other programs must be devised and effected before any new aircraft are received and placed in service. Furthermore, all these programs necessitate coordination and timing, since the failure of any part of this network of derivative plans means delay for the major program with consequent unnecessary costs and loss of revenues. Some of the programs, particularly those involving the hiring and training of personnel, can be accomplished *too soon* as well as too late, since needless expense results from employees being available and trained before their services are required.

Thus one seldom finds that a program of any importance in business planning stands by itself. It is usually a part of a complex structure of programs, depending upon some and affecting others. This interdependence of plans makes planning very difficult. The results of poor or inadequate planning are seldom isolated, for planning is only as strong as its weakest link. Even a seemingly unimportant procedure or rule, if badly conceived, may wreck an important program. Coordinated planning requires extraordinarily exacting managerial skill.

Budgets A budget as a plan is a statement of expected results expressed in numerical terms. It may be referred to as a "numberized" program. It may be expressed either in financial terms or in terms of man-hours, units of product, machine-hours, or any other numerically measurable term. It may deal with operations, as does the expense budget; it may reflect capital outlays, as does the capital expenditures budget; or it may show flow of cash, as does the cash budget.

Since budgets are also control devices, the principal discussion of them is reserved for the chapters on control. However, *making* a budget is clearly planning and is the fundamental planning instrument in many companies. A budget forces a company to make in advance—whether for a week or five years—a numerical compilation of expected cash flow, expenses and revenues, capital outlays, or man- or machine-hour utilization. The budget is necessary for control, but it cannot serve as a sensible standard of control unless it reflects plans.

Although a budget usually implements a program, it may actually be a program. One of the authors recalls a company in difficult financial straits installing an elaborate budgetary control program, designed not only to control expenditures but to instill cost consciousness in managing. A budget may also encompass the entire enterprise program, with all other programs reflected in it.

Grand Strategies "Strategies" is increasingly being used as a term to cover the over-all general plan of an enterprise or a major portion of it, or a major project within it. Thus Anthony[6] defines them as resulting from ". . . the process of deciding on objectives of the organization, on changes in these objectives, on the resources used to attain these objectives, and on the policies that are to govern the acquisition, use, and disposition of these resources." While such grand strategies may encompass or reflect competitive strategies, to be dealt with presently, they need not necessarily do so. Their main meaning and usefulness are to describe a type of planning program of a broad nature which gives over-all direction to the other and more detailed programs of an enterprise. The emphasis in grand strategies is on the pattern of basic objectives and goals and the major policies and plans for achieving them.

Thus, a company may have an objective of profitable growth at a certain percentage in, say, five years. Tied in with this and supportive to it will

[6] R. N. Anthony, *Planning and Control Systems: A Framework for Analysis* (Boston: Division of Research, Harvard Business School, 1965), p. 24.

be a determination that the company will be of a certain kind, such as a transportation company rather than a railroad company, or a container company rather than merely a paper box company. In addition, included in a grand strategy might be such major policies as one to market directly to industrial customers through its own sales organization and to seek to design and produce proprietary products with enough differentiation (real or, through marketing approaches, in the "beholder's eye") so as not to be exactly competitive with other similar products. The grand strategy might also include policies on whether the company would have a full product line, as General Motors decided to have years ago in the automobile business, or a specialized product line. It might further give direction to the extent of innovation and research the company intends to follow, its basic thinking on decentralization of authority to integrated divisions, how expansion will be financed, and other broad major policy matters.

The purpose of grand strategies, then, is to determine and communicate, through a system of major objectives and policies, a picture of what kind of enterprise is envisioned. They do not attempt to outline *how* the enterprise is to become this, since that is the task of countless major and minor supporting programs. But, as can be readily seen, a framework of the kind contemplated in grand strategies is a useful type of plan to guide company thinking. It really includes no new basic types of plans within it. It is actually a type of program. But the usefulness of the concept in practice and its importance in guiding planning justify its separation as a type of plan.

Competitive Strategies These may be regarded as interpretative planning, or plans made in the light of the plans of a competitor. Competition, as defined here, exists where two or more persons strive for the same goals under conditions in which not all can gain them. If a manager develops plans without regard to what his competitors are doing, he may find that even sound projections will go astray. In a sense, plans of competitors are part of the background against which a top manager must plan, but strategies become a special kind of plan because of being based on the projected action of competitors.

Obviously, the best kind of strategy can be developed when the manager has complete knowledge of his competitor's plans. He can then weigh his own plans in the light of his competitor's, modify them to take advantage of what his competitor is planning, and reach his own goals (say, maximum profits) with greater certainty. However, without a fairly thorough system of industrial espionage, the manager may not know his competitor's plans. He must then undertake to put himself in his competitor's place, develop a set of plans *for* his competitor, estimate this program in the light of objectives and the circumstances in which the competitor is operating, and then modify his own plans accordingly.

Although strategic planning is most apparent in competition between companies, many internal planning situations call for strategies. A manager may seek favorable treatment for a plan, such as to acquire a new production machine, only to find that he is competing with another manager, who wants to use capital funds for a new research laboratory. Since planning is often too inexact for a determination of whether one plan will help reach an enterprise goal better than another plan, opportunities arise for internal strategy.

THE IMPORTANCE OF PLANNING

Without planning, business decisions would become random, *ad hoc* choices, as though a pilot set out without knowing whether he wished to fly to London, Hong Kong, or Johannesburg. Four concrete reasons for the paramount importance of the planning function are: to offset uncertainty and change, to focus attention on objectives, to gain economical operation, and to facilitate control.

To Offset Uncertainty and Change   Future uncertainty and change make planning a necessity. Just as the navigator cannot set a course once and forget about it, so the business manager cannot establish his goal and let the matter rest. Comparative certainty may eliminate all but one alternative course of action and reduce planning to the minor function of confirming this obvious course. But the future is seldom very certain, and the further in the future the results of a decision must be considered, the less the certainty. An executive may feel quite certain that within the next month orders, costs, productive capacity, output, cash availability, and other factors of the business environment will be at a given level. A fire, an unforeseen strike, or an order cancellation by a major customer could change all this, but in the short run this is unlikely. However, as this manager plans further in advance, his certainty about the internal and external business environment diminishes. With increased uncertainty, possible alternative actions increase in number, and the rightness of any decision becomes less sure.

However, even when the future is highly certain, some planning is usually necessary. In the first place, there is the necessity of selecting, from among a number of alternatives, the best way to accomplish an objective. With conditions of certainty, this becomes primarily a mathematical problem of calculating, on the basis of the known facts, which course will yield the desired result at the least cost. In the second place, after the course has been decided, it is necessary to lay out plans so that each part of the business will contribute toward the job to be done.

Even when trends indicating change are easily discernible, difficult planning problems arise. The manufacture of kitchen stoves is a case in point. The change away from coal and wood burners did not take place overnight. The manufacturer of a half century ago had to determine what percentage of his production should be assigned to the new burners and what to the old and how to retain efficient production of both lines. There came a time when the declining business of old burners became uneconomical, an obvious cutoff point. However, the manufacturer could have chosen an entirely different course. Having satisfied himself of the certainty of change, he might have deliberately sacrificed old-burner business in order to concentrate on the design and development of new burners, with the hope of becoming the leader among gas- and electric-stove manufacturers.

When trends are not easily discernible, good planning can be even more difficult. Many businessmen missed the significance of heavy government expenditures, pent-up demand, extensive savings, and rapid population growth following World War II. The major recession they expected did not occur, with the result that—through underexpansion of capital facilities and lack of readiness for new markets—they missed opportunities for profit.

To Focus Attention on Objectives   Because all planning is directed toward achieving enterprise objectives, the very act of planning focuses attention on these objectives. Well-considered over-all plans unify interdepartmental activities and consequently restrict the area of freedom in the development of purely departmental plans. Managers, being typically immersed in immediate problems, are forced through planning to consider the future and even consider the periodic need to revise and extend plans in the interest of objectives.

To Gain Economical Operation   Planning minimizes costs because of the emphasis on efficient operation and consistency. It substitutes joint directed effort for uncoordinated piecemeal activity, even flow of work for uneven flow, and deliberate decisions for snap judgments.

The economy of planning is plainly seen at the production level. No one who has watched the assembly of automobiles in one of the larger factories can fail to be impressed with the way that the parts and subassemblies come together. From one overhead conveyor system comes a body and from others various appurtenances. Exactly the right engine, transmission, and accessories fall into place at the exact appointed time. This implies extensive detailed planning without which the manufacture of automobiles would be chaotic and impossibly costly. Although every manager sees the imperative economy of planning at the production level, planning of equal or sometimes greater importance in other areas is occasionally left to chance and too great individual discretion.

To Facilitate Control   The importance of planning for purposes of control has already been mentioned. A manager cannot check on his subordinates' accomplishments without having planned goals against which to measure. As a top executive told one of the authors, "After I leave my office at five o'clock in the evening, I will not care what happened today, for I cannot do anything about it; I will only care about what will happen tomorrow or the next day or next year, because I can do something about it." Perhaps this is an extreme position, but it emphasizes the point that effective control is that which looks to the future.

STEPS IN PLANNING

Although the steps in logical planning are presented here in connection with major programs such as the acquisition of a plant or a fleet of jets or the development of a product, essentially the same steps must be followed in any thorough planning. As minor plans are usually simpler, certain of the steps are more easily accomplished, but the following six practical steps are of general application. Obviously, the discriminating manager would not use 100 dollars worth of time to make a decision worth 50 cents, but what is shocking is to see 50 cents worth of time used to make a planning decision involving millions of dollars.

Being Aware of Opportunity Although preceding actual planning and therefore not strictly a part of the planning process, awareness of an opportunity[7] is the real starting point for planning. It includes a preliminary look at possible future opportunities and the ability to see them clearly and completely, a knowledge of where we stand and our strengths and weaknesses, an understanding of why we wish to solve uncertainties, and a vision of what we expect to gain. Setting realistic objectives depends on this awareness.

Establishing Objectives The first step in planning itself is to establish planning objectives for the entire enterprise and then for each subordinate unit. Objectives indicate the end points of what is to be done, where the primary emphasis is to be placed, and what is to be accomplished by the network of policies, procedures, rules, budgets, programs, and strategies.

Enterprise objectives should control the nature of all major plans, which, by reflecting these objectives, define the objectives of the major departments. Major department objectives, in turn, control the objectives of subordinate departments, and so on down the line. The objectives of lesser departments will be better framed, however, if subdivision managers understand the over-all enterprise objectives and the implied derivative goals.

Premising A second logical step in planning is to establish, obtain agreement to utilize, and disseminate critical planning premises. These are forecast data of a factual nature, applicable basic policies, and existing company plans. Premises, then, are planning assumptions, the future setting in which planning takes place—in other words, the environment of plans in operation.

Forecasting is important to premising: What kind of markets will there be? What quantity of sales? What prices? What products? What technical developments? What costs? What wage rates? What tax rates and policies? What new plants? What policies with respect to dividends? How will ex-

---

[7] The word "problem" might be used instead of "opportunity." But, in the view of the authors, a state of disorder or confusion and a need for a solution to gain a given goal can more constructively be regarded as an opportunity. In fact, the authors know of a very successful and astute company president who does not permit his colleagues to speak of problems, but only of opportunities.

pansion be financed? What political or social environment? Planning premises include far more than basic forecasts of population, prices, costs, production, markets, and similar matters.

Some premises forecast policies not yet made. For example, if a company has no pension plan and no policy with respect to one, planning premises sometimes must forecast whether such a policy will be set and, if so, what it will contain. Other premises naturally grow out of existing policies or other plans. For example, if a company has a policy of paying out 5 per cent of its profits, before taxes, for contributions and if there is no reason to believe that this policy will be changed, the policy becomes a planning premise. Or, if a company has made large investments in special-purpose fixed plant and machinery, this becomes an important planning premise.

As one moves down the organization hierarchy, the composition of planning premises changes somewhat. The basic process will be the same, but old and new major plans will materially affect the future against which managers of lesser units must plan. Superior plans affecting a subordinate manager's area of authority become premises for *his* planning.

Planning premises fall into three groups. There are noncontrollable premises, such as population growth, future price levels, political environment, tax rates and policies, and business cycles. There are semicontrollable premises, such as a firm's assumptions as to its share of the market, the character of labor turnover, labor efficiency, company price policy, and even industry legislative policy. And, finally, there are controllable premises, largely decided by company management and involving policies and programs such as expansion into new markets, the adoption of an aggressive research program, or the selection of a site for headquarters offices.

Because the future environment of plans is so complex, it would not be profitable or realistic to make assumptions about every detail of the future environment of a plan. Therefore, premises must, as a practical matter, be limited to those which are critical, or strategic, to a plan, that is, those which most influence its operation.

A difficulty of establishing complete premises and keeping them up to date is that every major plan, and many minor ones, become premises for the future. The plan to establish a factory in Kansas City, for example, becomes a premise for plans in which plant location is important. Or a Pacific Northwest railroad, for instance, would make little sense in premising future plans on Florida markets without reasonable expectation of expanding to the southeast. And when an airline equips its long-haul routes with one type of aircraft for which it builds maintenance and overhaul facilities, this becomes a critical premise for other plans.

It would be surprising if all members of a company's management at all levels agreed independently about the company future. One manager might expect world peace to last ten years, another, world war for the same period. One manager might expect prices to go up 10 per cent in five years, another, 50 per cent, and another might expect prices to drop.

Lack of planning coordination, through use by managers of different sets of premises, can be extremely costly to a company. The use of consistent premises should, therefore, be agreed upon. A single standard for the future is necessary for good planning, even though this standard includes several sets of premises, with the instruction that different sets of plans be developed on each. Some companies, for example, customarily develop plans in prospect of both peace and war, so that, regardless of what occurs, the company will be ready. Obviously, however, a plan actually put into operation for any future period can use only one set of premises.

Since agreement to utilize a given set of premises is important to coordinated planning, it becomes a major responsibility of managers, starting with those at the top, to make sure that subordinate managers understand the premises upon which they are expected to plan. These major premises are often the subject of careful study, sometimes including extensive economic and other research, so that the best thinking available in the company can be brought to bear upon them. It is not unusual for chief executives in well-managed companies to force top managers with differing views, through group deliberation, to arrive at a set of major premises that all can accept. But whether they are acceptable to all or not, no chief executive can afford to chance a situation where his lieutenants are planning their portions of the company's future on substantially different premises.

Established premises are useful only to managers who are aware of them, so premises must be appropriately disseminated throughout the organization. This does not mean that all premises should be communicated to all managers, but only that each manager should know of those premises necessary for him to do intelligent and coordinated planning in his area.

Having been led to believe that all planning should start at the bottom, a company president issued an instruction that all departments from the bottom up should develop their own budgets and submit them to his office. He was surprised and dismayed when he found out that they did not fit, and he had on his hands a complex of inconsistent budgets.

Determining Alternative Courses The third step in planning is to search for and examine alternative courses of action, especially those not immediately apparent. There is seldom a plan for which reasonable alternatives do not exist, and quite often, an alternative that is not obvious proves to be the best.

After reducing the number of available alternatives to those promising the most fruitful action or the best possibilities for mathematical analysis, the planner must next examine them. For a major plan, this examination may be very complicated, leading to the preparation of detailed forecasts of costs and revenues and of cash position, and to many other considerations of both a tangible and intangible nature. In deciding to build a new aluminum plant a few years ago, the American Aluminum Company not only studied the costs of electricity at various locations in the country, the availability of suitable sites, the costs of transportation of raw and finished materials, the costs of transmission of power, and other factors that could be reduced to figures but also analyzed such intangible factors as local opinion of the plant, the possibilities of suits from nearby farmers from real or supposed damage to their crops from fluoride fumes, and risking capital to build its own power-generating facilities.

Evaluating Alternative Courses   Having sought out alternative courses and examined their strong and weak points, the fourth step is to evaluate them by weighing the various factors in the light of premises and goals. One course may appear to be the most profitable but requires a large cash outlay and a slow payback; another may be less profitable but involves less risk; still another may better suit the company's long-range objectives.

If the only objective were to maximize profits immediately, if the future were not uncertain, if cash position and capital availability were not worrisome, and if most factors could be reduced to definite data, this evaluation should be relatively easy. But typical planning is replete with uncertainties, problems of capital shortages, and intangible factors, so evaluation is usually very difficult, even with relatively simple problems. A company may wish to enter a new product line primarily for purposes of prestige; the forecast of expected results may show a clear financial loss; but the question is still open as to whether the loss is worth the gain in prestige.

Because the number of alternative courses in most situations is legion and the numerous variables and limitations are involved, evaluation can be also exceedingly complex. Because of these complexities, the newer methodologies and applications of operations research and analysis, discussed in Chapter 8, are helpful. Indeed, it is at this step in the planning process that operations research and mathematical and computing techniques have their primary application to the field of management.

Selecting a Course   The fifth planning step, selecting the course of action, is the point at which the plan is adopted—the real point of decision making. Occasionally an analysis and evaluation of alternative courses will disclose that two or more are advisable, and the manager may decide to follow several courses rather than one best course.

Formulating Derivative Plans   At the point where a decision is made, planning is seldom complete, and a last step is indicated. There are almost invariably derivative plans to be constructed to support the basic plan. In the case mentioned above, in the section on programs, where an airline decided to acquire a fleet of new planes, this decision was the signal for the development of a host of derivative plans dealing with the hiring and training of various types of personnel, the acquisition and positioning of spare parts, the development of maintenance facilities, scheduling and advertising, financing and insurance.

Managers of each segment of the company make and execute the plans necessary for making a basic plan a reality, and this chain reaction must continue on down until there is a specific plan for each derivative activity of a main plan. To use again the airline example, this is where specific plans for recruitment and training of new people are made, where spare parts are ordered and shipping and warehousing schedules made, and where the final blueprints are prepared, contractors hired for the building, and arrangements completed for orderly occupancy of the new maintenance facilities.

The Planning Process: Rational Approach   As seen in the planning steps outlined above, planning is simply a rational approach to the future. The process can be diagrammed as shown in Figure 5.2. In this diagram, progress (toward more sales, more profits, less costs, and so forth) is on the vertical axis and time on the horizontal axis. X indicates where we are (at t_o) and Y where we want to be—a goal for the future (at t_n). Since we ordinarily have to study where we are in advance of t_o, particularly with the lag of accounting and statistical data, we may actually have to start our study of the future at X_1 (at t_{-n}). The line XY indicates the decision path which will take us from X to Y.

If the future were completely certain, the line XY would be easy to draw. However, in actuality, a myriad of factors in the environment in which a plan is to operate may push events away from the desired goal.

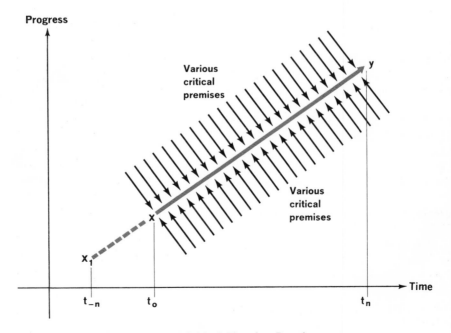

Fig. 5.2   Progress, Time, and Critical Planning Premises

These are the planning premises. Again, because we cannot forecast or consider everything, we try to develop our path from X to Y in the light of the most critical premises.

The essential logic of planning applies regardless of the time interval between t_o and t_n, whether five minutes or twenty years. However, the clarity of premises, the attainability of goals, and the lessening of other planning complexities are almost certain to be inversely related to the time span.

Decision making may be the easiest part of planning, although it involves techniques of evaluation and approach and considerable skill in applying these. The real difficulties arise primarily from sharpening and giving meaning (preferably verifiable) to objectives, spelling out and giving meaning to critical premises, seeing the nature and relationships of the strengths and weaknesses of alternatives, and communicating goals and premises to those throughout the enterprise who must plan.

THE PLANNING PERIOD

Shall plans be for a short period or a long one? How shall short-range plans be coordinated with long-range plans? These questions suggest a multiple horizon of planning—that, in some cases, planning a week in advance may be ample and that, in others, the desirable period may be a number of years. Even within the same firm at the same time, various planning periods may exist for various matters.

The National Industrial Conference Board, reporting on a survey of business planning some years ago,[8] disclosed, as might be expected, that businesses varied considerably in their planning periods. In some instances, long-range plans were confined to two years, while in others they spanned decades. But three to five years appeared to be most common for long-range planning, and few companies planned less than a year in advance. Later surveys showed more companies engaging in long-range planning, with the planning period being extended. A survey made by McGraw-Hill in 1956 disclosed that the number of large firms laying plans three to five years in advance had doubled in the prior few years and that even small and medium companies were increasingly undertaking long-range planning.[9] Approximately one-third of the companies interviewed had established their formal long-range planning programs in the previous two or three years. However, an increasing number of companies were laying their plans on forecasts of a future ten to twenty years ahead.

Long-range planning has continued to increase until today it is almost a badge of alert management to have some kind of long-range planning department. Yet, as late as 1962, a study by the American Management Asso-

[8] "Industry Plans for the Future," *Conference Board Business Record*, vol. 9, pp. 324–328 (August, 1952).

[9] "In Business, Everyone's Looking Ahead," *Business Week*, p. 113 (Jan. 5, 1957).

ciation reported that five years seemed to be the norm of long-range planning,[10] although planning periods ranging to twenty-five years and more did exist. In analyzing case studies, the AMA report concluded that companies seem to base their period on a future that can reasonably be anticipated. But there was some evidence that constant repetition of the Soviet government's Five Year Plan had had an influence. Moreover, even in more recent years evidence indicates that the normal time span of long-range planning has not changed materially, although we can find now more cases of spans longer than five years.[11] The AMA study also found the following factors influential in some companies: (1) lead time in development and commercialization of a new product; (2) time required to recover capital investments; (3) expected future availability of customers; and (4) expected future availability of raw materials and components.

The Commitment Principle   There should be some logic in selecting the right time range for company planning. In general, since planning and the forecasting that underlies it are costly, a company should probably not plan for a longer period than is economically justifiable; yet it is risky to plan for a shorter period. The answer as to the right planning period seems to lie in the "commitment principle," that logical planning encompasses a period of time in the future necessary to foresee, through a series of actions, the fulfillment of commitments involved in a decision taken now.

Perhaps the most striking application of this principle is the setting of a planning period long enough to anticipate the recovery of costs sunk in a course of action.[12] But since other things than costs can be committed for various lengths of time and because a commitment to spend often precedes an expenditure and may be as unchangeable as sunk costs, it seems inadequate to refer to recovery of costs alone. Thus a company may commit itself, for varying lengths of time, to a personnel policy, such as promotion from within or retirement at age sixty-five, or to other policies or programs involving commitments of direction and not immediately tangible in terms of dollars.

One can readily grasp the logic of planning far enough in the future to foresee, as well as possible, the recovery of capital sunk in a building or a machine. Since capital is the lifeblood of an enterprise and is normally limited in relation to the firm's needs, its expenditure must be accompanied by a reasonable possibility of recovering it, plus a return on investment, through operations. For example, when Lever Brothers sank 25 million dollars into a new factory on the West Coast, they, in effect, decided that the

[10] Stewart Thompson, *How Companies Plan*, Research Study No. 54 (New York: American Management Association, 1962), pp. 23–31.

[11] See, for example, E. C. Miller, *Marketing Planning* (New York: American Management Association, 1967), pp. 17–18.

[12] As a matter of fact, in the first edition of this book, this was referred to as the recovery-of-cost principle. See Harold Koontz and Cyril O'Donnell, *Principles of Management* (New York: McGraw-Hill Book Company, 1955), p. 442.

detergent business would permit the recovery of this investment over a period of time. If this period was twenty years, then logically the plans should have been based upon a projection of business for such a time. Of course, as will be discussed presently, they might have introduced some flexibility and reduced their risk (as they did) by spending extra funds to make the plant useful for other purposes.

What the commitment principle implies is that long-range planning is not really planning for future decisions but rather planning the future impact of *today's* decisions. In other words, a decision is a commitment, normally of funds, direction of action, or reputation. And decisions lie at the core of planning. While studies and analyses precede decisions, any type of plan implies that some decision has been made. Under these circumstances, then, the astute manager will recognize the validity of gearing all planning into present decisions. To do otherwise is to overlook both the basic nature of planning and that of decision making.

Application of the Commitment Principle The application of the commitment principle indicates that there is no uniform or arbitrary length of time for which a company should plan or for which a given program or any of its parts should be planned. An airplane company embarking on a new commercial jet aircraft project should probably plan this program some twelve years ahead, with five or six years for conception, engineering, and development and as many more years for production and sales in order to recoup total costs and make a reasonable profit. An instrument manufacturer might need to plan its revenues and expenses some six months ahead, since this may represent the cycle of raw-material acquisition, production, inventorying, sales, and collection of accounts. But the same company might wish to see much further into the future before assuming a lease for specialized manufacturing facilities, undertaking a program of management training, or developing and promoting a new product.

If a commitment appears to a manager to be for a longer period than he can foresee with reasonable accuracy and if it is not feasible to build enough flexibility at reasonable cost into a plan, the manager may decide arbitrarily to shorten his period of commitment. In many cases, particularly those involving capital expenditures, the actual recovery of cost is determined by accounting or tax practices. In these cases it is possible to decide (regardless of whether the tax authorities would agree for tax purposes) to write off an investment faster than would normally be the case. A West Coast aerospace manufacturer was faced with this situation a few years ago with the purchase of some special-purpose machinery for performance under a government contract. The machinery would normally be written off in ten years, but, in his opinion, the contract would probably last only two years, and the machinery had no apparent use for other purposes. He argued correctly and logically (but not successfully) with government contracting officers that he should be allowed to include in his costs a two-year write-off of the machinery. By doing so, he would shorten the commitment period for a highly inflexible investment to the length of time in which he could foresee fulfillment of his commitment.

The planning period will be longer or shorter depending not only upon the length of time it may take to recover costs from an investment or to discharge an obligation under commitment, but also upon the extent to which flexibility can be built into the plan. Thus, a company might be willing to lease a factory for ten years, even though it is impracticable to plan for longer than three, because of the possibility of getting out of this commitment through subleasing on a one- or two-year notice. But where there is no practicable flexibility, or where flexibility is costly, it is desirable to plan for the entire period of commitment. This almost surely explains why certain major oil companies have led the nation's business management in the excellence and length of their long-range planning, for there is probably no investment quite so fully committed as that of developing an oil field, building pipelines, and constructing refinery facilities.

Despite the clarity and importance of the commitment principle, the authors have found few managements that seem to be aware of it. Long-range planning is sometimes adopted because it's in fashion, whether the commitments justify it or not. In more cases, managements assume commitments without adequate planning, especially when—as with a personnel or management development plan—the capital investment aspect is remote.

Although this principle indicates that various plans call for various planning periods, depending on the commitment, the periods naturally used are often compromises. The short range tends to be selected to conform to quarters or years because of the practical need for making plans agree with accounting periods. And the somewhat arbitrary selection of five years or so for the long range is often based on the belief that the degree of uncertainty over longer periods makes planning of questionable value.

It is sometimes maintained that management should plan for periods longer than those covered by firm commitments and that looking ahead for ten or twenty years is justified by the desire to foresee what the world in which the firm will operate will then be like. From this standpoint, management may probe the future to see how it can best adapt its objectives and policies to the trends disclosed; but even this purpose in deciding upon the planning period seems designed to make sure that commitments currently being made fit the future, for even objectives and policies imply commitments.

Coordination of Short- with Long-range Plans Often short-range plans are made without reference to long-range plans. This is plainly a serious error. The importance of integrating the two can hardly be overemphasized, and no short-run plan should be made unless it contributes to the achievement of the relevant long-range plan. Many of the wastes of planning arise from decisions on immediate situations that fail to consider their effect on more remote objectives.

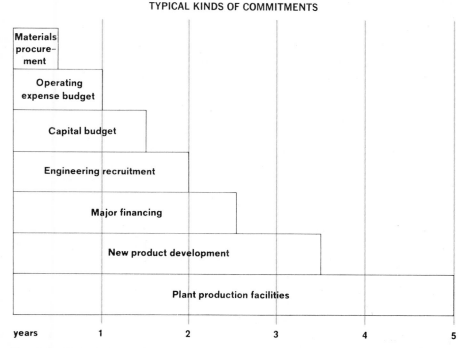

Fig. 5.3   Planning Areas and Time Periods . . . *Various management decision areas typically involve planning ahead for differing periods of time.
New plant facilities may be planned at least five years ahead. These periods
vary according to the kind of business. For instance, a large public utility
may plan new power-production plants twenty-five or thirty years into the
future while a small garment manufacturer may plan new production facilities only one year ahead. However, if acquired raw materials are bought,
used in making the product, and sold as finished product in six months, the
planning would logically be six months into the future.*

Sometimes these short-range decisions not only fail to contribute to a
long-range plan but actually impede or require changes in the long-range
plan. For example, if a small company accepts a large order without reckon-
ing the effect on productive capacity or cash position, it may so hamper its
future ability to finance an orderly expansion as to require a complex re-
orientation of its long-range program. Or, in another company, the urgency
of obtaining small additions to plant may utilize vacant property so hap-
hazardly as to thwart its longer-range use as the site for a large new plant.
In other instances, the decision of a plant superintendent to discharge
workers without adequate cause may interfere with the company's longer-
range objective of developing a fair and successful personnel program. The
short-range decision of Sewell Avery, chairman of Montgomery Ward, to

curtail expansion of the business after World War II, because of his belief that a serious recession was at hand, interfered with the long-range program of enhancing the profitability of the company.

Responsible managers should continually scrutinize immediate decisions to ascertain whether they contribute to long-range programs, and subordinate managers should be regularly briefed on company long-range plans, so that they will make consistent short-range decisions. It is far easier to do this than to correct inconsistencies, especially since short-term commitments tend to engender further commitments along the same line.

To say that short-range and long-range plans need to be coordinated is to recognize several basics. In the first place, what may appear to be a short-range plan may actually involve some longer-period commitments. Examples of this are pointed out above. In the second place, short-range plans usually contribute to or supplement long-range ones. To overlook this is to disregard the fact that plans are ordinarily a system of interacting or contributing elements. Another factor to bear in mind is that a short-range plan might actually interfere with a longer-range policy or objective. Thus, by planning long runs of a given product or size in this month's production schedule, the result may be interference with a marketing policy of serving customer orders quickly, or with an inventory objective of keeping finished goods inventory at a low point.

FLEXIBILITY IN PLANNING

The above discussion has indicated that the commitment principle must be considered in the light of flexibility of planning. In other words, if plans can be changed to meet future requirements which either were not or could not be foreseen, the planning period can be shorter than otherwise would be the case. Because of future uncertainties and possible error in even the most expert forecast, the ideal of planning is to be able to change direction when indicated by unexpected events, without undue cost.

There are two planning principles for use in effecting the change in direction, the flexibility principle and the principle of navigational change.

The Flexibility Principle According to this principle, the more that flexibility can be built into plans, the less the danger of losses incurred by unexpected events; but the cost of flexibility should be weighed against the risks involved in future commitments made.

To many managers, the principle of flexibility is the most important principle of planning. The ability to change a plan without undue cost or friction, to detour, to keep moving toward a goal despite changes in environment or even failure of plans, has great value. The greatest flexibility is required when the commitment is great and cannot be discharged in a short time (for example, in retrieving outlays for major capital facilities plus a return).

There are many inflexibilities other than financial to consider in planning. Inflexibilities of policies and procedures, psychological inflexibilities of workers and managers, and social and political inflexibilites are among those which often plague the manager who would change his plans.

Flexibility is possible only within limits. In the first place, a decision cannot always be put off long enough to assure its rightness, and an enterprise, like the proverbial donkey, can starve between two bales of hay while managers try to choose the best alternative. This is exemplified by the decision of the General Petroleum Company to build a refinery in the Pacific Northwest. The decision had to be taken some five years before the refinery was operated, and the financial point of no return was reached several years before the management could be completely certain that this would be an economic venture.

In the second place, built-in flexibility of plans may be so expensive that the benefits of hedging may not be worth the cost. Whether a company spends extra money to modify a special-purpose plant so that it can be used for other purposes, if the original program is not successful, will depend on the costs of doing so and the risks to be avoided. Some companies have felt, as apparently the top management of Montgomery Ward did for several years after World War II, that they could buy flexibility by keeping their resources in that most flexible of all assets—cash—only to have a competitor step forward with aggressive expenditures and capture much of the market.

Montgomery Ward, under the leadership of Sewell Avery, built up cash reserves exceeding 250 million dollars by 1953 but saw its share of the mail-order business fall from 40 per cent in 1942 to 28 per cent in 1952. Sears Roebuck, on the other hand, under the leadership of Robert E. Wood, adopted an expansionist program and increased its share of the mail-order business from approximately 50 to 66 per cent in the same period. Similar differences in position existed in the retail store field for the two companies. Sears also increased its profits relative to Ward's. Although Sears stock rose during this period, that of Ward fell. Had a depression occurred during this immediate postwar period, however, Montgomery Ward would have been in an excellent position to capitalize on its liquidity, and Sears might have been in a very vulnerable position.

The Principle of Navigational Change   The more planning decisions commit for the future, the more important it is that a manager periodically check on events and expectations and redraw plans to maintain a course toward a desired goal. This principle, unlike the flexibility principle, which applies to the adaptability of plans themselves, applies to flexibility in the planning process. Built-in flexibility does not automatically revise plans; the manager, like the navigator, must continually check his course and redraw plans to meet a desired goal.

It is sometimes erroneously believed that planning freezes future action. Commitment of funds or effort does bring elements of inflexibility into planning, and plans cannot always be modified with changes of the tides or winds of the future, but no able manager makes a single plan and then proceeds to put it into effect no matter what occurs. However, to the extent that a manager has been able to forecast the future accurately, establish long-range goals, and arrive at perfect planning decisions, plans may need very little change.

FOR DISCUSSION

1. "Planning is looking ahead and control is looking back." Comment.

2. If planning involves a rational approach to selected goals, how can one include goals or objectives as a type of plan?

3. Look at a typical statement of enterprise (business or otherwise) objectives, judge whether they are actionable, and, if not, determine how they could be made so.

4. Using the concepts of policies and procedures in this chapter, draw up a statement of policy and devise a brief procedure which might be useful in implementing it. How are you sure your policy is not a rule?

5. If all decisions involve commitments, and if the future is always uncertain, how can a manager guard against costly mistakes?

6. Taking a planning problem which is now facing you, proceed to deal with it in accordance with the steps involved in planning outlined in this chapter.

7. Using an example of a planning decision with which you are familiar, show to what extent, and how, the principles of commitment, flexibility, and navigational change apply to it.

SELECTED REFERENCES

Anthony, R. N.: *Planning and Control Systems: A Framework for Analysis,* Boston: Division of Research, Harvard Business School, 1965.

Davis, R. C.: *The Fundamentals of Top Management,* chaps. 3–4, New York: Harper & Row, Publishers, Incorporated, 1951.

Ewing, D. W.: *Long-range Planning for Management,* rev. ed., New York: Harper & Row, Publishers, Incorporated, 1964.

Fayol, H.: *General and Industrial Management,* pp. 43–53, 97–110, New York: Pitman Publishing Corporation, 1949.

Goetz, B. E.: *Management Planning and Control,* chaps. 1–4, New York: McGraw-Hill Book Company, 1949.

Koontz, H.: "A Preliminary Statement of Principles of Planning and Control," *Journal of Academy of Management,* vol. 1, no. 1, pp. 45–61 (April, 1958).

LeBreton, P. P., and D. A. Henning: *Planning Theory,* chaps. 1–6, Englewood Cliffs, N.J.: Prentice-Hall, Inc., 1961.

Newman, W. H., and C. E. Summer, Jr.: *The Process of Management,* chaps. 16, 18, 19, Englewood Cliffs, N.J.: Prentice-Hall, Inc., 1961.

Root, L. E.: "Development Planning for Management Decision," in *Organizing for Effective Systems Planning and Control,* Special Report No. 12, pp. 89–104, New York: American Management Association, 1956.

Scott, B. W.: *Long-Range Planning in American Industry,* New York: American Management Association, 1965.

Steiner, G. A., "Making Long-range Company Planning Pay Off," *California Management Review,* vol. 4, no. 2, pp. 28–41 (Winter, 1962).

————: *Management Long-Range Planning,* New York: McGraw-Hill Book Company, 1963.

————: "What to Do about Using Long-range Plans," *California Management Review,* vol. 2, no. 1, pp. 92–103 (Fall, 1959).

St. Thomas, C. E.: *Practical Business Planning,* New York: American Management Association, 1965.

Thompson, Stewart: *How Companies Plan,* Research Study No. 54, New York: American Management Association, 1962.

Urwick, L.: *The Elements of Administration,* chaps. 1–3, New York: Harper & Row, Publishers, Incorporated, 1944.

Warren, E. K.: *Long-Range Planning,* Englewood Cliffs, N.J.: Prentice-Hall, Inc., 1966.

objectives

Objectives are variously referred to as purposes, missions, goals, or targets. "Objective" or "purpose" might be used in connection with such ultimate things as profitable growth of a business enterprise. "Mission" is usually used in military enterprises and occasionally in such enterprises as churches or governments. "Goals" or "targets" often carry the connotation of specific qualitative or quantitative ends. However, because clear distinctions are not made in practice, these terms are used interchangeably throughout this book.

The identification of objectives is the first step in planning and requires careful consideration. No one can specify how he will accomplish a vague and indeterminate objective. Objectives must be identified in such a way that ultimate success or failure can be determined.

One would think that the need for good planning objectives would be thoroughly understood, but such is far from the case. Anyone who examines enterprise "plans" will find that many of them fail to qualify as true plans. The chief faults seem to lie in vague statements of objectives and in a misunderstanding of the planning process.

SOCIAL OBJECTIVES

When the objectives of a private enterprise conflict with the ends for which a society is organized, legal action, whether successful or unsuccessful, is usually taken to suppress or regulate the enterprise.

In History From the first, organized societies, whether villages, cities and city-states, or nations, have had specific objectives. Archeologists suggest that the earliest organized groups—the tribe or the village—had safety as their chief objective. Next, cities and city-states[1] required a relatively dense

---

[1] After R. Linton, *The Tree of Culture* (New York: Vintage Books, Random House, Inc., 1958), p. 37.

population, transportation facilities for bulk products, as well as provisions for security and an opportunity for extensive division of labor. The original objectives of the national state are not entirely clear, despite speculation by political historians stressing natural boundaries, common language, and community safety. The successful feudal lord and those who joined together to form some kind of federation expanded their power to a point where they were counterbalanced by a competitive and similarly motivated power. Then, the growth of nations may be due to the simple increase in social mass, to evolution through which societies grow and become integrated.[2]

In the United States, we do have in our possession statements of national purpose set forth in the Declaration of Independence and in the Constitution. Jefferson asserted that governments are instituted to secure to their peoples the rights of life, liberty, and the pursuit of happiness. The preamble of our Constitution states:

> We the people of the United States, in order to form a more perfect union, establish justice, insure domestic tranquility, provide for the common defense, promote the general welfare, and secure the blessings of liberty to ourselves and our posterity, do ordain and establish this Constitution for the United States of America.

Here we have a clear statement of the purposes of our society, and no institution, not even our Congress or the Presidency, is expected to adopt objectives which are at variance with it. Similarly, all subordinate enterprise—be it a school, church, hospital, government agency, business, or a local political organization—should have objectives which are harmonious with and supportive to national objectives.

Under Free Enterprise   In attaining social objectives in the United States, the reliance is largely upon free enterprise. In this system, entrepreneurs with privately owned property are generally free to organize cooperative effort to produce goods and services whose (ultimate) consumption contributes to national goals. The what, who, how, when, and why are left to individuals to decide within the confines of a free market. Not all enterprises organized in our system are intended to provide monetary profit. Many political, welfare, educational, religious, trade, and other organizations are nonprofit and exchange their services for income, either solicited or taxed, from contribu-

---

[2] As Herbert Spencer has said: "The many facts contemplated unite in proving that social evolution forms a part of evolution at large. Like evolving aggregates in general, societies show *integration,* both by simple increase of mass and by coalescence of masses. The change from *homogeneity* to *heterogeneity* is multitudinously exemplified; up from the simple tribe, alike in its parts, to the civilized nation, full of structural and functional unlikenesses. With progressing integration and heterogeneity goes increasing *coherence. . . .* Simultaneously comes increasing definiteness. . . . Thus in all respects is fulfilled the formula of evolution. There is progress towards greater size, coherence, multiformity, and definiteness." See *The Principles of Sociology* (New York: D. Appleton & Company, Inc., 1898), vol. II, book II, sec. 271.

tors or obtained from the sale of services. But every enterprise, regardless of its nature, has an objective of efficiency, that is, of obtaining the maximum of what is desired with the resources at its disposal.

While most enterprises are undertaken with a high degree of freedom, there has been an expanding area of cooperative action in which freedom is limited. Even originally, the Federal government obtained such exclusive rights as the maintenance of defense, administration of justice, levying of certain taxes, and conduct of certain businesses, such as the post office. These limitations on free enterprise have never been seriously questioned. On the other hand, through the decades, as critics of certain aspects of free enterprise behavior have gained political power, restrictions have multiplied in the form of antitrust laws, pure food and drug legislation, farm legislation, social security legislation, labor legislation, and so forth. The power to tax business income and its recipients at rates which many think are confiscatory indirectly limits free enterprise even more than does regulatory legislation. Be this as it may, we may have done well to retain as much freedom in enterprise as we have at present.[3]

Even somewhat limited private enterprise of whatever type must still aim to complement our social objectives. Enterprises which ignore this requirement risk losing all their resources: from a social viewpoint, this is as it should be.

Changing Objectives   Two sets of circumstances require objectives to be changed. One involves a change of direction, such as a switch from retailing to manufacturing or wholesaling. Another involves a change of environment, such as changes in the law, elimination of free enterprise in the field of the activity, radical technological innovations, changes in consumer living standards, reduction of the death rate, or higher literacy levels. Because our society is highly dynamic, it is incumbent upon management to review and modify objectives as indicated. Purposes must fit in with the cultural environment, because action to achieve them must take place in the economic, social, political, and technological stage of our culture.

It is the responsibility of the top managing group or the board of directors to establish and to review enterprise objectives. Those in control should make certain, first, that the objectives are consistent with social objectives without question. Their responsibility is to avoid antisocial objectives, whether direct or indirect. Furthermore, there is a need to review objectives occasionally to make certain that they conform with newly interpreted aspects of the social purpose. For instance, collusion is now forbidden in domestic trade but encouraged in foreign trade. Ambivalent as the social purpose is, in this connection, directors must ensure that enterprise objectives will be achieved within its confines and must keep alert to needed modifications as time goes on.

[3] See G. A. Steiner, *Government's Role in Economic Life* (New York: McGraw-Hill Book Company, 1953), chap. 14.

ENTERPRISE OBJECTIVES

In no other field of endeavor has the question of objectives of the enterprise as a whole been subject to more discussion than in business. This has been particularly true in a free private enterprise system where business is by nature material, rather than essentially socialistic or idealistic, and profit has often been attacked as being unsocial or immoral.

The Profit Objective in Business   A good argument can be made that in the United States all business enterprises have one and the same objective—to make a profit. This purpose is often obscured by platitudinous statements about service to the public and opportunity for employees. Not that these objectives are improper; certainly the profit-seeking enterprise will serve the public by producing useful and desirable goods and services at competitive prices. And a profitable, well-managed enterprise will provide good wages, security, and status for employees. But the common element in business enterprise, from the newsboy and peanut vendor to the largest bank or insurance company, is the pursuit of profit.

And yet, it seems inadequate to speak of profit as *the* motive of business, as though one merely said, "Business is business," when there have been so many cases of business owners with other incentives: power, social prestige, security, public acclaim, or any of the other strong motivations of human conduct. The business may be dominated by the desire to develop new things and try new ideas, as was the case of an engineering company with which one of the authors has worked; or to keep the business small, simple, and friendly—a sort of fraternal group; or to beat its nearest and larger competitor, as is held to be a principal objective of the Ford Motor Company. But in whatever terms objectives are stated, none is realizable without an actual profit.

Sometimes the motive of profit maximization gives way to that of enterprise value maximization. In other words, many businesses are operated mainly to increase their value in the long run, during which they pass by profits and pursue policies to increase capital value. Unquestionably, the principal reason for this kind of motivation is the tax structure, which places lesser taxes on capital gains than on profits or normal income. But many entrepreneurs receive satisfaction from seeing a business grow large, even though profits are passed by in the process. This may still maximize profits in the long run, although not always.

Another well-known variant of the profit objective might be called maintenance of management security. Although evidence cannot easily be obtained on this point, since the controlling managers of a business would hesitate to admit that such is their objective, the fact is that managers sometimes follow a conservative path, unwilling to take even normal risks to gain a profit, in order to protect their positions.

For example, a corporation president told one of the authors that he would not embark upon a certain expansion program, even though it promised great profits. He pointed out that, if he did not approve it and the company continued to make moderate profits, the stockholders would not feel dissatisfied. If his conservative path led to reduction in profits, the very fact that *he* had not done anything unusual would make it reasonable to blame external business or political conditions. On the other hand, if he took a moderate degree of risk for the promise of high profits and succeeded, stockholders would merely think he was doing a normal job, and, although content with it, would not especially reward him. But should he assume the risks of the expansion program and it did not turn out well, even through no fault of his own, stockholder reaction to losses might be quite adverse and he might lose his job. His reaction was, "Why take a chance? I like being president of this company!"

This attitude is not surprising, either, when enterprise directors cannot often reap the advantages of profiting through the assumption of risks. Maintenance of management security is probably more widespread as a planning objective than is generally realized and this attitude is not limited to executives; department heads may believe similarly.

Social Justification of the Profit Motive Although a business may have various objectives, making of profit must be a major one. A profit is simply a surplus of income over expenditures. And, since most businesses have the further objective of making this profit over a long period of time, profit making must be contemplated in fairly long-run terms. Those enterprises that endure profitably will, it is believed, be responsive to the economic needs and desires of customers and to the limitations that society places on them.

Business enterprises are economic enterprises. As such, they have a responsibility to society to produce the goods people want at the lowest costs practicable. To do otherwise would not fulfill their economic function, particularly in a social system dominated by extensive freedom of choice. There is a kind of underlying assumption that an enterprise will contribute best to social purpose if it furnishes goods or services at lowest practicable costs over a fairly long time. This assumption is based on the belief that stability and growth lead to efficiency. Except where monopoly has been found desirable, such as in public utilities, American society has placed heavy reliance on competition as a regulatory and driving force. Obviously, business enterprises are required to compete effectively and on a plane of ethically fair competitive behavior. To do otherwise would make necessary the intervention of government, which is believed not to be as responsive to individual wants, as aggressive in seeking innovation, nor as efficient in seeking the best means of production.

Making of a profit is the best proof in a free society that a business is actually meeting customer needs at reasonable costs, under competitive conditions. In other words, if there is real rivalry between firms, if entrepreneurs have a reasonable degree of freedom, and if buyers are free to choose between sellers, profit measures the success of free enterprise. Long-range profitability is also consistent with social purpose in that, through profits, a business can continue to produce, improve its product, and meet new customer needs. It is sometimes said that the objective of business is to create customers, but if this is done at the price of bankruptcy, it is difficult to see that the mere creation of customers is consistent with the social responsibilities of an economic enterprise.

Profit should also be an important objective of a regulated monopoly, such as a public utility. But here, in place of the spur of competition, government has found it necessary to impose price regulation to avoid excessive profits and service regulation to assure adequate customer service. Seldom does a regulated monopoly foster the aggressiveness and efficiency found in competitive enterprise. Difficulty arises also when firms, such as the railroads, lose most of their monopoly characteristics but public regulation of price and service continues. Here, the restrictions on the profit motive often result in a pronounced tendency toward stultification of economic growth and lack of responsiveness to customer requirements.

Reasons for Starting an Enterprise The great majority of people are employed by "going concerns." These people either shy away from an entrepreneur's risks or have not the capital, ability, or desire to found a business of their own. Yet in the United States each year several thousand enterprises are established. For what purpose? What is it that the entrepreneur, the prime mover, hopes to accomplish?

The new businessman may have a variety of reasons in mind. Immediately, of course, he must see a need for the enterprise, and unless he is correct, there is every prospect of failure. But probably most entrepreneurs see fulfillment of others' needs merely as a means of satisfying their own personal desires for a way to make a living, profit accumulation, freedom, and power.

Of course, nonprofit enterprises also provide an adequate standard of living for their employees, and—even though usually required by law to satisfy a health and welfare, charitable, religious, or educational purpose— they also sometimes provide freedom, power, and occasionally gain for the prime mover. And some men seem to prefer altruism to personal gain. Dr. Tom Dooley, Dr. Albert Schweitzer, and many other leaders of charitable, religious, medical, and welfare enterprises fall within this category.

Factors in Choosing an Enterprise An important factor in the choice of an enterprise is the *environment* in which it will operate. A total list of elements to be considered cannot be given here but would include the nature of the economic order, affluence of the society, national and international political stability, tax and tariff policies, and competitive practices. One would not design and manufacture fine furniture to be sold mainly to a have-not nation.

A second factor is *technical skill and knowledge*. People normally select an activity about which they know something, particularly where technology is important. A truck driver is not likely to found a university, nor a corner grocer to produce power plants for space travel. Of course, technical skill may be hired, but disparity between the technical knowledge of the founder and that required for operations is usually not as great as in the above examples.

It also is necessary that the technical ability required of employees be available and that satellite industries be convenient. Many firms have considered locating in seemingly favorable sites only to find that essential ancillary industry—whether it be power, raw materials, refrigeration, finance, or transportation—is not available.

A third factor concerns *creativity*. Creative enterprise entails risks as well as rewards and concentrates on such things as research, design, and development—risky because of the danger of creating unmarketable products, for one thing.

Multiple Objectives The plural form is used here to stress the fact that enterprises have multiple purposes. To say that the objective of an educational enterprise is to educate students is not enough. It may be, for example, much more accurate to state its objectives as being to attract qualified students; to train them in the liberal arts and sciences; to grant the Ph.D. degree to qualified candidates; to attract a highly regarded faculty; to discover new knowledge and organize it through research; to operate as a private school in the Spartan tradition; and to be supported principally by student tuition and gifts of alumni and friends. Similarly, a business enterprise might spell out its multiple objectives to include earning a competitive rate of profit and return on investment; emphasizing research to develop a continuing flow of proprietary products; developing publicly held stock ownership; financing primarily by earnings plow-back and bank debt; distributing products in foreign markets; assuring competitive prices for superior products; achieving a dominant position in the industry; and adhering, in all respects, to the values of our society. Such statements of objectives enable anyone to visualize the image the trustees or directors have in mind and establish planning premises useful for bringing the image to life.

SELECTING OBJECTIVES

Planning can be a useful managerial function only if objectives are properly selected. Improper selection or faulty specifications of objectives will vitiate planning time and cost, result in frustration, and make the entire planning activity futile.

Every enterprise should spell out its own precise objectives. The cost of failure to do this will be a helpless undertaking, battered by chance events because it can make no concrete plans. On the other hand, identification of objectives permits making plans to accomplish them. L. Gulick has stated,[4] "A clear statement of purpose universally understood is the outstanding guarantee of effective administration."

[4] *Administrative Reflections from World War II* (University, Ala.: University of Alabama Press, 1948), p. 77.

Objectives must represent hopes or wishes but must be reasonably attainable. Critical premises of the future environment and available alternative objectives must be considered. Also, because most enterprises have multiple goals, each must be established in the light of the others. They must fit. They must be consistent. It would, for example, be foolish to select as an objective an increase in sales volume that would undermine the profit objective or that would be impossible of attainment without a product as yet undeveloped.

Lack of Universality As to whether enterprise objectives have any universality, P. F. Drucker has asserted: [5]

> There are eight areas in which objectives of performance and results have to be set: market standing; innovation; productivity; physical and financial resources; profitability; manager performance and development; worker performance and attitude; and public responsibility.

This statement, while useful, raises questions, because such objectives are not independent of each other. Innovation has an important bearing on market standing, both may affect profitability, and success in any of these depends on manager performance. These objectives are seriously overlapping, to say the least.

Another difficulty of such generalizations is that different kinds of enterprises have different objectives, and purposes generally applicable to business enterprises may not be applicable to others. The long-suffering supporters of the New York Metropolitan Opera certainly have no objective in the area of profitability; the United States Air Force has no area of objectives concerned with market standing; nor are many small business operators directly concerned about their public responsibility. Thus, setting universal objectives for all enterprises is not valid.

These considerations lead to the conclusion that specific planning objectives must be deduced from broader enterprise objectives. To the extent that the latter vary from one undertaking to another, it is not possible to universalize specific objectives, and their selection will remain a matter of logic and sound judgment. This view is consistent with the statement, "One way to identify the areas in which a company should have basic objectives is to consider the factors the company influences that are necessary for survival." [6]

Need for Practicability In setting practical objectives, managers must face up to the decision to be conservative or expansive. For instance, should a firm set its five-year sales objective at a figure sure to be accomplished, or should it be optimistic? Much depends on what is occurring in the industry, what

---

[5] *The Practice of Management* (New York: Harper & Row, Publishers, Incorporated, 1954), p. 63.

[6] W. H. Newman and C. E. Summer, Jr., *The Process of Management* (Englewood Cliffs, N.J.: Prentice-Hall, Inc., 1961), p. 385.

competitors are doing, estimates of economic, political, and technological factors. Some managers feel that a conservative objective will avoid discouraging employees, or else that employees will work hard to exceed it. Other managers feel that a more optimistic objective will act as a challenge, and that better achievement results from striving for high goals. Most good managers believe that objectives should "stretch" an enterprise and cause people to "reach," but that they should be attainable.

Long-range Objectives and Enterprise Purpose   Against a forecast of probable environmental changes, a manager can spell out his long-range objectives in terms of sales, production facilities, financial position, and standing with vendors, customers, unions, and employees.

One obvious prerequisite to long-range planning objectives is that they must support enterprise purposes. It is as faulty to select a planning objective which makes no contribution to over-all enterprise purposes as it is to select one which conflicts with them.

The objectives, however, of long-range plans may be quite different from enterprise purposes, especially in timing and specificity. While the achievement of enterprise objectives may be a matter of decades or, indeed, one of continual striving, the accomplishment of long-range plans is a matter of specific time. A few firms—notably utilities—plan to build fixed assets whose life expectancy is twenty-five to a hundred years, but most long-range plans involve a shorter period.[7] Although long-range plan objectives may not be identical with enterprise objectives, the latter are valuable as long-range planning premises. The objective of the plan is merely a piece of the distant objective, as it were.

There must also be a logical relationship between long-range objectives and enterprise purpose. This is simply common sense, but in practical situations it is not nearly so clear. For instance, in pursuing the purposes of the educational enterprise described above (page 114), should the objective of the first five-year plan be to raise a fund, hire a faculty, or recruit students? A business firm whose objective is to double its sales in five years may not be able to do so entirely through internal expansion. But it may have such additional options as buying established firms, producing others' products under license, integrating vertically, or combining all of these. Which step to take first and how to coordinate them? If planners were sure, their paths would be strewn with flowers rather than weeds.

From Long- to Short-range Objectives   There must be an integral relationship between short-range and long-range objectives as there is between derivative goals and major goals, if planning is to be intelligent.

Long-range plans, drawn to specifications of objectives, are notably more vague for distant years than for the immediate future. This means that plans for the fifth year of a five-year plan are much more uncertain than

---

[7] For considerations in selecting the long-range planning period, see pp. 99–104.

those for the first, less certain than those for the fourth, and so forth. Short-range objectives, usually to be realized in the first year of a long-range plan, are likely to be both comprehensive and specific. The approach should always be from the distant (fifth) year to the present and not vice versa, because what is to be done the first year must provide a foundation for what is to be done each successive year, and this can only be guaranteed if short-range plans *are part of* the long-range plan.

The selection of short-range objectives proceeds from an evaluation of priorities relating to long-range objectives. Some things simply need to be done first, either because they are a prerequisite to doing other things or because of lead-time considerations. For instance, as a new firm is established, raising capital for fixed and operating expenses is likely to be a prime objective and may be the sole short-run objective. If so, short-range objectives visualized for succeeding periods might be hiring managers for engineering, production, and sales; leasing space and equipment; and manning the organization. At the same time, if a long lead time is necessary, say, for installing a piece of specialized equipment, then writing specifications and placing the order would also be a short-range objective.

Thus, for short-range objectives to help achieve intermediate and long-range objectives, it is necessary to draw a plan for accomplishing each objective and to combine these into a master plan for review in terms of logic, consistency, and practicality.

PROGRESS TOWARD OBJECTIVES

Once a master plan to achieve objectives is developed and approved, the derivative plans for derivative objectives are assigned to one or more subordinate managers for execution. For example, the objective of raising operating funds may reasonably be assigned to the finance manager, but objectives relating to public relations, manager succession, or quality of performance are clearly assignable to nearly every manager.

Assignment of Derivative Objectives   The first breakdown of the master-plan objectives into its parts is assigned to the chief executive's immediate subordinates. They, in turn, will assign objectives for *their* division or plant to *their* subordinates. This process continues on down to the level of the front-line supervisor. Thus, every manager has a group of assigned specific objectives to accomplish during a specified period, and for each of these he will develop specific plans.

Difficulties in Simultaneous Execution   Ideally, each manager would execute several plans simultaneously, making consistent progress toward several objectives. However, in practice this may not be done for several reasons. In the first place, the objectives are often quite diverse. For a sales manager, they may range from rearranging sales territories, recruiting salesmen, developing managers, reviewing and improving service, opening new markets, minimizing transportation and warehousing costs, and undertaking marketing research, to securing new engineering or product design. Simultaneous effort applied to these objectives would be difficult to accomplish. As a human being, the sales manager is likely to think he makes more progress by concentrating on one objective at a time, even though this throws out accomplishment as planned. Furthermore, every man invests more time in fulfilling objectives related to his peculiar interests, even though this leads, inevitably, to neglected objectives.

Managers also give prime attention to objectives in which their superiors show marked interest. The typical superior will inquire into sales regularly but perhaps never inquire into manager training from one year to another. The reaction of subordinate managers, then, is to attend particularly to the sales objective by stealing time from supervising the training of managers.

Then, too, unforeseen circumstances arise to unbalance the accomplishment of a group of objectives. The loss of a key subordinate, a fire, bankruptcy of a vendor, a strike, and other situations may jeopardize plans or force major revisions.

From these considerations, it may be concluded that maintaining balanced progress toward all objectives is almost insuperable. But this need not be true. A sophisticated manager counters his own weaknesses, understands that *all* assigned objectives are important—not always for their own sake but especially as prerequisites to the success of the longer-range objectives—accepts the responsibility resting upon his shoulders, and takes appropriate action.

MAKING OBJECTIVES ACTIONABLE

Objectives must be actionable, that is, meaningful to the manager who must plan to achieve them. A vague objective of "making profits," "expanding markets," "developing marketable new products," or "being a constructive corporate citizen" may be laudable, but it has no more than the vaguest meaning. The manager must know: How much profit? When? In what product lines? Distributing through what marketing channels? What kinds of new products? Meet what kind of public responsibilities and engage in what public activities? Objectives should lead to definite action.

Objectives and Goals Should Be Specific   Clearly, the most effective planning arises when the responsible manager knows for what definite end point to strive. It has meaning to him. It is something that he can develop programs to attain. He knows what resources may be required. And he knows whether the plan is succeeding in its operation. In addition, a specific objective should be made in the light of definite premises of the future since it must operate in this future. With specific objectives, the manager has a view of the risks he is assuming, the probabilities of success, the things to do, and the resources required to meet the critical premises of the future. He also knows the extent to which he is calling for "stretch" from his organization.

To be specific, objectives or goals need to be definite and accomplishment capable of measurement. Obviously quantified goals help planning. For example, one can set as objectives a specified increase in sales volume in a given number of years, a given profit percentage on the sales dollar or as return on assets, the introduction of a given number of new products in certain product lines, the improvement of quality by a given percentage, or an increase of capacity by a given amount. Many objectives, whether major and company-wide or applicable only to departments and projects, can be quantified.

Even objectives not immediately quantifiable can be given quantifiable meaning by indirection, that is, by using a quantifiable element that correlates with it. For example, absenteeism may correlate closely with employee morale, even though morale itself cannot be quantified. Hence, the specific objective of reducing absenteeism by 50 per cent in, say, a year, provides a substitute quantified objective for improvement of morale. Again, the percentage of qualified promotions made from within might indicate the effectiveness of manager development. Ideally, when a manager quantifies by indirection, he needs several indicators which correlate independently, so that he can verify the measurement. Through further research on underlying or correlated elements in unquantifiable objectives, many now vague and general objectives can be made significant for planning.

Objectives can also be made specific by relating them to programs that, while qualitative in nature, can be verified. For example, a president of a company is given by his board of directors the objectives of improving upper-level manager morale and stockholder support of the company. Among programs believed necessary for accomplishing these objectives are a bonus and stock option program, a divisional organization program, and a program of authority delegations; for the stockholders, a stockholder relations program with certain definite features. While these objectives cannot be quantified, they can be used as specific goals, the accomplishment of which can be verified. They thereby give real meaning to attempts by managers to attain them and become definite rather than vague.

Developing Verifiable Objectives   One of the most interesting and encouraging developments in business has been the increasing number of companies which are developing verifiable objectives. These programs have been spurred on primarily as a device to appraise managers by objectively measuring their progress against goals.[8] But they have had great operational impact on the same companies by forcing them to sharpen in a quantitative or qualitative way their whole structure of objectives or goals. At last, in these companies, managers are recognizing that people cannot work toward

[8] See chap. 22.

objectives expressed in vague, even though noble, generalities for the simple reason that there is no way to know whether a given program contributes effectively to them, and no way to know whether a company, a division, or a department, has actually accomplished them.

As was pointed out earlier,[9] the efficient and effective attainment of objectives is the goal of any manager at any level in any enterprise. While progress has been made in some businesses, it is the authors' impression that these still represent a small percentage of total business firms. And far too little progress—in many cases, not even any interest—is found in nonbusiness enterprises. That to attain objectives may be difficult is true. But the value of attempting to formulate objectives in a verifiable form in *any* enterprise and in *every* part of it is so great that no member of management can feel that he is doing his job unless he does all he can to accomplish this.

Objectives Must Be Planned   Although objectives or goals are the end points of planning, they must, of course, be planned. One of the dangers is that a board of directors or a top executive will set objectives which are in reality hopes and not attainable end points of enterprise operations. It is interesting that the same executive who would never think of setting a production department goal of manufacturing 1,000 units per week without taking into account whether this is possible with the resources and techniques available, may set a "dream" goal of a 20 per cent increase in sales per year without any investigation as to whether this is possible.

Objectives must be planned in the same way as programs. Those responsible for planning objectives, in effect, set as their goal the establishment of verifiable objectives which *can* be reached with a degree of "stretch" or "pull." In doing so, they must take into account the planning premises of the future. What are the company's opportunities? What are its strengths and weaknesses? What are its limitations? What are competitors doing? How much can be accomplished with the resources available and obtainable? These and other premises will necessarily shape the reality of objectives and the final decision of what can and should be accomplished. No one would think of establishing an objective of flying from New York to Hong Kong in an hour by 1975 *unless* the techniques, economics, and other premises indicated that this were attainable. Yet in more mundane areas, such as sales and profit increases, such thinking is not unusual.

Communication and Participation   Obviously, to be workable, objectives must be communicated to those charged with building plans to meet them. This requires not only a statement of the objectives, but, preferably, full disclosure of the premises underlying the objectives and the reasoning that led to them. An even better approach is to have the managers who will make the plans participate in defining the objectives, with the result that the ob-

[9] See above, p. 7.

jectives are likely to be more intelligently set. Such participation gears a manager to developing derivative plans. This is not to imply that subordinate managers should unilaterally set their own goals. They may be too remote from the over-all scheme of enterprise objectives and not in a position to reach high enough to get the necessary stretch required for progress. And it is even possible that a manager will reach too much, that he will set a goal that is unattainable or one that interferes with effective operation of another part of the company.

Understanding of objectives and their environment, plus participation, is the best assurance of loyalty to them. Managers are people, and people tend to distrust or lack enthusiasm for what they do not fully understand or what is foisted on them. Everyone likes to understand what he is doing and feel that he has had a part in choosing it. Although this applies to all managing, it is particularly true of setting objectives.

FOR DISCUSSION

1. Some writers stress the distinction between "quantitative" and "qualitative" goals. What do you think they mean?

2. Do you have an opinion on whether managers have a clear conception of their objectives? Make a list of the goals you wish to achieve in five years. Are they realistic, that is, accomplishable?

3. Concerning the preceding question, will you be able to determine, at the end of five years, the degree to which you have been successful in goal achievement?

4. Some people object to defining long-term goals because they think it impossible to know what will happen during the long run. Do you believe this is an intelligent position to take? Is there a difference between guessing what will happen and making certain that things will happen?

SELECTED REFERENCES

Ansoff, H. I.: *Corporate Strategy*, chaps, 3, 4, 9, New York: McGraw-Hill Book Company, 1965.

Branch, M. C.: *The Corporate Planning Process*, chap. 2, New York: American Management Association, 1962.

Drucker, P. F.: *Managing for Results*, New York: Harper & Row, Publishers, Incorporated, 1964.

————: *The Practice of Management*, chap. 7, New York: Harper & Row, Publishers, Incorporated, 1954.

Eells, R., and C. Walton: *Conceptual Foundations of Business*, chaps. 18, 19, 20, Homewood, Ill.: Richard D. Irwin, Inc., 1961.

Ewing, D. W. (ed.): *Long-range Planning for Management*, chaps. 16, 23, 25, 31, New York: Harper & Row, Publishers, Incorporated, 1958.

Goetz, B. E.: *Managerial Planning and Control*, chap. 5, New York: McGraw-Hill Book Company, 1949.

Grainger, C. H.: "The Hierarchy of Objectives," *Harvard Business Review*, vol. 42, no. 3, pp. 63–74 (May–June, 1964).

Huston, C. L., Jr.: "Setting Corporate Objectives," in *Targets for Management,* General Management Series No. 177, pp. 3–14, New York: American Management Association, 1955.

McConkey, D. D.: *How to Manage by Results,* New York: American Management Association, 1965.

Miller, E. C.: *Objectives and Standards: An Approach to Planning and Control,* New York: American Management Association, 1966.

Odiorne, G. S.: *Management by Objectives,* New York: Pitman Publishing Corporation, 1965.

O'Donnell, Cyril: "Planning Objectives," *California Management Review,* vol. 6, no. 2, pp. 3–10 (Winter, 1963).

Schleh, E. C.: *Management by Results,* chaps. 1–4, New York: McGraw-Hill Book Company, 1961.

Thompson, Stewart: *Management Creeds and Philosophies,* Research Study No. 32, New York: American Management Association, 1958.

planning premises

A fundamental requirement of coordinated planning is that it be undertaken against an established and accepted background of consistent planning premises which the planner understands and agrees to use.

A distinction should immediately be drawn between forecasts that are planning premises and forecasts that are translated into future expectancies, usually in financial terms, from actual plans developed. For example, a forecast to determine future business conditions, sales volume, or political environment furnishes premises on which to develop plans. However, a forecast of the costs or revenues from a new capital investment translates a planning program into future expectations. In the first case, the forecast is a prerequisite of planning; in the second, the forecast is a result of planning.

At the same time, plans themselves and forecasts of their future effects often become premises for other plans. The decision by an electric utility to construct a steam-generating plant, for example, creates conditions that give rise to premises for transmission-line plans, power-sales promotion programs, and other plans necessarily dependent upon the generating plant being built.

SELECTION

As was pointed out in Chapter 5, a manager must limit himself practically to the more critical or strategic planning premises.

In making this selection of planning premises, an enterprise must relate its basic program to those factors that bear materially on it. In virtually all business what happens with national and state gross product and income will be an important premise. Also, such elements of gross product as defense spending or personal services will be important to many businesses. In most businesses, the movement of the business cycle is a critical or limiting factor, although there may be some businesses, such as a water company in a small New England town, for which even this pervasive factor is unimportant. It is difficult to see how expected price-level movements can fail to be of importance to almost all businesses. And most businesses will be concerned with population growth and location.

On the other hand, there are many premises of strategic importance to one given industry and not to another. In the airline industry, for example, the availability of a limited number of airplanes of certain types becomes an important planning premise, since, unlike many other industries, an individual airline cannot easily develop a special type of machinery or plant for its own special operations. The passenger-load factor (ratio of seat-miles sold to seat-miles operated) also has strategic importance to the airline industry, because, unlike the manufacturing industry, an airline's output, the seat-mile, if unsold, cannot be stored for future use. Likewise, in a closely regulated industry, the policies and practices of the government have much more importance for planning premises than in a relatively unregulated business. Thus, the Civil Aeronautics Board's policies on new routes or rates are strategically consequential to an airline, whereas the toothpaste manufacturer has no such limitation on his market but will concern himself with premises critical to him, not the least of which is government regulation of price discrimination under the Robinson-Patman and Clayton Acts.

External and Internal Premises   Some premises for business planning lie outside the firm, others within it. Those premises external to the firm may be classified into three groups: the general business environment, which includes political, economic, social, technological, and ethical conditions; the product market, which includes conditions influencing demand for the firm's product; and the factor market, which has to do with land, location, labor, materials and parts, and capital.

Premises internal to the firm include the sales forecast, capital investment in plant and equipment, policies, major programs already decided, and many other factors that influence or dictate the type of planning to be done. Not the least important among internal planning premises are the beliefs, behavior, strong points, and weaknesses of the top executives or owners of the business and, often, of the employees.

Tangible and Intangible Premises   Occasionally, business managers forget that planning premises may be intangible, as well as tangible. Premises are tangible when they can be quantified, whether in dollars and cents, labor-hours, units of production, or machine units.

Of equal importance in planning are the many intangible factors normally encountered. These cannot be expressed numerically, but they are significant background elements in the planning scene. For example, it might be calculated that to produce and sell a new product would cost x dollars per unit and that it would sell at y dollars, leaving an attractive profit of z dollars. But the product may not fit the over-all strategy of the firm. If the firm's reputation has been built on high-quality luxury items and the product does not fit this category, the management may feel that the loss in prestige would offset the profits to be made. It may be argued that loss in prestige is really a tangible factor, for the management is really taking the position that the net profits of the firm as a whole will be enhanced by not producing the new product. If a way could be found to estimate quantitatively the loss in profits on other items, the factor referred to as intangible would become tangible.

FORECASTING

If the future could be forecast with accuracy, or, to put it in another way, if the businessman were operating under static conditions, business planning would be relatively simple. The manager would need only take into account his human and material resources, compute the optimum method of reaching his objective, and proceed with a high degree of certainty toward it.

Fayol speaks of *prevoyance* as the essence of management.[1] This looking ahead, according to Fayol, includes both assessing the future and making provision for it.

As a matter of fact, a half century ago Fayol referred to plans as syntheses of various forecasts, whether short- or long-term, special, or otherwise.[2] It is interesting, in this connection, that Fayol recommended yearly forecasts and ten-year forecasts, the latter being revised at least each five years and oftener if proved necessary by the yearly ones. Furthermore, each forecast was to include a wide variety of subsidiary or elemental forecasts, comprised of such data as capital, output, production costs, sales, selling price, and other factors.

In practice, forecasts vary considerably in length, breadth of coverage, and quality, from little more than a manager's hunch to a detailed analysis of the future made by a competent staff. As has already been indicated, some businesses need expert forecasts, of long periods, and others may be able to operate effectively with very short forecasts that reflect little more than the predilections of their managers. Furthermore, some businesses that need expert forecasts may be unable to afford more than the information that grows out of a manager's reading of economic predictions in numerous journals plus his own judgment of the situation.

Need for Forecasting   The need for adequate forecasting is apparent from the key role it plays in planning. But forecasting has values aside from its use in developing plans. In the first place, the making of forecasts and their review by managers compel thinking ahead, looking to the future, and pro-

---

[1] Henri Fayol, *General and Industrial Management* (New York: Pitman Publishing Corporation, 1949), p. 43. In this translation, the term is translated as "foreseeing."

[2] Fayol emphasized this usage in an interview published in the *Chronique Social de France* in January, 1925, quoted in Urwick's foreword to *General and Industrial Management*, p. xi.

viding for it. Also, the very act of forecasting may disclose areas where necessary control is lacking. For example, in a report submitting the results of a pessimistic forecast to his key executives, a president of a large company said: "The declining profit in this forecast is disappointing, but it is my impression that every forecast extending beyond a year has shown profits less than we have been able to procure as the result of determined efforts by all members of our management team. This picture should not dishearten us but should stimulate our efforts to improve it."

Forecasting, especially where widely participated in throughout the organization, may help to unify and coordinate plans. By focusing attention on the future it assists in bringing a singleness of purpose to planning.

Even though much emphasis is placed on forecasting, it must be recognized that all forecasts are subject to a degree of error, since the best analyses or judgments cannot result in true clairvoyance. Guesswork can never be omitted from forecasts, although it can often be reduced to a minimum. Sometimes the margin of error is considerable, although it can usually be brought within tolerable limits. Managers often expect too much from forecasts and fail to recognize the unavoidable margin of error which must exist in any prophecy. They also occasionally neglect to examine the underlying assumptions of a forecast to determine whether these are supported by facts, reasonable estimates, or accurate reflection of policies and plans.

Informed and intelligent "guestimates" made by experienced business executives and technicians are often extraordinarily prophetic. One of the authors, who has participated in much planning and many forecasts, has found the intelligent guess of a well-qualified executive to be an excellent check on the accuracy of forecasts made by a competent staff. Sometimes the specialist overlooks major policy and other matters which have a strong bearing on a forecast but whose influence may not be immediately apparent. A clairvoyant [3] quality is a rare gift, but many experienced managers have developed it, and where it exists, it is an excellent supplement to the work of the forecaster.

Essential Elements   From his experience as a management consultant, James W. Redfield [4] summarized some years ago the essential elements in the forecast process as follows:

1. *Developing the groundwork*—that is, carrying out an orderly investigation of products, company, and industry, in order to determine generally how each one of these has progressed in the past, separately and in relation to each other. In short, the aim is to build a structure on which future estimates can be based.

[3] As will be recognized, this "clairvoyant" quality is usually in reality the conceptual and computing ability of an exceptional mind.

[4] J. W. Redfield, "Elements of Forecasting," *Harvard Business Review*, vol. 29, no. 6, p. 82 (November, 1951).

2. *Estimating future business*—that is, following a clearcut plan for working out future expectancies in the form of a *mutual* undertaking with key executives and, after future business has been estimated in accordance with the predetermined step-by-step procedure, issuing an official statement of the resultant forecast. The key executives, by mutually developing the forecast, automatically assume co-responsibility and individual accountability for such later deviations of actual from estimated results as may occur.

3. *Comparing actual with estimated results*—that is, checking the attained with the anticipated status of the business periodically, tracking down reasons for any major differences. The forecast provides benchmarks for measuring unanticipated gains or losses. Once measured, the reasons for important variations can be investigated on the spot.

4. *Refining the forecast process*—that is, once familiarity with estimating the future of the business is gained through practice, sharpening the approach and refining the procedure. One must be reasonably tolerant with early forecasts, recognizing that proficiency with a new tool is not acquired overnight, and at the same time insist on constant improvement as experience with the process is gained.

THE GENERAL BUSINESS ENVIRONMENT: EXTERNAL PREMISES

In this section, certain of the main aspects of the general business environment will be outlined. Most of them will apply also to nonbusiness enterprises, but some aspects of environment not discussed here will be important if the enterprise is a church, a university, a charitable undertaking, or a political agency.

Political Stability The political environment in which a business operates is a premise of the utmost importance. Government, whether at the international, Federal, state, or local level, controls a number of elements in the environment of business. But political stability is perhaps even more important than the extent of government controls. In other words, if the political situation is stable, a business manager deals with a known condition in making his plans. But, as has been the case for more than a quarter of a century in the field of international politics, when an extraordinary degree of instability exists, business managers find it difficult to forecast. The questions of war, cold war, armed truce, or peace are usually uppermost in a planner's mind because of their permeating effect upon the business environment.

Political stability in domestic affairs is important also. In many countries internal political instability makes planning almost impossible. Even in the United States, the character of the national, state, or local administration and the degree of definiteness of policy of the various legislatures affect the general business environment.

Ethical Standards At various points in this book, it is emphasized that any enterprise, business or nonbusiness, must operate within and be responsive to the social and ethical norms of its environment. These are clearly important planning premises for a manager, although, perhaps unfortunately, they are not normally included in the formal structure of planning assumptions. It is usually assumed, of course, that managers interested in the long-run success of their enterprise will recognize this without any formal treatment.

But there have been a number of instances in recent years, such as price-fixing, conflict-of-interest situations, selling or buying through unusual favors, and even certain cases of outright bribery, which raise questions as to whether this premise is well understood. Nonetheless, the authors are confident that instances of unethical behavior are relatively rare and that businesses, like universities and churches, do operate against a background of, and are responsive to, ethical standards.

In fact, it is clearly in the best *selfish* interests of managers responsible for enterprises desiring successful growth and continuity to be so responsive. And there should be little need to make social responsibility a special area for teaching and premising. But for those who do not see this simple fact, it is well to emphasize the pervasiveness of this planning premise. Certainly, if a manager is not responsive to this aspect of his environment, society will soon find ways through application of present laws or new regulations to force his responsiveness.

Government Controls   A business must develop planning premises in accordance with the nature and extent of government controls and the freedom of limitation of its enterprise. Modern states are characterized by the extent to which private enterprises are prohibited, regulated, or subsidized. Moreover, controls continually change, largely in the direction of expansion, since government control has an inherent tendency toward the generation of more control in order to patch gaps, bring equality of regulation or subsidy, and strengthen original objectives.

The business manager must not only premise the immediate future of such controls but must forecast their probable character and effect for a longer term. Naturally, this difficulty is the greater the more a business is subject to controls and the less stable the controls. For example, the difficulty of forecasting what the government may do that will affect a long-range plan of a railroad is greater than the difficulty encountered by a toy manufacturer, if it can be assumed that detailed government controls will not be imposed on the toy industry. Both are concerned with the major regulatory and subsidy policies that affect business in general, but, in addition, the railroad company must reckon with the numerous special controls of the state commissions and the Federal Interstate Commerce Commission.

This difficulty is sharpened by the expanding position of the government in the product market. As many defense industries have found out, the government is no ordinary purchaser. As government purchases become larger and more specialized and as the government adopts greater safeguards against undue profits or against production departing from specifications, the business firm is increasingly at the mercy of official controls. These, in turn, are far more than pronouncements of the legislature or even of the department head and come to include the multitude of interpretations placed by commissions, boards, procurement officers, auditors, project engineers, and many others concerned with government supply.

Government Fiscal Policy   Closely related to the more direct problem of government regulation and purchasing is the effect of government financial and tax policy. When the Federal government spent less than 5 per cent of the national income, as it did four decades ago, the effect of government fiscal policy on business was considerably less than it has been in recent years, when the expenditures run to approximately 20 per cent. When the government plays a major role in income distribution, taxation, and investment, practically every manager in the nation must premise government fiscal policy in developing his plans.

The important role played by government fiscal policy has significant planning impacts beyond the over-all effects. The imposition of excise taxes on certain commodities or services, the allowance of exemptions for small-company profits, the operation of excess-profits taxes, special depreciation allowances for defense plant investment, and investment tax credits are among the important administrative devices for distributing the tax load. These are often difficult to forecast, and accommodation of plans to their effects is a formidable task. Could the passenger-transportation industry, for example, have known enough to plan on the basis of continuing the 15 per cent tax on passenger traffic, originally designed to discourage travel, years after a surplus of passenger service existed? In 1952, should a business have planned on the discontinuance of the excess-profits tax in 1953? In 1941, could a business planning expansion of capital facilities have foreseen whether there would be special allowance for accelerated depreciation and whether it would apply to wartime investment? And could a company have expected such treatment in the postwar period when the defense program was expanded in 1950? In 1962, should a business have planned on corporate tax relief and special tax benefits for new investment? How long and to what extent should a business plan on investment tax credits in 1968?

Population Trends   Among the best indicators of future markets for most businesses are population estimates, whether in terms of totals, composition, or location. While it is not always possible to translate accurately the effect of population changes on the market for a given product or for the output of an individual firm, there are a large number of products in which population is a major determinant of demand.

Population trends are subject to fairly accurate forecasting for periods up to five years and to tolerably accurate forecasting for much longer periods. For example, an estimate made in 1955 of population in the United

States forecast a rise from 165 million in 1955 to some 228 million in 1975.[5] Although population trends may be upset by such major calamities as wars and although such events as the extraordinarily large movement of population to the Southwest after World War II have been underestimated, population forecasts furnish a reasonably reliable and usable set of premises for most businesses.

Employment, Productivity, and National Income Fairly reliable premises for the future can be obtained from well-considered estimates of employment, productivity, and national income. Given a certain population trend, including some knowledge as to the age and sex composition of the population, and assuming that public policy will not permit more than a given level of unemployment, the total number of persons to be employed in all undertakings, both government and private, can be forecast. From employment data and estimates of annual increases in output per man-hour and of changes in the work week, one can mathematically calculate a gross national product for the future at the present level of prices.

Such a model has been produced for various periods in the future by government agencies, individual economists, and private organizations—for instance, the National Planning Association in 1952.[6] This interesting study, although it was claimed to be not a forecast but a model for full employment, summarized the basic features of an economy in the United States in 1960. It was based upon the assumption (1) that population would reach 175 million by 1960 and that the total labor force would be 69 million civilians; (2) that the United States government was committed to a policy of full employment, which assumed a maximum of 4.0 per cent of the civilian labor force as unemployed; (3) that the average work week would decline from 40.3 hours in 1951 to 39.0 in 1960; and (4) that the output per man-hour would increase at a rate of 2.5 percent per year. With a base of 1951 data, these assumptions furnished the means for calculating a 1960 gross national product of 425 billion dollars in 1951 dollars, against an actual 1951 figure of 329.2 billion dollars. By similar calculation, the National Planning Association calculated gross national products for intermediate years.

Moving from the calculation of gross national product, the report presented a series of alternative models of the American economy in 1960,

[5] As forecast by the U.S. Bureau of the Census, reported in *Economic Report of the President* (Washington: Government Printing Office, 1957), p. 97. Actually the estimate of the Census Bureau pointed to a range of 207 to 228 million in 1975, but this forecast was based on the probably too-conservative assumption that there would be no improvement in mortality experience after 1960. There has been a tendency in recent years for most population experts to underestimate population growth, and any estimate of this kind, although useful, particularly in the short term, must be revised as better indicators become available.

[6] Gerard Colm, *The American Economy in 1960*, Planning Pamphlet No. 81 (Washington: National Planning Association, 1952). See also Gerard Colm, *Long-range Projections for Economic Growth: The American Economy in 1970*, Planning Pamphlet No. 107 (Washington: National Planning Association, 1959).

based upon various analyses of trends and assumptions, including a major assumption of a level of national security expenditure of 40 billion dollars. Combining the various features of the alternative models in a way to give a "feasible and sustainable pattern of economic growth," the report outlined an "adjusted" model for full employment in 1960, as shown in Table 1.

Table 1 and the assumptions on which it has been based are an interesting example of the use of national-income techniques to determine what the total economy may be under a given set of conditions. To the extent that these conditions are accurately prophesied, the model becomes a forecast. But, in any case, it points up the determinants of the national economy and can be useful to any business in making its forecast.

As a matter of fact, this forecast for 1960 turned out to be surprisingly

TABLE 1   ADJUSTED MODEL OF PREDICTED GNP FOR 1960 COMPARED TO ACTUALS FOR 1951 (in billions of 1951 dollars)

	Receipts		Expenditures		Excess of receipts	
	1951 actuals	Adjusted model	1951 actuals	Adjusted model	1951 actuals	Adjusted model
Gross national product	$329.3	$425.0	$329.3	$425.0	0.0	0.0
Consumers	$225.0	$307.6	$208.0	$291.1	+17.0	+16.5
Business	33.0	46.9	58.5	55.9	−25.5	− 9.0
Plant and equipment	....	....	36.4	41.4		
Inventory increase	....	....	10.3	2.9		
Residential housing	....	....	11.8	11.6		
International	....	....	.2	2.5	− .2	− 2.5
Government	69.9	70.5	62.6	75.5	+ 7.3	− 5.0
Statistical discrepancy	1.4				+ 1.4	

	1951	Adjusted model
Assumptions		
Population	143.0 million	175.0 million
Labor force: total	66.0 million	72.5 million
Armed services	3.1 million	3.5 million
Civilian employed	61.0 million	66.2 million
Unemployed	1.9 million	2.8 million
Average weekly hours	40.3	39.0
Output per man-hour	$2.59	$3.24
Per capita consumption of disposable income	$1,348	$1,663
Per cent increase of per capita consumption	....	23.3%

source: Gerard Colm, *The American Economy in 1960*, Planning Pamphlet No. 81 (Washington: National Planning Association, 1952), pp. 43–65.

accurate. If adjustment is made for the change in price levels between 1951 and 1960, the difference in actual and forecast total gross national product (GNP) was only approximately 2 per cent. The components of GNP were likewise fairly accurately estimated, as were the year-to-year projections, which showed close correlation except in the recession year of 1954, and even then the variation was only 2.6 per cent.[7] It is, therefore, understandable that forecasters take seriously the National Planning Association projections for 1970, which show a GNP of 790 billion dollars (in 1959 dollars), a population of 214 million, civilian employment of 80.7 million, unemployment of 2.9 million, a work week of 37.5 hours, and an annual increase of output per man-hour of 3.4 per cent.[8]

While this is only one example of projections of national economic data, and there are many other available forecasts regularly being made by competent economists, it does show that long-range forecasts can reasonably be made. At the same time, forecasts cannot be expected to show up all the vagaries of the economy. However, they are a guide to long-range planning, particularly if it may be assumed that national economic and fiscal policy can successfully come to grips (and most economists believe that they can) with basic goals of full employment and growth.

In addition to studying broad projections of national economic trends, a company, of course, must translate them into impact on its industry and on itself. This requires, as Colm points out,[9] two estimating procedures. In one, the analyst moves downward from national data to industry group forecasts and perhaps to special industries. In the other, referred to as the "bottom up" projection, the analyst moves upward from individual company data and summaries of industry plans to the national economic data.

What is needed are refined breakdowns of basic economic data. One of the most promising approaches is the development of input-output tables. These show the relationships of industries to one another and their sharing of gross national product by calculating the purchases and sales made between industries. While some work on input-output analysis has been done by industrial and regional specialists, this lacks the accuracy and usefulness of an analysis on a national scale.

Developed by Professor Wassily W. Leontief of Harvard, input-output tables were first roughly utilized by him in 1945 and served to forecast the impending large demand in the postwar period for steel and other raw materials. The Federal government issued input-output tables for 1947 several years later. Unfortunately, because of lack of government appropriation, no analyses were again available until 1964. At that time, input-output

[7] See Gerard Colm, "How Good Are Long-range Projections of GNP for Business Planning?" *California Management Review*, vol. 1, no. 2, pp. 1–10 (Winter, 1959).

[8] Colm, *Long-range Projections for Economic Growth: The American Economy in 1970.*

[9] Colm, "How Good Are Long-range Projections of GNP for Business Planning?" *op. cit.*, p. 6.

tables for the year 1958 were published and, shortly thereafter, were updated to 1961 and 1963.[10] The availability of this powerful tool for forecasting is an encouraging development for businesses which now can have the derivative effects of national production and income factors reflected in their impact on a given industry.

There are, nonetheless, a tremendous number of industry studies available through government and industry sources, both of a forecast and a historical nature. Most Federal government departments with a business interest publish economic material useful for forecasting, as do trade associations, trade publications, banks, private research organizations, and professional associations. Certainly, in most industries, the manager who wants industry data can tap many sources.[11]

Price Levels One of the important premises to forecast is the course of future price levels and their effect upon the industry and firm. In the short term—approximately one to three years—through calculating the impact of deficit financing and the utilization of credit institutions, both government and private, the probable trend of prices is subject to a reasonably accurate estimate. But for periods beyond a few years, the course of price levels is not so clear. In some ways, however, the job of forecasting prices in general is not so difficult as it was several decades ago, since government fiscal policy plays such an important role in their determination. But the extent of deficit financing or the existence of surpluses, which may affect prices materially, is not too easy to premise.

Over the very long term, experience has proved that the business that bases its planning upon a rising price level has been right. While periods of price recession have occurred and have often presented serious problems, especially for businesses in which inventories are extremely important, the course of history has disclosed a relentless depreciation in the value of money in all economies. There seems to be no reason for expecting this trend to change in the future. But the fact remains that accurate price-level forecasting is largely a matter of prophesying government domestic and international policy.

Technological Environment In very recent years, business firms have been taking a closer and more systematic look at their technological environment, in addition to their general business environment. Since the pace of technical change is so rapid and since new products and processes may be keys to a

---

[10] Wassily W. Leontief, "Proposal for Better Business Forecasting," *Harvard Business Review*, vol. 42, no. 6, pp. 166–182 (November–December, 1964).

[11] An excellent bibliography for sources of market and economic forecasting information is R. N. Carpenter, *Guidelist for Marketing Research and Economic Forecasting*, Research Study No. 50 (New York: American Management Association, 1961). Also, see R. S. Reichard, *Practical Techniques of Sales Forecasting* (New York: McGraw-Hill Book Company, 1966), pp. 103–110. Reichard reports that the Federal government spends over 100 million dollars each year on statistical data collection.

company's future plans, an increasing number of companies are emphasizing regular and complete technological forecasts affecting their industry. In fact, developing premises from such forecasts may be as important to the company's planning and its future as are political, economic, or social premises.

Most companies that have gone far in developing planning premises from their technological forecasts have already made a considerable technical effort. What has been done in these instances is to encourage members of their technical staffs to be alert to future developments; to make frequent contacts with suppliers and customers with development staffs; to think in terms of the impact of current scientific developments on the future state of the technology; and to develop orderly forecasts of how these developments affect the company's products, processes, or markets. Executives who have asked their research and development staffs to undertake such an assignment have been pleasantly surprised at the enthusiasm with which these forecasts are prepared and presented. They have apparently found that scientists and engineers like to be a part of, and contribute to, basic company planning. These executives have also reported, not at all surprisingly, that these forecasts have been extraordinarily helpful in improving company planning.

Even smaller companies, without research and development staffs, can successfully make this forecast and include the future technological environment in their planning premises. A few scientists or engineers in a company, if encouraged, can do much to present an orderly picture of the company's technological environment. And many nontechnically qualified people, as well as those with special technical qualifications, can understand much of the technical literature in a periodical or report in the company's field. Moreover, suppliers especially and often major customers are willing to pass on to the discerning small businessman the results of their research and engineering ideas, if by doing so he becomes a larger-volume customer or a more alert supplier.

General Business Environment versus the Individual Firm   As is clear from the above discussion, a firm must translate general business environment into the probable effects upon its own problems and plans. This is an important and difficult step. But most managers are fairly familiar with the relationship of their firms to their industry, and if they can forecast industry behavior, they will have gone a long way in premising the future of their own firms. The difficult problem is often to discover the impact of the general business environment on the industry in which the firm operates.

The key relationships of any industry to national income, the work week, population, and similar factors of the general business environment, if properly studied and recognized, can often make it possible for the planner to interpret industry development in terms of changes in the nature of the national economy. Freight-transportation demand, for example, shows a strong correlation with gross national product, while passenger-transportation demand is correlated with national income. But the railroad manager who, in

1920, did not reckon with the private automobile and truck or who, in 1940, did not give attention to the impact of the airlines on passenger transportation could have been greatly misled by even the best estimates of national production or income. Hence the trends within broad categories of industry are important, as are new technologies, new products, and changes in public tastes.

Studies of industry trends, developed by astute planners in business, have bridged the gaps between broad industry forecasts and those for segments of an industry and, finally, those of the company concerned. There are no formulas available for making this transfer. But careful study of firm and industry trends can give forecasts within a tolerable degree of accuracy. It must ever be remembered that forecasting is not an exact science and that the further in the future a manager plans, the wider will be his margin of error. But one of the tasks of good planning is to recognize the width of this margin of error and to incorporate in plans the necessary safeguards, hedges, and flexibility, so that unavoidable error in prognostication will not lead to a crippling business loss.

PREMISES EXTERNAL TO THE FIRM: THE PRODUCT MARKET

The general business environment—especially such basic factors as national income, population, employment, and wage levels—obviously furnishes the principal key to the forecasting of the product market of a firm. The purpose of developing premises with respect to the product market is to determine the kind of market for its product or service that the firm faces.

Industry Demand For most industries, there are statistics available through government sources, trade associations, or special economic studies showing product output, prices, employment, and occasionally, costs. While these are usually of an historical nature, they often furnish a basis for forecasting industry demand, especially if factors such as new processes and techniques, shifts in customer tastes, national economic welfare, population changes, and similar items are considered. Moreover, for certain industries, comprehensive forecasts of demand have been worked out for the future. Such has been the case of key raw materials, a long-range forecast of the production and consumption of which was worked out in detail by the President's Material Policy Commission.[12] Similar studies have been made from time to time by government agencies for other industries.

Of course, the larger firms can afford to develop, in comprehensive detail and after careful study, forecasts of industry demand. These can be found in any large, well-managed firm and furnish an important planning backdrop against which the demand for the firm's products may be forecast.

In the understanding of industry demand, it may be worthwhile to

---

[12] See *Resources for Freedom* (Washington: Government Printing Office, 1952). This study forecasts selected material production and consumption through 1975.

emphasize again the importance of interindustry relationships. Input-output analyses, which portray how products move between industries, could be extremely helpful in forecasting industry demand, particularly for industries not primarily dependent upon the ultimate consumer for their market.

Individual Firm Demand   Few businesses, other than agriculture, operate in a market that closely approaches perfectly competitive conditions. Almost all businesses face a demand which has varying degrees of elasticity and which, although derived from industry demand, is sensitive to the actions of the competing firms. In other words, most business operates under conditions of imperfect competition. This requires special knowledge both of customers' desires and their ability and willingness to pay and of competitors' actions and strategies.

Customer data can be accumulated in many ways, although the time spent on them, their cost, and their value depend largely on the type of research and the intelligence with which it is undertaken. Every firm needs to know who its potential customers are, where they are, and what are the most effective means of selling them. Few firms are too small to take advantage of existing data, whether from government sources, publications available in libraries, or material collected by business associations.

If a firm cannot spend anything to find out about its customers, its best basis for premising plans will be to imitate competitors, on the assumption that they have discovered the proper outlets and means of selling them. A second method would be to experiment to a limited degree, to ascertain by trial what the best methods of sales are. But if the firm can afford to do so, clearly the best course is to engage in enough market research to make reasonably sure of the present and probable future market. This normally involves a considerable cost, and small firms that attempt to research any but the simplest markets may well find that market research, albeit desirable for good planning, is too expensive and must be engaged in sparingly. Even when research is done, it can hardly be more than a general estimate of a situation, the close watching of successful competitors to determine their policies, or a survey of major customers.

Those external planning premises relating to competitors also involve such factors as their production methods, costs and profits, the trend of their position in the market, and their reaction to a new entry into their market.[13] Such data are not easy to obtain, although business luncheons, cocktail parties, informal conferences, and similar channels can often give the astute observer fairly accurate information on which to premise his competitors' behavior. Furthermore, much can be inferred from the activity of competitors, from financial reports, and from studies of the market share of each firm. In addition, in certain industries data of this kind are in the official

[13] On this problem, see especially N. Kaldor's articles, "Market Imperfection and Excess Capacity," *Economica*, new series, vol. 2 (February, 1955), and "The Equilibrium of the Firm," *Economic Journal*, vol. 44, pp. 60–76 (March, 1934).

records. The so-called regulated industries—such as the railroads, airlines, and public utilities—file detailed reports with state and Federal commissions; these reports are public property, open to the use of any competitor desiring them. Moreover, even in some nonregulated industries, cost or production information or data on wage policies and payments are freely exchanged between firms or through the medium of trade associations.

PREMISES EXTERNAL TO THE FIRM: THE FACTOR MARKET

Among external premises necessary for effective planning are those dealing with the acquisition of goods and services. The factor market is that which the economist refers to as land, labor, and capital. It is preferable from the standpoint of business management, however, to refer to the factor market as applying to business location, the labor market, the source of materials and parts, and the availability of capital. Although not all aspects of these are external, the discussion at this point concerns those not within control, through internal decision, of the firm.

Business Location　The choice of physical location of a place of business is affected by several things that are generally uncontrollable by the enterprise, among which are transportation, the existence of complementary industry, the availability of special skills and services, and the local political environment.

Location, once decided upon, is not easily changed, because of the sunk costs in both property and trained local personnel. There are few more inflexible elements in planning than a plant site.

Transportation facilities and the costs involved are a primary consideration in location, and when the transportation of a given raw material important to a firm's production involves a large enough expense, this factor alone may determine the business's location. Or, as is more likely, location may be dictated by a balance between the cost of transporting raw materials and the cost of shipping finished goods.

In considering the existence of complementary industry, one has only to look at the concentration of the automobile industry in the Detroit area, the aircraft industry in southern California, or the steel industry in the Pittsburgh and Chicago areas to realize that a business intending to service these industries or to use their products would want to locate in their area. This is a matter not only of transportation but also of being near markets, of being in close communication with the industry, and of drawing upon the knowledge and skills that grow up in such locations. For example, many companies felt forced to establish West Coast branches in recent decades as their markets became concentrated there. One specific case was that of a manufacturer of very small electric motors used mainly in the aircraft and missile industries. Originally located on the East Coast and quite able without serious transportation disadvantages to ship its product to West Coast users, the company nevertheless found that certain customers preferred to work with

West Coast plants because of the ease of handling design improvements, inspection, and similar aspects of supply control.

The existence of complementary industry has a pronounced influence on the availability of skills. The development of a local labor force competent in the production of a given item may be a dictating premise upon which to plan expansion of that product. Until World War II and the subsequent expansion of defense production forced the training of skilled industrial workers throughout the country, there were industries in which virtually all the know-how was concentrated in a few cities. Although this concentration has been broken up somewhat in such fields as aircraft and electronics, where it still exists it is extremely influential, as in the garment industry, glovemaking, the textile industry, and even much of the heavy machinery industry.

Along with availability of skills, availability of local services is important. A plant dependent upon the services of tool and die firms, job machine shops, screw machine companies, and foundries, to mention only a few, would be at a serious disadvantage where they are not available.

Local political environment may be difficult to base future premises upon, but it is unquestionably significant for location. A city with a reputation for honest and fair dealing with business will be preferred by most businesses to a city riddled with machine politics and graft.

The Labor Market   In addition to the importance of availability of skills and services in selecting a location, the nature of the labor market is important in terms of quality, stability, and quantity. The quality of labor available for given kinds of operations varies between areas and between groups in an area. For example, an airline once found that the quality of maintenance mechanic labor on the West Coast was superior—probably because of the larger reservoir of trained workers—to that in the New York area. Furthermore, the quality of labor depends upon the type required. If financial training is a prerequisite to the jobs called for by a plan, this labor would be more available in and around the larger financial centers.

Labor stability also varies between areas and between groups. Some areas have records of work stoppages and difficult labor relations. In some industries, white-collar workers identify themselves with wage earners, dependent upon strong union leadership, while in other industries they ally themselves with company management.

Above all, of course, the quantity of labor available at a price is significant for planning. Although the growth of unionism and the widespread development of defense industry during and after World War II have had a leveling effect on wages, before World War II there were sharp wage differentials in different sections of the country. Even now some differences, though less extreme, exist, and they may be important in planning. For example, a company located in almost any larger city may have to pay somewhat higher labor rates and executive salaries than one that operates in a smaller or rural community.

Sources of Materials and Parts As pointed out in the discussion of business location, sources become of major importance when transportation costs are controlling factors in the economics of the firm. But even in cases where raw materials are heavy and transportation costs high, efficiency of transportation may keep the location of sources of supply from becoming a controlling factor. The steel industry has found that it can import Venezuelan ore efficiently, and a West Coast refinery found that it was not at a serious disadvantage when it had to obtain crude oil from the Near East rather than from the California oil fields.

Despite transportation efficiency, cost differentials in obtaining materials and parts do exist. Furthermore, the accessibility of a source makes it possible better to control design, quality, and delivery, and no transportation system can assure adequate supply of materials and parts. If the supply from outside is inadequate and the firm cannot produce a supply quickly enough, production can hardly be continued. Many of the early post-World War II television manufacturers failed to give enough weight in their planning to the availability of picture tubes; without this important part, they could not have reached volume production even if they had been able to solve all other problems of production and marketing.

Capital Availability Capital availability is often the controlling external premise of planning. It may commonly appear that a firm has many options in raising capital, such as bank loans, mortgages, factoring of accounts receivable, accounts payable, the securities markets, and direct and indirect government financing. And if a firm could actually choose from among all these possibilities, it would undoubtedly favor a low-cost source of funds with the minimum threat to financial control of the enterprise.

But despite the economists' reference to a "supply" of capital, which implies that capital can be had at a price, there are in fact serious gaps in the capital market. Particularly with small and medium-sized businesses, the limits to availability of capital are reached at a relatively low level and often far sooner than the enthusiasm of expansion-minded owners will admit. The writers have seen a number of small businesses reach the limit of their expansion, and often overreach it, because of the unavailability of capital. Moreover, the difficulty often is not that capital is not available but rather that providers of important capital properly wish to accompany their investment with a degree of control, a condition that may prove unacceptable to the firm's owners. A small firm whose owners do not wish to give up control usually has, as practical sources of capital, the capital of the principal owners, retained earnings, borrowing on real estate and other pledgeable assets, factoring accounts receivable, limited commercial bank loans (normally designed to finance operations and not investment), moderate loans from friends, and, occasionally, if a large special contract is involved, progress payments as money is spent in a contract. Even larger firms with established reputations and availability of public financing through sales of stocks or bonds suffer from some discontinuities in the capital market. There is almost always a limit to the amount of new financing that can be undertaken, either by debt or equity capital, and this limit varies, depending upon the fortunes of the company and the receptiveness of the market to new financing at any given time.

PREMISES INTERNAL TO THE FIRM: THE SALES FORECAST

As in the case of external planning premises, it will not be possible to deal here with all the various premises internal to an enterprise. Among those that deserve special attention, however, is the sales forecast. The sales forecast is the basic planning document of the typical firm. It is in a sense both a plan and a planning premise. It also may be regarded as partially external to the firm, in that it reflects external conditions as well as internal plans. But because it sets the framework on which most internal plans are constructed, it is regarded here as the dominant planning premise internal to the firm.

Nature and Use The sales forecast is a projection of expected sales, by product and price, for a number of months or years. It is, then, a kind of pro forma sales portion of the traditional income statement for the future. With a sales forecast over a long enough period in which it has some confidence, a management can usually do a good job in forecasting profits and cash flow. The revenue side of the future is usually the most difficult to forecast and the least subject to positive control by the firm. Given the revenue outlook, the firm can at least decide what it can afford to spend for operations. Moreover, since most operating expenses are within the control of managers to a major degree, the forecast of expenses can be more accurate than a forecast of revenues.

In any case, it is the sales forecast that is the key to internal planning. Business and capital outlays and policies of all kinds are made for the purpose of maximizing profits from expected sales. Although there are some enterprises that need to pay little attention to sales (for example, the small-city water company or the government defense contractor with a long-term order that has little chance of being canceled or modified), it is a rare business that can overlook the market for long. Even the farmer who, operating under support prices, may have a guaranteed market for a certain product for a coming year, can hardly ignore market influences as they affect succeeding years or alternative crops.

Since the sales forecast is so important a tool, there is scarcely a company that should not take the time and trouble to make the best one its resources will permit. Even the company with a fairly large backlog of orders for custom-made goods that need not go on the shelf as inventory needs such a forecast. One of the authors recalls a company that simply measured its future sales by the size of the total sales backlog. Although this backlog remained high, the managers were surprised to find one day that it was for a limited number of products for delivery over so long a period that the total dollar amount of the backlog would not permit capacity operation of the machinery and manpower then being employed.

Smaller companies often make the mistake of believing that sales forecasts are too expensive and of overlooking the variety of sources of data available at little or no cost. The purchasing agent, members of the sales staff, the treasurer, and the production manager are among those who may possess bits and pieces of information, which, gathered together, could make an acceptable forecast. Moreover, the wide range of information available from government and industry sources is neither difficult nor expensive to obtain.

There is some advantage in having the sales forecast made by as many key executives and staff personnel as possible. Since it becomes the basic internal planning premise of the firm, such participation may lead to more willing acceptance, as well as greater accuracy.

An indicator of the increasing importance being given planning is the rapid rise of sales forecasting in the past decade. Although better-managed companies long realized the value of good sales forecasting, the experience of World War II and the shortage years that followed led most managers to plan on the basis of maximum production rather than on the requirements of the market. With the return of normal business and strong competition, along with greater attention to the managerial job itself, managers have found that planning success depends largely upon the ability to forecast sales.

There has been a real swing away from the less formal methods, such as the managerial hunch, to more formal methods. A few years ago, a survey by the American Management Association of 297 firms showed a strong movement toward scientific sales forecasting.[14] This study indicated that more than one-sixth of the companies surveyed, many of which were rather large, had embarked upon organized programs of sales forecasting only in the past five years and that the number of companies centralizing primary responsibility for this forecasting had increased by 60 per cent in the same period. Another study, made for the Controllership Foundation by Sord and Welsch in 1958, found that, of 424 companies selected for a better-than-average quality of management, 93 per cent developed sales forecasts, 53 per cent estimated the company's share of the market, and 42 per cent developed forecasts of general economic conditions.[15] The publication of studies on sales forecasting since 1955 is an index of this trend.[16]

[14] *Sales Forecasting: Uses, Techniques, and Trends,* Special Report No. 16 (New York: American Management Association, 1956), appendix, "Survey of Sales-forecasting Practices," pp. 143–145.

[15] B. H. Sord and G. A. Welsch, *Business Budgeting* (New York: Controllership Foundation, Inc., 1958), p. 133.

[16] In addition to the American Management Association and Controllership Foundation reports cited, attention should be drawn to the following reports: American Management Association, *Company Organization for Economic Forecasting,* Research Report No. 28 (New York: American Management Association, 1957); National Industrial Conference Board, *Forecasting in Industry,* Studies in Business Policy No. 77 (New York: National Industrial Conference Board, Inc., 1956); the special report on "Business Forecasting" by *Business Week,* pp. 90–122 (Sept. 24, 1955); and the detailed analysis by the National Industrial Conference Board in *Forecasting Sales,* Studies in Business Policy No. 106 (New York: National Industrial Conference Board, Inc., 1963).

However, to obtain the impression that sales forecasting has become universal is erroneous. While a study published in 1966 did show continuing use of and enthusiasm for sales forecasts in larger firms, this situation was not found in smaller ones.[17] For example, the University of Minnesota found in 1961 that, in a sample of 106 small firms, only 21 per cent made formal sales estimates and even in firms having some 100 to 500 employees, less than 40 per cent did formal sales forecasting.[18] However, it is true that most of the smaller firms made some kind of forecast, usually an informal, unwritten forecast.

Methods of Sales Forecasting   Methods utilized in sales forecasting may generally be classified as the jury of executive opinion method, the sales force composite method, users' expectation method, statistical methods, and deductive methods.[19]

Jury of executive opinion method   The jury of executive opinion method is perhaps the oldest and simplest method of making sales forecasts, since it merely combines and averages the views, many of which may be little more than hunch, of top managers. In most cases, the final estimate is an opinion of the president, based upon his consideration of the opinions of other officers; in other cases, the poll of opinion leads to a rough kind of average estimate. In some cases, as the National Industrial Conference Board has pointed out, the process amounts to little more than group guessing; in other cases, it involves the careful judgment of experienced executives who have studied the underlying factors that influence their company's sales.[20]

This method has the advantage of ease and simplicity; it allows for pooling of experience and judgment; and it need not require the preparation of elaborate economic studies and statistics. An advantage not often cited is that, by forcing top managers to make an estimate, it may put pressure on

---

[17] R. S. Reichard, *op. cit.*, chap. 2.

[18] B. C. Hastings, "Forecasting and Small Business Planning," *Management Research Summary,* Small Business Administration (April, 1961), as quoted in R. S. Reichard, *op. cit.*, pp. 34–35.

[19] Much of this material is drawn from the NICB studies, *Forecasting in Industry* and *Forecasting Sales.* It is interesting to compare this classification of methods with those used by *Business Week* in its special report (Sept. 24, 1955, pp. 90–122). The *Business Week* report classifies forecasting techniques as "loaded deck" (in which the forecaster is working from known data, such as backlogs or inside information on customer plans), "oaks from acorns" (in which the forecaster operates on the premise that, although the future is not identical with the past, it is an outgrowth of it), and "test tube" (in which the future is forecast by studying the natural world, finding fundamental truths, and using them to predict behavior in the world of the future). A variant of the test tube, or systematic, technique of forecasting has been dubbed the "lost-horse" technique. This technique, credited to Sidney Alexander of the Columbia Broadcasting System, is based upon the old gag about the best way to find a lost horse: go where the horse was last seen and ask yourself where you would go if you were a horse. This technique is dealt with under the deductive methods outlined by the authors.

[20] *Forecasting in Industry,* p. 7.

them to develop pertinent data. On the other hand, such a method has serious drawbacks; forecasts are based on opinion rather than on facts and analyses; averaging opinions reduces responsibility for accurate forecasting; and forecasts are not usually broken down into products, time periods, or organizational units.

Sales force composite method One of the most commonly used methods of sales forecasting is to obtain from line salesmen and sales managers their combined view as to expected sales. The usual technique is to ask salesmen to forecast sales for their districts and have these estimates reviewed by the regional sales manager and then by the head-office sales manager. Sometimes salesmen are given guides in the form of company planning premises as to business conditions generally, and often the salesmen's estimates are reviewed by the product specialists, such as the company brand, sales and advertising managers.

Naturally, this method is based on the belief that those closest to the sales picture have the best knowledge of the market. Other advantages ascribed to this method are that it places forecasting, initially at least, in the hands of those who must make good on the forecast; it gives a broad sample that makes the total forecast more valid; and it allows an easy breakdown by product, customer, or territory.

On the other hand, the sales force composite method suffers from the fact that salesmen, and often even sales executives, are apt to be poor forecasters for any period except the immediate future, since they tend to give primary weight to present conditions. Where forecasts are desired for more than the short range, sales personnel normally are at a loss to make sound forecasts because of lack of knowledge of basic social, political, and economic trends. Moreover, under certain conditions—particularly where the forecasts are used for quota purposes—sales personnel incline to pessimism, while in other instances—especially when salesmen want more liberal allowances for expenses, promotion, or advertising—they are inclined to be rather optimistic. Furthermore, since sales forecasting is not their primary responsibility, sales personnel may neither be adept at it nor give it the time and thought necessary.

At the same time, most companies have found that forecasts submitted by the sales organization are useful and valuable inputs into the company forecasting effort. The National Industrial Conference Board study found that, when the sales force composite method is properly cross-checked by various other methods, such as review by head-office marketing and sales experts and constant check by salesmen of their estimates of past performance against actual results, it has furnished surprisingly good forecasts.[21]

Users' expectation method Many companies, particularly those serving industrial customers in industries comprised of a small number of companies

[21] *Ibid.*, p. 13.

or where a few large companies are dominant, find it useful to base their forecasts on expected purchases of these customers. Clearly, if a company can obtain an adequate and reliable information sample of what its customers will buy, even though the actual orders are not in hand, it will have a good basis upon which to develop a sales forecast.

This method requires careful solicitation and evaluation of desired information, usually a promise that individual customer intentions will be kept confidential, and an assurance that such information does not involve a commitment to buy. On the other hand, many companies have obtained useful forecast information at low cost by this method and have even gained customer good will by promising to use the information so as to be in a position to serve the customer better.

The users' expectation method has clear advantages where other ways of forecasting are inadequate or where the company cannot make a systematic forecast on its own, such as in small companies with limited resources for forecasting; in cases of new products where the market is known; or instances where a supplier is dependent on plans of major customers. This method is obviously difficult to use in cases where customers are numerous, or not easily located, or uncooperative. It is also subject to the difficulty of being able accurately to assess customer expectations, since the best of these are usually estimates of needs, and not commitments.

Statistical methods By far the most generally relied upon approach to sales forecasting is the application of various statistical methods. As mathematical techniques are improved and the electronic computing machine comes into wider use, so will statistics. These statistical methods may be divided into the trend and cycle, the correlation analysis, and the mathematical formula or model.

In approaching forecasting through an analysis of trends and cycles, the analyst summarizes a pertinent series of data that reflect dollar or unit sales, units per thousand population, or other basic indicators of sales volume. On the basis of his findings, he simply projects by extrapolation the directions indicated. This analysis is based on the assumption that what is past is prologue and that a trend will continue unless something happens to it. It is then up to the analyst to judge whether that "something" will happen. In fact, it is important to the user of a forecast to know whether it represents a mere projection of trends or a real forecast of what the forecaster expects *will* happen.

Although trend and cycle analysis leaves much to be desired and appears to have little scientific validity, it is, nevertheless, often accurate. One of the authors recalls making a five-year sales forecast for a company, using every available forecasting method plus considerable pooled judgment of the executives of the company. The result (which five years later proved to be within 1 per cent accurate) happened to fall exactly on a simple arithmetic trend line. In general, however, this method is used only to furnish one of several indicators for a final forecast.

The statistical method most widely used is correlation analysis, the measurement of the relationship between company sales and one or more other factors. What is usually desired is a close correlation between sales and some broad national index that can be used with a reasonable degree of accuracy, such as gross national product, national income, or consumers' disposable income. Such correlation, either directly or with a lag or lead of a given time period, can give a company a useful and highly reliable basis for sales forecasting.

Virtually every forecaster has found some accurate correlations in using this method. A coefficient of correlation between domestic freight ton-miles and gross national product in fixed dollars of some .98 over a thirty-year period is a persuasive fact. A drug manufacturing company, after considerable research, found that the total sales volume of the ethical drug industry bore an extremely close relationship to consumers' personal disposable income and that forecasts ultimately deduced from this relationship for periods fourteen months in advance fell within a range of 2 per cent of actual figures.[22] Other examples could be given, showing similarly close correlations. Many companies have found that *their* sales, aside from industry sales, bear a close relationship to some national index. The problem for the forecaster is, of course, to study the various relationships, with their leads and lags, to find one or more which serve as indicators of the company's sales.

The third statistical method, one which usually grows out of finding either a trend or correlation analysis relationship, is to develop a mathematical formula to depict the relationship of a number of variables to the company's sales. Often, sales for an individual company are subject to a number of variables. If the relationship of these can be ascertained with reasonable accuracy or if credible assumptions can be made to fill in statistical gaps, a mathematical model very useful to the forecaster can be constructed. Thus, the B. F. Goodrich Company found that total replacement passenger-car tire sales was given by taking the number of cars in use over two years, multiplying by four, correcting for the amount of wear tires receive, and further correcting by a factor giving effect to improved tire quality (1 per cent per year in the twenty-year period 1933–1953).[23]

Although statistical methods are good for sales forecasting from the standpoint of reliability, they are often subject to certain drawbacks for many companies. They require research and the use of statistically trained help, which may be too costly for smaller firms. It is not always possible to find reliable trends, correlations, or mathematical relationships. Many defense subcontractors have found, for example, that their sales potential is

---

[22] See K. F. Griffith, "Sales Forecasting at Eli Lilly," *Practical Techniques of Forecasting, Planning, and Control*, Manufacturing Series No. 216 (New York: American Management Association, 1954), pp. 10, 14. Lilly found that ethical drug sales increased or decreased 5 per cent with each increase or decrease of 10 per cent in consumers' personal disposable income.

[23] *Forecasting in Industry*, p. 35.

closely related to such vague factors as defense strategy, individual program expenditure level, and advances in the art of the industry, none of which bears a reliable correlation with predictable national or industry data. There is also a danger that managers may rely too heavily on statistical relationships and the results implied and thereby miss significant changes which intelligent judgment would have appraised. In any statistical method, it must be realized that the past is used only as a *basis* for prediction and that the future does not necessarily reflect the past.

Deductive methods No forecaster should overlook applying judgment and intelligent deduction from facts and relationships. Although this method bears certain similarities to the "lost-horse" technique mentioned on page 142, footnote 19, it has much validity. Generally, what is involved is to find out what the present situation is, where the sales are, and why, and then to analyze deductively, by resort to both objective factors and subjective judgments, the factors underlying sales. Although the indications so developed may be put into a mathematical model or merely left as an imprecisely correlated conglomeration of facts and value judgments, they are often a useful check on results arrived at through more scientific methods. After all, the state of the art of forecasting is such that independent, and often apparently intuitive, appraisal of the sales picture by an intelligent and experienced brain is still an input that no forecaster should overlook.

Combination of Methods in Practice In practice, there is a tendency to combine sales forecasting methods. This is as it should be. The importance of the final forecast for all aspects of company planning makes desirable a forecast system in which every possible input can be utilized. What warms the forecaster's heart and gives him a feeling of reliability is when several different forecast indicators, based upon independent approaches and data, all point to the same result. And, even if they do not, the disparity may serve as a warning that a single approach may have overlooked an essential factor.

Sales Forecasting in Practice To understand sales forecasting techniques, one might examine some typical examples of what companies do.

One large company approaches forecasting by having a staff prepare a forecast of general business conditions referred to as an "assumption about the future." From this premise of the external business environment is projected a forecast of product sales. The staff takes into account the various factors, both external and internal, that might bear upon sales—such as prices, production capacities, markets, technological changes, competition, and sales promotion plans—and combines them to bring about the forecast.

The basic assumptions for the future are arrived at by the staff after consideration, with upper managers, of levels of gross national product, disposable income, price indexes, and other basic economic conditions. Then, before the forecast is finished, a series of meetings is held with sales and other company personnel, to make sure that all factors have been properly considered. Conferences are also held with staff specialists in production, advertising, research, costs, and pricing. After the forecast weathers these discussions, it goes to the finished products committee of the company, which includes several vice-presidents. When this committee has approved or modified the sales forecast, it then becomes a guide for all managers in planning their budgets and operations.

In another typical case, the initial forecast is made by the salesmen in the field for each of their territories and then modified by the product managers and the sales vice-president to correct for known optimism or pessimism of certain salesmen. A second forecast is prepared by the company's economists after careful study of economic and market statistics, based on a combination of historical series and judgment of future conditions as they might affect the company's sales. Supplementing these two forecasts, sampling techniques are used to determine actual markets for their products, as disclosed by plans and practices of industrial and other customers. With these three forecasts, prepared independently, top management holds a conference at which the various predictions are appraised and modified. The resulting forecast becomes the basis for company planning and operations.

Another variant found in practice is for the company, as in the previous example, to have three sets of sales forecasts prepared. One set is prepared by industry specialists in home-office sales departments, another set by the commercial research department, and still another by the salesmen in the field. These sets are submitted to the sales manager, who presents all three, plus a forecast that reconciles differences, to the sales vice-president, who, in turn, checks or modifies the reconciled forecast and submits his approved forecast as the planning basis for company operations.

This procedure can probably better be shown in Figure 7.1.

OTHER PREMISES INTERNAL TO THE FIRM

Although the sales forecast is the primary blueprint for most business planning, there are many other premises internal to the firm. Precedents are set in various policy decisions as they are made day after day, year after year. The various commitments made for machinery, equipment, real estate, training programs, profit-sharing plans, or wage-incentive programs also establish sets of premises for planning. Some of these policy and program decisions need not influence plans, since changes in direction and policy do take place, but inflexibilities difficult to change often develop out of past actions. Other policy decisions, such as that involving investment in expensive single-purpose or limited-purpose machinery or equipment, may tie up so much capital as to constitute an inflexible premise for planning.

While internal planning premises are equal to the number of decisions taken in a business firm, the more important of them fall into the categories of capital investment, basic policies—past, present, and future—and supply factors, in addition to the market factors already discussed.

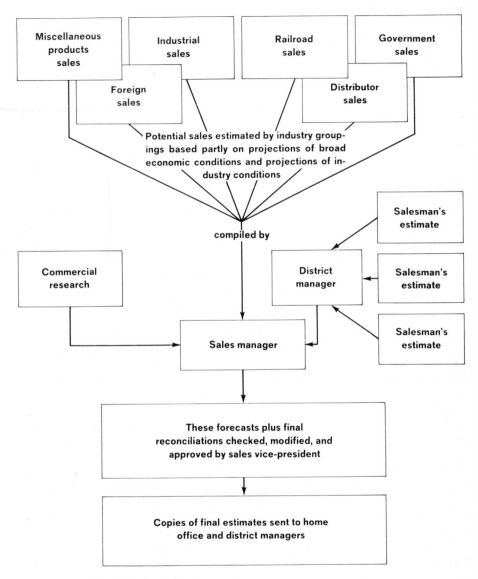

Fig. 7.1   A Procedure for Sales Forecasting

Capital Investment   A commitment made in a fixed area, such as land or capital, tends to have a long-run influence on planning, since this investment is normally only recovered through use over a period of time and by the write-off involved in depreciation allowances. Although capital so invested may be recovered by sale of the asset, this is often not a practicable alternative unless the asset has many uses, for the liquidation value of capital assets is usually well below original cost. As has already been indicated, the sunk nature of this investment will depend upon the limited or general use that can be obtained from the building, land, equipment, or machine. Consequently, in developing plans, a business must weigh carefully the commitments that have already been made in capital equipment and modify these plans to make the best possible use of this equipment. At the same time, the principle of disregarding sunk costs in planning is sound, even though the sunk nature of certain capital investments may place serious limitations on the firm's current resources.

Basic Policies Plans are also subject to conditions arising from basic policies, many of which are fixed and cannot be readily changed. A firm that decides to cater to the lower-quality trade and builds its product and distribution policies accordingly is ordinarily in no position to make a change to the high-quality market without considerable investment and time. A firm that has instituted a profit-sharing plan may find it difficult to change its direction. Or a firm that has built its reputation on undercutting its competition may find it practically impossible to depart from this policy. Policies such as these define the character of a business, the personality of the firm. Although they are, at least to some degree, controllable and can be changed, they nonetheless are an essential part of the internal planning background.

Supply Factors As discussed above, one of the significant premises external to the enterprise has to do with the sources of materials and parts. To some extent, however, these sources may be within the control of the firm and hence may be considered along with premises internal to the firm. A business sometimes has alternatives to the acceptance of supplies externally. These consist of integration or active cooperation with a source. The former alternative is a well-known practice in the large industrial empires so common to American industry. Less well known but increasingly evident in recent years is the alternative of discovering and taking care of desirable sources of supply. Many of the larger manufacturing enterprises have aided smaller firms to become reliable suppliers, and the large mail-order houses have had a definite program for developing reliable and well-managed sources. Hence, whether the sources of supply are obtained through integration or through conscious development, they furnish internal planning premises.

To summarize, planning is simplified if premises are clearly set forth; if these premises are accurate, planning will also tend to be accurate. Good forecasting lies behind good planning, and as forecasting techniques improve, that major portion of planning which depends upon forecasts will be improved. But complete premising is more than forecasting, since established and expected policies, facts as to capital investment, and other matters not connected with forecasting also affect planning.

ALTERNATE PREMISES FOR CONTINGENCIES

Because the future cannot be foreseen with accuracy, it is usually good planning to have alternative sets of premises and plans based upon contingencies so widely varying that no single plan can encompass them all—alternative plans based on such widely varying assumptions as war, peace, peace with large defense spending, full employment, prosperity, depression, recession, rising prices, falling prices, or other major political or economic events. In ideal business planning, alternative plans should be ready whenever basic premises change materially. However, at one time or another decisions that make planning less flexible must be made. A time comes when the manager can no longer wait to order construction of a new plant, hire and train a new staff of specialists, or embark upon a sales promotion campaign. When such decisions are made, the range of alternative plans narrows, as do the premises upon which they are based.

FOR DISCUSSION

1. Take a major decision problem facing you and outline the more critical planning premises surrounding it. How many of these are matters of knowledge and how many are matters of forecast? How many are intangible and how many are tangible? How many are within your control?

2. A sales forecast is often regarded both as a plan and as a premise. Comment.

3. Can objectives, policies, and procedures be premises in planning?

4. Examine how uniform premises aid in coordination of plans.

5. How should premises be developed and communicated?

SELECTED REFERENCES

Abramson, A. G., and R. H. Mack: *Business Forecasting in Practice*, New York: John Wiley & Sons, Inc., 1956.

American Management Association: *Company Organization for Economic Forecasting*, Research Report No. 28, New York: American Management Association, 1957.

———: *Practical Techniques of Forecasting, Planning, and Control*, Manufacturing Series No. 216, New York: American Management Association, 1954.

———: *Sales Forecasting: Uses, Techniques, and Trends*, Special Report No. 16, New York: American Management Association, 1956.

Business Forecasting: A Survey of Business Practices and Methods, New York: Controllership Foundation, Inc., 1950.

"Business Forecasting," *Business Week*, pp. 90–122 (Sept. 24, 1955).

Colm, G.: *Long-range Projections for Economic Growth: The American Economy in 1970*, Planning Pamphlet No. 107, Washington: National Planning Association, 1959.

———: *The American Economy in 1960*, Planning Pamphlet No. 81, Washington: National Planning Association, 1952.

Isenson, R. S.: "Technological Forecasting—Management Tool," *Business Horizons*, vol. 10, no. 2, pp. 37–46 (Summer, 1967).

Linden, F. (ed.): *Market Profiles of Consumer Products*, New York: National Industrial Conference Board, 1967.

National Industrial Conference Board: *Forecasting in Industry*, Studies in Business Policy No. 77, New York: National Industrial Conference Board, 1956.

————: *Forecasting Sales,* Studies in Business Policy No. 106, New York: National Industrial Conference Board, 1963.

Quinn, J. B.: "Technological Forecasting," *Harvard Business Review,* vol. 45, no. 2, pp. 89–106 (March–April, 1967).

Redfield, J. W.: "Elements of Forecasting," *Harvard Business Review,* vol. 29, no. 6, pp. 81–91 (November, 1951).

Reichard, R. S.: *Practical Techniques of Sales Forecasting,* New York: McGraw-Hill Book Company, 1966.

Spencer, M. H., and T. Mattheis: "Forecasting Sales of Consumers Durable Goods," *California Management Review,* vol. 4, no. 3, pp. 75–101 (Spring, 1962).

"Streamlining the Sales Forecast," *Dun's Review and Modern Industry* (August, 1953).

Wright, W.: *Forecasting for Profit,* New York: John Wiley & Sons, Inc., 1947.

decision making

Decision making—the actual selection from among alternatives of a course of action—is at the core of planning. Managers sometimes see it as their central job, because they must constantly choose what is to be done, who is to do it, when, where, and occasionally even how. Decision making must, however, be regarded only as a step in planning, even when done quickly and with little thought or when it influences action for only a few minutes. It is also part of everyone's daily living. Planning occurs in managing or in personal life whenever choices are made in order to gain a goal in the face of such limitations as time, money, and the desires of other people.

Rational decision making involves a concrete goal, for example, to reduce costs by a certain amount, get production back on schedule, speed a shipment, cut inventories, or reduce the unpleasantness or danger of a task. A cutting criticism made by a certain manager of his subordinate's decisions was not that the latter had made a mistake but that he did not know where he was trying to go. Moreover, a course of action can seldom be judged alone, because virtually every decision must be geared in with other plans of the firm. So the stereotype of the finger-snapping, button-pushing managerial mogul fades as the requirements of systematic research and analysis come into focus.

DEVELOPING ALTERNATIVES

Assuming known goals and clear planning premises, the first step of decision making is the development of alternatives. It is rare for alternatives to be lacking for any course of action; indeed, perhaps a sound adage for the manager is that, if there seems to be only one way of doing a thing, that way is probably wrong. What the manager has probably not done is force himself to consider other ways, to open his eyes and develop alternatives; unless he does so, he cannot know if his decision is the best possible. From the above adage appears a key planning principle, which might be referred to as the principle of alternatives. In every course of action alternatives exist, and effective planning involves a search for the alternative representing the best path to a desired goal.

One of the authors was with a firm that desperately needed certain capital equipment to build up its production to where reduced costs and expanded markets would turn losses into profits. Yet the losses had so depleted the company's capital and credit that the equipment could apparently not be financed. The single available course of action seemed to be to do nothing, but to do nothing was to assure bankruptcy. The officers of the company therefore sought out alternatives. A manufacturer was found who had the needed equipment, which he had not been able to sell and which had been financed by some banks. Inquiry of the banks disclosed that they would let the manufacturer sell the equipment without down payment and accept two-name paper instead of the single-name notes they held. In addition, a competitor of the firm needing equipment had new equipment on order and offered to sell, on a no-down-payment basis, his older machines. Hence, in an apparently hopeless situation two alternatives were found.

The ability to develop alternatives is often as important as making a right decision among alternatives. Ingenuity, research, and perspicacity are required to make sure that the best alternatives are considered before a course of action is selected. The development of alternatives, if thorough, will often unearth so many choices that the manager cannot possibly consider them all. Even with the latest mathematical techniques and electronic computers, the analysis of alternatives and their comparison with one another is almost impossible without some preliminary selection. Usually, this is not so difficult as it may seem because the experienced analyst develops a sharp sense of discrimination between a myriad of alternatives and is able to exclude the unsuitable ones.

THE PRINCIPLE OF THE LIMITING FACTOR

One of the most helpful principles of planning may be called the principle of the limiting, or critical, factor, stated as follows: In choosing from among alternatives, the more an individual can recognize and solve for those factors that are limiting or critical to the attainment of a desired goal, the more effectively and efficiently he can select the most favorable alternative.

In every area of decision certain factors are limiting in determining whether goals will be attained. These may be few or many, and they may change over a period of time. It is possible to make an error in a decision by concentrating on limiting factors, but the complexity of many managerial decisions makes it impracticable to consider every aspect of every problem, and the risk involved in overlooking the less important aspects is usually less than the risk of inattention to the strategic factor.

Chester I. Barnard, in his classic study, *The Functions of the Executive,* recognized the importance of this principle when he pointed out:[1]

> The analysis required for decision is in effect a search for the "strategic factors." . . . The theory of the strategic factor is necessary to an appreciation of the process of decision, and therefore to the understanding of organization and the executive functions as well as, perhaps, individual purposive conduct. As generally as I can state it, this theory is as follows:
>
> If we take any system, or set of conditions, or conglomeration of circumstances existing at a given time, we recognize that it consists of elements, or parts, or factors, which together make up the whole system, set of conditions, or circumstances. Now if we approach this system or set of circumstances with a view to the accomplishment of a purpose (and only when we so approach it), the elements or parts become distinguished into two classes: those which if absent or changed would accomplish the desired purpose, provided the others remain unchanged, and these others. The first kind are called limiting factors, the second, complementary factors.

Many examples of the principle of the limiting factor can be given. In the case of an automobile out of gasoline but otherwise in good condition, the limiting factor is, of course, fuel. The limiting factor in a house-lighting operation may be a fuse. If a machine fails to operate for lack of a screw, the screw is the limiting factor.

In decision making, the discovery of the limiting factor or factors may not be so easy, since these factors are often obscure and people and their reactions complex, but the principle is the same. For example, if a company were considering a profit-sharing program, the limiting factors might be tax deductibility and the attitude of employees toward the plan. In deciding whether to expand operations, one company might find its limiting factor to be availability of capital, another company, the diseconomies of size, still another, the attitude of the government antitrust authorities. In deciding whether to reorganize a subsidiary, the limiting factor might be the attitude of a key executive or two, the desirability of organizing to train managerial manpower, or the location of plants. In planning a price rise, the limiting factor might be the expected action of competitors, the reaction of customers, or long-term commitments already made.

The search for and recognition of limiting factors in planning never ends. For one program at one time, a certain factor or factors may be critical

---

[1] C. I. Barnard, *The Functions of the Executive* (Cambridge, Mass.: Harvard University Press, 1938), pp. 202–203. Note that Barnard states that he has borrowed the term "strategic factor" from John R. Commons. As one of the authors' students put it, when his automobile fails to operate, he has two basic choices. He might disassemble it part by part, lay all the parts out on a canvas, check each part, replace doubtful parts, reassemble it in accordance with manufacturer's specifications and prints, put gasoline and oil in it, and it would run. Or, he might try to locate the limiting factor and replace an ignition wire. As homely as this example is, it emphasizes the fact that many problem solvers, often very intelligent individuals, tend to be "automobile disassemblers" in their attempt to solve a problem.

to the decision; but, at a later time and for a similar decision, the limiting factor may be something relatively unimportant in the earlier planning, and these factors may shift abruptly. Thus, a company might decide to acquire new equipment when the limiting factor has been capital availability, only to have the limiting factor become delivery or, later, the training of operatives.

Discovery of the limiting factor lies at the basis of selection from alternatives and hence of planning. It is ordinarily not possible thoroughly to explore every problem and the solution of every limiting factor, so the business manager must exercise judgment in determining where and how research in this area can best be used.

THE PROCESS OF EVALUATION

Once appropriate alternatives have been isolated, the next step in planning is to evaluate them and select the one that will best contribute to the goal. This is the point of ultimate decision making, although decisions must also be made in the other steps of planning—in selecting goals, in choosing critical premises, and even in selecting alternatives.

Tangible and Intangible Factors   In most planning, there are certain tangible factors to be assessed in terms of dollars, man-hours, machine-hours, units of output, rates of return on investment, or some other quantitative unit, although these may carry a wide margin of error. There are other factors that can hardly be so quantified. However, both the tangible and intangible factors must be weighed in deciding upon a course of action.

Comparison of tangible factors   In most business decisions, the courses of action considered involve influence on profits, whether through effects on costs or through revenues. In many decisions, such as those involving an investment in plant, the concern may be the return on investment, rather than maximum profits. Thus, although greater *total* profits might result from a certain investment, analysis might show a greater percentage yield from a smaller investment. Even in this case, the goal would almost surely be maximization of profits, since use of the return-on-investment standard implies larger profits by use of capital in programs other than the one under consideration, or a decision to limit the total investment in the business.

The determination of maximum profits may depend upon comparison of various types of factors. Physical standards such as man-hours or units of output may be as revealing as standards expressed in dollars and cents. For example, in planning factory production, the loading of machines and the utilization of manpower may be the limiting factors in measuring the scheduling program. Yet they become so by virtue of their relationship to maximizing profits.

Wherever quantitative measurement can be given to the variables in a group of promising alternatives and where intangible factors do not unduly influence a course of action, the selection of an alternative on the basis of tangible factors can be relatively easy, in the sense of arriving at a mathematically demonstrable result. In certain major planning, it is customary to project income statements and balance sheets reflecting the various alternatives and showing clearly which is best for the firm. Even in less important planning, where the effect on the total enterprise is not felt, a comparison of expenses and revenues from the various alternatives can show clearly which course is most desirable.

However, there is the danger that analysts, making these comparisons and interpreting results, will forget that approximations, estimates, and forecasts usually lie at the base of their computations. Since the analysis must be made for the future, quantitative values given to the variables can rarely be exact and reliable. A detailed study may include tabular presentations of quantitative data, which will seem to the unwary to be more accurate than they really are. Judgment of the margin of error existing in basic data, and its effect on conclusions, is important in any evaluation. One of the authors recalls a case where a planning program was carefully analyzed by investment bankers to determine its validity, while certain underlying assumptions—which, if incorrect by even less than 10 per cent, could have diametrically changed the results of the entire program—were never questioned.

Comparison of intangible factors   The comparison of intangible factors is even more difficult. How does one compare the possibilities of good labor relations in one location against the state taxing situation in another? How is it possible to compare accurately a reputation for high quality with a reputation for aggressive competition and low prices? How can the advantages of offering high-grade service be compared to the expense of so doing?

The typical planning problem, too, is complicated by elements of sheer uncertainty. The importance to future activities of certain known factors can be little more than guessed. Other uncertain factors include those not even recognized when a decision is made but which are disclosed only with the passage of time. Thus, the possibility of a strike in the plant of a supplier should be weighed by a business planner, but, in most instances, he has no reliable basis upon which to weigh it. Or he may know that a new invention may make obsolete his most profitable product but be unable to estimate when. Or he may find years later that an event he had never considered, or could not reasonably have considered, has affected the success of his plans. The Vietnam conflict, which flared up with little warning in the 1960s, changed the fortunes of many businesses, making some bad decisions look good and some good decisions look poor.

To evaluate and compare the intangible factors in a planning problem and make decisions from them, the analyst must first recognize them, then determine whether a reasonable quantitative measurement can be given them. If not, he should then find out what he can about them, perhaps rate them in terms of their importance, compare their probable influence with the results disclosed from evaluation of the tangible factors, and then come to a decision. This decision may give predominant weight to a single intangible.

Such a procedure is, in effect, deciding upon the weight of the total evidence. Although it involves fallible personal judgments, few business decisions can be so accurately quantified that judgment is unnecessary. If every variable could be definitely measured, all that would be needed for intelligent action would be a mathematician and a computing machine. Decision making is seldom so simple. It is not without some justification that the successful executive has been cynically described as a person who guesses right.

Evaluating Alternatives: Marginal Analysis   Depending, of course, upon the importance of a decision and the time available to make it, the final selection of a course of action from the alternatives is a matter of weighing expected results against enterprise objectives, bearing in mind that a plan that might yield optimum results for a department or a division may not do so for an entire firm.

The evaluation of alternatives may utilize the techniques of marginal analysis. Marginal analysis emphasizes additional costs or revenues from additional quantities rather than averages. Thus, where the objective is to maximize profits, this goal will be reached when the *additional* revenues and *additional* costs are equal. *At any other point,* either more additional revenue could be obtained at less additional cost or additional revenue obtained would be less than the additional costs incurred; in either such case, profits would not be maximized.

Marginal analysis can be used in comparing factors other than costs and revenues. For example, to find the optimum output of a machine, one could vary inputs against outputs until the *additional* input equals the *additional* output. This would then be the point of maximum efficiency of the machine. Or the number of subordinates reporting to a manager might conceivably be increased to the point where incremental savings in costs, better communication and morale, and other factors equal incremental losses in effectiveness of control, direction, and similar factors.

Perhaps the real usefulness of the marginal approach to evaluation is that it accentuates the variables in a situation and deemphasizes averages and constants. Whether the objective is optimum profits, stability, or durability, marginal analysis will show the way.

Marginal analysis also emphasizes the importance of fixed costs, whether in the nature of sunk capital investment or of an established minimum of service and supervisory personnel. Depending upon the range of output considered (obviously, if an increase in output would require a larger plant or a larger overhead organization, these new fixed costs become marginal to the problem under consideration), fixed costs do not enter planning, except in emphasizing advantages of increased utilization of facilities and personnel.

The fact that marginal analysis does not normally reflect all costs, but only additional ones, also serves to show the importance of flexibility in business planning. If machines or people can be used for different products or different volumes of 'production, without loss in investment already incurred, the firm may be regarded as having perfect flexibility, so far as production is concerned. But it may have other inflexibilities. If, for example, it could not obtain additional working capital for expansion of operations, the flexibility of production machinery and personnel would allow changes in output only at a level permitted by the working capital.

Planning under Dynamic Conditions   Analysis of economic forces under static conditions is useful only to isolate the effects of uncertainty and thereby develop further tools for analysis. Static conditions do not exist in practice, and business planning is, therefore, undertaken under conditions of change and uncertainty. It is this dynamic character of the business environment that makes planning difficult.[2]

The central problem under dynamic conditions is the accuracy of a planner's estimate of the future. Since the future is uncertain—although the degree may vary widely as between products, markets, geographical and political areas, and times—when a business manager estimates a future situation, he necessarily makes certain assumptions as to what will happen. As he weights his contingencies in one way or another, he obtains different results. Suppose, for example, that a manager were planning a new plant and felt that he needed ten years to recover his costs. He might estimate the future with respect to markets, prices, labor costs, material costs, utilization of plant, labor efficiency, taxes, and other factors. Suppose further that he estimated six possible situations as being most likely to occur, created out of different sets of assumptions as to the future. These might bring completely different estimates of net profits, as shown in Figure 8.1.

As might be expected, all estimates for the first year or two are fairly close together, since the manager can be more certain of short-term than of long-term results. But as the planning period is extended, this or that contingency makes the estimates of accumulated profits vary from high, as in forecast A, through bare break-even (E), to projected loss (F).

Several observations may be made concerning this simplified model of planning under conditions of change and uncertainty. In the first place, the tools of marginal analysis are useful in arriving at these various estimates of possible situations. In each set of contingencies assumed, the planner would

[2] See Albert G. Hart, *Anticipations, Uncertainty, and Dynamic Planning* (New York: Augustus M. Kelley, Inc., 1951), pp. 25–27. Hart adds capital-market imperfections and other market discontinuities to uncertainty as major factors that distinguish the dynamic from the static. These are important factors, since the firm cannot practically add or subtract extremely small quantities of capital and since orders are often for minimum quantities. It is a fact that in most real business situations the schedule of supply of capital or the schedule of demand for a product does not represent smooth connected lines. Although these discontinuities have a significant bearing on planning and although other frictions exist (such as the desire of an owner of a small business not to use outside capital because of danger of loss of control), in this discussion simplification of the issues is obtained by dealing with the primary cause of dynamic conditions—uncertainty.

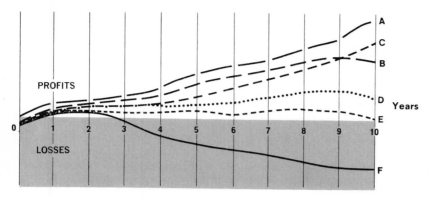

Fig. 8.1 Accumulated Profits from New Plant on Basis of Six Estimates of Future

attempt to maximize profits by assuring himself that additional costs are compensated by additional revenues and that, within the limits of divisibility of units of production, no opportunity for maximizing profits by increasing or reducing costs or revenues has been neglected.

In the second place, Figure 8.1 emphasizes the fact that the uncertainties over time, plus the alternatives available to accomplish results under each set of uncertainties, give alternative possibilities astronomical in number. Although only six forecasts are included here, the number could be infinite. In order for a manager to evaluate, therefore, especially where the subject is complex and the time period long, he must have some means of limiting his analysis to probable situations. In most cases, this is done by judgment and test. An experienced business analyst usually has a feeling for problems, growing out of familiarity with the underlying factors. If he can calculate his profits on basic estimates of what is most likely to occur, he will limit the alternative projections to a few most probable ones. At this point, a decision is likely to be based upon a weighing of the risks and benefits to be expected from these few probabilities, in the light of underlying uncertainties, the resources of the firm, and the ability and willingness to assume the risks involved.

BASES FOR SELECTION AMONG ALTERNATIVES

In selecting from among alternatives, three bases for decision are open to the manager—experience, experimentation, and research and analysis.

Experience   Reliance on past experience probably plays a larger part than it deserves in business decision making. The experienced manager usually believes, often without realizing it, that the things he has accomplished and the mistakes he has made furnish an almost infallible guide to the future. This attitude is likely to be more pronounced the higher in an organization a manager has risen.

To some extent, the attitude that experience is the best teacher is justifiable. The very fact that the manager has reached his position appears to justify his decisions. Moreover, the seasoning process of thinking problems through, making decisions, and seeing programs succeed or fail, does make for a degree of business judgment (at times bordering on the intuitive). If a certain program succeeded in the past and the same basic factors are present in a current situation, there is reason to believe that history will repeat itself; if a recognized mistake was made in the past and its causes analyzed, the same mistake is not likely to be made by the same manager again. Many people, however, do not profit by their errors, and there are managers who seem never to gain the seasoned judgment required by modern enterprise.

There is danger, however, in relying on one's past experience as a guide for future action. In the first place, it is an unusual human being who recognizes the underlying reasons for his mistakes or failures. In the second place, the lessons of experience may be entirely unsuitable to new problems. A general manager or company president is too likely to believe that the path he has trod is the right one. The difficulty is, of course, that even slightly different goals and premises call for at least slightly different paths. What successor to a retired manager has not found his predecessor's experience inapplicable? Good decisions must be evaluated against *future* events, while experience belongs to the past.

On the other hand, if experience is carefully analyzed rather than blindly followed, it can be extremely useful as a basis for decision making. A successful program, a well-managed company, a profitable product promotion, or any other business decision that turns out well may be used as an example by another business. Just as no scientist hesitates to build upon the research of others and would be foolish indeed to duplicate it, one business manager can learn much from others.

Making this experience reliable to managers is an important task. Many trade associations, government agencies, and luncheon and other social clubs act as vehicles for this purpose. The lessons of business history, as recalled by scholars and business reporters, are valuable grist for the manager's planning mill. And in the field of management itself, where managers learn much by comparing notes, a growing service has been performed by the American Management Association, the Society for Advancement of Management, and many other groups.

But as valuable as these aids are, the decision maker must watch that lessons from external as well as from personal experience are accurately applied. Small companies have tried, for example, to imitate the organizational policies and procedures of the General Motors Corporation, only to find that these, although eminently successful for that large firm, were too costly for them.

Experimentation   An obvious way to decide upon alternatives is to try them and see what happens. Such experimentation is used in scientific inquiry. It is frequently argued that it should be employed more often in business and that the only way a manager can make sure his plan is right—especially in view of the intangible factors—is to try the various alternatives to see which is best.

However, as Newman[3] has pointed out, "the experimental technique . . . should be utilized as a last resort after other planning techniques have been tried." It is clearly the most expensive of all techniques, especially where heavy expenditures in capital and personnel are necessary to try a program and where the firm cannot afford to prosecute vigorously several alternatives. Besides, there may be doubt, after an experiment has been tried, as to what it proved, since the future may not duplicate the past.

On the other hand, there are many decisions which cannot be made until the best course of action can be ascertained with experiment. Even the most accurate reflections of experience or the most careful research may not assure the manager of a correct decision. This is nowhere better illustrated than in planning a new airplane. The manufacturer may assiduously draw from his own experience and that of other plane manufacturers and of new plane users. His engineers and economists may make extensive studies of stresses, vibrations, fuel consumption, speed, space allocations, and other factors. But all these studies do not give every answer to questions about the flying characteristics and economics (although economics lends itself better to forecast through research) of a successful plane; therefore, some experimentation is almost always involved in the process of selecting from alternatives. Ordinarily, a prototype airplane is constructed and tested, and, on the basis of these tests, production airplanes are later designed and made. Even before the prototypes are constructed, numerous tests of fabricated subassemblies are made, and many three-dimensional mock-ups are constructed, at great cost, to make sure that dimensions are accurate.

Experimentation is used in other ways. A firm may test a new product in a certain market before expanding its sale nationwide. Organizational techniques are often tried in a branch office or plant before being applied over an entire company. An advertising program or a new brand promotion may be tested in a limited area before being employed widely. A candidate for a management job may be tested in the job during the incumbent's vacation.

Research and Analysis The most generally used and certainly a most effective technique for selecting alternatives, when major decisions are involved, is research and analysis. Although the lessons of experience may be drawn upon in analyzing alternatives and although experimentation may be undertaken to test hypotheses, research and analysis have many advantages for weighing alternative courses of action.

[3] W. H. Newman, *Business Policies and Management,* 2d ed. (Cincinnati: South-Western Publishing Company, 1949), p. 601.

In the first place, the solution of a planning problem requires that it be broken into its component parts and the various tangible and intangible factors studied. Research and analysis focus attention on the problem and each part and, in so doing, bring to the fore the critical factors of the various alternatives and their major components. Research and analysis thus apply the scientific method to planning.

In the second place, study and analysis are likely to be far cheaper than experimentation. Hours of analytical time and reams of paper usually cost much less than trying the various alternatives in practice. In the example of building airplanes mentioned above, if careful research did not precede the building and testing of prototype subassemblies and the final assembly, one can hardly imagine the failure and costs of planning that would result.

Research and analysis involve a search for the limiting variables and parameters and their placement in a logical causal relationship to each other as they affect goals. If all the important factors bearing on the solution in terms of a goal are known, if they can be seen in their relationship to each other and can be quantified, and if the goal is definite and subject to measurement, evaluation of various courses of action can normally be stated mathematically and the answer computed, unless, of course, the mathematics are too complex or the computing problem too great for even the most advanced modern computers. But even a problem involving unknowns can be expressed mathematically, particularly if simplified by concentrating on the most critical factors.

In fact, a characteristic of the research and analysis technique is seeing a problem and its relationships in mathematical terms. With its convenient use of symbols, mathematics need only to identify and recognize the relationships of unknown quantities. Being able to conceptualize a problem is a major step toward its solution. Placing it in a mathematical framework helps place the problem in a meaningful conceptual framework. The physical sciences have long relied on mathematics, and it is encouraging to see the mathematical methodology being brought into the area of managerial decision making.

Even where inputs cannot be quantified, clearer definition of a problem by mathematical approaches is illustrated by this oversimplified example: Assume that a supervisor instructed his production workers to paint the shop ceiling while work was slack and that they refused to do so. This problem might be expressed as follows:

$$X_a + Y_a + Y_l + P_m + P_n + P_o + R_{mno} = Z$$

where
X_a = authority of factory superintendent
Y_a = authority of immediate supervisor
Y_l = leadership ability of immediate supervisor
P_m = regular pay of worker m
P_n = regular pay of worker n
P_o = regular pay of worker o
R_{mno} = premium pay for workers m, n, o
Z = goal of getting the ceiling painted

As can be seen from this simple equation (and there would probably be other variables in an actual situation), none of the inputs alone was enough to get the ceiling painted. However, it is possible that if the authority of the superintendent or the supervisor had been greater, or the regular pay higher, or the leadership of the supervisor better, less premium pay might have been required; or, in reverse, with less of these, the premium pay required would have been greater. As simple as this problem is, putting it into mathematical form gives us an interesting view of it and forces recognition of its critical factors.

Even where facets of a business problem appear not to lend themselves to research and analysis techniques, the benefits of thorough analysis may be considerable. In most analyses of alternatives, there are intangibles which cannot be stated in terms of precise numerical units. They may include the attitude of employees or customers, the appeal of prestige, public acclaim for ethical behavior, or the attitude of a community toward a certain kind of business. Although it may be difficult or impossible to come to any very definite conclusions about these intangible factors, through research, careful analysis can highlight them and make the study of alternatives clearer.

For example, careful research might disclose that a certain airplane design is the safest and most economical an airline could select, but that another design, although equally safe and cheaper to build, is less economical to operate. However, a question might be raised as to whether the less economical design might have prestige or traffic advantages which could not be accurately measured but which might, in the judgment of top managers, offset the loss in economy. It can hardly be said that research would be useless here, simply because it could not accurately analyze important intangibles. It could still point out the intangibles that must be evaluated on the basis of business judgment; the ardent analyst must realize his limitations and be prepared to yield to judgment to a greater or lesser degree.

As was indicated earlier, the principle of the limiting factor may also apply to the amount of effort expended in deciding upon a plan. This is nowhere more applicable than in the case of research and analysis. Not every business decision can stand the cost or delay of careful analysis and weighing of alternatives, especially when the results of a wrong course of action may not be serious or costly. If a president or his board of directors, for reasons of their own, determine that a course of action must be decided upon by a certain date, the most avid researcher must tailor his explorations to fit the available time.

OPERATIONS RESEARCH AND PLANNING

One of the most comprehensive research approaches to decision making is operations research, or, as it is sometimes called, operations analysis or "management science." These terms, although sometimes given an aura of mystery by their mathematically inclined proponents, apply to the growing practice of applying the systems methodology of the physical sciences to management decision making.

To a considerable extent, operations research is a product of World War II, although its antecedents in scientific method, higher mathematics, and such tools as probability theory go back far beyond that period. The accelerated growth of operations research in recent years has followed the whole trend of applying the methods of the physical scientist and the engineer to economic and political problems. It has also been made possible by the development of rapid computing machines, particularly those using electronics, since much of the advantage of operations research depends upon the economical and feasible application of involved mathematical formulas and the use of data with complex relationships.

The Concept   There are almost as many definitions of operations research as there are writers on the subject.[4] Perhaps the most acceptable definition is that it is the application of scientific method to the study of alternatives in a problem situation, with a view to providing a quantitative basis for arriving at an optimum solution in terms of the goals sought. Thus, the emphasis is on scientific method, on the use of quantitative data, on goals, and on the determination of the optimum means of reaching the goal. In other words, operations research might be called "quantitative common sense."

Operations research, like accounting analyses or correlation analyses, does not provide decisions but develops quantitative data to help the manager make decisions. In most business situations, analyses cannot be so complete or conclusive that they constitute the decision. However, in a production planning or transportation problem, the goals may be so clear, the input data so definite, and the conclusions so workable as to point positively to the optimum solution.

Many operations researchers insist that with this tool the activities of an enterprise must be viewed as *a total system* in contrast to the usual attempts to solve isolated problems. In addition, it is often claimed that operations research requires the team approach in the solution of problems, that is, the use of a variety of talents such as those of the mathematician, the business specialist, the psychologist, the engineer, and the accountant. Although these conditions are desirable, neither seems to be essential to operations research.

Any top manager would appreciate having a problem area completely analyzed and its solution related to every other problem in his operation, but he recognizes the practical difficulties, if not the impossibility, of doing so. It does not seem realistic for the operations research experts to overlook the usefulness of their techniques in solving limited problems within a larger enterprise system. Even a total business enterprise is a subsystem of a larger system. And even suboptimization might be better than no system optimization.

[4] See comments in National Industrial Conference Board, *Operations Research*, Studies in Business Policy No. 82 (New York: National Industrial Conference Board, 1957), pp. 5–6.

This is not to say that enterprise-wide implications of solving an individual problem should be ignored; on the contrary, one often finds helpful answers in a related but separate problem area. But to include every possible ramification of a problem may require an expensive and time-consuming effort not justified by the results.

Again, the use of a team of experts with varying outlooks on a problem does not seem to be an essential, because many problems do not justify such thorough treatment. It is difficult to understand why such treatment should be *required* before it can be said that operations research techniques have been employed. Inputs from various experts are normally required as a matter of practice, but this arises from needs, not the method.

The Essentials Attempts have long been made to solve management problems scientifically, but operations researchers have supplied an element of novelty in the orderliness and completeness of their approach. They have emphasized defining the problem and goals, carefully collecting and evaluating facts, developing and testing hypotheses, determining relationships between facts, developing and checking predictions based on hypotheses, and devising measures to evaluate the effectiveness of a course of action.

Thus, the essential methods of operations research may be summarized as follows:

1. The emphasis on models—the logical representation of a problem. These may, of course, be simple or complex. For example, the accounting formula "assets minus liabilities equals proprietorship" is a model, since it represents an idea and, within the limits of the terms used, symbolizes the relationship among the variables involved.

2. The emphasis on goals in a problem area and the development of measures of effectiveness in determining whether a given solution shows promise of attaining the goal. For example, if the goal is profit, the measure of effectiveness may be the rate of return on investment, and every proposed solution will arrange the variables so that the end result can be weighed against this measure. Some variables may be subject to control by the manager; others may represent uncontrollable factors in the system.

3. The attempt to incorporate all the variables in a problem, or at least those which appear to be important to its solution, in an analysis.

4. The attempt to quantify the variables in a problem to the extent possible, since only quantifiable data can be inserted into a model to yield a finite result of value for prediction.

5. The attempt to supplement quantifiable data with such usable mathematical and statistical devices as the probabilities in a situation, thus making the mathematical and computing problem workable within a small and relatively insignificant margin of error.

Of all these methods, perhaps the basic tool and major contribution of operations research has been the construction and use of conceptual models for decision making. There are many types of conceptual models. Some assert logical relationships only, while others show quantity relationships between variables. Models may be referred to as descriptive if they are designed only to describe the facts of a problem and their relationships. But the models useful for business planning are referred to as decision models, designed to lead to the selection of a course of optimum action among the available alternatives.

In order to construct a decision model, it is necessary to express in some kind of terms the goals sought, to set forth the relationships of the variables as they influence these goals, and then to express these mathematically to determine the optimum relationship of the factors in terms of goals.

In typical management problems, there are usually a large number of variables. In fact, in some problems the variables are so numerous and their relationships so complex as to defy mathematical expression. The use of a model in a simple problem can be illustrated by the example of determining what is the most economic quantity of a product for a company to produce.[5] The major variables here might be the requirements for the product for a year, the unit cost, the inventory carrying cost, the setup cost per order, and the order quantity. The model so derived, expressed in terms of the measure of effectiveness—economic order quantity—is as follows:

$$Qe = \sqrt{\frac{2RS}{I}}$$

where Qe = economic order quantity
R = total yearly requirements
S = setup costs
I = inventory carrying cost per item

The experienced business planning analyst will recognize the ingredients of a decision model as those considerations he has long applied in coming to a recommendation for a course of action. He knows that in the process of evaluation, as indicated in the previous section, the various courses of action are weighed against the objectives sought. In fact, long before the term "operations research" came into use, the planning analyst constructed a model in the form of a forecast of costs, revenues, and profits, even though he did not develop a mathematical formula and hence probably restricted his analysis to a small number of most attractive alternatives, tested for profitability. The planning analyst will also be aware that, whatever the

[5] This model is drawn from R. G. Canning, *Electronic Data Processing for Business and Industry* (New York: John Wiley & Sons, Inc., 1956), pp. 230–231. For illustration of a large number of models and an explanation of model construction, see C. W. Churchman, R. L. Ackoff, and E. L. Arnoff, *Introduction to Operations Research* (New York: John Wiley & Sons, Inc., 1957).

results of his quantitative tests, he must temper his recommendations with consideration of intangibles.

Procedure Applying operations research involves six steps similar to those discussed in Chapter 5 on planning (see pp. 94–99).[6]

1. Formulate the problem As in any planning problem, the operations researcher must analyze the goals and the system in which the solution must operate. That complex of interrelated components in a problem area, referred to by operations researchers as a "system," will be recognized as comprising mostly the environment of a decision and representing planning premises. This system may comprehend an entire business operation or be limited to planning production for presses and lathes. It is still, however, an interconnected complex of functionally related human or material components. Obviously, unless the problem is greatly simplified by rigorous application of the principle of the limiting factor, the more comprehensive the system, the more complex the problem.

Since the purpose of formulating the problem is to determine the optimum course of action from among various alternatives, measures of effectiveness, as well as goals, must be clearly defined. Moreover, in the typical operations research problem, it is desirable to take into account as many goals as necessary and feasible. For example, in a production and distribution planning problem, the decision maker will probably wish to minimize operating costs, minimize investment in inventory, satisfy a level of consumer service, and optimize the use of capital investments. To measure effectiveness in reaching these goals and to formulate the problem so that multiple objectives can be satisfied on a balanced optimum basis—particularly in the light of a variety of inputs—can become a very complex conceptual and computational matter.

2. Construct a mathematical model The next step is to formulate the problem as a system of relationships in a mathematical model. For a single goal, where at least some variables are subject to control, the general form of the operations research model may be stated as follows:

$$E = f(x_i, y_j)$$

where E = measure of effectiveness of system
x_i = controllable variables
y_j = variables beyond control

3. Derive a solution from the model In arriving at a solution, there are two basic procedures. In the analytical procedure, the researcher employs mathematical deduction in order to reach, as nearly as possible, a

[6] Churchman, Ackoff, and Arnoff, *op. cit.*, pp. 12–15. The authors have drawn much of their material for this section from this excellent book.

mathematical solution before inserting quantities to get a numerical solution. This can be an exceedingly important contribution to complex decision making. Variables may be reduced or restated in terms of common variables. Certain variables (for example, sales) may appear in a number of places in a model and may be factored out or reduced. In other cases, a series of mathematical equations may be consolidated and simplified. The result of this analytical procedure is to place a complex series of relationships into as simple a form as possible. In addition, this analysis may disclose, mathematically, that certain variables are unimportant to a reasonable solution and may be dropped from consideration.

The second procedure is referred to as a numerical procedure. In this, the analyst simply "tries" various values in the variables subject to control to see what the results will be and from this develops a set of values which seems to give the best solution. The numerical procedure varies from pure trial and error to complex iteration. In iteration, the analyst undertakes successive trial runs which approach an optimum solution. In some complex cases, such as the iterative procedures used in linear programming, rules have been developed to help the analyst more quickly undertake his trials and identify the optimum solution when it is reached.[7]

4. Test the model   Because a model, by its very nature, is only a representation of reality and it is seldom possible to include all the variables, models should usually be tested. This may be done by using the model to solve a problem and comparing the results so obtained with what actually happens. These tests may be carried out by using past data, or by trying the model out in practice to see how it measures up with reality, or by simulating results.

5. Provide controls for the model and solution   Because a model, once accurate, may cease to represent reality adequately, or the variables believed to be beyond control may change in value, or the relationships of variables may change, provision must be made for control of the model and the solution. This is done in the same way any control is undertaken, by providing means for feedback of deviations so that significant deviations can be detected and changes made. In many complex models, such as those used for production or distribution planning, the effect of the deviations must be weighed against the cost of feeding in the correction or against the usually greater cost of revising the entire program. As a result, the researcher may decide not to correct the model or the inputs.

6. Put the solution into effect   The final step is to make the model and the inputs operable. In anything but the simpler programs, this will involve revision and clarification of procedures so that the inputs (including control

---

[7] For a clear application of this procedure, as applied to the simplex technique in linear programming, see the explanation in *ibid.*, pp. 304–316.

feedback information) are available in an orderly fashion, and this, in turn, often requires reorganization of an enterprise's available information. What many users of operations research have found as a major stumbling block is that no one is willing to undertake the hard work of revising the nature of basic information. Accounting and other data normally available in a company are often not adequate to the requirements of successful operations research. And many managers, intrigued with the possibilities of operations research, wish that some of the research effort of experts, now so widely employed in constructing models, could be channeled toward information reorganization.

Other problems in putting the solution into effect involve getting people to understand, appreciate, and use the techniques of operations research; deciding such questions as what computing facilities to use and how, and how the information outputs are to be made useful and understandable to those responsible for decisions. In this connection, operations researchers would do the manager a real favor by frankly admitting the type and margin of uncertainty in their solution.

All this is to say that the operations researcher is not nearly done with his task when his model is reduced to paper and tested. Mathematical gymnastics may be interesting to the pure philosopher, but the manager must make a responsible decision, and the operations researcher who would be useful to the manager must be more than a mathematical gymnast.

Operations Research and Simulation   A model is essentially an attempt to simulate reality, and simulation is sometimes regarded as one of the most powerful tools available for effective management planning and control. Not that simulation itself is new. Managers have long used it in such aids as training through role playing. Teaching business policy through cases is simulation; testing airplanes in a wind tunnel is likewise simulation. And war games long used by the military and the more recently popular business games are instances where individuals are given a kind of experience through simulating reality.

But the technique of simulation through use of mathematical models and the computer not only is relatively new but has interesting promise for the decision maker. If a manager can utilize a model to represent reality and, to the extent that a model can be constructed to represent reality (at least the more important variables and constraints), he has available a powerful means of testing various alternatives to see how they would work out, without chancing the commitments involved in a typical decision.

In other words, to the extent that a management problem can be reasonably simulated by the construction of a model, the better a manager can test the results of any proposed individual course of action. As a consequence, no modern manager, faced with a difficult or complex decision, should overlook the possibility of simulation. Even with its limitations, it might show results that would follow a decision which a manager had not anticipated, and this is a great deal less risky and less costly a way to experiment than through making decisions which are found later to have been costly mistakes.

As in the case of any model, a simulation need not be mathematical. But, in the typical business problem, the important variables and constraints are usually so numerous and the relationships so complex that mathematics and the computer are normally necessary. The number of cases where simulation can pay off through inexpensive experimentation are numerous. To mention a few, it is relatively easy to test a program for inventory control, to experiment with proposed programs of quantity discounts, or to simulate a new production line. While active use of simulation appears to be only in its infancy, at least in business management, although less so in military management, and virtually unknown in other types of enterprise management, the advantages appear to be very great. Even if there are considerable uncertainties, intelligent simulation of a course of action can at least give a manager some visibility of the size and nature of risks he must take in a decision.

Special Tools Although the construction of decision models is perhaps the central tool of operations research, it has been interesting how various mathematical and scientific techniques, generally developed in the study of the physical sciences, have had applications to the study of business problems.

Probability theory This is one of the special tools referred to. This important statistical device is based upon the inference from experience that certain things are likely to happen in accordance with a predictable pattern. Thus, if a coin is tossed a hundred times, it is probable, although by no means certain, that it will fall heads fifty times. However, the deviations from such a probability are within a fairly predictable margin, and consequently the probability becomes a workable substitute for data otherwise unknown. In an enterprise problem, where probabilities can be substituted for unknowns, the margin of error in the solution, although not removed, is limited.

Game theory This tool may be useful in the solution of business problems involving competitive situations. Although far too complicated to describe here, it is based upon the premise that a man seeks to maximize his gain and minimize his loss, that he acts rationally, and that an opponent will be similarly motivated. Under these circumstances, game theory attempts to work out an optimum solution in which an individual in a certain situation can develop a strategy which, regardless of what his adversary does, will maximize his gains or minimize his losses. Even though the mathematical development of game theory has not proceeded beyond the stage of the most simple competitive situations and there is little evidence that it has been very useful in actual planning, future development of this theory can have a remarkable impact on the scientific approach to strategic planning in competitive situations.[8]

Queuing, or waiting-line, theory This theory uses mathematical techniques to balance the costs of waiting lines versus the costs of preventing waiting lines by increased service. It is based on the premise that, although delays are costly, the cost of eliminating them may be even more costly. One of its interesting applications, often used as an example, was the case of the New York Port Authority, which used queuing theory to solve a problem involving the number of toll stations at the entrance to bridges and tunnels. Through the application of this operations research device, the Authority found it could reduce waiting lines and, at the same time, reduce the number of toll stations.

Linear programming A technique for determining the optimum combination of limited resources to obtain a desired goal, linear programming is one of the most successful applications of operations research to problems. It is based upon the assumption that a linear or straight-line relationship exists between variables and that the limits of variations can be well determined. For example, in a production shop, the variables may be units of output per machine in a given time, direct labor costs or material costs per unit of output, number of operations per unit, and so forth. Most or all of these may have linear relationships, within certain limits, such as machine capacity, and by solving linear equations, the optimum in terms of cost, time, machine utilization, or other objectives can be established. Thus, this technique is especially useful where input data can be quantified and objectives are subject to definite measurement. As one might expect, the technique has had its most promising use in such problem areas as production planning, shipping rates and routes, and the utilization of production and warehouse facilities to achieve lowest over-all costs, including transportation costs. Because it depends for its accuracy on linear relationships and many decisions do not involve these, newer and more complex systems of nonlinear programming have come into use.

Servo theory This is another important contribution of operations research to management problems. Originally used in the design of automatic or remotely controlled systems (for example, the thermostat), the feedback principle, by which information is fed back to correct for deviations, has become an important aspect of operations research. The dynamic characteristics of problems emphasize the necessity for correcting for changes in the inputs in a mathematical model. The servo theory also has implications for managerial control.

---

[8] One the most interesting and elementary expositions of game theory may be found in J. D. Williams, *The Compleat Strategyst* (New York: McGraw-Hill Book Company, 1954).

Other Tools There are, of course, many other tools of operations research. *Symbolic logic,* by which symbols are substituted for propositions or even programs, has led to a sharper analysis of complicated and sometimes ambiguous problems. *Information theory* has sharpened the evaluation of the information flow within a given system. *Value theory* assigns numerical significance to the value of alternative tangible choices. *Monte Carlo methods* put random occurrence in models, to simulate such occurrences as machine breakdown or customer arrivals.

Limitations In the enthusiastic embracing of the potentialities of operations research the existing limitations should not be overlooked. So far, it has been used, in practice, to solve only a limited number of problems.

In the first place, one is faced with the sheer magnitude of the mathematical and computing aspects. The number of variables and interrelationships in many business problems, plus the complexities of human relationships and reactions, apparently call for a higher order of mathematics than does even exploration of nuclear physics. The late mathematical genius, John von Neumann, found, in his development of the theory of games, that his mathematical abilities soon reached their limit in a relatively simple strategic problem. However, it can also be said that managers are a long way from using the mathematics now available.

In the second place, although probabilities and approximations are being substituted for unknown quantities and scientific method is quantifying factors heretofore believed to be impossible to quantify, a major portion of important managerial decisions involve intangible and unmeasurable factors. Until these can be quantified, operations research will have limited usefulness in these areas, and selections between alternatives will continue to be based on nonquantitative judgments.

Related to the fact that many management decisions involve unmeasurable factors is the lack of information inputs to make this tool useful in practice, even though, with adequate research, information desired might be obtained. By conceptualizing a problem area and constructing a mathematical model to represent it, variables are disclosed on which information, not now available, is required. What is needed is far more emphasis by those interested in the practical applications of operations research toward developing this needed information. At times it appears that, if the same intelligence now devoted to the building of models and their mathematical manipulation was applied by specialists to developing information inputs, the application of operations research would be greatly accelerated.

Still another limitation concerns bridging the gap between manager and trained operations researcher. Managers in general lack a knowledge and appreciation of mathematics, as the mathematician lacks comprehension of managerial problems. This is being dealt with, in a few instances, by the business schools, and, more often, by business firms that team up managers with operations researchers.

One of the outstanding specialists in operations research reported a few years ago in a rather pessimistic tone concerning the actual use of this important tool.[9] He had his graduate students write the authors of cases reported in the journal *Operations Research* over the first six years of its publication with a view to determining the extent to which recommendations of the studies had been carried out by practicing managers. His pessimistic report was that there was not sufficient evidence in any case that the recommendations had been accepted.

A final serious drawback of operations research—at least in its application to complex problems—is that analyses and the use of electronic computers are expensive, and many problems are not important enough to justify the cost.

Future Possibilities The future of operations research applied to management decisions warrants enthusiasm. By introducing more effectively than heretofore the methods of the physical sciences into managerial decision making, operations research concentrates attention on goals, recognition of variables, search for relationships and underlying principles, and—through use of the model, advanced mathematics, and computation—on optimum solutions from many more alternatives than ever before possible. The analyst of a few years ago ordinarily could study only a few alternatives because of the sheer size of the analytical task. With operations research techniques and the high-speed electronic computer, he can analyze the probable results of thousands or millions of alternatives.

This implies a revolution in the planning activities of the future decision maker. The ultimate goal of operations researchers is to be able to formulate such complete policy or decision models that every aspect of a problem, every significant variable, every probability, and every related decision made or likely to be made will be included. It is even hoped by some that this will extend to important decisions at all levels in the enterprise.

This very cursory explanation of operations research indicates that it will continue to influence managerial decision making. By improving the quality of planning, it should likewise improve the quality of managerial control. In fact, an increasing number of promising applications of operations research to planning and control systems are appearing. Some of these will be dealt with in Chapter 29. In the decades to come, managers cannot overlook this technique and the scientific attitude behind it, if they want to stay ahead in the competitive race.

On the other hand, it would be fatuous to believe that this means a new kind of management, a sort of management by mathematics and the machine. The limitations of operations research pointed out above must ever be borne in mind, along with the fact that such research is a tool of management showing the way to decisions rather than making them and, like any other tool, an aid to, rather than a replacement for, managers.

[9] C. W. Churchman, "Managerial Acceptance of Scientific Recommendations," *California Management Review*, vol. 7, no. 1, pp. 31–38, at p. 33 (Fall, 1964).

EVALUATING THE DECISION'S IMPORTANCE

Since the manager must not only make correct decisions but must make them as needed and as economically as possible, and since he must do this often, guidelines as to the relative importance of decisions are important. Decisions of lesser importance need not require thorough analysis and research, and they may even safely be delegated without endangering an individual manager's basic responsibility. Naturally, the importance of a decision depends upon the extent of responsibility, so that what may be of practically no importance to a corporation president may be of some importance to a section head. Yet there are useful criteria of importance.

Size or Length of Commitment   If a decision commits the enterprise to heavy expenditure of funds or to an important program, such as a program for management appraisal and training, or if the commitment can be fulfilled only over a long period, it should be subjected to suitable attention at an upper level of management.

Flexibility of Plans   Some plans can be easily changed; some have built into them the easy possibility of a future change of direction; and others involve action difficult to change. Clearly, decisions involving inflexible courses of action must carry a priority over those easily changed.

Certainty of Goals and Premises   If goals and premises are fairly certain, often the case in a company with a clear profit objective and a high firm backlog of orders, a decision resting on them tends to be less difficult than where they are highly uncertain.

Quantifiability of Variables   Where the goals and inputs, parameters and variables can be accurately quantified, as with definite inputs in a production machine shop, the importance of the decision, other things remaining the same, tends to be less than where the inputs may be difficult to quantify, as in pricing a new consumer product or deciding on its style.

Human Impact   Where the human impact of a decision is great, its importance is high. Plans that may be sound, feasible, and desirable in terms of a profit goal may not be practicable in terms of the attitudes of the people affected. For example, a decision to put payroll or purchasing procedures on an electronic data-processing machine may involve almost completely quantifiable data inputs, yet the unrest and resistance of the clerical force may make the decision difficult. In such cases, of which there are many in a typical enterprise, the decision should probably be rated up in terms of importance, since no action contemplated for a group of people can afford to overlook acceptance by the group.

THE POLITICS OF DECISION MAKING

Politics has been defined as the art of the possible. A good manager must be sensitive in his decision making to what he *can* do. It is not enough that a decision be logical and point to the best way of reaching a goal. As noted above, beliefs, attitudes, and prejudices of people must often be taken into account.

A few years ago, in one of the nation's major defense companies, the top management approved a commercial research project, largely to assuage the feeling of key scientific and engineering personnel that weapons development was unsocial and offered little long-range security to the enterprise. But further study disclosed both lack of resources to complete the project and a large commercial company already entrenched in the field. Faced by these facts, the board of directors soundly decided to abandon the project, but the president considered abandonment unthinkable without adequately preparing the people involved. Following a program of careful and complete information on the project and on the available alternatives given to a key committee of the people involved, the president was able to obtain the unanimous support of these scientific and engineering personnel for abandoning the project, when *they too* saw the practical logic of doing so.

The political environment of decisions thus rests largely on communication and is favorable when everyone is well informed about his particular planning area. While the "need to know" has limits, the limits should be set as broadly as company or national security and the costs of information will permit. Much carping at the "stupidity" of decisions is eliminated when they are explained to people affected by them. Furthermore, such information helps the subordinate manager make implementing decisions.

Political problems of decision making often disappear also with widespread participation in planning. The widest possible participation—whether in the form of consultation, contribution of analyses, or whatever—is the best assurance that good decisions will be reached and plans intelligently and enthusiastically administered.

FOR DISCUSSION

1. Why is experience often referred to not only as an expensive basis for decision making but also a dangerous one? How can a manager make best use of experience?

2. In a decision problem you now know of, how and where would you apply the principle of the limiting factor to it?

3. Taking the above decision problem, whether the variables are quantifiable or not, apply operations research methodology to it in as simple form as you can. What does this do for your understanding of the problem? Does it help you solve it?

4. Could you conceptualize an operations research problem in broad terms without the use of mathematics?

5. "Decision making is the primary task of the manager." Comment.

SELECTED REFERENCES

American Management Association: *Operations Research: A Basic Approach,* Special Report No. 13, New York: American Management Association, 1956.

————: *Operations Research Applied,* Special Report No. 17, New York: American Management Association, 1957.

Barnard, C. I.: *The Functions of the Executive,* chaps. 13–14, Cambridge, Mass.: Harvard University Press, 1938.

Beer, S.: *Decision and Control,* New York: John Wiley & Sons, Inc., 1966.

Charnes, A. W., W. Cooper, and A. Henderson: *An Introduction to Linear Programming,* New York: John Wiley & Sons, Inc., 1953.

Chorafas, D. N.: *Operations Research for Industrial Management,* New York: Reinhold Publishing Corporation, 1958.

Churchman, C. W.: "Managerial Acceptance of Scientific Recommendations," *California Management Review,* vol. 7, no. 1, pp. 31–38 (Fall, 1964).

————, R. L. Ackoff, and E. L. Arnoff: *Introduction to Operations Research,* New York: John Wiley & Sons, Inc., 1957.

Drucker, P. F.: "Management Science and the Manager," *Management Science,* vol. 1, no. 2, pp. 115–126 (January, 1955).

————: "The Effective Decision," *Harvard Business Review,* vol. 45, no. 1, pp. 92–98 (January–February, 1967).

Gore, W. J.: *Administrative Decision Making: A Heuristic Model,* New York: John Wiley & Sons, Inc., 1964.

Henderson, A., and R. Schlaifer: "Mathematical Programming: Better Information for Better Decision-making," *Harvard Business Review,* vol. 33, no. 5, pp. 49–58 (October, 1955).

Herrman, C. C., and J. F. Magee: "Operations Research for Management," *Harvard Business Review,* vol. 31, no. 4, pp. 100–113 (July, 1953).

Jones, M. H.: *Executive Decision-making,* Homewood, Ill.: Richard D. Irwin, Inc., 1957.

Kepner, C. H., and B. B. Tregoe: *The Rational Manager,* New York: McGraw-Hill Book Company, 1965.

Levin, R. I., and C. A. Kirkpatrick: *Quantitative Approaches to Management,* New York: McGraw-Hill Book Company, 1965.

McCloskey, J. F., and J. M. Coppinger: *Operations Research for Management,* vol. 2, Baltimore: The Johns Hopkins Press, 1956.

———— and F. N. Trefethen: *Operations Research for Management,* vol. 1, Baltimore: The Johns Hopkins Press, 1954.

Miller, D. W., and M. K. Starr: *Executive Decisions and Operations Research,* Englewood Cliffs, N.J.: Prentice-Hall, Inc., 1960.

Newman, W. H., and C. E. Summer, Jr.: *The Process of Management,* chaps. 12–15, Englewood Cliffs, N.J.: Prentice-Hall, Inc., 1961.

Williams, J. D.: *The Compleat Strategyst,* New York: McGraw-Hill Book Company, 1954.

policy making

As was pointed out in the discussion of the nature of planning in Chapter 5, policies are guides to thinking in decision making. They reflect and interpret objectives, channel decisions to contribute to objectives, and thereby establish the framework for planning programs. They thus establish limits to plans, as planning premises provide the operational background for them.

Policies may be thought of as a kind of plan. Like the selection of objectives or programs, they involve decision making. Were it not for the complexity of most enterprise operations, or were it possible for detailed action plans to flow immediately from the top manager without going through a hierarchy of subordinate managers, policy formulation could conceivably be limited to stating enterprise objectives. But, largely because all but the simplest forms of enterprise organization require levels of management, operating plans derive from a hierarchical series of decisions in which major programs are refined as they are broken into parts and moved down the organization structure.

Thus, major policies beget derivative policies to guide the decision making of subordinate managers. A policy may thus be as broad and major as that of financing growth from profits and as minor as the derivative policy of having foremen show their superiors economic justification for additional manpower.

Policies are made by someone at some time inside or outside the enterprise. Moreover, policy making is not reserved, as is often thought, to top management. Although the higher a manager is in the organization structure, the more important his role in policy making, policy is made at all levels. Though managers at the lower level must use policy furnished by superiors, there are very few managers who do not at some time make policy, however limited.

SOURCES OF POLICY - STRATEGIES

To understand the nature of policy, it may be useful to analyze its sources, classified as originated policy, appealed policy, implied policy, and externally imposed policy.[1]

Originated Policy   The most logical source of policy is that originated by top management itself for the express purpose of guiding managers and their subordinates in the operations of the business. Originated policy flows basically from the objectives of the enterprise, as these are defined by the top executive authority, whether board of directors, president, general manager, or other chief executive officer. This policy may be broad in scope, allowing key subordinates to give it clearer definition, or it may be promulgated so completely as to leave little room for definition and interpretation. The extent to which it is centralized or decentralized is obviously dependent upon the extent to which authority is concentrated or dispersed.

But whether centralized or decentralized, policy developed by managers for the guidance of subordinates is originated policy, and it may be originated at any level of management. Furthermore, characterizing a policy as originated does not necessarily imply that it is imposed by command. Many are the adroit managers who originate policy and obtain compliance by making unobtrusive suggestions. In fact, some skillful managers originate policy and secure compliance by allowing a subordinate manager to leave a conference believing that he himself originated the policy. But often the policy must be imposed upon subordinates with a force and clarity that permits no deviation. Thus, a company president might originate a policy of using sales agents on a commission basis, rather than full-time salesmen, by merely making indirect suggestions along this line to his sales manager; or, he might be positive and blunt in stating a policy that the company will not engage in sharp dealings to make a sale.

Appealed Policy   In practice, perhaps most policy in the typical enterprise stems from the appeal of exceptional cases up the hierarchy of managerial authority. If an occasion for decision arises for an executive who does not know whether he has sufficient authority or how this matter should be handled, he may appeal to his superior. As appeals are taken upward and decisions made on them, a kind of common law is established. Precedents develop and become guides for future managerial action.

Policies developed from appeals are sometimes incomplete, uncoordinated and confused. If decisions are made on a given set of facts, without regard for their possible effects on other aspects of the operation, or if unintended precedents develop from them, the resulting policies may not guide the thought and action of subordinates as really desired by top managers.

---

[1] For an excellent discussion of this development of policy and the use of most of these terms, see E. Petersen and E. G. Plowman, *Business Organization and Management,* 4th ed. (Homewood, Ill.: Richard D. Irwin, Inc., 1958), chap. 11.

Moreover, policies about which the top executives do not even know may be formulated.

The aimless formulation of policy arising from appeals explains in part why it is usually so difficult in business to know exactly what policies do exist. As analysts have come to find out in attempting to compile policy manuals, many managers simply do not know company policy in many areas. This arises partly because policy formulation is by nature complex, but it also arises because many managers dislike to meet issues until forced to do so and thereby delay policy making until a body of precedent from individual decisions accumulates.

Appealed policy *may* be foresighted and internally consistent, especially if the manager realizes that his decision constitutes policy. However, when he finds himself constantly making policy by appeal, he might well ask himself whether he has left too large an area of policy making to chance and whether his subordinates have understood the policy he has formulated.

Implied Policy It is not unusual for policy to develop from actions which people see about them and believe to constitute policy. Thus, a company may have a stated policy that it will only produce and sell high-quality products. But if in fact it does not discourage the production and sale of shoddy goods, those working for it will soon see what the real policy is. A company also might have a policy of plant cleanliness but, by having too few janitors, might tolerate a dirty plant. In that case employees will see that the company's stated policy is not the accurate one. Or, a company might have a stated policy of promoting from within, but if those in the company see promotional opportunities filled with outsiders, or the lack of an internal appraisal and development program in order to equip insiders for promotion, the implied policy will be understood to be quite different.

It may be that implied policy arises from instances where the stated policy is not enforced. This is often the case, but, probably as often, it is due to the fact that a company may desire a certain policy as a kind of image but be unwilling or unable to enforce it. However, it is probable that implied policies develop where no stated policy of any kind exists. Indeed, this is one of the difficulties with not having clear policies. Decision makers will consciously or unconsciously adopt their own guidelines. These guidelines, in the absence of anything better, will likely be those which they believe the company wants followed, based on individual interpretation of actions observed in the company.

The authors know of a company whose top management desired the development of profitable new products and earnestly solicited product ideas from its marketing and engineering groups, as well as from others in the company. However, as time went on and new product ideas were submitted, they were subjected to rather complex investigatory procedures and conservative standards, and those who had submitted ideas were never informed as to what happened to them. The result was that even key people in the company believed that it was the top management's policy not to go ahead with new products except for very low-risk items. The company had made no clear policy statement as to what its position on new products was and what kind of product suggestions would fit into its program. As a consequence, the imputed policy, which was actually not what the company had intended, became the guideline for decisions under which the company's new-product program severely stagnated.

Externally Imposed Policy   To a rapidly increasing extent, particularly in business organizations, policy is being externally imposed on the enterprise, notably by government, trade unions, and trade associations. Whether in the form of direct regulation, or the competition of government-owned or government-supported business, or the many conditions for accepting government aids or contracts, the result is to circumscribe and dictate many aspects of policy. As has already been noted, strong national unions, operating through collective bargaining and detailed labor contracts, have also imposed policy upon the business manager he might not otherwise make. Besides, 15,000 local, regional, and national trade associations have their effect in varying degrees on business policy. There are, too, other social groups—such as church, school, fraternal, social, and charitable organizations—that mold or dictate business policy.

All in all, few major business decisions are now made without regard to one or another type of externally imposed policy. Such policy is effected in two ways: sometimes outside forces dictate it; in other cases they merely influence it.

POLICY FORMULATION: PRODUCT

Since policy affects every type of activity undertaken by the firm, it is practicable to discuss but a few of the most common areas of policy formulation, classified into two broad groups. One group includes policies dealing with the managerial functions: planning, organizing, staffing, directing, and controlling. To a great extent, policy of this type is the subject of this entire book.

The other group of policies includes those dealing with the functions of the enterprise—characteristic behavior of business firms to gain their objectives. This type is largely the subject of this chapter, broken down into the areas of product selection and development, sales, production, finance, and personnel and public relations.

Product Selection and Development   This is an exceptionally important area of policy making. The nature of the product naturally determines the kind of production facilities and organization needed, gives shape to the financial problems involved, and furnishes the background against which all other policy questions must be determined. Rapid changes in technology and de-

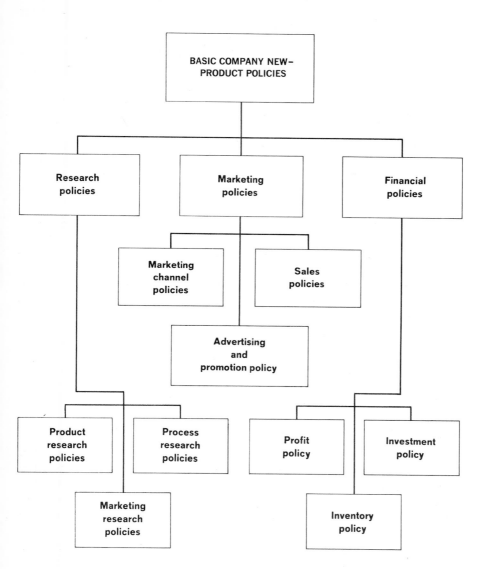

Fig. 9.1 The Hierarchy of Policy in New-product Development . . . *Policy generally exists in layers. For instance, basic company new-product policies are most often determined by top management. These, in turn, may affect or generate research policies, marketing policies, and financial policies. If top management does not itself generate derivative policy, managers at lower levels may develop policies governing product research, marketing research, advertising, and so forth. Basic company policy must be so logical and clear that derivative policy can be easily formulated.*

mand put company management on the alert to the quality of its product development. Furthermore, as Joel Dean has pointed out, product policy is the mainspring of economic progress and hence an important test of the company's social contribution.[2]

Product policy has to do with (1) selecting items and product lines, (2) developing and producing the items and lines, or services, (3) determining pricing, (4) selecting distribution channels, and (5) promoting sales. Of course, there are many attendant policy considerations, such as those dealing with the availability of financing, the effect of the product on the organization, the hiring and training of the necessary labor, the purchasing of material, and the acquisition of facilities. Also included in this area of selection are policies dealing with expected profits, fitting the product into product-line strategy, and the compatibility of the product with the firm's know-how, facilities, material sources, and distribution channels. Even though prospective profit may be of primary concern, these other factors cannot be overlooked.

Because of increasing recognition that products must be developed to supply a market and that product design and engineering are part of this, growing attention has been given to product development policies. A company may insist that its scientists and engineers develop products to fit a certain market, and this may require the product to be designed to a certain price or quality objective. The company policy may also dictate a design using the maximum number of standard parts. Or, product development policy might extend to organization, requiring—as many military contracts now do—product engineering to be set up under a project manager with integrated authority to manage all engineering talent and budget necessary to move the product from original concept, through preliminary design, to final engineering.

Other policies may require a development group to work closely with materials suppliers, to obtain engineering help from them; or they may require close liaison between development engineers within a company and production engineers, to assure the utmost of economic production potential in the final design. Or—as with General Motors' profit-oriented concept of a "family of cars"—styling policy may dictate that the product developed—in this case, cars—emphasize commonality of parts and tooling between different models. Except for the relatively few cases of basic research where only the most general of guidelines are given, technical developments tend more and more to be placed under policies that will assure low costs and market acceptability for the new product. Pouring money into research and development without practical guidance is no longer countenanced in the effective development of products.

Pricing   Pricing policy includes not only determination of base prices but

---

[2] For an excellent study of product policy and the considerations that enter its determination, see Joel Dean, "Product-line Policy," *Journal of Business,* vol. 23, pp. 248–258 (October, 1950). Much of the material of this section is drawn from his article.

also schedules of discounts and price differentials between products in a line. As almost all business has departed from conditions of perfect competition, with product differentiation and few sellers, pricing policy has become a key instrument of sales policy. Moreover, for businesses producing special goods and services, pricing policy is set less by sales competition than by a combination of costs and what the market will bear. However, even in these cases and despite the existence of price leeway, the pressure of competition is such that prices even of differentiated products must bear a close relationship. Despite imperfections in competition, there are few companies that do not feel in their pricing policy formulation the aggressiveness of existing or potential competitors.

Even where a seller establishes the policy of pricing his goods at fully allocated cost (that is, direct labor and material costs plus allocated overhead, sales, and administrative costs), he will find a wide variation of prices to suit this policy. Costs and cost allocations are seldom so accurate that somewhat less or somewhat more could not be included in them. This inability to allocate costs accurately, plus the usefulness of price variations for strategic marketing reasons, has made pricing policies of utmost importance in all businesses except those selling to a purely competitive market where the seller has no influence on price.

Price policy in most businesses must be continually studied because of changes in technology, new competition, new sales promotion programs of competitors, changes in demand, shifts in costs, and other factors.

Price policies vary in many ways. One company may have a policy of never undercutting competition; another may have a policy of always selling below competition. One company may have a policy of selling, even to the government, at fixed price; another may have a policy of selling on a cost plus fixed price; other companies may have both policies, applying one to a given line of products and another to a second line, the applications depending upon such environmental factors as the market and the risk involved in design and production. One company may have a policy of distributing nationally at one price; another may have a policy of varying prices between regions, depending on costs of delivery and regional competition. One company may have a policy of giving the utmost in quantity discounts; another may have a policy opposing such discounts. But virtually all companies have considerable policy imposed on them by the rigorous application of price discrimination laws of the Federal and state governments.

Moreover, pricing is often an instrument of sales promotion. If a firm's policy is to appeal to the mass market, price structure can make customers see the firm as a low-price source of goods and services. But the firm whose policy is to appeal to the prestige market will use price to enhance this appeal. Thus, a certain retailer handling high-grade men's clothing has a policy of selling suits at $100 or $150 and not at $99.95 or $149.95.

Sales Promotion Promotion policies may have to do with pricing, or with advertising, packaging, distribution, grading, sampling, or many other activities. But promotion goes far beyond the more obvious methods of selling.

A company's reputation for a good product, good service, or fair dealing may be sales promotion considerations. In the oil-drilling business, for example, it is well known that the availability of materials and supplies is more decisive than price, for a rig idled for lack of pipe or a drilling bit is very costly. As a result, supply houses and equipment manufacturers offering adequate field service and inventories get the business, regardless of small differences in price. Likewise, such apparently remote factors as a good market for resale materially affect sales, as indicated in the passenger automobile business by the fact that the largest manufacturers gain an edge from the better resale market of their cars.

Distribution Channels　In industries such as drug manufacturing, distribution channels are fairly clear-cut. In other industries, the use of jobbers, wholesalers, and retailers with fixed discounts is so standardized that little question of policy arises, aside from which distributors to select and how to sell them. But to many businesses, the selection of distribution channels presents difficult policy decisions. For example, a small laboratory equipment manufacturer had the choice of distributing by way of direct customer inquiry, field salesmen, manufacturers' agents, or established jobbers.

Policy on distribution channels is sometimes hard to change, once established. It is not easy to conceive of a very great change in practices affecting use of dealers to distribute automobiles, or advertising to sell proprietary drugs, or many other long-standing methods of doing business. On the other hand, certain types of enterprise—among them the chain stores, the supermarkets, many of the farm cooperatives, and the discount houses—have revolutionized distribution channels and methods.

POLICY FORMULATION: PRODUCTION

As with product, there are countless policy considerations connected with production, major examples of which follow.

To Buy or to Make　A policy question continually facing management is whether to buy or make a product or component of a product. Not only the small firm but many larger ones decide to buy a product or component rather than to tool up its own facilities for making it; in some cases, this decision is based on the specialized nature of the facilities or know-how required. Many of the larger firms do not, for example, do their own casting; others farm out their forgings; and many contract their screw-machine work. Furthermore, items that typically go into many products—such as steel and aluminum shapes, electric motors, wire, vacuum tubes, gears, bearings, and many others—are ordinarily purchased from companies specializing in them.

But the question as to whether to make or buy extends much further than to such components. Often a company has an entire product, or a major portion of one, made by another company. For example, Philco had its room air conditioners built by the York Corporation for many years. Radio Corporation of America bought its room air conditioners from Fedders-Quigan Corporation. International Harvester marketed a new type of body built by Fruehauf Trailer on its truck chassis. Even General Electric, which has followed fairly consistently the policy of making rather than buying, has bought its electric ironers from outside.

What would guide a company in the direction of buying rather than making its product? Obvious answers include lack of facilities or technique or lack of capital to expand into a particular new field. Other answers include timing, since a company might not be able to engineer a product, remove the "bugs," and get into production in time to take advantage of a market. Or a company might not wish to make a heavy commitment of capital and labor until it had amply tested the market. Furthermore, there are many products which a specialized or smaller company can make more efficiently than a more integrated larger company. In addition, especially as businessmen mistrust the stability of boom conditions, they may prefer not to have their capital so heavily committed. They may buy flexibility in planning, with a policy of buying rather than making.

Size of Run The size of the production run, where a company has an adequate backlog of orders, will normally be dictated by the economics of producing at capacity. But where, as is more usually the case, the company must produce on speculation for future sale, efficiency through large-volume operation runs the risk of creating an inventory too large either to finance or warehouse. Thus, the costs of tooling up for a run must be set against the risks of overstocking. At this point, of course, a reliable sales forecast can be the determining factor, although often competitive forces and the economics of volume production require a company to take the risk of overstocking in order for costs and prices to be low enough profitably to meet competition.

Production Stabilization Difficult policy decisions also arise in connection with timing production to market demands without upsetting stabilization of operations. The demand for many products is highly seasonal, and almost every product is subject to some demand variability. Some companies deal with this by merely producing to order, laying off and rehiring labor as needed. Other companies assume the risks of changing demands and price levels by producing for inventory. Still other companies make fill-in products, perhaps less profitable ones, to take up the slack of off-season facilities or labor. In the consumer goods market, the large chain mail-order and department stores often receive price concessions by contracting for off-peak production.

In service companies, such as transportation businesses, however, cyclical demands have a serious effect on costs. An unfilled boxcar or passenger seat is a perishable product and cannot be carried in inventory, with the result that operational stability and cost saving cannot be obtained by inventorying product. In such companies, there is usually no choice but to operate at times with unfilled or idle equipment and unused labor and at other times with unfilled or deferred demands. These peaks and valleys have been reduced somewhat by policy decisions in other areas, such as the sales policy of offering reduced family fares by air, or off-season fares, or encouraging people to take off-season vacations.

Inventory   Many production policies tie closely to inventory policy, and planning the economical level of inventories is one of the key decision areas of business. Inventories must be high enough to make products available as needed by the customer and as required by competition. And yet, too high inventories increase the cost of doing business and greatly magnify the risk of loss from price declines, or from changes in style, technology, or demand. Inventory size may also be influenced by the economics of production runs and will necessarily be limited by the financial capacity of the company.

Although the general principles governing inventory policy are fairly clear, the actual policy of a given company at a given time is not so simple. In one business, the time required to procure or make products may be a month, while in another it may be a year or, as with airplanes, three to five years. In one business, the customer may be willing to wait for months for a product, while in another, if the product is not immediately available, the sale will be lost. In one business, the market may be stable in terms of both demand and price; in another, both demand and price level may be mercurial. In one business, the inventory may be highly perishable; in another, everlasting.

Capital is the lifeblood of the firm. If this capital is tied up in slow-moving inventory, it cannot be used for business expansion or improved business economy. Therefore, most managers watch closely inventory size and turnover, for, in addition to risks involved in having resources sunk in unsalable merchandise or goods subject to price or quality deterioration, inventories require capital, one of the most strategically limiting factors in business enterprise.

POLICY FORMULATION: FINANCIAL POLICIES

The controlling importance of the financial aspects of business enterprise is recognized at many points in this book. A company's capital, whether furnished by its owners or borrowed, sets the limits to expansion and provides the means for obtaining those assets necessary to business operation. As with sales and production, policy making is much involved with financial considerations.

Capital Procurement   Polices dealing with capital procurement depend to a very great extent upon the size of the business and the willingness of its owners to draw upon outside capital. The point is often made that capital procurement depends largely upon the legal form of the business—that the individual proprietorship must depend upon the capital resources of the single owner, that partnerships must depend upon the resources of the partners, but that corporations can draw capital generally from the public through the sales of stocks and bonds. To an extent this is true, although there is no *legal* limit to the number of lenders who might help finance a proprietorship or a partnership, or to the number of partners who might join together. However, the corporate form, by creating the corporation as a separate entity, grants the stockholders limited liability and the corporation immortality.

Although the means for wide participation in investment are thus furnished, and it is difficult to conceive of the modern large enterprise without the features of limited liability and immortality, it does not follow that capital can be obtained thereby more easily than by other forms. A small business owned by a few persons gains little advantage in financing by incorporating. As a matter of fact, it has become customary for banks to require the principal stockholders in small businesses personally to guarantee a loan, along with the corporation. Furthermore, where a few individuals own the major interest in a small corporation, the lure of limited liability has little interest to an investor, since a minor equity in a small business would give him negligible control over his funds, and the smallness of the corporation would not guarantee a ready market for his stock.

In larger corporate enterprise, however, with a record of earnings, a well-managed operation, and an established market for stock, the limited-liability feature is clearly advantageous in inducing investment. Moreover, the assets and earnings of the business are likely to be large enough to support heavy borrowing without resort to the credit of its owners.

In developing policy for the procurement of capital, owners of a business must resolve a number of issues. Assuming that a realistic estimate of future capital requirements is available, policy questions arise as to the extent to which equity capital will be solicited from the public or from sources outside the principal owners. This raises questions, particularly for the small enterprise, about danger in the loss of control.

Furthermore, since a large portion of the ordinary company's funds comes from reinvesting profits, a policy question arises as to the extent to which profits should be retained or disbursed. This, in turn, raises numerous questions of dividend policy. The question of borrowing also requires decision. Should the firm's assets be mortgaged or otherwise pledged against loans? If so, upon what basis, with what kind of lender (bank, private lender, insurance company, factoring company, or other), for what term, with what provision for repayment, at what interest rate, and with what restrictions on operating and financial practices?

These and other questions bear on the kind of financial structure the company should adopt. It has been customary in American industry for railroads and public utilities to do a large portion of their financing with long-term borrowings, partly because these companies require heavy capital investment in relation to their sales, partly because they have found funds generally easier to obtain through borrowing, partly because of the belief that a certain stability of earnings exists that will support borrowings, and also because top managers have found in low-cost credit a means for pyramiding earnings on stock. On the other hand, industrial firms, generally with a much higher capital turnover and greater variability of earnings, have done far less long-term loan financing, obtaining their capital through the sale of stock and reinvestment of earnings. Short-term capital needs have been obtained through commercial credit.

For smaller corporate enterprises of all kinds, there is normally little room for decision as to capital structure. Long-term borrowing is usually out of the question, and the owner of the small business is generally limited in his capital expansion to obtaining funds through resources of himself and friends (and this seldom goes far, for even friends, investing any sizable amount of equity capital, want control commensurate with their investment) and through such working capital borrowing as may be obtained through commercial banks or factoring companies.

Cash and Depreciation Allowances Perhaps the largest single source of cash for going enterprises in recent years is the funds held in the business through depreciation reserve accounting. Although it is customary in business to speak of spending depreciation cash, every accountant realizes that depreciation charges do not *make* cash. A depreciation charge is a noncash expense, unlike most other expenses, and cash expenses are, therefore, overstated to the extent that depreciation (in addition to certain other noncash expenses) is charged. In other words, depreciation is a proper charge against earnings and is a real expense, but, because it is merely a write-down of asset values, it requires no cash outlays. Obviously, if the company takes in no cash beyond that for cash expenses, neither depreciation allowances nor book profits will give rise to cash. However, in most businesses, it is both accurate and customary to conclude that cash available from operations, even though used to finance such assets as receivables and inventories, is equal to book profits plus noncash expenses, notably depreciation.

The extent to which companies depend on cash "generated" through depreciation charges is indicated by the fact that many firms have relied on this source for a major portion of their capital expenditures. Consequently, in any policy having to do with capital sources, the reinvestment of funds arising because of depreciation charges plays a major role. Because of special tax dispensations in recent years, which have allowed accelerated depreciation, and because most businesses are anxious to accrue depreciation allowances as fast as possible, depreciation policy questions strike at the heart of capital planning.

To Own or to Lease One important source of capital, increasingly employed in recent years, is the lease. Businesses of all kinds extend their sources of capital by leasing plant and even machinery and equipment, thereby saving commitment of their scarce capital. Another important aspect of so doing, and one which has often become controlling, is the saving possible under tax laws. Lease costs are deductible for income tax purposes, so a firm can afford, particularly with high corporate income tax rates, to pay high lease costs and still have low net costs. If this same amount of capital were raised by equity sources, the equipment would have to earn much more to justify the expenditures.

Thus, high tax rates have affected the policy of owning versus leasing, as they have affected the entire economics of borrowing versus owning, so that the traditional risks of leasing or borrowing are greatly modified. Even when tax rates on marginal returns approximate 50 per cent, the corporate enterprise must consider taxes as a major factor in any decision to own or lease, or to borrow or invest equity capital. These financial policy considerations are no longer a simple matter of capital availability, risk, or absolute return on investment but are altered materially by the economics of corporate tax deductibility.

Working Capital   Working capital is generally defined as the excess of current assets over current liabilities and is thus that portion of current assets which has been supplied by the permanent investors of the business. Since assets are regarded as current if it is expected that they will be converted into cash in the normal course of the business (usually defined by accountants as within one year), and since liabilities are current if they will be liquidated in the same period, working capital becomes a measure of the ability of the business to meet its obligations. Adequate working capital, particularly that portion available in cash, is thus the first requirement for maintaining credit, meeting obligations promptly, and avoiding bankruptcy. It is the ability of the firm to pay its bills when they are due that assures continuance as a going enterprise, and not the size of the firm's surplus account, as many businesses have come to find out when a lack of liquid assets forced them to the wall. Inventories of unfinished or even of finished goods not readily marketable are an unacceptable substitute for cash for the creditor or the workman whose pay is due.

Working capital requirements and policies vary between companies. The electric utility company with regular cash collection needs less working capital than the manufacturer of expensive specialized machines. The company operating on a strictly cash basis will require less than a similar enterprise with predominantly credit sales. The company with the short-production cycle will need less than a similar company with a long-production cycle. These and other differences, then, affect seriously working capital policies.

Among the working capital problems that firms face are the extent to which current assets should be held in cash or easily marketable securities, the nature and liquidity of receivables and inventories, the nature and immediacy of current liabilities, creditor discounts, and other questions. Of course, of paramount significance are the size and adequacy of working capital and its variability as business operations expand or contract and as collections vary. Working capital policy understandably has a strong relationship to the firm's policy on credits and collections.

Working capital policies are also closely related to policies concerned with bank borrowing and the maintenance of a line of credit. The amount of credit line will reflect business variations, and the adequacy of invested working capital will be an important consideration in planning for periods when the firm can "clean up" its bank borrowings. Banks usually like to see credit used only for cyclical swings in working capital needs and not as a permanent source of these funds. Working capital planning is therefore primarily a function of cash planning, and cash planning, as will be seen in Chapter 10, reflects the entire planning program of the company.

Profit Disposition Profit disposition depends much upon policies adopted for the calculation of profits. Some firms, for example, charge off depreciation at rates much higher than the actual loss in value of the property depreciated, thereby reducing profits and retaining in the business funds that otherwise might be paid out in income taxes or dividends. Other firms understate or overstate profits through their policy of charging capitalizable research or tooling costs to current expenses. If a firm conservatively evaluates inventories, this may lead to understating profits. Consequently, policy questions arise as to the actual calculation of profits.

Regardless of how profits are determined, every firm must make policy decisions in connection with the disposition of profits. In the closely held company, this may be no problem, since the requirements of expansion and the desire to reinvest earnings, as well as the tax advantage of not paying dividends to well-salaried insiders, may make the policy choice clearly one of maintaining profits in the business. But in the typical large enterprise whose stock is widely held, difficult questions may arise. If the company wishes to develop an investment reputation for its stock, it may favor regular dividend payments. Even in this case questions arise as to how high dividends should be or what portion of earnings should be distributed in dividends. Or if a company prefers to rely on growth to make its stock attractive in the market, it will favor a policy of reinvestment of profits and the distribution of little or no earnings. Some investors even regard cash dividends as a sign of weakness in a "growth" company, an indication that it cannot profitably use its cash in the business. Clearly, the desirability of one policy or another will depend upon a number of factors, including (1) the desires of the stockholders, (2) the company's plan, if any, to raise additional funds through further stock flotations, (3) other available sources for obtaining capital, (4) the urgency of the need for additional capital, and (5) the profits possible from reinvesting the company's earnings.

POLICY FORMULATION: PERSONNEL AND PUBLIC RELATIONS

Company management must strive for loyal, intelligent, competent, and enthusiastic subordinate managers and employees. Therefore, in most companies, the largest group of policies are personnel policies. In addition, since the company must live and prosper within a community and since what the community thinks of it may greatly affect its success, it must develop a careful policy of public relations.

Personnel Selection and Training   Selection and training are at the base of personnel policies, as will be noted in Chapters 21 and 23, for these are the essential aspects of staffing. They involve a number of policy questions such as the following: In filling vacancies at the lowest rank, how much testing, interviewing, and other measurement should be taken of the prospective employee? Or should selection be rather casual, with a policy of ruthlessly weeding out the unfit after a short probationary period? What shall be the minimum educational requirements? How much experience or training should be required of an applicant, or should the company do its own training? Should company training be extensive, and, if so, through classroom procedures, conferences, committees, on-the-job coaching, or rotation through jobs? To fill positions of higher rank, should the firm adopt an ironclad policy of promotion from within or one of open competition from within and outside? What should be the policy on hiring relatives of present employees? Should religious, geographical, marital, or other personal factors be weighed in the selection or promotion of employees?

Compensation   Personnel policy gives rise to serious questions involving compensation, whether in terms of wages, profit sharing, bonuses, or other types of financial remuneration. These questions arise not only in connection with the absolute amount of the compensation, but also with the comparative amounts paid on jobs on the same general level, and with the relation of this compensation to pay scales vertically throughout the organization. Other questions arise as to the method of arriving at the compensation and the method of paying it.

Most companies adopt the policy of paying competitive wages and salaries, that is, equal to those paid by other companies employing the same skills in the same community. In the first place, such payments will probably attract the necessary personnel. In the second place, by not paying more, costs can remain competitive. Furthermore, as labor organizations have gained power and contracts are concluded with large national unions, wage scales among nonmanagerial employees approach uniformity in given industries and localities. However, many companies purposely adopt other policies when union or industry pressures permit them to do so. Some companies have adopted high pay policies to attract more competent workers, to lower costs by reducing turnover and increasing morale and efficiency, or to thwart union organization.

Within the firm both managers and workers react unfavorably if they find that in another part of the company others receive higher pay for work regarded as similar. Top-management members often delude themselves into believing they can avoid the problem of comparable compensation through the use of confidential payrolls and other devices to keep pay differences—particularly those of managers—a secret. Seldom, however, in practice do payrolls remain confidential, and it is unusual for managers not to find out what their colleagues are receiving. The best solution, of course, is to develop a job evaluation program, which will rate jobs fairly on the basis of importance, training and experience required, and nature of duties. Although no policy or practice can prevent all criticism of pay differentials, an open policy based upon objective evaluation will do much to solve the problem.

Employee Benefits and Morale   Personnel policy includes many decisions regarding employee benefits and other devices for improving morale: questions on vacations, sick leaves, leaves of absence, retirement pay, company cafeterias, and working conditions. In addition, most companies face policy questions of the extent and nature of recreational and social activities they should furnish, the kinds of insurance they should offer and how much the employee should pay, the kind of medical services they should offer, and the nature of employee publications. These questions require not only basic policy decisions on the extent to which the company should develop and support each program, but also detailed policy decisions on the nature of each portion of the program. Since many employees dislike the paternalistic approach in personnel programs—especially when they believe that the costs replace wages to which they might otherwise be entitled—intelligent top management can hardly delegate to a personnel department or a shop superintendent complete authority over the formulation of such programs but should carefully guide policy itself.

Union Relations   Earlier in the history of American business, top managers were in a position to make the serious decision as to whether to bargain individually or collectively with their employees. Since the rise of national unionism, under the protection of the National Labor Relations Act of 1935, this situation has changed. But there still exist many policy questions in union relations. A basic question has to do with the attitude of the company toward its labor organizations. In most cases, management has decided that a cooperative attitude saves trouble and money. In some cases, management has all but abdicated its leadership role, relying on union organization to serve as the primary channel of communication between the workers and the managers. But in most cases where employees are organized, the company has insisted, as a matter of policy and practice, on continuing an effective communication with employees.

In handling grievances, some companies adopt a policy of allowing almost any grievance to go through all established channels to an impartial arbitrator set up by the company-union contract. In these cases, the managers through whose hands the grievances go do little more than hear them and keep records. In other companies, however, there has been a fairly effective policy of encouraging managers at the very lowest levels to settle grievances, so that the grievance machinery is used only in the truly exceptional case. Of course, company policy in handling grievances is affected by union policy. Some unions seem to prefer pressing grievances to the utmost, while others obtain settlement at the lowest organizational level possible.

Public Relations Public relations policy making has become one of the major preoccupations of the typical chief executive. From a bygone attitude of secrecy and reticence, modern business policy is one of aggressively informing the public. This policy has been furthered by another relatively recent policy—that of news releases, speeches, and participation in outside functions by managerial personnel. Such control is designed to obtain a unified public relations program to ensure that the company presents the public image it desires.

In general, public relations policies of recent years have had certain definite manifestations. More complete and accurate financial and other information has been published. Businesses have taken a lead in supporting local and national charitable, educational, and other organizations. Management personnel has been encouraged to participate in community affairs and even to take governmental posts or run for political office. In more and more ways, business management has properly come to regard its job not only as that of offering a good product or service at a fair and profitable price, but also as that of making the public understand the importance of business to the community.

GUIDELINES FOR EFFECTIVE POLICIES *Strategies*

All companies have policies, whether they are written or unwritten, sound or unsound, followed or not followed, understood or not understood, complete or incomplete. It is virtually impossible to delegate authority without the existence of policy, since a subordinate manager cannot make decisions without some kind of guidelines.

It is surprising that so many companies neglect this powerful tool of management. Many companies do not have policy manuals, and of the increasing number of companies that do, many manuals are not kept up-to-date and the majority of them contain a mixture of policies, rules, and procedures. On the basis of analysis of a considerable number of policy manuals issued by well-managed companies, the authors have not been impressed with their quality or usefulness. And in companies without manuals, the fact that policy has not even been published is probably evidence that its formulation and use have serious shortcomings.

There is not space here to describe all the ways of making policies effective, but certain guidelines can be set down.

Polices Should Reflect Objectives and Plans If a policy does not further plans or make enterprise objectives more attainable, it has not done its job. No manager should ever be able to say: There's no good reason why we do it, it is just our policy!

Policies Should Be Consistent An obvious point, true, but often violated in practice. For instance, an ineffective sales program would surely result if the promotion for a product were based upon both a policy of product differentiation through heavy advertising and a policy of vigorous price cutting.

Policies Should Be Flexible   While many policies are, in effect, permanent, it should never be assumed that policies represent natural laws engraved on stone. If goals, premises, or major plans change, policies can likewise be expected to change to meet the new situation.

To be flexible as the situation changes is not to be casual in application. If current policies reflect objectives and plans and are consistent, they should not be regarded lightly and disregarded on slight pretext. This does not mean that exceptions should never be made to policies. It is sometimes impossible to make a policy to meet all conditions. But if a policy must be disregarded often, there is indication that it is not sound, is not applicable, or too tightly circumscribes a manager's area of discretion.

Policies Should Be Distinguished from Rules and Procedures   In Chapter 5, careful distinction was made between policies, rules, and procedures. This was done not to be petty in the semantics of management but because the understanding of this distinction is important to managerial functioning. The major criticism the authors have of company so-called policy manuals is that they are often a mishmash of policies, rules, and procedures.

Some policies are rules and not recognized as such; other so-called policies are really procedures designed to channel action, not thinking. The correct separation of these three types of guidelines is admittedly difficult, but it is important to good planning, workable delegation of authority, and even good human relations, and it can be accomplished. Some companies, albeit too few, have carefully distinguished between policies and procedures in their manuals by printing them on paper of different colors. It also helps to point out the policy to which each procedure is related.

Policies Should Be in Writing   Managers sometimes fear that written policies will lead to rigidity and lack of creative aggressiveness and will spoil a feeling of free teamwork. Other managers feel that policies must be so general or vague that they cannot be written. In companies without written policies, the position has often been that memoranda and bulletins which incorporate policy make formalized written policy unnecessary. While some top managers still oppose written policies, the attitude toward them has changed considerably in recent years.

If policies are to be used, they should be written. Putting a policy in writing does not make it a clear policy, but a policy that cannot be put in writing is, at best, an unclear one. The difficulty of communicating intentions and desires is reduced by precise communication in writing. Furthermore, the very act of writing policies has a way of forcing elimination of fuzziness and inconsistency. As one major management consulting firm has summarized the importance of writing policies:[3]

---

[3] As stated by Booz Allen and Hamilton, Inc., and quoted by Louis Cassels and Raymond L. Randall in "Written Policies Help Nine Ways," *Nation's Business,* vol. 47, no. 12, pp. 84–87 (December, 1959).

It builds on proved decisions of the past, conserving executive energy for new decisions; it creates an atmosphere in which individual actions may be taken with confidence; it speeds administration by reducing repetition to routine; it supports consistency of endeavor across a large group through the years. It stabilizes the enterprise. It frees top management so that more creative consideration can be given to the problems of today and the new programs of tomorrow.

In other words, putting policies in writing is the best way of putting them to work.

Policies Should Be Taught Written policies must be explained, interpreted, and taught. What people do not understand they cannot use correctly and are likely to distrust. No top manager may assume that the issuance of a written policy is enough. He must see that questions regarding it are answered and that subordinates comprehend its goal and why it has developed.

Policies Should Be Controlled Because policies have a way of becoming obsolete and because they may be misinterpreted or may not accomplish their purpose, they must be controlled. This means a regular and careful review of company policies to see whether they are up to date, whether they reflect goals and plans, whether they are consistent and flexible, whether they are distinguished from rules and procedures, whether they are understood, and whether they hamper the managers' legitimate activity.

To undertake this kind of control takes talent that companies are often unwilling to assign to the task. It is truly a top-management job. Administrative assistants and other staff personnel, unless on a high level in the company, cannot be expected to do it. One of the best programs of policy formulation and control that the authors have seen was carried out by a vigorous senior executive, nearing retirement. Not only did he have skill in writing and in teaching subordinates, but he was also thoroughly familiar with the company's operations and history and had the valuable experience and connection of having served on its executive committee. His qualifications give an idea of what it takes to properly assess, express, teach, and control policies.

COMPETITIVE STRATEGY AND POLICY

Polices are not made in a vacuum and are not often made unilaterally by one manager. In other words, plans and policies are made with the realization that they must be adjusted in accordance with the reactions of competitors, customers, suppliers, employees, subordinate managers, and others inside and outside the enterprise. The policy of a business firm may be clear and its plans well developed, but strategy may require some adaptation to meet the plans and policies of others.

In poker or chess, as in war or business, a carefully formulated plan may be upset by the action or strategy of an opponent.[4] The skillful player, therefore, shifts his plans in accordance with the moves and probable plans of opponents, although he will still lose if his opponent's "hand" or other situation is superior enough, of course, to outweigh good strategy and planning.

To borrow a term from military planning, "tactics"—the detailed steps by which a strategy is effected—also have an application to business planning. After a situation has been gauged and policy shaded to take it into account, a program of detailed action is required to implement the strategy.

Here are a few examples of business strategies.[5] A company may push a product that it would otherwise not produce and sell, to discourage a competitor. A finance vice-president may make discreet but carefully publicized inquiries about loans from other banks when his bank shows signs of becoming too severe about terms. A manager may voluntarily grant pay increases to his nonunion white-collar workers ahead of union-negotiated increases for the other employees. A purchasing agent may unduly encourage one vendor to obtain better attention and pricing from another. A top manager may deliberately avoid having anything to do with union negotiations until agreement is almost reached and then use his power and standing to close the deal by a last-minute intervention. Another top manager may purposely delay a needed reorganization of his upper-executive levels until the situation has become so serious that his subordinates will accept any solution of his rather than the existing situation. A manager opposing a course of action desired by his superiors may be converted by being put in charge of the activity or being appointed chairman of a committee to make recommendations regarding it.

Such examples of strategic shading of policies to gain objectives illustrate the flexible nature of policy formulation and execution. A basic policy and its objective may be clear, as may be the major derivative policies, but the reactions of persons affected by the policies must be taken into account, and here strategy can be decisive in the success of a policy.

FOR DISCUSSION

1. Select a policy in an enterprise with which you are familiar and, after determining that it is a policy, attempt to trace how it originated.

---

[4] The connection between strategy in games and in business is ably, although somewhat abstractly, described in J. von Neumann and O. Morgenstern, *The Theory of Games and Economic Behavior* (Princeton, N.J.: Princeton University Press, 1944). For a more popular treatment of this subject, see J. D. McDonald, *Strategy in Poker, Business, and War* (New York: W. W. Norton & Company, Inc., 1950); and J. D. Williams, *The Compleat Strategyst* (New York: McGraw-Hill Book Company, 1954).

[5] An interesting classification of business strategies was devised by the late Professor L. C. Sorrell of the University of Chicago. For a discussion of these, see W. H. Newman, *Administrative Action* (Englewood Cliffs, N.J.: Prentice-Hall, Inc., 1951), pp. 110–118. Some of these strategies, which businessmen will easily recognize, are "strike while the iron is hot," "time is a great healer," "bore from within," "in union there is strength," "divide and rule," "draw a red herring across the trail," "capitalize on apparent defeat," "pass the buck," and "conserve your gunpowder."

2. It has been found that most middle managers are anxious for a business firm to develop and publish clear policies. Can you see any reasons why this should be the case?

3. Should policies be permanent or subject to ready change?

4. Is policy making properly only the task of top managers in an enterprise?

5. How would you go about formulating a company's policies?

SELECTED REFERENCES

Anshen, M.: "Price Tags for Business Policies," *Harvard Business Review*, vol. 38, no. 1, pp. 71–78 (January–February, 1960).

Bachman, Jules: *Pricing: Policies and Practices*, Studies in Business Economics No. 91, New York: National Industrial Conference Board, 1961.

Buchele, R. B.: *Business Policy in Growing Firms*, San Francisco: Chandler Publishing Company, 1967.

Dean, J.: "Product Line Policy," *Journal of Business*, vol. 23, no. 4, pp. 248–258 (October, 1950).

Goetz, B. E.: *Management Planning and Control*, chaps. 6, 9, New York: McGraw-Hill Book Company, 1949.

Higginson, M. V.: *Management Policies I: Their Development as Corporate Guides*, New York: American Management Association, 1966.

————: *Management Polices II: Sourcebook of Statements*, New York: American Management Association, 1966.

Jamison, C. L.: *Business Policy*, chaps. 18–27, Englewood Cliffs, N.J.: Prentice-Hall, Inc., 1953.

Kline, C. H.: "The Strategy of Product Policy," *Harvard Business Review*, vol. 33, no. 4, pp. 91–100 (July–August, 1955).

McDonald, J. D.: *Strategy in Poker, Business, and War*, New York: W. W. Norton & Company, Inc., 1950.

Miller, E. C.: *Personnel Policies: Framework for Managerial Decision*, New York: American Management Association, 1966.

Newman, W. H., and J. P. Logan: *Business Policies and Central Management*, 5th ed., Cincinnati: South-Western Publishing Company, 1966.

Rowland, F. H.: *Business Planning and Control*, chaps. 3–8, New York: Harper & Row, Publishers, Incorporated, 1947.

Staudt, T. A.: "Program for Product Diversification," *Harvard Business Review*, vol. 32, no. 6, pp. 121–136 (November–December, 1954).

Steiner, G. A.: "Why and How to Diversify," *California Management Review*, vol. 6, no. 4, pp. 11–18 (Summer, 1964).

Tilles, S.: "How to Evaluate Corporate Strategy," *Harvard Business Review*, vol. 41, no. 4, pp. 111–121 (July–August, 1963).

von Neumann, J., and O. Morgenstern: *Theory of Games and Economic Behavior*, Princeton, N.J.: Princeton University Press, 1944.

Williams, J. D.: *The Compleat Strategyst*, New York: McGraw-Hill Book Company, 1954.

planning in action

When a plan is complete—with proper assignments made and understood—and it enters the phase in which the manager checks on actual execution, the function of the manager becomes one of control. But, as has been repeatedly emphasized, in practice these managerial functions blend into a single whole. The shift to control may be imperceptible, as exemplified in budgeting. Budget making is planning, while budget administration—the follow-up of planning—is control. Even in the course of planning, some follow-up is necessary; managers on each level of organization must make sure that their subordinates make and integrate derivative plans. Obviously, coordination of plans must precede their proper execution.

COORDINATION OF THE PLANNING PROGRAM

To coordinate plans, the manager must make sure that derivative plans are consistent with and timed properly to support the objectives and other decisions involved in the major plan. He must also set clear goals and clearly delegate authority, because people do better work when they know what is expected of them and what their area of discretion is.

Even so simple a plan as that to select a new piece of factory machinery may require many subsidiary, or derivative, plans. Arrangements must be made for its purchase, its shipment, and its payment; for the receipt, unpacking, inspection, installation, use, and maintenance; plans have to be ready so that it will be properly located and have the necessary power supply; production schedules must be modified, cost standards changed, and probably still other things must be done in connection with the installation and operation of the machine.

Managers seem often to forget how complex derivative planning is and how many delegations of authority must be geared into its making and execution. A great advantage of some of the new planning and control systems is that they force managers to consider these intricacies. Some of these new systems are discussed in Chapter 29 in connection with control. While such programs as PERT (Program Evaluation Review Technique) are often thought of as control programs, their real significance is in connection with planning, for they reflect basic principles of planning. For example, in one fairly simple project that one of the authors observed, the complex of derivative plans was so intricate that the project manager could not carry them in his head; the relatively simple problem of installation of a machine to make plastic bottles involved thirty-two distinct but closely related decisions necessary to coordinate derivative plans.

Timing Since the planning process is a complex of many major and derivative plans, and since plans are necessarily related to one another, it is important that they fit together, not only in terms of content and action but also in terms of timing. The principle of timing, then, reflects the fundamental truth that the more plans are structured to provide an appropriately timed, intermeshed network of derivative and supporting programs, the more effectively and efficiently they will contribute to the attainment of enterprise objectives. Part of the importance of planning premises, as discussed in Chapter 7, is to assure proper timing in fitting plans together. What is sometimes overlooked in planning is that timing is horizontal as well as vertical. Thus, a retirement plan must be timed vertically by properly meshing with it such derivative, or subordinate, plans as those of funding, insurance reserves, calculating benefits, and giving effect to past service. The plan must also be timed horizontally by being coordinated with plans for financing, for layoffs and leaves of absence, or for profit sharing.

A plan to purchase needed parts rather than to make them requires vertical timing in developing specifications and arranging for shipping and inspection. Horizontally, this plan may require changed timing of the fabrication program, a shift in inventory procedures, and organizational changes to strengthen the purchasing department or to make possible better coordination of engineering, purchasing, and manufacturing. Unnecessary costs are incurred if, for example, the purchasing agent obtains the parts much too early or much too late for use in assembling the final product, or if inspectors are hired and trained too early or too late; or if the traffic manager arranges for inbound shipment before facilities are ready to handle them.

As will be seen in later discussion of network analyses (Chapter 29), timing has as its essence the looking at programs as a network of supporting activities and events. It is obvious to a person viewing an automobile assembly line that events must fit from a timing point of view. In other words, the end result is not attained by doing very many things, other than the final assembly, in a sequential fashion. Instead, the components assembled represent a network of parts and subassemblies which have been accomplished in another time sequence, and each of them involves, in turn, a timed network which will vary considerably. Consequently, one should enlarge his thinking of the vertical and horizontal timing of supporting plans to more accurately encompass a network.

Timing is one of the most difficult problems of business planning, especially in assembly-line operations, where an entire operation may be held up for lack of a single small part. Sometimes, the need for timing is not apparent—as in working out an organization plan, initiating a personnel program, or planning a sales strategy—yet the costs of poor timing even in these areas may be considerable.

PLANNING COMMUNICATION

The often-encountered failure to plan on the part of managers at all subordinate levels is frequently not caused by inability or unwillingness to plan but rather by lack of knowledge concerning the firm's objectives, its planning premises, its major policies, and those plans made at higher levels in the organization structure which necessarily affect a subordinate's area of planning. An uninformed manager or employee is almost sure to be an ineffective one, no matter how sincere his wish to play his position on the team well. One reason production planning has been so well done in most American business firms is that factory supervisors and their employees understand clearly what they are required to do.

The Planning Gap   Because of the practical difficulties of furnishing adequate information, because many managers do not understand the importance of planning communication, and because in business internal security is necessary to avoid loss of information to competitors, the typical enterprise develops what might be called a planning gap. The top executives understand the company's goals and policies, and the workers in the shop understand what they are expected to accomplish in a day's work, but there exists a gap between the top and bottom, in which managers do not understand how their departmental goals and policies tie in with those of the enterprise as a whole. In a large, well-managed company with which one of the authors is familiar, a survey of the top fifty executives immediately under the vice-presidential level disclosed that their most pressing need was for knowledge of top-management plans. If this gap was that bad in the second level of command, one wonders how serious it was at lower levels.

That the planning gap exists in most organizations is apparent from observations made to one of the authors by a group of scientists in a military research laboratory. They remarked that, although they understood the basic objectives of the Defense Department and those of the service for which they worked, and although they understood the detailed plans for the projects assigned to them, they did not always understand the objective of these particular projects. Their feeling was that if they knew for what purpose their projects were to be used, they might be able to do a better job.

Planning Communication   The best planning occurs when everyone has access to complete information affecting the area for whose planning he is responsible. This implies that objectives, premises, policies, plans of others—whether superiors or colleagues—and other pertinent information which clearly affect their planning should ideally be available to managers concerned.

Information must be as specific and thorough as possible. The person executing a plan will do his best job if he understands his own assignment and the plan in its entirety—including its objective, the general and specific means of attaining it, and the jobs others are expected to do. In many cases, however, this is clearly impossible. The foreman in a large chemical plant can hardly expect to know top-management strategy in developing a new synthetic, the chemical engineering involved, how the finance department is making available capital funds, the tax planning, or the accounting procedures. There are limits to the information any manager or employee can gain concerning a specific plan. But the existence of limits relating to time, capacity to absorb knowledge, requirements of business secrecy, or other factors should not prevent top management from giving as much information as possible to help managers plan well and let them know, if at all possible, how their decisions contribute to major goals and plans.

Another problem of communication is connected with the manager interpreting and explaining plans to his subordinates. Often, halfhearted or even belligerent conformity to a management policy or program by employees results from lack of understanding. Much of the carping at the stupidity of the "brass" for a given policy or program might be eliminated by supplying employees with adequate information. Experience in many companies has shown that the gain of having a well-informed group of managers and employees offsets any losses—often greatly exaggerated—caused by a competitor's learning details of a plan. On the contrary, the authors have seen many cases where a company's competition knew the company's "secrets" and its employees charged with accomplishing a plan were uninformed.

PLANNING PARTICIPATION

A good way of assuring adequate knowledge of plans, with the extra dividend of loyalty to them, is to have as many managers as possible participating in planning. Plans are most likely to be enthusiastically and intelligently executed with the use of this technique. The best planning is done when managers are given an opportunity to contribute to plans affecting the areas over which they have authority.

Extent of Participation The informed participating manager should be encouraged to contribute suggestions which may be valuable to top managers. Another kind of participation sometimes possible to effect is that of consulting with managers in advance about plans they are to execute. Clearly, also, each manager participates by making the plans necessary for his department.

Participation in all planning affecting a manager's area of authority, through his being informed, contributing suggestions, and being consulted, leads to good planning, loyalty, and managerial effectiveness. Yet one may ask how, in a large plant, the hundreds of foremen and superintendents, sales and other managers *can* be consulted. One cannot imagine the top managers of the Ford Motor Company, for instance, consulting with their thousands of subordinate managers on plans for a new line of cars. Unfortunately, in such companies, this extent of participation is impossible, as much as it might be desirable.

Means Even so, there are means of wider participation of subordinate managers in planning for their departments. A planning staff, which spends time with key subordinate managers in developing plans and encourages these managers to discuss the plans with their subordinates, is one means of increased participation. In some companies, this practice has produced excellent results. Planning committees are another means. Although committees have limited administrative use, their appropriate establishment at various levels and points of the organization structure can improve communication by transmitting planning information, by eliciting suggestions, and by encouraging participation. They must be skillfully handled to avoid wasting time, but they can pay handsome dividends in helpful advice, improved understanding of objectives and programs, and loyalty.

Another means of increasing participation is what has been called "grass roots" budgeting. Instead of a budget for operations or capital expenditures being prepared at the company or departmental level, the smallest organization units prepare their budgets and submit them upward. Naturally, to be effective, these units must be aware of objectives, policies, and programs which affect their operations, must be given clear planning premises, and be furnished factors enabling them to convert work load into requirements for men, material, and money. If these budget requests are reviewed by departmental, divisional, and company management, and if the budget makers down the line are required to defend their budgets, this means of planning participation becomes real and purposeful. There probably exist no greater incentive to planning and no stronger sense of participation than those created in developing, defending, and selling a course of action over which the manager has control and for which he bears responsibility.

Still another helpful means employed successfully in some companies is the management club, an organization of all members of management, from the president to the foreman, which, in a large company, may be broken up into divisional or territorial clubs. At a specified number of meetings during the year the company president or a team of top managers conducts a meeting at which the planning and thinking of this top echelon are candidly reported to the club, and questions answered. The authors have noted that in several companies where this device has been tried, the lower-management group has responded avidly and gained a strong feeling of unity of objective with top management. Even the dullest financial matters thus become vital, and the most complicated plan interesting. What many top managers overlook is the simple fact that the rank and file of managers have a strong interest in enterprise planning, because their work is of paramount importance in their lives.

But no means of encouraging participation in planning will replace managerial deficiencies in other directions. The strength of top leadership, the example given to subordinate managers, clear delegations of authority, careful job descriptions, proper training, and competent direction and control cannot be replaced by any system of communication and participation.

THE REVENUE AND EXPENSE FORECAST

One of the essential tools of good planning is the forecast of revenues and expenses. This forecast may cover the enterprise as a whole or may be limited to a given project. It may also be used to evaluate alternative courses of action. It may be made for a short period of a month or two or for longer periods of one, three, or more years.

When made for the enterprise as a whole, this forecast is the same as an accounting statement of profit and loss, except that it is for a future period. It is useful not only for determining expected profits but also for anticipating effects of revenues, expenses, and profits on important balance sheet items, particularly cash.

Basic Estimates   A forecast of revenues and expenses for any project or for the whole enterprise can be made without difficulty if basic data are available. At the simplest, on the revenue side, these will include the number of units of a product that can be sold, when, and at what prices. The sales forecast, discussed in Chapter 7, is the primary source of these revenue data. On the expense side, the forecaster will require estimates of items basic to cost determination. These may include the number of man-hours required to produce an item at various quantities of output and at various times, the cost and quantity of materials required, the estimated factory burden, the sales and administrative costs, the capital equipment needed and its utilization and depreciation costs, and estimates of nonrecurring costs anticipated, such as training and special promotional expenses. What is needed, in other words, is precisely what the accountant later needs for a historical income statement.

When a forecast is broken into basic estimates, it becomes relatively simple and the process of compiling it is one of accounting arithmetic. However, the breaking down requires careful analysis to include all items affecting costs and revenues and to assure that the estimates are as realistic as possible. Often a small error in an important item can magnify the total results so much as to cause difficulties, especially in businesses where profit margins are slender and a few factors are critical.

Some of the basic estimates for a financial forecast—such as future markets, labor rates, material prices and availability, and interest costs—will be readily available. Other estimates must be made on the basis of internal studies, experience, or informed "guestimates." The lessons of experience, especially as interpreted by production or financial experts, are often extraordinarily valuable sources of basic estimates.

Hypothetical Forecast Perhaps the clearest way to describe the process of developing a revenue and expense forecast is to take a hypothetical case: A small business plans to produce and sell for the military market a mechanical device brought to it by the inventor, as it believes that this device is superior to existing units for muffling the noise of a small jet aircraft. After studying the market possibilities and the cost elements involved in producing these mufflers for a five-year period, the managers of the business arrive at the following basic estimates:

1. A total quantity of 1,000 units can be produced and sold in the first year at a price of $600 each; 2,000 units can be produced and sold in the second year at $500 each; and 3,000 units can be produced and sold during each of the third to fifth years of operation at a price of $450 each.

2. Operating cost estimates include the following basic items:

   a. Average direct labor costs for the five-year period will be $2.50 per hour.

   b. Direct labor hours will be 80 per unit in the first year, 64 per unit in the second year, and 48 per unit thereafter.

   c. Purchased materials will amount to $150 per unit during the first year and $140 per unit thereafter.

   d. Factory burden costs (excluding depreciation) will total $100,-000 during the first year, $175,000 during the second year, and $225,000 each year thereafter.

   e. Administrative and selling expense will total an additional $50,-000 beyond normal amounts already being spent by the company during the first year, $75,000 during the second year, and $100,-000 per year thereafter.

   f. During the first year of operations certain nonrecurring costs will be incurred for training, initial promotion, and expected losses due to high rejects during the period of learning, such costs estimated to amount to $50,000 for the first year only.

   g. Additional machinery, tools, and factory-space improvements are expected to cost $100,000 during the first year, an additional $75,000 in the second year, and $50,000 in the third year; the company decides to estimate costs on the basis of accelerated depreciation rates of 20 per cent per year.

   h. Interest costs for bank borrowings are estimated at $5,000 in the first year, $8,000 in the second year, and $12,000 per year thereafter.

On the basis of these estimates of revenues and expenses, the managers of the business make a forecast for each year and for the five-year period. This simple forecast is shown in Table 2. In most actual cases it would be set up more completely, with an outline of items similar to those required by the company's form of income statement.

It should be noted that the forecast includes, in addition to an item of net profit after taxes, an estimate of cash gain from operations. This is important for purposes of estimating a firm's cash needs and differs from the amount of profits indicated by the amount of those expenses that do not require the payment of cash. In the case used here, the only such items are assumed to be depreciation of machinery, tools, and factory space improvements. The cash gain from operations is consequently greater than profits after taxes by the depreciation charge of $20,000 in the first year, $35,000 in the second year, and $45,000 through the fifth year.

Although this hypothetical forecast is useful as a model, actual financial forecasts are usually divided into monthly periods, rather than yearly ones as shown; occasionally weekly or even daily periods are used. Forecasting for periods shorter than a year not only shows better the trend of revenues and expenses but also pinpoints the cash gains from operations. Furthermore, since financial forecasts often become budgets and are used for con-

TABLE 2   FIVE-YEAR FORECAST OF REVENUES AND EXPENSES FOR A SMALL BUSINESS

	First year	Second year	Third year	Fourth year	Fifth year	Five-year total
Revenues	$600,000	$1,000,000	$1,350,000	$1,350,000	$1,350,000	$5,650,000
Normal operating expenses:						
Direct labor	$200,000	$ 320,000	$ 360,000	$ 360,000	$ 360,000	$1,600,000
Materials	150,000	280,000	420,000	420,000	420,000	1,000,000
Factory burden	100,000	175,000	225,000	225,000	225,000	950,000
Depreciation	20,000	35,000	45,000	45,000	45,000	190,000
Administrative and selling	50,000	75,000	100,000	100,000	100,000	425,000
Total normal operating expenses	$520,000	$ 885,000	$1,150,000	$1,150,000	$1,150,000	$4,855,000
Nonrecurring expenses	50,000					50,000
Total operating expenses	$570,000	$ 885,000	$1,150,000	$1,150,000	$1,150,000	$4,905,000
Estimated interest expense	$ 5,000	$ 8,000	$ 12,000	$ 12,000	$ 12,000	$ 49,000
Net profits before taxes	$ 25,000	$ 107,000	$ 188,000	$ 188,000	$ 188,000	$ 696,000
Estimated applicable income taxes	8,000	53,000	93,000	93,000	93,000	340,000
Net profit after taxes	$ 17,000	$ 54,000	$ 95,000	$ 95,000	$ 95,000	$ 356,000
Cash gain from operations	$ 37,000	$ 89,000	$ 140,000	$ 140,000	$ 140,000	$ 546,000

trol, shorter periods furnish a more useful base for the manager, who would hardly wish to wait a whole year before ascertaining how close actual results are to those forecast.

The forecast shown here is not an over-all forecast of revenues and expenses for the entire company but is limited to the product being tested. In an actual case, similar forecasts would probably have been made for the most promising alternative courses of action.

Over-all Profit and Loss Forecast   The development of an over-all profit and loss forecast for a company's entire operations for a week, month, year, or longer would proceed on essentially the same basis as the special forecast outlined in previous paragraphs. In a motor trucking business, for example, the annual profit and loss forecast might be prepared by the following steps:[1]

1. Obtain from the sales department a forecast of the number of tons, the average revenue per ton, and the revenue to be expected on all outbound shipments from each terminal.
2. Determine the transportation service units necessary to handle this volume of traffic, such units being vehicle line-haul-miles, ton-miles, tons handled over each platform, man-hours for pickup, delivery, and platform, and the number of shipments.
3. Summarize operating expenses that do not vary with the volume of traffic or sales, such as salaries and expenses of officers, building rentals, and license fees.
4. Utilize performance and cost standards derived from experience and the various transportation service units found to be applicable in each case to complete the estimate of operating expenses by applying these standards to each primary expense account and appropriate secondary accounts. For example, maintenance expenses are found to vary largely with vehicle-miles, terminal expenses other than superintendence with tons and shipments handled, and line-haul expense with vehicle-miles and ton-miles.

In every business, there are statistical and financial factors that may reasonably be estimated from forecasts of sales volumes and used as bases for estimating expenses. Sometimes estimates made from such bases are extraordinarily accurate, particularly in such short-term periods as six months or a year. In other cases, careful analysis of experience will disclose improved methods and factors for making estimates. In all cases, if the statistical standards employed and their calculation are subjected to the intelligent judgment of well-informed production managers, sales managers, and other personnel familiar with a firm's operations, the results of revenue and expense forecasts can be extremely accurate. Some executives even speak of them as a method of planning specific profits.

[1] O. L. Doud, *Forecasting Financial Requirements of Motor Carriers* (Washington: American Trucking Association, 1952), pp. 2–3.

THE CASH FORECAST

An essential financial forecast for any business, large or small, is the forecast of cash. Profits are of questionable value if tied up in unsalable inventories or slow receivables. A profitable business may be hard pressed to pay its bills on time and to avoid forced liquidation if cash is not available, while an unprofitable business may be able to operate and even expand if it has cash to do so. A striking case of recent years was that of the commercial airlines after World War II. Virtually every airline lost heavily during 1946 and 1947, and many lost considerable money in 1948. Yet no airline was seriously threatened with bankruptcy (although a few had difficulty at times in paying bills). The reason was that depreciation charges have traditionally been high in this industry, and the cash developed on account of these charges made it possible for a company's cash position to be adequate, while its profit position was extremely weak. Obviously, long years of heavy losses must eventually take a real toll in cash as capital goods become fully depreciated, and losses cannot go on indefinitely without weakening a company through its inability to replace depreciated or obsolete assets.

A business with a suitable amount of cash can always meet its obligations when due, can afford to expand, and can replace worn-out or depreciated assets as required. Cash is also necessary to expand output even without the necessity for new machinery or other capital equipment. Expanded operations almost invariably require heavier working capital through the need of carrying larger inventories and more accounts receivable. Many is the business, particularly the small one, that has been "broke for cash" in the face of opportunities for profitable business expansion.

Elements of the Cash Forecast The forecast of cash is made up of cash sources and cash requirements. The sources include, in addition to revenues from operations, cash received from investment, borrowings, liquidation of assets, and others. Cash requirements arise not only from cash operating expenses but also from expenditures for capital equipment, investment in new buildings, working capital requirements, and from interest, tax, and dividend disbursements.

In order to simplify the cash forecast, however, cash operating revenues and expenses are usually summarized in the form of net cash gain or loss from operations. Since the revenue and expense, or profit and loss, forecast is necessary for making a cash forecast, the results of cash flows from or to the normal operations of the business need only be summarized.

Cash Forecasting a Matter of Timing as Well as Amount Since the availability of cash is so critical for successful business operations and since the flow of cash through a business is subject to many variations, cash flow, and hence cash forecasting, is a matter of timing as well as amount. For example, a forecast of revenues and expenses for a year may show a handsome cash gain, but if the flow of cash through operations were traced for each week, it might be found to be negative during the first eight or ten weeks of the year or in a period during a certain month; and the cash gain forecast for the year would represent a cash deficit of important proportions at some time during the year.

In the case of the jet muffler forecast outlined above, the estimated cash gain of $37,000 would undoubtedly present a different picture if the cash gain at the end of the fourth month of operation was shown. Most of the nonrecurring expenses would have been incurred in that period. Of the revenues expected during the year, probably very little would flow into the enterprise in the first months, before deliveries were made and receivables collected. In this case, then, it is probable that at the end of the first four months the cash loss from operations might be as much as $150,000.

This example emphasizes the importance of timing in cash forecasting. The ebb and flow of cash may be largely erased over a period of a year. But for a period of a certain week or month the cash need may be much greater or much less than that indicated by the longer period. Thus, the gross amount of cash needed to finance a business can be comprehended only by careful attention to timing.

A Simple Cash Forecast: A Hypothetical Case Using the hypothetical jet muffler program, many of the ingredients of a cash forecast for it are the same as those for its revenue and expense forecast. However, certain additional basic estimates would be required. Study of the program might, for example, disclose the following information:

1. Cash requirements other than for operations:
   a. New machinery, tools, and space improvements are estimated to cost $100,000 the first year, $75,000 the second year, and $50,000 the third year.
   b. Inventory levels are estimated at $150,000 the first year, $200,000 the second year, and $240,000 for succeeding years.
   c. Accounts receivable are expected to approximate $100,000 the first year, $160,000 the second year, and $210,000 for succeeding years.
   d. The higher cash balances needed to furnish operating cash (because of higher payrolls and other expenses) are estimated at $20,000 the first year, $35,000 the second year, and $50,000 for succeeding years.
   e. It is assumed that income taxes will be currently funded through tax-anticipation note purchases, so that income tax expenditures or withholding will not affect cash.
   f. A fund of $30,000 is believed to be ample for contingencies.
2. Cash sources other than from operations:
   a. The original $100,000 for new machinery and tools can be financed without carrying charges to the extent of $50,000, pay-

able in three annual installments of $20,000 for two years and
$10,000 for the third year.

b. Inventories and receivables can be financed through bank credit
to the extent of 50 per cent of their value.

c. Other cash requirements will be met by the owners of the business.

On these basic estimates, a five-year projection of cash flow on an
annual basis is shown in Table 3. As with the revenue and expense forecast,
an actual cash forecast might be broken into quarterly or monthly periods,
especially for the near future, rather than the longer periods shown, as cash
needs for a particular short period may vary considerably from those for the
year as a whole.

Such fluctuations might be considerable in the case of the muffler program.
Many of the cash expenditures—such as those for new equipment and
facilities, the establishment of a contingency fund, and promotion and training—would
be required in the first months. At the same time, while regular

**TABLE 3   FIVE-YEAR FORECAST OF CASH SOURCES
AND REQUIREMENTS FOR A SMALL BUSINESS**

	First year	Second year	Third year	Fourth year	Fifth year	Five-year total
Cash sources:						
Cash gain from operations	$ 37,000	$ 89,000	$140,000	$140,000	$140,000	$546,000
Borrowing on machinery and tools	50,000	....	....	....	....	50,000
Borrowing on inventory and receivables	125,000	55,000	45,000	....	....	225,000
Total cash sources	$212,000	$144,000	$185,000	$140,000	$140,000	$821,000
Cash expenditures and requirements:						
New machinery, tools, and improvements	$100,000	$ 75,000	$ 50,000	....	....	$225,000
Increases in inventory	150,000	50,000	40,000	....	....	240,000
Increases in receivables	100,000	60,000	50,000	....	....	210,000
Increase in operating cash	20,000	15,000	15,000	....	....	50,000
Payments on machinery loans	20,000	20,000	10,000	....	....	50,000
Contingency fund	30,000	....	....	....	....	30,000
Total cash expenditures and requirements	$420,000	$220,000	$165,000	....	....	$805,000
Net cash required: end of each year	$208,000	$ 76,000	($ 20,000)*	($140,000)*	($140,000)*	
Net cash required: cumulative	$208,000	$284,000	$264,000	$124,000	($ 16,000)*	($ 16,000)*

*These negative figures indicate an excess of cash available over the requirements.

operating expenses were being incurred, the company's pipeline of materials, goods in process, and finished inventory would be building up without any income from sales. In addition, lag exists between the time finished goods are delivered and the time they are paid for. The result would surely be to build up net cash requirements considerably beyond those indicated in an annual forecast, which necessarily includes in it some profits from operations after production is well under way. Indeed, if the net cash required from investment sources is $208,000 at the end of the first year, one would expect that they might reach $300,000 at the end of the third or fourth month.

Although a going business neither expanding nor contracting its operations might not be affected by wide cash-requirement variations, the expanding or contracting business will certainly be affected. If a business is expanding, the very fact of expansion causes temporary bulges in cash needs, while the business pipelines are being filled and a new level of operations (one in which the cash inflow becomes normal for that level) is being reached. If a business is contracting, the cash inflow caused from liquidating inventories and accounts receivable may result in an unusual increase in cash. It is these surges in cash requirements that make careful cash forecasting of exceptional importance, especially to the business with limited capital and limited sources for quick cash borrowing.

The Cash Forecast and Credit   A complete and realistic cash forecast is not only an essential instrument for careful planning of the business by its own managers but is equally important to creditors considering loans to the business. This is especially true of bank loans, since the primary concern of the lender is that the borrower be able to repay the loan when due. Ample collateral may secure a loan against loss, but the enforcement of rights against such collateral may involve bankruptcy proceedings, which are costly, subject to delay, and distasteful to all concerned. The best security for a loan is the ability of the borrower to repay promptly, and a good forecast will show whether the requisite cash will be available when needed. Consequently, banks are increasingly relying on such forecasts. To do so is sound practice, for the forecast not only shows the banker whether the loan can be repaid but also is evidence of careful financial planning.

Source and Application of Funds Statements   The cash forecast is often referred to as a "source and application of funds statement." Indeed, if this statement depicted cash flow and started and ended with cash rather than working capital, it would be the same kind of instrument as the simple cash forecast. A difference, however, is that it often starts and ends with working capital, the net of current assets over current liabilities. Since current assets may be tied up in receivables or inventories rather than cash, a forecast of working capital, though useful, may be illusory from the standpoint of the cash position of the firm and is not, strictly speaking, a cash forecast.

A typical statement of source and application of funds for several years in the future is illustrated by Table 4, a hypothetical forecast for a trucking

TABLE 4   SOURCE AND APPLICATION OF FUNDS STATEMENT FOR A SMALL BUSINESS

	1965	1966	1967
Income:			
Net operating revenue	$5,000,000	$5,500,000	$6,000,000
Net income before income taxes	370,000	395,000	435,000
Net income after income taxes	$ 181,000	$ 195,000	$ 215,000
Add back: depreciation	210,000	255,000	335,000
Funds provided by income	$ 391,000	$ 450,000	$ 550,000
Working capital at beginning of year	256,000	230,000	175,000
Total funds available	$ 647,000	$ 680,000	$ 372,000
Application of available funds:			
Payments on loans	$ 244,000	$ 371,000	$ 372,000
Down payments on new equipment	101,000	91,000	49,000
Facility improvements	33,000	15,000	7,000
Shop and garage equipment	4,000	6,000	4,000
Freight dock equipment	15,000	13,000	11,000
Furniture and office equipment	20,000	9,000	6,000
Total application of funds	$ 417,000	$ 505,000	$ 449,000
Working capital at end of year	$ 230,000	$ 175,000	$ 276,000

company. As will be noted, it follows the forecast principles outlined above, except that it starts and ends wtih working capital.

Pro Forma Balance Sheet Forecasts   The pro forma balance sheet forecast, although not a cash forecast, does reflect cash flow if made in proper detail; in addition, it depicts the flow of other assets and of liabilities and equity. Although somewhat difficult and complex to develop, it is, in effect, a succession of snapshots of the business for a series of selected times in the future, showing, in addition to cash position, the ratio of current assets to current liabilities, the ratio of debt to net worth, inventory and receivables levels, and other strategic guides to financial performance.

FORECASTS AND BUDGETS

From the above description of financial forecasts, it can be seen that a good forecast becomes the basis for a good budget. A realistic forecast of operating revenues and expenses reflects the expected financial results of a plan in operation and, therefore, becomes a sound and realistic budget. A cash forecast summarizes plans for the receipt and disbursement of cash, which, in turn, is translatable into a cash budget.

Since budgets are actually statements of plans, in financial or other terms, and therefore are standards against which performance is measured, they are usually considered an instrument of control. In succeeding chapters they will be discussed in this light.

To be sure, financial forecasts do sometimes differ from budgets, as a matter of policy. Company policy may make forecasts realistic, optimistic, or conservative, as the case may be, at the same time establishing budgets on other grounds. For example, a company might wish a somewhat optimistic forecast when making a case for liberal loan treatment, but a more conservative budget to influence expense control. In most instances, however, the manager will find that realistic financial forecasting and realistic budgeting should go hand in hand.

LIMITS OF PLANNING

A discussion of planning in action would be incomplete without special recognition of the limits of planning. These limits are not so great as to reduce seriously the possibility of making complete and adequate plans and should not interfere with bending every effort to plan. Nevertheless, awareness of them can remove many of the frustrations and inefficiencies of planning.

Difficulty of Accurate Premising   A limiting factor in planning is the difficulty of formulating accurate premises. Since these premises are the background against which a set of plans is made, they necessarily deal with the future. Since the future cannot be known with accuracy, premising must be subject to a margin of error. As was pointed out earlier, reliable forecasting is the basis of most planning premises. As forecasting techniques advance and as an enterprise gives more attention to careful prophecy, premises naturally improve.

One way of reducing the risks involved in future uncertainties is to have alternative sets of premises and alternative plans based on them, so that unexpected circumstances can be readily reflected in action, Another is to be ready with detours in planning to allow for unforeseeable events. The latter provides flexibility which may take the form of utilizing plant facilities for an operation not originally intended, shifting an advertising program in accordance with a revised sales policy, or changing radically a product line, to mention only a few examples.

Such flexibility is, however, possible only within limits. In the first place, an enterprise cannot always put off a decision long enough to make sure of its rightness in the light of the future. In the second place, built-in flexibility of plans may be so costly that the probable benefits are not worth the expense. Or, a company may keep so financially liquid in preparing for the right opportunity that the advantages of large cash reserves may be in substantial measure offset by the advantages presented by opportunities for expansion.

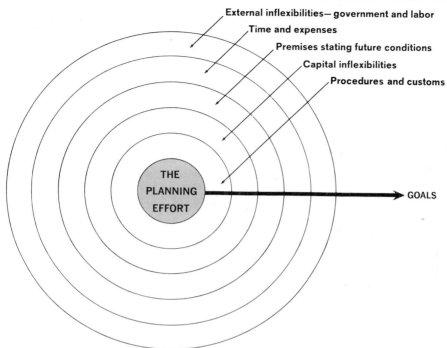

External inflexibilities—government and labor
Time and expenses
Premises stating future conditions
Capital inflexibilities
Procedures and customs

THE PLANNING EFFORT

GOALS

Fig. 10.1   Limitations on Planning Effort . . . *A manager's plans are directed at achieving goals. But a planning effort usually encounters limitations, hemming in the planning effort. Procedural inflexibilities and unwillingness to vary from customary procedures within the company often make it difficult to plan efficiently. Investment in fixed capital—plant, machinery, and other major investments—tends to limit a manager's area of choice. Premises, predicting the conditions under which plans will operate, usually present a whole series of limitations. Time and expense required for effective planning are also limiting elements. And there are many limitations imposed on managers by external factors such as government regulations and labor rules.*

Problem of Rapid Change   Another limiting factor in planning arises from business dynamics. In a complex and rapidly changing industry, the succession of new problems is often magnified by complications that make planning almost impossibly difficult. The planning problem in the first few years of expansion in the aircraft industry during World War II—when the growth of the industry from that of a few small businesses to that of very large companies was coupled with an exceptionally complex and rapidly changing product—was almost beyond comprehension.

Essentially the same kind of difficulty has existed in many other enterprises. The growth of the electronics industry after 1948, the defense program slowdown in 1957, and the space program expansion in recent years are noteworthy recent examples of highly dynamic situations in which planning has been exceedingly difficult. One might contrast planning in these areas with that of such stable businesses as a local water utility in New England or a flour mill in Minneapolis. Although all businesses are subject to some change, the degree of instability and complexity caused by business dynamics varies considerably from industry to industry and among firms within an industry.

Even in a highly dynamic industry, however, many problems are of a recurring nature. In every new problem, there may be the same elements, and a well-developed pricing formula may apply to widely different situations. Likewise, problems of manufacture and utilization of plant and machinery may have common elements despite differences in product. If the common elements in problems are sought out and separated, planning in a dynamic situation can be simplified.

Internal Inflexibilities   Major internal inflexibilities in business operations which may limit planning are related to human psychology, policies and procedures, and capital investment.

Psychological inflexibility   One of the important internal inflexibilities is psychological. Managers and employees may develop patterns of thought and behavior sometimes hard to change. A company may be so imbued with a tradition for operating flamboyantly or expensively that a program of retrenchment is difficult. For example, necessity for production at any cost in many war plants during World War II developed a psychological point of view difficult to overcome in the more competitive cost-conscious postwar era. Also, the attitude engendered by the excess-profits taxes during and after the war—that a dollar of expense was really only eighteen cents—became a serious threat to the efficient operation of many businesses after 1953, when the excess-profits tax law was repealed.

In other cases, particularly in old, established businesses, people develop patterns of thought resistant to change. Managers and employees may eschew new methods, new products, and organization changes. Or, close government regulation may bring about an attitude of so running the business as to avoid breaking the law rather than to seek low costs and high profits. Persons familiar with the railroad business, for example, cannot help being impressed by the efforts sometimes taken to assure that freight bills are completely accurate. The original price quotation made by the receiving agent may be audited by the delivering agent, then further audited by the regional accountant, again audited, at least on a sample basis, by the central office, and sometimes still further audited by representatives of the Interstate Commerce Commission. One of the writers has seen small bills audited and checked to the extent where the cost of making sure the charges were accurate must have far exceeded the amount of the bill.

Managers are often frustrated in instituting a new plan simply by the unwillingness or inability of people to accept the condition of change, and this is a difficult planning limitation to overcome. To do so requires patient selling of ideas, careful dissemination of information, aggressive leadership, and intentional development of a tradition of change among the members of the organization.

Policy and Procedural inflexibility Closely allied to psychological inflexibility are the inflexibilities inherent in policies and procedures. Once established, these become ingrained in the enterprise, and changing them becomes difficult. A way of doing things, a chain of reports or invoices, or the routine of employees in following out procedure may often be hard to modify. During World War II, for example, an aircraft company developed from a small operation to one of fourteen divisions and some 200,000 people. Procedures, paper work, and controls were developed for this large, far-flung operation. When the war ended and the company shrank to two divisions and 25,000 people, the wartime procedures lingered on. So drastic was the change in scale that a complete revamping of procedures was needed for guiding research and development, manufacture, and servicing of customers. Yet this would have required major overhaul of many aspects of operations and was believed to be impracticable. The result was a long and partially ineffectual program of gradual change of procedures, which certainly thwarted new planning of revised operations.

The resistance of policies and procedures to change was interestingly illustrated in the Hoover Commission study of the organization of the Federal government, begun in 1947.[2] The Commission found that essentially the same procedures were used for small government purchases as for large and that on over half of the 3 million purchase orders issued annually by civilian agencies the cost of paper work exceeded the cost of the purchases. It found that the disposition of surplus property was governed by more than 169 separate statutes, with new statutes being added until the weight of policy and procedure was stifling initiative and hamstringing efforts to solve the problem. The Commission also found most supply agencies overburdened with complicated statistical and other records, many of which were obsolete, though few agencies possessed all the data needed for their effective management.

One of the most convincing evidences of bureaucracy, whether in business or government, is the existence of complicated procedures designed to avoid mistakes. These procedures, which tend to become obsolete in established enterprises, seriously block the institution of new plans and the development of new ideas. Progressive planning requires an environment of change, with some reasonable degree of freedom and willingness to assume the risks of mistakes; this is prevented in an enterprise bound by the strait jacket of policy and procedural inflexibilities.

---

[2] The summary of the Commission's findings has been published as *The Hoover Commission Report* (New York: McGraw-Hill Book Company, 1949).

Capital investment   In Chapter 5, reference was made to the inflexibility inherent in invested capital. A new plant constructed or a new machine purchased and installed represents an investment of company resources that is, to varying extents, "sunk." Sometimes, when a company wishes to change its plans affecting such investment, it can sell the plant or the machine at a favorable price and thereby liquidate its investment. But in most cases, once capital is invested in a fixed asset, the ability to switch courses of future action becomes limited, and the investment itself becomes a planning premise.

Capital inflexibilities also exist where investment is sunk in items other than what is normally regarded as fixed assets. An investment in training of a particular kind or in building up a certain customer reaction to a product— through advertising, packaging, or otherwise—may become sunk. Unless the company can reasonably liquidate its investment or change its course of action or unless it can afford to write off the investment, these irretrievable costs may block the way of change. Although it may be a good axiom to disregard sunk costs in planning, since they represent money spent and nothing can be done about them, their existence does influence planning. A management that can retrieve any of them by bending its plans to recognize them gains an advantage, unless forgetting them entirely gains an even greater one.

External Inflexibilities   The manager has little or no control over external inflexibilities of business operations, because they are related to the social, technological, geographic, and economic environment. Whether these are subject to fast or slow change, they can stand in the way of planning. Three major external inflexibilities are briefly described below.

Political climate   Every business, to a greater or lesser degree, is faced with inflexibilities of the political climate existing at a given time. If the local, state, or national government actively regulates business, or if the national government adopts a high tariff or otherwise restricts trade, this must be taken into account in planning. Tax, antitrust, and fair trade policies also cause inflexibilities. Moreover, the basic attitude of government, as reflected in investigations of business practices, has significant effects. Furthermore, now that government has become business's largest customer, the procurement policies and programs of government agencies cause rigidities in business planning.

Labor organization   The existence of strong unions, particularly those organized on a national basis, tends to restrict freedom of business planning. The numerous wage- and working-condition provisions of union contracts and the influence of union policies on employee productivity and attitudes must be taken into account. In addition to being important environmental influences, they often give rise to definite inflexibilities. In the railroad industry, for example, management and unions entered into agreements in 1936, providing specific restrictions in the form of dismissal compensation and preservation of job rights and influenced by the thinking of the Great Depression. These agreements have been given the standing of law by the policy of the Interstate Commerce Commission of requiring such labor safeguards as a condition for approval of combinations or abandonments. The more recent resistance of the railroad brotherhoods to elimination of unneeded firemen and changing obsolete rules is also a case at point.

Technological change The rate and nature of technological change also present external limitations upon planning. There are perhaps few things as unyielding as the state of technological development. Not that technology does not change. It, of course, changes rapidly, and one new development begets another. But at any given time, the status of technical progress is relatively inflexible. The full use of the solution to a technical problem that has been solved may depend upon solution of a problem that has not been solved. In developing an electronic fire-control system, for example, guiding a projectile toward a target may be well understood and it may be possible to engineer the necessary circuits, but inadequate development of a single transistor or the susceptibility of another to vibration may delay accomplishment of the entire plan.

Time and Expense The effort that could be spent on forecasting, evaluation of alternatives, development of derivative plans, or other aspects of planning is almost limitless, the only effective brake being the cost to the firm and the time available to the manager.

From the standpoint of expense, the underlying principle applicable to planning is simple: no firm should spend more on planning than the value of the expected benefits. But the application of this principle is more complex, for a manager cannot easily know how much planning will be worth its cost. There are useful guides to planning expense, however.

In the first place, a large firm can almost certainly engage in more thorough planning than a small one, because the ratio of planning expense to operating expenses or to capital resources will be small. Since many planning problems which face the small firm are almost as complex and varied as those which face the larger firm, in the area of planning thoroughness and the resources to accomplish it the large firm has an important advantage.

In the second place, the more detailed planning becomes, the more expensive it will surely be. There is ever the danger, in large as well as small firms, that analysis of plans and formulation of the details of derivative plans may cost more than the benefits warrant. In modern engineering and production planning, a small project may receive the same attention as a large project. One of the authors recalls a project, undertaken by a large aircraft manufacturer, in which a minor modification of an airplane took some 3,000 man-hours of engineering and production planning for a job requiring 50 direct man-hours, when, had the job been done on a relatively unplanned basis, the planning time could have been reduced to some 30 man-hours, with only a doubling of the direct man-hours involved.

In the third place, the further into the future plans are projected, the more costly they are likely to be. If long-term forecasts are to be more than informed guesses and if long-term plans are to be worked out more than in outline form, the cost of investigation and of fitting plans together, with a tolerable margin of error, is likely to be extremely high. Here again, the critical factors are the importance of the plan to the future of the business and, in the light of this importance, the amount the business can afford to spend. To a large business and for major plans, planning for years in advance may justify heavy expenses. But for the small firm, costs may not justify doing more than careful planning for the short term, with reliance on hunches and judgment for the longer term.

In addition to the limit placed on planning by sheer expense, available time is a limiting factor. There comes a time when a decision must be taken, a course selected, and plans translated into action. Whether ready or not, the management may be forced to move. However, adequate planning done well in advance reduces the occasions when the manager may be forced into snap decisions under the pressure of crises or the necessity for fighting business fires.

ESTABLISHING A CLIMATE

In a period of change and world-wide rivalry, planning becomes a matter of great urgency for those who manage the resources of a department, an enterprise, or a nation. The following paragraphs summarize rules necessary for establishing a climate for planning.

Planning Must Not Be Left to Chance   Decisions should be soundly made as part of a fundamental planning process. As pointed out by an astute observer, planning must not only solve present problems but must discover and exploit longer-term opportunities in addition.[3]

Every superior manager should remove obstacles to planning and try to establish a climate in which his subordinates must plan. This involves, at each level of management, setting goals; establishing and publicizing applicable significant planning premises; involving all managers in the planning process; reviewing subordinate plans and their performance; assuring appropriate staff assistance and information. All this adds up to recognizing that planning will not occur unless it is forced and the facilities to undertake it are made available.

[3] For an excellent summary of this attitude, see Ralph M. Besse, "Company Planning Must Be Planned!" *Dun's Review and Modern Industry*, vol. 74, no. 4, pp. 46ff. (April, 1957).

Planning Must Start at the Top   Logically, basic goals from which others stem must be company-wide; therefore, these must be set at the top-management level. Since the example and drive of top management is the most important single force in planning, when top management rigorously reviews subordinates' programs, it naturally stimulates planning interest throughout an enterprise.

While the most effective planning must start at the top and must receive the support of those managers at the top, this does not mean that subordinates can do nothing. There is something to encouraging an "upward push" as well as a "downward press": superiors may be pushed into setting goals and premises and approving plans, if a well-reasoned program is presented to them. Top managers often *want* to make decisions and guide planning but simply have not sufficient knowledge, or assistance from their subordinates, to do so. Top managers have wistfully pointed out to the authors that they would like more subordinates to present solutions rather than problems to them. Certainly, no subordinate should be unduly critical of his superior without having come up with his program, recommended it, pressed for it, and been able to defend it.

Planning Must Be Organized   As will be shown later in this book, good organization structure—through appropriate grouping of activities and clear delegation of authority—establishes an environment for performance, including planning. Managers must be held responsible for planning within their area of authority. What is sometimes neglected is sufficient staff assistance. While no manager can delegate to a staff the responsibility for decisions that his job requires he undertake, most managers could improve their planning with help in gathering information and in its analysis.

Good planning organization, then, implies that planning and doing cannot be separated, even though staff assistance to a manager in planning is usually desirable. In other words, there is no practicable way that a manager can make decisions without taking part in planning since decision making is central to the planning process. Yet, one often sees in all types of enterprises special planning staffs working to develop programs which never become operative simply because those responsible for decisions make commitments without regard to such planning proposals. A planning staff is just that. Its task is to advise and assist those in an operating-line position in their making of decisions.

To avoid the error of separating planning from doing, it would seem wise for the manager to consult his planning staff by putting proposed decisions of any importance before it for the staff's analysis and recommendations—*before* he makes a decision. Also, the planning staff should be required to be knowledgeable of the realities of the situation on which its advice is sought. This means close informational contact with those who actively operate an enterprise in place of the ivory tower situation one often finds with such staffs. If staff advice in planning can be intermeshed with staff contact with reality, and if there is a clear recognition that decision making itself is central to planning and a plan is only a study or proposal until a decision has been made, the dangerous tendency in practice to separate planning from doing can be avoided.

Planning Must Be Definite Although some planning cannot be entirely definite, it need not even then represent little more than wishing. The need for verifiable goals has been repeatedly emphasized in this book, as has the requirement for a network of derivative goals throughout the structure of programs and organization. Also, the critical premises against which to make planning decisions must be definite, and vague or nonexistent policies are an invitation to unstructured, uncoordinated planning. Plans can eventually be made definite, include specific steps of action, and be translatable into needs for men, materials, and money. As has been indicated, the budget, by quantifying plans, may force this kind of definiteness.

If budgeting is carried down the line, related to goals at every level, made each manager's responsibility in his area, and reviewed and questioned by superiors to see whether it represents adequate plans for consistent goals, definiteness can be accomplished. Besides, there are few areas of planning in which—if the larger problem can be divided into steps or component parts—a manager cannot see what he must do, how long it should take, and how much it should cost. Recent experience in planning research and development projects, by breaking them down into a series of definite interrelated parts, has resulted in a marked increase in definite and meaningful planning.

Goals, Premises, and Policies Must Be Communicated Perhaps the greatest single cause for uncoordinated planning which the authors have detected in their experience and observation is the individual manager's lack of understanding of his verifiable goals and of the critical planning premises which affect his areas of planning. Likewise, high on the list of basic causes of planning failures is the lack of understanding of company policies in the area where a manager makes his decisions. It can readily be seen that, if a manager does not know his goals or whether an action will help him reach them, fails to understand the critical premises affecting his planning decisions, and is not aware of policy guidance where it is required to make his decisions contribute to company objectives, no amount of logical ability or analysis will lead him to a decision which supports and coordinates with the other plans of the enterprise.

Yet communication is a difficult process. But it is most difficult either when there is nothing to communicate or when what is available is general, fuzzy, or inapplicable to a manager's planning problems. Attention to developing clear goals, premises, and policies is within the competence of any intelligent group of managers. Also, as was pointed out above, there are a number of ways that these may be effectively communicated and, certainly, an astute manager can find others suitable to his purposes. At least, until enterprise managers have attempted to make sure that clear goals, premises, and policies are communicated to those who must have them, they are not doing what they can and should do to establish an environment for effective planning.

Long-range Planning Must Be Integrated with Short-range   Managers often focus attention on very short-range ("tomorrow") planning, if they plan at all, and regard long-range planning as not affecting their area of responsibility. Part of this difficulty stems from a lack of appreciation of what long-range decisions should cover. The commitment principle gives a practical guide on this problem. As applied to the usual business enterprise, those areas which are likely to involve long-range decisions are (1) new-product selection and development; (2) marketing channels and strategies; (3) facilities, particularly major capital facilities; (4) cash, particularly in a growing business; and (5) people and organization. Obviously, there are few day-to-day decisions not concerned with at least one of these, and a planning climate cannot exist when short-range plans and decisions do not contribute to or fit in with longer-range planning.

Planning Must Include Awareness and Acceptance of Change   Change is always necessary for enterprise survival. For enterprise success it may be necessary to forecast change in order to take advantage of the opportunities offered. Yet, since people resist change, it must be an objective of the manager to build in his organization an awareness of change and an ability to forecast it, and also to construct an attitude of welcoming change.

The distilled experience of the president of a large American company sheds light on this subject.[4]

> Change is more acceptable when it is understood than when it is not.
> Change is more acceptable when it does not threaten security than when it does.
> Change is more acceptable when those affected have helped create it than when it has been externally imposed.
> Change is more acceptable when it results from an application of previously established impersonal principles than it is when it is dictated by personal order.
> Change is more acceptable when it follows a series of successful changes than when it follows a series of failures.
> Change is more acceptable when it is inaugurated after prior change has been assimilated than when it is inaugurated during the confusion of other major change.
> Change is more acceptable if it has been planned than if it is experimental.

[4] *Ibid.,* pp. 62–63.

Change is more acceptable to people new on the job than to people old on the job.

Change is more acceptable to people who share in the benefits of change than to those who do not.

Change is more acceptable if the organization has been trained to accept change.

SUMMARY OF MAJOR PLANNING PRINCIPLES

Although a complete set of empirically proved, interrelated principles has not been discovered and codified, experience and observation of planning indicate certain fundamental planning principles.[5] As has been indicated earlier, management cannot progress as a science without a systematic theory. This, in turn, requires a conceptual scheme in which to arrange principles, not only for the benefit of the manager, but also as indicators of research areas. After all, one of the values of a conceptual scheme is that it makes visible what might otherwise remain unseen.

Major planning principles can be grouped around those dealing with (1) the purpose and nature of planning, (2) the structure of plans, and (3) the process of planning.

The Purpose and Nature of Planning The purpose and nature of planning might be summarized by reference to the following principles:

Principle of contribution to objectives The purpose of every plan and all derivative plans is to contribute positively toward the accomplishment of enterprise objectives.

Principle of efficiency of plans The efficiency of a plan is measured by the amount it contributes to objectives offset by the costs and other unsought consequences required to formulate and operate it.

Principle of primacy of planning Since managerial operations in organizing, staffing, directing, and controlling are designed to support the accomplishment of enterprise objectives, planning is the primary requisite of these functions.

The principle of contribution of objectives derives from the *raison d'être* of organized enterprise. The principle of efficiency of plans indicates the attempt to assure economical expenditure of individual effort to reach group goals. The principle of primacy of planning emphasizes that a manager can

---

[5] Drawn from H. Koontz, "A Preliminary Statement of Principles of Planning and Control," *Journal of Academy of Management*, vol. 1, no. 1, pp. 45–61 (April, 1958). This original formulation of principles was first presented to the Academy of Management in 1956.

hardly undertake the other functions of management without a road map of plans to guide him.

The Structure of Plans   Three major principles dealing with the structure of plans can go far in tying plans together, making derivative plans contribute to major plans, and assuring that plans in one department harmonize with those in another.

Principle of planning premises   The more individuals charged with planning understand and agree to utilize consistent planning premises, the more coordinated enterprise planning will be.

Principle of policy framework   The more policies, appropriate to guiding thinking in the direction of enterprise objectives, are expressed in clear form and are understood by managers charged with decision making, the more consistent and effective will be the framework of an enterprise's plans.

Principle of timing   The more plans are structured to provide an appropriately timed, intermeshed network of derivative and supporting programs, the more effectively and efficiently they will contribute to the attainment of enterprise objectives.

These principles indicate that guided knowledge is the key to a sound structure of plans. All who plan in an enterprise must proceed from understood goals and uniform premises, and the decisions which lead to plans cannot be accurately focused toward the enterprise objectives without a framework of policy. Both premises and policies are useless without proper timing; and information with respect to premises, policies, timing, and other factors is essential to the manager.

In practice, perhaps the greatest deficiencies of planning arise from poorly structured plans. This is largely due to ignorance. There is seldom a real lack of incentive to undertake plans that will contribute to enterprise goals, even though planning is almost invariably difficult intellectual work. However, one cannot expect a coordinated structure of plans if managers throughout the enterprise do not understand policies affecting their area of authority, the background of premises—including plans of others—in coordination with which they are to plan, and other facts necessary for decision making.

The Process of Planning   Within the process of planning, there are six principles, the understanding of which can help develop a science of planning.

Principle of alternatives   In choosing from among alternatives, the best alternative will be that which contributes most effectively and efficiently to the attainment of a desired goal.

Principle of the limiting factor   In choosing from among alternatives, the more an individual can recognize and solve for those factors that are limiting or critical to the attainment of the desired goal, the more easily he can select the most favorable alternative.

The principle of alternatives and the principle of the limiting factor are the essentials of decision making. The key to decision making is to solve the problem posed by alternatives, if possible, by seeking out and solving for the limiting, or strategic factor. To do otherwise is not only to sacrifice time and expense in examining every facet of a problem but also to risk giving too much weight to factors not critical to the decision.

The commitment principle   Logical planning covers a period of time in the future necessary to foresee, through a series of actions, the fulfillment of commitments involved in a decision.

Principle of flexibility   The more flexibility can be built into plans, the less the danger of losses incurred through unexpected events, but the cost of flexibility should be weighed against the dangers of future commitments made.

Principle of navigational change   The more planning decisions commit for the future, the more important it is that the manager periodically check on events and expectations and redraw plans to maintain a course toward a desired goal.

The commitment principle and the principles of flexibility and navigational change are all closely related. Although it makes sense to forecast and draw plans far enough into the future to make reasonably sure of meeting commitments, often either it is impossible to do so or the future is so uncertain as to make the fulfillment of commitments subject to undue risk. Under such circumstances, a manager might simply shorten his commitment, as, for example, he would do if he invested in a plant facility only if it could be liquidated through profits in a relatively short time. Or, as is often done, a manager might build into his plans an ability to change direction without undue cost in case future events make this wise. Thus, he might sign a twenty-year lease, even though he could not foresee events for that period, if he could obtain (normally, at a cost) the right to cancel the lease or to sublease the building.

The principle of flexibility deals with that ability to change which is built into plans. The principle of navigational change, on the other hand, implies reviewing plans from time to time and redrawing them if that is indicated by changed events and expectations. As is apparent, unless plans have built-in flexibility, navigational change is difficult or costly. If an inflexible plan cannot be completed efficiently because of changed circumstances, the manager may find that his best course of action is to junk his plan and take the loss. Certainly the lack of built-in flexibility is no reason for not taking repeated readings on plans and redrawing them if circumstances warrant.

Principle of competitive strategies The more the conditions under which a firm operates are competitive (that is, where others are striving for the same goals), the more important it is that plans be chosen in the light of what a competitor will or will not do in the same area.

It is not enough to build plans logically from goals in a competitive situation unless the plans take into account a rival's plans. There are several kinds of rivalry in enterprise operations. The usual kind is the competition of one firm with another. But rivalry certainly exists in dealings with representatives of organized labor, often with regulatory commissions, and even in obtaining scarce capital and human resources, either from inside or from outside the firm.

FOR DISCUSSION

1. It is sometimes said that cash planning is the minimum of planning since the enterprise that has cash to meet its obligations can continue. In order to do cash planning, what must an enterprise do?

2. If you were asked to take steps to make sure that adequate planning was accomplished in a company, what would you do?

3. How can a company plan in an orderly way for "business as usual" and at the same time for a contingency such as a major fire or the outbreak of war?

4. In organizing for long-range planning, the typical corporation has a central long-range planning staff. But it is generally recognized that planning is the task of each operating manager and that he must take responsibility for his plans and their execution. Can these kinds of approaches be reconciled in practice?

5. The job of good planning is to meet change successfully. How would you undertake to meet this problem in the light of the many inflexibilities and uncertainties involved in planning?

6. Show in what ways application of the major principles of planning clarifies the methods used and approaches in planning.

SELECTED REFERENCES

American Management Association: *A Program of Financial Planning and Controls: The Monsanto Chemical Company*, Financial Management Series No. 103, New York: American Management Association, 1953.

————: *Forecasting Financial Requirements*, Financial Management Series No. 87, New York: American Management Association, 1947.

————: *Modern Financial Planning and Control: The Johnson and Johnson Program*, Financial Management Series No. 110, New York: American Management Association, 1956.

Besse, Ralph M.: "Company Planning Must Be Planned!" *Dun's Review and Modern Industry*, vol. 74, no. 4, pp. 16ff. (April, 1959).

Busch, G. A.: "Prudent Manager Forecasting," *Harvard Business Review,* vol. 39, no. 3, pp. 57–64 (May–June, 1961).

Curran, N. J.: *Co-ordinating Budgets with Forecasting; Charting the Company's Future,* Financial Management Series No. 108, New York: American Management Association, 1954.

Doud, O. L.: *Forecasting Financial Requirements of Motor Carriers,* Washington: American Trucking Association, 1952.

Goetz, B. E.: *Management Planning and Control,* chaps. 5, 8, 10, New York: McGraw-Hill Book Company, 1949.

Jones, M. H.: *Executive Decision Making,* chaps. 10–14, Homewood, Ill.: Richard D. Irwin, Inc., 1957.

Mitchell, W. E.: "Cash Forecasting: The Four Methods Compared," *The Controller,* vol. 28, no. 4, pp. 162ff. (April, 1960).

Pflomm, N. E.: *Managing Company Cash,* Business Policy Study No. 99, New York: National Industrial Conference Board, 1961.

Steiner, G. A.: "Making Long-range Planning Pay Off," *California Management Review,* vol. 4, no. 2, pp. 28–41 (Winter, 1962).

Thompson, Stewart: *How Companies Plan,* Research Study No. 54, New York: American Management Association, 1962.

Tomb, J. O.: "A New Way to Manage: Integrated Planning and Control," *California Management Review,* vol. 5, no. 1, pp. 57–62 (Fall, 1962).

Welsch, G. A.: *Budgeting: Profit Planning and Control,* Englewood Cliffs, N.J.: Prentice-Hall, Inc., 1957.

Weston, J. F., and E. Brigham: *Managerial Finance,* 2d ed., chaps. 7–9, New York: Holt, Rinehart and Winston, Inc., 1966.

part three

ORGANIZING

In order to accomplish goals, carry out plans, and make it possible for people to work effectively, an intentional structure of roles must be designed and maintained. Activities must be grouped logically and grants of authority must be made so that conflicts and other frictions do not arise. The authors believe that the primary task of organizing must involve the grouping of activities necessary to accomplish goals and plans, the assignment of these activities to appropriate departments, and the provision for authority delegation and coordination. Thus, span of management, basic departmentation, decentralization, and proper understanding of line and staff patterns are a few of the important subjects covered in this part.

Chapter 11 deals with the nature and purpose of organization. In carrying out this function, the manager structures the task framework in which people perform. This does not mean that organization ignores people. It is the objective of organization to establish an activity-authority environment in which people can perform most effectively. In addition, the practical organizer is often faced with situations in which he must allow for the limitations, strengths, availability, and interests of people when he is structuring his organization. Moreover, as will be seen in the analysis of the functions of staffing and direction, people are central to these two functions of managing.

Although people operate in groups primarily to accomplish objectives that they cannot attain acting alone, the real cause of formal organization, as is pointed out in Chapter 12, is the limitations of the span of management.

Even though there is no definite and universally acceptable number of persons that a manager can effectively supervise, we do know that there is a limit to the number in individual cases. This limit, known as the span of management, is what makes levels of organization necessary and problems of delegation and policy making so important. In any given situation there are many underlying factors that determine the number of persons a manager can supervise.

Chapter 13, "Basic Departmentation," and Chapter 14, "The Assignment of Activities," deal with activity grouping in organization. To understand the material presented in these chapters quickly and with the least effort, it is important to understand that grouping has two aspects. One has to do with basic forms of departmentation which experience and logic have found useful. These forms and the advantages and disadvantages of each, along with their special uses in practice, are discussed in Chapter 13. The second aspect has to do with guides for assigning activities to existing departments within an existing organization structure. This is dealt with in Chapter 14. While most tasks are assigned on the basis of similarity to those in an existing department, others are assigned according to a variety of guides which experience and logic have found to be useful and important.

Chapter 15, "Line and Staff Authority Relationships," discusses two basic kinds of formal relationships that exist in organization structure: line and staff. The material in the chapter differentiates between the two and points out reasons for confusion. If the reader remembers that a person in a line capacity is one who bears responsibility for the performance of those who report to him and that a person in a staff capacity may only make recommendations or offer advice, he need not be disturbed by the complex reasoning behind this concept. This applies even to those hybrid functional authority positions which have some staff characteristics and some line characteristics. The chapter requires careful study because the line and staff concept is often confused in practice, and this confusion can cause severe organizational problems.

Chapter 16 deals with service departments. A point of possible confusion here arises from the fact that service departmentation itself has nothing directly to do with the question of line and staff relationships, although most service departments act in a staff capacity. Service departments are merely groupings of activities, usually quite specialized, which are concentrated in a given department for purposes of economy or control. For instance, a specialized typing and clerical service pool attached to the controller's department is a typical service grouping. In modern complex enterprises, service departments tend to proliferate. But as they have grown, operating problems have increased. In this chapter, special effort is given to presenting material on efficient operation of service departments.

Chapter 17 analyzes the problem of degree of authority dispersion in an enterprise. As management has become better understood and as enterprises have grown, it has become almost fashionable to "decentralize" authority. While authority must be dispersed in an organization structure, the degree and kind of decentralization are a source of difficulty and misunderstanding. The chapter undertakes to analyze the factors behind proper decentralization or centralization and to develop some theoretical and practical bases for this important organizational area. The authors believe that centralization or decentralization should not be regarded as desirable or undesirable trends in and of themselves, but that the actions of a company in this area must be determined by studying actual circumstances and needs in every case. Centralization and decentralization are, after all, simply means of achieving desired goals.

The committee form of organization is given special attention in Chapter 18. Uses and abuses and advantages and disadvantages are discussed with emphasis on methods of making the committee more effective.

In the final chapter, organization practice is analyzed from an over-all point of view. This chapter puts special emphasis on applying organizational principles.

nature and purpose of organization

"Organization" is variously used in management. Some theorists—particularly those who approach organization in the light of the behavioral sciences—regard it as simply the human relationships in group activity equivalent to social structure. Thus, the "organization" encompasses all formal and informal relationships, inside and outside the enterprise, which bear on the behavior of the employees.[1] Others use "organization" in the sense of "enterprise," an organized undertaking to accomplish goals.

As a function of managers, organizing and a resultant organization structure are concerned with the activity-authority relationships of an enterprise. It is thus the grouping of activities necessary to attain enterprise objectives and the assignment of each grouping to a manager with authority necessary to supervise it. Organizing, then, involves establishment of authority relationships with provision for coordination between them, both vertically and horizontally in the enterprise structure. Using organization as a structural system appears to the authors to be more realistic than other concepts of organization. Certainly, most managers believe they are organizing when they establish such a structure.

In viewing organization this way, the authors are not mechanistic, but rather, since people are a central concern of managers, consider that an organization must be so structured that *people can perform* in the environment it furnishes. Essentially it is the creation and maintenance of an intentional structure of roles.

Although the majority of group members may not be concerned primarily with the group's objectives, as will be seen in the chapters on the

---

[1] Chris Argyris refers to this as "the notion that an organization includes *all* the behavior of *all* the participants." See *Personality and Organization* (New York: Harper & Row, Publishers, Incorporated, 1957), p. 239.

managerial function of direction, the managers should maximize the satisfactions of individuals while striving toward department or enterprise goals. An organization structure should be designed to clarify the environment so that everyone knows who is to do what; to remove obstacles to performance caused by confusion and uncertainty of assignment; and to furnish a decision-making communications network reflecting and supporting enterprise objectives.

This view is not far from that developed by Wight Bakke, who, after considerable analysis, concluded: [2]

> A social organization is a continuing system of differentiated and co-ordinated human activities utilizing, transforming, and welding together a specific set of human, material, capital, ideational, and natural resources into a unique problem-solving whole engaged in satisfying particular human needs in interaction with other systems of human activities and resources in its environment.

FORMAL AND INFORMAL ORGANIZATION

Organization grows out of the human need for cooperation. As Chester I. Barnard[3] emphasized, human beings are forced to cooperate to achieve personal goals. Cooperation can be more productive and less costly, in most instances, with some kind of organization.

Taking the lead from Barnard and from the discoveries of the Hawthorne experiments,[4] many management people distinguish between formal and informal organization.

Formal People, their behavior, and their association belong to a large system of social relationships of which a single formally organized enterprise is but a subsystem. Barnard referred to an organization as formal when the activities of two or more persons are *consciously* coordinated toward a given objective. He found that the essence of formal organization is conscious common purpose and that formal organization comes into being when persons (1) are able to communicate with each other, (2) are willing to act, and (3) share a purpose. This definition is far broader than that used in this book, and few managers adopt it. In the first place, it covers any kind of group action with a common purpose and could apply to activities such as a

---

[2] "Concept of the Social Organization," in Mason Haire (ed.), *Modern Organization Theory* (New York: John Wiley & Sons, Inc., 1959), p. 37. In this article, Bakke outlines ten criteria for a concept of organization.

[3] *The Functions of the Executive* (Cambridge, Mass.: Harvard University Press, 1938), chaps. 6, 7, 9.

[4] The importance of human behavior independent of the structural considerations of formal enterprise organization was brought out by the researches of Elton Mayo and F. J. Roethlisberger at the Hawthorne Works of the Western Electric Company, beginning in 1924. For a comprehensive account of the experiments, see F. J. Roethlisberger and W. J. Dickson, *Management and the Worker* (Cambridge, Mass.: Harvard University Press, 1939).

card game or car pool,, which are not usually regarded by practitioners as formal organizations. In the second place, it goes beyond our activity-authority concept. No formal organization, as typically charted, can cover *all* human enterprise relationships. If authority lines map the course of responsible decision making, they are doing all that was ever intended.

As Wilfred Brown has declared, after managerial experience of many years and after participating in one of the most thorough research projects on organizational life ever undertaken:[5]

> Thus, I personally believe that the more formalization that exists, the more clearly we will know the bounds of discretion which we are authorized to use, *and will be held responsible for,* and [that] prescribed policies make clear to people the area in which they have freedom to act. Without a clearly defined area of freedom there is no freedom. This, in fact, is a very old story reaching down through the history of mankind: *there is no real freedom without laws.*

Unquestionably, some of the concern about the restrictive dangers in formal organization arises from poor organization practice. There should be room for discretion, for taking advantage of creative talents, and recognition of individual likes and capacities in the most formal of organizations. Yet, to assume that individual effort in a group situation can be completely unchanneled is to overlook the basic realities of any group activity.

There is nothing inherently inflexible about formal organization. On the contrary, if the manager is to organize well, his organization structure must furnish a constructive environment for individual performance, both present and future, contributing to group goals.

Although the attainment of some goals must be the reason for any cooperative activity, we must look further for principles to guide the establishment of formal organization, with its groupings of activities and assignments of authority.

Principle of unity of objective   An organization structure is effective if it as a whole and every part of it make possible accomplishment by individuals in contributing toward the attainment of enterprise objectives.[6] However, as will be presently discussed, an organization may gain enterprise objectives, even with every part contributing, without doing so efficiently.

---

[5] "What Is Work?" *Harvard Business Review,* vol. 40, no. 5, p. 127 (September–October, 1962). The research referred to is that undertaken first by the Tavistock Institute of Human Relations, London, in cooperation with Brown's Glacier Metal Company, Ltd. and after a few years by the company alone. This research project, started in 1948, is reported in Wilfred Brown, *Exploration in Management* (New York: John Wiley & Sons, Inc., 1960).

[6] Urwick referred to this as "the principle of objective," one of ten principles of organization. See also his *Notes on the Theory of Organization* (New York: American Management Association, 1952), pp. 18ff. Barnard (*op. cit.,* pp. 19ff.) refers to this principle as a matter of "effectiveness" of organization, making the point that an organization is effective, although not necessarily efficient, when it gains its objective.

Many companies have developed unnecessarily large and expensive organization structures.

The application of the principle of unity of objective implies, of course, the existence of formulated and understood enterprise objectives. If the objective is to make a profit over a period of time, then the organization pattern that helps to accomplish this conforms to the principle of unity of objective. Whatever the goals, or derivative goals, organization structure and action must be measured against the criterion of effectiveness in meeting them.

Principle of efficiency   An organization is efficient if it is structured to make possible accomplishment of enterprise objectives by people (that is, is effective) with the minimum unsought consequences or costs (going beyond the usual thinking of costs entirely in such measurable items as dollars or man-hours). Even though financial or material unit costs are important in measuring organizational efficiency, the principle of efficiency as employed here encompasses such matters as individual and group satisfactions and the contribution of the enterprise to the community. To an employee, an efficient organization is likely to be one that operates without waste or carelessness and makes for work satisfaction, an organization with clear-cut lines of authority and proper exaction of responsibility, that allows appropriate participation in problem solving, gives provision for security and status, and furnishes an opportunity for personal development and reasonably adequate pay rates.

The principle of efficiency must be applied judiciously. Too often, in establishing an organization structure, managers see the savings possible in setting up a service department, without ascertaining the complementary costs outside the department. For example, all activities dealing with statistics and their compilation may be assigned to a central statistical department; although this may produce statistics at low cost, they may not suit the needs of managers. Also, a customary way for the inexperienced efficiency engineer to save money is to establish secretarial pools. While these sometimes work efficiently for an enterprise or department as a whole, there are many occasions where efficient secretarial work is done at the cost of hours of executive time spent waiting to be assigned a secretary or for needed stenographic work to be done.

Efficiency may become a vague and variable criterion. One manager may measure efficiency by profit, while others may measure it in terms of survival, business status, public service, or business expansion. Or a company president may impatiently drive toward cost, market, and profit goals by tactics that create morale problems for subordinates.

But, however the standards of efficiency are applied, the principle of efficiency underlies the measurement of any organization. Difficulties may be encountered in selecting an appropriate standard of efficiency. Thus, one person may criticize the overlapping of activities in certain government departments, while another may feel that this overlapping is a necessary cost of gaining protection against the danger inherent in concentration of power. A president of a business may be criticized as inefficient in pressing too slowly for organizational changes, when this slowness may be justified by the benefits of having subordinates learn for themselves the advantages of such changes and therefore voluntarily embrace them more completely.

Informal Any manager can benefit from a study of informal organization behavior and interrelationships. Barnard regarded as informal organization joint personal activity without conscious joint purpose, even though possibly contributing to joint results. All manner of groups then fall within the sphere of informal organization, including an airplane load of passengers, or people walking down a street. Pursuing this thinking, informal organizations—relationships not appearing on an organization chart—might include the machine-shop group, the water-cooler clique, the production-engineering group, the sixth-floor crowd, the Friday-evening bowling gang, and the morning-coffee "regulars."

Informal organization fosters communication between people, so that they can perform as a group. It establishes patterns of behavior that enable individuals to perform in a group environment. One of these patterns is conformity—whether in speech, conduct, dress, or other behavior—which promotes smooth group operation, however stultifying if carried too far.

DEPARTMENTATION

"Department" designates a distinct area, division, or branch of an enterprise over which a manager has authority for the performance of specified activities. A department, as the term is generally used, may be the production division, the sales department, the West Coast branch, the market research section, or the accounts receivable unit. In some enterprises, departmental terminology is loosely applied; in others, especially larger ones, a stricter terminology indicates hierarchical relationships. Thus, a vice-president may head a division; a director, a department; a manager, a branch; and a chief, a section. This relationship of terminology to status is often found in the Federal government, where, in the typical executive department, the hierarchy runs from office or bureau to divisions, branches, sections, units, and subunits.

Indeed, in an enterprise requiring successive subordinate groupings, exact definitions may become imperative, since certain designations carry connotations of power, prestige, and salary. If the vice-president of production heads a *division*, the vice-president in charge of sales will hardly be satisfied to head a *department*. Some large organizations tend to run out of appropriate designations, especially when such terms as "bureau" may be unacceptable in business.

On the other hand, the terminology of departmentation in small-scale businesses, where there may be no departmental level lower than that supervised by the chief executive, may have little meaning. But some small businesses may be operated on the theory that titles can sometimes substitute for remuneration—a frequent practice in nonbusiness enterprises.

A valid department exists whenever a specialized group of activities is placed in charge of a manager. Obviously, if ever a managerial position—for whatever reason—is not staffed, the activities of the department should be regrouped and assigned to other executives.

Primarily, departments exist because of the inability of a single executive to manage an unlimited number of subordinates—in short, the span of management. As is discussed in Chapter 12, the span is not fixed but depends upon the type of work, the quality of management, the ability of subordinates, and other factors. Without departmentation, the president or owner of an enterprise would be the *sole* manager, to whom every employee would report directly. Many small businesses operate precisely on that basis.

The span of management explanation of departmentation must be distinguished from occupational specialization for the purpose of economizing. Grouping of workers into occupationally specialized units is practiced even in unorganized businesses. Thus, a small printing shop might find it economical to have two persons do nothing but typesetting, another two operate presses, one handle office work, and another handle design and sales. Departmentation, however, would not be justified until the boss's span of management was exceeded and the grouping of activities under subordinate managers found necessary.

The professor had just concluded a discussion of the formal- and informal-organization concepts. "It might be interesting to consider whether informal organizations precede rather than follow formal organizations in time."

"That is probably correct in a simple society," one student responded. Another suggested, "It would be especially true if the formal organization were not intended to last very long."

"In our society, I don't think it makes sense," contributed another. "Would you care to explain how that decision was reached?" asked the professor.

ORGANIZING AS A PROCESS

In looking at organization as a process, whereby a structure of activity groupings and authority relationships is formalized, it is apparent that several fundamental inputs must be considered. In the first place, the structure must reflect objectives and plans, because enterprise activities arise from these. In the second place, the structure must reflect the authority available to enterprise management; this depends upon such social institutions as private property, representative government, and the host of customs, codes, and laws that both restrict and sanction individuals in operating a business, a church, a university, or any group venture. Authority in a given organization is, then, a socially determined power; as such, it is subject to change.

In the third place, organization structure, like any plan, must reflect its environment. Just as the premises of a plan may be economic, technological, political, social, ethical, or psychological, so may be those of an organization structure. The structure must be designed to work, to permit contributions by members of a group, and to help people gain objectives efficiently in a changing future. In this sense, a workable organization structure can never be simply mechanistic.

Fourth, the organization must be manned with trained people. Obviously, the activity groupings and authority provisions of an organization structure must take into account people's limitations and customs. This is not to say that the structure must be designed around individuals instead of around goals and accompanying activities. But an important consideration—often a constraining factor for the organization architect—is the kind of people who are to man it. Just as the engineer considers the performance strength and weaknesses of materials going into his projects, so must the organizer consider his materials—people.

By Logic   There is a fundamental logic to organizing. Application of logical method to this process, in the light of the inputs outlined above, indicates the following steps: (1) establishment of enterprise objectives; (2) formulation of derivative objectives, policies, and plans; (3) determination of activities necessary to accomplish these goals, policies, and plans; (4) enumeration and classification of these activities: (5) grouping these activities in the light of human and material resources available and the best way of using them; (6) delegating to the head of each group the authority necessary to perform the activities; and (7) tying these groupings together horizontally and vertically, through authority relationships and information systems.

This logical process does not imply—as so many critics have declared it does—extreme occupational specialization, which in many instances makes labor uninteresting, tedious, and unduly restrictive. There is *nothing* in organization itself that dictates this. To say that tasks should be specific is not to say they must be limited and mechanical. Whether or not they should be broken down into minute parts—as on a typical assembly line—or be broad enough to encompass the design, production, and sale of a machine, is for the organizer to consider in light of the total results desired. In any organization, jobs can be defined to allow little or no personal discretion or the widest possible area of discretion, as a pure detail of operation or as the most creative of jobs.

In Practice   The logical pattern of organizing conforms to the usual practice of developing departmentation. The owner or promoter of a new, small business hires men as the size of his business requires. When the point is reached beyond which he is unable to employ, train, supervise, and control additional employees, subordinates are grouped into one or more sections, with a supervisor or manager appointed for each. Two organizational levels then exist. Further expansion of the labor force would give rise to more sections. When the chief executive can no longer properly manage the increasing number of subordinate managers, he will group them into departments and appoint a manager for each. Thus, three organization levels would be created, and the chief executive would be removed one step further from the nonmanagers.[7] Of course, in a going concern, the question of whether to build from the top down or from the bottom up does not arise. The organizing process is continuous, and the activities themselves and their grouping are simultaneously under consideration at all levels, in order to bring the enterprise into line with tested guides of association and assignment.

Two employees of a large, integrated enterprise were discussing in some amazement how it was possible for the same company to organize departments so differently.

"In our shop everything is organized like a tightly wound clock," one said. "The jobs are so broken down that I have only a small operation to carry on."

"It is not much like that in my department," replied the other. "We have several scientists in the laboratory who don't seem to be doing anything, and nobody seems to care."

"Well, when I come to think of it," replied the first employee, "there are a lot of office people who don't seem to be doing anything either."

"Our supervisor was giving us a pep talk the other day," began an employee in the machine shop. "He talked about some changes that would enlarge our jobs."

"Gosh," responded his auditor, "I don't want my job enlarged. I'm doing all I want to do anyway."

"Well," the first responded, "I don't think we will have to work harder. I think he meant that we will do less of what we are doing and more of some other work."

"I don't know if I would like that," was the comment. "It seems too complicated."

"I think it would be interesting for a change," the first employee concluded.

According to Drucker   In both logic and practice, the organizing process outlined here is similar to that emphasized by Peter Drucker,[8] who finds three ways to determine the kind of structure needed in a specific enterprise: activities analysis, decision analysis, and relations analysis. Drucker believes in finding out what an enterprise actually does—in terms of concrete activities necessary to attain objectives, rather than under such preconceived general headings as "engineering" or "selling."

Drucker points out that only by rigorous activities analysis can man-

---

[7] For an interesting case study of the process of departmentation, see Marshall E. Dimock, *The Executive in Action* (New York: Harper & Row, Publishers, Incorporated, 1945).

[8] See *The Practice of Management* (New York: Harper & Row, Publishers, Incorporated, 1954), pp. 194–201.

agers find out what work has to be performed, what work belongs together, and how each activity should be emphasized in the organization structure. His decision analysis determines what kind of decisions are needed, where in the organization structure they should be made, and how each manager should be involved in them. By relations analysis Drucker means knowing the contribution to programs that each manager must make, with whom he is to work, and what contribution other managers must make to him. His approach, then, is in accordance with what sound management practice has long recognized as logical and practical.

Organizing is, then, a process by which the manager brings order out of chaos, removes conflicts between people over work or responsibility, and establishes an environment suitable for teamwork. Implicit also is recognition of the human factor—that jobs must be designed to fit people, with all their strengths and weaknesses, and that people must be motivated.

BASIC QUESTIONS

In this book, the authors have found it useful to analyze the managerial function of organizing by answering, in succeeding chapters, the following questions:

1. What determines the span of management and hence the levels of organization?
2. What determines the basic framework of departmentation, and what are the strengths and weaknesses in the basic forms?
3. What determines whether activities should be assigned to a given department in this basic framework?
4. What kinds of authority relationships exist in organization?
5. How should authority be dispersed throughout the organization structure, and what determines the extent of this dispersion?
6. What place do committees have in organization?
7. How should the manager make organization theory work in practice?

The answers to these questions form a basis for a theory of organization. When considered along with similar analyses of planning, staffing, directing, and controlling, they are offered as an operational approach to management.

FOR DISCUSSION

1. Since people must occupy organization positions and an effective organization depends on people, it is often said that the best organization arises when a manager hires good people and lets them do a job in their own way. Comment.

2. A formal organization is often conceived of as a communications system. Is it? How?

3. Construct a diagram depicting the formal organization of some enterprise or activity with which you are familiar. How does this help or hinder the establishment of an environment for performance?

4. Using the same enterprise or activity as in the above question, chart the informal organization. Does it help or hinder the formal organization? Why?

SELECTED REFERENCES

Bakke, E. Wight: "Concept of the Social Organization," in Mason Haire (ed.), *Modern Organization Theory,* chap. 2, New York: John Wiley & Sons, Inc., 1959.

Barnard, C. I.: *The Functions of the Executive,* chaps. 6–9, Cambridge, Mass.: Harvard University Press, 1938.

Bennis, W. G.: *Changing Organizations,* New York: McGraw-Hill Book Company, 1966.

Bower, M.: *The Will to Manage,* chap. 5, New York: McGraw-Hill Book Company, 1966.

Brown, A.: *Organization of Industry,* Englewood Cliffs, N.J.: Prentice-Hall, Inc., 1947.

Brown, Wilfred: "What Is Work?" *Harvard Business Review,* vol. 40, no. 5, pp. 121–129 (September–October, 1962).

Dale, E.: *The Great Organizers,* chap. 1, New York: McGraw-Hill Book Company, 1960.

Drucker, P. F.: *The Practice of Management,* chaps. 16–18, New York: Harper & Row, Publishers, Incorporated, 1954.

Dubin, Robert: *The World of Work: Industrial Society and Human Relations,* chap. 16, Englewood Cliffs, N.J.: Prentice-Hall, Inc., 1958.

Gulick, L., and L. Urwick (eds.): *Papers on the Science of Administration,* chaps. 1–2, New York: Institute of Public Administration, 1937.

Hutchinson, J. G.: *Organizations: Theories and Classical Concepts,* chap. 1, New York: Holt, Rinehart and Winston, Inc., 1967.

Krupp, S.: *Pattern in Organizational Analysis,* Philadelphia: Chilton Company—Book Division, 1961.

Learned, E. P., and A. T. Sproat: *Organization Theory and Policy: Notes for Analysis,* Homewood, Ill.: Richard D. Irwin, Inc., 1966.

Litterer, J. A.: *The Analysis of Organizations,* chaps. 7–16, New York: John Wiley & Sons, Inc., 1965.

March, J. G., and H. A. Simon: *Organizations,* New York: John Wiley & Sons, Inc., 1958.

Pfiffner, J. M., and F. P. Sherwood: *Administrative Organization,* chaps. 2–6, Englewood Cliffs, N.J.: Prentice-Hall, Inc., 1960.

Stogdill, R. M.: "Dimensions of Organizational Theory," in *Approaches to Organizational Design,* J. D. Thompson (ed.), Pittsburgh, Pa.: The University of Pittsburgh Press, 1966.

Thompson, J. D.: *Organizations in Action,* chap. 11, New York: McGraw-Hill Book Company, 1967.

span of management

That the problem of span of management[1] is as old as organization itself is apparent from the passages of the Bible dealing with Moses organizing the exodus of the Israelites. The difficulties that Moses met and the departmentation he employed to meet them are recounted in Exodus 18:17–26, in which it is recorded that Moses' father-in-law, noting that Moses was spending so much time giving counsel to so many individuals, advised him as follows:

> The thing thou doest is not good. Thou wilt surely wear away, both thou and this people that is with thee: for this thing is too heavy for thee; thou art not able to perform it thyself alone. Hearken now unto my voice, I will give thee counsel. . . . Thou shalt provide out of the people able men . . . and place such over them [the people], to be rulers of thousands, and rulers of hundreds, rulers of fifties, and rulers of tens. And let them judge the people at all seasons; and it shall be, that every great matter they shall bring unto thee, but every small matter they shall judge: so shall it be easier for thyself, and they shall bear the burden with thee. If thou shalt do this thing, and God command thee so, then thou shall be able to endure, and all this people shall also go to their place in peace.

Moses thereupon followed his father-in-law's advice, with the result that he:

> . . . chose able men out of all Israel, and made them heads over the people, rulers of thousands, rulers of hundreds, rulers of fifties and rulers of tens. And they judged the people at all seasons: the hard causes they brought unto Moses, but every small matter they judged themselves.

[1] In much of the literature of management, this is referred to as the "span of control." Despite the widespread use of this term, the authors have preferred since the first edition of this book in 1955 to use "span of management," since the span is one of management and not merely of control, here regarded as a basic function of management.

HOW WIDE A SPAN?

In every organization it must be decided how many subordinates a superior can manage. Students of management have found that this number is usually four to eight subordinates at the upper levels of organization and eight to fifteen or more at the lower levels. For example, the prominent British consultant, Lyndall Urwick,[2] found "the ideal number of subordinates for all superior authorities . . . to be four," and "at the lowest level of organization, where what is delegated is responsibility for the performance of specific tasks and not for the supervision of others, the number may be eight or twelve." An experienced military observer has stated that he believes the proper number to range between three and six, with three likely to be best near the top of an organization and six near the bottom.[3] Others find that a manager may be able to manage as many as twenty to thirty subordinates.[4]

In actual experience, one finds a wide variety of practices, even among admittedly well-managed enterprises. General of the Army Dwight D. Eisenhower had three immediate line subordinates when he was Supreme Commander of the Allied Expeditionary Forces in World War II, and none of these had more than four line subordinates. Yet, at the same time, the Army Chief of Staff had reporting to him and his deputies at least fifteen major line and staff officers. In the General Motors Corporation in 1967, the president had reporting to him four executive vice-presidents, but one executive vice-president had eight key subordinates, and two group vice-presidents had eleven reporting to them. The president of a railroad generally regarded as one of the best managed in the industry had in 1967 ten top executives reporting to him, and one of these had eleven subordinates. Yet the head of another large carrier, not regarded as so well managed, had only seven major subordinates. The president of one well-managed department store had four key executives, none of whom had more than five subordinates, while an equally large and successful store showed twelve key executives reporting to the president and an equally large number of subordinates reporting to most of them.

In a survey of a hundred large companies made by the American Management Association in 1951,[5] the number of executives reporting to the presidents varied from one to twenty-four, and only twenty-six presidents

[2] Lyndall Urwick, "Axioms of Organization," *Public Administration Magazine* (London), pp. 348–349 (October, 1955).

[3] Sir Ian Hamilton, *The Soul and Body of an Army* [London: Edward Arnold (Publishers) Ltd., 1921], p. 229.

[4] J. C. Worthy, "Men, Management, and Organization," *Proceedings, Fifth Personnel Management and Industrial Relations Seminar* (Los Angeles: University of California at Los Angeles, Oct. 30, 1951; mimeographed). The term "subordinates" referred to in this section excludes personnel such as staff or administrative assistants, secretaries, clerks, and stenographers.

[5] As summarized in *Business Week*, pp. 102–103 (Aug. 18, 1951). Healey found similar variations in his study of 409 manufacturing companies in Ohio, although the median was six subordinates. See J. H. Healey, *Executive Co-ordination and Control* (Columbus, Ohio: Ohio State University Press, 1956), p. 66.

had as few as six or less subordinates. The median number was nine. In forty-one smaller companies surveyed, twenty-five of the presidents supervised seven or more subordinates, and the median was eight. Comparable results were found by White in 1963 in a study of sixty-six companies.[6] In a much more narrowly based study, using a random sample, Fisch, on the other hand, discovered in 1962 a tendency among very large companies (those with over 1 billion dollars of sales) for a span of management at the top to be more than twelve, with the span tending to be smaller as the company size decreases.[7]

In a very real sense, none of these studies is truly indicative of the span of management actually practiced. For one thing, they measure the span only at or near the top of an enterprise. This is hardly typical of what the span may be throughout the enterprise, particularly since every organizer has experienced the tremendous pressure for a large number of the functions of an enterprise to report to the top executive. It is probable that spans below the top executive are much narrower. Indeed, analysis of more than 100 companies of all sizes made by one of the authors discloses a much narrower span in the middle levels of management than at the top.

In addition, the fact that apparently well-managed companies have, as between them and certainly within them, widely varying spans indicates that merely counting what is actually done is not enough to establish what a span *ought* to be. And this is true even if it could be assumed that, through trial and error, each company has reached an optimum. It may only prove that underlying conditions vary.

PROBLEMS WITH LEVELS

There is a tendency to regard organization and departmentation as an end in themselves and to gauge the effectiveness of organization structures in terms of clarity and completeness of departments and department levels. Although grouping employees—to achieve the economies of specialization or to emphasize certain activities—has apparent advantages, proliferation of departments and levels creates economic and managerial problems. Division of activities into departments and hierarchical organization and the creation of multiple levels are not completely desirable in themselves.

In the first place, levels are expensive. As they increase, more and more effort and money are devoted to managing, because of the additional managers, staffs to assist them, and the necessity of coordinating departmental activities, plus the costs of facilities for such personnel. Accountants refer to such costs as overhead, or burden, or general and administrative, in contrast to so-called direct costs. Real production is accomplished by factory, engi-

[6] K. K. White, *Understanding the Company Organization Chart* (New York: American Management Association, 1963), pp. 60–61.

[7] G. G. Fisch, "Stretching the Span of Management," *Harvard Business Review*, vol. 41, no. 5, pp. 80–81 (September–October, 1962).

neering, or sales employees, who are or could logically be accounted for as direct labor. Levels above the "firing line" are predominantly staffed with managers who are not directly productive and the expenses for whom it would be desirable to eliminate, *if that were possible*. Most of the beautiful pyramid of organization usually represents costs only indirectly, and sometimes remotely, related to the basic functions of the enterprise.

In the second place, departmental levels complicate communication. An enterprise with many levels has greater difficulty communicating objectives, plans, and policies through the organization structure than does the firm in which the top manager communicates directly with employees. Omissions and misinterpretations occur as information passes down the scalar chain. Levels also complicate communication from the "firing line" to the commanding superiors, which is every bit as important as downward communication.

Finally, departments and numerous levels complicate planning and control. The plan that may be definite and complete at the top level as it is subdivided and elaborated at lower levels loses coordination and clarity. Control becomes more difficult as levels and managers are added, while at the same time the complexities of planning and difficulties of communication make this control more important.

OPERATIONAL SCHOOL POSITION

The so-called classical school approach to the span of management has tended to deal with generalizations embodying specific numbers of subordinates for an effective span. Empirical data do give support to the classical school consensus of an upper- and top-level span from three to seven or eight subordinates.[8] However, more recent operational management theorists have taken the position that there are too many variables in a management situation to conclude that there is any particular number of subordinates which a manager can effectively supervise.[9] It is concluded that there is a limit to the number of subordinates a manager may effectively supervise, but the exact number will depend upon underlying factors, all of which affect the difficulty and time requirements of managing.

In other words, the dominant current view is to look for the causes of limited span in individual situations, rather than to assume that there is a widely applicable numerical limit. If one can look at what it is that consumes the time of a manager in his handling of his superior-subordinate relationships, and also ascertain what devices can be used to reduce these time pressures, the analyst has an approach helpful in determining the optimum span in individual cases. He also has a powerful tool for finding out what can be done to extend the span without destroying effective supervision.

[8] A consensus as found by Healey, *op. cit.*, pp. 11–14.

[9] The authors of this book have taken this position since its first edition. Also see H. Stieglitz, *Corporate Organization Structures,* Studies in Personnel Policy No. 183 (New York: National Industrial Conference Board, Inc., 1961), p. 8.

There can be no argument that the costs of levels in supervision are such as to make it highly desirable for every individual manager to have as many subordinates as he can *effectively* supervise.

GRAICUNAS'S THEORY OF SUBORDINATE–SUPERIOR RELATIONSHIPS

In a paper first published in 1933, French management consultant V. A. Graicunas[10] analyzed subordinate-superior relationships and developed a mathematical formula based on the geometric increase in complexities of managing as the number of subordinates increases. Although the formula may not be applicable to a given case, it focuses attention upon the central underlying problems of the span of management perhaps better than any other device. Graicunas's theory identifies three types of subordinate-superior relationship: (1) direct single relationships, (2) direct group relationships, and (3) cross relationships.

The direct single relationships, easily understood and recognized, relate the superior directly and individually with his immediate subordinates. Thus, if A has three subordinates—B, C, and D—there are three direct single relationships.

The direct group relations exist between the superior and each possible combination of subordinates. Thus, a superior might consult with one of his subordinates with a second in attendance, or with all his subordinates, or with various combinations of them. If A has three subordinates, these relationships include:

B with C
B with D
C with B
C with D
D with B
D with C
B with C and D
C with B and D
D with C and B

Putting these nine direct group relationships in a mathematical form, with n the number of subordinates, amounts to

$$n(2^n/2 - 1) \text{ or } n(2^{n-1} - 1)$$

Although it may be objected that the relationship when A instructs B, with C in attendance, is no different from that when A instructs C, with B in attendance, Graicunas implies a difference. In any case, three additional di-

[10] V. A. Graicunas, "Relationship in Organization," *Bulletin of the International Management Institute* (Geneva: International Labour Office, 1933), in L. Gulick and L. Urwick (eds.), *Papers on the Science of Administration* (New York: Institute of Public Administration, 1937), pp. 181–187.

rect group relationships could have been included, as when A consults equally with BC, BD, and BCD, furnishing a different psychological situation from any of those noted above.

Cross relationships are created when subordinates must consult with one another. For B, C, and D, Graicunas gave six cross relationships:

B to C
B to D
C to B
C to D
D to B
D to C

The mathematical form for cross relationships Graicunas gives as $n(n-1)$. Although he did not acknowledge the possibility, the same line of reasoning would yield three more possible cross relationships by recognizing group conferences of BCD, initiated by any one of the three.

From this analysis of direct single, direct group, and cross relationships, Graicunas developed the following formula to give the number of all possible types of subordinate-superior relationships requiring managerial attention. Where n equals the number of subordinates, the number of all kinds of relationships will be represented by

$$n(2^n/2 + n - 1) \qquad \text{or} \qquad n[2^{n-1} + (n-1)]$$

The results of this formula are shown in Table 5.

Significance of the Formula The rapid rise in the number of relationships with the increase in number of subordinates is startling. Mathematically, but as will be seen below not necessarily in practice, an executive with four

TABLE 5 POSSIBLE RELATIONSHIPS WITH
VARIABLE NUMBER OF SUBORDINATES

Number of subordinates	Number of relationships
1	1
2	6
3	18
4	44
5	100
6	222
7	490
8	1,080
9	2,376
10	5,210
11	11,374
12	24,708
18	2,359,602

subordinates, by adding a fifth, increases the *possible* relationships for which he is responsible by 127 per cent (from 44 to 100), in return for a 25 per cent increase in subordinate working capacity. Clearly, an executive must think twice before he increases the number of his subordinates, even though this mathematical truism does not prove he should not do so.

Even in reducing the number of direct group relationships by saying it's the same when A consults B, with C in attendance, as when he consults C, with B in attendance, or that the cross relationship when B approaches C is the same as when C approaches B, the number of possible relationships is still large. And, as mentioned, Graicunas missed some that might logically have been included.

The usefulness of the formula is weakened because it does not deal with frequency or severity of relationships. Their total possible number is probably less important to a manager (as Graicunas recognized) than their frequency and their demands on his time.

The Graicunas theory emphasizes the complexity of managing more than a few subordinates. Yet any managerial action that will reduce the number and frequency of relationships requiring the manager's attention will increase his span of management and thereby reduce the costs and inefficiencies of an undue number of departments.

FACTORS DETERMINING FREQUENCY AND SEVERITY CF RELATIONSHIPS

In searching for the answer as to how many subordinates a manager can effectively control, one discovers that—aside from such personal capacities as comprehending quickly, getting along with people, and commanding loyalty and respect—the most important determinant is the manager's ability to reduce the frequency and time impact of superior-subordinate relationships. This ability naturally varies with managers and their jobs, but seven general factors materially influence the number and frequency of such relationships.[11]

Subordinate Training   The better the training of subordinates, the less the impact of necessary superior-subordinate relationships. A well-trained subordinate requires not only less time of the manager, but also fewer contacts with his superior.

Training processes call for time, energy, attention, and knowledge. The higher the management level, the harder it is to discover what to teach and how to do it. Thus, a supervisor in the lower levels of organization can normally manage a larger number of subordinates than managers in the upper levels, since the work at lower levels, being more specialized but less complicated, can be taught more easily. When one considers the relative difficulty of training a person to operate a punch press versus training him to

---

[11] One study found that nearly half of a top-level executive's time is spent in committees and direct personal conferences with subordinates. See Fred E. Case, "The Executive Day," *California Management Review*, vol. 5, no. 1, p. 68 (Fall, 1962).

manage an entire factory, the fact that more training effort has normally been expended at higher levels becomes understandable.

Training problems increase in new and more complex industries. Managers in the railroad industry, for example, would—after the long development of railroad technology—tend to be more completely trained than those in the aerospace industry. Similarly, the rapid changes in policy and procedures in the complex electronics and missile industries would increase training problems.

The necessity for training, however, is ever-present. Often managers, especially of old or static industries, make the mistake of assuming that subordinates who have been raised in the industry are well trained as managers. Such an attempt to maintain the *status quo* in managing overlooks the development of management principles and techniques, the impact of technical change, and the fact that the human relations problem—especially as affected by national unions and big government—no longer knows the boundaries of a single company or a single industry.

Delegation of Authority Although training procedures enable managers to reduce the frequency and severity of time-consuming relationships, the principal cause of the heavy time burdens of such relationships is to be found in poorly conceived and confused organization. This deficiency can both magnify the degree of training required of subordinates and the amount of time required for counseling, guidance, explanation, and correction of subordinates' mistakes and organizational misunderstandings.

The most serious symptom of poor organization affecting the span of management is inadequate or unclear authority delegation. If a manager clearly delegates authority to undertake a well-defined task, a well-trained subordinate can get it done with a minimum of the superior's time and attention. But if the subordinate's task is not one he can do, or if it is not clearly defined, or if he does not have the authority to undertake it effectively, he will either fail to perform it or take a disproportionate amount of the manager's time in supervising and guiding his efforts.

Planning Much of the character of a subordinate's job is defined by the plans he is expected to put into effect. If these plans are well programmed, if they are workable within his framework of operations, if he has the authority to undertake them, and if he understands what is expected, he will require little of his superior's time. Such is often the case of production foremen responsible for largely repetitive operations. Thus, in one volume work-clothing manufacturer's plant, production foremen operated satisfactorily with as many as sixty or seventy subordinates.

On the other hand, where plans cannot be drawn accurately and where the subordinate must do much of his own planning, his decisions may require considerable guidance. However, if his superior has set up clear policies to guide his decisions and make sure they are consistent with the operations and goals of the department, and if the subordinate understands them, there will certainly be fewer demands on the superior's time than if these policies are indefinite, incomplete, or not understood.

Adequate and clear authority delegations and planning, particularly in the area of policy making, will go far toward increasing the span of management. These fundamental conditions naturally vary widely in practice, both in their ease of accomplishment and in the ability of managers to accomplish them.

Rate of Change Obviously, certain enterprises change much more rapidly than others. The rate of change is important in determining the degree to which policies can be formulated and the stability of formulated policies maintained. It may, indeed, explain the organization structure of companies—railroad, banking, and public utility companies, for example—operating with wide spans of management, or, on the other hand, the very narrow span of management used by General Eisenhower during World War II.

The effect of slow change on policy formulation and on subordinate training is dramatically shown in the organization of the Roman Catholic Church. This organization, in terms of durability and stability, can probably be regarded as the most successful in the history of Western civilization. Yet the organization levels are few: in most cases, bishops report directly to the Pope, and parish priests to bishops, although in a few instances bishops report to archbishops. Thus, there are generally only three levels in this world-wide organization and a consequent wide span of management at the top. Even though it is unquestionably too broad, this extraordinarily wide span apparently works fairly well, partly because of the degree of training possessed by the bishops and even more because the rate of change in the Church is exceedingly slow. Changes in procedures or policies are developments of decades, and objectives have remained the same over almost two millennia.

Use of Objective Standards A manager must find out, by either personal observation or use of objective standards, whether subordinates are following plans. Obviously, good objective standards, revealing with ease any deviations from plans, enable the manager to avoid many time-consuming relationships and to direct his attention to exceptions at points strategic to the successful execution of plans.

Communication Techniques The status of the technology of communications and the effectiveness with which communication techniques are used also influence the span of management. Objective standards of control are a kind of communications device, but many other techniques reduce the frequency of superior-subordinate relationships.

If every plan, instruction, order, or direction has to be communicated by personal contact and every organization change or staffing problem handled orally, the manager's time will obviously be heavily burdened. Some executives use "assistant-to" positions or administrative staff personnel as a communications device in helping to solve their problems with key subordinates. Written recommendations by subordinates, summarizing pertinent considerations, frequently expedite decision making. The authors have seen busy top executives widen their span of management by insisting upon summary presentation of written recommendations, even when these involved enormously important decisions. A carefully reasoned and presented recommendation helps the executive reach a considered decision in minutes, when even the most efficient conference would require an hour.

An executive's ability to communicate plans and instructions clearly and concisely also tends to increase a manager's span. The subordinate who, after leaving his superior's desk or receiving his memorandum of instructions, is still in doubt as to what is wanted or what has been said is sure to increase the relationships that will sooner or later require the manager's attention. One of the pleasures of being a subordinate is to have a superior who can express himself well. A manager's casual, easy style may please subordinates, but where this easiness degenerates into confusion and wasted time, the effect is sharply to reduce the span of management and often morale as well. Clarity of instructions may appear to be unstudied and artless, but experienced managers know it to be a studied technique.

Modern communication techniques are of considerable variety. Some are mechanical and some are electrical, like the telephone, the dictating machine, and the buzzer. The electronic data-computing machine has made communications more expeditious, exact, and complete, and, if properly used, may considerably affect the span of management. Whatever techniques are used are subject to invention and discovery, so that what may be a limited span for a manager today may be less limited tomorrow.

Amount of Personal Contact　In many instances in management, face-to-face relationships are necessary. Many situations cannot be completely handled by written reports, memoranda, policy statements, planning documents, or other communications not calling for personal contact. The executive may find it valuable to him and stimulating to his subordinates to meet and discuss problems in the give-and-take of a conference. There may also be problems of such political delicacy that they can only be handled in face-to-face meetings. This is also true when it comes to appraising people's performance and discussing it with them. And there are other situations where the best way of communicating a problem, instructing a subordinate, or getting a direct "feel" as to how people really think on some matter is to spend time in slow personal contact.

However, it appears to the authors that far too much time is spent, particularly at upper management levels, in personal contact. One wonders whether the high percentage of executive time spent in conferences and committees might be reduced somewhat by better training, better policy making and planning, clearer delegation, more thorough staff work, better control systems and objective standards, and, in general, better application of sound principles of management. One wonders, also, whether much of the time spent in personal contact might not be much better spent in thought and study.

At the other extreme of management, many companies seem somewhat unaware of how newer personnel techniques affect first-line supervisors, many of whom appear to have spans far beyond their abilities to handle. Merit rating, insurance programs, grievance procedures, and other personnel matters now requiring the foreman's time in face-to-face relationships have perhaps reduced his traditionally wide span of management. This is not to say that these innovations are not worth their cost, but the span of management limitations must be evaluated in the light of the total picture.

OTHER SPANS

Among the limitations affecting the span of management are other so-called spans.

Time and Attention Spans   The span of time is a very real limitation, because it cannot be controlled.[12] Time is the most dynamic of the three basic resources available to the manager, the other two being human and physical. Except in time of war, when the last man and the last ounce of material may be used, the quantity at least—not to mention the quality—of human and physical resources are somewhat subject to managerial control. No one, however, can control the number of minutes in an hour.

The implications are profound. When managers live in harmony with the clock, they can develop more flexible plans and reduce the time lag between planning and execution. They also train subordinates to keep open the channels of communication, uncluttered by carelessness, repetition, lack of forethought, babble, or gossip. Managers can also insist that information be disseminated by successive stages throughout the organization without lost time.

Time is fast becoming the critical factor in enterprise. Automation implies heavy costs for interruptions of any sort, including time involved in planning, communication, and decision making.

Furthermore, psychologists have long recognized that people are limited by a span of attention—the number of things a brain can heed at any one time, plus the length of time it can concentrate on any one thing. Although this factor affects the span of management, it may be regarded as a refinement of the span of time.

Personality and Energy Spans   Spans of personality and energy are sometimes suggested as factors affecting the span of management. The span of personality includes whatever limitations a manager's personality may have in

---

[12] For an excellent discussion of this point, see C. W. Boyce, "Management Problems in the Factory of Tomorrow," *Transactions of the American Society of Mechanical Engineers* (Fall sess., 1953).

dealing with and influencing people. The span of energy is thought of as the amount of energy, physical and mental, that an executive may be able to apply to his job. Obviously, spans of personality and energy influence greatly the ability to manage numerous subordinates. One manager may have the personality and energy to handle far more than another.

However, although these are important qualifications of individual managers, neither seems to contribute much to the basic span of management. A wide span of personality may be a very real factor in executive success, but to regard it as a basic determinant of departmentation is to confuse executive qualities with factors of more general application. The span of energy is a refinement of the span of time. Energy limits are basically time limits. To be sure, one manager may seem to have an inexhaustible supply of energy, and another may tire quickly and easily. But this, like personality, is essentially personal. Practical men are interested in effective available time, and, of course, time should be used discreetly in terms of energy expended.

Span of Knowledge   It is sometimes contended that managers create departments and place them under subordinate managers to hide the fact that they themselves are not technically qualified to perform their duties. This, it is then argued, results in an increased number of subordinates reporting to a manager and increases the difficulties of direction and control.

If this happens, it is based on a fallacy. There is, of course, a span of knowledge. No one—not even the person who rises from office boy to company president—can be an expert in all things. But, the job of the manager is to get things done *through* people, and, to the extent that he does this, he need not be expert in all phases of the business.

WIDE VERSUS NARROW SPANS

Limitations affecting the span of management are what create levels in organization: the larger the enterprise or the narrower the spans, the greater the number of levels.

Organization structure laden with departments and levels causes complexity and losses. Experience with large organizations proves to anyone the frustrations of "layering," whereby authority, suggestions, questions, and instructions must flow up and down the chain of command. Although some of this may be allayed by understanding that requests for information need not follow the line of command, decision making—in which authority is required and used—does need to.

The losses caused by narrow spans and too many levels are not limited to expenses of supervision and losses of managerial efficiency. There are also losses in morale.[13] Individuals do not like to be regarded as cogs in a machine but want to have a feeling of belonging. When levels of organization make subordinate managers (and workers) feel too far away from top

---

[13] For an interesting discussion of this, see W. H. Newman, *Administrative Action* (Englewood Cliffs, N.J.: Prentice-Hall, Inc., 1951), pp. 267–268.

leadership, they are likely to misunderstand plans and policies and, indeed, to lose their desire to understand. Moreover, as one astute student of human relations has convincingly pointed out, the lower-level employee, submerged at the bottom of the organization pyramid, has few opportunities to develop self-reliance and initiative.[14]

The Sears, Roebuck Studies   An interesting study of the effect of organization levels on enterprise efficiency was made by Sears, Roebuck and Company.[15] Although the management of the company has been prejudiced for a considerable time in favor of short lines of communication and its organization has long reflected the attitude of Robert E. Wood, president or chairman of the board for many years, there was no evidence that this kind of thinking had been forced on the company's stores—at least not by the time the study of organizational efficiency was made.

In the course of this study, the operations of two groups of B stores (150 to 175 employees) in towns of approximately the same size were analyzed. In one group the managers had organized their stores with an assistant manager and some thirty merchandise managers in charge of departments. In the other group the stores were organized along more conventional lines, with an extra level of management between store managers and department heads. Analyses of sales volume, profit, morale, and lower-management competence all indicated that the stores with the "flat" type of organization were superior on all scores to those more conventionally organized.

The results—clearly violating the traditional limitations of span of management—were traced to several factors. The principal one appeared to be that managers having a large number of subordinate managers reporting to them had no alternative but to delegate adequate authority to these subordinates, who were thereby enabled to make important decisions. This not only improved their morale, but, because of the pressure placed on them to perform, actually improved the quality of their performance. By being forced to manage, they learned to manage. By the same token, the store manager, knowing that he had to delegate considerable authority, took greater care in selecting, guiding, and training his subordinates and also adopted efficient methods of objective control. In addition, the Sears study revealed that reducing the length of channels vastly improved communication between managers and subordinates, despite the large number of subordinates.

Other Widened Spans   As has already been indicated by reference to the American Management Association studies showing how many top execu-

---

[14] J. C. Worthy, "Organization Structure and Employee Morale," *American Sociological Review*, vol. 15, pp. 169–179 (April, 1950).

[15] *Ibid.* See also J. C. Worthy, "Factors Influencing Employee Morale," *Harvard Business Review*, vol. 28, pp. 65–67 (January, 1950); *Discovering and Evaluating Employee Attitudes*, Personnel Series No. 113 (New York: American Management Association, 1947); "Democratic Principles in Business Management," *Advanced Management* (March, 1949).

tives have fairly wide spans of management, industry is tending to pay more attention to the inefficiencies of extended levels of organization and less attention to those arising from wide spans of management. The International Business Machines Corporation, for example, cut out one entire level of middle management several years ago, thereby increasing the span of management of the remaining executives. As one organization expert has said: "You have a place in which good people can grow rather than stagnate when you discard this traditional idea of span of authority."[16]

This drive to shorten the line of command is a result not only of a realization of the disastrous effects of poor communications but also of the desire of many top managers to force authority down into the organization structure. The shortage, too, of managerial personnel in the middle and top levels of management, occasioned by the war years and the rapid expansion of industry, may have forced this kind of policy.

OPERATIONAL APPLICATION OF UNDERLYING–VARIABLES APPROACH

If, as the authors of this book believe, the number of subordinates that a manager can effectively supervise is not an exact number applicable generally but depends on underlying variables, it follows that managers should look at these variables for an answer to the span problem. Fortunately, such an experiment was undertaken a few years ago by the Lockheed Missiles and Space Company.[17]

The Underlying Variables   In the Lockheed program, the company identified a number of critical variables underlying the span of management. While the program was designed only to apply to the middle-management group of the company, where spans were found to be quite narrow (three to five), and while the underlying variables are not the same as those outlined by the authors above, there are many similarities. The company utilized for its analysis the following variables:

1. *Similarity of functions*   This factor referred to the degree to which functions performed by the various components or personnel reporting to a manager were alike or different.
2. *Geographic contiguity*   This factor referred to the physical locations of units of personnel reporting to a superior.
3. *Complexity of functions*   This factor referred to the nature of the task done and the department managed.

---

[16] Burleigh Gardner, formerly employee relations research director at Western Electric's Hawthorne plant, as quoted in *Business Week* (Aug. 18, 1951).

[17] For a report on this program see H. Koontz, "Making Theory Operational: The Span of Management," *The Journal of Management Studies*, vol. 3, no. 3, pp. 229–243 (October, 1966). See also, on the same problem, H. Stieglitz, "Optimizing the Span of Control," *Management Record*, vol. 24, no. 9, pp. 25–29 (September, 1962), and C. W. Barkdull, "Span of Control: A Method of Evaluation," *Michigan Business Review*, vol. 15, no. 3, pp. 25–32 (May, 1963).

4. *Direction and control*   This factor referred to the nature of personnel reporting to a superior, the amount of training required, the extent to which authority could be delegated, and the personal attention needed.

5. *Coordination*   This factor was related to time requirements of keeping an organizational unit keyed in with other divisional or company-wide activities.

6. *Planning*   This factor was designed to reflect the importance, complexity, and time requirements of the planning functions of the manager and his organizational unit.

Degree of Supervisory Burden within Span Factors   After identifying the underlying variables related to the span of management, the company spread each of them over a spectrum of five degrees of difficulty. For each span factor, also, weightings were given to reflect relative importance. Thus, the supervisory impact of coordination was thought to be three times as important as that of similarity of functions supervised, and that of direction and control three times as significant. The degrees and weights of the span factors are shown in Table 6.

It is worth noting that the weight values in these span factors were based on an analysis of 150 cases in the company at the middle-management and department-director levels. They were also checked against a number of comparative cases, the measuring standard being those organizational units which were regarded on the score of both reputation and performance as being well managed. Even though the weightings and values applied can be criticized as representing pseudo-science, there is evidence that they were

TABLE 6   DEGREES OF SUPERVISORY BURDEN WITHIN SPAN FACTORS (numbers show relative weighting)

Span factor					
Similarity of functions	Identical 1	Essentially alike 2	Similar 3	Inherently different 4	Fundamentally distinct 5
Geographic contiguity	All together 1	All in one building 2	Separate building, 1 plant location 3	Separate locations, 1 geographic area 4	Dispersed geographic areas 5
Complexity of functions	Simple repetitive 2	Routine 4	Some complexity 6	Complex, varied 8	Highly complex, varied 10
Direction and control	Minimum supervision and training 3	Limited supervision 6	Moderate periodic supervision 9	Frequent continuing supervision 12	Constant close supervision 15
Coordination	Minimum relation with others 2	Relationships limited to defined courses 4	Moderate relationships easily controlled 6	Considerable close relationship 8	Extensive mutual non-recurring relationships 10
Planning	Minimum scope and complexity 2	Limited scope and complexity 4	Moderate scope and complexity 6	Considerable effort required guided only by broad policies 8	Extensive effort required; areas and policies not charted 10

developed with care. Moreover, as in so many measurements applied to life, the breaking down of factors and assigning values to them did help in clarifying issues and giving visibility to the problem being analyzed.

Correction for Organizational Assistance After each position had been evaluated and the total of values from factor weightings had been added, corrections were then made by application of a reducing factor to each score to take into account the amount of organizational assistance that a manager had. Thus, a direct-line assistant with responsibility for certain portions of a manager's operations resulted in the application of a factor of 0.70, and a staff assistant in administering, planning, or controlling resulted in the application of a reducing factor of 0.75 or 0.85. A first-line supervisor with four lead men would have a factor of 0.40 applied to his score.

The Supervisory Index After scores for a given manager's position had been calculated and had been corrected by the organizational-assistance factor, they were compared with a standard. The suggested supervisory indexes are shown in Table 7. These were developed by using as a standard the cases of organizational units with wider spans which were generally considered to be effectively organized and managed. Thus, an individual manager could compare his own span factor ratings with the suggested standard span to determine whether he was below or above standard.

Results Results from this experimental program were interesting. Even though the program was not completely adopted in the company and was not too strongly pressed, there is evidence that it did lead to a widening of the span of management in the middle-management area and to a reduction of one complete level of supervision, with a consequent reduction in supervisory costs. Despite the rather crude methods necessarily used, they did give visibility to the problem of span of management and there is evidence that organizational effectiveness was improved. By identification of the problem through looking at underlying variables and making personnel in managerial posts aware of these, significant results were attained. The program thus indicates that material rewards in practice can follow the appli-

TABLE 7   SUGGESTED SUPERVISORY INDEX

Total span factor weightings	Suggested standard span
40–42	4–5
37–39	4–6
34–36	4–7
31–33	5–8
28–30	6–9
25–27	7–10
22–24	8–11

cation of theory to real problems, even where methods are not completely proved and basic data are inexact.

The Need for Balance There can be no doubt that, despite the Sears, Roebuck experience, the Lockheed program, and the tendency to flatten organization structures, the span of management is limited by real and important restrictions. A manager may have more subordinates than he can manage, even though he delegates authority, carries on training, formulates plans and policies clearly, and adopts efficient control and communication techniques. It is equally true that, as an enterprise grows, the span-of-management limitations force departmentation and organization levels.

What is required, of course, is a precise balancing, in a given situation, of all pertinent factors. Widening spans and reducing levels may be the answer in some cases; the reverse may be true in others. One must balance *all* the costs of adopting one course or the other—not only the financial costs but costs in morale, personal development, and the attainment of enterprise objective—in short, all the advantages and disadvantages. In military organization, perhaps the attainment of objectives quickly and without error would be most important; in department store operation, on the other hand, the long-run objective of profit may be best served by forcing initiative and personal development at the lower levels of the organization.

Much misunderstanding concerning the span of management has arisen from confusion. There is a tendency to regard the "theoretical" limits of effective span as being approximately three to seven or eight subordinates.[18] In fact, the practice of attempting positive numerical definition has led one writer to state that "the span of control (management) concept is not valid, since the supervision of the chief executive is much wider than that predicted."[19]

The correct principle of span of management is that there is a limit in each managerial position to the number of persons an individual can effectively manage, but the exact number in each case will vary in accordance with the effect of underlying variables and their impact on the time requirements of effective managing. This basic principle does exist, has not been superseded, and is useful in guiding managers toward ably managing more subordinates and simplifying organization.

FOR DISCUSSION

1. Some 750 line bishops and some 1,200 other persons report directly to the Pope. Urwick and other writers seem to say that at top levels the number should not exceed six. At one time in the Bank of America organization over 600 bank managers reported to the chief executive officer. How do you fit these facts with

[18] For a summary of the opinions of various authorities, see Healey, *op. cit.*, pp. 11–15.

[19] W. W. Suojanen, "The Span of Control—Fact or Fable?" *Advanced Management*, vol. 20, no. 11, pp. 5–13 (November, 1955).

the idea that there is a limit to the number of subordinates a manager can supervise?

2. At Lockheed Missiles and Space Company an attempt has been made to determine the span of managers by an arithmetic formula. Do you think this approach can be adopted in other enterprises? How?

3. When you become a manager what criteria will you favor to determine your span?

4. How would you determine the optimum span of management in a given situation?

5. Does the application of principles recommend, as many critics insist, a "tall" organization structure with a limited span of management?

SELECTED REFERENCES

Dale, E.: *Organization,* chaps. 1, 5, 8, New York: American Management Association, 1967.

————: *Planning and Developing the Company Organization Structure,* Research Report No. 20, pp. 49–60, New York: American Management Association, 1952.

Davis, R. C.: *The Influence of the Unit of Supervision and the Span of Control on the Economy of Line Organization Structure,* Research Monograph No. 26, Columbus, Ohio: Bureau of Business Research, Ohio State University, 1941.

Fisch, G.: "Stretching the Span of Management," *Harvard Business Review,* vol. 41, no. 5, pp. 74–85 (September–October, 1963).

Graicunas, V. A.: "Relationship in Organization," in L. Gulick and L. Urwick (eds.), *Papers on the Science of Administration,* New York: Institute of Public Administration, 1937.

Healey, J. H.: *Executive Co-ordination and Control,* Columbus, Ohio: Ohio State University Press, 1956.

Hill, L. S.: "The Application of Queuing Theory to the Span of Control," *Academy of Management Journal,* vol. 6, no. 1, pp. 58–69 (March, 1963).

Jaques, E.: "Too Many Management Levels," *California Management Review,* vol. 8, no. 1, pp. 13–20 (Fall, 1965).

Koontz, H.: "Making Theory Operational: The Span of Management," *The Journal of Management Studies,* vol. 3, no. 3, pp. 229–243 (October, 1966).

Newman, W. H.: *Administrative Action,* chap. 15, Englewood Cliffs, N.J.: Prentice-Hall, Inc., 1951.

Petersen, E., and E. G. Plowman: *Business Organization and Management,* 4th ed., chap. 4, Homewood, Ill.: Richard D. Irwin, Inc., 1958.

Stieglitz, H.: "Optimizing Span of Control," *Management Record,* vol. 24, no. 9, pp. 25–29 (September, 1962).

Suojanen, W. W.: "The Span of Control—Fact or Fable?" *Advanced Management,* vol. 20, no. 11, pp. 5–13 (November, 1955).

Urwick, L.: *Notes on the Theory of Organization,* pp. 53–57, New York: American Management Association, 1952.

————: "The Manager's Span of Control," *Harvard Business Review,* vol. 34, no. 3, pp. 39–47 (May, 1956).

Woodward, J.: *Industrial Organization: Theory and Practice,* London: Oxford University Press, 1965.

Worthy, J. C.: "Organization Structure and Employee Morale," *American Sociological Review,* vol. 15, pp. 169–179 (April, 1950).

basic departmentation

The limitation on the number of subordinates that can be directly managed would restrict the size of enterprises if it were not for the device of departmentation. Grouping activities and employees into departments makes it possible to expand organizations to an indefinite degree. Departments, however, differ with respect to the bases used to determine their specific activities. The nature of these bases and their relative merits are dealt with in the following sections.

DEPARTMENTATION BY SIMPLE NUMBERS

Departmentation by simple numbers was once an important method in the organization of tribes, clans, and armies. Although it is rapidly falling into disuse, it still has certain applications in modern society.

The simple-numbers method of departmentizing is achieved by tolling off a number of undifferentiated persons who are to perform certain duties at the direction of a manager. The essential fact is not what these people do, where they work, or what they work with but that the success of the undertaking depends upon simple manpower.

In many armies, portions of the infantry division are still organized upon the basis of numbers of men. Ground keepers for municipalities, universities, and large estates are often organized on this basis, as are house-to-house sales crews, collectors for community funds and membership drives, and common-labor crews.

Even though a cursory examination may impress an investigator with the number of people departmentized on a manpower basis, the usefulness of this organizational device has declined with each passing century. For one thing, labor skills have increased. Today, men operate machines, use tools, or exercise some other specialized skill. In America the last stronghold of common labor is agriculture, and even here it is restricted more and more to the harvesting of fewer and fewer crops.

A second reason for the decline of the manpower basis of grouping is the relatively new discovery that groups based on teamwork are frequently more efficient than those based on mere numbers. The reorganization of the defense forces of the United States on this basis is a case in point. Many ways have been found to combine men skilled in the use of different types of weapons into single units. For instance, the addition of artillery and tactical air support to the traditional infantry division makes it a much more formidable fighting unit than when each was organized separately.

A third and long-standing reason for the decline of departmentation by numbers is that it is only useful at the lowest level of the organization structure. At the middle- and higher-management levels activities tend to be grouped on a basis other than similarity. As soon as any other factor besides pure manpower becomes important, the simple-numbers basis of departmentation fails to produce good results.

DEPARTMENTATION BY ENTERPRISE FUNCTION *Sales, Finance, Production*

The grouping of activities in accordance with the functions of the enterprise is a widely accepted practice. The characteristic action of enterprises embodies what they typically do. Since all undertakings involve the creation of utility and since this occurs in an exchange economy, the basic enterprise functions consist of production (creating utility or adding utility to a good or service), selling (finding customers, patients, clients, students, or communicants who will agree to accept the good or service at a price), and financing (raising and collecting, safeguarding, and expending the funds of the enterprise). It has been logical to group these activities into such typical departments as production, sales, and finance.

Often, these particular terms do not appear in the organization chart. First, there is no generally accepted terminology: manufacturing enterprises employ the terms production, sales, and finance; a wholesaler will speak of his activities as buying, selling, and finance; and a railroad, as operations, traffic, and finance.

A second reason for variance of terms is that basic activities differ in importance: hospitals have no selling departments; churches, no production departments. This does not mean that these activities are not undertaken but merely that they are unspecialized or of such minor importance that they are combined with other activities.

A third reason for the absence of sales, production, or finance departments on many organization charts is that other methods of departmentation may have been deliberately selected, the functional basis being, after all, merely one way to organize. Those responsible for the enterprise may decide upon a product, customer, or territorial basis.

Functional departmentation is the most widely employed basis for organizing activities and is present in almost every enterprise at some level in the organization structure. When it is not widely used it may be found—say, as the finance department—beside or above a department based upon product, customer, or territory.

The characteristics of the selling, production, and finance functions of enterprise are so widely recognized and thoroughly understood that they are the basis not only of departmental organization but most often of primary departmentation. The managers of primary activities report to the executive general officer of the enterprise: the primary level is the first level in the organization structure below the chief executive. The designation is made without consideration of the question of the major or minor nature of the departments or the basis for grouping enterprise activities.[1]

Wherever activities are grouped into major functional departments, they will naturally be located in the organization structure at the primary level, while minor functional departments may be found almost anywhere below the first echelon.

The lawyer has no sales department, but he is actively engaged in selling his services at all times. The church is very much concerned about the number of its communicants, and it is always actively engaged in maintaining and increasing this number. Obvious emphasis is not placed on this activity because the institution is not desperate for clients or communicants or students, and because the social mores frown upon open selling activity in these areas as being unseemly. The conclusion to be drawn from these examples is that *all* enterprises have the same major functions, but these need not necessarily appear on the organization chart.

A hospital administrator approached a consultant on the subject of his organizational structure. "We have a lot of trouble here in coordinating our activities. Both the nurses and the doctors think they run the place but, of course, I really manage everything."

"Do you have someone acting as chief executive officer?"

"No, not really. You see, the Board just appoints the chief surgeon, the supervisor of nurses, and me."

"Do these represent the typical functions of your hospital?" asked the consultant. "For instance, where is the sales or business-getting function?"

"Oh," was the reply, "a hospital never sells its services."

"If there were a severe business depression, would the hospital be able to keep fully in operation?"

"No. I can still remember the depression of the thirties when hardly anyone was interested in hospital service. It was just not considered cricket to advertise."

Minor Functional Departments   In minor functional departments are grouped those activities which, although important to the enterprise, nevertheless lack

---

[1] W. H. Newman, *Administrative Action* (Englewood Cliffs, N.J.: Prentice-Hall, Inc., 1951), p. 279. Newman thinks of primary departments as major operating divisions, while Petersen and Plowman think of primary departments as those based upon territories, commodities, and functions. See E. Petersen and E. G. Plowman, *Business Organization and Management*, 3d ed. (Homewood, Ill.: Richard D. Irwin, Inc., 1953), p. 254.

the supremacy of major departments. What may be major in one enterprise, or at one time, may be minor at another. For example, in many enterprises during World War II, sales departments suddenly sank from major to minor importance because the firms had no sales problems other than that of rationing.

The choice of customer, territory, or product departmentation does not eliminate functional activities, but it diffuses and subordinates them. The structure may then be likened to the roots of a plant. Each root performs an essential function, but each, regarded singly, is subordinate in that its loss would not endanger the life of the plant. However, all the roots, combined, are of major importance.

Major Functional Departments The term "major" may be used by various writers to identify departments with large budgets, many employees, or an importance related to the very existence of the enterprise. Large budgets and many employees are obviously a result, rather than a cause, of departmentation. The major functional departments in any organization structure are those which carry on its characteristic activities.

Without exception, every organization is engaged in creating utility in goods or services, exchanging this wealth at a price for purchasing power, and managing the cash flow which is entailed in the operation. This means that every organization has a production, sales, and financing function. Of course, every one may not use these terms. A university must produce educational services, it must attract students, and it must finance its operations; a religious organization must provide services, it must have worshippers, and it must also finance its operation. A lawyer offers services to his clientele for a price; a public accountant likewise proffers services to clients for a fee.

In each case, the services proffered are often divided between major departments. A university will offer services within groups of activities that may be called liberal arts, engineering, law, medicine, and business. A church may divide its services under such heads as general, Sunday school, missions, etc. If special departments covering any of these activities are not organized, it merely means that the state of the market does not require maximum effort to be exerted.

Derivative Functional Departments Derivative functional departments are established when the manager of any functional devision feels that his span of management is too broad. For instance, when an enterprise is small, the production manager may have only workers reporting to him. With the expansion of activities it may be necessary to split off the buying function and place a purchasing agent in charge. The new purchasing unit is a derivative functional department; it would appear on an organization chart at the second level, if production is a primary division. A typical grouping of functional activities into derivative departments is suggested in Table 8.

There are several points of interest here. First, the titles assigned to activities are not intended to represent standard practice, for none exists. They do, however, conform to rather widespread custom. Second, the suggested departmentation does not follow the practice of any single firm, since the stage of departmentation depends upon the span of management peculiar to each firm. A third point is that some types of enterprises, such as department stores, do not organize all primary functional departments directly into subordinate functional groups. The merchandise manager is in charge of the total buying and selling activity of the store, but the people who report to him are product-line buyers, who, in turn, do organize their activities into derivative functional groups. Some derivative functional departments, finally, are in turn subdivided into a second derivative functional grouping.

Advantages The most important advantage of functional departmentation is that it is a logical and time-proved method. It is also the best way of making certain that the power and prestige of the basic activities of the enterprise will be defended by the top managers. This is an important consideration among functional managers, for they see on every side the encroachments of staff and service groups, which sometimes threaten the security of the principal line executives. A third advantage is that functional departmentation follows the principle of occupational specialization, thereby making for efficiency in the utilization of manpower.

Disadvantages In spite of the advantages of functional departmentation, there are times when the claims of other methods seem even stronger. The size of the geographical area over which an enterprise operates may call for territorial grouping of activities; the production or purchase of numerous product lines, or of products designed for certain buyer classifications, may call for grouping along product or customer lines. In addition, functional departmentation may tend to deemphasize the enterprise objectives as a whole. Accountants, production experts, and salesmen, growing up in specialized departments, often have difficulty seeing the business as a whole, and coordination between them is frequently difficult to achieve. Another disadvantage is that only the chief executive officer can be held responsible for profits. In small firms, this is as it should be, but in large firms the burden becomes too heavy for one man to bear.[2] What is perhaps most important is that, since the first *general* managerial position is that of the president or the executive vice-president, the functionally organized company is not the best training ground for promotable managerial manpower.

DEPARTMENTATION BY TERRITORY

Departmentation based on geographical areas is a rather common method for physically dispersed enterprises. The principle is that all activities in a given area or territory should be grouped and assigned to a manager. From a superficial viewpoint such a rule appears eminently sound.

[2] See Cyril O'Donnell, "Gladding, McBean & Company," in *Cases in General Management* (Homewood, Ill.: Richard D. Irwin, Inc., 1961).

**TABLE 8   DERIVATIVE FUNCTIONAL DEPARTMENTS
OF TYPICAL ORGANIZATION STRUCTURES**

Primary functional department	*Derivative functional departments*
In a manufacturing organization	
Production	Manufacturing: 　Fabrication 　Assembly 　Tooling Purchasing Production control: 　Scheduling 　Materials control Quality control
Sales	Selling: 　Selection 　Training 　Operation Advertising Sales promotion
Finance	Capital requirements Fund control Disbursements Credit Accounting
In a department-store operation	
Publicity	Advertising Display Media public relations
Merchandising	Buying (organized by product line): 　Budgeting 　Merchandise control 　Sales promotion 　Sales force
General superintendent	Supplies Customer service Store protection Warehousing Receiving, marking, delivery
Finance	Financial management: 　Cash control 　Credit Accounting
In a wholesale organization	
Sales	Buying (organized by product line): 　Budgeting 　Merchandise control 　Sales promotion 　Sales force

Extent of Use   Territorial departmentation is especially attractive to large-scale enterprises or other enterprises whose activities are physically or geographically spread. A plant may, however, be local in its activities and still assign the guards in its protection department on a territorial basis, placing

Primary functional department	Derivative functional departments

General superintendent	Warehousing:
	  Receiving
	  Will call
	  Shipping
	  Stockroom

Finance	Money management Credit and collections Accounting
In a service organization (airline)	

Operations	Engineering:
	  New equipment
	  Modification of equipment
	  Communications engineering
	Maintenance:
	  Line maintenance
	  Overhaul
	Ground operations:
	  Station management
	  Food and commissary
	Flight operations:
	  Flying
	  Communications
	  Dispatching

Traffic or sales	Administration:
	  Reservations
	  Schedules
	  Tariffs
	Sales:
	  Passenger sales
	  Cargo sales
	  Sales promotion
	Advertising:
	  Direct mail
	  Newspaper and periodical
	  Radio and television

Finance	Financial management:
	  Cash control
	  New financing
	  Foreign exchange
	Accounting:
	  Revenue
	  Disbursements
	  General ledger

two men, for instance, at each of the south and west gates. Department stores assign floorwalkers on this basis, and it is a common way to assign janitors, window washers, and the like. Business firms resort to this method when similar operations are undertaken in different geographic areas, as in automobile assembly, chain retailing and wholesaling, and oil refining. Many government agencies—the Internal Revenue Service, the Federal Reserve Board, the Federal courts, and the Post Office Department, for example— adopt this basis of organization in providing like services simultaneously across the nation.

Reasons for Use   Although it is important for the enterprise considering territorial departmentation to base its decision on the right reasons, frequently the choice is made for the wrong reasons.

The wrong reasons   Poor communication facilities are often advanced as a reason for territorial departmentation. At one time, this reason was good, and in many parts of the world it still is. In general, communication is now so easy that this reason is not so forceful. With telephone, telegraph, and television, an associate many miles away can sometimes be reached more quickly than can the man in the next office.

The need for taking prompt action in a given area is also cited as a good reason for territorial departmentation. The assumption is that the local officer will be prompt. But if promptness is desired, nothing should hinder the distant officer's being prompt. Nor is so-called ease of coordination and control on a local basis sufficient reason for territorial grouping. Fumbling will give poor results, whether perpetrated by local officers or by central office managers.

Further, those who advocate area grouping for the above reasons miss the point, developed in the next section, that not all the enterprise activities are actually associated on a territorial basis anyway. Concentrating attention on those which are locally grouped overlooks the serious management problems created when different organizational methods are employed simultaneously.

The right reasons   Territorial departmentation is proper when its purpose is to avoid absenteeism and to take advantage of certain economies of localized operation. As the term is used here, absenteeism means that the officers of an enterprise ignore local factors in decision making. Many enterprises, as a matter of policy, practice absenteeism in some or all phases of their activities. On the other hand, the managers of many firms, with great or little fanfare, denounce absenteeism and do their very best to avoid it.

The firm that makes allowances for local elements in a situation will find many opportunities to do so. Firms which can tie in their product with such local phenomena as fishing facilities, skiing opportunities, sunbathing, or the occurrence of smog can use local appeals in their advertising. Sometimes supplies are ordered on a local basis, as when managers of chain retail stores tie in with local businesses for construction, supplies, and services.

Sales managers look with favor upon the local recruitment of salesmen. Familiar with area factors that outsiders would have to learn, such men are not required to uproot their families and are presumed to know how to deal with area customers. Men recruited elsewhere may be better men, but they will require adjustment to local factors.

Although the great improvements in communication have largely eradicated differences in custom, style, and product preferences, many enterprises still consider these differences important enough to treat on a local basis. Even language differences or weather can influence vitally the success of a distribution program. And there is a closely related issue here. If it is enterprise policy to heed local factors, territorial departmentation provides the area with a manager who has the prestige essential for getting results. Middle- and high-level managers may not be ready to listen to the bleat of a distant salesman, but they will listen to the representations of a regional executive. They may even act promptly. Finally, good as mechanical and electronic communication is becoming, there is really nothing that takes the place of face-to-face discussion. More time can be allowed for this type of interchange, and a deeper and fuller understanding is achieved, both about the person and the subject matter being discussed. The very lack of this opportunity is the chief reason why more authority is delegated to the distant executive than to the nearby man on the same organizational level.

The economic reasons for selecting territorial departmentation concern the cost of getting things done. Plants for the manufacture and assembly of parts may be located so as to reduce transportation costs. The proper location of warehouse facilities will reduce the time required for delivery, a factor that may affect booking the order. Any arrangement of salesmen's routes to reduce traveling during their best hours for sales will likewise reduce the expense of distribution.

The district, region, or branch has long been recognized as an excellent training ground for managers. It is made to order for giving them essential experience at a place in the organization structure and at a time in their careers most valuable to them and least risky for the firm. This is not to say that a firm should organize territorially in order to permit subordinate managers to gain essential experience, but it is a factor to consider in deciding upon the type of departmentation.

Application in Functional Areas   The reasons for departmentation on a territorial basis do not apply with equal force to all enterprise activities. Neither are they applicable at the same organization levels within different departments. The place and the point in an organization structure at which the strength of these reasons overpowers other considerations are so highly variable that there are few rules to guide the organizer.

An extreme view of territorial departmentation envisages the grouping on this basis of all enterprise functions. The Eastern division of a firm would then be composed of the production, sales, and finance functions essential to carrying on enterprise activity in that region, while the Western and Southern divisions would likewise be complete operating units, with nothing whatever to hold them together. They would be wholly independent of one another and of any "headquarters" activity set up to serve them. No known enterprise exists on such a basis, although the public utility holding company in recent times and the international trading companies of the fifteenth and sixteenth centuries did approach it.

Each of the three primary functional areas of enterprise activity may now be analyzed from the point of view of the proper reasons for regional grouping. In the production department, the proposal for organizing on a regional basis would mean the establishing of plants, to be engaged in manufacturing, mining, refining, or assembling the *same* product, in various areas. By catering to local factors, the production activity would gain certain advantages: the good will produced by providing jobs for local labor, for instance. But the chief gains would be economic: lower freight rates, lower rent, and lower labor costs.

The advantages of territorial organization of the sales activity may include attention to local preferences and local pride, economic gains, and the opportunity granted its men to acquire managerial experience. No general rule can be developed because the various advantages carry different weights with every firm. Some enterprises make a product that must be sold by sales engineers appealing to customers on the basis of operating economy. Others make a product such as electric lighting fixtures, the sale of which is affected by quality or terms rather than local preferences. Each enterprise will find it necessary to assess for itself the net influence upon sales of grouping activities on an area basis.

The reasons for area departmentation apply with little or no force to the finance function of enterprise. The development of sources of funds, their care, disbursement, investment, property management, record keeping, and controls—typical activities of a finance department—reflect no gains from catering to local factors. On the other hand, the economies of centralization of these activities are so pronounced that all enterprises strive for them.

Neither is a general rule applicable to the level within the department at which territorializing should be considered. Decisions depend upon the facts in each case. It would be purely a coincidence if both the sales and the production activities would reap net advantages from area grouping at the same levels. Also, the likelihood that all derivative functional departments should be departmentized on an area basis is extremely remote. This question will be considered later.

Derivative Territorial Departments The subdepartmentation of an area activity into smaller area groupings is a common practice. Indeed, some enterprises utilize the territorial basis for establishing several orders of derivative departments of the same type. The railroad companies are typical. Large-scale firms subdivide sales or other operations into regions, and these are successively subdepartmented into such derivative forms as divisions, districts, and sections or branches. Or a region may be subdivided into state, county, and township derivatives.

The span of management is an important factor in such practices. The grouping of activities on an area basis may mean establishing a thousand districts, the managers of which cannot report directly to the general sales manager. Since his span of management may be limited to eight or ten subordinates, he would have to have the thousand managers report to about a hundred superiors at the branch level, who would in turn report to ten or so regional managers. Three territorial *levels* within the sales department would thus be established.

Net Gain from Territorial Departmentation   The area basis of grouping activities has three fundamental advantages. First, there may be gains, even above immediate efficiency, to be achieved by catering to the good will of local people. Second, there may be lower cost of territorial operations, which may offset any increases in the cost of coordination and control at headquarters. Third, territorial departmentation provides numerous managerial positions at levels where the firm can afford to permit employees to gain experience. Many minor supervisory positions are also available when other bases of departmentation are chosen, but few give the breadth of experience a branch or district manager receives.

DEPARTMENTATION BY PRODUCT

The grouping of activities on the basis of product or product lines is steadily growing in importance in multiline larger-scale enterprises. It is an evolutionary process. Typically, the enterprises adopting this form were originally organized functionally. With the growth of the firm, production managers, sales and service managers, and engineering executives encountered a growing inflexibility. The managerial job became intolerably complex and the span of management limited their ability to increase the number of immediate subordinate managers. At this point, reorganization on a divisional basis was indicated. This strategy permits top management to delegate a division executive extensive authority over the manufacturing, sales, service, and engineering functions that relate to a given product or product line. It matters not whether the plant is located near the head office or far away so long as it is organized around a product and not a territory.

Advantages   Product or product line is an important basis for departmentation because it facilitates the employment of specialized capital, makes easier a certain type of coordination, and permits the maximum use of personal skills and specialized knowledge. For instance, the sales effort of a particular man may be most effective when confined to lubricants, or conveyors, or power plants, each of which is best sold by the expert thoroughly familiar with his product. Where the potential volume of business is high enough to employ fully such a salesman, the advantages of product departmentation are significant.

This basis of grouping activities also permits, although not exclusively, the employment of specialized capital goods. If production of an item, or closely related items, is sufficiently large to employ specialized facilities fully, strong pressure will be felt for product departmentation, in order to realize economic advantages in manufacturing, assembly, or handling.

If it is important for activities relating to a particular product to be coordinated, then product departmentation may be preferred. Better timing and customer service can thus sometimes be provided. If sales and engineering effort also emanates from the plan, cooperation with production can be exceptionally good. Other factors that may reduce this advantage will be considered presently.

There is a managerial advantage that can be very important. In an attempt to gain the economic advantages of specialization, engineers, for instance, are frequently divided into departments devoted to pure research, design, and application (sometimes called production engineering). These men, however, may be very narrow in their viewpoints, and their supervisor may be equally narrow, with little appreciation of the problems in other sections. Many firms, therefore, organize in terms of projects (a type of product departmentation), wherein all types of engineering skills are required. Similarly, in department-store operations, activities can be rearranged so that the section manager, rather than being confined to supervising sales of one or a few related items, will be also responsible for buying, credit, selection of personnel, and other functions, all the activities necessary to work on a given "project."

Finally, profit responsibility can be exacted from product department managers. Where they supervise the sales, production, engineering, service, and cost functions, they may be required to achieve predetermined profit goals. They share the responsibility of producing a profit along with other similarly organized groups and thus enable a general manager to evaluate intelligently the contribution of each product line to total profit.

Employment in Functional Areas The product basis for grouping activities has proved successful in all functional areas except industrial relations and finance. In the former, where the enterprise must deal with a single national union, and especially with its national officers, it is usually essential that administration be centralized. This permits the employment of skilled managers to negotiate with unions and to make authoritative interpretations of the agreement. The centralization of authority over finance enables top managers to economize in the use of a very scarce resource, and, by this means, hold the enterprise together.

All other functions can be successfully organized on a product basis. Such a well-known grouping as Buick, Cadillac, Chevrolet, and other divisions of General Motors rests upon the product basis. The buyers who report to the merchandise manager of a department store are known by their product lines. Hospitals departmentize on the basis of such services as surgery and radiology, and relief organizations include such "product" departments as food, clothing, shelter, and medical care.

Sales managers of enterprises that manufacture numerous items group them on the basis of their similarity. Wholesalers do the same thing. Examples: a linen department; a period-furniture grouping; an electronics department, including condensers, contacts, switches, tubes, and similar items. This departmental structure permits the salesmen to gain a broad and deep product knowledge. A commercial bank, too, is quite likely to subdivide its loan activities into commercial, industrial, and personal loans, and its investment activities into securities, real estate, and trusts.

Derivatives Regardless of the level at which the first product department is located within the organization structure—a problem that will be considered later—it is not uncommon to continue subdepartmentation at least one step further on the same basis. When the first derivative is concerned with a plural product, two or more second-derivative product departments may be expected, and from that point the manager will subdepartmentize on a functional, territorial, customer, or other basis. For instance, in the sales department illustrated in Table 9 the manager of the processed food section will normally find it desirable to subdepartmentize on a product basis, thus

TABLE 9   DERIVATIVE PRODUCT DEPARTMENTS OF TYPICAL ORGANIZATION STRUCTURES

Primary product department	Derivative product departments
A meat packer (production department)	
Dairy and poultry	Butter, cheese, hatcheries, ice cream, eggs, poultry, dried milk
Beef, lamb, and veal	Calf buying, cattle buying, lamb buying, hides and skins, wool
Branch-house provision (functional department)	Casing, hog buying
By-products	Hides and fats, cleanser, gelatin, glue, industrial oils, soap and glycerine, tallow
Plant food	Insecticides and fungicides, phosphate rock
Agricultural research	Canned foods, margarine, table-ready meats, vegetable oil, dog and cat food
A container manufacturer (sales department)	
Food industries	Processed food, prepared food, coffee, dairy
Drug and chemical	Pharmaceutical and proprietary, household and chemical, prescription
Closure and plastics	
Beverage industries	Beverage, brewery, liquor
An insurance company (finance department)	
Investment (a functional derivative)	Mortgages, private placements, public utility, transportation, industrial, government

developing second-derivative product groups. A comparable move is unlikely in the dried milk derivative of the dairy or the poultry department of the meat packer.

Limitations This method of grouping activities encounters certain difficulties in coordination and may lead to instability of the organization structure. Where the production department is organized in this way, there is a strong tendency to force a similar grouping in sales, buying, shipping, accounting, and credit control, since it is difficult otherwise to synchronize these activities with those of production. This often provides ambitious production managers with a good argument for having all related activities transferred to them. They would thus gain in power to the point where they might rival the president. Firms like General Motors, which have transferred such power to division heads, have also introduced safeguards in the form of a general staff and centralization of finance and major policy determination.

CUSTOMER DEPARTMENTATION

The grouping of activities to reflect a paramount interest in the customer is commonly found in a variety of types of enterprises. The customer is the key to the way activities are grouped when the things an enterprise does for him are managed by one department head. The industrial sales department of a wholesaler who also sells to retailers is a case in point.

There are close decisions to be made in separating some types of customer departments from product departments. For instance, in the great central cash markets for agricultural products, the loan officers of commercial banks frequently specialize in fruit, vegetables, and grain, and even to such a point that they will make loans only on wheat or oranges. This is a clear case of customer departmentation, because loan service is provided by type of customer. On the other hand, a grouping such as sales, manufacturing, engineering, and cost accounting, all of which are concerned with serving a single customer type, such as public utilities, would likely be called functional departmentation even though the special customer is identifiable.

Extent of Use Customer departmentation is utilized in many types of enterprises. Businessmen frequently arrange activities on this basis to cater to the requirements of clearly defined customer groups; and educational institutions offer regular and extension courses to serve different groups of students.

Reasons for Use The special and widely varied needs of customers for clearly defined service impel suppliers to departmentize on this basis. The manufacturer who sells to both wholesalers and industrial buyers frequently finds that the needs of the two outlets can best be met by specialized salesmen. The wholesaler requires a product of dependable quality, available on a continuous reorder basis, and suited to the ultimate consumer. The industrial buyer wants a product that will save money, which frequently calls for high quality, plus a service that includes survey of needs, installation and repair of the product, and the specific training of employees.

Producers sometimes can best cultivate sales when customers are classified on such bases as age, sex, or income. Department-store operators departmentize into such groupings as children's, women's, and men's shoes; and they have bargain basements to appeal to low-income customers.

Nonbusiness groups follow similar practices. The extension work of universities is arranged, with respect to time, subject matter, and sometimes instructors, to appeal to an entirely different group of students from those who attend on a full-time day basis. The operations of a Community Chest drive are arranged on the basis of different "customer" classifications. And departments of the Federal government are set up to care particularly for farmers, businessmen, industrial workers, old people, and others.

Employment in Functional Departments   Customer departmentation is often found to be useful for grouping the sales activity of those who cater to different classes of customers. For instance, it is not unusual for a manufacturer with only an industrial market to divide his customers into large and small accounts. On the other hand, manufacturers may not develop derivative customer departments in their production function. A manufacturer of typewriters does not specialize his production facilities in terms of university students and insurance-company customers. Even when separating the manufacture of standard and electric typewriters, the resulting departmentation is on a product and not on a customer basis.

Independent wholesalers and retailers combine their sales and production functions and then subdepartmentize them according to product. Sometimes, however, they organize customer departments. For instance, department stores often carry similar merchandise in the bargain basement and on an upper floor, organizing the two departments under two buyers. This is customer departmentation, since it assumes that different income groups patronize the two areas. Wholesalers such as mill-supply houses often organize their buying-selling activities under two specialized buyers who cater to the needs of industrial customers and retail stores, respectively.

The finance departments of manufacturers, wholesalers, and retailers have no need for customer departmentation, since they are operated with a view to the welfare of the enterprise rather than to the needs of customers.

Derivative Customer Departments   As in the case of product departmentation, there are no derivatives of customer departments unless the original classification combines two or more customer groups. There may be a need for subdepartmentizing a plural classification into further customer refinements, but the limited customer department is most likely to be subdepartmentized on a functional basis.

Disadvantages   Customer departmentation is not enjoyed without certain drawbacks. There is, for instance, the difficulty of coordination between this type of department and those organized on other bases, with constant pressure from the managers of customer departments for special treatment.

Another disadvantage is the possibility of underemployment of facilities and manpower specialized in terms of customer groups. In periods of recession some customer groups may all but disappear, for example, machine-tool manufacturers; in periods of expansion the unequal development of customer groups is characteristic.

⑦ *Marketing Channels*

⑧ PROCESS OR EQUIPMENT DEPARTMENTATION

The grouping of enterprise activities about a process or a type of equipment is often employed by manufacturing establishments, especially at the lowest levels of organization. Such a basis of departmentation is illustrated in a paint or electrolytic-process grouping or in the arrangement in one plant area of punch presses or automatic screw machines. Manpower and materials are brought together in such a department in order to carry out a particular operation.

The purpose of such departmentation is to achieve economic advantages, although it may also be required by the nature of the equipment involved. For instance, the electrolytic process requires heavy specialized capital, since it is not possible to utilize economically small units of this apparatus. In the case of equipment departments such an arrangement is purely a matter of economy and convenience. The machines themselves may be placed with respect to other equipment in such a way that a series of operations on material is feasible. But where there is a large volume of single (or a few) operations to be performed on material, which then may be sent to stockroom or sold to customers, specialized supervision and full employment of setup men and operators offer definite economies.

⑨ *Temporariness*

EVALUATION OF ALTERNATIVES IN SELECTING DEPARTMENTATION

Departmentation is not an end in itself but is simply a method of arranging activities to facilitate the accomplishment of the enterprise objective. It is not even an unmixed good, for the separation of activities on any basis creates problems of coordination difficult to solve. Each method has its advantages and disadvantages. Consequently, the process of selection involves a consideration of the relative advantages of each type at each level in the organization structure. In all cases the *central question* concerns the type of coordination that the manager wishes to achieve.

Primary Departmentation At the primary level the claims of the functional basis of departmentation are especially strong. This method most closely conforms to the activities of every enterprise, and it permits the coordination by one person of each of the basic functions. With all production activity under one person, sales under someone else, and finance under another, the chief general officer can concentrate on the coordination of staff and service departments with functional areas without being himself involved in the internal affairs of production, sales, and finance.

Many enterprises, for a number of reasons, have established primary departmentation on some other basis. There may have been pressure from a powerful product department head, or some special reason for developing a market in a particular customer classification; again, such organization may be temporary, pending the discovery and development of a good functional manager. Exceptions to the general practice are usually difficult to justify except in multiproduct firms or enterprises selling or servicing widespread geographic areas; even here, coordination along functional lines is often provided for by staff executives. On the other hand, there should be no hesitancy in employing any basis if a legitimate case can be made for it.

Although there may be occasions when functional sales and production departments will not be organized at the primary level, there are almost never circumstances that justify a similar abandonment of the functional finance department. Indeed, the finance division occupies a unique place in enterprise. As a function, finance must be represented at the primary level, because the corporate handling of and accounting for funds must be coincident with the general management of the corporation as a whole. This is not to say that all financial and accounting *activities* must be carried on in a functional finance department reporting at a primary level, but rather that there must be such a central function summarizing and controlling the accounting for those activities on an over-all corporate basis.

Intermediate Departmentation   Intermediate departmentation includes all the grouped activities that appear in the organization structure between the primary departments at the top and the departments at the bottom of the hierarchy. It is in the choice of bases for departmentation at such levels that managers find decision making most difficult. There are no general rules. It is certain, however, that below the primary functional departmentation the claims of most of the other methods of grouping activities become more insistent. And it is probable that at secondary and lower levels these claims may best be satisfied.

In the production function the claims of product departmentation exert heavy pressure at the secondary level whenever there is marked diversity of product or of product lines or a geographic dispersion of operations. The functional production manager of a firm manufacturing various electronic items normally will establish product-line departments. But if only condensers were made, no product departmentation would take place. Consideration might then be given to the claims for territorial departmentation at the secondary level.

Sometimes it is possible to secure advantages of two or more methods at the same level, as when the establishment of a secondary-level product department permits a firm to locate the plant where it can also reap the economies of territorial departmentation.

The functional sales manager is faced with strong claims of territorial departments at the secondary level. This is true even of firms that narrowly confine their distribution. City department stores open branches to serve suburban territories; salesmen's territories are commonly established even within cities. Where the product basis has strong appeal, the coordination of activities is greatly facilitated if this departmentation is organized at the secondary level. Similarly, customer departmentation usually occurs at the secondary level if at all.

There is no virtue in attempting to maintain a mechanical similarity in choosing the bases of departmentation. Although strong claims of functional departmentation may result in functional grouping at the primary level, the secondary level in a sales department may be composed of a territorial or customer grouping, the production department may have a product classification, and the finance department may utilize derivative functional groupings. It is on the ground of net advantage to the functional department executive, not that of parallelism, that the basis is selected.

MIXING DEPARTMENTATION

In the evaluation of the alternative methods of departmentation it was made clear that each method yields certain gains which are reduced by difficulties in coordinating different departments, and that the achievement of parallelism in the intermediate departmentation of the functional divisions is not a proper organizational objective.

Another point to be highlighted concerns the mixing of departmentation within a functional area. For instance, a wholesale drug firm has grouped the buying and selling activities relating to beverages in one product department but has grouped, on the same level, all other selling activities on a territorial basis. A manufacturer of plastic goods has territorialized both the production and sale of all of its products except dinnerware, which is a product department. A functional department manager may, in other words, employ two or more bases for grouping activities on the same organizational levels. Such practices may be justified on logical grounds, because the objective of departmentation is not to build a rigid structure, balanced in terms of levels and characterized by consistency and identical bases. The purpose is to group activities in the manner which will best contribute to achieving the enterprise objective. If variety of bases does this, there is no reason why any manager should not take advantage of the alternatives before him.

The logic of this view is frequently ignored by the heads of organization service or staff departments in large-scale enterprises whether of a public or a private nature. For some reason, possibly aesthetics or control, it is insisted that all departmentized activities below the primary level of organization be grouped in exactly the same manner. For instance, the organization structure of the Internal Revenue Service at the regional and district levels is exactly the same despite tremendous variation in district sizes. Firms with multi-plants organize them in the same way; thus, the same departments will be found in virtually all stores of Sears, Roebuck and Company.

The aesthetic reason for identical organization structure of similar enterprise groupings is really not at all persuasive. The organization planner may think it "looks better," but this is clearly a poor reason for organizing in a particular way. The control reason, however, is quite different. There may be very important reasons for comparing the operation of similarly organized plants, stores, and agencies. They all may be comparable profit centers; their managers can be more readily compared within this organization structure. Even though these, and others, are important arguments for similarity of organization structure, it must be remembered that no one organizes to control; he organizes to produce efficiently and effectively. If the latter purpose is sacrificed for the former, the cost of control is too great to bear.

The Principle of Division of Work   The mixing of departmentation in practice is, then, merely a reflection of the operation of the principle of division of work. Originally noted by Fayol as the first of his fourteen principles of management,[3] his principle might be stated as follows: the more an organization structure reflects the economic division of work in an enterprise through grouping of activities in departmental form, the more efficiently and effectively it will tend to aid performance contributing to enterprise objectives. It concerns what has been called the primary step in organization, the determination and establishment of "the smallest number of dissimilar functions into which the work of an institution may be divided."[4] As Fayol indicated, this is the principle of specialization; it is the "division of work to produce more and better work with the same effort."[5]

It should be emphasized that division of work—in the sense of occupational specialization—is an *economic* principle and *not* a management principle. In other words, it has been found in many cases that when work is specialized, people learn the task more easily and perform it more efficiently. It may well be that in many cases work has been over-specialized, with resultant loss of both motivation and a sense of accomplishment. Job enlargement may often be a highly desirable thing. But the organization designer is given certain economies and other conditions. Given these, his primary task is to design a structure of roles which will help individuals contribute to objectives. Not that he should remain silent if he feels that other con-

---

[3] Henri Fayol, *General and Industrial Administration* (New York: Pitman Publishing Corporation, 1949), p. 20. It should be pointed out that the authors' list of principles of organization vary from those of Fayol. A number of them are essentially the same, such as Fayol's principles of division of work, authority and responsibility, unity of command, unity of direction, centralization (balance), and scalar chain. Other Fayol principles apply to such managerial functions as direction. Still other principles expressed by Fayol, such as equity, initiative, and *esprit de corps*, seem to refer only to problems of leadership or characteristics of planning, control, or direction and are therefore not included in the authors' list.

[4] H. A. Hopf, *Organization, Executive Capacity, and Progress* (Ossining, N.Y.: Hopf Institute of Management, 1945), p. 4.

[5] Fayol, *op. cit.*, p. 20.

siderations, such as occupational specialization, force an unworkable organization structure from the point of manning it. But the *management organization* principle of division of work implies that: Given a system of tasks or activities required economically to attain enterprise goals, the better an organization structure reflects a classification of these tasks and assists in their coordination through creating a system of interrelated roles, and the more these roles are designed to fit the capabilities and motivations of people available to fill them, the more effective and efficient it will be.

FOR DISCUSSION

1. Sociologists tell us that organization is a social invention. What do you think they mean? Do they imply that there is a "right" and "wrong" way to organize? What test would you prefer?

2. Some managers feel that a firm should not "mix up" its basic departmental forms. Would you agree with them? What is your opinion of an organizational philosophy of requiring all activities to be organized in the same manner?

3. Some managers are not satisfied with the alternatives they have in basic departmentation. Propose some additional ideas for them to consider.

4. Take as an example the organization of a typical engineering or research and development department. How is it organized? Why?

SELECTED REFERENCES

Allen, L. A.: *Management and Organization,* chaps. 4–5, New York: McGraw-Hill Book Company, 1958.

Davis, R. C.: *The Fundamentals of Top Management,* chap. 10, New York: Harper & Row, Publishers, Incorporated, 1951.

Gulick, L., and L. Urwick (eds.): *Papers on the Science of Administration,* chaps. 1–2, New York: Institute of Public Administration, 1937.

Holden, P. E., L. S. Fish, and H. L. Smith: *Top-management Organization and Control,* part B, secs. 1, 2, New York: McGraw-Hill Book Company, 1951.

Knudson, H. R., Jr.: "Enter the Personnel Generalist," *Personnel,* vol. 37, no. 2 (March–April, 1960).

McNulty, J. E.: "Organizational Change in Growing Enterprises," *Administrative Science Quarterly,* vol. 7, no. 1, pp. 1–21 (June, 1962).

Newman, W. H.: *Administrative Action,* chaps. 8, 16, 17, Englewood Cliffs, N.J.: Prentice-Hall, Inc., 1951.

Petersen, E., and E. G. Plowman: *Business Organization and Management,* 3d ed., chap. 8, Homewood, Ill.: Richard D. Irwin, Inc., 1953.

Sorrell, L. C.: "Organization of Transportation and Traffic Activities," *Traffic World,* vol. 46, nos. 24–26; vol. 47, nos. 2, 4 (1930–1931).

"Splitting a Company Lets It Move Faster," *Business Week* (Apr. 6, 1957).

Stieglitz, H.: *Corporate Organization Structures,* Studies in Business Policy No. 183, New York: National Industrial Conference Board, 1961.

Thompson, V. A.: *Modern Organization,* chap. 3, New York: Alfred A. Knopf, Inc., 1961.

Tosi, H., and H. Patt: "Administrative Ratios and Organizational Size,' *Academy of Management Journal,* vol. 10, no. 2, pp. 161–168 (June, 1967).

the assignment of activities

In the preceding chapter two subjects were considered in some detail: the alternative methods of grouping activities and the factors influencing a manager's decision to utilize one or more of these alternatives. But the type of departmentation is only part of the problem, for, regardless of the types that exist in an organization structure, the manager must still decide where to assign a new activity or where to shift an old one. The principles of basic departmentation do not answer such questions as whether customer claims, traffic, shipping, or warehousing should be assigned to a functional department or to a customer, territorial, or product department.

THREE ISSUES IN ASSIGNING ACTIVITIES

There are three fundamental issues involved in assigning activities to a particular department.[1] First is the need to recognize and identify an activity in order to place it in its proper niche. But how is this done? A method of analysis is required.

Recognition of Activities   One approach is to view the enterprise in terms of employee skills. This would result in a count of the people having an identifiable skill, for example, thirteen chemists, eleven process engineers, or thirty typists.

Since the issue involves the assignment of activities, it is best to analyze directly what people do. An activity may be defined in terms of what people

---

[1] The original systematic examination of the issues involved in assigning activities was made by the late L. C. Sorrell, "Organization of Transportation and Traffic Activities," *Traffic World*, vol. 46, nos. 24–25 (November–December, 1930). The authors have followed Dr. Sorrell's approach.

do that is essential to the realization of the enterprise objective. There are three levels from which such action may be viewed. The first concerns an analysis of enterprise activity in terms of its basic functions, such as production, sales, and finance. The second is concerned with what the people in the enterprise are doing. For instance, if they were asked, the answers would be "adjusting claims," "receiving and shipping," "buying supplies," "operating a truck," "copy writing," and so forth. The third level is the job-analysis approach, wherein the important question is: What do you do when you carry on your job?

The assignment of activities is concerned with the second level. To know what functions to recognize, one may proceed along inductive lines, observing what people are doing in a large number of instances and classifying the results under such headings as calling on customers, delivering orders, negotiating with finance houses, buying raw materials, or assembling parts. On the basis of the generality of such activities, one may conclude that these are the proper functions to recognize.

But the investigator may also start with an exact definition of the enterprise purpose and deduce that its realization depends upon the creation of utility in goods or services and the exchange of the latter for purchasing power. He can then enumerate the activities that make a net positive contribution to the production, sales, and finance functions. For instance, in the case of the production of goods or services, the derivative activities logically fall under such heads as acquiring the factors of production, production control, and the manufacturing operation. Each of these may in turn be analyzed in the same way. The deductive method has two important virtues: it provides a classification system that omits nothing, and it guards against the inclusion of activities unrelated to the enterprise purpose. But a total reliance need not be placed upon it; conclusions reached by this procedure should always be checked against direct observation.

The second procedure is considerably superior to the first. It can be applied to the organization problems of a new enterprise and will prove useful for the firm already organized, whether the purpose is an audit of the enterprise structure or the determination of the need for a proposed activity.

Need for Combining Activities   The second issue in the problem of assigning activities involves the necessity for combining the activities recognized. As was seen in Chapter 13, the coordination of numerous activities can best be achieved by grouping them into basic and derivative departments.

Need for Guides   The third issue in the problem of assigning activities, and the one with which the following material is concerned, involves the considerations in response to which activities are combined. It is one thing to recognize the activity of receiving shipments; it is quite another to know where to locate it in the departmental structure. The guides useful in this respect relate to similar activities and intimate association of activities.

ASSIGNMENT BY SIMILARITY OF ACTIVITY

The practice of grouping together similar activities is both apparent and logical. Its wide usage emphasizes the need for understanding its advantages and the bases upon which it rests.

Basis for Recognizing Similarity The search for a basis of classifying activities that leads to the association of those which are similar eventually brings the organizer to the skills of people. At first, he may be persuaded that the important element is the object to which labor is applied. But that which results from labor depends upon the skills applied to it. After determining what needs to be done and what skills are required, the organizer can then group them under such heads as typing, chemical analysis, process engineering, and accounting. In this way people who perform similar activities can be grouped in one department, and the advantages of occupational specialization realized.

Several illustrations of this procedure may be cited. Research engineers, salesmen, file clerks, and machine schedulers are commonly grouped in the research and development department, sales department, general office, and production control department, respectively. Sometimes it is also convenient to group together people who operate similar equipment or who undertake the assembly of a product.

Business, the defense forces, public-works projects, universities, churches, and charitable enterprises all find in similarity of activity or skill a convenient method of combining some of their activities. However, the fact that similar activities are not always combined suggests that there are some limitations in practice.

Activities Not Assigned by Similarity Similarity as a basis for combining activities is used most frequently at the lower levels of the organization structure—the levels of punch press operators, salesmen, janitors, and clerks, whose activities are routine and very limited compared to the widely varied ones of a major department head. Many firms, however, get along without a general office, and typists and file clerks are assigned separately to the several departments. Process engineers work best not grouped together but assigned to production departments. Even the vanishing common laborer is not ordinarily part of a group but is assigned to work with people who have different activities. Thus, diversity as well as similarity is a factor in grouping activities.

GUIDES FOR ASSIGNMENT BY INTIMATE ASSOCIATION

The association of activities merely on the ground that they are diverse would, of course, be foolish. The diversity must be of a particular kind, and there must be very good reasons for using it as a basis for grouping. Such reasons are found in the guides for assignment by intimate association, which occurs when diverse activities are so closely related in the achievement of departmental purposes that they are carried out most effectively when grouped in the same organizational unit.

Most Use This guide suggests that an activity for which a manager has the most use should normally be assigned to him. Such functions as traffic, engineering, and shipping are often located in either the sales or production departments. In manufacturing establishments, the traffic function, which includes such activities as the purchase of transportation services, the use of equipment for transporting materials to the plant, in-plant movement of materials, and warehousing, is often assigned to the production manager. Since his department uses traffic services much more than do others, he would endeavor to manage them efficiently. Other departments are not thereby deprived of the service, for the production manager can operate it for the benefit of all departments.

The assignment of engineering may also be determined in accordance with the principle of most use, depending upon the particular emphasis a firm gives to this activity. Where the basic need is to fit a product to customer requirements, there is strong pressure to assign engineering to the sales department. But where the engineering problems are most closely associated with production, they may be assigned to that department.

Shipping may be similarly assigned. Perhaps the sales department is most sensitive to the efficiency of the shipping department. Meeting delivery dates, rush handling, and carrying out packing and handling instructions so that the products arrive in good condition are important in the sale of commodities. When, on the other hand, the product is made to customer specification, is destined for industrial users, or is largely undifferentiated, shipping may be assigned to the production department. Firms that manufacture heavy equipment, refine oil, or produce lumber look upon shipping as a natural extension of the manufacturing process.

Executive Interest An activity may be assigned to a particular manager if he is especially interested in it and has the capacity to direct it intelligently. In the early stages of growth, business firms often operate without directly undertaking certain ancillary activities, either paying no attention to marketing research, product planning, economic forecasting, budgetary control, and similar activities or else employing outside consultants to handle them. As the firm grows, becomes more conscious of its future, and faces competitors alert to innovation and technological developments, influential managers may be expected to urge that these activities be undertaken by full-time specialists. Such an activity frequently will be assigned to the manager chiefly interested in promoting it.

Or again, there may be a recognized need for marketing research. The sales manager may not know what such an activity can do for him, or his limited knowledge of research might make it difficult for him to manage the activity efficiently. The president could then attach the activity to one of his own staff groups. Such an action is contrary to the guide of "most use," but it is probably better than either neglecting the activity or changing sales managers.

In many manufacturing and service enterprises, real estate activities are assigned to the general counsel's office. A large manufacturing company may have many real estate leases and a fair number of real estate sales and purchases. These are often not important enough to justify establishing a separate functional department nor do they logically belong in any existing department. The problem is solved by assigning them to that executive who has an interest in them—most likely, because of the extensive legal and contractual work involved, the chief legal officer.

Competition Often a desired activity does not flourish because various executives fear it, because its possibilities are not recognized, or because it fails to receive vigorous direction. The cure for a wilting activity is sometimes the application of the guide of competition. For instance, American universities attempted, in the early 1920s, to meet the growing demand for business instruction by offering a few courses such as corporation finance, marketing, and accounting in the department of economics. Since there were few economists with much interest in or knowledge of the subject matter, there was definite hostility in their departments against such instruction. The insistent demand was met by splitting off the business from the economics courses and establishing a competitive department. Since then, departments of business administration have achieved equal stature and have surpassed the parent department in numbers of students, facilities, and budgets.

It is still quite a common practice for business firms to direct almost their entire attention to the domestic market, although inquiries from foreign sources are answered and unsolicited orders may be shipped. Often, when foreign interest persists, a clerk is placed in charge of the activity, but he has no voice, no influence with the sales manager or even the packing engineer, and very little budget. Then there comes a time when foreign sales are regarded as important. It may then be decided that sales abroad require the attention of a separate manager, free to fight for a larger budget, for favorable attention from the production department, and for respect in the shipping department—in other words, someone placed on a parity with the manager of domestic sales and expected to compete with him in contributing to the profitable operation of the total enterprise.

Encouraging competition between departments, divisions, and other units enables the firm to make comparisons that greatly aid in control. For instance, in the above example, similar measures of efficiency can be applied to the domestic and foreign sales departments. From such records as costs of sales, gross profit per net sales dollar, and sales per dollar of effort, the president is able to compare the relative efficiency of the two managers.

Suppressed Competition As its title implies, this guide is the exact reverse of the one that encourages competition, and, naturally, applicable under a different set of conditions. As the advantages to be reaped from competition become fully realized, the president of the firm may feel a growing need for greater coordination between two functions, for more cooperation and less competition. To achieve this, he need only change the place in the organization structure where the two activities are coordinated.

For instance, in the example of the starved foreign sales department, the cure was found by having both the domestic and the foreign sales managers report directly to the president. This worked out so well that no further discriminatory practices were evident. At this point, the guide of suppressed competition becomes applicable. The two sales departments are now reorganized on a functional rather than a territorial basis. To this end, the heads of each sales department report to a new officer, a vice-president in charge of marketing, who would report to the president, with the result that coordination is now achieved on the level of the marketing executive rather than on that of the president.

Policy Control Policies, which are guides to thinking in managerial decision making may be variously interpreted. General intentions—such as to compete on a price basis, not to advertise on Sunday, or never to sue a customer—rarely encounter differences of managerial opinion, but other policies, such as those relating to credit, customer claims, and returned goods, may suffer from a lack of clear specifications, permitting variations in interpretation. In such instances, it might be important that the policy be enforced by that manager who would best reflect the intention of the group that originally adoped it.

The customer claims activity of department stores, for example, is generally recognized as necessary and important. The typical policy relating to this activity is one of fairness to the store and to the customer. But the very vagueness of what fair dealing is makes possible sincere but widely different attitudes. The manager makes the decision. If customer claims are assigned to the merchandising manager, his interpretations may favor the customers because of his desire to keep their good will and continued patronage; furthermore, he is in a position to shift any blame for the cost of the activity to department buyers. If the activity is placed in the several departments, however, the buyers will be torn between pleasing the customer and taking the blame for buying the unsatisfactory product in the first place, and there may be as many interpretations of policy as there are buyers. The accounting department, finally, might administer the activity on a coldly factual basis that would alienate both customers and department buyers. All these alternatives have been tried in independent department-store operations. Since each might endanger the original policy, it is a growing practice to assign the activity to the general superintendent, the official in charge of the store building, receiving and delivery, warehousing, and safety. Store executives feel that this manager is in the best position to execute the claims policy in the way it was originally designed.

The administration of credit policy also causes considerable difficulty because of the impossibility of establishing objective rules for time purchases. Credit managers rightly insist that every such rule needs to be interpreted on an individual basis. But to whom should a credit manager report? A sales manager would prefer a liberal interpretation in order to facilitate selling. A production manager would obviously have no particular interest or skill in directing the credit activity. It is likewise beyond the proper scope of accounting. Credit really belongs in the treasurer's department because of its vital effect upon working capital and the financial safety of the enterprise.

Another illustration concerns the proper assignment of claims in a railroad enterprise. The fact that this activity has been variously assigned to the traffic, operating, accounting, and legal departments is evidence, not only of experimentation, but also of competition between these department managers to secure jurisdiction in the matter. The head of the traffic department may argue that the way in which claims are handled affects the good will of patrons and that claims should therefore be assigned to him. The operating manager may ask for the activity on the ground that his department is responsible for claims arising in the first place. But the operating department may be too severe with patrons who have damage claims, an attitude that would adversely affect good will. The legal department manager, finally, may declare that liberal settlements are one way of giving a rebate, possibly unlawfully, and that he should have jurisdiction. This battle usually has been settled in favor of the legal department, a development that might suggest that railway presidents are more afraid of going to jail than of losing business.

The important point is that activities be assigned to that manager who will interpret policy in a way satisfactory to those drafting it. It is their *intention* which needs to be reflected in policy applications. So important are the virtues of accuracy and consistency that policy control often can be vital to enterprise welfare.

Lack of a Clean Break Sometimes difficulties are encountered in assigning activities that would logically be placed in separate departments but are, for some conflicting practical reason, best undertaken together. In a sense, this is a perennial problem that arises the moment an enterprise is organized. Although the one-man operation is particularly efficient for coordination of activities and this effectiveness may continue so long as activities can be broadly grouped into functional classifications, the organizer always runs into some difficult problems in assigning activities that normally would be located in separate divisions but are yet managed best by a single official.

Students of independent department-store operations are frequently surprised to learn that a department manager, called the buyer, is responsible for *both* purchasing and selling merchandise. The assignment of both activities to the buyer results from the close relationship of sales volume to what is bought for resale, and when one manager is assigned both activities, it is easy to fix responsibility for results. On the other hand, chain department-store operations separate the two, partly because the chain enterprise is not engaged in fashion merchandising and because it soon runs into the limitations of the span of management.

The assignment of the traffic activity in a manufacturing establishment also illustrates the lack of a clean break. Whereas the production department is interested in receiving and on-plant transport, the sales department insists upon prompt shipments to customers. In the interests of economy, both departments may use the same equipment. The organizer faces the choice of assigning the activity to production or to sales or to a separate traffic department. In practice, all three solutions are used, with the first and last alternatives the more successful. But success is due, not to whichever department is selected, but rather to the fact that divided control is not permitted.

These illustrations emphasize the fact that arbitrary decisions to divide control of an activity may be impractical, resulting in unworkable assignments of parts of functions to several managers. If for any reason the activities in question refuse to break clean, even though their nature may make it appear logical to do so, the appropriate guide is to avoid forceful separation.

Coordination at a Given Point   The coordination of enterprise activities involves two factors: the activities must be properly timed, and the effort placed behind each activity must be integrated with the other. Thus, if advertising effort is to be coordinated with personal selling, it must be timed to help the salesmen most; and the effort placed behind both advertising and selling should be integrated so that the marginal expenditure upon each will produce the same volume of sales.

The coordination guide involves the question of where, *in the organization structure,* given activities should be integrated. If everyone in a firm reports to the president, it is clear that all coordination takes place at his level. If the managers of sales, advertising, sales promotion, and research report to the chief marketing executive, all selling activities will be coordinated at the first level of the organization structure. The old-fashioned foreman used to coordinate production, hiring, promotion, wage determination, firing, and maintenance; such activities are now coordinated at the level of the production executive. In American railroad organization, operation and traffic functions are normally coordinated by the president, while the British combine these functions under the managers responsible for freight and passenger departments.

The organization structure, therefore, plays an important part in achieving coordination of activities. Once the organizer decides where coordination of a particular function is to be achieved, there is no trouble in modifying the organization structure accordingly. But the reasons for deciding that coordination should take place at a particular point are another matter entirely. They may be found in the personal idiosyncrasies of the executives; in social demands for speed, convenience, or taste; in a desire to exact a particular kind of responsibility from a given manager; or in the determination to make a new policy work. Whatever the reason, the coordination guide will dictate the method of assigning activities to give the desired results.

However, since all organization has an objective of coordination, the coordination guide to assignment by intimate association must be carefully distinguished. It involves the grouping of activities in such a way as to obtain coordination at a *point* in the organization structure where such coordination would not otherwise exist.

Separation   The successful operation of enterprises of all types requires that certain activities be undertaken purely as a check upon the effectiveness and propriety with which functions are carried out. It is not desirable to assign them on the basis of most interest, lest the very purpose of their creation be jeopardized. They must rather be carried out by a manager independent of the executive whose work is being evaluated.

Manufacturing firms, for example, commonly provide for the quality control of purchased materials and goods in various stages of production, in order to see that those who are responsible for purchasing and manufacturing are meeting quality specifications. This activity could clearly be subverted if its personnel were responsible to the purchasing agent or the plant superintendent.

Similar issues are involved in the employment of an outside auditor and in the separation of accounting from the finance function. The certification of financial records could hardly be made by a subordinate in the treasurer's department. And since accounting activities are useful checks upon the treasurer, who controls the enterprise funds, they could serve no such purpose if the chief accountant reported to the treasurer, or vice versa.

The principle of separation—that, if an activity is designed as a check on another activity, the individual charged with such activity cannot adequately discharge his responsibility if he reports to the department whose activity he is expected to evaluate—is a valuable and invariable rule. The organizer is on firm ground when he applies this principle, both when a new activity is created and when he carries out his examination of the organization structure.

Functional Interest   Functional interest,[2] although it does not have the general applicability of other guides, is efficient in grouping activities that are closely related in terms of purpose. For instance, a publicity manager may have such functions as institutional advertising and publicity assigned to

---

[2] Related in some respects to this concept is the category of the "common objective," described in W. H. Newman, *Administrative Action* (Englewood Cliffs, N.J.: Prentice-Hall, Inc., 1951), p. 136.

him. These are functionally related because both concern the impact on the general public of the firm, its policies, practices, and personnel. This is important particularly to large-scale firms, all of whose outside communications should be consistent and in good taste. Practically all large firms, as a result, not only require that executives clear their speeches with the publicity department but often supply publicity personnel to write them.

APPLICATION OF THE GUIDES FOR ASSIGNMENT OF ACTIVITY

The application of the guides for assigning activities presents many problems to the organizer. They cannot be followed like directions for assembling a radio, because they present alternatives, the selection and use of which require good judgment. Nevertheless, a conscientious effort to follow the guides is part of good management practice, and many problems are simplified, if not eliminated, by this means.

Similarity and Intimate Association as Alternatives   Perhaps the first choice that the organizer faces is that between the similarity of activity and the intimate association guides. The advantage of grouping assignments by similarity of function lies in economy of supervision and equipment use. Assignment by intimate association, on the other hand, has the advantages of the task-force method of grouping different but closely related activities. Its employment is mandatory at the top echelon of the structure but becomes less of a necessity in middle and lower levels.

Evaluation of Guides   There is much to be said for the idea that if an objective is clearly understood, the selection of the way to achieve it is made easy.[3] This is particularly apropos in the organizing function, since the kind of coordination that activities receive depends largely upon where they are assigned.

   In allocating activities, the organizer experiences pressure from two directions. The external forces arise from the desire and even the insistence on the part of other managers to have certain functions assigned to a particular department. Their interest may derive from a wish to build empires, a conviction that the assignment they suggest is appropriate, or an ambition to head a new department. The internal pressures arise from the several guides themselves, each calling for recognition in particular circumstances. However, in many situations two or three guides may point to the same conclusion, a helpful factor lending assurance to the decisions made.

Conflict in Guides   One of the difficulties in applying the guides for assignment of activity is that some of them are in open conflict. This does not mean that any is wrong but that under some circumstances in the life and

---

[3] For an excellent discussion of this topic as applied to the traffic, shipping, and receiving activities, see L. C. Sorrell, *Traffic World*, vol. 47, nos. 6–8 (1931).

growth of enterprise some of the guides are clearly inappropriate. Small firms may have difficulty in using guides for similarity of activities, because they may not be able to realize fully the economies of specialization. No firm, moreover, could encourage and discourage competition at the same time for the same activity. Consequently, in the application of guides, the organizer must keep in mind the stage of growth and the size of the enterprise, on the one hand, and the purpose to be achieved, on the other.

Jurisdictional Disputes   All enterprises experience more or less disagreement among managers in connection with the assignment of certain activities. Few top managers have not been present at discussions about assigning engineering to production, credit to accounting, public relations to personnel, or receiving to purchasing. These and similar discussions consume hours of the time of expensive personnel, and, unfortunately, most of the discussion is futile, because it is not about the *right issues*. Circumstances of this nature open wide the door for aiding friends, hurting colleagues, or grabbing power.

The guides for assigning activity are sharp weapons to use in these controversies. Attention to them avoids overtones of personal bases for decision making and focuses attention upon both the main problem and the selection of the appropriate method to solve it. In such an atmosphere few jurisdictional disputes will be permitted to cause more than a ripple of concern. This does not mean that the nonlogical motivations of employees can be ignored. But it does mean that outlets for them need to be sought in directions that do not interfere with the essential wisdom of assigning an activity appropriately in the organization structure.

The Right to Change the Assignment of Activities   An assignment, once made, does not carry with it the sacrifice of all rights to make a subsequent change. In fact, just the opposite is true. The organizer makes the best assignment possible under the circumstances. He puts the allocation into effect with the view of letting it rest until future developments raise the question again. Enterprises, even the most static, are forever changing their emphasis, and consequently their organization structures are likely to burst at the seams unless pressure is relieved by reallocating activities. Assigned activities should be shifted in the manner dictated by purpose, time, and circumstance.

In view of these inevitable changes, it is important to realize that no person acquires a vested interest in any activity. First things come first. In an enterprise, first things are the objective to be realized and the activities that further its realization. If these activities can be furthered by a shift in the assignment of activities, managers are within their rights to undertake the change.

Quality of Organizational Activity   The degree to which the guides for assigning activity are appropriately applied at a given time is an index of the quality of organization. The correctness of the guide chosen and the good judgment with which it is applied inevitably lead to good organization structure. It is, unquestionably, a fruitful way to facilitate good management.

The logic of this situation points directly to the fact that audits of the organization structure may be made directly. The consultant need not waste time inferring the existence of structural defects by identifying the results thereof. He is in a position, as is any manager, to evaluate directly the skill with which the enterprise is structured, by referring to the application that was made of the guides for assignment.

FOR DISCUSSION

1. It has been argued that business is so dynamic that no rules for assigning activities can be applied. Do you agree?

2. Until recently the transportation function has generally been assigned to manufacturing or to sales. It is now argued that the activities are much broader, including getting goods into the plant, moving them to storage, through the production process to shipping, and thence to warehouse or customer. Therefore, say these advocates, transportation (or physical distribution as it is now called) should be a major function reporting on a par with sales, production, finance, etc., to the executive vice-president. What guides or principles underlie these viewpoints?

3. What becomes of the guides to assigning activities if a firm "organizes around people"?

SELECTED REFERENCES

Newman, W. H.: *Administrative Action*, pp. 131–143, Englewood Cliffs, N.J.: Prentice-Hall, Inc., 1951.

Petersen, E., and E. G. Plowman: *Business Organization and Management*, 4th ed., chap. 9, Homewood, Ill.: Richard D. Irwin, Inc., 1958.

Simon, H. A.: *Public Administration*, chap. 7, New York: Alfred A. Knopf, Inc., 1950.

Sorrell, L. S.: "Organization of Transportation and Traffic Activities," *Traffic World*, vol. 46, no. 25; vol. 47, nos. 6–8 (1930–1931).

"Splitting a Company Lets It Move Faster," *Business Week* (Apr. 6, 1957).

line and staff authority relationships

The reason for departmentation and the guides for assigning activities to departments have been discussed. We now consider another essential organization question: What *kind* of authority is allocated in the organization structure? The question has to do with the nature of authority relationships— the problem of line and staff.

Without coordinated allocation of authority to department heads, the various departments cannot become a smoothly working unit properly harmonized for the accomplishment of enterprise objectives. Authority relationships, whether perpendicular or horizontal, are the factors that breathe life into an organization, harness departmental activities, and bring coordination to the enterprise.

LINE AND STAFF CONCEPTS

Much confusion has arisen both in literature and among managers as to what line and staff are; as a result, there is probably no area of management which causes more difficulties, more friction, and more loss of time and effectiveness. Yet line and staff relationships are important as an organizational way of life, and the kind of authority relationship that a member of an organization has must necessarily affect his part in the coordination of group activity.

One widely held concept of line and staff is that "line functions are those which have direct responsibility for accomplishing the objectives of the enterprise," and that staff "refers to those elements of the organization that help the line to work most effectively in accomplishing the primary objectives of the enterprise."[1] Those who hold to this view almost invariably classify production and sales (and sometimes finance) as line functions, and purchasing, accounting, personnel, plant maintenance, and quality control as staff functions.

The confusion arising from such a concept is immediately apparent. It is argued that purchasing, for example, is auxiliary to the main goals of the business in the sense that, unlike the production departments—such as heat-treating or parts assembly—it is not directly essential. But is purchasing really any less essential to the gaining of company objectives? Could the company not store up heat-treated or assembled parts and get along without these departments as well as it could without purchasing? And could not the same question be raised as to other so-called staff departments such as accounting, personnel, and plant maintenance? Moreover, there is probably nothing that could stop satisfactory production and sale of most manufactured goods more completely than the failure of quality control.

The Nature of Line and Staff Relationships A more precise and logically valid concept of line and staff is that they are simply a matter of relationships. In line authority, one finds a superior and a subordinate with a line of authority, running from the former to the latter. As Mooney[2] so aptly recognizes, this gradation of authority is found in all organization as an uninterrupted scale or series of steps. Hence this hierarchical arrangement has been referred to as the scalar principle in organization, which is: the more clear the line of authority from the ultimate authority for management in an enterprise to every subordinate position, the more effective will be the responsible decision making and organization communication. In many large enterprises, the steps are long and complicated, but even in the smallest, the very act of organization introduces the scalar principle.

The nature of line authority, therefore, becomes apparent from the scalar principle as being that relationship in which a superior exercises direct supervision over a subordinate—an authority relationship in direct line or steps.

The nature of the staff relationship is advisory. As Mooney[3] has stated, staff is auxiliary, and although "it may suggest that the structure of organization is like a double-track railroad, consisting of line and staff as two coordinate functions . . . there could be no more erroneous conception." For, as he points out:[4]

---

[1] L. A. Allen, *Improving Line and Staff Relationships*, Studies in Personnel Policy No. 153 (New York: National Industrial Conference Board, Inc., 1956), pp. 12, 20. See also similar definitions in L. A. Appley, "Staff and Line," *Management News*, vol. 29, no. 5, p. 1 (May, 1956), and R. C. Sampson, *The Staff Role in Management* (New York: Harper & Row, Publishers, Incorporated, 1955), pp. 42–44.

[2] J. D. Mooney, *Principles of Organization* (New York: Harper & Row, Publishers, Incorporated, 1947), pp. 14–15.

[3] *Ibid.*, pp. 34–35.

[4] *Ibid.*, p. 35.

The structure of organization is single track only, and can never be anything else. What is known in military organization as line is synonymous with what we have called the scalar chain, and there can be but one chain of line authority. Any duty in organization that cannot be identified as an actual link in the scalar process is an auxiliary function, adhering to the line like sidings along the main track. This means that every staff function must adhere to the line in some dependent relation, and could not otherwise exist. If we find in staff organization a counterpart of the same scalar gradations that appear in the line, this is implicit in the fact of its adherence. It must of necessity follow the gradations of that to which it adheres.

Line and Staff: Relationship or Departmentation?   Frequently, line and staff are regarded as types of departments. Although it is true that a department may stand in a predominantly line or staff position with respect to other departments, line and staff are distinguished by their authority relationships and not by groupings of activities.

The public relations department, for example, being primarily advisory to the top executives, may be thought of as a staff department. But within the department are line relationships; the director will stand in a line authority position with respect to his immediate subordinates. On the other hand, the vice-president in charge of production may be regarded as heading a line department, since his department usually stands in a scalar relationship to the organization as a whole. His job is not primarily advisory to the chief executive officer. If, however, he sits with other top officers to counsel the chief executive on over-all company policy, his relationship becomes one of staff. Furthermore, within the production department there may be many subordinates and among them a number having an advisory role and, therefore, having a staff relationship to the whole department or its parts.

When one looks at an organization structure *as a whole*, the general character of line and staff relationships for the total organization emerges. Certain departments are predominantly staff in their relationship to the entire organization. Other departments are primarily line.

Figure 15.1 portrays the skeletal organization of a manufacturing company. The activities of the director of research and the director of public relations are apt to be mainly advisory to the main stream of corporate operations and are consequently often referred to as staff activities. The finance, production, and sales departments, which have activities generally related to the main corporate functions—with direct delegations of authority and supervisory relationship leading to the ultimate accomplishment of enterprise purpose, through handling money, production, and sales—are consequently ordinarily referred to as line departments.

Although it is often convenient and correct to refer to one department as a line department and another as a staff department, *their activities do not so characterize the departments.* Line and staff are characterized by relationships and not by departmental activities. Should research be a principal function of the company—as in aircraft manufacturing, where the

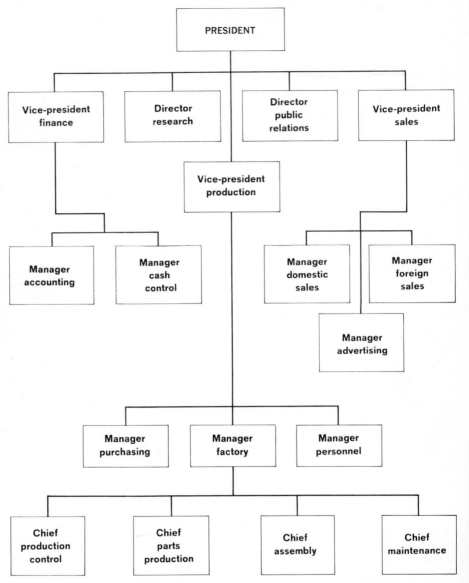

Fig. 15.1   So-called Line and Staff Organization of a Typical Manufacturing Company

engineering department produces ideas for sale to military and commercial customers—it will stand in an operating relationship to the organization as a whole and take on the authority characteristics of a factory department in a typical manufacturing enterprise.

Some of the tendency to regard line and staff as types of departments arises from confusing service departments with line and staff. Service departments represent grouping of *activities* for the purpose of control or economy arising from specialization. Thus, purchasing, accounting, or certain personnel activities may be separated from other departments and grouped in service departments. As service departments, they may be auxiliary to the principal operations of sales or production. To be sure, because service departments are comprised of specialists, their advice is usually sought by company managers, and, at such times, they stand in a staff relationship to the rest of the company. Nevertheless, the line authority within these departments is as real as that in a production or sales department.

Line and Staff: Specialization of Managerial Functions?   Although recognizing the inherent nature of line and staff as one of authority relationships, many students of management have attempted to distinguish between them on grounds that they represent a specialization of managerial functions. Some express the distinction by asserting that it is the line executive's function to *act* and the staff executive's function to *think*.[5]

The implied distinction between line and staff in terms of a division of managerial functions may possibly be traced to Frederick W. Taylor's attempt to separate planning from performance. It will be recalled that Taylor, in his quest for specialization of functions, advocated the division of the functions of foremen into eight groupings and these, in turn, into a planning level and a performance level.[6] This principle has never had wide application in industry nor been regarded as workable, for it involves, in part, the subdivision of managerial functions. The fact is that no manager can manage unless he has the authority to plan, organize, direct, staff, and control, although the degree to which he may be called upon to engage in these several functions may vary.

Nevertheless, staff officers do assist line officers in carrying out their

[5] L. Gulick, "The Theory of Organization," in L. Gulick and L. Urwick (eds.), *Papers on the Science of Administration* (New York: Institute of Public Administration, 1937), p. 31. Gulick observed that "when the work of the government is subjected to the dichotomy of 'line' and 'staff' there are included in staff all those persons who devote their time exclusively to the knowing, thinking, and planning, and making suggestions to superior officers. They cannot operate otherwise. But this does not make them staff officers. Those also in the staff are *doing* something; they do not merely sit and twiddle their thumbs. But they do not organize others, they do not direct or appoint personnel, they do not issue commands, they do not take responsibility for the job. Everything they suggest is referred up, not down, and is carried out, if at all, on the responsibility and under the direction of a line officer."

[6] F. W. Taylor, *Shop Management* (New York: Harper & Brothers, 1911), p. 99. Taylor believed that efficiency would be gained if the job of the shop foreman were subdivided into the following activities and duties: (1) order of work and routing, (2) instruction, (3) time and cost, (4) gang boss, (5) speed boss, (6) repair boss, (7) inspector, and (8) disciplinarian. He thus distinguished planning and performance levels, placing the first three functions on the planning level and the remainder on the performance level.

managerial functions. Staff assistants most often specialize in planning assistance, but they also assist in other managerial functions. On every hand, one can see departments engaged actively in planning, in examining organizational problems, in drawing up instructions or commands for the use of superiors, and in staffing studies. These are truly staff activities, not because they represent planning instead of performance but because they represent counsel and advice.

It is thus often stated that staff officers are assigned an "authority of ideas" and line officers an "authority to command."[7] Although this appraisal is accurate and can be helpful in dramatizing these relationships, it must not be taken to mean a splitting of the managerial functions. The manager may benefit greatly by ideas, but he cannot delegate his job as a manager.

Importance of Understanding Line and Staff   In view of the confusion about line and staff, the distinction is sometimes assumed to be meaningless. It is argued that these are obsolete concepts, carried into industry from military organization, and that modern firms have obliterated them by new organizational devices so that they no longer have any meaning.

The distinction seems important, however, as a way of organizational life. Superior and subordinate alike must know whether they are acting in a staff or a line capacity. If in a staff capacity, their job is to advise and not command: their line superiors must make the decisions and issue the instructions through the scalar chain.

A case in point is that of a competent young staff assistant, with unusual industrial experience as controller and internal auditor of several large business enterprises, who was hired by the executive vice-president of an expanding company. The assistant's charge was clear—to bring to the attention of the executive vice-president means and places for reducing costs of operations, expending scarce capital wisely, and achieving growth in orderly fashion. But some uncertainty must have existed in his mind as to whether he was limited to a staff position or whether he had line authority from the vice-president to see that these things were done. In any event, he gathered together many statisticians, production-efficiency experts, planners, economists, budgetary-control personnel, and organization specialists. With their help, he readily and accurately discovered numerous places where costs could be reduced, production and service improved, management bettered, and money efficiently expended; yet the entire program failed, and the executive vice-president was forced to abandon it. The reason was simple: his assistant had not understood that he was to act in a staff capacity, that he could not force his findings and policy determinations on unwilling line executives but must instead sell his ideas to them. The line executives resented

---

[7] E. Petersen and E. G. Plowman, *Business Organization and Management*, rev. ed. (Homewood, Ill.: Richard D. Irwin, Inc., 1948), p. 259. A similar idea is expressed by Mooney (*op. cit.*, p. 34), who notes that "the line represents the authority of *man;* the staff, the authority of *ideas.*"

the intrusion of this staff officer, as well they might, since he was, in effect, stripping from them their power to manage. The result was not only complete lack of cooperation by the line officers but their insistence that the staff position be abolished. Faced with a choice between supporting his chief line lieutenants and supporting a staff officer who had not confined his activities to investigation and recommendations, the executive vice-president could only favor the line.

Many other examples could be given of the importance of understanding line and staff relationships. Not only must the staff executive recognize that his job is to counsel, but the line executive must not confuse such counsel with the power to make decisions. Authority to manage must rest with the executive who stands in a line relationship with his subordinates. Failure to understand this is a common cause of friction.

DEVELOPMENT OF THE STAFF CONCEPT

The staff concept is probably as old as organization itself. Since organization almost certainly developed first in political and military areas of social existence, the first traces of staff are found in those areas. Mooney found that the pure staff function of the boule of ancient Athens was to prepare measures for the consideration of the ecclesia,[8] and that the early Roman senate first exercised a pure staff function but later changed to a line function. In the age of feudalism, too, and on to the present, the importance of staff counsel has ever been recognized, even though the emphasis of early organization was clearly on the development of line relationships.

Application of the Staff Principle in the Catholic Church   Mooney finds that the use of staff provides one of the "most notable lessons" furnished by the long history of Catholic Church organization, where staff service has taken forms unknown in other areas. The most obvious instance is in the central administration of the Church, consisting of two major institutions, the Sacred College and the Roman Curia. During the entire history of these institutions, they have been regarded as advisory to the pope, who delegates none of his final authority to them and has no obligation to adopt their advice.

One of the institutionalized organization principles of the Catholic Church has been described by Mooney as "compulsory staff service." This principle operates to force the superior to *listen* to his subordinates. While the line decision rests with the superior, he cannot refuse to listen. This principle—at least as old as the Rule of St. Benedict, promulgated in the sixth century—originally required the abbot of a Benedictine monastery to consult the elder monks, even on minor matters, and is now applied to some extent throughout the Church.

[8] For his excellent description of organization in antiquity, see *ibid.*, chap. 7; chaps. 8–20 include other pertinent material; chaps. 14, 17, and 18 deal with the development of staff. Much of the material presented in this section has been drawn from Mooney.

Another interesting principle Mooney calls "staff independence." In Catholic organization staff advisors are often independent of superiors with respect to both tenure and position. Advice is thus unweakened by the fact of dependence. As Mooney so well reflects on the lack of this in military, civic, and business organization:[9] "The weakness of many forms of staff service is that the counselor is dependent on the man whom he counsels, and hence is subject to the danger of sinking to the level of a 'yes' man."

The Army General Staff Although the staff concept can hardly be called a military invention, the terms "line" and "staff" appear to have had their origin in military organization. The modern concept of the army general staff is usually traced to the seventeenth century, when emphasis was placed upon a staff of experts by Gustavus Adolphus of Sweden. The Mark of Brandenburg is given credit for the evolution of the general staff organizations of the Prussian and German armies. The Prussian general staff, as organized by Scharnhorst in the early nineteenth century, was a completely organized advisory service coordinated under a single head, the chief of staff. Scharnhorst saw the dangers of separation of line and staff personnel and required that, periodically, all staff officers assume line duty and all line officers be given staff assignments.

This practice of rotation was overlooked in the organization of the French general staff of the nineteenth century, with the result that the line neither understood nor paid attention to the counsel of the staff. The tradition of staff counsel and its acceptance, so well formulated by Scharnhorst and developed by such successors as Clausewitz and von Moltke, was the basis of the German staff of World Wars I and II. It has been copied and improved upon by all great military machines of the present day.

The reason for the efficiency of staff in the military organization of modern times is not difficult to understand. A general commanding a large number of men cannot possibly develop all the information needed for sound decisions and balance; as division, battalion, and regiment commanders face, to some extent, similar problems, the general staff idea has been carried down into lower echelons.

The importance of effective staff work was brought forcefully to the attention of the United States Army as the result of the Spanish-American War. Men were ordered to Cuba without adequate planning for necessary equipment and armament, without adequate intelligence information as to the armament of the foe, and without other requirements of a well-planned and coordinated attack. Because of this lack of staff planning, men were sent to a tropical climate in woolen uniforms, transport ships had little information about the depth of channels and the nature of harbors, and little was known of the proper routes to take upon landing.

As a result of this experience and the brilliant report of Elihu Root in 1902,[10] the American army adopted the general staff device that is the basis

---

[9] *Ibid.*, p. 122.
[10] *Report of the Secretary of War* (Washington: Government Printing Office, 1902).

of its organization today. Root's report is a classic on the need for a general staff with no other duties than gathering information, presenting alternative plans, and preparing the details of selected plans.

Staffs in Business   The development of the staff in business can probably be traced simply to the use of assistants to handle details of a managerial job, to furnish information needed for decisions, and to offer advice in making plans. The separation of planning and performance, recommended by Frederick W. Taylor and his disciples, gave impetus to staff organization, even though Taylor's objective was not staff assistance as such but rather functional specialization.

Widespread use of staff in American business developed only in the twentieth century, particularly after the Great Depression of 1929–1932. The emphasis on planning and control, with their requirements for information, the growing complexities of labor relations, the expansion of government regulations, and the difficult legal and accounting problems arising from tax legislation have argued for staff assistance. The development has been accelerated by the growth of large business, in which the problems of managing approach those of any army and require specialized information of a breadth and complexity unknown to smaller operations.

The proliferation of staffs in business takes many forms. Few indeed are the top managers who do not have staff assistants in law, taxes, accounting, and perhaps research. Executives of large companies add staff assistants in public relations, personnel, engineering, or budgets. Staff assistants are so widely used that a sales or production manager may have from one to a half dozen. In large-scale enterprises, for example, the sales managers may have staff men separately assigned to such activities as the selection and training of salesmen, sales strategy, research, quotas, budgets, traffic, and warehousing. Moreover, some large companies are reminiscent of the army general staff. In the General Motors Corporation, for example, there exists an operations staff of seven key managers—each in charge of a staff group devoted to such important activities as distribution, engineering, styling, personnel, and public relations—plus financial and legal staffs.

On the other hand, many corporation presidents studiously avoid having many staff assistants or staff departments, choosing instead to have staff men report to the managers in the major line departments. Their purpose is to place the staff assistance at the point in the line where it can best be used, and to avoid undermining the line officers by concentrating staff assistance at the top level. Furthermore, many staff agencies are not really staff in nature, as will be explained below, but have been given line authority over certain activities in other departments.

STAFF RELATIONSHIPS

The basic nature of staff as an advisory relationship amply characterizes the nature of staff authority. Although the staff officer exercises line authority over the subordinate in *his* department, he has no other line authority. The information he furnishes or the plans he recommends flow upward to his superior, who decides whether they are to be transformed into action.

Thus, the assistant to the president of a corporation may be a staff official with the duty of recommending policy and procedure. The fact that the president normally accepts and implements these recommendations may give them exceptional weight. But if the assistant confines himself to the authority inherent in his position, he will never allow line subordinates of the president to take his recommendations as policy decisions of the president until the latter has specifically approved them as *his* policy. The flow of staff authority is, then, upward to the president, who subsequently exercises line authority in putting recommendations into effect, as may be seen in Figure 15.2.

Should the assistant, after study of a problem of product line, recommend the manufacture of a new item, and should this recommendation be

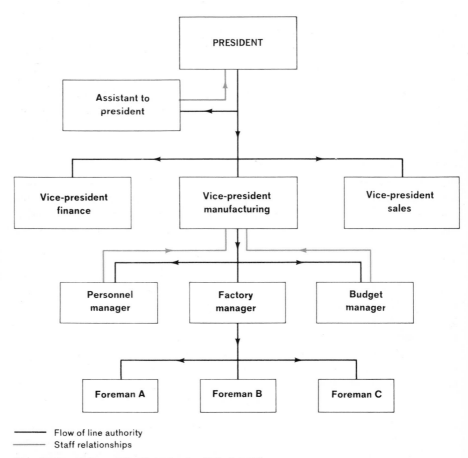

———— Flow of line authority
———— Staff relationships

Fig. 15.2   Line and Staff Authority Relationships

accepted and a decision—either by the president or the board of directors—
made in accordance with it, the president, as a line officer, would then issue
appropriate instructions to his line subordinates. Likewise, as illustrated in
Figure 15.2, if the personnel and budget managers are in a staff relationship
to the vice-president for manufacturing and the vice-president requested
personnel and budgetary recommendations for the new venture, the staff
relationship would flow upward to the vice-president. Adopting the recommendations, he would, as line officer, issue instructions to his line subordinate, the factory manager.

As was apparent from the discussion of authority in Chapter 4, the
president has the power to *order* his line vice-presidents to act, and the
vice-president for manufacturing has a similar power over his factory manager. Successful administration and good personnel relations require that
line subordinates understand and accept policy decisions. The staff assistant should consult line officers and have them, if possible, agree to his
recommendation *before* it goes to his superior. A line superior is more likely
to follow a staff recommendation if it already meets the approval of subordinate managers who must implement it. A well-sold recommendation is
likely to be accepted, whereas a recommendation developed secretly, without
the assistance of line managers, not only places on the superior the responsibility of evaluating it but often brings down on the head of the staff
assistant the understandable suspicion—and often resentment and opposition
—of those asked to administer a program on which they had not been consulted.

FUNCTIONAL AUTHORITY

Functional authority is that power which an individual or department may
have delegated to it over specified processes, practices, policies, or other
matters relating to activities undertaken by personnel in departments other
than its own. If the principle of unity of command were followed without
exception, authority over these activities would be exercised by line managers, but numerous reasons—including lack of special knowledge, lack of
ability to supervise processes, and danger of diverse interpretations of policies—explain why they occasionally are not allowed to exercise this authority.
In such cases, the line manager may be deprived of this limited authority,
and a manager in another department may be delegated specialized, that is,
"functional," authority to carry out the activities properly.

Functional authority is not restricted to managers of a particular type
of department. It may be exercised by line, service,[11] or staff department
heads, more often the latter two, because they are usually comprised of
specialists whose knowledge becomes the basis for functional controls.

---

[11] Some so-called staff departments are service departments. Since the latter reflect
a special grouping of activities and since this discussion is concerned with line and staff
authority relationships, the analysis of service departments as a special organizational form
is postponed to Chapter 16.

Development of Functional Authority The successive steps by which a line manager gradually gives up his authority over particular activities make an interesting study. As has already been emphasized, the pure staff specialist offers advice or recommendations to his line superior, who may issue them as instructions to be filtered down the organization hierarchy. The first modification of this relationship ordinarily occurs when the superior delegates authority to the staff man to transmit information, proposals, and advice directly to the former's subordinates. For example, a personnel assistant might be permitted to transmit directly to the operating department heads information and advice on the handling of labor grievances, instead of presenting them first to the president for transmission to the line organization. Obviously, this saves the president time and trouble and expedites the spread of the information.

A second modification might be to allow the staff specialist not only to transmit information and advice to the line managers but to consult with with them and show them how the information should be used or how the recommendations should be put into effect. For instance, the personnel assistant might be asked to advise line personnel on procedures to eliminate mishandling of grievances. It will clearly be advantageous to all concerned if the staff man can instruct the persons responsible for this activity. Here, there is no question of his ordering them; the agreement of the line executive concerned is needed; should this not be forthcoming, he can only appeal to his superior to issue the requisite instructions. And even with the variations outlined above, the specialist is still operating wholly in a staff capacity.

The transition to functional authority is accomplished when the assistant is delegated specific authority to *prescribe* processes, methods, or even policy to be followed in all subdivisions of either staff or operating departments. The personnel assistant, for example, who once could only advise, now may be given limited authority to supervise a special function or process of the line organization. He no longer merely advises his superior or the line organization concerning handling grievances. Now, he may issue instructions prescribing procedures. Or, to use another example, a corporation controller may be given authority, not to recommend, but to prescribe the kind of accounting records to be kept by the sales department, the sales division, or the sales district, as well as by the manufacturing departments.

By limiting this authority to function, the factory manager—handling his labor grievances in accordance with procedures prescribed by the personnel manager—and the district sales manager—keeping his records according to instructions of the controller—are still primarily subject to the orders, supervision, and control of their line superiors. The extent of their control by the staff officer is governed by the latter's functional authority.

Functional Authority Delegation Functional authority can perhaps be better understood if it is regarded as a small slice of the authority of the line superior. A corporation president, for example, has complete authority to manage the corporation, subject only to limitations placed upon him by such superior authority as the board of directors, the corporate charter and by-laws, and government regulations. In the pure staff situation, his advisers on personnel, accounting, purchasing, or public relations have no part of this authority, their duty being merely to offer counsel. But when functional authority relationships exist, the president delegates some of his authority to these advisers to issue instructions directly to the line organization as shown in Figure 15.3.

As illustrated, the four staff executives have functional authority over the line organization with respect to procedures in the fields of accounting, personnel, purchasing, and public relations. What has happened is that the president, feeling it unnecessary that such specialized matters be cleared through him, has delegated functional authority to staff assistants to issue their own instructions to the operating departments. Likewise, of course, the various operating managers and their line subordinate managers could themselves set up staff assistants with functional authority, as when a factory

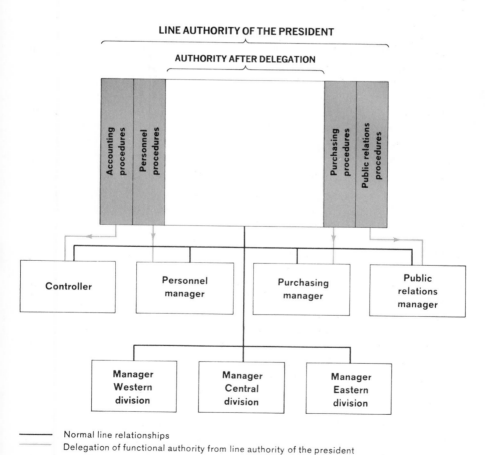

Normal line relationships

Delegation of functional authority from line authority of the president

Fig. 15.3   Functional Authority Relationships

superintendent sets up cost, production-control, and quality-control supervisors with functional authority to prescribe procedures for the foremen.

Functional Authority as Exercised by Operating Managers Operating department heads sometimes have good reason to control some method or process
of another line department. For example, the vice-president in charge of
sales may be given functional authority over the manufacturing executives
in scheduling customer orders, packaging, or making service parts available.

Where a company is organized along product lines, the exercise of
functional authority over the product division managers by other executives
is rather commonplace. For purposes of administrative convenience, particularly coordination at a point in the organization structure, all functions
of sales, production, finance, or other so-called line functions (that is, "line"
to the enterprise) may be placed under a division or product manager
reporting directly to the president, or, as is sometimes the case, to the vice-
president in charge of operations. In either case, certain top line officials in
charge of a major function of the business might not have a direct line of
authority over the product managers. But, to make sure that sales or financial
policy is properly followed in the divisions, these officers may be given
functional authority, as illustrated in Figure 15.4.

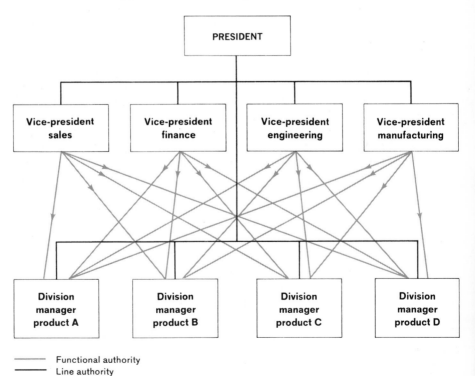

Fig. 15.4 **Functional Authority of Line Departments**

The Area of Functional Authority   Functional authority should be severely restricted authority. The functional authority of the purchasing manager, for example, is generally limited to the procedures to be used in divisional or departmental purchasing. Although he may *conduct* certain purchasing activities of an over-all company nature, he is thereby acting either as a direct line officer over a portion of purchasing or as head of a service department. The functional authority of the personnel manager over the general line organization is likewise ordinarily limited to the prescription of procedures for handling grievances, for sharing in the administration of wage and salary programs, and for handling vacation procedures and matters of a similar nature.

Functional authority is usually limited to the area of "how" and sometimes "when" and seldom applies to "where," "what," or "who." The reason for this limitation is not found in any logical demarcation between normal line authority and functional authority, since the latter *can* be made to apply to any aspect of operations. It is rather that the functionalization of management, if carried to extremes, would destroy the manager's job. As will be recalled from an earlier discussion, whenever a manager loses his authority to plan, organize, staff, direct, and control the activities within his department, he can no longer manage.

To some extent, this occurs when a staff or line executive has functional authority over some part of another manager's job. Even when the personnel manager requires the factory manager to follow seniority in layoffs or to grant employees definite pay and vacation allowances, he is interfering with some of the factory manager's prerogatives. When the accounting department requires district sales managers to file their expense accounts in a certain form, it is, to some extent, interfering with the authority of the general sales manager over his subordinates.

Therefore, well-managed concerns recognize that functional authority should be used sparingly and only where a real necessity exists. This necessity comes often from both outside and inside influences. On the outside are such requirements as those of government agencies and labor union contracts that must be interpreted and administered by specialists. On the inside some matters are of such importance or complexity that the best possible grade of uniform action is required, necessitating in turn that the expert be given sufficient authority to carry out desired procedures. A rather thin line sometimes divides what should be controlled by the expert and what should be under the jurisdiction of the operating manager. Where there is doubt, good practice would seem to favor limiting the area of functional authority so that the operating manager's position is not weakened.

Unity of Command and the Flow of Functional Authority   Limiting the area of functional authority is, then, important in preserving the integrity of the managerial position. If a company had, as some do, executives with functional authority over procedures in the fields of personnel, purchasing, accounting, traffic, budgets, engineering, public relations, law, sales policy, and real estate, the complications of authority relationships could be great indeed. A factory manager or a sales manager might have, in addition to his immediate line superior, five, ten, or even fifteen bosses. Although much of the multiplication of command is unavoidable because of the demands for specialist prescription in complex areas, it is obvious that it can precipitate serious, and frequently intolerable, confusion and dispersal of responsibility.

Some semblance of unity of command can be maintained by requiring that the line of functional authority shall not extend beyond the first organization level below that of the manager's own superior. Thus, in Figure 15.5 the functional authority of the personnel or public relations director should not extend beyond the level of the vice-presidents in charge of finance, sales, and manufacturing. In other words, functional authority should be concentrated at the nearest possible point in the organization structure, to preserve the unity of command of the line executives.

The manner in which this concentration of functional authority can be effected in large companies with a number of levels of organization is apparent from Figure 15.6. The manager in charge at each level has concentrated in him the functional authority lines of the principals at each level above him. While these lines of functional authority may seem complicated—and, as any regional manager knows, this intricacy is as real as it is apparent—the complications would be increased many times if the functional authority were not concentrated at each level.

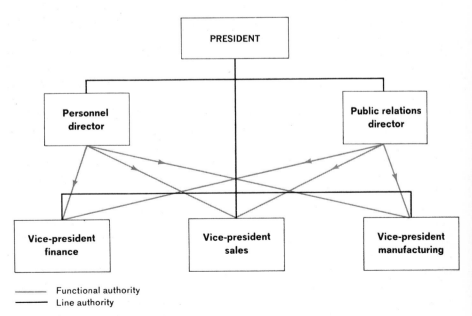

Fig. 15.5 Line and Functional Authority

Nevertheless, the actual lines of authority do not operate in this manner, even though they were intended to. From Figure 15.6, one would expect that the general manager of the Eastern division would pass on all instructions from the vice-president of sales to the division sales manager, and that the manager of the New York region would relay instructions of the division sales manager to the regional sales manager. In practice, these instructions would often be relayed without the divisional general manager's or the regional manager's ever having looked at them. But the fact that they are transmitted *through* these managers gives a basis for unity of command that could not be retained if the general line managers at each level were bypassed.

This principle is often violated. Top managers with functional authority sometimes issue instructions directly to personnel throughout the organization. Where the policy or procedure determination is so important that there must be no deviation, both the prestige of the top manager and the necessity for accurate communication may make it necessary and wise to issue such instructions. Issuing them to the responsible line subordinate, as well as to the functional counterpart at the lower level, does not seem seriously to increase the multiplicity of command. As will be noted later, there are forces of centralization of authority that may make this kind of exercise of functional authority unavoidable.

Clarifying Functional Authority Almost certainly the best means of avoiding some of the problems, confusions, and frictions of functional authority is to make sure it is clarified. There is always the danger that any specialist will see virtually everything in a company through the eyes of his specialty. Thus, it is not enough to say that a division or plant manager is "administratively responsible" to his line superior and "functionally responsible" to the controller. If the controller, like a few the authors have known, regards his functional authority over accounting matters to extend to all expenditures of funds, there is a built-in situation for undue conflict through multiplication of command. Or if a personnel manager interprets his delegation to cover anything concerned with people, the conflict potential is obvious. Likewise, if an operating manager regards the controller as being "staff" with no authority even to prescribe the form and nature of the company's accounting system, the controller cannot discharge his responsibility.

It is surprising how many companies, even those otherwise well managed, fail to define the exact nature of functional authority which a manager may have. Study of authority delegations in a large number of companies shows that adequate clarification in this area is rare. Yet nowhere is clarification more important, particularly in the light of the apparent inevitability of functional authority, the numerous instances where it is used, and the number of "dotted" lines which may converge on a given operating manager. (By "dotted" we refer to lines usually not shown on charts because they would make the chart look confused, even though their existence in practice

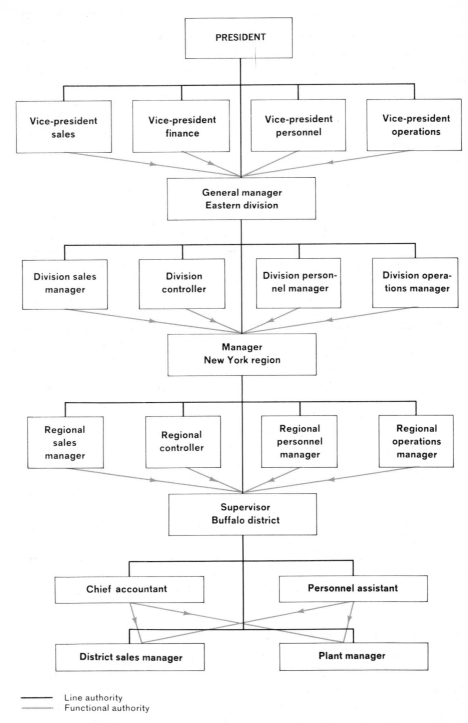

Fig. 15.6 **Conception of Functional Authority of the Various Levels of an Organization**

can be even more confusing to the person who receives these instructions.)

In order to obtain clarity, it appears to be imperative that the exact functional authority delegated to a manager or to a department be clearly spelled out. This is necessary not only from the standpoint of the bearer's use and understanding of this specialized type of authority, but also for those operating managers who are on the receiving end of such authorized instructions. An example of one company's attempt to define the authority of the vice-president–controller is the following specific delegations to that officer, which delegations were thoroughly discussed with him and with key operating managers over whom he was expected to exercise such powers of authority.

1. Authority to prescribe the corporate chart of accounts and the division's charts of accounts so far as they are supportive to and necessary for the corporation chart of accounts; authority to direct the development and maintenance of necessary procedures to insure the integrity of the company's accounts and statements; authority to see that the company's accounting policies and procedures are followed in the divisions.
2. Authority to prescribe policies and procedures in the handling of cash, including banking arrangements, methods of handling receipts and disbursements, and the requirements for bonding throughout the company.
3. Authority to prescribe policies, standards, and procedures with respect to inventory control matters which affect the integrity of accounting records.
4. Authority to prescribe the necessary form, procedures, and timing for the preparation and submission of profit plans.
5. Authority to require from the various divisions and departments of the company financial, accounting, and statistical reports and forecasts in a form and at times believed to be necessary for proper company planning and control.
6. Authority to approve the selection of the chief financial officer of any division or affiliate.
7. Authority to prescribe and undertake a program of internal auditing of financial, cash, credit, and accounting transactions, and an audit of corporate and divisional financial and accounting policies and procedures.

LINE AND STAFF IN PRACTICE

The essential character of line and staff relationships becomes readily apparent in the study of well-managed enterprises. Although the semantics of management occasionally mislead the student (and, more often, those managing and being managed), a clear statement of authority relationships will identify the kind of authority—whether it be line, staff, or functional authority.

For example, in an organization analysis prepared by one of the nation's leading industrial management firms for a fast-growing enterprise, territorial divisions for major line operations and a staff of top executives to control over-all policy were established. In the organization manual, the treasurer's scope of authority was spelled out as follows:[12]

> The Treasurer has line authority over and is responsible for directing activities of such personnel as he requires to establish system policies and procedures for the functions under his jurisdiction and to administer system treasury and accounting functions which are reserved for his department. He has no direct line authority over the day-to-day activities of accounting personel in the divisions and regions except as specifically delegated by division or region managements. He is responsible for developing and interpreting budgeting, accounting, and financial policies, for assisting the division organizations in carrying out such policies, and for satisfying himself that such policies are correctly and ably administered in the field.
>
> At the request of division managements, or voluntarily when system welfare is materially concerned, the Treasurer shall make recommendations concerning the employment, promotion, dismissal, or change in compensation of supervisory personnel engaged in activities within his functional responsibility. Final action on such matters shall be taken by division managements when mutual agreement has been reached with system staff department heads concerned.

This general description of authority is supplemented by a list of duties making clear that the treasurer's major duties are establishing budgetary policy and procedures for the divisions and instituting accounting policies and procedures for maintaining division records and such other procedures as might be necessary for the discharge of his duties. The description and list make clear the line, staff, and functional authority relationships of the treasurer: He has line authority over his own department, staff relationship to top and divisional managers, and functional authority to require the major operating departments, the divisions, to follow good budgeting and accounting procedures.

Standard Oil Company of California   A large and well-managed company is the Standard Oil Company of California. For some four decades it has paid special attention to organization, with a department of organization in the top echelon of management. This emphasis is an outgrowth of a preoccupation with the preparation of job descriptions. Attempts to describe managerial jobs, with their intangible and undefined aspects, resulted in one of the most interesting analyses of organization ever made. Published over a period of years as *The Management Guide*,[13] the manual describing the

---

[12] From a confidential organization report by a major management consulting firm.

[13] G. L. Hall, *The Management Guide*, 2d ed. (San Francisco: Standard Oil Company of California, 1956). Although the first edition of the guide was clearly an exposition of the company's actual organization structure, the revised edition, probably because of organization changes that took place in 1956, became a statement of "principles" and the chart and positions used were referred to as "hypothetical."

underlying principles of the Standard Oil Company's organization structure has widely influenced other enterprises.

In general, these principles are consistent with those outlined in this chapter. An interesting variation of Standard Oil practice is the use of the concept of "functional guidance" instead of functional authority. The so-called staff departments are generally given, in addition to their staff status, authority to furnish functional guidance to various managers on matters within staff specialization. Thus the job description of the organization department is as follows:[14]

> Furnishes functional guidance to the heads of the organizational components of the company by advising and assisting in the development, maintenance, and improvement of plans of management embracing: organization structures and complements; functions, responsibilities and authority, and relationships; control over wages, salaries, operating expenses, and manpower; and company, department, and division policies on these matters.

This seems to imply that this department, like most staff departments, has a staff relationship to the president and functional authority over department and division managers, for whom it also operates as a service department. However, the company attempts to preserve the integrity of its line organization and avoid problems of multiple command by describing functional guidance in the following terms:[15]

> This does not mean that staff members issue orders, supervise activities, or control any portion of the operating groups. Each staff man recommends policies to the head of the enterprise for his approval. Once these policies are approved, procedures in line with the policies are established, in some cases by the staff member concerned, and in other cases by the top position upon recommendation of the staff member.
>
> After establishment of a procedure, the staff man within whose particular province the particular procedure falls furnishes the appropriate operating component chief with technical or specialized advice and assistance in the application of the procedure. The staff man is responsible for furnishing this functional guidance, and is accountable to his principal for the fulfillment of this responsibility. The chief of the operating component is responsible for the application of the functional guidance which he receives, and is accountable to *his* principal for the fulfillment of *his* responsibility. In no case is the chief of the operating component subject to the orders, supervision, or control of the staff man, nor can he ever be held accountable to the staff man for fulfillment of his responsibilities.

Briefly, this hybrid type of line and staff organization permits help and guidance to be given to the operators by the specialists; at the same time it ensures that an individual has only one person to whom he reports.

[14] *Ibid.*, p. 42.
[15] *Ibid.*, p. 36.

Ford Motor Company   In handling the distinctions between line, staff, and functional authority relationships, the organizational practices of the Ford Motor Company[16] has had three levels of specialized staff, dealing with such areas as industrial relations, law, manufacturing, finance, engineering, public relations, and governmental relations. Although not every staff operation was present at all levels, there were specialized staff agencies at the corporate, division, and plant levels.

At the corporate level, the responsibility for managing the company clearly rests with the chairman of the board and the president, but a staff of specialists advise and assist these line officers and perform certain administrative and technical services. Some of the staffs primarily serve the divisions and plants as well as the entire company; others serve in the dual capacities of (1) advising on the establishment of over-all company objectives, policies, plans, and programs, and (2) assisting staff groups at the division level to carry these out through "functional supervision." Functional supervision is a mixture of pure staff and functional authority, since the Ford Motor Company regards it as an extension of the office of the president with a view to assuring the following actions:

1. Formulating major company objectives, policies, plans, and programs for line management approval.
2. Establishing necessary controls, such as company standards, systems, and procedures, and implementing policies, to ensure the carrying out of major company objectives, policies, and programs.
3. Measuring performance within a particular field of activity through the medium of reports and the review of divisional plans, programs, and operations.
4. Concurring in the selection and change in assignment of key personnel.
5. Furnishing administrative and technical advice and services to the divisions.

Although the staff specialist is regarded as having no authority for line operations and is expected to obtain acceptance of his ideas on their merit, there is clearly an implication of line-type authority, especially when the specialist operates under approved policies and plans. It is interesting, too, that in the Ford organization the specialist on the central office staff exercises his functional supervision directly over his counterpart in the division organization, unless a problem involves over-all operations, in which case he exercises it through the division general manager.

The Army Staff   The top organization of the United States Army provides an

---

[16] The information included in this section was drawn from Allen, *op. cit.*, pp. 81–87.

example, from which other enterprises have borrowed extensively, of the uses of line and staff and of the virtually unavoidable functional authority relationships that develop as organization becomes complex. As seen in Figure 15.7, the principal line authority in the Department of the Army is from the Secretary and his assistants to the Chief of Staff and then to the various field commands. With the exceptions of the Vice-Chief of Staff and the Secretary of the General Staff—as well as certain rather definite line functions of the Assistant Secretary (Financial Management)—the head-quarters organization is comprised mainly of staffs and service departments. This large staff organization is not essentially different from that of the Navy Department or the Department of the Air Force. The Administrative Assistant, the General Counsel, the Chief of Public Information, and the Chief of Legislative Liaison act in a staff and service capacity to the Secretary. Other agencies stand in a staff or service capacity to the Chief of Staff and, through him, to the Army as a whole. Together, the staffs comprise the Army Staff, whose duties have been prescribed as follows:[17]

(a) The Army Staff shall furnish professional assistance to the Secretary, the Under Secretary, and the Assistant Secretaries of the Army.
(b) Under the direction and control of the Secretary, the Army Staff shall—
(1) prepare such plans for the national security, for employment of the Army for that purpose, both separately and in conjunction with the naval and air forces, and for recruiting, organizing, supplying, equipping, training, serving, mobilizing, and demobilizing the Army, as will assist in the execution of any power, duty, or function of the Secretary or the Chief of Staff;
(2) investigate and report upon the efficiency of the Army and in its preparation for military operations;
(3) prepare detailed instructions for the execution of approved plans and supervise the execution of those plans and instructions;
(4) act as agent of the Secretary and the Chief of Staff in co-ordinating the action of all organizations of the Department of the Army; and
(5) perform such other duties, not otherwise assigned by law, as may be prescribed by the Secretary.

The above description of duties of the Army Staff, as well as the job descriptions of the staff heads, discloses few instances of pure staff authority. All the heads of staff departments have advisory authority and, of course, line authority within their departments, but, in almost every case, the department heads also have some functional authority over various Army operations.

Considering the necessity for uniform policy and procedures in many areas in a complex organization and the wisdom of having specialists de-

---

[17] *Organization and Functions: Department of the Army* (Washington: Department of the Army, Army Reg. No. 10–5, May, 1957), pp. 8–9.

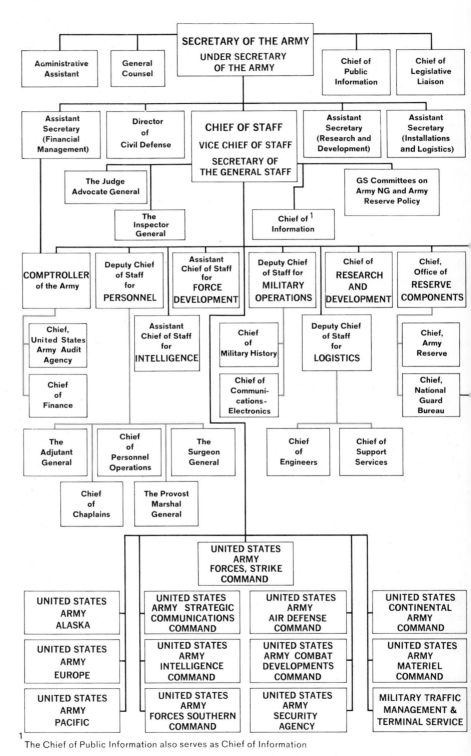

The Chief of Public Information also serves as Chief of Information

Fig. 15.7   Organization of Headquarters, Department of the Army, 1967

velop and supervise both policy and procedure, it is not difficult to understand the extensive use of functional authority. In the Army, as in business, an attempt is made to protect the unity of command by having instructions go to the field commander and from him to his line subordinates. But—again in the Army as in business—the pattern of the top staff is duplicated in the upper echelons of the line command and, as a practical matter, specialized instructions issued by the top staff officers filter through the organization by following a functional path through the staff assistants in the line command.

In recent years, descriptions of Army Staff jobs have distinguished between those which carry the authority to plan and advise and those which include the exercise of line command and functional supervision. Technical staff and services are also more carefully defined as service agencies and their staff relationships clearly separated from line-type service authority. For example, the 1957 regulations state that "the heads of technical staff agencies provide advice and assistance" and "are also heads of the technical services, in which capacity they command troops, organization, activities, and installations." The regulations go on to explain that "the two functions of staff and command, although vested in a single head, are separate and distinct in that each involves different responsibilities and duties; the exercise of one is not to be confused with the exercise of the other."[18] Business firms would do well to duplicate this accurate instruction.

As the result of a study made in 1961,[19] the Army General Staff was considerably streamlined in 1962. The Staff had long been comprised of staff assistants assigned to the Secretary of War, a General Staff (Comptroller, Operations, Personnel, and Logistics), a special staff (Finance, Military History, Information, Chaplains, and Provost Marshal), and the technical staffs and services (Surgeon General, Chief of Ordnance, Chief of Engineers, Quartermaster General, Chief of Transportation, Chief Signal Officer, and Chief Chemical Officer). In the reorganization of 1962, the staff was reduced to reflect mainly advisory activities. While the Staff remains important and strong, many service activities were placed in the field commands for which they were designed, and much of the previously overgrown functional authority was eliminated.

One reason for the reorganization was to relieve the General Staff of "command-like and operating functions" so that it could more responsively emphasize planning, programming, policy making, and general supervision of defense. The reorganization was aimed to return the General Staff to a more clearly defined staff position and to place greater line authority in the major operating commands.

General Motors Corporation One is not surprised to find a system similar to the Army Staff in the world's largest privately owned industrial enterprise,

[18] *Ibid.*, p. 18.
[19] *Report on the Organization of the Department of the Army* (Washington: Department of the Army, December, 1961).

the General Motors Corporation.[20] This firm employed 745,000 people in 1967, had 1,418,000 stockholders, sold over 20 billion dollars worth of goods, and operated through thirty-nine operating divisions, with plants over the entire United States and in several foreign countries. Despite its size, this industrial empire has an enviable record of managerial excellence, profitable operation, and service to many countries. Its size and the scope of its activities pose tremendous organizational problems. Although its organizational success is due primarily to good management and the decentralization of authority discussed in a later chapter, its utilization of line and staff has been an interesting and important managerial accomplishment.

The top organization of the General Motors Corporation is illustrated in Figure 15.8. At that level there are an operations, a financial, and a legal staff, the latter being separated from the operations staff in order to keep financial operations and related legal activities separate from manufacturing and sales. As will be discussed later, good management, particularly of a far-flung enterprise, dictates that control of finances should be highly centralized.

Most of the staff departments are headed by a vice-president, and all report to an executive president. All heads of the staff departments act as advisers to both divisional and corporation executives. They also formulate policy recommendations and, in limited cases, have some functional authority over the line divisions.

The policy-formulation function of the staff departments is important to the successful operation of General Motors. The staff departments make recommendations of major policy to the executive and finance committees. The engineering staff, for example, works on future policies and coordinates the product-development programs of the divisions, presenting its studies to the top committees. The styling staff develops advanced automobile and truck styles and works with the various body divisions in presenting new models.

Since these staffs recommend policy to top management through the executive and finance committees and since they participate either on these committees or on specialized subcommittees, the operating divisions unquestionably find cooperation with the staff good practice for expeditious policy formulation. A line divisional manager is not *ordered* to cooperate or take advice from a staff department, but failure to do so might be to his detriment when the recommendations go to top management. By the same token, if the staff did not sell its ideas to the line and cooperate with line managers, the result would be a divided program at the top committee level.

[20] A good description of the General Motors Corporation organization may be found in *GM and Its People* (Detroit: General Motors Corporation, 1949) and in *The Development and Growth of General Motors: Statement before the Subcommittee on Antitrust and Monopoly of the United States Senate Committee on the Judiciary* (Dec. 2, 1955). See also P. F. Drucker, *Concept of the Corporation* (New York: The John Day Company, Inc., 1946), especially chap. 2.

Not that differences do not occur. But the built-in need for staff and line cooperation in formulating major policy compels cooperation at the lower levels. Staffs can do more than merely assist the line to obtain a favorable decision. Their specialized knowledge and their freedom to engage in long-range research give them a standing that makes their services appreciated and sought.

The need for centralizing controls over such matters as labor relations, public relations, procurement, real estate, research, and accounting leads to giving staff specialists some functional authority to prescribe methods and techniques for their counterpart functions in the operating line divisions. At the same time, the evidence available indicates that General Motors has limited functional authority relationships to the most urgent matters requiring central control, such as the interpretation of union contracts, the interpretation and administration of dealer contracts, and the basic chart of accounts. Apparently, the company finds it best to rely upon a kind of acceptance of staff assistance, which its organizational environment encourages, as a result of their system of policy making.

Unavoidability of Functional Authority In all the examples above, in virtually every large enterprise, and in many smaller enterprises, some delegation of functional authority to staff departments seems unavoidable. Even though a manager may abhor and try to avoid a hybrid combination of line and staff authority, as does the Standard Oil Company of California, most major staff departments have some functional authority. This practice is largely due to the necessity for expert interpretation of policy and for formulation of procedures by specialists, which, in turn, results from the need for varying degrees of uniformity in accounting, labor, public relations, and other activities.

Of course, the line executive could maintain the separation of line and staff authority relationships in his organization structure if he were to insist on issuing all the instructions relating to matters requiring specialized staff assistance. As a matter of fact, some corporation and division executives have done so. However, in most enterprises, this either taxes unduly the line manager's span of management or, if he automatically accepts his staff's recommendations, makes the apparent avoidance of functional authority a meaningless pretense.

STAFF AND THE SMALL BUSINESS

Since the staff type of department represents a refinement in specialization resulting from division of labor, the appearance of staffs is usually proportional to the size of the enterprise. Just how large a business firm must be before it will gain by regrouping certain activities into staff departments cannot be stated generally. It can be stated, however, that it need not be very large before it feels the necessity for specialized assistance on such

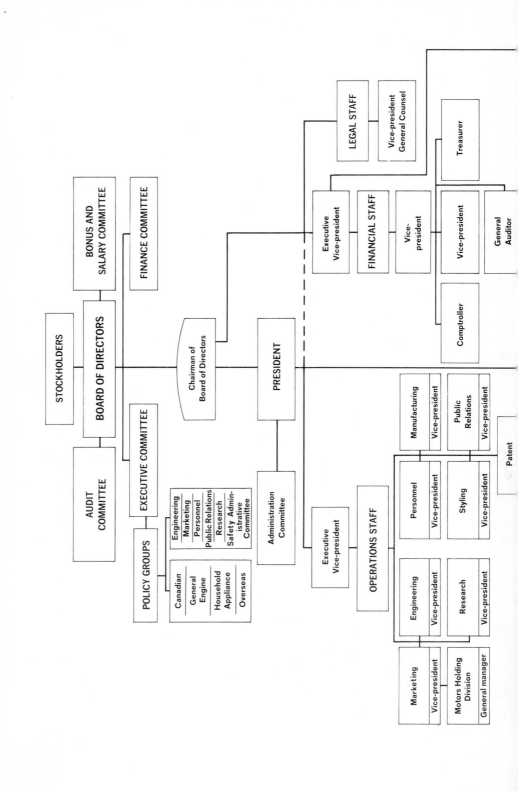

STOCKHOLDERS

BONUS AND SALARY COMMITTEE

FINANCE COMMITTEE

AUDIT COMMITTEE

BOARD OF DIRECTORS

EXECUTIVE COMMITTEE

POLICY GROUPS

Canadian
General Engine
Household Appliance
Overseas

Engineering
Marketing
Personnel
Public Relations
Research
Safety Administrative Committee

Chairman of Board of Directors

PRESIDENT

Administration Committee

LEGAL STAFF

Vice-president General Counsel

Executive Vice-president

FINANCIAL STAFF

Vice-president

Comptroller

Vice-president

Treasurer

General Auditor

Executive Vice-president

OPERATIONS STAFF

Marketing
Vice-president

Motors Holding Division
General manager

Engineering
Vice-president

Research
Vice-president

Personnel
Vice-president

Styling
Vice-president

Manufacturing
Vice-president

Public Relations
Vice-president

Patent

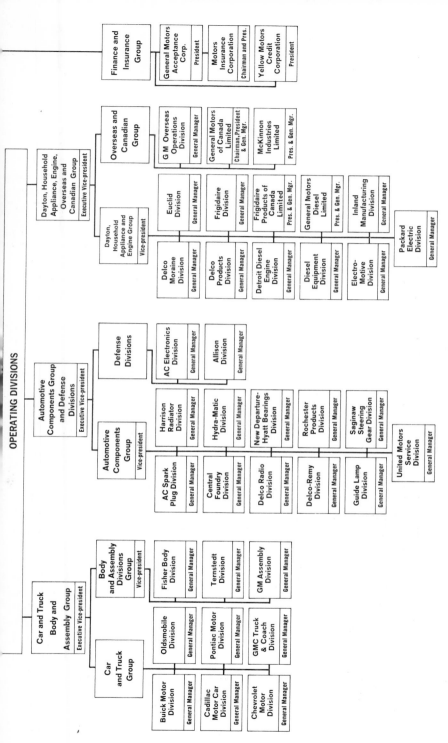

OPERATING DIVISIONS

Fig. 15.8   Organization Chart of General Motors Corporation, 1967

matters as taxation, government procurement, personnel policy and procedures, accounting, financing, contracts and legal matters, and even management itself. The web of government, union, and other controls and complexities in which even the small business finds itself has blurred many of the old sharp distinctions between the small and larger business.

Naturally, the specialized assistance of staff officers and departments is most fully developed in the large company; in fact, the ability of such a company to hire the best staff counsel is one of its principal advantages. But relatively few firms are large. One study disclosed that of the business establishments in the United States only 0.12 per cent, or some 3,600 firms, could be classified as large—having 500 or more employees.[21] In comparison with the United States Army or General Motors Corporation, these firms are very small.

However, even without being able to develop extensive staff departments, the small company can benefit from staff assistance in many ways. Indeed, in the present economic, social, and political environment, the price of error in such matters as the determination of costs and taxes, the maintenance of labor relations, and planning and control is so great that the small firm cannot afford to do without the best possible counsel. Heads of companies of thirty or even fewer employees can frequently afford a general staff assistant to study business policy. No matter how small the company, one of its essential costs is for legal and tax advice on a retainer, per diem, or job basis. Any company can receive accounting counsel at reasonable cost from its auditing firm, and audit of a company's books is usually a necessity in connection with income taxes and bank loans. Other advisory services include those of bankers and those relatively untapped but available in universities and colleges. Just as medical schools contribute to the community—particularly that part of the community which cannot afford the services of a high-priced specialist—so can university staffs be available, at a reasonable cost, to small businesses in such areas as engineering, accounting, economics, and management. The small corporation, furthermore, can use its board of directors as a source of advice and assistance. Sitting on boards of directors has attractions for men challenged by the opportunity for interesting service and for strengthening the free enterprise system.

In the small firm managers often operate in both line and staff capacities. The production manager may be the president's chief adviser on present and future costs and even on product design. The treasurer or controller may be the counselor on taxes, prices and availability of materials, or wage levels. But this fact does not change the essential nature of line and staff relationships, which are the same in small as in large firms. However, a staff organization suitable for the General Motors Corporation would bankrupt a medium-sized company, and a staff organization suitable for the latter would be too expensive for a small firm. Thus, one of the arts of good

---

[21] A. D. H. Kaplan, *Small Business* (New York: McGraw-Hill Book Company, 1948), p. 21.

managing is to tailor the application of the various management devices to the resources available.

LIMITATIONS IN USING STAFF

Although staff departments are necessary to an enterprise and can do much to make it successful, the nature of staff authority and the difficulty of understanding it lead to certain limitations, some of the more important of which are briefly discussed here. Knowing these limitations, both the line executive who is creating a staff and the staff personnel may be better able to skirt them.

Danger of Undermining Line Authority Staff personnel are usually viewed with skepticism by operating executives, who see in them a high potential for harm. Observation of the fortunes of staff departments in many enterprises gives evidence that their prestige ebbs and flows. Too frequently, a president brings in a staff executive, clothes him with authority (frequently very vague), and commands all other managers to be cooperative. The proposals of the staff man are received by the president with enthusiasm, and pressure is brought to bear upon the managers involved to put them into effect. What is actually taking place here is that the authority of the department managers is being undermined, yet, grudgingly and resentfully, the proposals will be accepted, because all will recognize the high tide of the staff's prestige. A continuation of this situation might harm or even destroy the operating departments. Capable managers, not willing to submit to indignity or wait until the tide ebbs, would be snapped up by competitors, and the operating departments would gradually fall into inept hands. The denouement would be for the board of directors to fire the president or, as is more probable, for the president to discharge the staff.

Frequently, the tidal prestige of the ill-conceived or ill-operated staff department, rather than swelling, will only ebb. There are a multitude of ways in which other managers are able subtly to sabotage staff proposals, even those with the imprimatur of the president. Rather than be completely stubborn, the president may then suggest to the staff executive a restudy or tabling of his recommendations. Above all, no president of an enterprise should ever allow the authority of his major department heads to be undermined.

These operating departments represent the main line of the enterprise and their heads gain a degree of indispensability. If a staff adviser forgets that he is to counsel and not to order, if he overlooks the fact that his value lies in the extent to which he strengthens the line manager, and if—worse yet—he should undermine line authority, he risks becoming expendable. If there is a supernumerary in an organization, it is likely to be the staff executive.

A personnel manager recently extended his service activities and advisory functions to encompass control over the actual staffing and much of the actual supervision of subordinates in line departments. For a time, the line managers welcomed his assistance with their personnel problems. But when they realized they no longer controlled their subordinates and when the personnel manager was unwilling to relinquish his control, the resultant outcry forced the president to request the resignation of the personnel manager.

Lack of Responsibility of Staff Advisory departments only propose a plan. Others must make the decision to adopt it and put it into operation. This creates an ideal situation for recrimination and the shifting of blame. The staff will claim that it was a good plan and that it failed because the operating manager was inept, uninterested, or intent on sabotage. The manager who must make the plan work will claim that it was a poor plan hatched by inexperienced and impractical theorists.

Thinking in a Vacuum The argument that a staff position gives the planner time to think is appealing, but it overlooks the possibility of thinking in a vacuum. The weakness of impracticality has resulted, in business and government alike, in friction, loss of morale, and sabotage.

Another weakness in the assumption that planners must be set off from line departments in order to think is the implication that operating managers are without creative ability. They may, indeed, be without specialized knowledge, but this can be furnished them by properly hired and utilized staff assistants. Good operating managers can analyze plans, see long-range applications, and spot fatal weaknesses far better than most staff assistants. An intelligent manager will not delegate his managerial functions, and it is fatal to his managership to strip away real responsibility for activities such as planning and to assign them to a staff assistant.

Management Complication Throughout the discussion of line and staff relationships, reference has been made to the importance of maintaining unity of command. It is not easy for a department head to be responsible to two or three people; at the worker level it is disastrous to attempt multiple responsibility. Some disunity in command may be unavoidable, since functional authority relationships are often unavoidable. But the manager should remain aware of the difficulties of multiple authority and should either limit them—even at the cost of some uniformity or loss of the fruits of specialization—or else establish authority lines to guarantee unity of command at every possible point in the organization structure.

Furthermore, too much staff activity may complicate the line executive's job of direction and control. A corporation president may be so busy dealing with the recommendations of a large number of staff assistants and straightening twisted lines of authority that he may not be able to give requisite time and attention to his operating departments; or the business may become so oriented to making policy and setting procedure that there is little time left to make shoes or give transportation service.

MAKING STAFF WORK

Observation of many business, government, educational, and other enterprises leads the authors to the belief that the line-staff problem is not only one of the most difficult that organizations face, but that it is also the source of an extraordinarily large amount of inefficiency. Solving this problem requires high managerial skill, careful attention to principles, and patient teaching of personnel.

Understanding Authority Relationships Before the problems of line and staff can be solved, the nature of line and staff relationships must be understood. So long as line and staff are regarded merely as groups of people or are confused with groupings of activities—as when service departments are confused with staff—this understanding is lacking. It must be recognized and emphasized that line and staff are relationships and that most managerial jobs have elements of both.

Every manager and his subordinates must understand the purpose of their tasks and whether they operate in a line or in a staff capacity. This understanding must be accompanied by inculcation of the idea that line authority means making decisions and acting on them, while staff authority implies only the right to advise and counsel. The line may tell, but the staff must sell.

Making Line Listen to Staff If staff counsel and advice are justifiable at all, the reason must be found in the complexities of enterprise operation and the need for assistance either from experts or from those freed from more pressing duties to give such assistance. Obviously, if staff help is not used, it would be prudent to abolish it. Line managers should realize that the competent staff assistant offers suggestions to aid and not to undermine or criticize. Although most line-staff friction probably arises from ineptness or over-zealousness on the part of staff people, trouble also arises because the line executive too carefully guards his authority and resents the very assistance he needs.

Line managers should be encouraged or forced to consult with staff. Enterprises would do well to adopt a variation of the practice of compulsory staff assistance found in the Catholic Church, whereby the pope or a bishop must *listen* to staff, even though he can make a contrary decision. In General Motors, the product division manager consults with the staff divisions before proposing a major program or policy to the executive committee. He may not be *required* to do so, but he is likely to find smoother sailing for his proposal if he has done so; and if he can present a united front with the staff division concerned, there will unquestionably be a better chance for its adoption.

Keeping Staff Informed Common criticisms of staff are that specialists operate in a vacuum, fail to appreciate the complexity of the line manager's job, or overlook salient facts in making recommendations. To some extent, these criticisms are warranted because the specialist cannot be expected to know all the fine points of a manager's job. So the specialist must take care that his recommendations deal only with matters within his competency; and the operating manager should not lean too heavily on a recommendation if, as is often the case, it deals only partially with a problem.

However, many criticisms arise because the staff assistant is not kept informed on matters within his province, and even the best assistant cannot advise properly in such cases. If the line manager fails to inform his staff of decisions affecting its work, or if he does not pave the way—through announcements and requests for cooperation—for his staff to obtain the requisite information on specific problems, it cannot function as intended. In relieving his superior of the necessity for gathering and analyzing such information, the staff assistant largely justifies his existence.

Completed Staff Work   Many staff persons overlook the fact that to render the most and best assistance, their recommendations should be complete enough to make possible a simple positive or negative response by the line manager. The staff assistant should be a problem solver and not a problem creator. He creates problems for the manager when his advice is indecisive or obscure, when his conclusions are erroneous, when he has not taken into account all the facts or consulted the persons seriously affected by the proposed solution, or when he does not point out to the manager the pitfalls as well as the advantages in a recommended course of action.

Completed staff work implies the presentation of a clear recommendation based upon full consideration of a problem, clearance with persons importantly affected, suggestions about avoiding any difficulties involved, and, often, preparation of the paper work—letters, directives, job descriptions, and specifications—so that the manager can accept or reject the proposal without further study, long conferences, or unnecessary work. Should he accept the recommendation, thorough staff work provides him with the machinery to put it into effect.

Although many staff problems do not lend themselves to thorough work and some managers may wish detailed work on all problems, the staff man should nevertheless keep uppermost in mind that his job is to assist. Many time-consuming conferences could be avoided or materially shortened if staff work were truly complete.

Staff Work as an Organizational Way of Life   Understanding staff authority lays the foundation for an organizational way of life. Wherever staff is used, its responsibility is to develop and maintain a climate of favorable personal relations. Essentially, the task of the staff assistant is to make the responsible line manager "look good," to help him do a better job. A staff assistant should never attempt to assume credit for his ideas. Not only is this a sure way of alienating his line colleague, but the operating manager who accepts the idea actually bears responsibility for his action. The staff must sell and keep selling itself to other executives. Note that this is selling the staff service and the persons engaged in it and not a particular idea. No discerning manager wants a biased selling job done on the ideas and recommendations of the staff specialist. It is as important that a manager responsible for a decision understand the disadvantages as that he understand the factors in favor of taking a certain course of action.

Even under the best of circumstances, it is difficult to coordinate line and staff authority, for men must be persuaded to cooperate. The staff officer must gain and hold the confidence of his colleagues. He must keep in close touch with the operating departments, know their managers and staffs, and understand their problems. He must, through precept and example, convince his line colleagues that his prime interest is their welfare, and he must deprecate his own contributions while embellishing theirs. He will have "arrived" when line executives seek his advice and ask him to study their problems.

FOR DISCUSSION

1. Select four articles or books in which the terms "line" and "staff" are used. How are they defined? To what extent do the concepts you find agree or disagree with those in this book?

2. Why is it there has been a conflict between line and staff for so long and in so many companies? Can this conflict be removed?

3. Take as examples a number of positions in any kind of enterprise (business, church, government, or elsewhere). Classify them as line and staff.

4. If the task of a person in a purely staff position is to offer advice, how can a person receiving this advice make sure that it is competent, independent, and true?

5. How many cases of functional authority in organization have you seen? Analyzing a few, do you agree that they could have been avoided? If they could have been, would you have eliminated them? If they could not have been avoided or you would not have wanted to eliminate them, how would you remove any possible difficulties which might arise?

SELECTED REFERENCES

Allen, L. A.: *Improving Line and Staff Relationships,* Studies in Personnel Policy No. 153, New York: National Industrial Conference Board, Inc., 1956.

————: *Management and Organization, chaps.* 10–11, New York: McGraw-Hill Book Company, 1958.

Baker, A. W., and R. C. Davis: *Relations of Staff to Line Employees,* Research Monograph No. 72, Columbus, Ohio: Bureau of Business Research, Ohio State University, 1954.

Dale, E.: *Management and the Managers,* chap. 18, New York: McGraw-Hill Book Company, 1965.

————: *Planning and Developing the Company Organization Structure,* Research Report No. 20, part 1, pp. 61–83, New York: American Management Association, 1952.

Fisch, G. G.: *Organization for Profit,* chap. 5, New York: McGraw-Hill Book Company, 1964.

Gulick, L., and L. Urwick (eds.): *Papers on the Science of Administration,* pp. 49–88, New York: Institute of Public Administration, 1937.

Longenecker, J. G.: *Principles of Management and Organizational Behavior,* chap. 10, Columbus, Ohio: Charles E. Merrill Books, Inc., 1964.

McFarland, D. E.: *Co-operation and Conflict in Personnel Administration,* chaps. 2, 4, New York: American Foundation for Management Research, 1962.

Mee, J. F.: "Organization Ideals and Realities," in D. M. Bowman and F. M. Fillerup (eds.), *Management: Organization and Planning,* pp. 53–66, New York: McGraw-Hill Book Company, 1963.

Mooney, J. D.: *The Principles of Organization,* rev. ed., chaps. 3–5, 14, 16–18, New York: Harper & Row, Publishers, Incorporated, 1939.

Myers, C. A., and J. G. Turnbull: "Line and Staff in Industrial Relations," *Harvard Business Review,* vol. 14, no. 4, pp. 113–124 (July, 1956).

Newman, W. H.: *Administrative Action,* 2d ed., chap. 12, Englewood Cliffs, N.J.: Prentice-Hall, Inc., 1963.

—— and C. E. Summer, Jr.: *The Process of Management,* chap. 5, Englewood Cliffs, N.J.: Prentice-Hall, Inc., 1961.

Sampson, Robert C.: *The Staff Role in Management,* New York: Harper & Row, Publishers, Incorporated, 1955.

Schleh, E. C.: "Make Your Staff Pay Its Way," *Harvard Business Review,* vol. 35, no. 2 (March–April, 1957).

Spriegel, W. R., and J. K. Bailey: "The Staff Function in Organization," *Advanced Management,* vol. 17, pp. 2–6 (March, 1952).

Urwick, L.: *Profitably Using the General Staff Position in Business,* General Management Series No. 165, New York: American Management Association, 1953.

CHAPTER SIXTEEN

SKIP

service departments

The concept of a service department is distinct from that of line and staff authority relationships. Such terms as "service," "facilitating," "auxiliary," and, more simply, "support" have been employed to convey the nature of service activities. A service department is an auxiliary activity that facilitates the operation of other departments, contributing to their efficiency. Service departments represent *grouping of activities* and thus involve the performance of an operating function.

A distinction between the service department and others lies in the occasion for its appearance. Although the span of management is the limitation that ordinarily makes departmentation necessary, such is not the case with respect to service activities. One basis for their departmentation is economy of performance: net savings determine the setting up of the particular service department grouping. Another basis may be the desire to gain a single, clear, and definite control of policy and procedure throughout the organization. Thus, service departments are comprised of a concentration of facilitative activities, which, for reasons of operating economy or policy control, are separated from other types of departments.

DEVELOPMENT OF SERVICE DEPARTMENTS

Persons familiar with the large, smoothly operated service department of a large-scale business may overlook such departments in embryo form—for instance, the maintenance, accounting, or personnel departments created in a new college, bank, public utility, or department store. The *reason* for organizing activities in this way may be more clearly observed in connection with the establishment of a small enterprise and in its subsequent growth. Such a metamorphosis of service departmentation is illustrated in Figure 16.1.

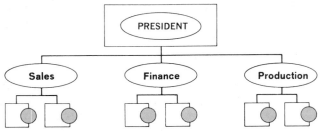

A. Organization without specialized service department.

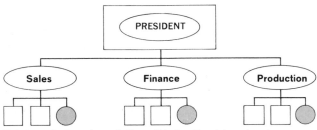

B. Independent service activities within functional departments.

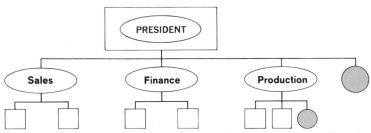

C. Company-wide service department reporting either to the president (1) which is typical of accounting or to the production manager (2) which is typical of maintenance and sometimes personnel.

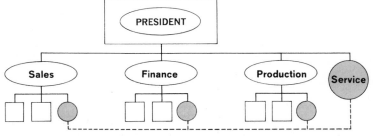

D. Specialized service department with functional authority over decentralized units reintroduced into functional departments.

⊙ Shaded areas represent a kind of service activity.

Fig. 16.1   Metamorphosis of Service Departmentation in a Factory

Origin in Economies of Specialization There is no question, of course, of division of labor in a one-man business, but with the addition of one or more employees the owner shifts some nonmanagerial duties to his subordinates. In the case of a grocery store, the clerks may be expected to receive and check goods against invoice, to price and display goods on shelves, to assist customers, and to contribute to the neat appearance of the store. Continued growth, accompanied by additions to the clerical force, enables the clerks to perform specialized activities. More specific titles are then used to describe their functions, such as cashiers, janitors, stock boys, and the like. Further expansion will force the owner, in accordance with the limitations of the span of management, to organize the enterprise by grouping activities and personnel under grocery, meat, and produce department managers, who will be engaged in assigning subordinates to do paper work, maintenance activity, and line work.

Paper work—such as orders, invoices, pay records, and asset records—is typically assigned to the office of the owner, who may employ a part-time bookkeeper to undertake the accounting function. When the volume of work will support a full-time accountant, such a person will probably, though not necessarily, be hired. Similarly, the work that the part- or full-time maintenance clerks perform may be accomplished more economically if it is split off from the duties of the department managers and regrouped into a single department, the head of which may report to the owner or to the grocery manager. On the other hand, even so large an enterprise as a supermarket may not have a personnel department if adding one would entail considerable overhead and if its staff would be underemployed.

The bases for economy in specialization of service activities are rooted in the use of personal skills and specialized equipment, in the full employment of personnel, and in the potential improvement in the quality of service. The existence of a volume of work sufficient to occupy an employee's full time permits the employment of a skilled individual; hence, a trained accountant is ordinarily hired as soon as a full-time job exists for him. Such a situation is portrayed in Figure 16.1A, where each department services itself with the aid of a few part-time or full-time specialists.

The consolidation of the accounting or maintenance activity in line departments will often permit the economical employment of small specialized equipment, such as computing machines or floor waxers. At the same time, several part-time jobs may be consolidated into a few full-time jobs, to be undertaken by employees able to render prompt service. Centralization to this extent is illustrated in Figure 16.1B, where the shaded department in the sales, production, and finance divisions may represent grouped activities relating to recruiting and training employees.

As a firm continues to grow, further economies may be reaped in the manner suggested in Figure 16.1C. The centralization of all accounting activities into a department whose head reports directly to the chief executive can be justified on the basis of economical use of specialized personnel and equipment and on the easy access to information required for developing budgets, controls, and plans. Alternatively, it is common factory practice to consolidate maintenance service in a department subordinate to the production manager, thus permitting the economical employment of specially trained labor and specialized equipment in a new service department ready to perform services for all departments.

The final stage in the development of service departmentation is illustrated in Figure 16.1D. In this instance the firm has grown to the point where a certain lack of effectiveness is felt from the degree of centralization achieved in Figure 16.1C. These drawbacks become important where mere size destroys the freedom of quick communication, with a consequent deterioration in the quality of service. In response to such a situation it is not uncommon for a firm to reestablish within the important functional divisions a subdepartment whose duty it is to render specialized service. For instance, the main accounting or personnel department may, as a result of delays, misunderstanding of needs, or other problems, be forced to agree to the opening of a cost or a personnel subdepartment in the sales and production divisions, respectively. But, in doing so, they still retain functional authority over the subdepartment head—authority to specify how, but not when or where, he shall undertake his assigned duties. In many cases, the subdepartment head will be trained and appointed to his position by the main service department manager.

Origin in Need for Policy Control   Although service departments usually develop because of a need for the economic advantages of specialization, they are organized occasionally from the need for assuring policy control; in other cases of service departmentation the economies of specialization are buttressed by considerations of policy control. There are many modern service departments where the control influence can be seen. With complicated union agreements and extensive labor legislation requiring uniform interpretation, many companies have been forced to concentrate the handling of such matters in a personnel or industrial relations department. To be sure, economies are gained merely from having specialists work with these problems, but perhaps more important to the firm is the assurance of uniform policies and interpretations.

A comparable situation is illustrated by the important role of a purchasing department, particularly at times when prices are fixed and materials allocated under government control. During the price-fixing days of World War II and the Korean War, many larger businesses even found it wise to establish service departments with the sole function of making sure that price regulations were properly reflected in business practice. Policy control has also had an influence in the organization of a tax department in many companies, a matter requiring close and careful control, although economies from specialization have perhaps been an equally strong motive. Moreover, companies doing much business with the armed forces, such as aerospace and electronics firms, have found it necessary, in the interest of uniform policy, to consolidate contract interpretation and surveillance into a service department.

Difficulty of Evaluation Neither in the literature nor in the recorded experience of business managers can one find substantial information on the importance of service departments. What proportion of the total expense budget should be allocated to service departments? What percentage of total employment should one expect to find in the service groups? Can service departments grow too large? And, if so, what is their optimum size?

The answers to these questions and the practice of business firms in finding such answers may be revealed in future research. An analysis of such practices, the influence of time and circumstance upon them, and the way they differ between types of enterprise may result in the development of practical norms. Although these can never produce absolute answers, they will permit comparison of a given enterprise situation with normal practice in the same industry and thus provide guides for management. The theoretical approach to this problem will give absolute answers if measurable data exist, since the service department justifies its existence by savings in the cost of getting a job done. For instance, proposals for the enlargement of a service activity should be accompanied by analysis of the costs of alternative ways of providing the service or of the cost of not having the service. Thus a proposal on the part of the maintenance department to build a carpenter shop could be analyzed to show anticipated net savings.

However, practical factors ruin all attempts to make successful analyses along these lines. There is the hurry at budget time that prevents proper substantiation of proposals; there is the host of assumptions made by proponents of the expansion, for example, that in the long run it will pay, that morale will be improved, that other firms have benefited by this step, or that better service will be available. In the face of such a barrage of arguments, it is easy to see why the relative size of service departments grows during periods of expanding net profits, when resistance is low. There is little worry in the short run that overhead is creeping upward, that breakeven points are skyrocketing. But this is, of course, the point of great danger. It takes a long depression to reduce effectively the overhead of service groups. Even relatively small decreases in business activity can quickly become embarrassing and create a risky situation for those firms which have succumbed to expanding appropriations for service groups.

There is another reason for the expansion of service activities, emphasized by Holden, Fish, and Smith.[1] These writers make the point that service departments are *expected* to respond to any request with speed and adequacy of performance on the pain of suffering considerable criticism. As a consequence, service departments tend to expand their facilities in order to

[1] P. E. Holden, L. S. Fish, and H. L. Smith, *Top-management Organization and Control* (New York: McGraw-Hill Book Company, 1951), p. 175.

avoid this type of criticism, only to run into equally devastating criticism of their cost.

FUNCTIONS OF SERVICE DEPARTMENTS

The functions of service departments, even those with the same titles, vary widely from time to time and from firm to firm. All personnel departments do not carry on the same activities, and wide variations in function are typical of departments of accounting, real estate, law, traffic, general office work, engineering, maintenance, and purchasing. To determine first the exact function of a particular service group, it is necessary to learn what duties have been assigned and what authority has been delegated to its manager.

Service to Other Departments   Service departments would hardly exist if they were not to perform a service for major divisions. The maintenance department, for example, may furnish for all departments heating, ventilation, repair of the business premises, installation of equipment, and janitorial service. But whether this department should also be responsible for redecorating, internal modifications of the building, the purchase of small motors and their installation, relocation of power outlets, salvage, or equipment repair depends entirely upon the exact assignment of duties. Questions of precedence of the various departments in receiving service might be determined in the same way.

One of the problems encountered in service departments is that the quality of the service performed for the several divisions within the firm may vary. It may be difficult, for example, to persuade the accounting department to provide for the sales or market research department a cost service similar to that which it offers the manufacturing division. Or the centralized stenographic department may offer ample service to a top executive but feel less inclined to be as alertly useful to a minor manager.

The organization of a department for the purpose of performing certain services for all other departments is almost always accompanied by an edict that its service must be used. This makes sense, because the cost of a service department is a burden and underemployment results in undue cost. Many managers object to granting any department a monopoly of the service to be performed and are quick to complain of poor results and high costs. This dissatisfaction is a continuing source of contention in enterprises. Frequently it results in improvement, but it can also result in the decentralization of the service activity or its abolition in favor of buying the service from independent entrepreneurs.

It is not unusual for certain advisory duties to be assigned to service groups. When these functions are undertaken, they are performed in the same manner as that in which a staff group would undertake them. A maintenance or a traffic department frequently carries out an investigation and makes a recommendation to the proper authorities for the purchase of machinery, trucks and trucking facilities, or transportation facilities at one location rather than another. A personnel department may be assigned the duty of investigating and reporting on the practices of leading business firms with respect to executive training programs. The legal department may be required to study and recommend action relating to workmen's compensation. The general office manager may be asked to make a recommendation about the best method of reproducing forms. And the real estate department may be charged with the duty of making recommendations with respect to the prospective purchase of a warehouse.

The chief difficulty arising from service departments acting in a staff capacity results from a misunderstanding of the kind of authority delegated. Service departments make decisions that facilitate the operations of other departments. A manufacturing department may want to place a machine in a second-floor location, but a maintenance department can veto such action on the ground that the weight and vibration of the machine will create a hazard. A legal department will determine how the clauses in a sales contract shall read; a traffic department will establish its own routes and select its own equipment; and an engineering department will write a bill of materials. In all these areas, the authority to make the decision is delegated to the service department. But when the same departments act in a staff capacity, they do so with authority to investigate and recommend, but not to decide.

There may be certain instances in which the distinction is not clear. For example, who is to decide what colors will be used in redecorating an office? Clearly, the maintenance department is responsible for repair and upkeep. But does this also involve the selection or even the recommendation of a color scheme? Many arguments have arisen over such matters.

A different problem is created where a power-oriented manager of a service department also has a staff function. Despite his originally restricted power, he will reach out for decision-making authority and frequently obtain it by default. He may be especially energetic and efficient, in which case others may be content with whatever action he may take. Or he may gloss over situations where an overt act may create opposition. Or, as often happens, he may encounter the devastating opposition of operating managers, who can hardly let the service department in a staff relationship run the business.

Functional Authority Relationships   In many instances it is convenient to delegate functional authority to a service department. In such cases it is given a prescriptive right over certain phases of an activity being performed in other departments. For instance, the accounting department may have the functional authority to train and assign cost men for the factory. *How* their work is done may be the responsibility of the accounting department, but in every other respect the cost men work for the plant manager, are paid by him, and conform to the same working conditions as other factory employees.

The grant of functional authority to service departments often works well, although there is one exception. This involves the problem of divided loyalties. In case of a dispute, in the above instance, between the factory and the accounting department, the cost man has a difficult time deciding where he stands. He is serving the factory in a manner that the parent service department disapproves and, consequently, may be expected to stand with the factory in matters of improving service facilities. On the other hand, his promotion may be in the hands of the service department. Smoothing out these situations is truly a job for a diplomat, although diplomacy may not have been regarded as a qualification when the man was originally employed.

Two managers were heard talking about the support departments in their agency. "I cannot put up with the overbearing attitude of that facilities manager. I can't get any service out of him. He is always saying 'No!' to every request I make."

The second manager was very surprised. "I don't have that trouble at all. Since his service is free to me anyway, I have him and his people down here every chance I get. I invite them to study my problem and help me get my requirement for facilities into my budget proposal on time. Of course, I don't get all I ask, but I'm doing very well."

"Well," the first manager responded, "maybe the fellow just wants to know that he's appreciated."

"On that point I propose a new management principle," replied the second manager. "Staff and support groups want to be loved."

Nonmanagerial Aspects of Service Departments   As in the case of all other grouped activities, many of the functions of service departments are entirely nonmanagerial in nature. Carpenters, clerks, painters, and typists work as they would if they were employed in a production, sales, or finance division. In their own departments, service managers undertake the same managerial functions of planning, organizing, staffing, directing, and controlling as do managers of line departments. But the *activity* of serving the operating departments is entirely nonmanagerial in nature. Record keeping, repairing, calculating, and transporting, undertaken purely as an aid to other departments, are simply "work." Since the essential feature of service departments is the *grouping* of activities, the actual work is exactly the same as that which would be required in the total absence of service departments.

PLACE IN THE ORGANIZATION STRUCTURE

So long as service activities remain undifferentiated or are scattered throughout the organization structure, questions of good organization practice in respect to them either do not arise or are relatively minor in importance. But at the point where the economies of grouped performance or the desirability of policy control begin to weigh heavily, managers must determine not only whether to create a service department but also where to assign it in the organization structure. When the problem of servicing geographically separated units arises, a further complication ensues.

Independent versus Subsidiary Department   The practices of business managers in locating a service department in the organization structure are so widely diverse that no general rule can be derived. Personnel departments are found within production divisions or at the first level of departmentation. Accounting may be found within the treasurer's division or at the level of the functional departments. Legal departments may be independent and report to the chief executive, or they may be found within the controller's office or in the finance division. Maintenance and traffic may be assigned to the production or sales departments or they may be independent of both. In the face of such varied treatment of service groups, can anything be said about the desirability of a given practice? Recourse to the principles of intimate association will aid in differentiating between good and poor practice in many cases. The following skeletonized charts, showing the major functional departmentation and the location of important service departments, illustrate good organizational structuring in important areas of enterprise activity.

The independent medium-to-large department store   The most usual departmentation of service activities in a retail store of this type includes accounting, maintenance, personnel, and customer service. Good practice would dictate the arrangement in Figure 16.2. Accounting is here shown as independent of the other functions, with the chief accountant reporting to the controller, who is normally assigned the duties of maintaining the financial records and developing information required by other managers. To the general superintendent, an important officer in department-store structuring, fall the duties of maintaining the physical facilities of the firm, managing the warehouse, making purchases of operating supplies, and supervising store protection. It is customary to assign to him such additional service activities as personnel, shipping and receiving, and customer service. All these activities are intimately associated in the sense that they contribute to the success of the main business of the firm, that is, to sell merchandise. The inclusion of customer service is a happy solution of a difficult problem, since it lends confidence that the policy governing the return of merchandise will be carried out impartially and with justice to both the firm and the customer. The inclusion of the personnel activity reflects a decision that this function should be coordinated at a level just below that of the chief executive rather than in his office.

The independent full-service wholesaler   Good organization practice for this type of enterprise, as illustrated in Figure 16.3, does not differ materially from that proposed for the independent department store, because both types of enterprise are in the business of buying for resale. Consequently, each requires the services of a merchandise manager, a controller, perhaps a treasurer, and a superintendent.

The terminology that different types of wholesale firms employ to identify the departments suggested above varies widely. The terms em-

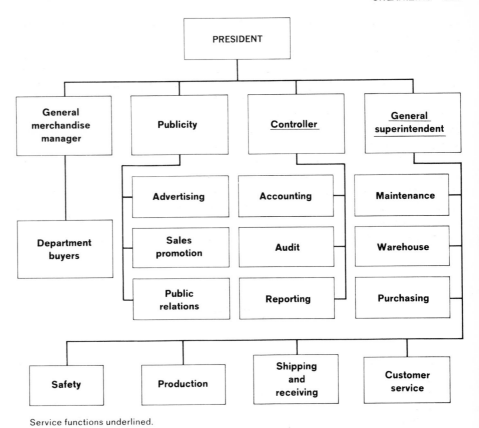

Service functions underlined.

Fig. 16.2 Typical Service Departmentation in a Department Store

ployed here indicate the activities normally assigned to the several departments. It is important to separate the controller from the treasurer because each is a check upon the other. Consequently, the heads of these departments should report to the same superior. The service manager is assigned those activities that relate to the smooth operation of facilities. It may be wise for the president to have the responsibility for these functions centralized. Depending upon the number of employees and whether they are unionized, the assignment of the personnel service will normally be made either to the service manager or to an independent department. The latter solution is a good one if the director also has charge of negotiations with the union and undertakes the myriad activities relating to employee welfare; if neither of these situations obtains, the personnel activity will ordinarily be the responsibility of the service manager.

The manufacturing establishment The important service departments in manufacturing establishments are accounting, industrial relations, and maintenance. Their assignment in a typical organization structure is shown in Figure 16.4. For reasons already stated, the accounting service is best separated from the activities of the treasurer. Since the heads of these departments should report to a common superior, smaller concerns coordinate them at the level of the president, but larger ones frequently install a vice-president in charge of finance to undertake this activity. The usual practice of assigning maintenance to the production manager rests on the fact that most maintenance activity is performed for his department. Since the person in charge of manufacturing has the greatest interest in making certain that maintenance is carried out efficiently, he is likely to give it adequate supervision; it is probable that the other department heads, for whom the maintenance group also peforms service, would neglect such an activity if it were assigned to them. Manufacturing enterprises have tended, in recent years, to detach the personnel department from the factory and require its head to report to some general officer. This is particularly likely to occur if

Service functions underlined.

Fig. 16.3   Typical Service Departmentation in a Wholesale Enterprise

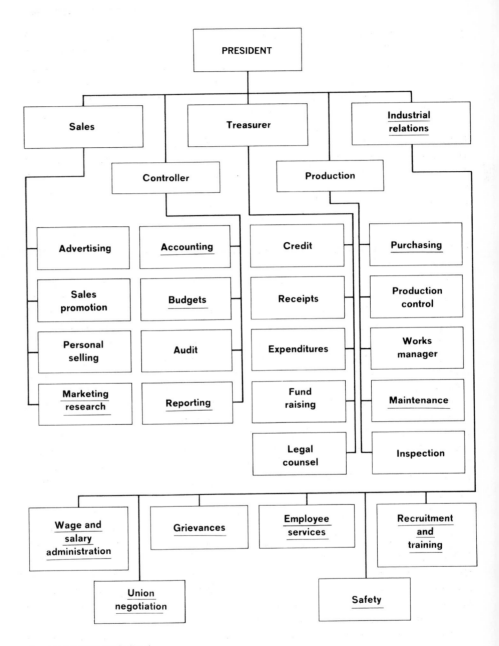

Service functions underlined.

Fig. 16.4 Service Departmentation in a Manufacturing Enterprise

the personnel director is also assigned the duty of negotiating with trade or industrial units and handling grievances. If he is merely concerned with record keeping, recruiting of labor, employee services, and plant safety, he will still quite properly report to the production manager, for the same reasons as were suggested for the maintenance service activity. In such a case, the production manager would carry on negotiations with the union.

Relationship between Central and Divisional Service Departments In Figure 16.1 the successive steps by which a centralized service department emerges are illustrated in sections A, B, and C. Section D, however, illustrates a reversal of this trend. It shows an independent service department, together with subsidiary groupings in the major divisions of the enterprise structure. This development is exceedingly important in large-scale enterprises.

Reasons for Decentralization of Service Departments The same calculus that pointed strongly to the economies of specialized service departments will yield a somewhat different answer when applied to very large enterprises. As a firm grows in size, the net advantage progressively favors an increasing degree of centralization in the service activity until an optimum is reached. When line department heads, however, find themselves charged with sharply rising costs for sustaining the accounting, personnel, and maintenance services, they are likely to question their value. And if, in addition, they feel that these services are ineffective, that attention to their particular needs is lacking, or that reports required for their operations lag, pressures to decentralize the service departments arise. It is important to note, however, that throughout this period of growing criticism no one is able to place a finger on the total cost of alternative ways to provide the necessary service. Even an accurate measure of observable costs fails to tell the complete story because of the many intangibles involved. One of the most interesting of these is the attitude of line and staff department heads toward service bureaucracies.

Businessmen are quick to recognize a striking parallel between the operating tendencies of service departments and the costly, rigid formalism in government. The private bureaucracy reaches its terrifying size, not in one fell swoop, but by minute accretions of function and procedure. It is here that the "empire builder" is seen at his best. The heads of these departments are quite free to propose further "services" from time to time, each of which is viewed marginally and evaluated in terms of its particular contribution rather than in terms of the complete service the department was created to perform. Many added services can readily be created by an accounting, a personnel, an industrial engineering, or a traffic department. The critical issue is their net help to the major departments. The basis for measuring such aid is its cost as compared with its over-all value. Viewed in this light, few bureaucracies could flower. Thus, the lack of adequate top-level supervision of service departments on an over-all basis and the lack of adequate service standards create a no man's land wherein he who asserts that a service is needed is rarely opposed. The executive who criticizes the cost of the service knows full well that the whole department cannot be eliminated. Since he does not know just where the cuts should be made, he is inclined to favor a type of decentralization that will give him some control over the amount and cost of the service for which he pays.

Bases for Decentralization   The bases upon which a centralized service department should be decentralized and its functions scattered among other departments are complex. Such an undertaking involves at least three areas of investigation: (1) Should a given service activity be decentralized among *all* other departments? (2) Should all the services performed be decentralized? (3) If not, what should be the relationship between the decentralized services and the remainder of the centralized service departments? One must turn to economic and management principles for a proper analysis of these issues.

Quite patently, the fragmentation of such service activities as traffic, purchasing, personnel, and maintenance among *all* departments is undesirable. The chief argument against this procedure is economic. For instance, the centralized recruitment of nonmanagerial personnel permits the economical use of advertising, the employment of skilled interviewers, and the full employment of centralized effort. The centralization of traffic permits full employment of high-cost equipment rather than the use of less desirable apparatus. These are the economic reasons why company doctors and nurses are not assigned to finance, engineering, or sales departments and why company-owned automobiles are not assigned to persons in the production, personnel, or accounting departments.

On the other hand, the assignment of decentralized service activities to *some* departments is feasible. A company that operates with a head office and two or more branch plants may have no centralized maintenance, personnel, or traffic department. Distance, time, and variations in the labor market may point to the economy of decentralization in these instances.

The problem of discriminating between the services of a given department for the purpose of decentralizing some services but not others raises issues involving the quality, as well as the cost, of the service. Few would deny the need to establish a centralized general accounting department. This service activity involves financial and tax accounting for the firm as well as the recording and reporting of information internally useful for decision making. Financial accounting should remain centralized in view of realizable economies; the lack of direct interest in, and understanding by, the several department heads; the greater ease in achieving proper policy interpretations; and the relative ease of coordinating it with other functional areas. On the other hand, it is probable that cost accounting should be decentralized, at least to the extent of the sales and manufacturing divisions. The typical deplorable lack of production and sales cost data can be explained by the centralization of cost accounting in a separate department, where the needs of major departments for accurate and timely information are not always understood. Although it is not unusual for some types of cost reporting to be decentralized in the production division, it is extremely rare for this to be permitted in the sales division. It is little wonder that distribution costs remain indeterminate in so many manufacturing, wholesale, retail, and service establishments.

Upon reading the above paragraph, the computer enthusiast remarked to the consultant, "These problems no longer exist. We now have electronic data processing. We simply program operating data and send appropriate slices of it to operating managers."

"The only thing you have really changed is the place where the data are summarized," remarked the consultant.

"I don't see why cost men are still required in the operating departments," observed the specialist. "Let the managers read the reports."

"Have you ever met a manager who did read them?" responded the consultant.

Similar issues are resolved in favor of decentralized service when the recruitment of salesmen is undertaken by the sales division rather than by the personnel department; when the traffic department buys and services but does not control the use of automobiles for sales personnel; and when the production division trains and assigns service personnel to the sales division but does not control its activities.

Elimination of centralized service and centralization of service represent the two extremes in the organization of these activities. Partial decentralization, contemplated in the grant of functional authority, is middle ground; but it is an unstable compromise, giving rise to recurrent shifts in the degrees of authority over the decentralized service. The delicacy of the makeshift is beyond question.

Advantages of Partial Decentralization   The right kind and degree of partial decentralization of service activities can be attractive from several points of view. Complaints about poor service are usually forestalled. The decentralized unit comes to understand the importance of time and works with good will to provide quick service. Or, even where there is little improvement in the time factor, the operating executive can be made to understand the reasons for the delay.

However, the allocation of service department overhead to an operating division is a source of continuous irritation. Comparisons are made, frequently on a subjective basis, between the uncontrollable charge and the value of the service, much to the disadvantage of the former. Operating department heads admit the need for the service but are frustrated by lack of control over its cost. Consequently, when decentralization does take place, service personnel are in a position to emphasize their contribution to operations in a much more direct and forceful manner. And skill in doing this can result in allaying dissatisfaction with the amount of the service charge in the operating department budget.

A closely related yet distinct advantage of partial decentralization lies in the importance to the major department managers of getting control over the service function. The successive splitting off of activities which occurs in the centralizing process is viewed with grudging concern by line executives. Aside from losing power, they worry about the inevitable decline in the quality of coordination. When their feeling is confirmed by experience with the central service setup, the move to decentralize, even on a basis entirely different from the original one, is greeted with much satisfaction. For once again direct control over much of the activity will be established; and this way of doing things is one that operating men like.

There is still another advantage in partial decentralization. The operating manager may confidently look forward to obtaining a special pleader in the centralized service department. For instance, the frustration that production and sales managers feel toward the controller's office is proverbial. The men often fail to understand one another, and the operating man often feels that he cannot get needed information from the accounting department. The decentralization of the cost function often results in the "friend-at-court" situation. The cost personnel come to understand the production or distribution problems of the operating executive, evaluate the necessity for reports containing different content and better explanations of accounting practices, and become, perhaps, the best group to represent the operating department in the centralized service department. This is a great advantage for those operating managers—and they are legion—who are not trained in accounting and who are at a loss to deal with the man who creates the figures.

Dangers of Partial Decentralization Partial decentralization of service activities is not without its disadvantages, several of which have been suggested. Functional authority relationships give rise to potential conflicts between the managers of service and operating departments in question. The difficulty becomes clear as soon as a service is divided. After decentralizing cost accounting, the controller may draw up instructions relating to what cost data to gather and how and when to report them. But who appoints the cost representative? Suppose the production manager demands entirely different reporting of data, or new data? Who decides questions of pay rates and promotions of the cost representatives? And who terminates them? These matters, usually ignored when decentralization is decided upon, inevitably lead to recurring controversies.

There is also the danger that, once started, the trend toward decentralization of service will be permitted to go beyond the bounds dictated by savings in time and cost and by improvement in service. The initial exuberance in establishing division service groups is sufficient to discourage a careful analysis of the complete cost picture. Consequently, underemployment of personnel and equipment and the use of inferior equipment are encountered in a discouraging number of cases.

Finally, there is the danger that the divided loyalties of the decentralized personnel will not only lead to instability of the function but will also result in disaster for the personnel. The fact that, whenever contentions arise, such people are caught between the upper and nether stones of central service and operating division underscores the human cost of decentralization. Also, the ease or difficulty in getting pay raises and promotions must be fully considered by the employee as he considers whether he prefers to work in a service or in an operating department.

THE ECONOMICS OF SERVICE DEPARTMENTS

Business managers have a continuing concern with the economics of service departments. The relationship of service activities to other departments and to the total activity of the enterprise is never settled. Circumstances that favor the growth of service activities can change radically when the enterprise must trim its sails in face of the changing economies of war, defense, and peace; of the cyclical stages of business activity; of revolutionary innovations in products and their uses; and of technological and organizational changes in the economic structure.

Costs and Benefits The manager must balance the costs of service departments against the benefits they provide and decide whether the firm stands to gain from modifying their scope and duties.

Measurable and unmeasurable costs The costs of operating a service department can rarely be set down in a neat row and summed. Much to the discouragement of cost analysts, many unmeasurable elements—among them poor communication, delays, failures to act, and simple arrogance— must somehow be evaluated. The separation of service from other functions inevitably leads to reduced understanding of each other's needs on the part of the personnel concerned. Accounting departments, primarily concerned with the record keeping that facilitates their reporting of financial and tax information, often overlook the needs of other departments for cost data. This particular situation develops from failure to realize that an accounting department should perform a tax and financial service for the total enterprise *and* provide data in the form most useful to the other departments and their managers. Some firms solve this by creating a new service department to perform the functions of reporting, analysis, and internal auditing.

Accounting departments are by no means the only service activities that show up the cost of poor communication. Many are those who have taken part in arguments between a department requesting better lighting and the service manager who maintains that his meter shows that lighting is normal. Or consider the personnel manager who insists upon interviewing salesmen despite the sales manager's obvious lack of confidence in the results. In these and many other situations, the service activity is fighting for what it considers its prerogatives, while the line department criticizes the value of the results.

A second type of cost of service departments involves delayed performance. Every executive is conscious of the "poor" service he receives. This feeling is induced by delays in the receipt of cost or budget reports, by failure of the personnel department to maintain an active roster of immediately available candidates, and by the frustrations of postponed installations or repairs of equipment by the maintenance department. Rarely is the cost of these delays actually calculated. Indeed, they may not be measurable at all, but this does not make them less costly.

Sometimes confusion arises concerning who should act in a given situation. Lack of clarity in the assignment of duties can be an expensive mistake when a job is neglected because no one is certain he should undertake it— a situation comparable to a ball dropping between two fielders because each thought the other would catch it. Efficient recruitment of employees with certain skills may be neglected because both the personnel and the line department heads thought the other was following through. And the production manager may complain that the maintenance department is not servicing a new machine when no budget provision was made for this activity, the manufacturer having sold the equipment on a service basis in the first place.

A further type of unmeasurable cost involves a frequently encountered characteristic of bureaucracies—arrogance. It is unfortunate but true that personnel in service departments occasionally develop an overbearing attitude toward other activities, a result usually of the political power of the service head within the organization structure. Lordly attitudes breed suspicion and opposition which disrupt the basic activity of service to the line.

Finally, there is the measurable cost of overhead. A basic theory of service specialization is that the centralized department can perform an activity more economically than decentralized departments. But few indeed are the departments that are established *after* a careful study of relative costs. The savings are taken for granted. With the passage of time, moreover, service departments tend to acquire further areas of service, with attendant provisions in the budget. Starting with few duties, a personnel department grows by the successive additions of other activities such as interviewing, interdepartment transfers, safety, cafeterias, and recreation. A maintenance department soon blossoms out with a machine shop of its own, a carpenter's repair shop, an electric shop, and storage facilities. These accretions are requested and approved, one by one, on the ground that other companies have these things or that higher morale or better service will result. Such assertions often are not documented. And in the rush to get the enterprise budget approved, the top managers often fail to insist upon cost data to substantiate claimed savings. No one stops to consider the *total* outlay for service or the relative growth of service to line departments. Indeed, there is little use in doing so, since no one knows how large a service department should be permitted to grow. But the effect of growth is certain. It lies in the burden charged to operating departments.

Benefits Since service departments may be justified on the basis of savings in cost as compared with other methods of servicing, the evaluation of benefits is exceedingly important. Benefits include skilled service, adequate attention to service, and smoothing out of fluctuating needs.

Centralization of service permits the employment of specialized skills and group activities that would otherwise be scattered through the organization structure. For instance, the centralization of recruiting, interviewing, and testing in a personnel department brings to one place a volume of work that makes it economical to employ experts on a full-time basis, in contrast with the sporadic, part-time, seasonal attention given these activities by personnel employed mainly for entirely different purposes. Thus it is probable, although unproved, that centralized performance of these activities by specialists costs less, compared with the value received, than would diffused personnel work.

Getting adequate attention paid to the performance of a given service through the centralization of the activity is a complex idea, for what is "adequate" is difficult to define. Generally, the service department has the manpower and the time to carry out properly services within its province. For instance, it is said that a personnel department can give adequate attention to testing, whereas other departments would probably neglect this work. But the matter is not disposed of so easily. It is clear that any department that had the budget for this function could give as much attention to it as the personnel department. This is also true of such other factors as the amount of time spent on a specific task and the timeliness of such attention.

Finally, the benefit received by ironing out uneven demands for certain types of service can be exceedingly valuable. The maintenance department in a factory is a good example. Seasonal changes in weather lead to changing emphasis on certain types of work performed by maintenance. Winter calls for attention to heating, humidity, and lighting service. Summer permits an emphasis on painting, cleaning, and construction. If the same work force can be utilized to carry out both groups of activities, steady annual employment can be furnished to a given complement of men.

Evaluation The importance of making a determined effort to weigh the cost and benefits of a given service cannot be stressed too much. Haste in approving expansive budgets for service departments permits specious arguments, generalizations, and hazy references to savings to go unchallenged. Such haste is particularly likely during a succession of good business years, when the enterprise can afford luxuries, or during periods of excess-profits taxes, when businessmen may be tempted to approve expanded service budgets purely because they can be financed on a "cheap" dollar.

Just because intangible costs and benefits make accurate evaluations literally impossible, every proposed expansion should be analyzed with great caution. Otherwise, overhead may grow to the point where the firm has to do an enormous business just to stay even, and heavy fixed costs will cause undue embarrassment to the firm in the face of even moderate recessions.

Purchased versus Owned Services Up to this point, attention has been directed to the internal problems involved in the organization of service activities. Various ways of handling these activities have been considered, with the emphasis on tangible and intangible savings and on policy control.

There is, however, an additional alternative available, that of purchasing the service from another firm. Consideration of this alternative requires an analysis of the possible net savings that may be realized.

Analysis of savings through purchased services   In analyzing the purchase of services, there are several measurable costs to be considered. One is the savings in the direct cost of operating a service as compared with hiring another firm to operate it. Since current or projected service department expense and capital budgets are readily available, they may be directly compared with the bids of outside firms, so that there can be no room for doubt about the realizable savings, if any.

One factor in direct cost sometimes overlooked is the maintenance and operator-training service provided for in the purchase contract with suppliers and included in the price of the equipment. This often occurs in the sale of expensive machines; consequently, the cost of training employees to use the equipment and the cost of maintaining it should be omitted from all considerations of service costs in purchasing such machines, whether provided in-plant or bought outside.

Some argue that purchased service involves heavy losses when it involves waiting time for the agency to come and repair defective equipment. Basically, this is a question of the value of lost time and the quality of service available. The proper approach is to determine whether in fact there are greater delays in purchased service than in owned service and then calculate the value of the net loss in time. This reasoning is particularly appropriate in the case of maintenance service on production equipment. It is claimed that, when the machines go down, a whole section of productive activity stops and that this is expensive. It is by no means always certain, however, that an internal maintenance department would actually be on the job sooner than the purchased service. Maintenance groups make appointments and develop time schedules for providing service, and while production may carry top priority, this does not mean that service can be given promptly, since the men may be involved in other assignments or may have to wait for parts. Also, business firms habitually purchase certain kinds of service—that for typewriters and electronic equipment, for example—on a stand-by basis. Once the net differential in lost time can be calculated, it is an easy matter to figure the cost of the net loss. Unless this is substantial, it does not provide a proper basis for preferring owned service.

Another calculable cost savings between owned and purchased service lies in the frequency of the required service. For instance, legal counsel needed but a few times a year is much too expensive to provide within the firm. Some enterprises have little use for transportation equipment except at odd times. An owned service must, at a minimum, be needed sufficiently to occupy the full time and attention of at least one person from one year to another. Full employment for short periods is not enough. If it is argued that full employment is unnecessary, because personnel may be assigned other tasks, the answer is that such skills are likely to compare very unfavorably with those available from outside firms, and therefore the quality of the internal service is likely to suffer.

A final measurable cost concerns the burden of service expense, an overhead cost if the service is owned. As explained in previous sections, it is difficult to control the growth of owned service and to cut down an overhead of this nature. The firm that purchases service is not hampered at all with this problem. The kind and amount of service is contracted for; it is an operating, and not an overhead, cost of doing business; and it can readily be dispensed with or postponed whenever indicated. Thus, as a firm approaches a cutback in its business, it is indeed in an enviable position if it has purchased services rather than owned them.

There are, on the other hand, certain unmeasurable costs of purchased service that require mention. These include the matter of divided attention of the service firm, the danger of not knowing what service to ask for, and the question of relative managerial skill. In the first place, the service available from outside firms usually does not belong to any one customer. For instance, an enterprise selling accounting service to other firms is interested in having several customers. The complaint made against such service is that customers fail to receive adequate attention from the specialists. This complaint may be quite legitimate, but the entailed loss is probably unmeasurable.

The second matter involving unmeasurable costs involves the firm not knowing what to ask a service to do. This is by no means unusual. The managers of nearly all enterprises are in a quandary at one time or another, not knowing what to expect of a personnel, accounting, legal, traffic, or other service group. In the main, this difficulty is the result of a lack of understanding of what the service is capable of doing and of how to use it effectively. For instance, through lack of training, relatively few business managers understand the important services that a controller can perform. Unfortunately, the controller may not know, either. Unless division managers know what to ask for in the way of form and content of reports, they may not get them. On the other hand, a manager can probably always get the purchased service he needs by knowing what he needs and insisting upon getting it.

Third, it may be considered strange that there are differences in skill between the managers of owned and purchased service. Nevertheless, the firm that wants to provide its own service may have great difficulty in finding a manager as skilled as the managers of outside service firms. This is frequent in the case of legal, insurance, tax, real estate, and other services and also with respect to certain aspects of personnel, maintenance, and accounting. In any case, the value of the relative managerial skills is largely incalculable.

Practical application   There are no general rules that can be summoned for a quick solution of the problem of whether to own or purchase service. It is not possible to say that any particular service should be purchased. Each instance requires individual analysis and should be decided on its merits. But the framework of the correct *procedure* is both clear and applicable to all kinds of service activities. The first step involves the careful calculation of the measurable costs of owned versus purchased services and the determination of the net savings to the firm. The second step consists of the painstaking analysis of the unmeasurable relative costs of the alternatives. The third step requires the comparison of the results of the first steps and a decision in the best interests of the firm.

In the situation where the contemplated service is *in addition to* activities currently performed by either an owned or a purchased service, the same scientific approach is essential but with a difference in the nature of the costs. The important costs here are marginal and should be calculated in terms of the added expense of each alternative. For instance, a firm with an owned personnel department may need a training service. The question arises whether to add this activity to the department or purchase it outside. On the basis of the relative costs involved, the decision may go either way.

FOR DISCUSSION

1. What kind of authority or authorities do you believe a controller exercises?
2. Very few managers distinguish between staff and service groups. What are the advantages of making the distinction?
3. Many managers feel that service departments "run the business." What faults in assigning activities and in communication may explain this situation?
4. How do you think the budget for a service department should be fixed?

SELECTED REFERENCES

"Contracting Out Maintenance Jobs Is Getting to Be a Corporate Habit," *Business Week* (Nov. 1, 1958).

Dale, E.: *Planning and Developing the Company Organization Structure,* Research Report No. 20, pp. 72–73, New York: American Management Association, 1952.

Holden, P. E., L. S. Fish, and H. L. Smith: *Top-management Organization and Control,* part C, sec. 2, New York: McGraw-Hill Book Company, 1951.

Newman, W. H.: *Administrative Action,* chap. 9, Englewood Cliffs, N.J.: Prentice-Hall, Inc., 1951.

Organization of Staff Functions, Studies in Personnel Policy No. 165, New York: National Industrial Conference Board, Inc., 1958.

"What Should Maintenance Cost?" *Factory,* vol. 111, no. 1 (January, 1953).

decentralization *Philosophy of delegation of Authority*

of authority

Whether authority should be concentrated or dispersed throughout the organization is a question not so much of *what kind* as of *how much* authority. Decentralization of authority is a fundamental phase of delegation; to the extent that authority is not delegated, it is centralized. Absolute centralization in one person is conceivable, but it implies no subordinate managers and therefore no structured organization. Consequently, it can be said that some decentralization characterizes all organizations. On the other hand, there cannot be absolute decentralization, for if a manager should delegate *all* his authority, his status as manager would cease; his position would be eliminated; there would, again, be no organization. Centralization and decentralization are, therefore, tendencies; they are qualities like "hot" and "cold."

As one management expert[1] has explained the nature of decentralization, the degree of decentralization is greater:

1. The greater the number of decisions made lower down the management hierarchy.
2. The more important the decisions made lower down the management hierarchy. For example, the greater the sum of capital expenditure that can be approved by the plant manager without consulting anyone else, the greater the degree of decentralization in this field.
3. The more functions affected by decisions made at lower levels. Thus companies which permit only operational decisions to be made at separate branch plants are less decentralized than those which also permit financial and personnel decisions at branch plants.
4. The less checking required on the decision. Decentralization is greater

---

[1] E. Dale, *Planning and Developing the Company Organization Structure,* Research Report No. 20 (New York: American Management Association, 1952), p. 107.

349

when no check at all must be made; less when superiors have to be informed of the decision after it has been made; still less if superiors have to be consulted before the decision is made. The fewer people to be consulted, and the lower they are on the management hierarchy, the greater the degree of decentralization.

"Centralization" has been used to describe tendencies other than the dispersal of authority, as in centralization of performance (discussed below on page 356). This is a problem of geography: a business characterized by centralized performance operates in a single location or under a single roof. Centralization often refers, furthermore, to departmental activities: service divisions centralize similar or specialized activities in a single department. But when centralization is discussed as an aspect of management, it refers to withholding or delegating authority and the authority dispersal or concentration of decision making.

Although closely related to delegation of authority, decentralization is more: it is a philosophy of organization and management, implying both selective dispersal and concentration of authority. It requires far more than simply handing authority to subordinates. As companies find when they begin to decentralize, it requires careful selection of what decisions to push down into the organization structure and what to hold at or near the top, specific policy making to guide the decision making, selection and training of people, and adequate controls. Indeed, decentralization encompasses all areas of management.

FACTORS DETERMINING THE DEGREE OF DECENTRALIZATION OF AUTHORITY

A manager cannot ordinarily be for or against decentralization of authority. He may *like* to delegate authority, or he may *like* to make all the decisions himself. A well-known despot in a certain large enterprise in this country, who would like to make all the decisions, finds that he cannot. Even the autocrat in a smaller enterprise is often forced to delegate some authority.[2]

Although the temperament of individual managers affects the extent of authority delegation, other factors also affect it. Most of these are beyond the control of the individual manager. One manager may resist their influence, while another recognizes them and delegates accordingly, but no successful manager can ignore them.

Costliness of the Decision   Perhaps the overriding factor determining the extent of managerial decentralization is, as in other aspects of policy, the criterion of costliness. As a general rule, the more costly the action to be

---

[2] *Business Week*, pp. 182–194 (Sept. 6, 1952), ran a feature story on the president of a $50,000,000-a-year rayon converter who apparently disproves "what the books say" by not delegating decision making. Yet, even though he makes a surprising number of detailed decisions, the article quotes him as disposing of callers by saying, "See my advertising manager," or "Talk to Marty."

decided upon, the more probable it is that the decision will be made at the upper levels of management. This cost may be reckoned directly in dollars and cents or in such intangibles as the company's reputation, competitive position, or employee morale. Thus, an airline decision to purchase airplanes will be made at the top levels, while the decision to purchase desks may be made in the second or third echelon of an operating department. Quality control in drug manufacturing, where a mistake might endanger lives, to say nothing of the company's reputation, would normally report at a high level, while the quality inspection in toy manufacturing might report much lower.

The fact that the higher the cost of a mistake the less likely that decision making will be decentralized is not necessarily based on the assumption that top managers make fewer mistakes than subordinate managers. They may make fewer mistakes, since they are probably better trained and in possession of more facts, but the controlling reason appears to be the weight of responsibility. As already discussed, delegating authority is not delegating responsibility; therefore, the manager typically prefers not to delegate authority for crucial decisions.

On the other hand, this concept must be applied cautiously and, in large companies, sparingly. Some managers fear to delegate *any* authority for decision making, exaggerating the dangers and costs of mistakes by subordinates. An overburdened manager who does so may incur greater costs, from delay or indecision, than he hopes to avoid by withholding decision-making power. Although it cannot be proved statistically, experience supports the conclusion that it may cost more to centralize too much authority, thereby permitting subordinates to drift without clear-cut decisions, than it would to risk subordinates' mistakes.

The need for top control depends on the area of decision. In the typical large business, top management may reasonably feel that it cannot delegate authority over the expenditure of capital funds. Reference to the organization chart of the General Motors Corporation, shown in Figure 15.8, discloses that the financial aspects of that company's operations are well centralized under an executive vice-president, who reports to the chairman of the board of directors rather than to the president. This is a living example of the importance of centralization in this area.

Uniformity of Policy Another, and somewhat related, factor favoring centralization of authority is the desire to obtain uniform policy, and those who value consistency above all are invariably in favor of centralized authority, since this is the easiest road to such a goal. They may wish to ensure that customers will be treated alike with respect to quality, price, credit, delivery, and service; that the same policies will be followed in dealing with vendors; or that public relations policies will be standardized.

Uniform policy also has certain internal advantages. For instance, standardized accounting, statistics, and financial records make it easier to compare relative efficiencies of departments and keep down costs. The administration of a union contract is facilitated through uniform policy with respect to wages, promotions, vacations, dismissals, and similar matters. Taxes and government regulation entail fewer worries and chances for mistakes with uniform policies.

Yet many enterprises go to considerable length to make sure that some policies will not be completely uniform. When a firm organizes on a product or territorial basis or opens plants in other parts of the country to take advantage of situations with respect to labor, customers, sources of supply, or trade practices, it obviously prefers at least some nonuniformity in certain important policies. And when a company decentralizes authority to encourage individual initiative, certain business policies may be as varied as the individual managers make them. Many companies encourage this variety in all except major matters, hoping that out of such nonuniformity may come managerial innovation, progress, competition between organizational units, improved morale and efficiency, and a supply of promotable managerial manpower.

Economic Size   The larger the firm, the more decisions to be made, and the more places in which they must be made, the harder it is to coordinate them. The larger the firm, the greater the number of departments and levels. These complexities of organization may require policy questions to be passed up the line and discussed not only with many managers in the chain of command but with many managers at each level, since horizontal agreement may be as necessary as vertical clearance.

In the case of an American railroad, a local freight traffic representative saw an opportunity for the carrier to make a handsome profit transporting race horses in special cars on fast passenger trains. The horse owners were concerned not so much with cost as with fast and convenient service. But since there were no procedures for this, the local trainmaster would not take responsibility for interfering with passenger-train movement. The proposal, therefore, had to be discussed locally with the passenger traffic and operations managers and then referred upward through the echelons of the operations and traffic departments to a point where a decision could be made—in this case, by the president of the railroad. One might contrast the simplicity of decision making of the owner-operated trucking company, which, incidentally, obtained most of the business that this particular railroad lost.

Slow decisions—slow because of the number of specialists and managers who must be consulted—are costly to large business. To minimize this cost, authority must be decentralized wherever feasible. Indeed, the large enterprise that prides itself on the right kind of decentralization is recognizing the inevitable, although the extent and effectiveness of decentralization may differ widely among companies, depending largely upon the quality of their management.

Diseconomies of large size may be reduced by organizing the enterprise into a number of nearly autonomous units. Considerable increases in efficiency are likely to result from making the unit small enough for its top executives to be near the point where decisions must be made. This makes possible speedy decisions, keeps executives from spending time coordinating their decisions with many others, reduces the amount of paper work, and improves the quality of decisions by reducing their magnitude to manageable proportions.

Exactly what this size is cannot be arbitrarily stated. Some astute managers believe it to be 1,000 persons, others believe it to be closer to 100 or 250, and some would hold that 2,500 employees can be grouped into manageable divisions, each with considerable decentralized authority.[3] In any case, there is evidence that, where the unit exceeds a certain size, the distance from top to bottom may impair the quality and speed of decision making.

Also important to the size of major and subordinate decision-making units is the character of the unit. For decentralization to be thoroughly effective, the unit must possess a certain economic and managerial self-sufficiency. Functional departments such as sales or manufacturing ordinarily cannot be as independent as product or territorial departments. A department of 1,000 engineers or salesmen usually cannot be the independent unit that product or territorial departments of the same size can be, encompassing as they do nearly all the functions of an enterprise. It therefore follows that, if the uneconomic aspects of size are to be reduced by decreasing the size of the self-contained decision-making unit, it is preferable to departmentize along product or territorial lines.

In the zeal to overcome the disadvantages of size by reducing the decision-making unit, certain shortcomings of decentralization should not be overlooked. When authority is decentralized, a lack of policy uniformity and of coordination may follow. The branch, product division, or other self-sufficient unit may be so preoccupied with its objectives as to lose sight of those of the enterprise as a whole. What headquarters executive has not had the feeling that a division or a branch is at times "running away with the company"? Independence may mean, too, that the talents of top line and staff officials and specialists—whose experience and training are expensive business assets—and their departments are not sufficiently used by the subordinate managers in the decentralized units.

History of the Enterprise Whether authority will be decentralized frequently depends upon the way the business has been built. Those enterprises which, in the main, expand from within—such as Marshall Field and Company and International Harvester Company—show a marked tendency to keep authority centralized, as do those that expand under the direction of the owner-founder. The Ford Motor Company was, under its founder, an extraordinary case of centralized authority; Henry Ford, Sr., prided himself on having no organizational titles in the top management except that of president and general manager, insisting, to the extent he could, that every major decision in that vast company be made by himself.

---

[3] For a discussion of this point, see *Problems and Policies of Decentralized Management,* General Management Series No. 154 (New York: American Management Association, 1952).

On the other hand, enterprises that represent amalgamations and consolidations are likely to show, at least at first, a definite tendency to retain decentralized authority, especially if the unit acquired is operating profitably. To be sure, this tendency not to rock the boat may be politically inspired rather than based on pure managerial considerations. Certainly, the claim of autonomy of the once-independent units is especially strong, and a full managerial generation may have to pass before the chief executive of the amalgamation dares materially to reduce the degree of decentralization.

On the other hand, the first influence of an amalgamation may be toward increased centralization. If the controlling group wishes to put in its own management or take immediate advantage of the economies of combined operation, the requirements of policy uniformity and quick action may necessitate centralization.

Management Philosophy   The character of top executives and their philosophy has an important influence on the extent to which authority is decentralized. Sometimes the top manager is despotic, brooking no interference with the authority and information he jealously hoards. At other times, the top manager keeps authority, not merely to gratify a desire for status or power, but because he simply cannot give up the activities and authorities he held before he reached the top or before his business expanded from an owner-manager shop.

But some men find decentralization a means to make big business work. In those cases, top managers may see decentralization as a way of organizational life that takes advantage of the innate desire of men to create, to be free, and to have status. And many successful top managers find in it a means to harness the desire for freedom to economic efficiency, much as the free enterprise system has been responsible for this country's remarkable industrial progress. As an example of this attitude Robert E. Wood, former chairman of the board of Sears, Roebuck and Company, said:[4]

> We complain about government in business, we stress the advantages of the free enterprise system, we complain about the totalitarian state, but in our industrial organizations, in our striving for efficiency, we have created more or less of a totalitarian organization in industry—particularly in large industry.

The problem of retaining efficiency and discipline in these large organizations and yet allowing people to express themselves, to exercise initiative, and to have some voice in the affairs of the organization is the greatest problem for large organizations to solve.

Desire for Independence   It is a characteristic of individuals and of groups of individuals to desire a degree of independence. A region may resent various aspects of absentee control. Observe the hostility of the Chicago Board of

[4] Quoted in Dale, *op. cit.*, p. 116.

Trade and the Chicago newspapers toward the absent managers of its railroads during the fifty years prior to World War I; the establishment of twelve Federal Reserve banks to meet regional banking needs; the frequent exasperation of branch managers with their head offices.

Individuals may become frustrated by delay in getting decisions, by long lines of communication, and by the great game of passing the buck. This frustration can lead to dangerous loss of good men, to jockeying by the office politician, and to resigned inertia by the less competent seeker of security.

These are evidences of the desire for recognition, for status, for autonomy. They comprise, as one astute observer has pointed out, "the need for personal purposefulness," a desire of "all normal individuals to make some kind of meaningful contribution to the betterment of their environment."[5] Even pure vanity or a desire for self-assertion or power often requires some delegation of authority.

Availability of Managers Managerial manpower shortage necessarily limits the extent of decentralization of authority, since dispersal of decision making assumes the availability of managers. But too often the mourned perennial scarcity of good managers is used as an excuse for centralizing authority; the executive who complains that he has no one to whom he can delegate authority is sometimes merely trying to magnify his own value to the firm.

There are managers, also, who believe that a firm should centralize authority because it will then need very few good managers. Indeed, if this can be well done, savings will result. One difficulty is that the firm that so centralizes authority may not be able to train managerial manpower to take over the duties of the centralized top managers, and external sources must be relied upon to furnish any necessary replacements.

The key to safe decentralization is adequate training of managers. By the same token, decentralization is perhaps the most important key to training. Many large firms whose size makes decentralization a necessity consciously push decision making down into the organization for the purpose of developing managerial manpower because they feel that the best training is actual experience. Since this usually carries with it chances for mistakes by the novice, it is good practice to limit the importance of his decisions.

Control Techniques Another factor affecting the degree of decentralization is the state of development of control techniques. One cannot expect a good manager at any level of the organization to delegate authority without some way of knowing whether it will be used properly. Not knowing how to control often explains unwillingness to delegate authority and makes valid the manager's belief that it takes him more time to unmake mistakes or oversee a job than it would to do the job himself.

---

[5] P. E. Mills, "Making Decentralization Work: One Company's Experience," *The Management Review*, vol. 46, no. 6, p. 69 (June, 1957).

Coupled with the manager's need to understand and use appropriate control techniques is the state of their development. Improvements in statistical devices, accounting controls, and other techniques have helped make possible the current trend toward extensive managerial decentralization. Even the most ardent supporters of decentralization, such as General Motors, du Pont, and Sears, could hardly take so favorable a view without adequate techniques to show management, from the top down, whether performance is conforming to plans. To decentralize is not to lose control, and to push decision making down into the organization is not to abdicate responsibility.

Decentralized Performance This is basically a technical matter depending upon such factors as the economies of division of labor, the opportunities for using machines, the nature of the work to be performed (thus, a railroad has no choice but to decentralize its performance), and the location of raw materials, labor supply, and consumers. Although this kind of decentralization may be geographical or physical in nature, it influences the centralization of authority.

Authority tends to be decentralized when performance is decentralized, if for no other reason than that the absentee manager is unable to manage, although there are exceptions. For example, some of the large chain-store enterprises are characterized by widely decentralized performance, yet the local manager of a store may have no authority over pricing, advertising and merchandising methods, inventory and purchasing, or product line, all of which may be controlled from a central or regional office. The head of a local manufacturing plant of a large organization may have little authority beyond the right to hire and fire, and even in these cases he may be circumscribed by company policy and procedure and by the authority of a centralized personnel department. At the same time, the decentralization of performance limits the ability to centralize authority. The most despotic top manager of a national organization cannot completely supervise his San Francisco plant as closely as he could if it were adjacent to his New York office.

It does not follow that when performance is centralized authority is centralized as well. True, authority can be more easily centralized if performance is, and if a company wishes tight control over decision making, centralized performance will aid this. But there are too many other factors to give geographical concentration a controlling influence in centralization.

Business Dynamics The dynamic character of a business also affects the degree to which authority may be decentralized. If a business is growing fast and facing complex problems of expansion, its managers, particularly those responsible for top policy, may be forced to make a disproportionate share of the decisions. But, strangely enough, this very dynamic condition may force these managers to delegate authority and take a calculated risk on the costs of error. Generally this dilemma is resolved in the direction of delegation, and, in order to avoid delegation to untrained subordinates, close attention is given to rapid formation of policies and accelerated training in management. An alternative often adopted is to slow the rate of change, including the rate of that tempting change, expansion. Many top managers have found that the critical factor limiting their ability to meet change and expand a business is the lack of trained personnel to whom authority may be delegated. Often, also, authority is delegated to untrained and undirected hands in order to meet the requirements of change, with the recognized future task of taking in the reins and rectifying mistakes when the pace of change has slowed.

In old, well-established, or relatively static businesses, there is a natural tendency to centralize or recentralize authority. Where few major decisions must be made, the advantages of uniform policy and the economies of having a few well-qualified persons make the decisions dictate that authority be centralized. This may explain why in many banks and insurance companies and in certain railroads, decentralization is not extensive. Nevertheless, in static businesses too much centralization may carry danger. New discoveries, vigorous competition from an unexpected source, or political change are only a few of the factors that might introduce dynamic conditions, and, if this occurs, the overcentralized firm may not be able quickly to meet a situation requiring decentralized decision making.

Environmental Influences   The determinants of the extent of decentralization dealt with so far have been interior to the firm, although the economics of decentralization of performance and the character of business dynamics include elements well beyond the control of an enterprise's management. In addition, there are definite external forces affecting the extent of decentralization. Among the most important of these are government controls, national unionism, and tax policies.

Government regulation of many facets of business policy makes it difficult and sometimes impossible to decentralize authority. If prices are regulated, the sales manager cannot be given much real freedom in determining them. If materials are allocated and restricted, the purchasing and factory managers are not free to buy or use them. If labor may be worked only a limited number of hours at a minimum rate of pay, the local division manager cannot set hours and wages.

But the restriction on decentralization goes further: top management itself no longer has authority over controlled aspects of policy and cannot, therefore, delegate authority it does not have. Nevertheless, government regulations are ordinarily not so detailed as to take *all* authority over the matters controlled but only to set certain maximum and minimum limits over them. Much authority could still be decentralized. But the manager often does not dare trust subordinates to interpret government regulations, especially since the penalties and the public opprobrium for breaking the law are so serious and since the interpretation of laws is a matter for the specialist. Therefore, the manager is often forced to centralize this portion of authority.

In the same way, the rise of national unions in the past four decades has had a centralizing influence on business. So long as the departmental or divisional manager may control the terms of the labor contract, either by dealing with company unions or with employees directly, authority to negotiate may be delegated by top management to these subordinates. But where a national union enters into a collective-bargaining contract with headquarters management, with the terms of the contract applicable to all workers of a company wherever located, the company can no more chance decentralization of certain decision making than it can in the case of government controls.

Although designed for revenue rather than for regulatory purposes, the tax system of the national, state, and local governments has had a marked regulatory effect on business. The tax collector, especially the Federal income tax collector, sits at the elbow of every executive who makes a decision involving funds. As a matter of fact, with high rates applicable to corporate income, the impact of taxation is often a policy-determining factor that overshadows such traditional business considerations as plant expansion, marketing policies, and economical operations. Uniformity of tax policy becomes a consideration of primary importance to company management. This spells centralization, because the manager without appropriate tax advice cannot be expected to make wise decisions involving profits. It may even require a central tax department acting not only in an advisory capacity and as a tax service agency but also with a degree of functional authority over matters with tax implications.

RECENTRALIZATION OF AUTHORITY

As was pointed out earlier in this chapter in discussing the control factor, once a decision is made to decentralize authority, it is important simultaneously to establish controls. Otherwise, the superior cannot know soon enough to take action just what use is made of the delegated power, and this places him in an insecure position. If, on the other hand, a control report, summarizing effectively actions taken by the subordinate under his new power, is required periodically, the insecurity is reduced. Budgetary control illustrates this: If a program has been budgeted, authority to implement it can be more easily delegated because of the built-in controls that reflect actual achievement compared with program goals.[6]

At times an enterprise can be said to recentralize authority—to centralize authority once decentralized. This process is normally not merely a reversal of decentralization, for the authority delegations are not wholly withdrawn by the managers who made them. What occurs is a centralization of authority over a certain type of activity or a certain kind of function, wherever in the organization it may be found.

[6] For a more detailed explanation of the application of this principle, see chap. 28.

Thus, the growing importance of taxes, the requirements of uniform labor policy, and the realities of government regulation may dictate that authority over these areas be recentralized or managed by a department with functional authority over them. This recentralization may also occur when, through growth and extensive decentralization, top managers feel that they have lost control over the business. Or if a business falls on difficult times, managers may wish to reinforce their authority over the expenditure of funds, the level of costs, or the character of sales effort. In these cases, top managers may establish a control staff with functional authority over certain kinds of decisions of subordinate managers. Such recentralization, sometimes intended to be temporary, often becomes permanent. Many top managers take pride in their cost control, budget, or internal auditing departments and in the authority of these departments not only to advise but to supervise many previously decentralized prerogatives of lower managers.

DECENTRALIZATION AND ENTERPRISE FUNCTIONS

As will be recalled, the principal functions of any business enterprise are the creation of utilities (production), the exchange of utilities (sales), and the financing of this exchange and of the enterprise itself (finance). In addition, through the need for specialization, there have been split off such functions as personnel, accounting, statistics, purchasing, and traffic and distribution.

A study by the American Management Association has thrown interesting light on the decentralization in these several functions.[7] Although the study was made some time ago and was limited to relatively few companies, its findings may be regarded as typical; they agree with other findings, the observations of the authors, and normal expectancy in business. The following paragraphs are based on them.

Production   Authority over production is usually the first to be delegated by the chief executive of a company, although the extent of this delegation varies with such factors as the nature of the product, the scale of production, markets, and supply of labor and materials. As the production scale increases or as the processes become more complex, authority is likely to be further decentralized. However, even in large companies where authority over manufacturing is widely dispersed, budgets and controls exert a centralizing influence, as also do the functional staff departments made necessary by internal and external factors discussed above.

Sales   Authority over sales is also likely to be decentralized early. As soon as the geographical area covered by salesmen becomes extensive, or salesmen numerous, the sales department begins to feel strongly the advantage

[7] Dale, *op. cit.*, appendix C, pp. 188–195.

of decentralization. As a matter of fact, delegation of decision-making authority in most aspects of sales is usually greater than in any other enterprise function. Even where there may be considerable centralization of authority over other functions, decentralization of sales is probable.

The reason for this is easy to find. When customers are geographically scattered and require much individual attention from the salesman, authority over sales performance can hardly be centralized. Sales effort must be brought to the customer, and the branch or district sales manager and his staff need a wide area of discretion in handling him. This decentralizing is usually accentuated when a manufacturer has several product lines. Despite strong centralization policies, the Ford Motor Company, when it introduced the Lincoln and Mercury lines years ago, was forced to establish new sales divisions with delegated authority to direct sales effort somewhat differently from that used for the Ford.

Although selling is usually greatly decentralized, connected staff or service activities are not so likely to be. For example, advertising and market research may be centralized, mainly because of the need for specialized talent, economy, and the requirements of uniform policy. Also, especially with regulation of price discrimination, pricing decisions are not likely to be decentralized.

Finance   The finance department is ordinarily the last—and, in a large business, frequently the only—stronghold of highly centralized authority. Even when a company has widely adopted a policy of decentralization, the finance function is far less decentralized than any other.

The reason for this is simple. Enterprise objectives almost always include profitability and stability. Profitability is measured by the return made on funds available to the business. These considerations give rise to the need for central control of such funds and for accurate accounting of their use. However, in addition to this need for centralized financial control at the top of the enterprise, many treasurers and controllers mistakenly assume detailed control over the *activities* of spending, purchasing, and accounting. The important considerations revolve around control of the proper use of funds, in accordance with approved plans, and control to assure that the accounting system gives an accurate and honest record of amounts received or spent.

Centralization is customarily exerted through budgetary controls over both expenses and capital expenditures, those over the latter usually being stricter than those over the former. In a large company, for example, the production manager may be given authority to approve operating expenditures to a fully budgeted sum amounting to hundreds of thousands of dollars each week and may be permitted to approve a single expense item of $50,000, yet possess authority to approve only $1,000 of capital expenditure. The authors know of a sales manager who could sign sales contracts to $5,000,000 but could not approve a capital expenditure of more than $100. The reason for this distinction is usually that sales and operating expenses can be more easily budgeted and that more effective corporate controls can be placed over them (such as price setting, delivery schedules, control over hirings, and uniform contract terms). Capital expenditures, on the other hand, are difficult to budget accurately and to coordinate properly, and they represent a commitment of scarce resources. At the same time, there is a growing awareness that closer centralization of authority over both sales and operating-expense commitments should be made, since overextension of operations can soak up a corporation's capital lifeblood as readily as can uncontrolled capital expenditures.

Personnel Certain areas of personnel activities are highly centralized. One of these is the collective-bargaining contract and its administration, the centralization of which has been forced on companies as the result of such contracts and government regulations. Other sensitive areas are wage and salary administration, job evaluation, and managerial selection and appraisal. Except for these areas, which have been expanding and growing in importance, the personnel function should be as decentralized as is managership, since all managers must be responsible for their personnel. Managers should have the widest kind of authority over their people, a fact often overlooked by the too zealous personnel specialist.

Accounting and Statistics With the eyes of top managers fixed on the necessity for over-all controls and with the economies of concentrating acounting and statistics, the predominant trend of recent decades has been to centralize authority over these functions, except, of course, in the actual gathering of data. More recently, however, alert managements have begun to decentralize a large portion of this activity.

Central control of accounting and statistics may be most economical and serve top managers well, but the managerial group on the firing line—the group that can really control costs, production, and sales—have often been denied information necessary to their jobs or have received it too late. As a consequence, industry has developed a kind of centralized decentralization, with centralization of authority over the accounting and statistical activities necessary for top management and for accumulating those data, but with decentralization of data gathering and report making for the lower levels. Some companies have consciously assumed the costs of some duplication of effort in order that subordinate managers may have the necessary information.

Purchasing It is difficult to generalize with respect to decentralization of authority over purchasing. The purchase of capital equipment and the acquisition of major materials that comprise a large share of costs are almost invariably handled centrally. So are almost all other purchases in single-plant enterprises and companies having several plants in a fairly small geographical area, as well as in those firms where purchasing problems are rather simple. When a company, however, has many plants or branches geographically dispersed or where it has departmentized along product lines, purchasing decisions, particularly over less important items, are likely to be within the province of decentralized departments but subject to the functional authority of the central purchasing department. Likewise, for purposes of efficiency and control, authority over national contracts will almost always be centralized.

Traffic and Distribution Traffic functions are likely to be subject to centralized authority in cases where, as in vertically integrated plants, a steady flow of work depends upon a unified and efficient system of routing materials among various plants and suppliers. In most companies, such traffic functions as studies of transportation rates, negotiation with carriers, and the establishment of basic shipping policies also are subject to centralized authority. Again, in companies in which the cost of transportation constitutes a major element in the total production cost, the traffic function is usually centralized. On the other hand, in enterprises whose transportation costs are a small portion of total costs, the traffic function may be widely dispersed, although, even in these cases, the need for special handling leads often to centralization. In recent years, with the development of planning and control of physical distribution as a logistics system, there has been a definite trend toward centralizing authority in this area.

DECENTRALIZATION AND THE GENERAL MOTORS CORPORATION

One of the most successful examples of management and one with a well-publicized philosophy of decentralization is the General Motors Corporation,[8] whose organization chart was shown in Figure 15.8. It is interesting not as a typical American business—its size and phenomenal development are hardly typical—but because its organizational philosophy and practices have been thoroughly tested by the rugged standards of more than four decades of competitive and dynamic enterprise.

The officials of General Motors see in its policy of decentralization advantages for both the large corporation and the independent small business. The division manager may operate his division much as an independent businessman, but, unlike the manager of the small business, he has the financial resources and the staff facilities and know-how of the large enterprise.

[8] Material for this section has been freely drawn from *GM and Its People* (a description of the company organization written originally for employees); P. F. Drucker, *Concept of the Corporation* (New York: The John Day Company, Inc., 1946); Dale, *op. cit.*, pp. 98–106; D. Brown, *Centralized Control with Decentralized Responsibilities*, Annual Convention Series No. 57 (New York: American Management Association, 1927); H. H. Curtice, *The Development and Growth of General Motors, Statement before the Subcommittee on Antitrust and Monopoly of the United States Senate Committee on the Judiciary* (Dec. 2, 1955); and W. M. Collins, *The Organization of General Motors Corporation* (Detroit: General Motors Corporation, 1966) as well as one of the author's personal interviews with company executives.

GM's Philosophy of Decentralization   Referred to by Peter Drucker as an "essay in federalism,"[9] General Motors' policy provides decentralized operations and authority, with coordinated control by top management over the semiautonomous divisions. This means, according to the company, that "subject to broad corporation policy the operating divisions into which our business is organized are left pretty much on their own" and that "each division makes its own decisions within the framework of over-all corporation policy."[10] This philosophy was described many years ago by Donaldson Brown as "centralized control with decentralized responsibilities."[11] Or, as more recently expressed, this company operates on the basis of "decentralized operations and responsibilities with coordinated control," which is translated into simpler terms as "give a man a clear-cut job to do and let him do it."[12] It should be noted that the emphasis on "coordinated control" and "a clear-cut job" unmistakably implies that subordinate managers are not given autonomy and that ample decision-making authority on major policies and programs exists at the top of the company.

Aims of Decentralization   In his study of General Motors, Drucker interviewed a number of the company's executives and summarized their views as to the aims of decentralization, for which the following advantages were claimed:[13]

1. Speed and lack of confusion in decision-making.
2. Absence of conflict between the top management and the divisions.
3. A sense of fairness in dealing with executives, confidence that a job well done would be appreciated, and a lack of politics in the organization.
4. Informality and democracy in management.
5. Absence of a gap between the few top managers and the many subordinate managers in the organization.
6. The availability of a large reservoir of promotable managerial manpower.
7. Ready visibility of weak managements through results of semi-independent and often competitive divisions.
8. An absence of "edict management" and the presence of thorough information and consideration of central management decisions.

How Decentralization Works   How the concept of decentralization of General Motors works in practice is best illustrated by reference to the operation of the various divisional managements. These divisions—such as Chevrolet, Buick, Allison, and Frigidaire—operate much as independent businesses, always subject, of course, to over-all corporate policy, the formulation of which will be described presently. Each division designs, develops, manufactures, and merchandises its own products; purchases its own parts and

[9] Drucker, *op. cit.*, p. 46.
[10] *GM and Its People*, p. 8.
[11] Brown, *op. cit.*, p. 1.
[12] Collins, *op. cit.*, p. 2.
[13] Drucker, *op. cit.*, pp. 47–48.

materials from other divisions of the company or from the outside—wherever it can find the most suitable product at the best price; hires and trains its own employees and develops and maintains its own staff and line organization; and decides upon its own manufacturing processes and methods. In fact, Drucker found that the managers of several divisions estimated that 95 per cent of all decisions affecting their operations fell under their own area of authority.[14]

In principle, the philosophy of decentralization extends also into the divisions, and appropriate authority is pushed further down into the organization. But the very fact that the divisional managers have been given so much independence means that authority is not as decentralized in some divisions as in others. Central management does not dictate organizational practices of the divisions, a fact that has occasionally resulted in more centralization of authority at the division level than for the corporation as a whole. However, the philosophy of decentralization tends to permeate the organization—largely because of the strong leadership long held by Alfred Sloan—and to be reflected in the actions of managers promoted to high positions. At the same time, the divisions vary in size from 1,000 employees to more than 50,000, and one could not expect the degree of decentralization to be the same for all divisions. Moreover, in certain divisions performance is considerably decentralized while in others it is highly centralized, and the effect of this as well as other pertinent differences naturally affect the extent of decentralization.

The diffusion of decentralization throughout the organization is encouraged by the training of executives to be promoted to the posts of division managers and higher. Drucker found that many of these had come from plants and divisions where authority had been fairly well decentralized and that there was a feeling in the company that persons with well-rounded experience in managerial matters at lower levels were most likely to be promoted to the top.

Centralized Top-policy Formulation   One may receive an erroneous impression of the degree of independence of GM division managers, since the 5 per cent of decisions reserved for top management may be extraordinarily important. General Motors has interesting machinery for the establishment of central policy. It will be noted from Figure 15.8 that, at the top of the organization, there is an executive committee and a finance committee that report to the board of directors. In addition, reporting to the board are an audit committee and a bonus and salary committee. Indeed, all members of these committees are directors. And working with and reporting to the executive committee are nine policy groups, somewhat in the nature of subcommittees, which do much of the preparatory policy-determination work in a number of specialized fields. This committee organization, with the

---

[14] *Ibid.*, p. 56.

board of directors as the top committee of all, plus, of course, the top-management group, the operations, financial, and legal staffs, and the division managers, represents the top policy-making machinery of the company.

Thus, it can be seen that major policy and program decisions are sharply centralized in the top level of the organization, although ample channels for communication to the divisions are established. In general, the line executives dominate the policy-formulation machinery, with the staff departments having an active role primarily at the advisory and study level of the policy groups attached as subcommittees to the executive committee.

Centralized Control Although General Motors practices and preaches decentralization, it realizes that no division of a company and no department of any division can be given *complete* freedom and autonomy. Complete decentralization would permit a division to bankrupt a company or a department to succeed even at the cost of failure of the entire enterprise. Yet it is interesting to note how often lack of managerial understanding causes regional and divisional managers in all types of enterprise to chafe under the necessary controls of central management and to mistake a policy of decentralization for an untenable policy of complete independence. The facts of business life are simple. No subdivision of a business can be given so much authority that the central management of the entire enterprise lacks authority to accomplish its objectives.

Combining decentralized authority with the degree of centralized authority necessary to accomplish control is one of the major reasons for the success of General Motors. As a matter of fact, careful study of this company's authority delegation brings to light the importance and extent of centralization of selected areas of decision making and not the company's emphasis on decentralization. Perhaps the most important of these centralized controls relates to finance. Auditing controls are placed at the very highest level, in a position independent of the management at other levels. Accounting controls—including the methods of accounting to be followed in the divisions, cost comparisons, and the measurement and comparison of rate of return in each division—are functional matters under the jurisdiction of the executive vice-president in charge of the financial staff. Each division and plant controller, for example, not only reports to his line superior, the division manager, but also has a clear line of responsibility to the comptroller of the corporation, to whom he sends income statements, balance sheets, cost comparisons, and other financial data, prepared in accordance with instructions of the central office. Indeed, one can say that the financial and accounting areas in this company are highly centralized.

Centralization of financial controls is also closely geared to centralization of top-management programming. The top managers of the corporation, in consultation, of course, with division managers, establish major planning goals, production and sales policies, and performance standards that fit into centrally determined long-range plans. These major goals and plans are converted into capital and operating budgets, so that, even though the division managers enjoy considerable freedom of decision, top management has not lost control over the finances of the enterprise.

In addition, certain definite authority limitations are imposed on division managers. These include such matters as capital expenditures, product line and price, union contracts, salary changes above a certain level, and bonuses. Decisions on these matters, regarded as basic to the successful operation of the company as a whole, are centralized in top management.

Besides, there are the centralizing effects of the headquarters staff departments. Although these staff activities may be largely advisory, the policy-determination machinery of the company, as has been noted, operates so as to ensure consideration of staff recommendations by division managers. Through the committee framework and various personal contacts between members of central staff departments and line managers and their staffs, planning recommendations, techniques and practices, and new policies suggested by the central staff are likely to have company-wide application. In some cases, such as personnel and finance, the functional authority of the staffs forces the divisions to listen. In any case, staff operations have a controlling effect on the company's many divisions.

Recentralizing Trends   As in other businesses, a study of General Motors discloses trends toward recentralization of authority. The expansion of functional authority in personnel, public relations, and tax policy is evidence of the centralizing influence of national unionism, government control, and a system of corporate taxation that makes tax aspects often a controlling consideration in decision making. Increasingly, regardless of its desire for decentralization, a company must draw back from the division managers and their subordinates much authority that would otherwise be delegated to them.

Keys to Success of GM's Decentralization   It cannot be denied that General Motors has been one of the most successful industrial enterprises and that much of this success is due to the quality of management it has enjoyed for over four decades. To present such a record of financial success, alert and progressive management, and increasing dominance in so dynamic and competitive an industry, it must, despite its size, have found a successful organizational formula. This formula is a kind of centralized decentralization in which authority is decentralized to an enormous extent yet with major planning and control centralized to yield continuity, coordination, and uniformity.

The keys to the success of this formula are not hard to find. In the first place, the leadership of the company, in encouraging decentralization, has arranged for a combination of independence and coordination and has furnished the machinery for centralization of top policy and control, with decentralization of all but major matters. Moreover, the policy of giving executives authority and then holding them to high standards of performance has a way of teaching people to manage, and manage well. This policy, in conjunction with that of careful selection and broad training of executives, brings men of courage and ability to the top.

Another major key to the success of decentralization is the conscious policy of General Motors to make upper-level managers as independent as possible. A debilitating influence in business is the development of "yes" men in the middle and upper levels of management. It is only natural that a person reaching the top of an organization should develop a feeling of infallibility as to the wisdom of his decisions and of the course he followed to reach his position; indeed, many top executives forget that they reached their position by soliciting criticism and seeking out the truth. To make sure that subordinates with decision-making power will utilize it carefully and courageously to make decisions with a view to their wisdom rather than to precedent or to acquiescence, a feeling of independence must be developed. Much of this can be accomplished by sheer force of leadership. But perhaps a better way is to make a manager sure that he does not have to consider his job security before making each decision. It has, therefore, been a policy of General Motors to be generous with managers and, through stock and cash bonuses and stock options, ensure that by the time a man becomes a division manager, and usually well before, he will be financially independent. Also, men who do not fear each other cooperate the best. And when, as in General Motors, these men have a stake in the success of the enterprise, their cooperation is likely to further enterprise objectives.

Perhaps another key to the success of GM's practice of decentralization is competition between divisions. One of the problems of large businesses is that department heads tend to be in a protected monopoly position *within the company*. The manager of factory A, which produces parts, has a monopoly position with respect to the manager of factory B, who *must* use these parts, regardless of cost or quality, to manufacture his assemblies. It is exactly here, in breaking down the monopoly position of one division with respect to another and in making the divisions meet the competition of outside firms, that General Motors forces on the division manager a high standard of performance. Furthermore, the market test is extended to the completed product, so that the manager of an automobile division, for example, is measured by central management not only on the basis of his costs and profits but on the basis of how well he has done against outside competition.

Another key to the success of GM decentralization is the way in which the corporation has centralized control and major planning. Without such effective policy formulation and follow-up and without the highly centralized control over money, the company would degenerate into a number of too-independent island empires. The resultant disintegration of coordination would, of course, be at the cost of some of the most important advantages of the large firm, such as the specialized services of engineering, marketing, public relations, and financial experts. Lack of control would also soon result in dissipation of the financial resources necessary for expansion, development, and market aggressiveness.

OBTAINING THE DESIRED DEGREE OF DECENTRALIZATION

Underlying the discussion to this point has been the assumption that managers can obtain the degree of decentralization upon which they have decided. In other words, the emphasis has been upon how much decentralization, rather than on whether the desired degree can be realized and maintained.

Many managers who believe that authority should be pushed down in an organization as far as it will go are faced with the practical problem of how to push it down there. It is a rare top manager who does not find in his organization somewhere an authority hoarder who simply will not delegate. One of the authors had occasion once to observe a division controller whose office was piled high with major policy matters requiring his attention, while he engaged in minute examination of employees' expense accounts, excusing himself with the statement that none of this work could be entrusted to his subordinates.

In obtaining the degree of decentralization desired, an understanding of the concept of decentralization is essential. This concept is based upon the knowledge that decentralization cannot mean autonomy, that it implies establishment of policies to guide decision making along the desired courses, that it requires careful delegation of authority by managers who know how and want to delegate, and that, not being an abdication of responsibility, it must be accompanied by controls designed to ensure that delegated authority is used to further goals and plans. Although the art of authority delegation lies at the base of proper decentralization, and the manager who would decentralize successfully must clearly understand this art, it is apparent that the mere act of delegation is not enough to ensure decentralization.

No manual can indicate how to ensure authority being properly decentralized or appropriately withheld, but several techniques may be used with some chance of success. One of these is merely a technique of organization, the provision of a statement of each manager's duties, the degree of authority delegated to him, and his responsibility. Besides being clear and, preferably, written, the statement should be issued in such a way that all employees may know what it contains. This can serve a vital purpose in settling jurisdictional squabbles and excursions beyond the authority area of a given manager.

Another important technique to obtain a desired degree of centralization lies in the example and teaching of the superior, starting at the top of the organization. As has been pointed out, the character of top leadership in an enterprise permeates any organization. There are in every firm of any size those who will reach out for power, impinge upon activities assigned to others, and bully the nonbelligerent. Rules and job descriptions are often subject to differences in interpretation, which can be conveniently stretched or circumscribed, depending upon the political environment. Their unreliability, despite their obvious usefulness, stands as a warning to executives that the most dependable foundation for achieving the desired degree of decentralization is the education of subordinate managers in the rights of others—teaching them restraint as well as aggressiveness.

One of the best means of forcing delegation of authority, particularly in middle and lower levels of organization, is to require managers to have a large number of subordinates, and, at the same time, hold them to a high standard of performance. In the Sears, Roebuck and Company studies[15] it was found that, when a manager's span of management was stretched, he had no alternative but to delegate authority. At the same time, in order to protect his own performance, the manager with so many subordinates found it essential to obtain good subordinate managers, train them well, establish clear-cut policies, and find efficient means of control. Thus, Sears discovered that widening the span of management reduced levels of supervision, shortened communications, resulted in decentralization of authority, required better management, and forced managerial training.

Another technique used to force decentralization has been the policy of promoting managers only when they have subordinates trained to take their places. To accomplish this training and assure themselves that the subordinates could take over, managers have no alternative but to delegate authority. Moreover, this policy removes a major cause of hoarding authority, the desire of a manager to gain indispensability by making sure that his duties cannot be handled by any of his subordinates.

Occasionally the problem concerns how to retain a predetermined degree of authority. Division and branch managers—because they are far away from the home office, wish to build empires, or want to do a complete job—may assume too much authority and resent the outside auditor, sabotage centralized controls, and fight attempts of central management to limit their expenditures. The answer, of course, to this problem is primarily one of leadership, clear policy determination and authority delegation, and proper training of subordinate managers. But perhaps the principal answer lies in the character of the top executives. If they temporize, do not support the authority delegations they have made, ignore the organization structure, condone serious deviations from policy, and neglect in other ways to do a thorough managerial job, little can be done to retain any predetermined degree of decentralization.

CLARIFYING DECENTRALIZATION

As in so many areas of managing, conflict, friction, and inefficiencies result from lack of clarification of individual roles. This is nowhere more true in

---

[15] J. C. Worthy, "Organizational Structure and Employee Morale," *American Sociological Review,* vol. 15, pp. 169–179 (April, 1950). Information was also obtained directly from Mr. Worthy.

practice than in clarifying the extent and nature of decentralization. This problem can be greatly simplified and clarified by means of a chart of executive approval authorizations, a tool which every company, large or small, with any significant delegation of authority should utilize. The chart of executive approval authorizations is a technique by which, normally on a single sheet of paper or chart, the various authority delegations of a company are outlined and clarified. Since most of these delegations have to do with the right to commit the company for money, most of the chart has to do with expenditure limits. However, there are other matters, such as policies and programs, which can be and are often shown on such a chart.

An example of a chart of approval authorizations for a small to medium-sized company is shown in Fig. 17.1. It will be noted that a list of major decision areas appears on the left-hand side of the chart. It was found useful in this company to group these decision areas under the classifications of those concerned with personnel, operating expenses, capital expenditures and commitments, prices and sales commitments, major programs, and general. Across the top of the chart are listed those various managerial levels which have approval authority, along with certain staff personnel who have functional authority in a decision matter or whose consultation is required for advice or information.

In the development of a chart, it is apparent that the authority and responsibility for doing so must rest at the top of a company. And because it even distinguishes between decision matters that the board of directors reserves for itself and those delegated to operating management, the board must necessarily be called upon to approve at least this area of delegation. But the effective board may wish to do more. If its organizational policy is really one of decentralization, with centralized decision making in certain matters at the top, it may wish to approve the entire chart, at least enough so as to perceive that its policy is being followed in practice.

In addition to clarity to individuals with authority, the chart of executive approval authorizations has other advantages. It acts as a medium of communication of the entire structure of decision making in a company so that people down the line, or in departments whose coordination in a decision is necessary, can see what the decision-making relationships are. Also, in a multi-division company, by having separate divisional charts, as well as a corporate chart, authority may be delegated in varying degrees. Thus, in a large division, more authority will be delegated; or in a division manned by less experienced managers a smaller degree of authority could be delegated. A further advantage is that authority delegations can be changed with greater ease than where they are included in a number of individual-position descriptions. By having the position description refer merely to the chart of executive approval authorizations, it becomes easy to change any part, or all, of the authority structure of a company by the mere issuance of a new chart.

Although the chart of approval authorizations is only a tool, it is regarded by the authors as an essential one. But if this tool, like any other

Fig. 17.1 Chart of Approval Authorization*

Nature of transaction	Department manager	Staff manager	Division director	President (corporate and domestic) Chairman of the board (international)	Board of directors
1. Personnel Employment of new personnel:					
Hourly	All	Personnel manager to process and review for consistency with company policy	All exceptions to company policy		
Salaried	All	Personnel manager to process	All over $800 per month	All over $1,200 per month	All over $2,000 per month
Wage and salary increases:					
Hourly	All	Personnel manager to process and review for consistency with company policy	All exceptions to company policy		
Salaried	All	Personnel manager to process	All	All resulting in salary over $1,200 per month	All resulting in salary over $2,000 per month
Moving expenses	.....	To be processed by controller	All	All over $2,000 in cost	
Leaves of absences	All	To be processed by personnel manager	All	All over 30 days	All over 90 days
2. Operating expenses Procurement of materials and services (approval of manufacturing and engineering schedule by vice-president manufacturing and engineering):					
In accordance with approved schedules	Manager of purchasing on all				
Not in accordance with approved schedules	.....	Vice-president of manufacturing and engineering on all. Controller on all exceeding $5,000	All		
Consultation services	.....	.....	All	All corporate services	All contracts or retainers over $5,000 per year

371

Fig. 17.1 Chart of Approval Authorization* (continued)

Nature of transaction	Department manager	Staff manager	Division director	President (corporate and domestic) Chairman of the board (international)	Board of directors
Supplies and maintenance materials and services	All	....	All over $5,000		
Travel and entertainment requests and reports	All those reporting to him	....	All those reporting to him	All those reporting to him and all over $1,000	
Advertising and public relations:					
In accordance with approved program	Manager of advertising and sales promotion on all				
Not in accordance with approved program	....	....	General sales manager on all	All outside total budget	
Contributions:					
Budgeted	Controller				
Nonbudgeted	....	....	....	Chairman of the board	
Memberships and subscriptions	All	....	....	Chairman of the board on all except technical magazines and books	
Research and development projects	All	....	Director of research and development on all	All involving new product lines	
Miscellaneous expenses	All	Controller on all	All over $1,000	All over $5,000	
Tax payments and adjustments	....	Controller on all	....	President and corporate secretary where law requires	Tax adjustments over $15,000
Guarantees and replacements	....	General sales manager and controller on all	....	All over $5,000	All over $10,000
Contract cancellations	....	General sales manager and controller on all	....	All involving more than $10,000	
Leases:					
Temporary, not to exceed $1,000 in total commitment	All	Controller on all	All		
Other	....	Controller and secretary-treasurer on all	All	All	All
Operating expense budgets: basic variable budget	....	Secretary-treasurer on all	All	All	All

(President and chairman of the board approved by board of directors)

3. Capital expenditures and commitments

Capital expenditures:					
In accordance with approved budget	.....	Controller to check for budgetary accuracy	All	All individual items exceeding $5,000	All items exceeding $25,000
Not in accordance with approved budget	.....	Secretary-treasurer on all	All	All items over $1,000	All items exceeding $5,000
Capital expenditure budgets	All	Secretary-treasurer on all	All	All	All
Disposal of capital assets	.....	Secretary-treasurer and controller on all	All	All over $5,000	All over $100,000
Patent applications, licensing and patent agreements	.....	Secretary-treasurer on all	All	All	All basic policy

4. Prices and sales commitments

Sales price formulas	.....	Secretary-treasurer on all	All	All	
Sales commitments:					
Catalogue standard items	Manager of sales service on all	Controller on all acceptance of credit	General sales manager on all orders exceeding $100,000	All exceeding commitment of $20,000	All exceeding commitment of $100,000
Nonstandard items	Manager of sales service on all	Controller on all acceptance of credit	General sales manager on all exceeding $10,000	Inform president of variations in excess of 10% on orders exceeding $10,000	
Variations from standard prices	Manager of sales service on all	.....	General sales manager on all over $5,000. Vice-president of manufacturing and engineering on all over $15,000		
New product lines	.....	.....	General sales manager on all	All	All
Contracts with sales representatives	.....	Form approved by legal counsel	General sales manager on all	All nonstandard contracts	Basic items of commitment in standard form

5. General

Bank loans for company operations:					
Line of credit	.....	Secretary-treasurer on all	.....	All	All
Loans within line	.....	Secretary-treasurer on all	.....	All	All
Loans for buildings and land	.....	Secretary-treasurer on all	.....	All	All
Acquisition of financial interest in or loan to any company	.....	Secretary-treasurer on all	.....	All	All

* A person required to approve transactions as outlined in the above chart may authorize another person to sign for him in his absence. The person so authorized must affix the proper signature, showing his initials under such signature.

SOURCE: H. Koontz, *The Board of Directors and Effective Management* (New York: McGraw-Hill Book Company, 1967), pp. 46–49.

one, is to work, it must be made a way of life in an enterprise, must be updated whenever there is any significant change in organization structure or authority delegation, and must be communicated wherever decision-making relationships exist. It seldom, if ever, includes matters that should be held confidential. And along with position descriptions and the formulation of verifiable goals for each position in an enterprise, it gives necessary meaning to the organization by helping define the roles which individuals must fill.

SOME CONCLUSIONS

It is difficult to find principles to apply to decentralization of authority that are not merely principles of delegation of authority, which were discussed in Chapter 4. Naturally, any program of decentralizing authority must reflect principles of authority delegation if the practical pitfalls that these principles predict are to be avoided. In addition, however, when a company wishes, for size or other reasons, to decentralize, there are a number of matters to be considered.

Decentralization of authority has so grown in recent years that the management that does not subscribe to it may appear outmoded. This development is understandable, because if enterprise efficiency lies in the coordination of people, it is logical that those responsible for this coordination should have requisite authority to manage and that this authority, in turn, should suitably be pushed down into the organization.

Furthermore, the present focus on the development of managerial manpower emphasizes that one must manage in order to learn to manage, and it is least risky to begin this apprenticeship at the lowest organization levels.

In addition, the very size of business makes decentralization of authority necessary. Top managers increasingly realize that the functions of managing extend through the organization to the foreman level and that they must decentralize authority accordingly.

At the same time, extensive decentralization is not to be blindly applied. In the first place, in many organizations the size and complexity of operations do not require it, and the losses in policy uniformity and other costs of decentralization may not make it worthwhile. In the second place, decentralization is not without costs, even in larger companies. In addition to the dangers from nonuniform policy and the problems of control, there are often real financial costs of decentralization. As authority is decentralized, the manager becomes more and more an independent operator of a small business. He may acquire his own accounting force, his own statisticians, his own engineering staff. Indeed, he may soon be duplicating specialized services of the top company organization, with resultant increase in cost but with lower quality of staff and service department activities than the parent enterprise maintains.

Perhaps the principal problem of decentralization is loss of control. As was discussed above, no enterprise can decentralize to the extent that its existence is threatened and the achievement of its enterprise goals frustrated. If organizational disintegration is to be avoided, decentralization must be tempered by selective centralization of certain areas of vital major policy. For example, the company with well-balanced, centralized decentralization will probably centralize decisions at the top on such things as financing, over-all profit goals and budgeting, major facilities and other capital expenditures, important new-product programs, major marketing policies, basic personnel policies, and selection, evaluation, compensation, and training of key managerial personnel. The key to effective decentralization is the proper balance between centralization and decentralization.

What is unduly limiting decentralization of authority is not the managers of American business nor their understanding and use of management principles, but, rather, forces largely external to business. Political centralization, with widespread controls of business concentrated in the national government, forces recentralization of decision making. Likewise, the rise of national unions, with so much concentration of authority in their officers, forces recentralization. And business managers themselves, through their delegation of some element of authority to numerous trade associations and their willingness to abide by industry policies formulated by them, are—probably necessarily, although perhaps unwittingly—participating in limiting decentralization of authority in American industry.

FOR DISCUSSION

1. Why has there been so much written and said, in the last twenty years, in favor of decentralizing authority?

2. What is the distinction between decentralizing "some of all authority" and "all of some authority"? What is actually done?

3. In many foreign countries very little authority is decentralized. What reasons do you think would explain this phenomenon?

4. If you were a manager, would you decentralize authority? State several reasons for your answer. How would you make sure that you did not decentralize too much?

5. There is considerable justification for the position of some top managers that they do not have a free choice in deciding upon the extent of decentralization of authority. Comment.

6. Should authority be pushed down into an organization as far as it will go?

SELECTED REFERENCES

Allen, L. A.: *Management and Organization*, chaps. 8–9, New York: McGraw-Hill Book company, 1958.

Baker, H., and R. R. France: *Centralization and Decentralization in Industrial Relations*, Princeton, N.J.: Industrial Relations Section, 1954.

Brown, D.: *Centralized Control with Decentralized Responsibilities*, Annual Convention Series No. 57, New York: American Management Association, 1927.

Collins, W. M.: *The Organization of General Motors Corporation*, Detroit: General Motors Corporation, 1966.

Controllership Foundation, Inc., *Centralization and Decentralization in Operating the Controller's Department,* New York: The Controllership Foundation, 1954.

Cordiner, R. J.: *New Frontiers for Professional Managers,* New York: McGraw-Hill Book Company, 1956.

Dale, E.: *Organization,* chap. 6, New York: American Management Association, 1967.

————: *Planning and Developing the Company Organization Structure,* Research Report No. 20, part 1, pp. 98–119, New York: American Management Association, 1952.

Davis, R. C.: *The Fundamentals of Top Management,* chap. 9, New York: Harper & Row, Publishers, Incorporated, 1951.

Drucker, P. F.: *Concept of the Corporation,* part 2, New York: The John Day Company, Inc., 1946.

GM and Its People, Detroit: General Motors Corporation, 1949.

Litterer, J. A.: *The Analysis of Organizations,* chap. 19, New York: John Wiley & Sons, Inc., 1965.

Newman, W. H.: *Administrative Action,* chap. 12, Englewood Cliffs, N.J.: Prentice-Hall, Inc., 1951.

———— and C. F. Summer, Jr.: *The Process of Management,* chaps. 3–4, Englewood Cliffs, N.J.: Prentice-Hall, Inc., 1961.

Problems and Policies of Decentralized Management, General Management Series No. 154, New York: American Management Association, 1952.

Self, H.: *Problems of Decentralization in a Large Scale Undertaking,* London: British Institute of Management, 1951.

Sloan, A. P., Jr.: *My Years with General Motors,* Garden City, N.Y.: Doubleday & Company, Inc., 1964.

Stieglitz, H.: "What Limits on Limits of Authority?" *The Conference Board Record,* vol. 2, no. 3, pp. 7–16 (March, 1965).

Worthy, J. C.: "Organization Structure and Employee Morale," *American Sociological Review,* vol. 15, pp. 169–179 (April, 1950).

committees

One of the most ubiquitous and controversial devices of organization is the committee. Whether referred to as a committee, board, commission, task force, or team, its essential nature is the same, for the committee is a group of persons to whom, as a group, some matter is committed. It is this characteristic of group action that sets the committee apart from other organization devices.

THE NATURE OF COMMITTEES

Because of variation in authority assigned to committees, much confusion has resulted as to their nature.

Some committees undertake managerial functions, and others do not. Some make decisions; others merely deliberate on problems without authority to decide. Some have authority to make recommendations to a manager, who may or may not accept them, while others are formed purely to receive information, without making recommendations or decisions. The writers have, for example, heard top business executives object to being appointed to "advisory" committees of government, educational, and trade organizations on which their only function is actually to receive already developed plans incorporating decisions previously made.

A committee may be either line or staff, depending upon its authority. If its authority involves decision making affecting subordinates responsible to it, it is a plural executive and a line committee; if its authority relationship to a superior is advisory, then it is a staff committee.

Committees may also be formal or informal. If established as part of the organization structure, with specifically delegated duties and authority, they are formal. Most committees with any permanence or standing fall into this class. Or they may be informal, that is, organized without specific delegation of authority and usually by some person desiring group thinking or group decision on a particular problem. Thus, a manager may have a problem on which he needs advice from other managers or specialists outside his department and call a special meeting for the purpose. Indeed, this kind of motivation, plus the occasional need for gathering together in one room all the authority available to deal with an unusual problem, gives rise to many of the numerous conferences in organizational life.[1]

Moreover, committees may be relatively permanent, or they may be temporary. One would expect the formal committees to be more permanent than the informal, although this is not necessarily so. A formal committee might be established by order of a company president, with appropriate provision in the organization structure, for the sole purpose of studying the advisability of building a new factory and be disbanded immediately upon completion of its task. And an informal committee set up by the factory manager to advise him upon the improvement of quality or to help coordinate delivery dates with sales commitments might continue indefinitely.

However, the executive who calls his assistants into his office or confers with his department heads is not creating a committee. It is sometimes difficult to draw a sharp distinction between committees and other group meetings. But the essential characteristic of the committee is a group charged with dealing with a specific problem. The committee is in wide use in all types of organization. In government, one finds a large number of standing and special committees of every legislative body; indeed, state and national legislatures are committees, as are the cabinets of the chief executives of the Federal and state governments. Committees manage many government agencies such as the Tennessee Valley Authority, the Atomic Energy Commission, the Federal Deposit Insurance Corporation, and the Export-Import Bank. Even the courts make liberal use of the device.

In education, faculties of great universities, jealous of academic freedom and distrustful of administrative power, traditionally circumscribe the authority of presidents and deans with a myriad of committees. In one large university more than 300 standing committees share in administration or advise on policy, ranging from the academic senate and the budget committees, to committees on committees, coordinating committees, and committees on alumni records, university welfare, and maintenance of order during examinations.

---

[1] "Formal" and "informal" are not used here in the sense in which Chester Barnard in *The Functions of the Executive* (Cambridge, Mass.: Harvard University Press, 1938), chaps. 6–9, employs the terms in discussing formal and informal organizations. It will be recalled that Barnard refers to any organization as formal when the activities of forces of two or more persons are *consciously* coordinated toward a given objective. The essence is joint purpose. Informal organizations, on the other hand, are "the aggregate of personal contacts and interactions and the associated groupings of people" without any specific joint purpose (pp. 114–115). As used here, a formal committee is one formally provided for by the organization of an enterprise, while an informal committee is one for which no such provision is made; both, however, are cases of conscious coordination toward a joint purpose.

Religious institutions likewise lean heavily on committees, partly to encourage active participation by members and partly to delimit the authority of leaders. Although their authority may vary widely, depending upon the traditions of the sect, committees—ranging from the church board to the committee in charge of a church supper—are ever-present.

Committees are also prevalent in business. The board of directors is a committee, as are its various constituent groups such as the executive committee, the finance committee, the audit committee, and the bonus committee. Occasionally, one finds a business managed by a management committee instead of a president. And almost invariably under the president will be a variety of management or policy committees, planning committees, wage and salary review committees, grievance committees, task forces for particular projects, and numerous other standing and special committees. Moreover, at each level of the organization structure, one or more committees are likely to be found.

REASONS FOR USE

One need not look far for reasons for the widespread use of committees in organization. Although the committee is sometimes regarded as having democratic origins and as being characteristic of democratic society, the reasons for its existence go beyond mere desire for group participation. Committees are found even in authoritarian organizations, as in the Russian state and in Communist China.

Group Deliberation and Judgment Perhaps the most important reason for the use of committees is the advantage of gaining group deliberation and judgment—a variation of the adage that "two heads are better than one."[2] A group of people can bring to bear on a problem a wider range of experience than can a single person, a greater variety of opinion, a more thorough probing of the facts, and a more diverse training in specialized aspects. Few indeed are important business problems that fall entirely into a single area such as production, engineering, finance, or sales. Most problems, on the contrary, require more knowledge, experience, and judgment than any individual possesses.

It should not be inferred that group judgment can be obtained only through use of committees. The staff specialist who confers individually with many persons expert in a given phase of a problem can obtain group judgment without the formation of a committee, as can the executive who asks key subordinates or other specialists for memoranda analyzing a problem and making recommendations thereon. Often group judgment can thus be obtained more efficiently, in terms of time, without the long deliberations of a committee. The keen manager can usually grasp ideas and the reasoning behind them more quickly from a concise written memorandum than from an oral presentation.

[2] Even though, as the Scots add, "one is a sheep's head."

However, one of the advantages of group deliberation and judgment, not to be obtained without an actual meeting, is the stimulation resulting from oral interchange of ideas and the cross-examination techniques of the committee meeting. Leading, as it does, to the clarification of problems and the development of new ideas, this interchange has been found to be especially enlightening in policy matters.[3] There are also several studies indicating that sometimes the results obtained by group judgment are superior to those obtained by individual judgment.[4]

Fear of Authority Another reason for the widespread use of the committee in organization is the fear of delegating too much authority to a single person. This fear, especially pronounced in government, dictated to the framers of the American Constitution not only the establishment of a two-house legislature and a multimember Supreme Court but also the division of the powers of government among the Congress, the Supreme Court, and the President. However, despite this fear of centralized authority, the founders of the American Republic placed the administration of laws in the hands of a single top executive, recognizing the advantages of this system.

Fear of delegating too much authority to the individual has been felt in all levels and activities of government, as evidenced by the numerous boards, commissions, and other instances of the plural executive. It is also experienced in educational organizations and in charitable and religious enterprises. In the latter, however, the willingness of people to be bound by the authoritarianism of faith and the religious interpretation of individual leaders has led to such concentration of authority as is found in the head of the Roman Catholic Church. However, in the various Protestant denominations, one finds far less willingness to trust the single executive, and the bishops or other church heads are usually well circumscribed by the authority of committees or conferences that dictate denominational policy.

This fear has had less influence in business than in other types of organization. Business enterprises have, for one thing, developed primarily from small beginnings within the institution of private property, with its implications of authority of the owner; workers, too, have been free to avoid abuse of power by moving from one company to another; and the overriding importance of efficiency, finally, has favored the single manager. At the same time, the traditional existence of a board of directors as the top managing

---

[3] The Ansul Chemical Company, which has experimented with group management (notably in the top executive team, consisting of the president, sales vice-president, production vice-president, and treasurer), found this to be one of the advantages of their use of a management committee at the top of the firm. See R. C. Hood, "Group Management—The Ansul Plan," in M. J. Dooher and V. Marquis (eds.), *The Development of Executive Talent* (New York: American Management Association, 1952), pp. 122–131.

[4] E. Dale, "Group Organization and Output," *Management News* (Spring, 1949); Hood, *op. cit.;* and C. P. McCormick, *Multiple Management* (New York: Harper & Brothers, 1938). See also report on du Pont's management committee in W. H. Mylander, "Management by Executive Committee," *Harvard Business Review*, vol. 33, no. 3, pp. 51–58 (May–June, 1955).

group of the business corporation may be traced, to some extent, to the fear of property owners of delegating too much authority to a managing director.

This motive has likewise influenced the formation of many internal business committees. A committee may be established to make recommendations on a problem largely because the president or department head does not wish to take full responsibility for making a decision or to trust the decision to a subordinate. Bonus committees often result from such motivation, and major financial and capital investment policies are developed by committees, partly because of unwillingness to trust a single individual with a complete authority to make so important a decision.

Representation of Interested Groups The desire to have various interested groups represented in policy matters, which played an important part in the organization of the United States House of Representatives and the Senate, makes itself felt in all branches of government where either law or tradition requires that the two major political parties, various sections of the country, or various pressure groups be represented.

Representation plays a part, too, in the establishment and manning of committees in business. Boards of directors are often selected on the basis of groups interested in the company and, perhaps more often, on the basis of groups in which the company has an interest. Thus, a large national company may select as members of its board men prominent in various geographical sections and representing banks, insurance companies, newspapers, and large customers. When an executive has a particularly difficult internal problem involving managers and specialists in various departments and activities, he may choose committee members in such a way as to give these interested parties representation. He may ostensibly do this in order to get a more balanced group judgment and a more diversified point of view, but he may actually be doing it to ensure that these groups will be represented and will thereby feel a sense of loyalty and commitment to the decision reached.

Coordination of Plans and Policies Committees are also useful for coordinating planning and the execution of programs. The dynamics of modern enterprise place a heavy burden on its managers to integrate plans and activities. With complications, change, and numerous specialized departments, it is difficult to coordinate every activity, every subordinate plan, and every expenditure with others, not only in time but also quantitatively.

A committee permits the individuals concerned not only to obtain firsthand a picture of over-all plans and of their place in them but to contribute suggestions on the spot for improvement of plans. The committee also furnishes a place where agreement may be reached on the steps in coordination. Furthermore, the committee, as a coordinating device, may be valuable for pooling authority to plan a program involving several departments.

Transmission of Information The committee is useful for transmission of information. All parties to be affected by a mutual problem or project can learn of it simultaneously, and decisions and instructions can be received uniformly with opportunities for clarification. The time thus saved may be considerable; and the spoken word, with its possibilities for overtones and emphasis and the opportunities for clarification, may carry its point better than even carefully written memoranda.

Consolidation of Authority A manager in a department, branch, or section often has only a portion of the authority necessary to accomplish a program. This is known as splintered authority. Good organization practice normally provides managers with the power appropriate to their position. However, this is not possible in every kind of problem, and some matters call for the exercise of authority that the manager at the level concerned does not possess.

One way to handle problems of this sort is to refer them upward in the organizational hierarchy until they reach a point at which the authority requisite for a decision exists. But this place is often in the office of the president, and the problem may not be of sufficient importance to be decided at that level. Suppose, for example, that a customer of a machine-tool manufacturer wished a slight but unusual change in design in a piece of equipment. He would approach the sales department, which, if there were no established procedure for handling this change, could not act without the authority of the engineering department, the production department, and the cost estimating department. In this case, the sales manager might establish a special-purpose committee to study the problem, to agree on the nature and cost of the change, and to use its combined authority to approve the request. In this way, the president would be spared the time and effort of dealing with the problem or working out special machinery to handle something that might not ever come up again.

This informal use of the committee gives much flexibility to organization. However, consolidating splintered authority through a committee should be watched carefully to ascertain whether the organizational structure itself might not be changed to concentrate in one position the appropriate authority to make recurring decisions. There is danger that splintered authority will become so much the rule rather than the exception that the purpose of the organization—to coordinate tasks with the least cost in personnel and time—will be defeated. As will be noted below, committees are expensive and time-consuming and must be weighed in this light.

Motivation through Participation Committees permit wider participation in decision making. Persons who take part in planning a program or making a decision usually feel more enthusiastic in accepting and executing it. Even slight participation can be helpful.

An intelligent manager will, therefore, at times appoint a committee to come up with a recommendation or a decision on a matter in which group deliberation is not necessary, a matter he has already decided or to which there is but one good answer. By skillful leadership or by the sheer force of facts, the group can be brought to a foregone decision. If the manager can avoid the appearance of "railroading," he is likely to obtain a stronger motivation toward acceptance and successful prosecution of a plan than if he had announced it to his subordinates without their participation. Even those who disagree with the decision may feel compelled to loyalty by the sheer weight of group opinion.

The use of committees to motivate subordinates to get behind a program or decision requires skillful handling. It is by no means certain that deliberations of this kind will result in enthusiastic support, for they can also result in the deepening of existing divisions among participants. Should this occur, this use of a committee may be a mistake. On the other hand, there are people who seem to be against every move unless they have been previously consulted. One of the authors recalls a college president who had on hand a surplus of Federal government funds. He had concluded an agreement with the government representatives to use these funds for the construction of a Greek theatre. At this stage the president announced the coup to his faculty. Taken by surprise and therefore hurt (being easily bruised, anyway), the faculty forced the abandonment of the project and the return of the surplus moneys to the government.

Avoidance of Action It cannot be denied that committees are sometimes appointed by a manager when he does not want any action to ensue. As will be noted presently, the committee device has many drawbacks, among them costliness in time and the difficulty and delay of getting a group to agree. One of the surest ways to delay the handling of a problem and even to postpone a decision indefinitely is to appoint a committee to study the matter, particularly if its membership is carefully selected with delay in mind. In organizations of all kinds, skillful chairmen or managers resort to this delaying action when they see fit.

DISADVANTAGES OF COMMITTEES

Certain dangers of committees have been so widely publicized that many managers make little use of them. Disparaging attitudes are reflected in such definitions as "a committee is made up of the unfit selected by the unwilling to do the unnecessary," or "a place where the loneliness of thought is replaced by the togetherness of nothingness."

High Cost in Time and Money The cost of committee action in time is likely to be considerable. A committee may require members to travel some distance to reach a meeting. During the meeting, each member has the right to be heard, to have his point of view discussed, to challenge and cross-examine the points of view of others, and to go over grounds for a considered group conclusion. The spoken word, though valuable for emphasis and clarification, is seldom concise, and the "thinking out loud" that takes place is sometimes a waste of time for those who must listen. If the committee must reach a unanimous or nearly unanimous decision, the discussion is likely to be lengthy. And if a decision can be reached quickly, the meeting may have been unnecessary in the first place.

The monetary cost of committee discussion can also be very high. One must consider not only the cost of executive time (which for a $25,000-per-year executive runs to $15 an hour) but even more the cost to the company of the time lost by the executive from his principal job.

This cost in time and money becomes all the more disadvantageous when a committee is assigned a problem that could as well, or better, be solved by a single individual, or by an individual with the help of a smaller and lesser-paid staff. Thus, the advantages of committee action must be considerable to offset the costs.

Compromise at the Least Common Denominator Where committees are required to come to some conclusion or to reach some decision, there is danger that their action will be watered down or even meaningless. If the matter under consideration is so simple that differences of opinion do not exist, the use of committee time is wasteful. If differences of opinion exist, the point at which all or a majority of the committeemen can agree will tend to be at the least common denominator of group agreement. Most often this is not as strong and positive a course of action as that undertaken by an individual who has only to consider the facts as he sees them and then reach a conclusion. Because of the necessity for seeking out common ground, committees often take innocuous action or defer action entirely.

The danger of compromise at the level of the least common denominator of agreement grows as the percentage of agreement felt necessary for committee action increases. Even committees whose authority delegation requires only majority agreement sometimes develop traditions of unanimity. Small groups of people frequently seek—from feelings of politeness, mutual respect, and humility—to reach conclusions on which all can agree. Since committee members are ordinarily picked from organization equals, the reluctance to force a conclusion on a recalcitrant minority is understandable, increasing thereby the probability of weak decisions.

This danger is largely eliminated when the committee is used solely as a forum or to transmit information and the decision is made by the chairman. It is also reduced when a skillful chairman leads the committee along a preconceived path. But a committee operated in either of these ways ceases to be a true decision-making group.

Indecision Another disadvantage of committees is that the time required for thorough deliberation, the discussion of peripheral or tangential subjects, and the difficulty of reaching agreement often result in indecision.

Tendency to Be Self-destructive Also, the indecisiveness of committees gives the chairman or a strong member opportunity to force the committee into a decision, for it is a rare group of men who can participate in the exercise of authority on a team basis. Almost invariably, one man emerges as the leader. But when an individual becomes dominant, the nature of the committee as a decision-making group of equals changes, and there actually emerges an executive with a group of followers or advisers.

In other cases, the members join in combat until one wins his point or until the group is disbanded by a superior authority. Even when the committee operates smoothly, one individual usually dominates. Executives often delude themselves into believing that committees operate on group-management principles with a group of equals, when, as a matter of fact, the "team" is composed of subordinate advisers or even yes-men following the superior's leadership.

To some extent, even when a committee does not make decisions it often disintegrates into an assembly dominated by a leader or leaders of two or three opposing factions. When the committee ceases to operate as a group of equals, and especially when it becomes a battleground for warring camps, the politics of the situation may lead to decisions or recommendations worse than those weak ones based on the least common denomination of agreement.

Splitting of Responsibility   When authority to study, make recommendations, or arrive at a decision is delegated to a group, the fact is that the authority is dispersed throughout the group. Thus, the individual member hardly feels the same degree of responsibility that he would feel if he personally were charged with the same task. This splitting of responsibility is one of the chief disadvantages of a committee. Since no one can practically or logically feel accountable for the actions of the group, no individual feels personally responsible for his action within it.

Minority Tyranny   As was pointed out above, committees tend to seek unanimous or near-unanimous conclusions or decisions. Minority members are, therefore, in a strong position. By their insistence upon acceptance of their position or of a compromise position, they exercise an unwarranted tyranny over the majority. The minority members of a jury have such power. The authors recall an important committee of nine members in which a tradition for unanimous agreement developed. One member actually controlled the committee, not through force of leadership but through power to withhold his vote. The matters which he blocked or on which he forced a watered-down conclusion fell in the area of committee authority and responsibility; the committee, though having failed because of his tyranny, provided cover for him. Had he borne individual authority and responsibility for his actions, he could hardly have been the obstructionist he was.

THE PLURAL EXECUTIVE

Most committees found in business are nonmanagerial in nature. However, there are many groups that are given the power to make decisions and to undertake some or all of the managerial functions of planning, organizing, staffing, directing, and controlling. It is this latter type of committee that is referred to as the plural executive. And it is to this type that most of the disadvantages of committee action apply.

Origin   The plural executive may be established by law, or it may result from a managerial decision.[5] Examples of the former are the board of directors of a corporation and the plural executive (commission, board) established by the various legislatures to operate one of their agencies. In the case of the corporation, legislatures have traditionally required that the board be elected to act for the stockholders. State and Federal legislatures have, especially in recent years, provided for direction of most government agencies by a single manager, but in many instances a plural executive is still operating.

Location within Organization Structure   When the plural executive is required by law, its location within or at the head of an organization structure is, of course, clearly defined. But internal committees may be found from the foreman level of management, where schedule committees are of particular importance, to higher levels, where broader issues are involved.

Authority   The extent of authority to manage and to make decisions held by a plural executive is not always easy to ascertain. Some, such as the board of directors, clearly have this power, although they may not exercise it. Some companies, like the Standard Oil Company (New Jersey) and the du Pont Company, are managed from the top, on a day-to-day or weekly basis, by a plural executive. In Standard the plural executive is the inside members of the board of directors meeting weekly, with an executive committee meeting daily; and in the du Pont Company an executive committee, comprised of the president and eight vice-presidents, meets weekly to make major decisions.[6]

There are, however, many executive committees which potentially have the power to manage but which actually do not, since decisions are made by a prominent stockholder or a strong leader in the group. Usually, the president is the dominant figure, with the other members little more than advisers. In other words, the plural executive is not always what it seems, and a single executive often in reality makes the decisions. Then there are other committees established with advisory authority only. Sometimes these actually operate as plural executives if, through tradition, weakness of leadership, or insistence of the chairman on agreement before a decision is made, they actually make decisions or undertake managerial functions as a group.

---

[5] For a history of the corporate executive, see C. O'Donnell, "Origins of the Corporate Executive," *Bulletin of the Business Historical Society*, vol. 26, no. 2 (June, 1952).
[6] Mylander, *op. cit.*

Role in Policy Making   The plural executive is often found in the field of policy making. Many companies have an executive or management committee to develop major plans and adopt basic policy. They go by various names: General Motors has its executive and finance committees, United States Rubber Company its operating policy committee, the Sun Chemical Company its management committee, Lockheed Aircraft Corporation its corporate policy committee, and the Koppers Company its policy committee.

The extent of authority of these and other policy-making or planning committees varies considerably, although their influence on decision making is perhaps greater in this area than in any other. These committees also engage in control, for their concern with policies and plans must be followed up to make sure that events conform to decisions.

Furthermore, these committees often decide organizational matters which are important in planning, because the adequacy of the organization structure may affect and be affected by planning. This function is especially useful in the settlement of questions of organizational jurisdiction. The plural executive is an ideal arbitrator of this kind of dispute, since the determination of a group will usually be accepted by contesting parties as more impartial than that of a single arbiter. Besides, personality clashes in a given organizational situation are more easily submerged in group action.

Where committees are successful in policy formulation, however, they are dependent upon accurate and adequate staff work. A committee can hardly develop a proposal, forecast probable profits and costs from alternative courses of action, or investigate the numerous tangible and intangible factors influencing a basic decision. These are matters for study, and the committee is a notoriously poor study or research device. Therefore, if group deliberation is to be productive, facts and estimates must be developed and presented so that the members need not grope for material upon which to base conclusions. The decisions of a policy or planning committee are no better than the caliber of staff work that presents the problems and recommended solutions for consideration.

Role in Policy Execution   Many companies and management experts distinguish between policy making and policy execution. It has been said that the former is concerned with "the establishment of broad principles by which administration is guided," while the latter is concerned with "the daily conduct of the company's affairs—setting standards and procedures to guide and govern execution of policies, establishing controls to insure adherence to standards, solving interdivisional disputes, improving interdivisional coordination, and meeting various emergencies as they arise."[7]

In companies where this distinction is made, special committees are established in functional areas—such as engineering, distribution, manufacturing, public relations, and labor relations—to deal with the more special-

---

[7] E. Dale, *Planning and Developing the Company Organization Structure*, Research Report No. 20 (New York: American Management Association, 1952), pp. 96–97.

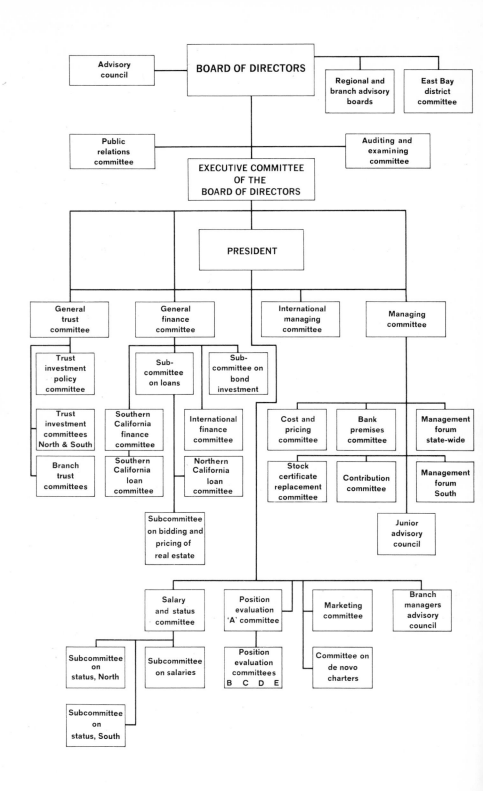

Fig. 18.1   Committee Organization in the Bank of America . . . *This bank, largest private bank in the world, supplements its management organization structure with a large number of committees and subcommittees. All these groups exert influence on management policy and decision, and certain committees, such as the Position Evaluation Committee, actually make decisions. Others, such as the Advisory Council of the Board of Directors and the Regional and Branch Advisory Boards, operate only in an advisory capacity. Likewise, the General Trust Committee concerns itself only with policy decisions, while the Trust Investment and Branch Trust Committees make actual trust decisions. Most of the committees have as their members senior or other key managers from all the important departments and divisions of the company. The Junior Advisory Council, however, consists of lower level managers or those about to be placed in a managerial capacity. While it carries on important analyses and projects and advises senior management groups, its primary purpose is training junior managers for future increased responsibilities in the bank.*

ized and technical aspects of planning; such committees may make recommendations to policy committees or may bolster basic policy with detailed enabling plans and programs.

In reality, there is little difference between policy-making committees and those which are thought of as executing policy. Both committees are engaged primarily in planning. The difference between them is one of degree, with the former usually engaged in major planning and the latter in less important planning. But because the latter are often facilitative and involve technical tasks requiring specialists, use of the committee in these areas is sometimes far less effective than the single administrator. Nevertheless, where the specialized deliberations can proceed from carefully prepared staff work and the committee need only consider matters requiring judgment, the plural executive can be effective in basic policy formulation.

Occasionally, committees are used to direct the accomplishment of plans, to assign tasks and authority, to select staff, and to follow up work. A committee is at a severe disadvantage in undertaking these managerial functions because of the disunity of command and it is seldom as competent as the individual manager.

PLURAL VERSUS INDIVIDUAL EXECUTIVE

Committees without managerial authority are far more numerous than those which are true plural executives. While much experience exists in organization with committees and with plural executives, the benefits of group management, as compared to individual management, have not been widely studied.

AMA Survey   One attempt to measure the merits of group versus individual management was made by the American Management Association.[8] Through

[8] *Ibid.*, pp. 92–93.

interviews with executives and analysis of records of some twenty representative companies, the Association found some interesting results. Breaking down management activity into twelve functions, the survey roughly estimates the proportion of each function that can (1) be exercised effectively by committee action; (2) be exercised effectively by committee action but more effectively by individual action; (3) be exercised by individual action, though helpfully supplemented by committee action; or (4) be effectively exercised only by individual action.

The results of this survey are summarized in Table 10. Although the sample is small, the breakdowns rough, and the percentages no more than approximate, the survey shows what a group of top executives in some well-managed companies think of group, as compared to individual, executive action. In three classifications the individual executive is considered superior to the plural executive, although in the two middle classifications committee action is deemed possibly helpful. This survey indicates a strong preference for the plural executive only in the settling of jurisdictional questions, with a prominent place in the formulation of objectives, and some usefulness in planning, control, administration, and communication. But the emphasis on the superiority of individual action in practically every function of management is pronounced. Even where committee action was found effective (the first two classifications), though not in all cases as effective as individual action, the score in favor of committees, with one exception, is still not particularly high.

TABLE 10   RELATIVE EFFECTIVENESS OF INDIVIDUAL AND
COMMITTEE ACTION IN FUNCTIONAL ACTIVITIES, PER CENT

Management function	Can be exercised by committee effectively	Can be exercised by committee but more effectively by individual	Individual initiative essential but may be supplemented by committee	Individual action essential; committee ineffective
Planning	20	20	25	35
Control	25	20	25	30
Formulating objectives	35	35	10	20
Organization	5	25	20	50
Jurisdictional questions	90	10		
Leadership			10	90
Administration	20	25	25	30
Execution	10	15	10	65
Innovation	30	20	20	30
Communication	20	15	35	30
Advice	15	25	35	25
Decision making	10	30	10	50

Evaluation Growing out of the foregoing discussion of the plural executive are certain clearly defined impressions. The plural executive succeeds fairly well in helping to coordinate the activities of managers. It has a high potentiality for aiding in defining objectives, selecting alternative ways of achieving them, and measuring the success attained. In terms of managerial functions, the plural executive is thus especially useful in planning and in certain of the broader aspects of control. However, all the disadvantages of the committee form apply with special force to the true plural executive.

BOARD OF DIRECTORS: TOP PLURAL EXECUTIVE

One of the most interesting organizational devices of the business management scene, established in the form of a plural executive, is the board of directors. Its importance to American business management is sometimes underestimated. An organization devoted to the study and rating of managerial effectiveness has made this surprising statement about boards:[9]

> The Institute, after study of thousands of corporations, is convinced the greatest single weakness in American business organization lies in the composition of the average board of directors. . . . In fact, more than one-half of the correspondence of the American Institute of Management, in answer to inquiries from the outside, is now concerned with matters regarding directors.

State laws under which corporations are established almost invariably require that the corporation be "managed" by a board of directors comprised of at least three members. The logic behind the requirement is that the corporation is an artificial entity, established by a sovereign power through contract with a group of owners (the stockholders), and therefore must have real persons responsible for managing.

Observation of boards of directors, however, shows that many of them actually do not manage, and corporate boards have often been criticized for this. Instead, managing, in its usual sense, is given completely to the president and other chief officers.[10] The separation of ownership and management sometimes makes the inside managerial group all-powerful and the board of directors a legal sham. Prominent stockholders, often controlling with a minority interest, occasionally make boards of directors approve their wishes. Yet boards of directors have an important managerial job to do. Under the corporation laws they are charged with the duty of managing the entire corporation for the stockholders, who are often too numerous and unorganized to take part in policy determination. Moreover, directors are definitely liable for their conduct, particularly under the Securities Act of

[9] American Institute of Management, *The Corporate Director*, Special Issue No. 15, p. 4 (December, 1951).

[10] W. O. Douglas, "Directors Who Do Not Direct," *Harvard Law Review*, vol. 47, pp. 1305–1334 (June, 1934).

1933 and the Securities Exchange Act of 1934. The criticism of American business in the decades after 1933, coupled with increasing legal liabilities and rising interest in the quality of managing, has reawakened interest in the board and its proper functioning in the modern corporation.

Functions   Some of the functions of the board of directors will be discussed briefly in this section.

Trusteeship   Probably the most important function of the board of directors may be summed up in the term "trusteeship," the husbanding of the corporation assets for the benefit of the stockholders. Even the most ineffectual board cannot escape this obligation.

Sometimes, especially in the large, publicly held corporation, the concept of trusteeship will extend beyond obligation to the stockholders to include obligation to the public, without whose support a corporation, as a social institution, could not endure; obligation to the employees of the corporation, whose efforts are necessary for its success; and obligation to the customers, who buy its products.[11] The position may be taken, on the other hand, that a director has the duty to operate exclusively for the benefit of the stockholders because it is their funds that he manages. To manage them for the benefit of other groups might then be interpreted as misappropriation of private property. At the same time, it can prove to be in the interest of the stockholder to administer for the benefit of employees and the public generally. With the lessening of privacy of the large corporation, the importance of labor relations forced on management by unionism, and in particular an enlightened attitude toward the human factor in business, such is often the case. Nevertheless, when directors forget that their first obligation is to the corporate owners whose funds they manage, there is a real question as to whether they are living up to their trust.

Determination of enterprise objectives   Another major function of the board of directors is the establishment of the general objectives of the business. Although making profit is properly the primary objective of all business, this must be translated into clearly understandable enterprise goals and into basic policies by which to achieve these goals.

Selection of executives   The board's function in selecting the chief executive of the corporation is a planning matter with long-run implications.[12]

Basic policy making and the choice of an executive are both functions of the board of directors, and in fact they are closely related. Every action

---

[11] See Chapter 32 for more detailed analysis of the social responsibilities of enterprise managers.

[12] See H. Koontz, *The Board of Directors and Effective Management* (New York: McGraw-Hill Book Company, 1967), pp. 26, 66–68.

by a board regarding the choice of a chief executive involves basic policy examination. If the man chosen is expected to follow the course of his predecessor, that action is a reaffirmation of the predecessor's policies and a decision to proceed as before. When a board maps out a new course preliminary to the choice of an executive, or when it accepts policy changes as conditions of acceptance stipulated by a candidate, the board of directors is making a long-run major planning decision.

In numerous ways, therefore, the effects of the decision reached by a board of directors in choosing a new executive will be apparent for a long time in the future.

While boards of directors actually elect other corporate officers, most directors regard it as the job of the president to nominate them. This is as it should be. The president is the operating head responsible to the board and if he cannot select his lieutenants, he can hardly be held responsible for the successful operation of the corporation as a whole. On the other hand, a responsible board must satisfy itself as to the quality of the company's entire management team and certain powers of *approval*, rather than *selection*, of top managers should be reserved to the board.

Check on plans and results Directors, by establishing corporate objectives and formulating major policies, are of course doing basic planning. But this is not enough. Being responsible for seeing that the company is well managed, the board should assure itself that the operating managers are making adequate plans. Thus, a board should review, or be informed of, management programs in such areas as new products, marketing approaches, personnel, organization, management development, and finance. The very presentation of such programs is often assurance that adequate planning is being done.

A board should also see that results are being accomplished in accordance with plans. Such evaluation means more than a study of financial statements and the audit reports. In the financial area, it means a careful review of forecasts and expected performance. In the area of organization, reports on actual organization practice, as dictated by board policy, should be submitted to the board. Similar reports should be made in the other areas of board interest. Too often, boards of directors approve planning programs and then forget them.

Approval of budgets Final approval of budgets is usually a key function of boards of directors. Whether applying to cash, revenues, expenses, capital expenditures, or number of employees, budgets are planning instruments whereby anticipated results are reduced to numerical terms. After adoption, they become the standard against which performance is measured for a given future period. To the extent that they are focused on over-all corporate affairs, as in the case of budget summaries, or matters of major corporate concern, such as cash and capital expenditures, they are properly subject to board approval.

Securing a long-range stability An often-overlooked function of the board of directors is securing long-range business stability in a changing environment. Barnard[13] has remarked that, although formal organization is "omnipresent and inescapable . . . successful cooperation in or by formal organizations is the abnormal, not the normal, condition." Even though people have a natural propensity to organize and many organizations exist at one time, few survive for a long period, since most fail to adjust their objectives and plans to a changing environment. From the standpoint of business, these changes include new technology, markets, and tastes; varying political, ethical, and economic conditions; and the growth of new business institutions.

Experienced directors, detached from everyday company operations, can call to the attention of management the need for changes in objectives and techniques. As Copeland and Towl[14] have pointed out, a competent board, operating as a group, has "a vitality which transcends that of the individual directors."

There are those who feel that securing long-range stability is the fundamental function of a board of directors. One authority has written, "Board and management alike are in the business of avoiding calamity, of preserving the company, maintaining its personality, ensuring its continuity."[15] In other words, as the corporation form is designed to furnish immortality, so the duty of the board is to accept responsibility for survival.

Distribution of earnings Another major function that must be exercised by directors—at least to meet the requirements of corporation law and the obligation to stockholders—is the distribution of earnings. Directors must decide whether earnings should be distributed as dividends, retained in the business for expansion, or used to eliminate outstanding indebtedness.

This decision is of exceptional importance. If a director decides that earnings should be distributed, he is taking the position that the owner would rather have immediate earnings in hand than invest in future earnings of the business or in capital gains. Should he decide to keep the earnings for expansion, he is, to some extent, forcing owners to reinvest funds in the corporation. If earnings are to be used to retire debt, the director is once more exercising his trusteeship of the investor's funds. The distribution of earnings is, to the stockholder, second in importance only to the actual utilization of his original capital investment.

Checking on plans and operations through discerning questions A director should ask discerning questions, an activity that does not depend

---

[13] Barnard, *op. cit.*, pp. 4–5.

[14] M. T. Copeland and A. R. Towl, *The Board of Directors and Business Management* (Boston: Division of Research, Harvard Business School, 1947), p. 24.

[15] H. Maurer, "Boards of Directors," *Fortune*, vol. 41, no. 5, p. 130 (May, 1950).

upon a detailed familiarity with the affairs of a business. Such questions force the proponents of a proposal, usually the corporation's executives, to defend it with facts and analysis or considered judgment. Questions seek to make sure that all facets of a problem have been explored, that all facts have been considered, and that alternative courses of action have been properly analyzed and rejected.

The ability to ask discerning questions comes from experience in decision making; consequently, some of the best corporation directors are not those who know every detail of a company's operation but those who have had experience in a variety of situations. Such persons often develop an intuitive feeling about business problems and know what is likely to affect them.

Perhaps more important than the effect of discerning questions on a board's deliberations is their effect on the study and preparation of a proposal before it is submitted to the board. Although questions are not designed to represent cross-examination or to discredit management, they frequently embarrass managers. The executive who knows he will be questioned will naturally try to anticipate it, and his assistants will take far greater care in briefing their superior to prevent his embarrassment by a failure on their part.

Boards in Small Corporations Boards in smaller businesses are often mere legal forms, with the owner or owners and members of their immediate families as directors. Indeed, it is not unusual for the necessary minutes of such boards to be prepared by legal counsel to cover matters required by state laws, while the actual operation of the board is practically nonexistent. At the same time, many small businesses have found the board of directors useful for improving the quality of their management, and studies have indicated that the board has an important place in the small corporate business.[16]

A dominant reason why the typical small corporation owner does not attach much importance to the board of directors but makes it a family board is his distrust of outsiders. Having built his own business from a garage machine shop or a basement office in his house, he often regards it as his offspring, his life, and his prized possession. Moreover, he may feel timid about asking a banker or lawyer or a management consultant, who he feels would not have this interest, to serve on such a board, and he may feel that the business could not make it worth their while to give their time. On the other hand, many public-spirited business and professional men see in the small business the heart of the private enterprise system, a

---

[16] An excellent study of this subject has been reported by M. L. Mace in *The Board of Directors in Small Corporations* (Boston: Division of Research, Harvard Business School, 1948). This study, which should be read by every owner of a small corporate business, has been used in this section to supplement the authors' own experience.

challenge to professional experience and ingenuity, and a means of being of genuine service in the building of well-managed business enterprise.

A small corporation may not be able to afford specialized talent, managerial and technical, yet its problems are the same, except in degree and scope, as those of the large corporation. The owner-manager of the typical small corporation frequently has several limitations, both in education and in experience. The outside director can be extremely useful in at least partly eliminating them.

An outside director can assist materially in basic policy making in the small corporation. Such policy is often overlooked by the small business manager, who becomes overburdened by recurring operating problems and details that could easily be handled by reference to an established policy.

Managers of small businesses often fail to plan. Sales and production dips come without warning. Income taxes come due without enough cash on hand. Inventories build up and working capital becomes frozen before the manager realizes what is happening. The temptation to accept orders without thought of the capital required to meet them sometimes causes the owner to become overextended in the midst of promise of profits. An outside director, whose approach to the business is uncluttered by day-to-day problems, can often bring the necessary foresight to this kind of situation.

Again, the review and reestablishment of company objectives in the light of new technical, political, or economic developments may be overlooked by the harassed owner-manager but will be natural subjects for consideration by the more detached outside director. Problems of management succession become especially important to the small business, which normally has no ready supply of understudies trained to take over active management. Misunderstandings or jealousies between owner-managers and their key subordinates may reach exaggerated proportions if left unsolved. The interests of minority stockholders may be overlooked by the ambitious owner of a majority of the stock in a small corporation. These and other problems, although not peculiar to the small corporation, are likely to be aggravated in it. Their solution requires skill, tact, and an objective point of view—qualities that can be found in the well-selected outside board member. In addition to these specific functions, the board member of the small corporate enterprise also can serve the business valuably in the many ways any director serves any corporation.

Revitalization of Boards Although subject to the various inherent drawbacks of the plural executive, boards of directors stand at the apex of the pyramid of corporate organization. The character of the business leadership, the tone of managerial policy, and the basic direction of the enterprise are among their far-reaching concerns. There are signs that the authoritative position of boards is coming to be better recognized and their independence encouraged. Special surveys of board effectiveness made in 1955, 1962, and 1964 disclosed that more outsiders were serving on boards, more boards were made up of specialists, more was being expected of directors, more and longer meetings were being held, and directors were being paid more.[17]

This revitalization of corporate boards results from several factors. The rise in stockholder interest in corporate affairs and the instances of stockholders ousting company managements have led many top managers to seek the protection and help of an effective board. The larger holdings of institutional investors in corporate stocks and the fact that these investors have become a major source of capital funds have likewise contributed to the establishment of more effective boards with more outside members. Also, the increased tempo of business competition has caused company officers and prominent stockholders to secure more outside specialists on the board and to seek their counsel in major policy matters.

In place of the former resentment of interference by outsiders on the board, there is a rising realization by top corporate managers that major decisions call for thorough analysis and deliberation on the part of the best available management brains, that some of this can come from outside the corporation, and that advantages may offset disadvantages in group decision making. With recent searching studies and the focus of attention upon corporate responsibilities, a further revitalization of boards as molders of business policy may be expected.

MISUSE OF COMMITTEES

The committee form has often fallen into disrepute through misuse. The five following abuses should be avoided when committees are set up.

In Place of a Manager   The weakness of the committee as a managing device has already been noted. Leadership is essentially a quality of individuals. If decision making is to be sharp, clear, prompt, and subject to unquestioned responsibility, it is better exercised by the individual, as is the direction of subordinates.

There are times, it must be admitted, when managerial effectiveness is not an overriding consideration. In certain government agencies the danger of putting too much authority in the hands of an individual may be so great as to supersede questions of pure efficiency. As a matter of fact, before criticizing the waste, duplication, and inefficiency of governmental manage-

---

[17] "Directors; Doing More Directing," *Business Week,* pp. 101–104 (Mar. 12, 1955). See also John R. Kinley, *Corporate Directorship Practices,* Studies in Business Policy No. 103 (New York: National Industrial Conference Board, Inc., 1962); J. D. Thompson and F. J. Walsh, Jr., "Directors' Compensation, Fringe Benefits and Retirement," *Conference Board Record,* vol. 2, no. 2 (February, 1965); G. C. Thompson and F. J. Walsh, Jr., "Selection of Corporate Directors," *Conference Board Record,* vol. 2, no. 5, pp. 8–16 (May, 1965); and J. Bacon, *Corporate Directorship Practices,* Studies in Business Policy No. 125 (New York: National Industrial Conference Board, Inc., 1967). See also "What It Takes to Make a Board," *Business Week,* pp. 93–94 (Mar. 12, 1966).

ment, one should face the question of whether these costs are a fair price to pay for curtailing abuses of authority. Similarly, in business, a certain area of decision might be so important to the welfare of the company and the dangers of abuse of authority in that area so great that no individual should be entrusted with this power. But this would be an exceptional case.

One can hardly say that a committee has no place in management. But, as was noted in the analysis of types of committees, the advantages of group thinking and participation in policy questions can be gained in most cases through advisory committees. Most business committees function this way, leaving the real decision making and managing to the line executives to whom they report. As Ralph Cordiner, former President of the General Electric Company,[18] has said, "We have no committees to make decisions that individuals should make."

For Research or Study A group meeting together can hardly engage in research or study, even though it may well weigh and criticize the results of these. When the solution to a problem requires data not available to a committee, no amount of discussion or consideration can turn up the missing information. This is essentially an individual function, even though, of course, individuals may be coordinated into a team with individual research assignments. Most committees, therefore, need a research staff, providing at least analyses of alternative courses of action, historical summaries, or well-considered forecasts.

For Unimportant Decisions Even where the committee is clothed with advisory authority only, the disadvantages of this device should dictate that its use be limited to important matters. Moreover, no intelligent specialist or manager can help chafing as a result of the time wasted by a group deliberating at length on trivial subjects. This impatience reaches its frustrating climax when a committee member finds himself considering a question upon which a certain decision is a foregone conclusion.

For Decisions beyond Participants' Authority Where committees are used for decision making, if committeemen with authority attend the meetings or send duly empowered representatives, and if the agenda deals with matters within the competence of the members, no authority problem will be encountered. But, altogether too often, the executive with the requisite authority cannot or does not attend the meeting and sends in his place a subordinate who has not been delegated his superior's power or who hesitates to bind his superior. The result is that the committee cannot function as was intended. Delay results while the substitute refers questions to his superior, and much of the advantage of group decision making and deliberation is lost.

[18] Quoted in H. Maurer, "Management by Committee," *Fortune*, vol. 47, no. 4, p. 192 (April, 1953).

This misuse is probably the most usual reason for failure of the well-constituted committee. In a sense, it is inherent in the system. The committee is most useful in major policy determination, which is ordinarily the province of relatively few upper-level executives. If the same executive belongs to many committees, he cannot afford time to attend all meetings and must send subordinates. Yet he hesitates to delegate binding authority, a situation that causes many executives to be critical of committees. The way out of this dilemma is twofold: careful preparation of the agenda, so that the delegant knows precisely what will come up and can give his subordinate the authority necessary for the meeting; and careful advance study of proposals, so that the executive can offer his opinions intelligently even by proxy.

There are other cases of committee misuse where the committee as constituted includes members whose authority does not fit the decision or discussion area. Often, to spread committee memberships, reduce the load of committee work, or increase the training and informational advantages of participation, individuals are chosen to represent points of view in areas over which they have no authority. Thus, a committee might be constituted to establish advertising policy. Although it might be entirely proper for the sales promotion manager and the market research manager to be members, unless one of them can speak for the marketing department as a whole, the committee may be unable to come to a conclusion and may result in a wasteful use of manpower.

To Consolidate Divided Authority A disadvantage of departmentation is that authority is so delegated that, in some cases, no executive except the chief officer has adequate authority to do what must be done. Even within departments or sections, authority may be so splintered that group meetings are necessary to consolidate authority for making decisions.

A degree of splintered authority is unavoidable, and since the alternative to committee action might be the submission of too many problems to higher executives, the committee is useful for consolidating such authority. At the same time, if divided authority can be eliminated by changing the organization structure and the delegations of authority, recourse to a committee is certainly a misuse of the device. Whenever a committee must be continually used to concentrate authority, the organization structure probably needs revision.

SUCCESSFUL OPERATION OF COMMITTEES

The costs and other drawbacks of a committee system, as well as its frequent misuse, call for more managerial attention than is usually forthcoming. Moreover, the democratic tradition in American social life, plus increasing emphasis on group management and group participation in business affairs, makes this problem of great importance to management. Despite the acknowledged disadvantages, there is evidence that the use of committees in business continues to increase.[19] This calls for fresh attention to improving their use.

Need for Well-defined Authority and Scope   Unless a committee's authority is carefully spelled out, the members may not know whether they are responsible for a decision, a recommendation, or merely inconclusive deliberation from which the chairman may gain some insights. The members should also know the exact scope of subjects the group is expected to consider. A great inefficiency of committee action is wandering from the subject or the chairman's introducing subjects that are beyond the committee's scope. In some cases, the committee may roam so far afield that it must be disbanded and a new committee appointed.

Furthermore, with authority and scope clear, committee members are better able to gauge whether they are meeting their responsibilities to the organization. Some companies make extensive efforts to review committee work, dissolving or consolidating those whose work is no longer justified. Some companies have an evaluating committee that continually analyzes other committees in this way.[20]

Determining Size   No precise conclusions can be drawn here. As a general rule, a committee should be large enough to promote deliberation and include the breadth of expertness required for its job but not so large as to waste time or foster indecision. This is thought by some to mean as large as five or six members but no larger than fifteen or sixteen.[21] It is obvious that the larger the group, the greater the difficulty in obtaining a "sense of the meeting," and the more time necessary to allow everyone to make his contribution.

If a committee is to have all interested parties participate in its deliberations, the number may be too large, and the group may be incompatible. If all interests are not represented, the committee's work may be subject to criticism. Where representation is important, the answer may be

---

[19] See, for example, "Business Probes Its Own Structure," *Business Week* (Apr. 12, 1952), in which the statement is made (partly, but certainly not completely, on the basis of Dale's study, *Planning and Developing the Company Organization Structure*), "As companies get bigger, it is almost certain that committees will play a bigger role, again lightening top management's burden. Most companies already have some kind of group thinking, whether formal or not." A study made in 1957 supports this conclusion. See "Committees: Their Role in Management Today," *Management Review*, vol. 46, no. 10, pp. 4ff. (October, 1957).

[20] For a discussion of this committee, see Dale, *Planning and Developing the Company Organization Structure*, pp. 186–187.

[21] *Ibid.*, p. 90. W. H. Newman, in *Administrative Action*, p. 234, believes, however, that a committee should be held down to three or four members. C. J. Berwitz, in "The Work Committee—An Administrative Technique," *Harvard Business Review*, vol. 30, pp. 110–124 (January, 1952), suggests a maximum of seven members. A study made by the American Management Association in 1957 found that sizes of major committees in more than half the companies surveyed varied from six to ten members, with far more committees below five members than above ten. See "Committees: Their Role in Management Today," *Management Review*, loc. cit.

found in a structure of subcommittees, with the problems to be considered properly broken down for their action. However, in many instances, the need for representation is overstressed. The true purposes of committees are often accomplished by complete staff preparation for scrutinizing the various facets of a problem, and by limiting the membership to individuals who can look at the problem as a whole rather than regard their membership as a means of protecting a narrow interest.

Selecting Members For a successful committee,[22] the members must be suitably representative of the interests they are intended to serve and possess the requisite authority, and they must be able to perform well in a group. Not everyone has the temperament, verbal and analytical ability, and capacity for working with others to do this. Although members should be able to express themselves clearly and easily, even some able executives find this difficult.

Members should also have the capacity for reaching group decisions by integrating group thinking rather than by compromise or by conclusions forced by position or political strength. Committees are more likely to reach agreement without weak compromise or power politics if the members are friendly, known to one another, and mutually respectful of one another's positions and interests. This means that the participants should generally be on approximately the same organizational level and independent enough of one another not to fear reprisal. Where committees are used as the forum of the traditional dissenter or as the rostrum of the ambitious climber anxious to use his talents, waste of time may be the sole result. Again, some individuals feel a need to engage in hypothetical discussions achieving no concrete results. It is a rare and enjoyable committee that does not have the committee bore among its members.

Selecting Subject Matter Committee work must be limited to subject matter that can be handled in group discussion. As mentioned above, the committee is not a good medium for research and study or for exercising managerial functions. Certain kinds of subjects, therefore, lend themselves to committee action while others do not. Other than jurisdictional questions, where the prestige and impersonal nature of group action are definitely superior, the best area for group action is policy formulation or major planning. Along with planning, subjects for committee action lie in the area of control, especially over managers responsible for implementing major plans.

The way subjects are presented is also important. Proposals made before the committee should be sharply presented. Unless the questions raised are appropriate to the deliberations desired, a well-prepared agenda is not helpful. Ideally, an agenda should be circulated to members well in advance of the meeting, so that they may know what will be discussed. Even the cleverest and best-informed committee member can hardly be expected to

[22] For suggstions on membership selection, see C. O'Donnell, "Ground Rules for Using Committees," *Management Review*, vol. 50, no. 10, pp. 63ff. (October, 1961).

have a considered opinion on important matters without some notice of what to expect. Masses of carefully prepared recommendations available for cursory study at the member's place at the table seldom meet this need. Yet it is common for directors and other committee members to receive their first glimpse of the material to be discussed neatly stacked on the committee table. The results are as might be expected. Often the meeting time is consumed in laborious study of the reports or in listening to various members think aloud; or else the reports are meekly accepted by the members and the results railroaded by the chairman; or the meeting may be postponed to a later date after the members have had an opportunity to study the proposals.

Importance of the Chairman The success of a committee will never be greater than the skill of the chairman. A good chairman can avoid many of the wastes and drawbacks of committees by planning the meeting, preparing the agenda, and seeing that it and the results of research are available to the members ahead of time, arranging definite proposals for discussion or action, and conducting the meeting efficiently.

The chairman sets the tone of the meeting. He may wish it to be formal or informal, the argument to be casual or pointed. By anticipating objections and playing the devil's advocate, he may completely undermine many objections. When the subject matter is especially open to contention, the chairman may lead the discussion so that members are not forced into a position, at least until the subject has been fully discussed. Human nature being what it is, individuals who take a premature position are likely to defend it to the end. Since a committee is after results of group deliberation, lines should not be too sharply drawn, at least early in the discussion.

It usually falls to the chairman to integrate committee deliberation. Integration of ideas, as contrasted to compromise, builds a point of view, often quite new, from the basic positions of the group. If the chairman is weak or not fully familiar with the subject or the way individual members think, integration of ideas is unlikely to result. When leadership is assumed by a committee member, that member often becomes the *de facto* chairman of the meeting.

The chairman, also, must keep discussion from wandering. This often takes great skill, especially when the committee includes persons who enjoy the sound of their own voices or who lack ability to recognize essentials and to speak of them concisely. The chairman must handle the meeting firmly, without imposing his own opinions or thwarting freedom of discussion, yet without yielding his powers of chairmanship.

As a government administrator who has had long experience in the operation of committees has put it: [23]

[23] Berwitz, *op. cit.*, pp. 112, 122. Among some of the difficult personalities Berwitz mentions as problems for the chairman are the genius, the frustrated man, the "inferiorated," the lazy man with ability, the cocky oversimplifier, the stubborn man, and the "lone wolf." The experienced chairman will recognize these problem types immediately.

The chairman must be able to organize and guide thinking. He must know the objectives of the organization and the nature and extent of the problem to be solved. He must understand his superior executive's attitudes and be able to predict what he will or will not approve. He must know the operating organization's problems and attitudes and be able to predict staff reaction to any solution reached, if only so the findings will be understandable by those who did not have the benefit of working with the committee.

While the committee functions, the chairman establishes the sequence of elements to be discussed, makes assignments to committee members, coordinates and integrates subcommittees or members working independently. During discussion, he will often find it necessary to resolve conflicts and opposing viewpoints on the basis of his own knowledge and experience or, if he has no reference points, through his ability to sense the emergence of the more "correct" approach. Sometimes he will have to stimulate thought when none is forthcoming voluntarily. All this calls for ability to cajole, reprimand, and soothe; for qualities of alertness, aggressiveness, calmness, objectivity; for a knack of envisioning theory and projecting it against practice. And, needless to say, no chairman can be really successful unless he commands the respect of his colleagues.

I am, of course, describing a "wonder boy." Success is not dependent on securing such a man, but success is the more likely the nearer these specifications are met. . . .

The pleasant, firm, capable leader with knowledge and ideas, who can open and close debate at will, who recognizes and capitalizes on the strengths and weaknesses of his committee, who accepts majority opinion wherever possible, generally fares the best. For through his ability and skill he wins the respect and admiration of the group, and at the same time he is able to sense and control any of the arch-personalities the moment danger signs appear.

Thus, the chairman of a committee must be chosen with great care. On his shoulders falls most of the responsibility for assuring that the committee acts effectively. Obviously, it is a great help if the members and subject matter have been well selected. Even a skilled chairman can hardly make up for the deficiencies of a poorly constituted committee.

Checking Conclusions The use of a committee allows a group of people to participate in the solution or discussion of a problem and to be informed simultaneously concerning it. Yet individuals may walk away from meetings with varying interpretations as to what was accomplished. To avoid this, it is well to take careful minutes of the meeting, circulate them in draft for correction or modifications, and then have the final copy approved by the committee. This procedure has the advantage of forcing committee members to agree or disagree upon the results of the discussion and the further advantage of supplementing oral discussion with the written word.

Checking conclusions also provides for a follow-up of committee actions. Good management practice demands that control be undertaken to assure committee operation. If a committee makes a recommendation to a superior manager, the group should be informed as to the action, if any, which is taken; if the recommendation is not followed, some explanation to the committee is in order, to preserve committee morale, as well as educate its membership on management policy. Even if a committee makes neither decision nor recommendation but merely explores ideas, some report to the membership on its results is of value.

Follow-up on committee operations is important to a feeling of participation, and individuals become better-trained committee members if they know how their deliberations were used and how and why they were modified.

The Committee Must Be Worth the Cost   Above all, in measuring the success of committee operation, one must continually question whether the committee's benefits to the company are worth its cost. It may be difficult to count the benefits, especially in such intangible forms as morale, enhancement of status, teamwork, and training. But the committee can be justified only if the costs, which are often considerable, are definitely offset by tangible and intangible benefits.

FOR DISCUSSION

1. A prominent novelist-critic of the management scene has said:
"I don't think we can go on very much longer with the luxurious practice of hiring 10 men to make one man's decision. With all its advantages, professional management tends to encourage bureaucratic corpulence." Comment.

2. Distinguish among a "committee," "team," and "group."

3. Where in an organization would you suggest, if any place, committees should be used? Why?

4. Boards of directors legally have the responsibility to "manage" a corporation. How should they do it?

5. If you were asked to develop a course of study to train committee chairmen, what would you put into this course?

6. Compare, in organization terms, the typical formal business organization with the usual committee with which you are familiar, the usual athletic team, and a symphony orchestra.

SELECTED REFERENCES

Bacon, J.: *Corporate Directorship Practices,* Studies in Business Policy No. 125, New York: National Industrial Conference Board, Inc., 1967.

Baker, J. C.: *Directors and Their Functions,* Boston: Division of Research, Graduate School of Business Administration, Harvard University, 1945.

Bates, G. E.: "The Board of Directors," *Harvard Business Review,* vol. 19, no. 5, pp. 72–87 (October, 1940).

Berwitz, C. J.: "The Work Committee—An Administrative Technique," *Harvard Business Review,* vol. 30, pp. 110–124 (January, 1952).

Bienvenu, B. J.: "Boards of Directors Revisited," *Business Horizons,* vol. 5, no. 3, pp. 41–50 (Fall, 1962).

Blair, W. T.: "Appraising the Board of Directors," *Harvard Business Review*, vol. 28, no. 1, pp. 101–113 (January, 1950).

Charlton, J. M.: "Directors: The Duty to Manage," *Mississippi Valley Journal of Business and Economics*, vol. 1, no. 2, pp. 36–51 (Spring, 1966).

Chiles, E. A.: "Use and Limitations of Committees," *Handbook of Business Administration*, pp. 2–87, 92, New York: McGraw-Hill Book Company, 1967.

Copeland, M. T., and A. R. Towl: *The Board of Directors and Business Management*, Boston: Division of Research, Harvard Business School, 1947.

Dale, E.: *Planning and Developing the Company Organization Structure*, Research Report No. 20, pp. 83–97, New York: American Management Association, 1952.

"Directors: Doing More Directing," *Business Week*, pp. 101–104 (Mar. 12, 1955).

Douglas, W. O.: "Directors Who Do Not Direct," *Harvard Law Review*, vol. 47, pp. 1305–1334 (June, 1934).

Juran, J. M., and J. K. Louden: *The Corporate Director*, New York: American Management Association, 1966.

Kinley, John R.: *Corporate Directorship Practices*, Studies in Business Policy No. 103, New York: National Inlustrial Conference Board, Inc., 1962.

Koontz, H.: *The Board of Directors and Effective Management*, New York: McGraw-Hill Book Company, 1967.

Lohman, M. R.: *Top Management Committees*, Research Study No. 48, New York: American Management Association, 1961.

Mace, M. L.: *The Board of Directors in Small Corporations*, Boston: Division of Research, Harvard Business School, 1948.

Maurer, H.: "Boards of Directors," *Fortune*, vol. 41, no. 5, pp. 107ff. (May, 1950).

————: "Management by Committee," *Fortune*, vol. 47, no. 4, pp. 145ff. (April, 1953).

Mylander, W. H.: "Management by Executive Committee," *Harvard Business Review*, vol. 33, no. 3, pp. 51–58 (May–June, 1955).

O'Donnell, C.: "Ground Rules for Using Committees," *Management Review*, vol. 50, no. 10, pp. 63ff. (October, 1961).

Smith, E. E.: "Put the Board of Directors to Work!" *Harvard Business Review*, vol. 36, no. 3, pp. 41–48 (May–June, 1958).

Vance, S. C.: *Boards of Directors: Structure and Performance*, Eugene, Ore.: University of Oregon Press, 1964.

Watson, J. H., III: *The Corporate Directorship*, Studies in Business Policy No. 63, New York: National Industrial Conference Board, Inc., 1953.

making organizing effective

Perhaps organization is the most fully developed area of management theory. Its importance was recognized before that of the other management functions and its principles have been more completely explored, developed, and tested. Although some that the authors regard as principles may not be as fully tested in practice as others and some important truths of organization are probably yet undiscovered, fundamental truths, distilled from long practice, can be applied to make organization structure aid in the effective and efficient performance of individuals.

Organization is essentially an intentional structure for performance, a network of decision communications centers from which to secure coordination of individual effort toward group goals. Yet to make organization work, certain common mistakes—certain inflexibilities and conflicts which arise in practice—must be avoided, the organization must be understood, and principles put into practice.

SOME MISTAKES IN ORGANIZING

Despite their obviousness and their thwarting of personal and enterprise goals, the persistence of certain mistakes of organizing is striking evidence of either the difficulty of managing or the lack of sophistication of managers, or both. Following is a discussion of a dozen common mistakes to be particularly avoided.

1. Failure to Plan Properly It is not unusual to find an enterprise continuing a traditional organization long after its objectives, plans, and external environment have changed. For example, a company may keep its product research department under manufacturing division control long after the business environment has changed from being production-oriented (as in a typical sellers' market) to being marketing-oriented (as in a typical buyers' market). Or a company may continue its functional organization when product groupings and the need for integrated, decentralized profit responsibility demand an organization decentralized in its product divisions.

Also, a company may need managers of a kind not currently available, or, just as likely, may find that certain managers have not grown with the company or do not fit current needs. Small, growing businesses often make the mistake of assuming that original employees can grow with the company, only to find that a good engineering designer, made a vice-president, can no longer fill the larger role of the company officer; or that a once-adequate production superintendent cannot head a larger manufacturing department.

Such mistakes occur when an enterprise fails to plan properly toward a future materially different from the past or present. By looking forward, the manager should determine what kind of organization structure will best serve future needs and what kind of people will best serve this organization.

Another failure in planning involves organizing around people. Organization structure must normally be modified to take people into account, and there is much to be said for trying to take full advantage of employee strengths and weaknesses. But organizing primarily around people overlooks several facts. In the first place, there can never be assurance by so doing that all bases will be covered, that all the necessary tasks will be undertaken. In the second place, there is danger that different people will desire to do the same things, resulting in conflict or multiple command. In the third place, people have a way of coming and going in an enterprise—through retirement, resignation, promotion, or death—which makes organizing around them risky and their position, when vacated, hard to determine accurately.

2. Failure to Clarify Relationships The failure to clarify organization relationships, probably more than any other mistake, accounts for friction, politics, and inefficiencies. Since the power to do a job and the responsibility for doing it are critical in organization, lack of clarity here means lack of knowledge of the part employees are to play on an enterprise team. As has been pointed out many times in this book, clarity of assignment and of authority implies neither a detailed and minute job description nor that people cannot operate as a team. Although business leaders have prided themselves on having a team of subordinates without specified tasks and authority lines, any sports coach could tell them that such a team is likely to be a group of jealous, insecure, buck-passing individuals jockeying for position and favor.

The mistake of failing to clarify relationships is illustrated in the case of line, staff, and functional authority relationships. As was pointed out in Chapter 15, much of the problem of line and staff—as well as that of the complex hybrid of functional authority—can be traced to people not knowing who is responsible for what. And, not knowing, they tend to undermine their effectiveness, as the staff assistant does in issuing orders for activities not under his command or in taking credit for the action of a line manager who uses his advice. In the case of functional authority, it is likewise clear that, if neither the holder nor the object of functional authority understands its nature and extent, the authority may be misused, be ignored, or become cause for resentment and conflict.

3. Failure to Delegate Authority A common complaint in organizational life is that managers are reluctant to push decision making down into the organization. In some small businesses, where uniformity of policy is necessary and decision making can be handled by one or a few managers, there may be neither need nor desire to decentralize authority. But bottlenecks of decision making, excessive referral of small problems to upper echelons, overburdening of top executives with detail, continual "fighting fires" and "meeting crises," and underdevelopment of managerial experience in the lower levels of organization give evidence that failing to delegate authority to the right extent is usually a decided mistake.

4. Failure to Balance Delegation Another mistake made in organizing is failure to maintain balanced delegation. In other words, some managers—in their zeal for decentralization—may take literally the organizational bromide to "push decision making down in the organization as far as it will go." Obviously, to do this pushes it down to the very bottom of the structure and develops a system of independent organizational satellites. Even without going to this extreme, not maintaining authority suitable for the various levels of organization has caused many organizational failures.

As was pointed out in Chapter 17 on decentralization, top managers must retain some authority, particularly over decisions of company-wide impact and at least enough to review the plans and performance of subordinates. The manager must not forget, then, that there is authority he should not delegate, either because he can make certain decisions most effectively and efficiently himself or because, by their nature, they should not be made at a lower level. Nor should he overlook the fact that he must maintain enough power to make sure that authority delegated to his subordinates is being used to discharge his own responsibility.

5. Confusion of Lines of Authority and of Information The problems and costs of levels of organization and departmentation can be reduced by opening wide the channels of information. Unless information is confidential (and businesses, as well as other enterprises, overdo this classification) or is unavailable except at too great expense, there is no reason why lines of information should follow lines of authority. Information gathering should be separated from decision making, as only the latter requires managerial authority. Enterprises often force lines of information to follow authority lines, when the only reason for following a chain of command is to preserve the integrity of authority for decision making and the clarity of responsibility.

6. Authority without Responsibility A significant cause of mismanagement is the granting of authority without exacting responsibility. Authority delegation is not responsibility delegation; the delegant remains responsible for the proper exercise of authority by his subordinate. Any other relationship would lead to organizational anarchy. Moreover, anyone to whom authority is delegated must be willing to be held responsible for all his actions. Too often the division or regional manager remembers only the authority delegated to him and forgets that headquarters officers have the right and obligation to hold him fully accountable for its use.

7. Responsibility without Authority A common complaint of subordinates is that superiors hold them responsible for a duty without giving them the authority to accomplish it. Some of these complaints are unjustified and based on misunderstanding the fact that few subordinates can have unlimited authority in any area, because their actions must be coordinated with those in other areas and must remain within defined policies. Subordinates often see their jobs as all-encompassing and forget that their authority must be limited to their own departmental boundaries and within controlling policies.

Too often, however, the complaints are justified; managers, sometimes without realizing it, do hold subordinates responsible for activities they have no power to accomplish. This does not happen as frequently where organization lines and duties have been clearly set forth, but in an uncharted organization, where relationships are not spelled out specifically, it does occur.

8. Careless Application of the Staff Device There are many valid reasons for using the staff assistant or the staff specialist and even building entire advisory departments. However, there is danger that the staff person will be used to undermine the authority of the very managers he is intended merely to advise. A manager in charge of a department or a president responsible for managing a company may assign a policy problem to his staff and then assume unconsciously that this action constitutes a decision, although no authority has actually been delegated.

The undermining of managerial authority may extend to subordinate line managers. There is an ever-present danger that a top manager may surround himself with staff specialists and so preoccupy himself with their work as to exclude from his schedule the time and attention needed for his line subordinates; or he may assign problems to his staff that should be more appropriately assigned, often with specially delegated authority, to his line lieutenants.

In other instances, staff personnel exercise line authority which has not been delegated to them. It is easy to understand the impatience of a staff specialist who sees clearly how a situation should be handled, while the line officer in charge of it seems to be dilatory or clumsy. The very quality that makes a staff specialist valuable—his specialized knowledge—also makes him impatient to command. Yet if he were to have this authority without clear delegation, he would be not only undermining the authority of the responsible line official but breaking down unity of command.

9. Misuse of Functional Authority Perhaps even more perilous to good managing than the careless application of the staff device are the dangers in undefined and unrestricted delegation of functional authority. This is true especially because the complexities of modern business often create cases where it is desirable to give a predominantly staff or service department functional authority over activities in other parts of the organization.

In the quest for the economies of specialization and for advantages of technically expert opinion, managers often unduly exalt staff and service departments at the expense of line operating departments. Many line officers—from the vice-president in charge of operations to the foreman—feel, with justice, that the business is being run by the staff and service departments. While the specialist and the specialized department often are essential for business efficiency, sometimes because of external influences bearing on the enterprise, they are meant only to assist and facilitate the central activities of the business; functional authority—creating conflict and confusion, as it may—should be used sparingly and defined carefully.

10. Multiple Subordination The principal danger of too great proliferation of functional authority delegations is the breakdown of unity of command. One has only to look at the various departments of a typical medium-sized or large business to see how such a breakdown occurs. The controller prescribes accounting procedures throughout the company. The purchasing director prescribes how and where all purchases are to be made. The personnel manager dictates (often according to union contracts or government regulations) how employees shall be classified for pay purposes, how vacations shall be scheduled, and how many hours are to be worked. The traffic manager guides the routing of all freight. The general counsel insists that all contracts bear his approval and be made in prescribed form. The public relations director requires that all public utterances of managers and other employees be cleared through him or meet a prescribed policy line. And the tax director reviews all policy decisions for clearance on their tax aspects.

Thus, with all these staff and service specialists having some degree of line authority over other parts of the organization, plus counterparts often in divisions and regions, the key operating manager finds himself subject to the direction of a number of people with functional authority in addition to his principal superior, who usually has the final decision on his pay scale and chances for promotion. One frustrated general foreman of a factory subdepartment informed the authors that he just did the best he could to satisfy everyone and that, when he did not have time and energy to satisfy all, he resorted to the "decibel" principle of management, satisfying those who made the most noise.

Multiple subordination results not only from delegations of functional authority, but also from faulty organization and from instances of plural executives. Wherever found, multiple subordination tends to cause confusion, undermine the definiteness and effectiveness of authority, and threaten organizational stability.

11. Misuse of Service Departments   As was pointed out in Chapter 16, service departments group specialized activities into one department for purposes of efficiency or control, or both, when these activities might otherwise logically be assigned to the departments needing the services. (They are not, therefore, in themselves, staff in the sense of an advisory relationship.) These departments are often looked upon as not much concerned with the accomplishment of major enterprise objectives, when they are in fact just as immediately concerned as any operating department. This confusion also sometimes results in people, particularly in so-called line departments, regarding a service department as relatively unnecessary, unimportant, and therefore something to be ignored when possible.

On the other hand, many service departments mistakenly look upon their function as an end unto itself rather than a service to other departments. Thus, a purchasing department may not realize that its purpose is to purchase efficiently items ordered by authorized departments; or a statistics department may forget that it exists to furnish data desired by others rather than to produce reports of its own choosing.

Perhaps the greatest misuse of service departments is summed up in the words "efficient inefficiency." When managers establish service departments, looking more to their cost savings rather than to the efficiency of the entire enterprise, a highly "efficient" service may do an inefficient job of serving. For example, little is gained in putting out low-cost reports not useful to managers, nor is it sensible to set up a low-cost central recruiting section if the employees recruited do not meet enterprise needs.

12. Overorganization   When an enterprise overorganizes, tasks can be spelled out in so much detail that no room is left for discretion in carrying out a job in the incumbent's *own* way and under circumstances not anticipated when his position was established. Or organization can be overdone by creating too many levels, centralizing staff and service activities better left in operating departments, creating unnecessary line assistant positions, and otherwise unduly complicating the structure.

Of course, overorganization usually results from failure to put into practice the concept that the activity-authority structure of the enterprise is merely a framework for efficient performance of people. Unduly complicating the structure through too many levels ignores the fact that efficiency demands that a manager supervise as many subordinates as he well can. Narrow spans may reflect misunderstanding of the span of management principle, managerial inability to minimize the time requirements of his necessary human relationships, or lack of time to manage—a lack often caused by poor assignments and authority delegations. Likewise, the multiplication of staff and service activities or departments may be caused by inadequate delegation to line subordinates and the tendency to regard service specialization and efficiency so narrowly that larger enterprise operations are overlooked.

Managers also overorganize by having unnecessary line assistants (for example, assistant or deputy managers). Having a line assistant is justified when a manager wishes to devote his time to matters outside his department, during his long absences from the office, when he wishes to delegate line authority in a given area such as engineering, or during a limited training period for a subordinate to whom full managerial status is soon to be given. Otherwise, the separation of the manager from his other subordinates and the confusion as to who is really the superior officer in a department lead the observer to conclude that this form of overorganization should rarely be undertaken.

Sometimes, excessive procedures are confused with overorganization. Overorganization—particularly if interlaced with functional authority—can lead to excessive procedures. But much of the "red tape" often blamed on overorganization really results from poor planning. The failure to regard procedures as plans—and to treat them with the respect given other areas of planning—often results in bewilderingly complex procedures.

Similarly, too many committees, sapping the time and energies of managers and their staffs, are often blamed on overorganization rather than on *poor* organization (particularly when committees make decisions better made by individuals). Excessive committees often result from splintered authority or vague delegation that forces pooled decisions. Such excess of committees may actually point to underorganization.

AVOIDING MISTAKES BY PLANNING

As with the other functions of management, establishment of objectives and orderly planning are necessary for good organization. As Urwick has said, "Lack of design [in organization] is illogical, cruel, wasteful, and inefficient."[1] It is illogical because good design, or planning, must come first, whether one speaks of engineering or social practice. It is cruel because "the main sufferers from a lack of design in organization are those individuals who work in an undertaking."[2] It is wasteful because "unless jobs are clearly put together along lines of functional specialization it is impossible to train new men to succeed to positions as the incumbents are promoted, resign or retire."[3] And it is inefficient because, unless based on principles, management becomes based on personalities, with the resultant rise of company

[1] L. Urwick, *The Elements of Administration* (New York: Harper & Row, Publishers, Incorporated, 1944), p. 38.
[2] *Ibid.* In this connection Urwick quotes the following lines from Browning:
"It's an awkward thing to play with souls
And matter enough to save one's own."
[3] *Ibid.*

politics, for "a machine will not run smoothly when fundamental engineering principles have been ignored in construction."[4]

Need for Objectives Organization cannot be designed without enterprise objectives. Over-all goals will determine basic organization structure, while departmental goals will decide the character of such units as production, sales, finance, personnel, or public relations. For example, one large manufacturer, in planning a reorganization, discovered that it was necessary to go back to the basic goals of the company in order to find where to begin.

The relationship between objectives and "organizational consequences" is interestingly shown in the following approach of A. C. Gilbert Company.[5]

Over-all Objectives
1. Preservation of the American Way of Life (opposing monopoly in any form, whether in industry or labor unions)
2. Being a good citizen in communities of operation, assuming a share of community responsibilities
3. Research, development of know-how and an ever-advancing technology
4. Making the company a better place to work; getting enjoyment out of work; good wages; fair play; recognizing the dignity of the individual; maintaining a progressive personnel program
Organizational Consequences
1. A limit to the expansion of the organization; absence of tie-in agreements and other organizational devices which might aid monopoly
2. Establishment of a "Department of Relationships"
3. Establishment of a separate research department
4. Establishment of a personnel department

Financial Objectives
        The company should make enough profit to
1. Continually improve plant facilities and working conditions so that production may become more efficient and work more pleasant
2. Provide a reasonable return to common stockholders
3. Aim toward maintaining the soundest financial structure possible, with particular emphasis on maintaining a good liquid position
4. Consider banks as friends and as absentee members of the company; their interests to be recognized in the financial policies
Organizational Methods of Accomplishing These Objectives Include
1. Capital budget procedures and follow-ups
2. A centralized department for the establishment of accounting, cost and budget controls with additional decentralized advisory departments and control agencies
3. A centralized fund and bank loan procedure

[4] *Ibid.*
[5] As reported in E. Dale, *Planning and Developing the Company Organization Structure*, Special Report No. 20 (New York: American Management Association, 1952), pp. 24–25.

Sales Objectives
1. Highest quality products
2. Sales exclusively through company organization
3. Maintenance and improvement of the firm's market position (percentage share of sales in major product markets)
Organizational Consequences
These objectives led to the organizational establishment of
1. A quality control department
2. An extensive sales organization with branches in different parts of the country
3. Centralized market research, marketing budgets, and closely centralized control of results

Public Relations Objectives
Managerial co-workers shall do their share of worthwhile civic activities and strive to further the good name of the company in all walks of life. In the conduct of their personal lives they shall do nothing to bring censure or discredit to the company.
Organizational Impact
This led to the establishment of a separate public relations function.

Production Objectives
1. Emphasis on diversification: through diversity in products, seasonal peaks and valleys can be minimized and unfavorable changes in public acceptance of any one product hedged against.
2. In order to provide full employment, existing plant facilities shall be utilized fully and sub-contracting done systematically only when found advisable for reasons of capacity, economy, or lack of specialized machinery and know-how.
Organizational Consequences
1. Division of production work into different product departments
2. Establishment of production and engineering control departments
3. Co-ordination of production and sales through a committee of the executives concerned

Planning for the Ideal Much organizational planning centers on people instead of focusing, as is proper and logical, on enterprise objectives, finding the best possible structure to accomplish them, and then making necessary modifications for the human factor. Obviously, an organization built around specific people, with their shortcomings, can hardly reflect logical grouping of activities and allocations of authority. Moreover, such organization perpetuates problems raised by individual personalities, even after the individuals have dissociated themselves from the enterprise.

Essential to organization planning, then, is the search for an ideal form of organization to reflect enterprise goals. This entails charting the main lines of organization, considering the organizational philosophy of the enterprise managers (for example, shall authority be as centralized as possible, or should the company break its operations down into semiautonomous product or territorial divisions?), and sketching out consequent authority relationships. The ultimate form established, like all plans, seldom remains unchanged, and continuous remolding of the ideal plan will normally be necessary. Nevertheless, an ideal organization plan constitutes a standard, and, by comparing present structure with it, enterprise leaders know what changes should be made when possible.

In planning ideal organization structure, planners should keep abreast of the best thought and practice on the subject, objectively test the soundness and adequacy of every phase of their plan, and design specifications for each level of management and each key job. Besides, there is need continually to reexamine the philosophical basis for organization. Otherwise, there is danger of decentralization of authority becoming such a fetish as to cause top managers to overlook the importance of centralizing certain policies and controls; or there may be the danger of taking for granted the necessity for a limited span of management, while inefficiencies generated by too many levels are overlooked.

The organizer must ever be careful not to be blinded by popular notions in organizing, because what may work in one company may not work in another. Principles of organizing have general application, but the factual background of each company's operations and needs must be considered in applying these principles. Organization needs to be tailor-made.

Modification for the Human Factor   Despite objective application of principles and the formulation of ultimate organizational plans without regard to specific persons, these plans must ever take into account the human factor. If available personnel do not fit into the ideal structure and cannot or should not be sidetracked, there is no alternative but to modify the structure to fit individual capabilities, attitudes, or limitations. Although this smacks of organizing around people, the difference is that it is organizing *first* around the goals to be met and only *then* making modifications for the human factor. In this way, planning will be available to eliminate further compromises with principle whenever changes in personnel occur.

Advantages of Planning   The basic advantage of organization planning, like that of all aspects of planning, is improvement of management through orderly coordination of human endeavor in the face of change. Good organization can go far to make up for deficiencies in leadership by furnishing a support for available abilities. Such a support increases managerial efficiency by cutting down on meetings to determine who has the authority to do what, or how this program or that policy is to be implemented, and relieves the manager of constantly correcting subordinates on the nature of their functions, responsibilities, or authority.

Planning the organization structure also helps determine future personnel needs and attendant training programs. Without knowing what managerial personnel will be needed and what experience to demand, an enterprise cannot intelligently recruit and train men.

Furthermore, organization planning can disclose organization weaknesses. Duplication of effort, unclear lines of authority, too long lines of communication, too much red tape, and obsolete practices show up best when desirable and actual organization structures are compared.

AVOIDING ORGANIZATIONAL INFLEXIBILITY

One basic advantage of organization planning is avoidance of organizational inflexibility. Many enterprises, especially those which have been in operation for many years, become too rigid to meet the first test of effective organization structure—adaptation to changing environment.

Signs of Inflexibility Some of the older companies provide ample evidence of these inflexibilities: an organization pattern no longer suited to the times; a district or regional organization that could be either abolished or enlarged because of improved communications; or a too highly centralized structure for an enlarged enterprise requiring decentralization. Some of the railroads remained organized in territorial divisions originally determined by the daily mileage of a steam locomotive long after the diesel locomotive had made such divisions obsolete. Some of the defense plants of World War II still held fast to the complicated structures of their war-swollen industrial empires although their postwar operations were reduced by as much as 90 per cent. The Ford Motor Company lost much of its efficiency and market before new management, under the founder's grandson, dispersed the centralized authority demanded by the late Henry Ford, Sr. Countless examples of organizational inflexibility could be cited, but they all express the inability or reluctance of managers to change an organization structure to reflect change in their internal or external environment.

Reasons for Reorganization Although ordinarily the main reason for reorganization is to meet changes in the enterprise environment, there may be other compelling reasons. Those related to the business environment include changes in operations caused by acquisition or sale of major properties, changes in product line or marketing methods, business cycles, competitive influences, new producing techniques, labor-union policy, government regulatory and fiscal policy, or the state of current knowledge about organizing. New techniques and principles may become applicable, such as that of developing managers by allowing them to manage decentralized semiautonomous units of a company; or new methods may come into use, such as that of gaining adequate financial control with a high degree of decentralization.

Moreover, a new chief executive officer and new vice-presidents and department heads are likely to have some definite organizational ideas of their own. Shifts may come merely from the desire of new managers to make changes from ideas formulated through their previous experience, or because their methods of managing and their personalities require a modified organization structure.

Furthermore, reorganization may also be caused by demonstrated deficiencies in an existing structure. Some of these arise from organizational weaknesses themselves: excessive spans of management, too many levels, inadequate communication, poor interdepartmental coordination, excess committees, lack of uniform policy, slow decision making, or failure to accomplish objectives, as well as through inability to meet delivery schedules, excessive costs, or breakdown of financial control. Other deficiencies may stem from inadequacies of managers. Lack of knowledge or skill by a manager, who for some reason cannot be replaced, may be avoided by organizing so as to move much of the authority for decision making to another place. Personality clashes between managers also may be solved by reorganization. Staff-line conflicts may develop to such an extent that they can be resolved only by reorganization.

Need for Readjustment and Change   In addition to impelling reasons for reorganization, there is a certain need for moderate and continuing readjustment merely to keep the structure from developing inertia. "Empire building" is not so attractive when everyone knows that his position is subject to change. As a company president told his subordinates: "Don't bother to build any empires, because I can assure you that you won't be in the same position three years from now." Some enterprise managers, realizing that an organization must be a living institution, make structural changes merely to accustom subordinates to change.

Much can be said for developing a tradition of change. People used to change tend to accept it without the frustration and demoralization that result when need for reorganization is allowed to reach the stage at which change must be revolutionary. On the other hand, too much organizational change strikes at the motivational core of much human conduct—status and security. A company continually undertaking major reorganization may so damage morale as to harm the enterprise by losing key personnel. Also, organizational turmoil causes inefficiency as people in all ranks spend much of their time wondering what will happen to them.

Somewhere between these extremes is the desirable degree of change in which morale and efficiency are not harmed but helped. This will depend upon the quality of leadership, the effectiveness of communication (people fear change unless they understand it and its probable positive effect upon them), and the soundness of the revision. Managers tend to underestimate the ability of subordinates to accept a reorganization that makes sense in the light of business facts and enterprise objectives. When morale is damaged by reorganization, the fault may be ascribed to lack of understanding of the need, an ill-conceived organization plan, or poorly qualified executives.

AVOIDING CONFLICT BY CLARIFICATION

A major reason why conflict develops in organizations is that people do not understand their assignment and that of their co-workers. No matter how well conceived an organization structure, people must understand it to make it work. Understanding is aided materially by proper use of organization charts, accurate job descriptions, the spelling out of authority and informational relationships, and the introduction of specific goals to breathe life into positions.

Organization Charts   The organization chart is widely used and appropriate for making organization principles work. Every organization can be charted, even a poor one, for a chart merely indicates how departments are tied together along the principal lines of authority. It is, therefore, somewhat surprising occasionally to find top managers taking pride in not having an organization chart or feeling that the charts should be kept secret.

Advantages   A prominent manufacturer once informed the authors that, although he could see some use for an organization chart for his factory, he had refused to chart the organization above the level of factory superintendent. His argument was that charts tended to make people overly conscious of being superiors or inferiors, tended to destroy team feeling, and gave persons occupying a box on the chart too great a feeling of "ownership." Another top executive informed the authors that, if an organization is left uncharted, it can be changed more easily, and it also encourages a competitive drive for higher executive positions on the part of the uncharted middle-management group.

These reasons for not charting organization structures are clearly untenable. Subordinate-superior relationships exist not because of charting but rather because of essential authority relationships. As for any too-comfortable feeling engendered and a lack of drive for those who have "arrived," these are matters of top leadership—of reorganizing whenever the enterprise environment demands, of developing a tradition of change, and of making subordinate managers continue to meet adequate and well-understood standards of performance. The manager who believes that team spirit can be engendered without clearly spelling out relationships is deluding himself and preparing the way for politics, intrigue, frustration, buck passing, lack of coordination, duplicated effort, vague policy, uncertain decision making, and other evidences of organizational inefficiency.

Since a chart maps lines of decision-making authority, sometimes merely charting an organization shows inconsistencies and complexities and leads to their correction. A chart also reveals to managers and new personnel how they tie into the entire structure.

Charts, therefore, not only help avoid conflict by clarification but are also useful in decision making and in teaching how a company is organized. It has been generally found that those firms which have comprehensive organization charts appear to have sound organization structures.

Limitations   Although organization charts are useful and often revealing, they are subject to important limitations. In the first place, a chart shows only formal authority relationships and omits the many significant informal and informational relationships. Nor does it picture how much authority exists at any point in the structure. While it would be interesting to chart an organization with lines of different widths to denote varying degrees of formal authority, authority is not subject to such measurement. And if the multiple lines of informal relationships and of information were drawn, it would so complicate a chart that it would lose its value. At the same time, something of this nature can be achieved by accompanying organization charts with clear descriptions of the authority and duties of each management job.

Furthermore, many charts show structures as they are supposed or used to be, rather than as they really are. Managers hesitate or neglect to redraft charts, forgetting that organization is dynamic and that a chart should not be allowed to become obsolete. If charts do not reflect the actual structure and if the pattern is intended to be as charted, it is the job of effective management to see that the actual organization conforms with that desired. Charts cannot substitute for good organizing nor take the place of spelling out authority relationships, outlining assignments, or defining responsibilities.

Another limitation of organization charts is that they may, in the absence of good leadership and a tradition of change, foster inflexibility, although there is no reason why they *should* do this. If organization is changed to meet new needs and if charts soon reflect these changes, flexibility can be maintained. Moreover, the very existence of charts gives managers something graphic to consider in connection with continuous organization review.

Still another difficulty with organization charts is that individuals may confuse authority relationships with status. The staff officer reporting to the corporation president may be depicted at the top of the organization chart, while a regional line officer may be shown one or two levels lower. Although good charting attempts to make levels on the chart conform to levels of enterprise importance, it cannot always do so. This problem can be handled by clearly spelling out authority relationships. As is well known, even though field commanders in the military are shown on organization charts below staff officers, they do not object to this placement so long as their rank is equal or higher and their duties reflect their position. And no one is likely to hear that the general manager of Chevrolet in General Motors feels a sense of inferiority because his position on the chart is below that of the patent section director.

Position Descriptions Every managerial position should be defined specifically, although perhaps not in the detail customary for job descriptions for assemblers and mechanics. A good managerial position description informs the incumbent and others about what he is supposed to do and helps determine what authority must be delegated in order to carry out the job. Without such a description, it is difficult to know what to hold a manager responsible for.

A soundly conceived position description is not a detailed list of the duties a manager undertakes and certainly does not specify *how* to undertake them. Rather, it states the basic function of the position, its major duties, its scope of authority, and, often, the major authority and information relationships to be observed. For example, the basic function of one vice-president in charge of marketing was described as being responsible to the president for effectively and efficiently planning, organizing, staffing, directing, and controlling company activities in market research, consumer public relations, advertising and promotion, and sales. He was given authority, among other things, to hire, dismiss, or change the rates of pay (in accordance with the established salary program and the chart of executive approval authorization) of his subordinates. One of his major relationships was to keep the general manager of the international division informed of domestic marketing plans.

Besides, managerial position descriptions should formalize each managerial position in such a way as to reflect analysis of what must be done to attain company objectives. And the descriptions should not be strait jackets but should be broad enough to permit changing plans and situations.

Such descriptions have many benefits. As jobs are analyzed, attendant duties and responsibilities are brought into focus and areas of overlapping or neglected duties come to light. The authors have found these results of forcing people in an organization to consider what should be done and who should do it to be more than worth the effort. Further benefits of job descriptions include their guidance in training new managers, in drawing up candidate requirements, and in setting up salary levels. Finally, as a means of control over organization, the position guide furnishes a standard against which to judge whether a position is necessary and, if so, its organization level and exact spot in the structure.

Need to Define Relationships   As mentioned above, some statement of authority and information relationships is often included in position descriptions. People often do not cooperate because they do not know with whom their cooperation is required. People often do not communicate—not because they have nothing to say or don't know how to say it—but because they do not know to whom their message should be directed for the purpose of helping the enterprise program move ahead.

By showing up vague authority, inappropriate or misunderstood communication lines, and inefficiencies of organization levels or management spans, spelling out a position and its relationships is a major step toward removing conflict. And, as with organization charts, the very spelling out furnishes a standard against which effectiveness of organization can be measured.

Perhaps the most powerful tool for defining and clarifying relationships is the chart of executive approval authorizations, discussed above in Chapter 17. By spelling out clearly what organizational positions have the responsibility of approving actions involving commitments and where final approvals lie, as well as what managers are to exercise functional authority, the whole system of authority relationships may be made clear. This clarity extends not only to the manager who is given approval authority but, if proper publicity is given to the chart, can be made available to other persons who are involved. As was pointed out earlier, also, the use of such a chart has advantages of ease in changing delegations and avoids the necessity of going into authority delegations in detail in position descriptions. Moreover, there is no reason why the chart cannot be expanded to include decision authority in policy matters and also important places where informational relationships or consultations are believed to be necessary.

Goal Definition Managerial position descriptions need to be bolstered by specific goals. Thus, a manager's major duty may be to develop plans for field sales, but this duty has no concrete meaning without goals in terms of the kind of plans and of a time element.

In other words, a position description indicates the area of a manager's work, but goals—and accompanying plans—indicate what is expected of him in this area. The position description is not in itself enough to describe completely what is expected of a manager. While goals and some elements of plans could be incorporated in the description, and sometimes are, it is usually better practice to separate them, since immediate goals and plans may change from month to month or quarter to quarter.

ASSURING UNDERSTANDING OF ORGANIZING

To be made to work, organization structures must be well understood by its members. This requires teaching. Also, it must be remembered, formal organization, as conceived in this book, does not cover all organizational relationships but is supplemented by informal organization, which plays a part in making formal organization work. Since this is so, members of an organization must understand the general working of informal as well as formal organization.

Teaching the Nature of Organizing Many soundly conceived organization plans fail because organization members do not understand them. To be sure, a well-written organization manual—containing a statement of organization philosophy, programs, charts, and an outline of position descriptions—goes far toward making organizing understandable. Certainly, if an organization structure is put into written word and charts, it has a better chance of being clear than if it is not. However, because even the best written word and charts do not always clearly convey to every reader the same meaning, the effective manager cannot stop with written clarification. He must teach those in his operation the meaning of the organization structure, their position in it, and the relationships involved.

This may be done by individual coaching, through staff or special meetings, or by simply watching how the structure works. If subordinates pass decisions up the line when they should be making them, the manager can take this opportunity to clarify authority. Likewise, if communication between members of a group seems to be inadequate, the manager can look for causes either in a poorly conceived organization or a poorly understood organization structure. Too many group meetings or too much committee work is a signal for the manager to do some investigating. Thus, the manager is obligated continually to teach the fundamentals of organization, for if he does not, his enterprise or department is likely to fail.

Recognizing the Importance of Informal Organization Another way of making the formal organization work effectively is to recognize and take full advantage of informal organization. Since formal organization is a social tool for the conscious coordination of activities toward a goal, informal organization, as Barnard has pointed out,[6] necessarily precedes it. Before coordination and structure can be given to group behavior, there must be communication, association, and a concrete goal. People seek associations and the satisfactions that arise from them. This gregarious impulse and association to accomplish goals that an individual alone cannot gain form the basis for formal organization. When the group is coordinated, with a conscious joint purpose and a structure to gain this purpose, it becomes a formal organization.

Formal organizations, according to Barnard, create additional informal organizations. Interrelationships of authority that cannot be charted, unwritten rules of organization conduct, the necessity for "learning the ropes," and other typical phenomena lead to informal organization.

The grapevine One of the most interesting and significant informal relationships, almost always supplementing formal organization, is referred to as the "grapevine." This relationship is generally quite structureless but comes to life when members of the formal organization who know each other well enough pass on information in some way connected with the enterprise. In the typical enterprise—the members of which spend many hours a day deriving both material security and status from it—the desire for information concerning the company and its people is strong enough so that such information is rapidly transmitted between persons who know and trust each other.

The grapevine, of course, thrives on information not openly available to the entire group, whether because it is regarded as confidential, because formal lines of communication are inadequate to disperse it, or because it is of the kind (for example, scandal) that would never be formally disclosed. Even a management that conscientiously informs employees through company bulletins or newspapers never so completely or expeditiously discloses all information of interest as to make the grapevine purposeless.

Some executives worry unduly about the grapevine. The authors recall one company president who did his utmost to destroy it and fretted con-

---

[6] *The Functions of the Executive* (Cambridge, Mass.: Harvard University Press, 1938), chap. 9. Also see discussion of informal organization above, p. 235.

stantly over his inability to do so. Despite his best efforts to get pertinent information completely, clearly, and quickly to his employees and thereby make the grapevine unnecessary, the grapevine continued to thrive. He should not have expected it to do otherwise.

Since all informal organization serves essential human communication, the grapevine is inevitable and valuable. Indeed, the intelligent top manager would probably be wise to feed it with accurate information, since it is very effective for quick communication. There is much to be said for the manager gaining a place—personally or through a trusted staff member or secretary—on the company grapevine.

Benefits The grapevine emphasizes the use of informal organization to make formal organization work. As Barnard has emphasized, informal organization brings cohesiveness to formal organization. Finally, it brings to the members of a formal organization a feeling of belonging, of status, of self-respect, and of gregarious satisfaction. Barnard observes in this connection that informal organizations are rather an important "means of maintaining the personality of the individual against certain effects of formal organizations which tend to disintegrate personality."[7] Many managers, understanding this fact, consciously use informal organizations as channels of communications and molders of employee morale.

SUMMARY OF MAJOR PRINCIPLES OF SOUND ORGANIZING

Although no one would claim that the science of organizing has developed to the point where principles are infallible laws, it is surprising how much unanimity there is among management scholars and practitioners as to the existence of a number of principles of organizing. These principles are truths of general application, although the generality of their application is not so precise as to give them the exactness of the laws of pure science. They are more in the nature of criteria for good organizing. They are, as Urwick has pointed out,[8] "a beginning, if only a beginning, of a comprehensive philosophy of the task of administration, whether in business or elsewhere."

In its survey of organization, published in 1952, the American Management Association found nine criteria used most frequently in the organizational process.[9] To a very great extent the criteria are the principles enunciated by various outstanding scholars of management, especially Barnard,

---

[7] *Ibid.*, p. 122.

[8] L. Urwick, *The Need Is Urgent to Make Leadership a Reality* (Toronto: Manufacturing and Industrial Engineering, 1952), p. 34. This monograph is a series of six lectures given by Urwick at the University of Toronto in 1951.

[9] The results of this survey were published by Ernest Dale in *Planning and Developing the Company Organization Structure*, Research Report No. 20 (New York: American Management Association, 1952). The criteria of sound organization are found on pp. 138–144.

Fayol, Taylor, Dennison, and Urwick. It is interesting that the principles developed by these scholars should be those most generally applied by well-managed American business firms. These criteria, as modified and supplemented, have become the basis for the organization principles discussed in the previous chapters.[10]

In order to summarize the major principles of organizing and to see them in a logical framework, the authors propose an outline in which the principles may be grouped under the following aspects of organizing: the purpose of organizing, its cause, the structure of organization, and the process of organizing. Or, to state these aspects as principles, it might be said that the attainment of an objective is the purpose of organizing, span of management the cause, authority the cement, departmentized activities the framework, and effectiveness the measure in supporting performance.

The Purpose of Organizing   The purpose of organizing might be summarized by the following principles:

Principle of unity of objective   An organization structure is effective if it as a whole, and every part of it, make possible accomplishment of individuals in contributing toward the attainment of enterprise objectives.

Principle of efficiency   An organization is efficient if it is structured to make possible accomplishment of enterprise objectives by people (that is, effective) with the minimum unsought consequences or costs.

Thus, a structure must be effective, as Barnard has emphasized, in furnishing individuals *as a group* the organizational means for gaining enterprise objectives. And every division, branch, department, or section should be judged in the light of how well it contributes to the attainment of enterprise objectives. But the fact that an organization may be effective in gaining enterprise objectives, with every part contributing to this end, does not imply that it does so efficiently. Certainly the concepts of effectiveness and efficiency must be considered together. Moreover, both principles imply the existence of formulated and understood enterprise objectives.

The Cause of Organizing   One finds the basic cause of organizing, in the sense of groupings of activities and delegation of authority, in the span of management principle. Certainly, if there were no such limitation, one could have an unorganized enterprise with only one manager.

Span of management principle   There is a limit in each managerial position to the number of persons an individual can effectively manage, but

[10] Included in this summary are certain principles of organizing dealt with in Part I. An increasing number of companies are summarizing principles of organizing and incorporating them in their organization manuals. See, for example, *Preparing the Organization Manual,* Studies in Personnel Policy No. 157 (New York: National Industrial Conference Board, Inc., 1957).

the exact number in each case will vary in accordance with the effect of underlying variables and their impact on the time requirements of effective managing.

Much confusion has arisen in the statement and application of this principle because of the tendency to make a specific law of it through attaching some maximum number of subordinates. This is, of course, erroneous. The number of subordinates a manager can effectively manage may be few or many, depending upon his job and basic factors that influence the frequency and severity of the relationships he must supervise. But there can be no doubt that there is a limit to an individual's span of management in any given case. The determination of the exact limit in each instance and the undertaking of methods to extend the limit, in order to reduce levels, must be determined in each instance in the light of the various underlying factors involved.

The Structure of Organization: Authority   As has been pointed out, authority is the cement of organization, the thread that makes it possible, the means by which groupings of activities can be placed under a manager and coordination of organizational units can be promoted. It is the tool by which a manager is able to create an environment for individual performance. Authority furnishes the primary line of communication in an enterprise, since it deals with those communications which are comprised of decisions. One finds, as might be expected, that some of the most useful principles of organization are related to it.

The scalar principle   The more clear the line of authority from the ultimate authority for management in an enterprise to every subordinate position, the more effective will be responsible decision making and organization communication.

Principle of delegation   Since authority is intended to furnish managers with a tool for so managing as to gain contributions to enterprise objectives, authority delegated to an individual manager should be adequate to assure his ability to accomplish results expected of him.

Principle of responsibility   The responsibility of the subordinate to his superior for authority received by delegation is absolute, and no superior can escape responsibility for the organization activities of his subordinate.

Principle of parity of authority and responsibility   The responsibility exacted for actions taken under authority delegated cannot be greater than that implied by the authority delegated, nor should it be less.

Principle of unity of command   The more completely an individual has a reporting relationship to a single superior, the less the problem of conflict in instructions and the greater the feeling of personal responsibility for results.

The authority-level principle Maintenance of authority delegation requires that decisions within the authority competence of an individual manager be made by him and not be referred upward in the organization structure. Don't pass the buck!

The Structure of Organization: Departmentized Activities
The framework of organization, in the sense of activity groupings, is furnished by departmentation. This aspect of organization involves both the departmental framework itself and the problems of assigning activities to these departmental units. Although a number of fundamental truths might be summarized in this area, there are three that appear to be of major importance.

Principle of division of work Given a system of tasks or activities required to attain goals, the better an organization structure reflects a classification of these tasks and assists in their coordination through creating a system of interrelated roles; and the more these roles are designed to fit the capabilities and motivations of people available to fill them, the more effective and efficient an organization structure will be.

The principle of division of work has at times been incorrectly interpreted to mean that activities should be thoroughly specialized. In this instance, it has been confused with the economic principle of occupational specialization. Formal organization, rather than economic specialization, has consequently been blamed by some persons for the existence of highly specialized and limited tasks. It is true that Fayol's discussion of this principle perhaps implies this;[11] but it is likewise true that Fayol wisely recognized that "division of work has its limits which experience and a sense of proportion teach us may not be exceeded."

The principle of division of work should be distinguished from occupational specialization in its detailed and ultimate sense. Division of work does imply that an enterprise will gain from specialization of tasks. But this specialization can be in the broad area of sales or accounting, or it can even be in a project form in which a variety of fairly specialized tasks are aimed at the accomplishment of a special integrated project. The point of the principle is that the activities of an enterprise should be so divided and grouped as to contribute most effectively to objectives. In some cases, this might mean a department with the specialized task of doing nothing more than fuel accounting; or it can mean an engineering project section working to design a complicated piece of electronic gear.

Particularly with respect to the principle of division of work, further principles might be noted as means for explaining the effectiveness and efficiency of the activity groupings in meeting objectives. The various guides

[11] *General and Industrial Administration* (New York: Pitman Publishing Corporation, 1949). Fayol says (p. 20), "Division of work permits of reduction in the number of objects to which attention and effort must be directed and has been recognized as the best means of making use of individuals and of groups of people."

and advantages and disadvantages in using functional or product or territorial bases of departmentation are cases in point. Also, attention has been
given in a previous chapter to the guides for associating activities that are
tools for the manager to use when the easier and more general criterion of
similarity is found to be inapplicable or unsuitable.

Principle of functional definition   The more a position or a department
has clear definition of results expected, activities to be undertaken, organization authority delegated, and authority and informational relationships with
other positions, the more adequately individuals responsible can contribute
toward accomplishing enterprise objectives.

Principle of separation   If an activity is designed to be a check on the
activities of another department, the individual charged with such activity
cannot adequately discharge his responsibility if he reports to the department whose activity he is expected to evaluate.

The Process of Organizing   In a real sense, the various principles of authority delegation and of departmentation are fundamental truths dealing
with the process of organizing. But they deal with phases of the two primary aspects of organizing—authority and activity groupings. There are
other principles that appear to deal with the process of organizing as a
whole. It is through their application that one gains a sense of proportion or
a measure of the total organizing process.

Principle of balance   The application of principles or techniques must
be balanced in the light of the over-all effectiveness of the structure in
meeting enterprise objectives.

The principle of balance is common to all areas of science and to all
functions of the manager. Perhaps, however, its application is more dramatic
in the case of organizing than with the other functions. To expect all principles to pull in exactly the same direction in every environmental situation
is to overlook the facts of life in complex situations. Although a principle is
a fundamental truth of general applicability and of predictive value in a
given set of circumstances, there are often varying sets of circumstances in a
single complex social (or physical or biological) system. Certainly a physicist
would not argue that the principle of gravitation is void merely because it
might be offset by principles of centrifugal force. Yet there are those who
argue that a principle of management may be invalid because another principle, or a group of forces, tends to offset it.

In every structure there is need for balance. For example, there
must be balance in centralizing and decentralizing authority. Many matters
require adequate authority at the level of the foreman or the district manager. Other matters, such as control over capital expenditures and the
over-all level of operating expenses, may properly be centralized in the
upper levels of management. Moreover, the inefficiencies of broad spans of

management must be balanced against the inefficiencies of long lines of communications. The losses of multiple command must be balanced against the gains from expertness and uniformity in applying functional authority to staff and service departments. The savings of occupational specialization in departmentizing in accordance with enterprise function must be balanced against the advantages of better management obtained by establishing profit-responsible, semiautonomous product or territorial departments.

Principle of flexibility　It being the task of managers to provide for attaining objectives in the face of changing environments, the more provisions are made for building in organizational flexibility, the more adequately organization structure can fulfill its purpose.

This principle has to do with building into every structure devices, techniques, and other environmental factors for change. Every enterprise moves toward its goals in a changing environment, both external and internal. The enterprise that develops inflexibilities, whether these are resistance to change, too complicated procedures, or too firm departmental lines, is risking inability to meet the challenges of economic, technical, biological, political, and social change.

Moreover, one of the obligations of the manager, and one of the roles structures are designed to perform, is the perpetuation of the enterprise. Part of this task has to be accomplished through changing objectives and the plans that derive from them. Structures might assist in accomplishing this purpose in many ways. One is to provide flexibility in organizational arrangements; another, to provide a ladder of positions, with increasing scope, so as to make available logical and practicable training steps. Even the best management development program cannot operate well unless opportunity is given for managerial candidates to gain experience in positions of increasing diversity and responsibility.

Principle of leadership facilitation　The more an organization structure and authority delegations within it make it possible for a manager to design and maintain an environment for performance, the more it will facilitate his leadership abilities.

Since managership depends materially upon the quality of leadership of those in managerial positions, it is important for the organization structure to do its part in creating a situation in which the manager can most effectively lead. In this sense, organizing is a technique of promoting leadership. If the authority allocation and the structural arrangements create a situation in which the head of a department tends to be looked upon as the leader and in which his task of leadership is facilitated, structuring has accomplished an essential task. But if the department head is buried in detail or if the actual authority for planning, organizing, directing, staffing, or controlling his department is out of his hands, the organization structure has overshadowed and thwarted its managers.

It is no accident that organizations are usually charted in pyramid form.

The pyramid itself implies a situation in which the head of the pyramid and of each subordinate pyramidal part is the leader of a group. But it is necessary that there be more support for the leadership situation than the ability to chart a pyramid. The authority delegations and relationships must be such that the structure of organization actively supports the leadership position of the manager.

FOR DISCUSSION

1. Many psychologists have pointed to the advantages of "job enlargement," whereby tasks are not so specialized that an individual loses a sense of doing things which are meaningful. Assuming that a manager wishes to limit specialization of tasks and "enlarge" jobs, can he do so and still apply the basic principles of organizing?

2. Taking an organized enterprise with which you have some familiarity, can you find any of the deficiencies commonly found in organization structures?

3. It is sometimes stated that the typical hierarchical organization chart is an undemocratic device that emphasizes the superiority and inferiority of positions. Comment.

4. What, in your judgment, makes an organization structure "good"? How does "good" organization structure support leadership?

5. What would you need to know to plan an organization structure? How far ahead would you plan it? How would you go about making such a plan?

6. A prominent scholar has forecast that a system of well-defined organizational hierarchy will give way to one of democracy in organization. What do you think?

SELECTED REFERENCES

Allen, L. A.: *Management and Organization*, chaps. 13–14, New York: McGraw-Hill Book Company, 1958.

Andrew, G.: "An Analytic System Model for Organization Theory," *Academy of Management Journal*, vol. 8, no. 3, pp. 190–198 (September, 1965).

Bailey, J. K.: "Organization Planning: Whose Responsibility?" *Academy of Management Journal*, vol. 7, no. 2, pp. 95–108 (June, 1964).

Bakke, E. W.: *Bonds of Organization*, chaps. 4, 6, 7, New York: Harper & Row, Publishers, Incorporated, 1950.

Barnard, C. I.: *The Functions of the Executive*, chaps. 5–9, Cambridge, Mass.: Harvard University Press, 1938.

Bennis, W. G.: *Changing Organizations*, New York: McGraw-Hill Book Company, 1966.

Brown, A.: *Organization of Industry*, pp. 1–26, Englewood Cliffs, N.J.: Prentice-Hall, Inc., 1947.

Brown, Wilfred: *Exploration in Management*, New York: John Wiley & Sons, Inc., 1960.

Daniel, D. R.: "Reorganizing for Results," *Harvard Business Review*, vol. 44, no. 6, pp. 96–104 (November–December, 1966).

Fayol, H.: *General and Industrial Management*, chaps. 4–5, New York: Pitman Publishing Corporation, 1949.

Hall, G. L.: *The Management Guide,* rev. ed., San Francisco: Standard Oil Company of California, 1956.

Learned, E. P., and A. T. Sproat: *Organization Theory and Policy,* Homewood, Ill.: Richard D. Irwin, Inc., 1966.

Litterer, J. A.: *The Analysis of Organizations,* New York: John Wiley & Sons, Inc., 1965.

March, J. G., and H. A. Simon: *Organizations,* New York: John Wiley & Sons, Inc., 1958.

Millman, R. W.: "Some Unsettled Questions in Organization Theory," *Academy of Management Journal,* vol. 7, no. 3, pp. 189–195 (September, 1965).

Mooney, J. D.: *Principles of Organization,* rev. ed., chaps. 1–5, New York: Harper & Row, Publishers, Incorporated, 1947.

National Industrial Conference Board, Inc.: *Preparing the Company Organization Manual,* Studies in Personnel Policy No. 157, New York: National Industrial Conference Board, Inc., 1957.

Stogdill, R. M.: "Some Dimensions of Organization Theory," in J. D. Thompson (ed.), *Approaches to Organization Design,* pp. 3–56, Pittsburgh: University of Pittsburgh Press, 1966.

Thompson, J. D.: *Organization in Action,* New York: McGraw-Hill Book Company, 1967.

Urwick, L.: *Notes on the Theory of Organization,* New York: American Management Association, 1952.

————: *The Elements of Administration,* chaps. 1, 4, 5, New York: Harper & Row, Publishers, Incorporated, 1943.

————: *The Need Is Urgent to Make Leadership a Reality,* Toronto: Manufacturing and Industrial Engineering, 1952.

White, K. K.: *Understanding the Company Organization Chart.* AMA Research Study No. 56, New York: American Management Association, 1963.

Whyte, W. H.: *The Organization Man,* New York: Simon and Schuster, Inc., 1956.

Woodward, J.: *Industrial Organization: Theory and Practice,* Fair Lawn, N.J.: Oxford University Press, 1965.

part four

STAFFING

Every enterprise should be vitally concerned about the quality of its managers. These men are its only guarantee that its objectives will be achieved, or at least, that the objectives will be striven for as intelligently and efficiently as possible. The best-staffed organization will see that the other four management functions are carried out effectively.

Part 4 includes a chapter on appraisal and another on the development and training of managers. This is one evidence that modern business does not regard the staffing job of top management as selection alone. Managers must be developed and trained for organization positions; the key to an effective job here is adequate appraisal so that training and development needs can be properly determined.

Material on selection and development and training of nonmanagerial employees is not included. These subjects are adequately dealt with in books on personnel administration.

A chapter-by-chapter orientation to this part of the text seems unnecessary because the subject matter dealt with under each chapter title is fairly well understood. However, if the reader gains only an understanding of good selection, appraisal, development, and training techniques and comes away with no other message, he has missed the most important point. The first chapter of the part stresses this. The managerial job in staffing is often neglected because top management has "more pressing" tasks—usually the immediate direction of day-to-day affairs. Often such a company suddenly finds that *all* its important managers are sixty years of age or over and that a desperate staffing crisis is *now* on hand. At that point, of course, it's almost too late to find a remedy.

the managerial job

The efficient manager is an enterprise possession whose value is incalculable. He can make even poor organization structures operate effectively; his vision of objectives to be attained is often a substitute for more formal planning and control; he unerringly selects and develops competent subordinate managers; he is an inspiration to all employees; he can and does carry the weak and mediocre managers; and in the meantime he takes pains to ease his burdens by improving the quality of professional management within the firm as far as his efforts can reach. This kind of manager makes the difference between a brilliantly successful firm and a desultory enterprise about to expire. Some one or a few managers within a firm are often responsible for successful operations over long periods of time; when these men are gone, these same firms have started down the long road to bankruptcy.

There was a famous university that decided to establish a business school. A dean was selected. He first concentrated upon staffing the positions established in his budget. He did not look for professors with an established reputation; instead, he searched among graduate students who were nearing their doctorate. These were appointed assistant professors in marketing, industrial relations, production, accounting, finance, and transportation. They, in turn, were gradually helped by new appointees as the enrollment required. Within ten years this man had developed the very best business school in the nation. The dean left after about eighteen years of service, and his position was filled by a succession of deans who vainly sought to stop the declining reputation of the school, a phenomenon brought on by poor appointments to the staff.

A corporation was established in Los Angeles to produce and sell to the Navy a weapons device of great importance. The inventor, who was president, found himself in high favor with the customer, and large orders flowed in. To handle this business, functional managers threw together in helter-skelter fashion space, materials, and people. Finance was a neglected function; budgets were approved as requested; cost control did not exist; contract deadlines were not met. Though the cash flow was large, profits were very elusive.

After three years of operation the corporation was ripe for acquisition. A new president was appointed with the order to make a profit. His first concern was to establish financial control; his next was to evaluate and remove at once those managers who were unable to operate under the new regime. They were replaced by men selected by the new president. It took two years to make the turnaround. Profits are being earned on an expanding sales program and morale is high. Quality staffing saved this firm.

Students of business history can supply many more examples of this phenomenon. It is abundantly clear that the quality of the manager makes most of the difference between success and failure. Consequently, it is of critical importance to every enterprise to achieve success in staffing management positions.

Before selecting a person for a position, as much as possible must be known about its nature. Just what are managers asked to do? Some time ago Barnard described the nature of the job in these words:[1]

> . . . for executives, . . . the world of the future is one of complex technologies and intricate techniques that cannot be adequately comprehended for practical working purposes except by formal and conscious intellectual processes. To understand the formal aspects of a complex organization; to analyze formal relationships between organizations; to deal appropriately with combinations of technological, economic, financial, social, and legal elements; and to explain them to others so manifestly call for ability in making accurate distinctions, in classification, in logical reasoning and analysis, that the point requires no argument.

Management is a most difficult activity, and men in these positions must be effective decision makers. They are often called upon to decide issues on short notice, and management issues tend normally to be very complex in terms of all the factors which affect them. The manager must recognize these elements, weigh them correctly, formulate sets of simultaneous equations, and often solve them while the person who requests the decision awaits the answer. And the answer had better be correct, because on it may hang profit or loss, an industrial strike or peace, a facilitated or blighted career of a subordinate, a bold or timid response to challenge, a helping or a dead hand in making free enterprise work, an assist in achieving cultural values or a disregard of them which could help to destroy civilization. All these factors are grist in management decision making. Correct choices are of crucial importance to the enterprise and conceivably to our way of life.

The managerial job is complex, even in small firms. No way has ever been found to place an enterprise in a laboratory. The engineer, the physi-

---

[1] Chester I. Barnard, *Organization and Management* (Cambridge, Mass.: Harvard University Press, 1949), p. 197.

cist, and the chemist are aided in their quest to discover the nature of a force or an element by the facility with which they can control the test environment. The scientist is able to exclude the influence of factors not currently being studied, either by creating a situation in which they cannot intrude or by permitting them to exert an unvarying influence. The manager cannot do this. His decisions must not only take into consideration such forces as the stage and trend of the business cycle, the political, economic, and social policies of government in its national and international phases, trends in the markets, and his immediate and future competitive situation, but he must also evaluate all these forces simultaneously. For him there is no easy assumption as to "other things being equal" or "other factors remaining constant."

The quality of executives needed is affected by the social responsibility of the enterprise. It is a premise of great importance that no firm will exist in the long run unless it contributes positively to the general welfare, for, after all, it is the preponderant majority of the people of a democratic society who determine what activities shall be cultivated and what activities shall be stamped out. Private enterprise contributes its share to the general welfare by providing goods and services to improve the standard of living, by adopting approved employee-relation practices, and by facilitating the purposes of the community. It is essential that the business manager understand these responsibilities and their harmony with profit seeking, so that he can develop and carry out policies that will fulfill both.

WHAT IS A MANAGER?

When it is necessary to ask, "What is a manager?" we surely have reached the extremes of the dilemma of language that has frustrated management scholars for so long. The manager is so clearly the focus of the events of organized activity that one would expect him to be known. But common terms have numerous meanings: the struggle of management to become a science is blunted in the first instance with its terminology and the things that writers do with it.

Some Individual Views In reading Herbert Sonthoff's article[2] one is reminded of a childhood fable:

> There were six men of Hindustan
> With learning much inclined
> Who went to see an elephant
> Though all of them were blind

Each learned with a high degree of accuracy about that part of the elephant's anatomy that he touched, but the descriptions of the animal by these six men were irreconcilable. The writers in the field of management seem to

[2] "What Is the Manager?" *Guideposts to Executive Growth* (Cambridge, Mass.: Harvard University Press, 1956–1965), pp. 50–56.

have equally conflicting views of the manager. No wonder it is difficult to see the whole man!

There are those who assume that managers must have certain qualities or traits if they are to be successful. No scientific basis is laid for this deduction. One merely looks around and decides that a rather long list of (frequently) overlapping characteristics is just what the successful manager must have. He achieves this state of excellence through knowing what qualities he should have and acquiring them through practice. Few would deny that most enterprises would benefit from being managed by such godlike creatures, but many would question the correlation between each of the qualities and enterprise success. The ability to pour oil on troubled waters would have a low correlation quotient if the manager did not permit the waters which oil can soothe to become troubled. Even more serious is the problem of acquiring these qualities. Managers are exhorted to practice them. This is good advice insofar as behavior can be learned. Whether it is really worthwhile in terms of enterprise success, and whether we have efficient means of changing behavior, are quite other questions.

Those who are concerned with the operation of research enterprises look upon the manager in quite a different light. Knowing that scientists want to report to technically competent men, many individuals specify that the research manager must be respected for his scientific capability as demonstrated by his engaging part-time in personal research and spending the rest of his time in crystallizing the creative ideas of his subordinates, in advising with them about approaches to their problems, and in smoothing away the administrative clutter that scientists are presumed to dislike so much. This view of the laboratory manager is certainly quite common among scientists; it is extraordinarily narrow from the viewpoint of the superior managers or contractors who must pay the bills. Both the scientists and those who employ them are results-oriented. The latter are in addition time- and cost-oriented. The manager who is solely a technical catalyst is no manager at all.

In his *The Managerial Mind*, David W. Ewing[3] draws a fundamental distinction between the front-line and middle-level managers, who are primarily concerned with the execution of the managerial functions, and the top manager, who cultivates—like a gardener—his enterprise that it may live and grow. The latter will use the productive factors with a skill that rests upon a deep knowledge of technical factors and of human nature, and he will observe the external scene with a view to taking both defensive and offensive action. This is a useful view of the manager because it draws the distinction between the man who looks upon the execution of the manager's functions as an end and the man who looks upon those functions as the means to achieve a healthy and growing enterprise. The implication that there is a necessary distinction between managerial levels with respect to this view of the top manager is, however, highly questionable.

[3] (New York: The Free Press of Glencoe, 1964).

After examining *Role Development and Interpersonal Competence*,[4] Sonthoff deduces that its authors look upon the manager as a friend. They stress the importance of the individual's total role performance, indicating that the manager must necessarily be aware of behavioral patterns within the context of individual development and the conditions in which significant change and learning can take place. Indeed, not only must he be aware: he must do something about it. This would require the manager to become counselor, teacher, and therapist. The underlying presumption seems to be that the growth in interpersonal competence somehow is "good" for the enterprise as well as for the individual. It is certain that if this is the total concern of the manager, he does not understand *his* role.

When Abram T. Collier[5] looks at the manager, he sees a man who is concerned about the enterprise in its total complexity. He has established for the manager's guidance five sets of values. The "A" values are comprised of self-teaching, the virtues of hard work, self-realization, personal responsibility, and the search for justice and honor. The "B" values include organizational skills, sales techniques, administrative genius, communication power, and the integration of mental and physical health. Among the "C" values are professional training, desire for facts, legal realism, and historical objectivity. The "D" values relate to people-centered teaching, customer-oriented selling, service, participative management, and self-transcendence. Finally, the "E" values are ultimate values: the capacity to adapt to change, ability to integrate viewpoints, and the power to go beyond the above four value structures. In essence, Collier thinks that a man must be able to look at the results of his work and call them "good." The enterprise is thus not looked upon merely as a profit-making[6] organization but as part of the existence of the manager.

---

[4] By David Moment and Abraham Zaleznik (Boston: Division of Research, Harvard Business School, 1963).

[5] *Management, Man and Values* (New York: Harper & Row, Publishers, Incorporated, 1962), chap. 11, pp. 226–227.

[6] The voices of those who would attack the profit system grow louder. Businessmen do indeed have a complex value system, and this system certainly does include profit making. It should be obvious to everyone in the community that in a free enterprise system profit is essential to keep a business alive. It should also be obvious to academic men who seek contributions from business that the only source is profit; to ministers of the gospel who seek donations from businesses, that these must come from profits; and to students who look to business firms for a job, that none can exist if the firm does not make a profit. Perhaps these critics of the profit system do not see because they will not see. Or perhaps they would feel better living in a society without free enterprise.

In our society the profit maker is typically the small businessman, such as a farmer, a restaurant owner, and so forth. The men who choose to make a living this way do so by means of trying to keep income in excess of expenses. Just why he is to be castigated for choosing to make a living this way rather than by getting a job on a farm, in a factory, in a university, or in the church is difficult to see. In large-scale enterprise, gross profit is distributed to managers and nonmanagers as salary and wages, to stockholders as a return on investment, to landowners as rent, and to the government as taxes. The managers don't make profit for themselves: they work for pay like most everyone else.

The manager has also been looked upon as a technician.[7] He operates an open system, seeking his objectives through an organization which functions in an extraordinarily complex environment. He protects the enterprise through decision making that reflects the changing laws of the land, shifting markets, and many pressures exerted by unions, competitors, politicians, and educators. He also maintains his internal system by evaluating the pressures of technology, financial forces, and the social interrelationships of his employees. He develops an operating system which provides for feedback and review.

Sonthoff's review of the differing views of the manager is interesting and valuable because it highlights the widely varying assumptions that are hidden so deeply when the term "manager" is used. On the other hand, there is no indication whether he considers the cited authors to be representative of important groups. Without the group implication there is no reason to stop at a listing of so few; with the group implication there are perhaps other ways of classifying authors on the basis of what they think a manager is.

Some School Views The student will be more at home if the classification is made on the basis of management "schools." This approach does require generalizations of the viewpoints of authors who prefer to be grouped in specific schools of management, and to this extent perhaps no statement exactly reflects any individual view. But as a summary technique it provides an opportunity to state clearly the different but widely held concepts of the manager as reflected in the management science, behavioral, and operational or process schools.

The management science group includes authors who view managers as decision makers. They utilize mathematics, models, and computers to aid managers to make optimum decisions. Of course, the issues that can be solved best by these means are relatively few, even though considerable effort has been made to apply these techniques to both measurable and heuristic problems.[8] The important aspect of the attitude under consideration here is not, however, the limited uses to which these techniques are helpful; it is that the manager is viewed as a person whose function is to make decisions. No wonder the writers in this group sometimes forecast that computers will eventually replace the manager!

The behavioralists take quite a different point of view. They are primarily concerned with personal and interpersonal behavior of nonmanagers in enterprise, and with the conditions which encourage the expression and growth of their capabilities. They seem to look upon the manager as the one who inhibits this process. He is depicted as having little knowledge of or

---

[7] Leonard R. Sayles, *Managerial Behavior* (New York: McGraw-Hill Book Company, 1964), chap. 14.

[8] See Jerome Wiest, "Heuristic Programs for Decision Making," *Harvard Business Review*, vol. 44, no. 5, pp. 129–143 (September–October, 1966).

interest in the human resources he hires, and therefore treating them as a purchased factor of production. Proper behavior on his part requires those modes that encourage the growth of competence in his subordinates. Coursing through the writing of certain behavioralists seems to be the basic assumption that enterprises should not be managed for any reason but to permit and encourage personal and interpersonal competence to flower. The manager must be a therapist; other aspects of his functions are usually overlooked.

Whereas some management science people do not seem to understand the functions of the managers, and certain behavioralists seem to very well understand but not like what they are, the authors of this book—who are best described as of the operational, or process, school—insist on full understanding of all of his functions as he proceeds to achieve objectives through organized effort. The fundamental assumption of the operational school is that enterprises of all kinds are to be operated efficiently and effectively. The manager is exactly what the term has always implied; he is the one who employs resources in organized activity to secure known objectives. The objectives must be chosen with a view to their contribution to social needs; the decisions made must square with the ethics of society; the welfare of the enterprise must be cultivated; efficiency and effectiveness are achieved through the application of both knowledge and skill to the selection and combination of the best means to maximize the contribution of the factors of production. Thus, the manager is not merely a friend, guardian, technician, catalyst, owner, or actor. He is an intelligent man who utilizes his knowledge to select the best application of economic resources, the most effective means of motivating his subordinates, and the best techniques for problem solving so that his enterprise can make a significant contribution to society.

If he is to manage in an outstanding fashion, such a man certainly needs the broad knowledge of external affairs that Barnard insists upon. He must guide his enterprise in a competitive world so that it will grow and flourish. If he is successful, the undertaking will make an important contribution to national and social purposes. Internally, the manager needs to be skilled in the execution of his functions. It is necessary for him to see to it that scarce resources are effectively applied and, in so doing, he has a need to be aware of technological change, of the appropriate use of the contributions of management science, especially to the functions of planning and control. Above all, he wants productive subordinates, because this is critical to efficiency. In approaching this problem it is absolutely essential that he be familiar with the knowledge of human beings that is developed by behavioralists. This knowledge he will put into practice with a view toward encouraging everyone to operate at the peak of his capability. His means are many: he may delegate authority or withhold it; he may utilize participative techniques; he will certainly want to develop an operational motivational system; and he will be keen to improve his leadership skills.

This manager is a compulsive consumer of knowledge, whether it is derived from mathematicians, philosophers, psychologists, sociologists, economists, or historians.

The Manager and Organization Levels   Up to this point we have been examining the manager in general. It is pertinent to inquire whether the generalized description is applicable to all the managers in an enterprise. This book is concerned with the management of *organized* enterprise, whether this be a government, a university, a hospital, or a business. All of these enterprises are organized in a formal and, therefore, similar way. There are many writers who seem to object to any formal organization because they feel that it requires conformity, the treatment of people as things, the stultification of personal and interpersonal growth. And yet none of these critics has a substitute to offer for the formal organization. The manager of an enterprise resorts to formal organization because, so far, it is the most effective way to integrate the efforts of large numbers of people toward the accomplishment of enterprise objectives. It is certain that when a better means of doing this comes along, the manager will adopt it.

The inevitable result of the formal organization process is to structure activity in such a way as to take advantage of specialized skills. Since the span of management limits the number of persons who can be effectively supervised by a single manager, it is inevitable that there will be levels of managers. The front-line managers, typically called supervisors, stand between the nonmanagers and all superior managers. The top managers include the general officers and those men who report to them. The middle managers—a poor name for some remarkable people—stand between the front-line and top managers. Does the generalized concept of the manager apply equally well to the men at these three levels?

For the front-line manager, there are many elements of the position which are inflexible. He has little leeway in adjusting to external factors; organization structure tends to be fixed; there is little he can do about employment practices. In particular instances, there may be other important constraints. Yet the front-line manager is deeply concerned about efficiency, especially in the use of resources; he has an important planning and control function to carry out; and he is deeply involved in guiding, training, communicating with, motivating, and leading his subordinates. Even at this level, he should not look upon his job description as a kind of black box within which he operates and outside of which he does not dare to tread. He is not merely an executor of policies and procedures, making a series of decisions within well-known premises. He should visualize his function as one in which he not only leads men toward productive effort, but one in which he also is innovative in finding ways in which his group can make an enlarged contribution to the enterprise for which they work.

All other managers manage managers. The number of levels of middle managers obviously depends upon the size of the enterprise in terms of number of employees. Their chief concern is with perfecting their skills in the execution of the managerial functions. Much of their time is spent on planning for the accomplishment of objectives, refining the control process, making certain that organizational problems are solved or minimized, selecting subordinate managers, appraising their work, and leading them effectively. They are also concerned with some external factors, especially with legislation that affects their operations and with changes in competitive conditions. They are accountable for the performance of a larger share of work than are front-line supervisors, and they feel their responsibility intensely. Consequently, they too should not look upon their jobs as routine decision making in frustrating circumstances. Rather, they should be thinking about how they can broaden their contribution to enterprise welfare without impinging on the activities of their peers. To do this, they need to keep current on new knowledge and practices, new technology, and new ways of utilizing resources, and to urge the application of this information, wherever it is deemed useful, upon their superiors.

The generalized manager referred to earlier is obviously identifiable with top managers. Only they think of the enterprise as a whole. They want to be certain that it is efficient and vigorous so that it can contend effectively with the external environment. Innovation and creativity are at a premium, although these must be applied constructively for the benefit of social welfare and within generally accepted ethical restraints. Top managers are no narrow decision makers: they are indeed strategists[9] who guard their enterprise in a complex and changing world.

In order to understand better the manager's job, the student may look upon it as a system. In Fig. 20.1, the nature of this system is depicted. The manager, in this case the controller, has a charter[10] which specifies what his superior expects him to do. In order to accomplish this, it is necessary to identify the end products which, if properly conceived and efficiently produced, will make certain that his charter will be accomplished. Since such a state of affairs is hardly ever experienced, the controller is always in a position of striving for achievement. This he does by identifying short-term goals toward which he strives through the execution of the manager's functions in the utilization of his available resources of men, equipment, and space. Since this is a dynamic world, the controller will find that his charter is always being refined or modified, as are the instruments he produces to achieve it.

Perhaps from the foregoing sections the student will be able to grasp both the critical part played by managers in organized enterprise and will achieve some insight into just what a manager is. One can only conclude that there is no question more important than who will be selected to manage. This brings us face to face with all the problems that focus on making sure that able men manage our enterprises.

---

[9] Cf. William H. Newman, "Shaping the Master Strategy of Your Firm," *California Management Review*, vol. 9, no. 3, pp. 77–88 (Spring, 1967).

[10] For an extended explanation of the manager's charter, see chap. 21.

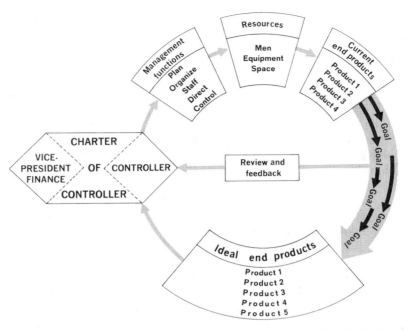

Fig. 20.1 Controllers Management System . . . *Design by J. R. Pelamati, Manager, Logistics Department, Librascope Group, General Precision, Inc.*

Logic of Staffing

IMPORTANCE OF THE STAFFING FUNCTION

Staffing is the executive function which involves the recruitment, selection, compensating, training, promotion, and retirement of subordinate managers. The board of directors undertakes a staffing function by hiring a president; a manufacturing vice-president discharges this function when he employs his immediate subordinate managers; and a superintendent likewise is engaged in staffing when he selects and trains his foremen. Only the front-line supervisors, among all managers, do not select subordinate managers, for, by definition, they compose the first link between enterprise management and the nonmanagers who work for them—the work force. The staffing of nonmanagement positions is a complicated function in its own right, which has been treated extensively in books on personnel administration. The scope of the staffing function treated here is limited to management positions.

Staffing Involves People Every manager performs, to some extent, all the managerial functions, so the question of priority of activities in time and importance can scarcely arise. And yet it may be instructive to consider that while a manager must plan, control, and organize effectively, these functions may be viewed as essentially objective and even mechanistic in the sense that their processes yield rather easily to logic and principle. On the other hand, the functions of staffing and directing are concerned almost completely with people, a fact which introduces enormous complexities that do not yield so well to the efficacy of logic. The uncertainties in the selection and direction of people create baffling problems in general management and as such will probably continue to be not only a source of intense frustration to managers everywhere, but also of prime importance when measured by the cost of failure.

Responsibility for Staffing Since staffing is one of the functions which all managers undertake, the immediate responsibility for its efficient execution rests upon every manager at all levels. For many managers this requirement is not agreeable, for while they would not like to have others select subordinates for them, still they are timid and dilatory in taking action in an area where the responsibility is so heavy. As a consequence, it is much too common for managers to neglect their staffing function.

Such neglect is compensated for in some enterprises by permitting the personnel department to select managers. This solution is attractive to those executives who wish to dump an ill-understood function in the lap of someone else. But neither the personnel department nor any other service group is the proper place for this function. The development of future executives, for one thing, cannot be routinized. There is a need for direction from top policy makers. And decisions about the identity of persons to be developed are so far-reaching and are tinged with so much judgment that few people would trust any one individual to make them.

The responsibility for staffing rests upon the chief executive officer and those of his immediate subordinates who compose the internal policy-making group of executives. They also have the duty of developing policy, assigning its execution to subordinates, and making certain that it is being properly carried out. In policy making they must consider how to develop a staffing program, whether to promote from within or to secure managers from without, where to seek candidates, which selection procedures to follow, whether training should be formalized, and what promotion and retirement procedures to follow. Once staffing policies have been set, putting them into effect may be assigned to any department head. Normally the personnel director is selected, because he has the facilities and procedural knowledge.

Need for follow-up The need for top-level follow-up is as essential for the staffing program as for any other. Numerous types of resistance will be encountered: managers will resent the loss of promising subordinates, routed, for the sake of broadening experience, to other departments; staffing may not seem pressing and be neglected; and there may be certain changes in the routines. The prestige of top officials is therefore necessary in carrying out the program according to plan.

A further and overriding reason for placing the ultimate responsibility on the shoulders of the chief general officer is that the staffing function is carried out with an eye to the future of the enterprise. The board of directors may properly look to the president to assure the future of the business being in the safe hands of able managers. Although directors are responsible to the stockholders for the future as well as the present welfare of the enterprise, they cannot directly undertake the staffing function, beyond the appointment of a president and corporate officers and perhaps the approval of nominations for other top executives.

Relation of organization structure to staffing The number of managers needed in an enterprise depends not only upon its size but also upon the complexity of the organization structure, its plans for expansion, and the rate of turnover in managerial personnel; and the ratio between the number of managers and the number of employees does not obey any law of proportion. It is possible, by enlarging or contracting the delegation of authority, to modify organization structures so that the number of managers in a given enterprise will increase or decrease.

The rate of annual appointments to executive positions can be readily determined by a review of past experience and future expectations. Analysis will also reveal the relative importance of retirement for age and vacancies created by ill health, demotions and separations, the national defense effort, and the steady demand of other enterprises for able young subordinates whom the firm has trained but is unable to hold.

Need for Job Descriptions Although there is a managerial job to be done, there is no standardized managerial position.[11] This fact is traceable to variations in assigned duties and to semantic difficulties. The common usage of such terms as sales manager, personnel director, and president implies that these positions are standardized, yet nothing could be further from the truth. A person entitled "president" may devote his time entirely to engineering; he may grant a title to a subordinate but assign to him few, if any, of the duties implied in the title; or he may create a responsible position without a title.

Position titles may be both misleading and unrevealing. The organization structures of department stores provide several examples of these two difficulties. One store may have a position with the title of sales manager. There is no way of determining from the organization chart just what this title implies, and it is not comparable to the commonly accepted title of merchandise manager, because the product-line merchandise manager reports to the president. Four stores may employ four different titles for the manager in charge of publicity, display, and advertising—publicity manager, advertising manager, manager of sales and publicity, and publicity director.

In order to communicate more specifically about the activities associated with a position title, enterprises have long relied upon job descrip-

---

[11] M. L. Mace, *The Growth and Development of Executives* (Boston: Division of Research, Harvard Business School, 1950), pp. 20ff.

tions. A great deal of frustration has always accompanied this technique because it is clearly impossible to identify all of the activities associated with a position, because it is most difficult to make a written delegation of authority to go with assignment of duties, and because the description is almost always out of date either because of dynamic changes in the environment or because various occupants of the position view it quite differently. As a consequence, there is much to be said for dropping entirely the description technique and merely using the broad statement of the manager's charter as suggested in Chapter 21.

THE SHORTAGE OF MANAGERIAL MANPOWER

Enterprise managers are becoming more and more aware that potential executive personnel are extremely scarce. Evidence of this awareness may be seen in current literature on this subject and in the intensive efforts of firms to discover and develop candidates. The reasons for this situation are both complex and far-reaching.

Modern Industry and Managers   The growth in size of modern business has increased the demand for persons with managerial skill. Whereas small firms often cannot fully enjoy the economic advantages of the division of labor between manager and nonmanager, large enterprises profit from specialization. The roles of foremen, front-line supervisors, office managers, and the numerous department heads, as well as the general officers, are filled with people who engage primarily in carrying out managerial functions. Consequently, a clear-cut demand for managers is felt in all large-scale enterprises.

Yet the risks involved in decision making have underscored the scarcity of good managers. Since the decisions made by numerous firms have a profound impact on the owners, the employees, the community, and the government, able managers are required to make certain that the impact will contribute to the social welfare rather than injure it. The risk to society in employing mediocre executives to wield immense power is insuperable.

Tardy Recognition of the Problem   Tardy recognition of the problems of staffing is evidenced by the tentative steps that business managers have taken to develop suitable candidates, although uncertainty has characterized the formal programs. Part of this uncertainty can be explained by the relatively recent growth of large enterprises. There have been, of course, a few huge enterprises with long histories—armies and navies, the Catholic Church, and governments, for example—but little recognition of the common application of the managerial functions to these enterprises and to business.[12]

Another reason for delaying attention to staffing has been slowness to

---

[12] A major contribution to the understanding of the commonality of the executive functions in diverse types of enterprises was made by J. D. Mooney and A. C. Reiley in *Onward, Industry* (New York: Harper & Row, Publishers, Incorporated, 1939).

understand what a manager does. So long as it was believed that a manager just "managed" and that whatever this entailed was indistinguishable from the exercise of technical skills, there was very little chance that the importance of the staffing function would be realized. Before any of the functions of executives could be studied with profit, it has been necessary to identify them, define them, and understand their relationship to enterprise objectives.

A third reason for the tardy recognition of the managerial staffing problem is the late discovery that the qualifications for executives are, in part, psychological in nature and that success in staffing depends, therefore, upon the development of ways of measuring such factors as intelligence, personality, leadership potential, and judgment. Psychologists have thus far been unable to help much, and there is, consequently, an understandable hesitancy on the part of business managers to proceed with assurance in the selection of potential candidates.

Lack of Managerial Teaching   The lack of managerial teaching in educational institutions was deplored by Henri Fayol as early as 1916,[13] but little or no attention was paid to his views at that time. Indeed, despite the development of business schools, there have been few academicians interested in the subject until recent years. Such inattention may be largely responsible for the highly developed educational activities of the American Management Association, an organization whose membership is predominantly drawn from business executives.

The inadequacy of university teaching in the area of management theory stems from two factors. One is that skilled teachers in this area need to be mature persons with a combination of academic training and business or other management experience. To some extent, businessmen are trying to remedy this fault through internships for university professors, lasting from a week or two to three months. Such firms as Boeing, Swift, and du Pont have been pioneers in this movement.

A second reason for the lack of managerial teaching concerns the nature of the subject: clearly, the universities cannot teach management in the same sense that they teach chemical research, accounting, and engineering calculations. The manager must work through *people*, and the ability of the potential manager to do this cannot be discerned without on-the-job experience. However, there is one thing that can be done by the universities. This is to transmit to the student an understanding of the managerial functions and the principles underlying them and to provide him with a background of knowledge and skill in the application of scientific methodology. From this point on, it is largely the responsibility of the employer to give managerial candidates an opportunity to learn through experience.

Uncertainties of Businessmen   Further causes for the shortage of executive manpower may be found in the uncertainties that plague businessmen.

---

[13] Henri Fayol, *General and Industrial Management* (New York: Pitman Publishing Corporation, 1949), p. v.

Many executives hesitate to do anything about the development of managers because they are not sure just what they want them to do. Many are uncertain, too, about their future needs for managers. Here the question is really one of how farsighted an executive should be. Those who are concerned mainly with the immediate and short-term problems of an enterprise are often inclined to delay attention to the flow of future managers. And for firms which find the expense of training able managers high, delays are understandably not uncommon.

Executives have been slow to realize their personal responsibility for the development of future managers. There are too few firms that assign to their officers the specific duty of training subordinate managers. This duty is, of course, clearly implied. But it is easily neglected by men who consider themselves too busy to execute it, who shy away from the expense of development—especially when candidates are free to leave the enterprise after their training—and who themselves were brought up by older men who trusted to chance and experience and believed in an innate ability to hire good outside executives when needed (and when there was no shortage).

Finally, businessmen contribute to the shortage of future managers through their uncertainty about the proper training methods to use. Many executives who recognize the need for managers and conscientiously accept their responsibility for developing them are stymied, because principles of training are yet unsettled. Universities, business consultants, business associations, and individual business firms are experimenting in this area. Until conclusions are reached, the cautious businessman will move slowly in adopting a formal program of managerial training.

QUALIFICATIONS OF MANAGERS

Since success in staffing rests firmly upon a clear understanding of what the enterprise expects of each manager, this target must be kept in view when planning to select and train able future executives. As was pointed out in Chapter 3, the essential nature of the managerial job does not vary with the type of enterprise or with the organizational level, yet no two jobs are alike. Consequently, if one looks for a neat set of qualities which successful managers must have, he will look in vain. After many years of effort to prove that certain specific qualities should be possessed by managers, the task has been virtually abandoned. Problems of identification and semantics were insurmountable; more important, the variations of the "mix" comprised of knowledge, experience, and personality of successful managers defied pinpointing. Different mixes produce equally successful managers.

However, there is one quality common to successful managers—that of leadership. A manager may plan what others are to do, group subordinates effectively, staff managerial positions, supervise and guide subordinates, and measure results to determine how his plans are working out. But unless his subordinates work as a team, efficiently and with zeal, to perform their essential separate activities, he will have mediocre success in achieving his purpose. He must motivate his subordinates to enjoy their willing cooperation; he must, in other words, show them that through cooperation they will best be able to achieve their personal objectives. Thus leadership molds individuals into a team and creates the environment for the flowering of initiative, innovation, discovery, and new techniques.

Despite the lack of a generally accepted list of qualities which potential managers should possess and despite the scarcity of appropriate manpower, the executive must, nonetheless, select and appraise candidates. Chapter 21 is devoted to developing a procedure which, it is hoped, will result in the identification of candidates with real management potential.

SOURCES OF MANAGERIAL PERSONNEL

Although there is a shortage of managerial manpower, those who feel the shortage most may have failed to develop all the available sources. This is not merely a question of overlooking certain sources; it can also result from not knowing how to use them.

Promotion from Within   The phrase "promotion from within" has had such wide currency for about half a century that its meaning has long since lost precision. It has even acquired an emotional content that contributes to its indiscriminate use. In its original and literal meaning, promotion from within implied that advancement into managerial positions proceeded from rankers, or workers, into front-line supervisory positions and thence upward through the organizational hierarchy. Thus, the firm was pictured as receiving a flow of nonmanagerial employees from among whom future managers emerged.   ↑MORALE

So long as the matter is considered theoretically, there is little question but that employees overwhelmingly favor a policy of promotion from within. The proscription of outsiders places severe limits on the competition for positions and gives employees of the firm an established monopoly on managerial openings. Employees come to doubt the wisdom of the policy only when they are confronted with a specific case of selection of one of their own number for promotion. This feeling is present at all levels of the organization. Indeed, the difficulty of selecting a general officer from among the sales, production, finance, or engineering managers, or a dean from among a group of professors, grows so large that managers are inclined to choose the easier way and select an outsider.

The attitude of managers toward a policy of promotion from within is conditioned by similar conflicts of interest. To placate the employees, the firm is likely to publicize bravely its adherence to this policy. William B. Given, when president of the American Brake Shoe Company,[14] wrote, "It is our policy to give our own people the benefit of advancement as openings occur. We believe that unless we have no one who can possibly qualify it is not fair to our people to hire an outsider." Even more emphatic is the

[14] "Experience in the Development of Executive Leadership," in Marvin Bower (ed.), *Development of Executive Leadership* (Cambridge, Mass.: Harvard University Press, 1951), p. 79.

position taken by Sears, Roebuck and Company. In a booklet given to prospective employees is the statement, "At Sears the policy of 'promotion from within' is not just a phrase or a slogan. It is a fact, insured by specific administrative measures to make sure that it happens." Similarly, General Petroleum Corporation stated that its policy was to fill all jobs, whenever possible, from within; and Procter & Gamble asserts that its policy of promotion from within is strictly adhered to.

Such statements by managements on the internal source of managerial candidates probably represent the general and official attitude of corporate executives. There can be little question that they place heavy emphasis on the policy for the purpose of encouraging prospective nonmanagerial candidates to accept employment, with the view of long-run commitment and of bolstering employee morale. It is unknown whether these same firms give similar assurance to their middle and top functional executives. The saving phrase "whenever possible" is quite sufficient to provide an escape.

Making promotions from the personnel within the firm not only has positive values relating to morale and the reputation of the firm, but it also permits the firm to take advantage of the presence of potentially fine managers among its personnel. Even though these positive but unmeasurable values are important, their pursuit should not blind executives to the dangers of either overemphasizing this source or relying upon it exclusively.

The assumption underlying the policy of promoting from within is either that new employees are hired with a view to their managerial potential or that from among the new and old employees there will emerge a sufficient number of qualified candidates for promotion. The latter assumption is unsafe for modern business enterprise. It is increasingly dangerous as a population becomes differentiated in the degree to which its members seek education, since well-educated persons are more likely than the less well-educated to be the successful candiates for managerial positions.

The assumption that all employees are hired with a view to their managerial potential is contrary to fact. Indeed, most employees are hired for their acquired skills as machinists, electricians, PBX operators, typists, accountants, engineers, or statisticians. Those who are wanted because of their skills are not refused because they may have low managerial potential.

An exclusive policy of promoting from within leads to inbreeding, which is the selection of persons for promotion who have prepared by imitating their superiors. Inbreeding is not a fault if only the best methods, routines, and viewpoints are cultivated. But such a circumstance is likely to be an unapproachable ideal. Enterprises depend upon new blood to introduce new ideas and practices, the very elements that competition forces the firm to cultivate. Consequently, there is every reason to avoid a policy that contributes to inbreeding.

Reliance upon a policy of promotion from within enhances the monopolistic position of current employees with respect to managerial openings and denies to the enterprise the benefits of open competition. Since there is neither a legal nor a moral obligation to promote employees, it is incumbent upon those who manage a firm to decide whether the benefits of such a policy outweigh its shortcomings. There are forthright reasons for implementing the principle of open competition. It gives the firm, in the final analysis, the opportunity to secure the services of the best-qualified candidates. It counters the shortcoming of inbreeding, permits a firm to adopt the best techniques in the recruiting of managers, and eliminates the complacent heir apparent. To exchange these advantages for a part-time morale factor would appear to be questionable. It should be noted that the dangers of inbreeding and the creation of monopolistic advantages for existing employees can be avoided in a large, diversified firm even though it follows a policy of promotion from within. Promotion from within in these companies can provide competition over a fairly broad area of activity if the policy of the firm permits it. Unfortunately, many diversified firms confine selections for promotions to candidates in the requesting department. In so doing, they encounter the same evils of promotion from within as much smaller firms.

Exclusive reliance upon a policy of promotion from within is, therefore, dangerous to the welfare of the firm. As one of several sources of managerial personnel, the current roster of employees is, indeed, important. No executive would consider ignoring this area, for it unquestionably contains many individuals who are promising candidates and who possess the further advantage of being identified with the firm and knowing its personnel, history, problems, and objectives. Other things being equal, employees can and do compete successfully with outsiders. For the superior candidate, competition with all others from whatever source holds no hazards. At the same time, the enterprise confirms its freedom to seek the best managers wherever they may be.

Selection of Key Executives from Outside   The key executive is the one who supplies the force that sparks a program and carries it to completion. These executives may be identified at all organizational levels. They may be the men who make the functional, service, and staff departments operate with vigor and efficiency. But more probably, the key executive will be found at or near the top of the organization structure. He provides the tone, imagination, and judgment with which the enterprise attains its objective. Since subordinate managers tend to reflect the attitudes of their superior, their contribution to a program may often be ascribed to the inspiration of the dominating personality.

The negative reason for recruiting key executives from the outside has already been suggested—the morale problem of dealing with grumpy, frustrated, uncooperative executives who have not been selected for a given promotion. Rather than create such conditions, which are extremely disagreeable, it is not uncommon for an enterprise to recruit a key man from outside, though he may be superior in no way to the internal candidates for the position.

Often there are positive reasons for selecting a key executive from the outside. In such cases, the outside candidate is considered superior to the internal contenders for one or more reasons. For instance, when firms reach a position in their development where the outstanding need is for their energies to be directed vigorously toward the solution of marketing problems, they almost certainly will turn to the outside. Promotion of inside men would be unthinkable, since they have brought the enterprise to its stagnant position. Indeed, this is the situation that faced many firms during the 1920s, when key sales executives were brought in to guide firms through a highly competitive period. For similar reasons, production men were imported during the nineteenth century; and engineers have more recently been brought into conspicuous positions with firms in the aerodynamics, electronics, and plastics industries. Here the factor being sought is vision, new ideas, and new applications.

Trend toward Formalizing Managerial Development The policy of deliberately recruiting managerial candidates for the purpose of developing them into successful executives is of recent origin but has an increasing number of practitioners. In some respects it is a last resort, adopted because other methods of recruitment have developed serious shortcomings. However, this practice still awaits expansion of knowledge about managerial functions and the identification of managerial qualities; when this is forthcoming, recruitment will give better results than those obtained from the trial-and-error methods of earlier decades.

Several factors are at work in bringing businessmen around to managerial development programs. Many firms have been startled by the gap between junior and senior executive age groups. They are inclined to blame this situation upon the lack of hiring that characterized the 1930s. But the difficulty is more fundamental. Even in earlier periods these firms were relying upon the random appearance of employees with managerial potential. They were quite unaware that such reliance was sadly misplaced.

Some have turned to managerial development programs only after belatedly realizing the importance of the managerial functions. Others have waited for the development of successful selection and training techniques before embarking upon such programs. And still others have been prodded by futility in securing managerial personnel. There are, of course, many enterprises that still hire from without because they do not know how to develop managers, consider it too costly, or have found other enterprises that can be relied upon to produce candidates. These firms, knowingly or unknowingly, live a precarious existence. The source of their future managerial candidates may dry up at any time. More likely, the personnel in the management-training groups will become so superior to the imported type that the firms relying upon the latter may be at serious competitive disadvantage. As this lesson is realized, even the parasitical firm will turn to its own development programs.

LONG-TERM OBJECTIVES

Concentration upon the qualifications of managers and the sources of suitable candidate obscures the point that managers do not work for enterprises: they work for *an* enterprise. Hence, the firm is faced with persuading the prospective candidate to select it from among all others competing for his services. This situation is essentially new. Before World War II, few firms sought the individual. It was the seeker of work who bore the entire burden of searching out a prospective and usually unenthusiastic employer. Since then, businesses have scrambled for candidates with managerial potential, persuaded to do so by growing awareness that the manager's functions are different from others, and that there is a shortage of promotable candidates for executive positions.

But what incentives should be offered the candidate? Such a question could not be answered until something was known about motivation. The motive of monetary income in an era of prosperity was not enough. Firms that paid good salaries often failed to attract good candidates. Gradually they learned that statistical averages and general observations obscure the fact that every individual has desires and requirements that do not square with those of the "average" man. Consequently, a successful approach to motivating prospective managerial candidates must be broad enough to encompass dominant human desires and still be personal enough to cover individual needs. Some progress has been made in understanding human incentives: we feel we have a better understanding of the manager.

Managerial candidates differ widely in age, economic position, and maturity. Nevertheless, it may be helpful to consider the potential executive as one who begins his career with no other assets than innate drive and a good education. And he wants many things—opportunity, income, power, prestige, and respect. A lifetime may not be long enough to satisfy in some measure all these desires. Circumstances undoubtedly deprive many potential managers of opportunity; few, indeed, succeed to positions of power. Perhaps in this may be found the reason for the human tendency to imbue with gradations of status every occupation, every department in a firm, every enterprise, and every classification of enterprises.

Opportunity for a Progressive Career   The main concern of a managerial candidate who stands on the threshold of his career is to find an enterprise that will give him maximum opportunity to gain breadth, as well as depth, of business experience. He is aware that he lacks practical experience and that the only way to fill this void is through employment. A job, he knows, is not enough to qualify him for a supervisory position. He requires a variety of work broad enough to make him understand the total operation of the enterprise and the departmental interrelationships as well as internal problems, handicaps, limitations, and merits.

As he scans the business horizon, the candidate will be assessing the opportunities for promotion after such experience has been acquired. Clearly, preparation for advancement is no end in itself. It is at this point that the prospective employer, because of poor communication, is likely to lose patience with a candidate "who wants to be a top manager." The only assurance the firm can give, and the only one sought by the candidate, is in terms of the average number of promotions made by the firm per year and its future plans. The candidate will favor the firm which annually fills many supervisory positions over the firm that has a record of promoting few employees.

Financial Reward   The young candidate thinks in terms of financial security as soon as he feels confident that he can gain experience toward an opportunity to compete for future promotions. It is at this point in his career that his family expenses usually begin to rise, he develops a keen desire to live in the manner of his colleagues, and he achieves a realistic conception of the importance of laying a solid foundation for financial independence. These considerations will be high on the list of incentives for much of his active life.

Power   By the time he may become swayed by the motive of power, the manager will already have proved his ability to settle issues of enterprise policy, demonstrated he can get things done, developed judgment, and gained the confidence of his superiors. At this point a freer rein can be given to exercising the power that enables him to influence people and events in the direction in which he wishes them to go. In business, power is derived from the authority to use both material and human resources. Hence, the manager who has reached this stage has considerable leeway in changing policies, practices, products, objectives, and public relations. There is a strong element of creativeness in such changes. The manager wants to try out new ideas, improve the orientation of the firm in the industry, and be able to point with pride to his handiwork.

Prestige   As the desire for power becomes less important, the desire for prestige becomes greater. The manager comes to value more highly that ascendancy which is derived from the admiration of his fellow human beings, whether they be his superiors, subordinates, or individuals unconnected with the enterprise. Such admiration may spring from the estimation of a man's worth based upon his reputation; it may reflect acceptance by peers; it may arise from the favorable opinion of subordinates; or it may adhere to the executive who occupies or succeeds to a position surrounded by an aura of prestige. Whatever its source, the desire to acquire the satisfaction of being well thought of by other human beings can become intense. The top executive may then feel that he has arrived at the stage when he can afford the motivation of seeking actively the approbation of mankind. Like our Presidents, he begins to think of his place in history. The enterprise in which he has made his career in business may not afford opportunities for such an experience of prestige. Consequently, he may turn to the broad field of public service, employing his talents in diplomacy, government, research, philanthropy, or education.

NEED FOR A PHILOSOPHY OF MANAGERIAL TRAINING AND APPRAISAL

All managers must train and eventually appraise candidates selected for jobs and, later, eligible for promotion. This is one field of action in which too often the manager mounts a horse—the horse of managerial training—and rides off in all directions. During the past decade businesses have spent millions of dollars in a riot of training. They have followed every means from junior boards of directors through various junior executive development plans, functional training courses, American Management Association seminars, university conferences and courses, and in-plant courses to human relations and "sensitivity" programs. The mood of businessmen has been to spend and train in the hope that "something" positive will occur, because of not knowing what should be measured or how it should be accomplished. The time has come to reassess the techniques of training and appraisal for management. Managers need a philosophy which embraces both theoretical and practical knowledge of management; better ways of communication, in general, and of interviewing, in particular; and means of developing all phases of managerial competence and for measuring success in training.

PROBLEMS OF EXECUTIVE COMPENSATION

The problem of retaining managers, once they are selected and trained, bulks large in the considerations of superior managers. It will not be solved by overweening attention to such specific factors as morale, physical environment, hours, opportunity, or power. All of these are subsumed in the executive market. Consequently, compensation becomes a prime factor. It behooves every enterprise to take a mature view of this matter and to develop a compensation system that will ensure the attraction and retention of the quality and number of managers essential for its success. The key questions are: (1) What compensation should be paid? and (2) How should it be paid?

Amount of Compensation   The determination of executive salary depends upon the demand and supply of managers. In preceding sections the supply aspect was considered in some detail. The demand aspect of the equation is very complex. Consideration must be given to the type, size, and location of the enterprise; the esteem in which it is generally held; the urgency of the need; the level and responsibility of the position to be filled; the internal relationships of the enterprise salary structure; and the prospective period of employment.

In order to obtain current information on competitive salary levels, enterprises commonly resort to surveys. For top-management salaries, businessmen look to the Security and Exchange Commission reports and proxy statements, the reports of Arch Patton,[15] occasional studies of the National Industrial Conference Board, and the surveys of the American Management Association. For front-line managers such as supervisors and foremen, salary

[15] Published annually for several years in the *Harvard Business Review*. The most recent appeared in vol. 44, no. 5, pp. 94–97 (September–October, 1966). The danger of "averaging" salaries in such surveys is stressed by Patton in "What Is an Executive Worth?" *Harvard Business Review*, vol. 39, no. 2 (March–April, 1961).

administrators, careful in selecting comparable firms, may successfully conduct private surveys of going salaries. For middle-management positions there are no reliable salary data available, and firms make little effort to survey this area because the elements of these jobs are simply not comparable. As a consequence, a salary structure is developed for these positions by fitting in rational ranges between the known top and bottom levels.

Salary ranges, rather than specific salaries, are now common. Applied to middle- and front-line management positions, they provide the needed flexibility with which salary administrators may take into account such differences between men holding similar positions as age, experience, value to the firm, leeway in negotiation, and in-range rewards for performance. Ranges are rather uncommon for general executives because of the difficulty of determining their value to a firm and because other forms of compensation are usually tied in with salary. In general, the normal practice is to negotiate a salary at the time of employment and to move the figure up in subsequent years, depending upon the performance of the firm and of the individual.

Form of Compensation The selection of forms of compensation for managers is a major enterprise decision, because it must satisfy the interests of both employee and employer. The former needs cash income, protection of earning power, a chance to accumulate an estate, and financial security after retirement. The first two needs are of utmost importance to younger men who are establishing families; with the passage of time, these needs gradually give way to those of estate building and retirement income.

The enterprise makes an effort to supply these different forms of compensation because qualified managers *must* be attracted and retained. But in so doing, the interest of the owners must be safeguarded. Particular attention is paid to the protection of the owners' stock interest, executive incentives, the enterprise cash requirements, and tax laws. Obviously, the form of compensation must not in any way affect adversely the ownership interest of stockholders and must stress the common interest of manager and owner in expanding the earning power of invested capital. Large outflows of cash for executive salaries are not only an expensive form of compensation for the firm, but they have little incentive value beyond limited levels under the current income tax structure.

For these reasons, enterprises have developed very complicated forms of executive compensation, including cash income to meet current needs; fringe benefits, such as group insurance and perquisites, to protect earning power and lessen the need for cash; incentive compensation, such as bonuses and stock options, to tie in the common concern of both stockholders and managers to expand profit; and retirement pay, such as pensions and deferred-income agreements, to support a manager in his postproductive years. Large, publicly owned firms often adopt the full array of these forms, emphasizing one or the other. Individual proprietorships and institutional enterprises are more restricted in their practices. In any case, superior managers must be cognizant of the variety of forms and develop that which best meets its need for able managers.

SOCIAL RESPONSIBILITY OF MANAGERS

The superior manager cannot afford to overlook the effect of managerial actions on society. In a free enterprise or in a mixed economy such as we have in the United States, the freedom of a manager—in government; in educational, religious, medical, and other "social" institutions; and in business—to make decisions affecting people is extraordinarily great. His power is so pervasive that he can and sometimes does take action in ways which adversely affect our social values. Well-known examples come to mind, such as violation of antitrust laws, misleading advertising, dishonesty, and personal prejudice in dealing with people. Few of these acts are challenged, and these lie almost entirely in the area of legal redress. The innumerable inequities in the treatment of employees of a business, a university, or a government bureau result from emotional rather than logical decision making, and they are rarely redressed.

In terms of our total society, important managerial decisions affect relatively small segments. If, for instance, a regulatory agency were to make a decision to remove a subsidy for carrying mail, beyond the few people concerned with the firms in question, who really cares? Even though an agency makes a questionable decision affecting social values, the probability of achieving redress is insignificant because too few people are affected. The administration of a democracy may be unpopular, yet it can make decisions adverse to our liberties. By action or inaction, by control of funds or information, a manager makes decisions affecting social welfare. In what directions can people look for safeguards from arbitrary action? There are at least three: the diffusion of power among managers, the forces of competition, and the determination on the part of managers to make decisions which will contribute to the enhancement of our social values.

So long as we remain free to contest arbitrary decisions, to develop and broadcast information, and, as consumers, to select our schools, hospitals, and the products of business enterprise, we have a positive foundation on which to maintain these safeguards. In so doing we need managers who discharge their social responsibilities by knowing and prizing the values of our society and making decisions which support and enrich these values. To staff with this idea in mind is a top-management function not to be lightly undertaken.

FOR DISCUSSION

1. What differences do you see in the problem of staffing for managers and for nonmanagers?

2. It is sometimes argued that good managers can make even inefficient enterprises effective and, therefore, that staffing is the most important managerial function. What are the issues involved?

3. Most observers of American institutions would agree that good managers seem to be very scarce. What explanation of this situation seems acceptable to you?

4. Although it is usually assumed that managers are mobile, a survey by *Fortune* indicated that top managers typically have worked for only two firms. Does the survey refute the assumption?

SELECTED REFERENCES

Cassell, F. H.: "Management Incentive Compensation," *California Management Review,* vol. 8, no. 4, pp. 11–20 (Summer, 1966).

Collier, A. T.: *Management, Men and Values,* New York: Harper & Row, Publishers, Incorporated, 1962.

Ewing, D. W.: *The Managerial Mind,* New York: The Free Press of Glencoe, 1964.

Knowles, H. P., and B. O. Saxberg: "Human Relations and the Nature of Man," *Harvard Business Review,* vol. 45, no. 2, pp. 22–40, 172–178 (March–April, 1967).

Lawler, E. E., III: "The Mythology of Management Compensation," *California Management Review,* vol. 9, no. 1, pp. 11–20 (Fall, 1966).

Mace, M. L.: *The Growth and Development of Executives,* Boston: Division of Research, Harvard Business School, 1950.

McGuire, J. W.: "Management Concepts: Fads and Fancies," *Dun's Review,* vol. 87, no. 3, pp. 47–48, 80–84 (March, 1966).

Monsen, R. J., B. O. Saxberg, and R. A. Sutermeister, "The Modern Manager: What Makes Him Run?" *Business Horizons,* vol. 9, no. 3, pp. 23–34 (Fall, 1966).

Odiorne, G.: "How Do Managers Make Things Happen?" *Michigan Business Review,* vol. 13, no. 5, pp. 25–29 (November, 1961).

Patton, A.: "Impact of Taxes on Executive Compensation," *Business Horizons,* vol. 9, no. 1, pp. 91–96 (Spring, 1966).

Petit, T. A. "Making Socially Responsible Decisions," *Academy of Management Journal,* vol. 9, no. 4, pp. 308–317 (December, 1966).

Sayles, L.: *Managerial Behavior,* chap. 8, New York: McGraw-Hill Book Company, 1964.

Sonthoff, Herbert: "What Is the Manager?" *Guideposts to Executive Growth,* pp. 50–56 (Cambridge: Harvard University, 1956–65).

Summer, C. E., Jr.: "The Managerial Mind," *Harvard Business Review,* vol. 37, no. 1, pp. 69–78 (January–February, 1959).

Urwick, L. F.: "Organization and Theories about the Nature of Man," *Academy of Management Journal,* vol. 10, no. 1, pp. 9–15 (March, 1967).

Logic of Staffing

selection of managers

If it is not too much to say that the well-being of an enterprise depends largely on the quality of its managers, then it may also be said that no enterprise activity can be more important than that of choosing these managers.[1] Since the maturing of these men is a long process involving training, practice, and the creation of developmental opportunities, it is critical for the future of the enterprise to identify, if possible, these men at all levels in the organization structure. To the problems involved in this task the present chapter is devoted.

Three general difficulties should be kept in mind when judging the qualifications of managerial candidates. First is the variation in management positions from front-line supervision through middle to top posts. Second is the variation in what is known about a candidate's past managerial experience; whereas the candidate for front-line supervision normally will have had no management experience, the candidate for higher-level positions will probably have had such experience, but records of it, even if available, are likely not to be comparable or adequate. Third, variation occurs in the matter of who makes the selection; this can run the gamut from immediate superior to a series of committees at several levels in the management hierarchy.

THE RECRUITMENT PROBLEM

The execution of a policy of developing managerial personnel logically proceeds from an understanding of the sheer magnitude of the job. The firm

---

[1] See P. F. Drucker, *Concept of the Corporation* (New York: The John Day Company, Inc., 1946), p. 31. Or, as L. F. Urwick remarked, ". . . businesses are made or broken in the long run not by markets, or capital, patents or equipment, but by men. . . ." See *Sixteen Questions about the Selection and Training of Managers* (London: Urwick, Orr & Partners Limited, 1958).

must know how many candidates need be considered each year in order to provide the requisite number of selections. There must also be an understanding of the meaning of recruitment. To some firms this term will be confined to the college graduates selected for management development each year. To others, it may be expanded to include those who are selected from among the ranks. Still others will include the selection of experienced men from both within and without the firm to fill middle- and higher-level positions.

Scope of a Recruitment Program   A recruitment program rests upon a definition of the jobs to be included and the source of candidates. On the basis of the argument developed in the preceding chapter, the program should embrace the recruitment of candidates from all available sources.

Definition of the jobs to be covered can be troublesome. Specifically, shall the program include front-line supervisors? There are many reasons— relating to their educational qualifications and the nature of their jobs—for excluding them. The front-line supervisor, whether a foreman, a section chief, or an office manager, requires considerable technical skill in the operation of machinery or equipment, or of the activities supervised, in order to evaluate the quality of work turned out. He also needs this foundation to be able to teach new hands and to direct all subordinates in the work group. To obtain this skill and knowledge, he may be most efficiently trained in a nonmanagerial position and promoted thereafter from the ranks.

At this point the critical question is whether particular persons with managerial potential should be assigned to nonmanagerial jobs for the purpose of acquiring these technical skills and knowledge, or whether enterprise executives should depend upon the random appearance of potential front-line supervisors among their work crews. It is unfortunately true that production and sales executives generally follow the second alternative.[2] In so doing they run into serious educational deficiencies in prospective candidates. The nonmanagerial employee may have finished his high school training and, in some cases, may have completed vocational training in commercial schools, but he is unlikely to have the facility in communication and scientific methodology and the broad educational background essential for successful upper-level managers.

Even though these deficiencies tend to set apart candidates for front-line supervision from candidates for higher-level jobs, there appear to be good reasons for including front-line supervisors in the management selection program. Although they may be operating under an educational handicap at first, this shortcoming can be repaired by those who have the necessary foresight, interest, and drive. Also, because these men are older, on the average, than the college graduate, they are often superior in experience. If the enterprise executives do not wish to deprive themselves of potential

[2] L. F. Urwick, *Management Education in American Business* (New York: American Management Association, 1954), pp. 60–61.

managers drawn from the ranks, the recruitment program must be sufficiently broad to include all positions from front-line supervisor to president.

How Many Selections?   The actual magnitude of the recruitment program is affected by several factors. The first step in arriving at a reasonable figure for the average number of selections to be made each year is to count the number of managerial positions that currently exist. Such a task is easy for any firm that maintains its organization chart in a complete and up-to-date manner.

The next step is to estimate the turnover in managerial personnel. A better estimate can be obtained if the immediately preceding five-year period is considered as a sample, rather than a shorter span. The purpose is to arrive at a stable figure that represents the annual average number of appointments made to management positions. It is most useful to express this average in the form of an index or as a ratio.

At this point a careful inventory of the current position of the firm with respect to its existing managers should be made. This is developed by classifying managers as (1) prospects for promotion, (2) those who should be retained in their jobs but are not promotable, (3) those who should be replaced, and (4) those who are about to retire. This information, supplemented by a time and position schedule for each promotable manager, is useful for determining whether the demand for selectees will be greater than average for the next year. The firm following such inventorying consistently will be able to forecast its needs quite accurately.

Since it is necessary to determine the number of selections to be made for the succeeding year, it is important to allow for any foreseeable changes in the organization structure. This requires an evaluation of plans made by the officers for the expansion or contraction of enterprise activity, and translation of these plans into the number of managerial positions that will exist in the next year. Application of the turnover index to this total will yield the probable number of changes to be made in managerial personnel during the succeeding year.

The final step involves the determination of the number of trainees to be selected. Enterprises vary widely in their practices here. Some follow the conservative 1 to 1 ratio between the number of selections and the number of probable openings. Others adopt ratios of 2, 5, and even 10 to 1.[3] Every firm runs into an attrition rate of large or small proportions. Selectees leave the firm for many different reasons.

There are other factors involved in this problem. Businessmen know that the number of people who can be interested in their firm also depends

---

[3] Urwick urges four, on the basis that by the time they are sixty years old one-quarter will be dead, one-quarter will have fallen by the wayside, and there should be at least two qualified for each position. See *Sixteen Questions about the Selection and Training of Managers*, p. 13.

upon such factors as climate, geographical distances, and personal interests. It is for reasons of this nature that New England firms are reluctant to recruit in California. They can keep down the number of separations by drawing upon potential managers from nearby localities, because the personal ties of these people condition them to local employment.

As a consequence of all these factors, the individual firm can gradually develop a group of specific sources, whether they be universities, other firms, or their own ranks. Many even rely on college faculty people to recruit for them from among promising students in graduating classes. Whatever practices are followed must yield the requisite number of bona fide candidates.

The Recruitment Process   When outside personnel are sought, it may be for several reasons. In most cases, college graduates are recruited for their technical abilities, with little attention given to their managerial potential, although with hope that somehow enough of the recruits will eventually succeed as managers. On the other hand, some firms recruit college men in the hope that their broad educational background will serve them in becoming good managers. In either case, enterprises assign such recruits to nonmanagerial positions from which they may eventually become candidates for front-line supervision.

A second reason for recruiting outsiders is to fill an immediate need for a supervisor or superintendent, a department, division, or functional manager, or, indeed, to fill the presidency of a firm. Such people are normally put through the same recruitment processes described below.

There are three steps in this activity. First, the discovery of potential candidates involves initial screening for intelligence, age, and maturity. Every enterprise has certain minimum requirements in these areas, and it saves money to find out, as early as possible, whether the prospects can meet them. Secondly, persuading potential managers to become candidates sometimes involves selling the firm to them. Thirdly, each candidate receives an extended guided interview.

Screening   Since the need for men with fairly high intelligence is pressing, the candidate is usually given a standard intelligence test by the personnel department. If he is a college graduate, he may perhaps skip this on the assumption that he would qualify. Candidates should be informed by the company representative that acceptance will depend on either superior grades or a proportionally good test score.

Age is of general significance for managerial candidates. Good training programs emphasize the importance of an early start. They contemplate one or two years to be spent on nonmanagerial tasks; another two to five years in front-line supervision; and some fifteen years beyond this point for the development of full managerial potential. Since the "typical" executive of a successful enterprise is selected in his early twenties by the firm in which his career is built, it is advantageous to place an upper age limit for inexperienced managerial candidates at roughly twenty-seven years.

Maturity is an elusive quality that defies quantitative measurement. It is certainly not highly correlated with age or experience. The managerial candidate may reflect his maturity by the scope of his past experience and what he has learned from it, by his present general knowledge and breadth of view, by the common sense of his objectives and the means by which he proposes to achieve them, and by his sense of personal responsibility. The detection of such things is a heavy, but critical, burden to place upon the recruiting officer.

Selling the firm Men found eligible in terms of intelligence, age, and maturity may need to be sold on the firm, and the recruiting officer should pursue this objective with the same vigor and imagination that the salesman employs in selling the firm's products to customers. He is the key salesman; his product is the enterprise, its location, size, prestige, prospects, incentives, and morale. His success depends on persuading qualified but hesitant men to *want* to work for the enterprise. The candidates are then requested to complete an application form, at their leisure, and to appear for an extended interview *on a given date*. (It is as important to set a date immediately for the interview as it is to get a deposit on an order from a buyer.)

Interviewing Candidates who qualify on the basis of the screening process and the information carried on the application form are ready to be interviewed, preferably at the plant site, both intensively and extensively. The candidate is passed along from one manager to another on a pre-arranged schedule, the smooth operation of which reflects good planning and a respect for the value of time to all concerned.

Mistakes in Selection Techniques Ever since one man employed another, candidates have been subject to selection techniques. In the second half of the twentieth century the gradual acceptance of the concept that managers have distinct functions has encouraged both employers and students of management to take a careful look at executives to try to find out why some succeed where others fail, and to apply such knowledge to techniques for selecting good managers.

Three rather common misconceptions about the selection of managers are ordinarily encountered at the level of the "practical" man, who suffers a lack of training in the basic tenets of scientific procedures. Such men may turn away from the problem, rely on random candidates, or overemphasize their own practical experience.

Ignoring the problem More than a few persons behave as if problems solve themselves if they are simply ignored. These individuals either lack foresight or procrastinate. They create a grave risk for the enterprise if, when suddenly struck down by accident or time, they leave it with no capable successors.

There are other managers who are conscious that it is desirable to develop able successors but who deliberately turn their backs on the issue. These individuals have no confidence that either they or anyone else can successfully select able successors, and, consequently, they adopt a fatalistic attitude and do nothing.

Real problems that are ignored simply fail of solution. Nothing will be learned about selection techniques until managers face the problem and analyze it.

Reliance on random development There are executives who recognize the problems involved in selection and, having no confidence in current practices, are content to rely upon the random appearance of acceptable managers. This is a do-nothing policy which involves the misconception that in the ordinary course of enterprise activity, candidates who possess management potential will "obviously" emerge from the ranks in sufficient numbers and at the right time.

There are two reasons which negate this assumption. First, potential managers must enter at the nonmanagerial level if they are to emerge eventually. But do they? Certainly some do, especially those who advance to front-line supervisory positions. However, confidence in this exclusive source of managerial personnel is difficult to maintain in the face of the current insistence upon a high educational level for executives and the common competitive practice of recruiting potential managers both from colleges and from other firms. If well-managed and progressive enterprises do not rely upon the random appearance of potential managers from the labor ranks, there must be a reason why.

Second, even if a firm could rely upon this source, there still remains the question of recognition of these men. What, after all, is "obviously" apparent about them? If they have leadership qualities which set them apart from their co-workers, those qualities must be appraised. Indeed, some executives deliberately wait to see which subordinate will rise to a dominating position over his colleagues before making a selection for promotion. The executive who denies that anything is known about how to evaluate candidates forgets that he is himself evaluating them the moment they become "obvious" to him.

Dependence on practical experience Dependence on their own practical experience is the trap into which fall those executives who "know how" to pick their subordinate managers, although the bases for such subjective selections are conspicuous for their variety. The executive may thus select a subordinate because he wears the same school tie, is a good athlete or an admirable physical specimen, is obsequious and given to flattery, or has red hair.

Despite their self-confidence, these executives are victims of the misconception that competent selection is a simple process. When everything points to the complexity of this process and to the expensive procedures installed by leading firms for carrying it out, it is simply naïve to act as though personal experience and taste are significant in identifying potential managers.

Misuse of Common Practices   Three rather common misuses of selection techniques involve interviewing, group estimates, and testing.

Questionable interview techniques   Interview techniques run the full gamut from ridiculous to productive practices.

The busy executive often does things that, although perhaps not deliberate, are unproductive. He will make an appointment to see a candidate, permit the allotted time to be absorbed by other matters, hurry from his office on his way to another appointment, and, as he does so, shake hands with the candidate while telling him that no opening exists just now. Or he will keep his appointment but permit the interview to be fragmented between numerous phone calls. Whatever else may be said about this executive, he is operating under a misapprehension if he thinks that his interviewing responsibility is being discharged. As for the candidate in such cases, he is well advised to shun an employer who operates in this way. An applicant is as worthy of his interview as an employee is worthy of his hire.

Executives of some large corporations are giving attention to interviews with the wife of the candidate, the idea being to assess whether the applicant is married to a woman who is socially adaptable and who has the potentiality to mature with her husband. The "interview" is commonly made by the executive's wife, a practice that adds hazard to an unscientific procedure.

The guided interview has received considerable attention in recent years. Its protagonists are looking for some method of counteracting the common practice of permitting the conversation to drift into inconsequential fields and to dwell too long on too few items. To combat this, the interviewer is provided with a list of subjects to be covered, including such things as a man's background environment, associations, ambitions, achievements, aptitudes, interests, and attitudes. Sometimes the interviewer will be provided with a rating scale for each subject in order to make certain that the coverage is complete.

To the extent that the guided interview does elicit the desired information, there is no question of its superiority over any haphazard procedure. But there are two issues capable of rendering the interview quite valueless. One relates to the importance of training the interviewer. This skill is not innate. It implies a knowledge of what the questions purport to bring out, the imagination to ask related questions, and the ability to evaluate the answers. A second difficulty is that however well "guided," the interview can be carried out without yielding the needed data.

Superficial group estimates The practice of the group estimate is based on the theory that a common judgment is needed in order to be certain that a man is well suited for the position. Thus, a government bureau or business firm will list several managers who can spare the time to interview a candidate. Each in turn informs the applicant about his area of operation, learns something about the applicant, and reaches some opinion about his acceptability. This opinion is communicated to the individual who arranged the interviews, and he takes action in accordance with the evaluations.

The group estimate will do one thing well. It will reveal a man's social personality. After he has been passed around to three or four managers and taken to lunch, cocktails, or dinner with several of his potential colleagues, there will be a consensus as to whether the man has charm or is a bore. The temptation to decide upon a candidate on this basis is very great. Are the interviewers supposed to do more than evaluate the candidate's personality? If so, the group estimate is open to all the criticisms leveled at other techniques considered in this section. Furthermore, how is the executive who has arranged for the group estimate to evaluate the opinions he receives? Often a negative position taken by one interviewer is permitted to outweigh the positive opinions of all the rest. Sometimes the reports may all be favorable but no manager wants the candidate. Can such a technique be more than superficial?

Overreliance upon tests Perhaps the greatest impetus to psychological testing was received during World War I, when the United States Army administered an intelligence test to its personnel. These tests were originally developed for use in schools. The postwar period saw a great increase both in the types of tests and in the fields of application. Exaggerated claims about the efficacy of testing have grown into a strong chorus as the procedure has become commercialized.

Business executives have responded to these claims in a variety of ways; some exhibit profound bewilderment; many rely implicitly on the tests; others administer them for fear they might otherwise be missing a bet; and still others have nothing to do with them.

Although by now there are several hundred "standard" tests, they may be readily classified in four groups:

1. Intelligence tests, designed to measure mental capacity and test memory, speed of thought, and observation of interrelationships
2. Proficiency and aptitude tests, constructed to discover, respectively, existing skills and the potentiality for acquiring such skills
3. Vocational tests, designed to discover the most suitable occupational area
4. Personality tests, last to be developed, designed to measure potentiality for leadership

On the basis of present knowledge, certain conclusions with respect to the use of psychological tests can be reached.[4] In the first place, the writers on the topic of testing almost universally fail to distinguish between tests for nonmanagerial and managerial positions. Important claims are made for tests for certain types of nonmanagerial jobs. For instance, Schein refers to the success of testing in the selection of Air Force pilots and insurance salesmen. Other applications include aptitude, intelligence, specific skills, comprehension, interests, attitudes, and personality testing.

In the second place, psychologists have yet to develop reliable tests for use in selecting managers. Despite many attempts made, the basic reason for their failure is that the managerial job or, more accurately, the qualities on which managerial success rest, are extremely difficult to isolate. Without knowing for what one is testing, there is no expectation, except perhaps by coincidence, that a successful test can ever be developed. As Schein says, ". . . selecting managers, for example, has been much more difficult because of the problem of describing the managerial job and reliably judging relative performance." He cites other technical difficulties in developing such a test, but these are scarcely important in view of the fundamental problem.

Having outlined a number of mistakes common in dealing with the selection of managers, in the succeeding sections we shall suggest how enterprises may effectively establish a selection program. First the basic difference between selecting a candidate for front-line supervision and for middle- or upper-management positions must be remembered: in the former case, nothing can be known about the candidate's managerial ability, because he has had no management experience; in the latter case, all candidates will normally have had several years of such experience. This fundamental distinction requires a different approach to the selection of the two types.

SELECTION OF FRONT-LINE SUPERVISORS

Every supervisor needs guidance in the difficult and risky task of selecting from among his nonmanagerial subordinates a candidate to fill a vacant or potentially vacant supervisory position. Neither time-honored practices nor psychological tests will help him because they are not discriminative enough in identifying potential management ability. He would be able to make the selection efficiently if he knew (1) what qualities were required; (2) in what degree each was essential; (3) what combinations of qualities were required and in what degree; and (4) how to identify the required qualities in candidates.

The inductive approach to these issues has been barren, and such an approach may be impractical in view of the nature of the managerial job. But a deductive approach has much to commend it. From a thorough

---

[4] Edgar H. Schein, *Organizational Psychology* (Englewood Cliffs, N.J.: Prentice-Hall, Inc., 1965), chap. 3.

knowledge of the executive functions and the environment in which they are discharged, certain qualities important to success should be identifiable. Knowing what a front-line supervisor will be asked to do, his success, it is believed, will depend directly on the degree to which he wants to manage, his intelligence, his analytical and communication abilities, and his integrity. He will also require leadership ability, but this quality can best be assessed as management is practiced. Based upon available records and especially upon observation and personal knowledge of subordinates, the supervisor can evaluate those who aspire to management positions. For purposes of summary, he might consider Figure 21.1 useful.

Factors in Selecting Front-line Supervisors Some of the most important managerial qualities are discussed briefly below.

Desire to manage Perhaps the most pervasive requirement for successful performance of the managerial function is an intense desire to manage. There is a close correlation between good managerial performance and the possession of a driving desire to achieve purposes through the teamed efforts of subordinates. Too many people drift into management because they are attracted by its rewards in terms of salary, status, and perquisites and fail to understand that it has its frustrations and responsibilities. Those who select supervisors must probe beneath the superficial reasons of candidates for promotion and search for individuals who will derive a basic satisfaction from accomplishing objectives through the teamwork of their associates. These men, in all likelihood, will have the drive and determination essential in effective managers.

Intelligence An estimate of the candidate's intelligence level can be a simple matter. If he is a graduate of a university known for its high standards, the transcript of his scholastic record will provide the requisite information. In case of doubt about the reliability of the grade index or if the candidate is in some other category, the supervisor will probably evaluate intelligence on the basis of performance of work assignments.

Analytical ability The supervisor has many opportunities to assess the facility of a candidate in the use of analytic methods. Subordinates are often given special assignments beyond the routine of their jobs, such as reporting on a new proposal, a change in policy or procedure, or a marketing program. If the supervisor learns to assess not only the recommendation in the report but the investigative procedure used in making it, he will have a good measure of the candidate's analytical ability as well as of his ability to proceed logically.

Ability to communicate The supervisor can judge the candidate's ability to transmit ideas from his written reports, letters, oral discussions, and any committee assignments in which he may participate. These ac-

FIG. 21.1   Supervisor Selection Form

This form to be used in weighing the managerial potential of nonmanagerial candidates for supervisory appointments.

Policy

The future of this company is largely dependent upon its ability to attract, select, and develop personnel with superior managerial potential.

This form, when completed, becomes an important instrument in the selection of our future supervisors. It becomes part of the permanent personnel record of those who are accepted.

Detailed instructions

This form is to be completed by the immediate supervisor of each candidate. Read the definition and explanations of each characteristic before selecting the degree to which it is possessed by the candidate.

Attention should be devoted to a single characteristic at a time.

Personal data:

Name:_____

Age:_____

Date:_____

Supervisor:_____

1.   The desire to manage

This quality can be recognized only by knowing a candidate well. Discussions about management, its problems, and the candidate's reasons for desiring a management career are probably essential in coming to a considered opinion.

Candidate:

Wants to manage ☐

Is not sure ☐

Prefers technical work ☐

tivities will reflect his facility in choice of words, organization of thought, phrasing, sentence structure, paragraphing, and over-all clarity and forcefulness of expression.

Integrity   Our social system demands that managers be morally sound and worthy of trust. They exercise considerable authority, they cannot be closely supervised, and they are responsible for numerous actions which could compromise the enterprise. Integrity in managers means many things. It goes beyond a conception of honesty in money and material matters and in the use of time, important as these are. It requires a subordinate manager to keep his superior fully informed, to adhere always to the full truth,

2. Intelligence

This quality may be determined from the transcript of the college record of the candidate and/or from observation of him as he performs his tasks.

Grade point_____ Graduate of_____ Degree_____

	Low			High
Estimate of Intelligence:				
	1	2	3	4

3. Ability to make a logical analysis

Consider the candidate's performance of work assignments and special projects in terms of his logical approach and indicate your judgment of his facility with scientific methodology.

	Low				High
Check one:					
	1	2	3	4	5

4. Ability to communicate

Evaluate the candidate's facility with language. Note particularly grammar and spelling, choice of words, flow of words, clarity of thought and expression, and ability to maintain interest while conveying information.

	Low				High
Check one:					
	1	2	3	4	5

5. Integrity

Consider the candidate's honesty and responsibility in using time, company equipment, in reporting expenses and use of funds, in reporting both positive and negative factors concerning his performance of assignments, and his moral soundness.

	Low				High
Check one:					
	1	2	3	4	5

especially in briefing superiors, and to have the strength of character to live and act in accordance with the moral standards of our society.

While it is not an easy matter to evaluate the integrity of a subordinate, close acquaintance with him in the work environment provides the best opportunity for a correct assessment. His use of time and expense reports, his dealing with co-workers and other business associates, his probity in handling assignments, his sincerity about his work, and his attitude toward life combine to give the observing superior many opportunities to evaluate integrity.

Many managers, in selecting a candidate for front-line supervision, may wish to consider additionally such other factors as cooperation, ability to lead others, imagination, and appearance. There is no particular reason to dissent from such elaboration and no doubt that such qualities are important to a manager.

Who Shall Select?   The immediate supervisor is in the best position to nominate candidates for promotion from among his subordinates. He should know them well in work situations; he has trained and coached them. If he can show that he has evaluated them objectively on the basis of the qualities set forth in the preceding section, his judgment is very important.

From among such candidates the common superior of the supervisors—usually the department head—should make his selection. When he decides who will work for him, he can be held responsible for the performance of his department and will be deprived of the alibi that someone else selected his subordinates.

Limitations of the Selection Process   The program outlined in this section is not without its limitations, which must be understood along with the positive features. Only then may the value of the program be judged.

The recommended program rests upon two premises, considered in the preceding chapter. First, there is no known way positively to identify potential managers in advance. Second, certain qualities, deduced from the nature of managing, will improve the chances of becoming an efficient manager. Whether the man *really* can manage remains unknown until he can be judged on the basis of performance. Mistakes in selection at the front-line level are numerous. For this reason it is only fair that the successful candidate be forewarned of the risk of eventual failure and be told frankly that if he is not successful he will be removed. Superiors have a moral responsibility to make this clear so that candidates may choose their course of action intelligently. The timid may decline promotion while the confident will risk it, and both these reactions will be in the best interest of the enterprise.

SELECTION OF MIDDLE- AND UPPER-LEVEL MANAGERS

The program suggested for selecting middle- and upper-level managers is entirely different from that recommended for front-line supervision. First, the functions of managers are the same at all levels; second, all candidates for promotion at this level have management experience behind them; and third, the most reliable forecast of a manager's future is his past accomplishment *as a manager*. Since selection is made from among candidates *who have achieved*, the process can be largely results-oriented. The critical question becomes, to what degree has the candidate measured up to the requirements of his job? In order to answer this question, it is first necessary to have a clear concept of what that job is.

A Manager's Charter[5]   The purpose of any organized undertaking is to achieve specific objectives in an efficient and effective manner. As an essential requirement, each enterprise selects a manager,[6] who establishes a formal organization at the top level. By this means the manager divides the work to be accomplished in accordance with some principle. He may select a functional basis, as does the President of the United States in his organization of the Cabinet and a business manager in carving out areas of activities such as production, marketing, and finance. He may select a service basis, as does the hospital manager in dividing activities between surgery and internal medicine, or a product basis, as when activities are divided between group executives who are concerned about ground systems and aerospace systems. He may decide upon still other methods of grouping activities. The essential point is that the work of realizing the ultimate objective is divided up (specialized). As is illustrated in Figure 21.2, the manager of each division is assigned a charter or mission to produce certain goods or services, under appropriate conditions of time, cost, and quality, which, with proper integration with the charters of other peer managers, is designed for accomplishment of the enterprise objectives. To do this properly, each manager, depending upon the amount and variety of resources placed at his disposal, will subdivide activities within his command and establish a charter for each subordinate manager. Thus, the manager's charter reflects what he is supposed to accomplish; the simultaneous accomplishment of the charters of peer managers will thereby achieve the charter of their common superior. The essential feature of this concept is that *the manager is responsible for accomplishing his charter* within the broad limitations of the law, acceptable public practice, and ethical principles. This, and this alone, is his job.

To illustrate these relationships, we may turn to a firm in the aerospace industry. Its objective is to maintain a corporate image as a cost-conscious, efficient, advanced-technology enterprise as it strives for profitable growth. Its organization structure breaks into product and functional divisions. Each of these divisions has a charter. For example, one product division conceives, designs, sells, manufactures, installs, and supports its (specified) systems and subsystems. Each department and section within this division also has its charter. One department provides logistic support for division products. In total, the accomplishment of all subordinate organizational charters will add up to the achievement of the product division charter,

---

[5] This section and much of Chapter 22 are based on Cyril O'Donnell, "Managerial Training: A System Approach," *Training and Development Journal,* vol. 22, no. 1 (1968).

[6] There must be a "top" to secure unity of command, despite the rather fuzzy experimentation with divided authority by some corporations. See "Management Problems of Tomorrow," *Dun's Review,* vol. 89, no. 2, pp. 24–26, 78–79 (February, 1967), and Pearson Hunt, "Fallacy of the One Big Brain," *Harvard Business Review,* vol. 44, no. 4, pp. 84–90 (July–August, 1966).

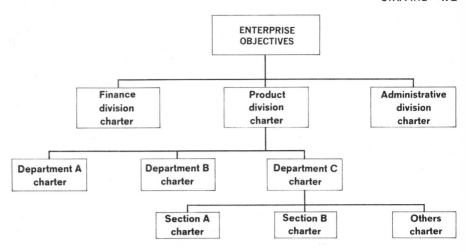

Fig. 21.2 Relation of Managerial Charters to Enterprise Objectives

and this, added to similar accomplishment on the part of peer divisions, will enable the enterprise to accomplish its objectives.[7]

In order to accomplish its charter, each organizational unit will produce certain *end products*. As the term implies, an end product may be hardware, paper (reports), or service produced by the unit in question and turned over to other organizational units or directly to a customer. For instance, a logistics department has an end product comprised of engineering service to be performed according to a contract which spells out skills, man-hours, location, cost, and other constraints. A controller's end products are comprised mainly of specific reports, such as balance sheets, profits and loss statements, financial forecasts and analyses, and reports to government agencies.

It is especially important to distinguish between charter and end products. These are by no means the same. The end products are the means by which the charter is accomplished. This may be readily understood if one considers the ubiquitous controller. It is commonly understood that his charter is to keep safe the assets of the enterprise.[8] One of the means by which he accomplishes his job is to produce a series of reports for the use of others outside his department.

The Selection Process Every manager's job is to accomplish his charter. To do this he identifies and produces certain end products which, in terms of scope, content, cost, quality, and timeliness, conform to his (and his su-

[7] See George S. Sanders, "The Management of Research," *Chemistry and Industry,* pp. 2076–2079 (Dec. 25, 1955).

[8] Technically this is inaccurate, because the controller can only develop reporting procedures which become the basis for decisions by his superior. Thus, the responsibility for safeguarding assets is his superior's and not the controller's.

perior's) concept of appropriateness. Since he lives in a dynamic world, both charter and end products are likely to change with time. So also will standards for measuring the quality of his ultimate accomplishments. At a moment in time, these standards may be contained in a contract which is being fulfilled. Sometimes they are established in the plan of operation (including physical and budgetary plans). Sometimes they are extremely vague, as in the case of the end products of administrative divisions where there are no standard services, or costs thereof, except those that may be agreed upon between the hierarchy of divisional managers.

Since every manager has established a record which reflects his progress in achieving the charter for which he has been accountable, it becomes possible to weigh his potential for promotion.[9] Actual achievements, conceptual skill in visualizing the best means of charter accomplishment, skill in anticipating the need to modify and enlarge his charter in the interests of the enterprise, and the resulting need to improve the end products can be assessed with varying degrees of accuracy. Although we may regret our inability to reach more accurate assessments, at least we take comfort in knowing that we are assessing the correct data.

Implications One of the implications of the foregoing process is that there will be differing views held about a candidate by different evaluators. This is, of course, inevitable in view of the nature of the evidence. The comforting aspect is that the selectee has to work for one man, and it is this man's opinion that is critical to the candidate and to the enterprise. One needs only to look about him to realize that many mistakes are made in interpreting the data used as a basis for selection.

Another factor that is very important is the degree of risk one is running by selecting a man who will "top out." This is a widely apparent phenomenon. There are managers who succeed well, though perhaps not brilliantly, in assignments involving a few subordinates but simply fail when promoted to a level where larger numbers of employees are in the total group supervised. No one currently knows why this happens, but it is certainly one of the important reasons for an unhappy experience.

A somewhat related problem concerns the promotion of an assistant manager. The training that such an employee has received is of critical importance in the assessment of his qualifications for full responsibility. There are some assistants who are inadequately trained by their managers. One, for instance, was used entirely for staff investigations and never did become a line assistant concerned about the direction of employees in accomplishing department objectives. When he was promoted to manager of a peer department, he failed promptly and was dismissed. On the other hand, the managers who use their assistants for departmental operational duties give them appropriate training and experience and, thus, establish a basis for properly assessing their candidacy for promotion.

[9] See Chapter 22 for appraisal data useful for selection purposes.

Another factor in the problem of selection concerns the probability that the selectee will be able to operate effectively at a higher level. For instance, what is the likelihood that a promising department manager will be effective as a division manager? One will, of course, look at his record as a manager. But over and above this record is the question whether the man can be effective not only in managing larger affairs, but also in his relationships with other division and major functional managers. Involved in this situation are all the personality factors which result in peer acceptance, admiration, respect, and deference. Unless the candidate "seems" to have the ability to compete with future peers, he would probably be a poor choice.

Available Candidates Availability is an important practical factor in the selection process. It is often assumed that every qualified candidate is available. This is scarcely ever true. In the first instance, there is the question of the breadth of the search for candidates. Alfred[10] complains that those who have an appointment to make look narrowly within their own organizations for candidates. He seems to feel that this practice gives undue scope to political relationships, whereas the "best man" would more likely be found by an enterprise-wide search. There is no discounting the *theory* of enterprise-wide searches. If everything works out right, the best man within the firm will most often be selected. The practice, however, is quite different. First, there is the wide disparity between the information one has on his own candidate and the information he can secure about stranger candidates. It cannot be presumed that one's own candidate will have the advantage. He certainly will if the politics of the situation are right; he certainly will not otherwise. Men who fail of appointment often say that too much was known about them. This cannot be true, of course, but what is meant is that when *what is known* is not outstandingly favorable, the candidates outside the organization have the advantage. Too little is ever known of the latter, and for this reason they often receive appointments for which they are not qualified.

There is another practical aspect of the enterprise-wide search idea. Managers who have really tried this technique complain about the number of candidates who turn up. Unless the requirements are mainly technical, it is possible that in a large-scale enterprise, such as the Internal Revenue Service or General Electric Company, dozens and perhaps hundreds would become candidates. The appointing manager is overwhelmed by such response and wants to be shielded from it. It seems that not only the time factor but also the sheer number of decisions that must be made lead the manager to conclude that the degree of improvement in the prospect for a good appointment is infinitesimally small when more than a few are considered.

Another aspect of availability is the question whether a likely candidate

[10] Theodore M. Alfred, "Checkers or Choice in Manpower Management," *Harvard Business Review,* vol. 45, no. 1, pp. 157–169 (January–February, 1967).

can really be spared from his present appointment. This difficulty is frequently encountered. It is one thing to say that a manager cannot really become a candidate unless he has a trained successor available; it is quite another to actualize this requirement. A very practical problem faces the appointing manager. He must judge whether a man is available. He usually is if there is no other alternative to follow; he is usually not available if he has no successor and if other candidates stand on the horizon.

Finally, a further word may be said about the political factor in selection. Very many writers in this field seem to be keenly aware of the political basis for appointments from within an enterprise and to oppose them for this reason. Indeed, they are almost pathological in their concern. They are the first to point out that human beings rather rarely make decisions on rational bases and tend to make very many of them on emotional bases. In an enterprise a political appointment is made emotionally; the manager wants to select a person he likes for a number of different reasons. The selection may be made because it is popular, because the person will do the will of the manager, because the candidate has useful connections inside and outside the enterprise, and because he enjoys the company of the candidate. Nothing can or ever will be done about eliminating these factors from the selection decision. It is simply part of our human nature to be concerned about these factors. Certainly it is not a poor basis for selection, provided always that the candidate has been successful in managerial positions. Indeed, it probably portends the very best for the manager's career.

When Is a Manager Promotable?   The process of getting a man ready for promotion is considered in Chapter 23. Just when he is ready is a judgmental issue. One thing that can be said is that the candidate must have demonstrated that he is skilled in carrying out *all* of the managerial functions as he uses resources of men, space, and equipment in achieving his charter. Many times it is apparent that men are promoted who have discharged their accountability in an acceptable way but have "succeeded" because much of their job was carried out by their superior, because they had inherited able subordinates whom they kept hidden from view, because their ineptitude in some of the functions was overshadowed by the strength of subordinate personnel, or owing to the overriding importance of company policies and procedures. These several reasons give rise to the question: Just what results was the candidate alone responsible for? It is a difficult question to answer.

An assistant manager of a well-run division was selected as head of another division. He encountered trouble from the beginning—trouble in becoming familiar with the information required by the executive vice-president, trouble with the subordinates he inherited, and trouble in really understanding that he was in trouble. Within a year he was terminated.

The man who selected him was concerned about how he came to make such a mistake. He analyzed the situation carefully, and concluded that when the selectee was an assistant manager he was not trained to operate the division. His then superior simply used him as a staff man and kept him completely excluded from division operations. The assistant certainly "looked" good to all, but he was merely reflecting the reputation of the well-run division.

A prominent department manager was being considered for promotion to assistant division manager. His was a strong personality; he ran a tight shop; he clearly discharged his responsibility; he was known as a "good" manager. Upon closer inquiry, it became clear that this candidate was "carrying" all his section heads; they were weak yes-men and none was remotely able to succeed the department manager. The candidate was not appointed because it was feared that he would be unable to manage a whole division, as it would be too large for him to run by himself.

All candidates for promotion should be replaceable. It is not that there must be trained and identified subordinates on hand; it is that there should be someone, somewhere in the organization, available to succeed the successful candidate. If the candidate is not replaceable, it may be too risky to appoint him to another post. Enterprises need effective managers in all positions and there are few who would figuratively cross their fingers and appoint an unknown quantity to fill an empty post.

A final consideration is the stature of the candidate. This is a vague concept. It has aspects relating to the appearance of the candidate, the respect he commands, his personality "fit" with potential peers, the aura of success that surrounds him, and the sand in his blood. No amount of technical accomplishment will overshadow these factors. They should be uppermost in the minds of all appointing officers.

John was an assistant department manager. He was originally appointed on the basis of his technical skill. He had been promoted through the ranks in a technical department and knew very well all aspects of the operation.

The division manager was looking over candidates to head a department. John was considered well qualified from the point of view of his knowledge of management principles and practices and of the operations.

"Why don't you select John?" the division manager was asked.

"He just wouldn't fit," the division manager responded. "The man is just impossible. Look at the way he dresses. Think of that silly grin on his face. Have you noticed those crooked spectacles he wears?

"In my division, a man has to look like a manager as well as be one."

Balancing Managerial Skills   There are situations in which managers are concerned about balancing the abilities of a manager and his assistant manager, or the abilities of the president and the executive vice-president. Sometimes the relationship envisaged pairs the technically oriented and the managerially oriented; at other times the pairs are skilled in different functions. For instance, there are many presidents who are adept at planning and public relations. They usually see to it that the next in command is skilled in operations.

"I know it looks peculiar," a well-known director of a public agency re-marked. "I don't like the planning function and I am very poor in public relations. So, I have just reversed the traditional role. I take care of operations and have my line assistant undertake my normal activities."

In Germany, the typical organization structure often establishes the technical man on the same level as the administrative man. They report to a common su-perior. This arrangement is generally used only at the top level.

The issue that managers face in these circumstances is that the job is structured in a manner that makes it too large for one man to handle. One apparent advantage of solving it in this manner is that it takes less time to prepare a manager to handle part of a job than to prepare him to do the whole. However, the disadvantage of trying to find a second-in-command who actually complements his superior is immense. But even more difficult is the role that must be played by the subordinate. He is by no means an independent operator, even though the job description says so. The superior still feels a total responsibility because the one aspect of the job influences the other. Thus, the subordinate will be insecure (unless he indeed domi-nates his boss). He finds himself in the position of making decisions in the light of both aspects of the total job, of knowing his superior so well that he automatically makes the same decision his superior would in the same circumstances, and of keeping his own subordinates from going around him to the over-all superior.

So difficult is it to operate in this fashion that some companies find a different answer. They do not create a job too large for one manager to carry out. It is probable that they encounter heavier overhead costs by choosing this method. On the other hand, there is no question but that operations are streamlined and each manager can effectively be held ac-countable for his total activity.

Balancing the Age Factor   It is not too uncommon to see a company manned by people in the same age group. The vice-presidents may cluster about the age of forty or fifty-five or sixty, depending upon the history of the firm. Similarly, the middle managers approximate the same age. Inattention to this factor can be very embarrassing to any enterprise. When several man-agers on the same level retire within a short period of time, a serious gap in operating effectiveness is likely to occur. Furthermore, if a level of man-agers grows old simultaneously, they put an effectual cap on the promotion process for their subordinates. These difficulties can readily be avoided by paying close attention to the age factor when appointments are originally made.

A summer conference was held for the front-line supervisors of a large gov-ernment agency. Upon the morning of the first assembly, the instructor walked into a room that was crowded with fifty men. Their average age was forty-eight; the range was from forty to fifty-five.

Gray heads nodded rhythmically to the points made by the dedicated instructor, but stopped on dead center when the latter remarked, "Why are *supervisors* so old?"

"What factors do you look for in the selection of a manager?" This question was posed during a conference with the president of a large corporation.

"Well, after one is sure that the candidates have the technical qualifications, I look for four things. They must have demonstrated under fire a capacity for using *common sense*. They must have *integrity*. They must reflect *drive* and *aggressiveness* in developing their careers, and they must not deviate from any of these in their *behavior under pressure*."

Who Selects?   It is an undeviating rule that the manager to whom the successful candidate will report should make the selection. This requirement is paramount because the selector will be held accountable for all events in his department or division. This rule works very well in practice, but it is frequently challenged by those who prefer a "committee" approach. There are several reasons for rejecting the committee technique. It obviously reduces the authority, and therefore the responsibility, of the superior manager. Even if the committee is designated as advisory, it can and does wield considerable power by talking the appointment to death, by overemphasizing the factors that certain members want stressed, and by intimidating the prospective superior.

The committee process is widely prevalent in making university appointments, as it is in some government agencies. It seems to have the widest application in those enterprises where accountability for results is ephemeral. Certainly no competitive enterprise could stand the strain of group deliberations on candidacies for promotion. This is not to say that opinions of others who have had a working relationship with the candidate should not be solicited. Indeed, they should. The major responsibility, however, is the unequivocal right of the candidate's prospective superior.

At the same time there are likely to be cases where approval of a superior's selection may not be desirable. In fact, many companies, particularly for upper-level appointments, follow this practice. They do it for two basic reasons. In the first place, they wish to assure themselves that the superior is selecting an adequately high-caliber subordinate. Second, it is often recognized that from a man's subordinates will likely be selected his replacement or the replacement for others at the level of the superior. While this exercise of the approval function is understandably wise as a matter of assuring that the best quality of manager will be hired, it still is unwise if the actual selection is made by any person other than the immediate superior.

FOR DISCUSSION

1. Do you see any relationship between the selection process and the scarcity of good managers?

2. Although top managers are fond of saying that a liberal arts education is preferable for potential managers, their recruiters look for particular skills. What seems to be wrong?

3. What factors would influence you to prefer a policy of free competition for managerial positions?

4. What are the factors which make it difficult to select effective front-line supervisors?

5. Delay in identifying potential successors to managers often leads to quick and inadequate selection when a position suddenly becomes vacant. Discuss the steps which might be taken to avoid this problem.

SELECTED REFERENCES

Alfred, T. M.: "Checkers or Choice in Manpower Management," *Harvard Business Review*, vol. 45, no. 1, pp. 157–169 (January–February, 1967).

Bower, M.: *The Will to Manage*, chap. 6, New York: McGraw-Hill Book Company, 1966.

Brice, M. H.: "The Sales Manager's Alter-Ego," *Dun's Review*, vol. 88, no. 5, pp. 59; 111–114 (November, 1966).

England, G. W.: "Personal Value Systems of American Managers," *Academy of Management Journal*, vol. 10, no. 1, pp. 53–68 (March, 1967).

Learned, E. P.: "Problems of the New Executive," *Harvard Business Review*, vol. 44, no. 4, pp. 22–28; 166–176 (July–August, 1966).

McKenzie, C.: "Incompetent Foreign Managers?" *Business Horizons*, vol. 9, no. 1, pp. 83–90 (September, 1966).

Schein, E. H.: "Identifying and Developing Managers: World-wide Shortages and Remedies," *The Conference Board Record* (Quarterly International Survey of Business Opinion and Experience), vol. 2, no. 6, pp. 21–48 (June, 1965).

————: *Organizational Psychology*, chap. 3, Englewood Cliffs, N.J.: Prentice-Hall, Inc., 1965.

appraisal of managers

To appraise means to evaluate or estimate. Appraisal has ever been the lot of man and beast, as well as of inanimate things. It is really a condition of life from which there is no escape except through a total withdrawal from society. It is quite probable that men do not want to be appraised unless they know in advance that the estimate will be sufficiently favorable as to improve their prestige. The superiors who eagerly appraise subordinates, whether these be children, students, or the employed, are themselves much less enthusiastic when their own turn comes. It is often said, especially by the subordinates, that they *want* to be appraised so that they may improve their performance. It is feared that observations of this kind apply only to the very few who can and do profit through criticism. The others who so contend don't really mean it. It is a posture that they have learned.

It is, of course, quite clear that evaluation requires a benchmark. There must be some kind of standard against which the appraisal is to be made. This requirement is very troublesome because there are so few reliable bases for measuring anything. In the physical world we do best. In the human world we do very poorly. Those who appraise students presumably have benchmarks. If the appraisal concerns knowledge of physical sciences and mathematics, the standard is objective and clear; but in appraising the students in areas requiring subjective measures we really have few benchmarks. Both the appraiser and the appraisee are largely unknown variables. The lack of objective standards gives the one who appraises full rein to vent the spleen of his biases and prejudices. The sad thing is that he often does so, and that there is no way to judge the job he does. Those who produce objective things in the process of making a living are appraised, and this can be done objectively. Output, for them, is measurable. But for the quality of the teacher, of the supervisor, of the diagnostician, of the preacher—how unreliable have been our benchmarks!

An assistant professor, newly appointed to teach a class in a social science, appeared to be both humble and sincere when he asked the students to give him the benefit of their criticism of the course. Being wise in the ways of professors, most students knew that the grades were not yet determined, and therefore they appraised the instructor publicly as a truly inspired man, etc. Two students took the professor at his word and voiced the view that the course had no purpose, the material was ill-organized, and that students thought the whole thing was a waste of time. This view penetrated the moral armor of the professor; he promptly failed the temerarious two and balanced the record with high grades for the wise.

As applied to managers, appraisal is the process of estimating the potential effectiveness of a man in achieving certain results through the utilization of human and other costly resources. The results in question are really amazing in their variety. Managers are appraised for their image, for the way they deal with people at all levels, for the results produced by the cooperative effort of their subordinates, for promotion, for the contracts they bring in, for their skill in financial negotiation, for the morale of their subordinates—the list is almost unending. If it is possible to bring science to our aid in the appraisal process, it must be through our ability to classify the results wanted and to establish standards for performance.

If managers were left to their own devices, it is altogether probable that no formal system would be used. They feel very comfortable with the technique of continuous, informal appraisals and with the judgment of peers whom they trust. They feel very uncomfortable with formal appraisal systems which personnel departments force upon them, largely because they have no confidence in specific systems. Much can be said for this reluctance when one considers the variety in which proposed techniques have been presented over the last thirty years. These have run the gamut from personality factors to the present interest in management by objectives. Variety and change certainly do not develop confidence; rather, they imply experimentation based upon unstated assumptions.

Another aspect of this reluctance to use a formal system of appraisal is the natural distrust of managers of any system that implies rational bases for evaluation. There is a strong, perhaps intuitive, feeling that rational systems are inadequate. Managers think not only of mere ability to produce results: they are also deeply concerned about the way results are produced, the short- and long-term implications of the methods used, the interpersonal interaction of managers. They are deeply certain that life is really not worth the struggle if effort cannot be coordinated in pleasing ways. It is thus clear that the apparently objective and rational evaluation systems proposed by academicians fail to encompass the full scope of factors which managers deem of utmost importance.

PERIODICITY OF APPRAISALS

A basic distinction needs to be made between continuous and periodic appraisal of managers. The former is a *sine qua non* in management, while the latter is a useful addendum.

In day-by-day practice the superior continuously appraises his subordinates, experienced as well as new. Assignments are checked, reports and letters read and corrected, problems discussed, advice given, scopes of work and authority reassessed, initiative encouraged, objectives reviewed and clarified, and orientation deepened. The close contact implied in these relationships is an educational experience beyond price. It provides the superior with opportunities to watch the progress of his subordinates and shows the latter that they are important to the enterprise and that their development is of concern to higher management.

Cooperative enterprise simply could not prosper if this type of relationship did not exist. If nothing else, it provides management with a strong basis for appraising subordinates. In fact, if one had to choose between continuous and periodic appraisal, the former would be the more essential.

There are, nevertheless, certain dangers in sole reliance upon continuous appraisals. Managers are exceedingly busy and in the pressure of work are likely to give too little attention to needed explanations and coaching. They may fail to look behind the work to the man doing the work. They may neglect important areas of development because these are not immediately significant to the job at hand. Failure inevitably comes to their attention while success may pass unnoted; in thinking about subordinates, they may remember the failures only. Being human, they will seek to spend time with compatible personalities to the neglect of others. In general, the daily appraisal lacks summation and objectivity. To overcome these deficiencies, managers have turned to periodic appraisal.

PERIODIC APPRAISAL

Most enterprises provide for an annual or semiannual formal appraisal of employees. Sometimes no effort is made as far as nonmanagerial people are concerned; the system is not always applied to top managers. It is the supervisors and middle managers who are consistently appraised. As distinguished from informal assessments, the periodic appraisal assumes that an over-all estimate is made of the effectiveness of the manager in producing results. Implied is that elements of strengths and weaknesses will be laid bare; a vision of the total man in his environment is presumed to emerge.

Purposes   Periodic appraisal can assist the superior in judging the degree of trust he can place in his subordinate—trust in his character, trust in his judgment, and trust in his punctual and effective performance.

Periodic appraisal is used to determine how much a subordinate's responsibility should be expanded. His success in carrying out limited assignments hopefully indicates his probable success in more responsible situations. The impression he has made on managers in other divisions may suggest whether he is ready for expanded responsibility. His behavior in unsupervised assignments is an index to his readiness for added responsibility in situations which limit close supervison.

Periodic evaluation can help the future development of the subordinate. With a desire to improve his efficiency, a basic requirement for development, he will be made aware of weaknesses and his superior can give special attention to them by close supervision, coaching, or other appropriate training.

Inevitably, periodic evaluations will be used in the promotion process. The effectiveness and efficiency with which an employee has carried out his assignments are the critical bases for candidacy; the means he has used and the skill which he has applied are diagnostic tools which help to explain the results achieved.

Variety of Periodic Appraisals Many enterprises have no periodic appraisals; others stick to them with extreme tenacity. Some firms use simple forms listing but a few activities or characteristics; others use formal systems requiring numerous decisions in many categories. As is ever the case, when no science exists, the way is open for everyone to be an expert. Enterprise managers respond with everything from skepticism to enthusiasm, and employees tend to believe that whatever the system, it works against them.

Unfortunately, in many instances, the wrong questions are raised by the wrong people in the wrong environment. Take, for instance, the subject matter of appraisal forms. An appraisal form is likely to include a rating of personality, cooperativeness, leadership, intelligence, knowledge of work, clarity of objectives, output, absences, honesty, profit achieved, productivity, and planning ability. What is the matter with such lists? First, why stop with ten elements? Or ninety-six? There is simply no basis for knowing what or how much should be included. Second, numerous overlaps will be inevitable. Third, many such elements are unmeasurable. Fourth, it may be unnecessary to inquire into such factors as personality, intelligence, and leadership, because these traits were explored when the men were chosen for front-line supervisory positions. Now the subject matter appropriate for consideration is their proved record of performance.

Another shortcoming of current appraisal practices concerns the interview between the superior and the subordinate. This is generally recognized as the most unsatisfactory phase of appraisal programs. Superiors are not trained for this ordeal and their ineptness often harms their relationship with subordinates. The ratings depend largely on subjective evaluations of unmeasurable factors. Of course, subordinates evaluate themselves differently, and the stage is set for unprofitable argument.

In enterprises where several superiors on the same level evaluate subordinates, an effort is frequently made to array the results for such purposes as salary adjustments, promotion, etc. These efforts are almost sure to be misleading because different superiors use different standards. Thus attempts to code or compare results are unfair to subordinates and dangerous for the firm.

In firms where periodic appraisals are tied in with salary adjustments or merit raises, a further problem is encountered. The superior may rate in accordance with his wishes to reward or penalize a subordinate. Or he may take the easy way and be liberal with all subordinates. Salaries have nothing directly to do with appraisals of performance; although raises may *result* from such appraisal, they should not be permitted to deflect attention from the appraisal on its own terms.

Finally, the distastefulness of appraisal to both superiors and subordinates frequently results in superiors giving every subordinate one of the two top grades or omitting the interview altogether. In nonprofit enterprises it is nonsensically common to rate everyone either "excellent" or "superior." In business firms—where more attention is given to grade levels—the interview may be omitted. Both of these practices are regrettable. The first is no appraisal at all; the second may fail to help subordinates in overcoming weaknesses.

It is difficult to be proud of achievements to date in the appraisal of managers. Knowledge and logic seem often to be absent, and the results are sometimes chaotic. Yet the reasons for periodic evaluation are still with us, and there is a way to enjoy its fruits.

MANAGEMENT BY OBJECTIVES: PREMISES

At a moment of time, the position of a manager may be illustrated as in Figure 22.1. The manager's charter and the end products which will ensure its accomplishment may be idealized as shown on the right. Much as he strives, they may not ever be fully realized because performance lacks perfection and because the ideal changes through time. At any moment, the manager is usually far from operating at the ideal level. Although his charter is the same, his end products are not. They fall short in terms of scope, frequency, and probably cost and quality. It is imperative that the manager move from his current position toward the improved position, and this

Fig. 22.1 Typical Relationship between Existing and Ideal End Products (in an assumed controller's department)

Charter	Current end products	Ideal or approved end products	Charter
To safeguard the Corporate Assets	1. Annual balance sheet	1. Quarterly balance sheet	To safeguard the Corporate Assets
	2. Monthly profit and loss statement	2. Monthly profit and loss statement	
	3. Annual financial forecast	3. Semiannual financial forecast and analysis	
	4. Corporate budget	4. Variable budgets by organizational unit	
		5. Estimating data	

Time →

process is facilitated if he utilizes the supervisory device of "management by results."[1]

This concept has been widely heralded and is practiced in a limited way now. However, aspects of it have been widely used in some way though perhaps not in a formalized fashion. It embraces the practice of setting near-term goals for a subordinate manager, reviewing accomplishment at an appropriate time, and repeating this process indefinitely. The presumption is that successive efforts to accomplish established goals will gradually move a manager's end products from the position at the left of Figure 22.1 toward the ideal at the right. In the application of this technique, the superior manager will make certain that goals are set in quantitative or qualitative terms, a specific time for the completion of the goal and one for its review are set, and adequate authority to perform the task is delegated.[2] Taken as a whole, the process becomes a supervisory technique: if records are kept, they will become the best evidence for subordinate appraisal whenever measurement is required.

Clarification of Objectives   The superior, with his subordinate managers, has certain objectives to accomplish. Too often these are vaguely assigned, which results in either diffused or unconstructive effort. If a manager's objectives are not set forth clearly by his superiors, it is incumbent upon him to define his own objectives and have them confirmed. Then it becomes possible for him to agree upon specific objectives with each of his subordinate managers and to measure their performance against these.

Succession of Specific Goals   Most progress to a distant goal is made by setting and achieving specific, integrated, short-run objectives along the way to it. It is most difficult otherwise to maintain the long-range energetic action necessary. People respond with ease to a short-run goal, established by themselves or by others, because it may be accomplished comparatively quickly, within their span of attention and will power, and because they can enjoy small successes on the way to the larger one. For example, it is difficult for a new employee to maintain steady and economical progress toward the goal of becoming a general officer in an enterprise. But if his subsidiary goals along the way are defined and achieved in succession, he is likely to develop the knowledge, ability, and opportunity required to realize his ulti-

[1] Here again terminology varies widely and is itself a source of confusion. Several writers use such phrases as "management by objectives," "management by results," and "managing for results." The trouble with these phrases is that they all convey the impression that each is the sum total of the managing process. It could be pointed out that we also manage to achieve zero defects, manage for a profit, and even manage to stay alive. To escape from these misconceptions, it is surely much better to drop all reference to "managing with, by, for, and to." Men manage only to achieve their charters—this is their sole job. To learn if they are doing this, it is only necessary to compare performance with established goals.

[2] For an excellent statement of the whole process see E. C. Schleh, *Management by Results* (New York: McGraw-Hill Book Company, 1961).

mate goal. Like the rungs in a ladder which permit the achievement of a distant goal by single, successive steps, so by accomplishing limited, integrated objectives, one makes progress to distant ends.

Delegation by Objectives It is difficult to delegate specific authority when objectives are vague or absent. The usual practice is to state that the subordinate has the delegated authority to accomplish his duties. However, if duties are assigned in terms of the results to be achieved, authority becomes specific. For example, let us assume that the results expected by the department-store merchandise manager of his furniture buyer for a particular period, say one year, include: (1) increase of sales by 10 per cent, and (2) maintenance of a 40 per cent gross margin. Both objectives must be achieved within company policies relating to quality of product and service, employee relations, credit, etc. The buyer who manages the furniture department will develop detailed plans for accomplishing these two concrete purposes, budget them, and get his superior's approval. At this point, specific authority can be delegated to the buyer to operate within budgetary limits. This permits him to make all necessary decisions for carrying out his plans, including those concerning advertising, supervision, space and layout, personnel, and purchase orders.

Freedom to Act Provided with a clear objective, specific goals along the way to it, and the authority to achieve them, the subordinate manager gains the freedom to act and to exercise the full scope of his initiative. As he watches his plans materialize, he can make adjustments as necessary: shift funds from one type of a program to another, give training where needed, reassign personnel, improve the zeal of employees, travel when necessary, and ensure vendor support. He has flexibility. He is captain of his own ship and has maximum freedom to bring her into port.

Verifiable Results To clarify and achieve objectives, it is best to quantify them. It is impossible to measure achievement of objectives stated in such general terms as "improve morale," "increase sales," "operate efficiently," or "cut down expenses." Appraisal cannot be implemented in these terms. But if the results desired are quantified, such as "reduce absenteeism by 20 per cent," "increase sales by 15 per cent," or "reduce travel costs by 10 per cent," there can be no question of the degree of achievement when results are compared with targets. Realistic appraisal becomes possible.

Although goals that can be expressed in quantitative terms are the most clearly verifiable, specific verifiable goals can also be expressed in qualitative terms. For example, if a manager agrees to undertake by a certain date a program to tailor control information to the needs of his subordinates, to encourage subordinate self-education through taking advanced university courses, and to improve the quality of engineering personnel through instituting a recruitment program with certain definite features, he has a set of qualitative goals that are nonetheless specific. In other words, while accomplishment of such goals cannot be measured numerically, whether the agreed-upon program has been undertaken or concluded can be verified objectively; even many of the aspects of quality of the program can be given objective measurement. While the emphasis on such qualitative goals does tend to be on the question of "how well" rather than "how much" and may therefore have subjective elements, the emphasis is still on specific and reasonably verifiable performance.[3]

Thus, with a set of quantitative and qualitative goals, as specifically set forth as possible, and with agreed-upon target dates, both the superior and the subordinate manager have an objective program which becomes the standard against which performance can be judged.

Clear Communication   The basis for clear communication is established when a subordinate is given verifiable results to attain and the authority to achieve them. There is no place for doubt or indecision. This eliminates the confusion in situations where the superior is heard to say, "My department managers let me down," or subordinates say, "I wish the boss would tell me what he wants me to do." Communication is complete when objectives are specific, agreed upon, and budgeted. Only then will subordinates be motivated to put forth the effort and imagination essential for success.

Shared Responsibility   Cooperative determination of the results to be achieved provides the basis for a feeling of increased responsibility to attain them on the part of _both_ superior and subordinate. Experimental evidence[4] shows that when either party determines goals alone, there is less feeling of responsibility for achievement and the person with less power feels less responsible. When the superior alone specifies results to be obtained, there is a question whether he can gain the support of his subordinates. On the other hand, the subordinate feels that he is working in a vacuum if he attempts to establish the results he wants to obtain without the concurrence of his superior.

Personal Accountability   Appraisal has no meaning unless personal accountability can be established. Assignment of duties cannot be used as a basis for accountability if the nature of the duties is vague. But if assignment by results is made and the necessary authority delegated, personal accountability becomes clear and definite.

Improved Management Ability   At each interval in the routine appraisal program, the results to be achieved require the subordinate's concentration on the weaker areas of his performance. As these become corrected, new tar-

---

[3] For an excellent article summarizing this approach, see Arch Patton, "How to Appraise Executive Performance," *Harvard Business Review,* vol. 38, no. 1, pp. 63–70 (January–February, 1960).

[4] R. R. Blake and J. S. Mouton, *Group Dynamics: Key to Decision Making* (Houston: Gulf Publishing Company, 1961), pp. 34–35.

gets are selected. Consequently, over a period of time, attention is directed to specific activities which are to be improved. Growth in the general ability of a subordinate to manage can be confidently predicted.

The above premises upon which management by objectives rests are derived from knowledge of how people respond to certain stimuli and of what is expected of managers in circumstances which cloud or clarify their functions. It is now possible to construct an appraisal procedure which rests squarely upon these premises. Appraisal by results is the other side of the coin of management by objectives.

APPRAISAL BY RESULTS: PROCEDURE

Sooner or later the superior manager will turn his attention to the problem of establishing goals for each of his subordinates. In most cases, all the managers have been working together for some time and considerable progress has been made in communication and understanding. At the time when a new subordinate is selected, it is important to review the operation with the latter, analyze it carefully, and set certain goals toward which special effort is desired.

Identifying Desired Results   As the superior considers a subordinate's operation, he becomes aware of both satisfactory and less satisfactory elements. Consideration of weaknesses will bring them into focus and enable the

	Results	
Activity to be improved	Sought 4-1-67	Achieved 7-1-67
1. Reduce absenteeism	25%	35%
2. Submit plan for reorganization	plan	approved
3. Develop plan for equipment maintenance	plan	approved
4. Realized cost savings	$15,000	$5,000

Fig. 22.2   Agreement for Appraisal by Results in a Production Department . . . *After an exchange of memoranda in which superior and subordinate list the most important objectives each feels should be accomplished in the next few months, both parties agree in conference on the specific work needed to reach these goals and come to agreement on exact, attainable targets. At the end of the period, both examine the results and repeat the process for the succeeding period. This technique is superior to the more common annual reviews or rating periods. It makes agreement on objectives possible before action is taken. The subordinate knows what he will be measured against and can judge his own progress. Thus he is never surprised when the superior is dissatisfied. The written memoranda furnish data for annual reviews. This system gives the superior more frequent opportunities to coach his subordinate than those provided by the usual system.*

superior to specify those which, if eliminated, will most strengthen the department—perhaps excessive cost, submarginal profit, poor housekeeping, or high employee turnover.

The superior is now ready to send a memorandum to the subordinate which will (1) invite him to confer, at a specific time, on the results to be obtained in the next period; (2) enumerate the elements which the superior thinks should be considered; and (3) suggest that the subordinate bring a list of the elements he would like to have considered—perhaps excessive overhead, need to raise salaries or to recruit better qualified employees, or improvement of staff meetings.

As the two men sit down to their conference their purpose will be one, namely, to agree upon specific results to be obtained in the ensuing period. They will examine and compare the two lists calling for improvement, noting items which they agree upon; items about which one may have specified an area for improvement and the other a method of achieving it, namely, reducing turnover and raising salaries; and items not mentioned by the one or the other. Exchange of viewpoints will result in agreement on areas for concerted attention and on verifiable results to be obtained in each. For instance, the high cost of operations would be dealt with by a detailed examination to identify which costs are out of line. The result to be obtained might then be stated: reduce overtime by 25 per cent.

An apparent divergence of views on the reason for turnover would be explored extensively. If the superior feels it is due to more driving than leading on the part of the subordinate, and the subordinate thinks it is due to low salaries, they cannot agree without data showing that salaries are in line and without carefully analyzing the subordinate's technique in motivating his employees. Then it is possible to spell out an attainable result during the succeeding appraisal period, such as to reduce turnover by 10 per cent.

As this process of goal formulation proceeds, it is important to check out each objective on several points. First, is the target a result to be achieved or a method of reaching a result? It should normally be the former, leaving methods to the ingenuity of the subordinate. Second, can the target be achieved completely within the authority of the subordinate? If not, the extra authority should be delegated; otherwise, the subordinate will be in the uncomfortable position of being responsible for a result which he has no authority to accomplish. Furthermore, if the necessary authority for accomplishing the target is, in part, beyond the power of the superior to delegate, then the projected goal must be modified to overcome this defect. And, third, can the subordinate be held accountable for realizing the target, or will someone in another department be partially able to influence the result? All targets should be drawn in terms of personal accountability.

Thus will be developed jointly a document containing three or four items to be improved by a specific, measurable degree, in a given period of time. This requires considerable analysis, discussion, and time. Superior and subordinate will emerge each with his original list much modified, and each will have a much better understanding of the operation, its relation to the total enterprise, and of each other. The cost in time is a small price to pay for these results, let alone for the targets agreed upon.

Appraisal Review and Projection of Goals   At the appointed time, superior and subordinate consider the degree to which the projected results have been achieved. There is no question about the success or failure of the subordinate, because data exist to measure actual against planned results. As is ever the case when anticipating accomplishment in the future, the data on accomplishment will differ from the goals, exceeding or falling short, but rarely agreeing exactly with them. Both superior and subordinate will be pleased to see the targets equaled or exceeded, but little time will be spent on congratulations. Instead, the men will analyze in detail the instances in which targets were missed in marked degree, to determine the cause. Detailed objective consideration will reveal whether the target was attainable, whether it was carelessly fixed, or whether inadequate performance was due to uncontrollable circumstances.

A review of this nature is a satisfying experience for both parties. The achievement of verifiable results signifies an improved operation, a credit to both men. Increase in the subordinate's ability and in the superior's confidence in him are other gains.

During the review conference, projected goals for the next appraisal period are established. Much the same techniques as described above are used. Except for the retention, with any agreed-upon modification, of any underachieved targets, the new goals will most likely be different, because of changes in the priority of attention. For instance, if satisfactory cost control and labor relations were achieved in the appraisal period just ended, they would have low priority in the new period, compared with marked deficiencies such as the lack of a trained successor or the need for improved long-range planning. Thus, a group of new comparative weaknesses will be defined and from them will emerge measurable goals for the succeeding appraisal period.

This periodic shift in targets from one period to the next does not mean that either the superior or the subordinate will neglect the "old" targets. Having achieved satisfactory cost control, it would be dangerous and wasteful to ignore cost thereafter. Both parties hold steadily to good performances while shifting emphasis to the pursuit of the new goals. This gradually improves over-all performance, whereas inattention to retaining former gains may result in no over-all improvement in operational efficiency.

Periodic Appraisal and the Annual Review   Periodic appraisal of the degree to which specific results have been achieved is distinct from the annual or semiannual review. There may be several appraisals within a total review period. Furthermore, the purpose of the appraisal is to improve the efficiency of the subordinate, whereas the annual review is meant to measure his over-all efficiency at a given time. The targets of each appraisal might be concentrated on only one or two functions of the manager, whereas the annual review evaluates his over-all proficiency.

Successive periodic appraisals help the superior complete the annual review. Since the appraisals show up the subordinate's weakest areas, for purposes of both appraisal and review these will receive close attention. Furthermore, the review, under these circumstances, will not tend to over-rate or underrate the subordinate and therefore will become a more reliable document than heretofore.

MANAGEMENT BY OBJECTIVES AND APPRAISAL BY RESULTS

Management by objectives and appraisal by results rest upon assumptions which, taken as a whole, spell out a partial philosophy of management. The process implies a reliance upon subordinates to accomplish the tasks of cooperative enterprise and an acceptance of the principle that men respond better to the achievement of a few short-range measurable goals than to a long-range target. The very purpose of cooperative enterprise is to accomplish goals beyond the capability of a single individual, and this requires that the joint effort be well integrated.

Negative Advantages In management by objectives and appraisal by results there are certain negative as well as positive advantages. These negative advantages arise through the avoidance of error inherent in other techniques.

Avoidance of vagueness Vagueness is a serious deficiency in setting goals or trying to appraise performance, and it arises when targets are stated in unmeasured or unverifiable terms such as "improved production," "higher profit levels," or "improved personality." There is no way in which to measure such improvement nor any specification of the acceptable degree of improvement. Furthermore, such terms make it impossible to communicate clearly to a subordinate the basis for his eventual appraisal. Any attempt to appraise under these conditions is bound to result in argument and dissatisfaction on the part of both superior and subordinate.

Management by objectives avoids all this, because agreed-upon verifiable goals replace the indeterminate and the unverifiable. Communication is clear and complete. There is no basis for misunderstanding.

Avoidance of subjective evaluations Superiors, as well as subordinates, often face the appraisal interview with deep misgivings. There would be no reason for this if performance could always be rated excellent, but any rating at lower levels must be justified to the subordinate and accepted as accurate by him. This is beyond possibility when uncertainty is present and objective proof is lacking. The door is then open wide for charges that the superior is arbitrary, prejudiced, and unfriendly. Even more discouraging, such appraisals do not contribute to the development of the subordinate or to the efficiency of the operation.

Appraisal by results avoids these deficiencies. Superior and subordinate approach the process on firm ground. Neither may like the results, but each is confident of their accuracy. This allows moving directly to objective analysis of the results, with the conviction that problems yield to logical solution and that management ability will be sharpened by experience—especially bitter experience.

The generally poor performance of superiors in situations involving subjective measurements and the probability of unfair charges has led many firms to provide superiors with special training to handle appraisal interviews with more success. This crutch is not only expensive, it is ineffective. The training does not yield the expected results, because sufficient knowledge for the purpose is nonexistent. Fortunately, enterprise managers need not wait for the development of such knowledge, because appraisal by results requires neither the knowledge nor the training. Here, appraisal carries over from a prior agreement on objectives, and the latter provides the basis for joint interest in measuring results and discovering why some were or were not achieved. Thus, the vague and subjective are replaced by the verifiable and objective, which eliminates the need for special training to improve interviews.

Positive Advantages   The positive advantages which can be enjoyed when techniques of management by objective and appraisal by results are faithfully practiced benefit both the enterprise and its employees.

Benefits to the firm   The objectives established for subordinate accomplishment are meant to improve the efficiency of his segment of the enterprise as well as to improve his skill as manager. Every goal falls within the framework of a manager's functions. Since positive effort is directed at the correction of deficiencies in a continuous manner, enterprise efficiency can only improve.

As was stated earlier in the chapter, successive appraisals by results are valuable for annual review purposes. This review assesses the subordinate's ability to manage. Simple referral to the degree in which successive results have been accomplished provides indisputable evidence of the quality of a subordinate's performance in that area. One or two such appraisals would be inadequate evidence for the first annual review, yet no other technique provides more information. The longer appraisal by results has been in operation, the sooner the annual review will rest upon a solid base.

Benefits to the subordinate   The advantages to the subordinate manager are several. He knows exactly where he stands with his superior. Without this knowledge, he is uncertain of his position and of his future. Appraisal by results tells him the degree to which he has overcome his known weaknesses. Furthermore, as each appraisal period is reached, his progress is recorded.

Appraisal by results, by pinpointing operational and personal activities most in need of improvement, provides a sound basis for management development. With the passage of time, attention will be given to submarginal and marginal performance of the several aspects of planning, controlling, organizing, staffing, and directing. Since proficiency in these should be the goal of every manager, it is indispensable for promotion. The fact that the manager knows he is being made ready for promotion in this way should give him assurance and satisfaction.

Finally, the subordinate manager is provided with a technique for use in improving the performance of *his* subordinates. The process of managing by objectives and of appraising by results is educational for any subordinate. Each manager may gradually develop the techniques which work best for him. He is then in a position to develop his own subordinates with skill.

Potential Pitfalls There are several things which could limit the effectiveness of management by objectives and appraisal by results.

First, it is assumed that superior and subordinate will detect correctly the areas in need of improvement. This is no easy matter in an activity as complex as management. It is one thing to identify unsatisfactory results; it is quite another to identify correctly their causes. And the causes must be clear before any program of correction can be initiated. For instance, declining sales can be readily recognized, but a vague attempt to increase them will not do. The situation must be analyzed to determine *why* sales have declined. The decrease may not be due to inadequate coverage of territory, decline in engineering design budgets, new competition, or lower tariffs; it may be due to poor customer service. In this case, the chosen target for the subordinate will be in the service area, and, specifically, it might encompass a revision of the guarantee under which the product is sold. Failure to identify correct causes of poor performance is the greatest danger to success in management.

The second pitfall concerns the amount of time which the superior will give to the process of appraisal by results. It is much easier to be vague and to shift blame to others than it is to take seriously the duty of analysis and discussion of specific targets for the next appraisal period, not to mention the appraisal itself. Superior managers are busy men, much involved in daily problems, and they may put off managing by objectives. This technique requires a thorough respect for the manager's functions, farsightedness, and will power, qualities which are not common.

A third pitfall relates to the problems of interdependence of goals and the need to retain past gains as future gains are sought. The essence of the first problem may be illustrated by a situation in which an output goal is attained at the expense of credit losses or loss in quality. Clearly, it is essential that a sales goal be attained without jeopardizing the quality of accounts receivable; that production goals be attained without suffering a loss in quality; or that a profit goal be realized without short-run economies in new-product development expense.

Related to the second problem is the situation where an objective, attained in the last appraisal, will be sacrificed to achieve an agreed-upon new goal. For instance, a subordinate might have been complimented in the last appraisal period for realizing a given reduction in overhead. The superior and subordinate then agreed to improve visibility (that is, ready availability of information on operations) and to this end two additional weekly reports are to be issued. However, the increased work load calls for adding an indirect employee (an employee whose salary is not charged against any specific job or contract) to the payroll. Thus, the gain from the previous appraisal period may be lost in the current period. Unless previous gains are "pegged" and are not permitted to slip, management by objectives could degenerate into a net balance of gains and losses. From the point of view of operating efficiency, nothing would be gained beyond proving that the subordinate manager is resourceful in meeting, willy-nilly, new challenges to his way of life.

Evaluation Experience in the practical application of this supervisory technique makes possible further refinements of the practice to the point where it becomes a very valuable tool. These include certain technical operations of the plan, the source of goals, analytical procedures, and the transition from an operating procedure to manager appraisal.

Managers do not like an inflexible plan whereby goals are set to be accomplished simultaneously. They prefer to set a time for each goal to be accomplished in its natural period, which may be every two weeks for one, quarterly for another, or contract reporting for another. They think that the establishment of the same completion time for every goal is artificial and simply makes for unnecessary work. Neither do managers like the simultaneous periodic review of goals which theoreticians or in-plant staff usually require. Managers feel that it is much more effective to review *progress toward* goal accomplishment as well as to compare performance with goal on the date set. Review thus becomes part of the normal supervisory process rather than an additional, and strange, procedure. Finally, the selected goals must be clearly related to the enterprise plan of operation (sometimes called profit plan). This requirement is especially important, not only because the sole reason for employing any manager is to secure the contribution of his job to the enterprise objectives, but also because it is through this means that the subordinate becomes committed to goal achievement. Commitment is important in the manager's view because he is relying upon the assumption that commitment will result in a subordinate performing at or near his capability. The problem is, how to achieve commitment? Psychologists[5] seem to feel that if the enterprise objectives are under-

[5] See Douglas McGregor, "Do Management Control Systems Achieve Their Purpose?" *Management Review*, vol. 56, no. 2, pp. 4–18 (February, 1967).

stood by the employee, and if he perceives them as supportable, he will then work at full capability toward their achievement. Managers are not this naïve. They feel that commitment not only requires an understanding of the enterprise objectives and their approval by subordinates (as measured by their willingness to work for them), but also a recognition of the personal objectives of the subordinate and the effort to secure complementarity between the two through leadership techniques.

Discovery of Goals   Perhaps not strange, but certainly surprising, is the difficulty some managers have in casting about for goals. They are as likely to select in accordance with some personality defect or a misapplication of management principles as they are to relate near-term goals to desired end products. Of course, there can be no question but that the place to look is the efficiency and effectiveness of end products. It is a two-step process. The first step requires the manager to identify the ideal end products. This is by no means an easy task. The ideal is difficult to state in terms of comprehensiveness and timing in their relationship to cost effectiveness. And since this is a changing world, the end products will change through time because they certainly will be affected by expansion of knowledge, broadening conceptions of work, technology, and enterprise size. The second step requires a comparison between the current output of end products and the ideal. It is among the discrepancies found that goals must be sought.

This whole process is illustrated in Figure 22.3. Certain short-term goals have been selected. They are few in number and the periods of their achievement are short. They are related to certain of the ideal end products as shown by the common numbers. For instance, item 5 in each case may be accounting procedures; item 2 as an end product may be the annual budget but, as a near-term goal, it may call for the approval of new procedures required to shift from a quarterly budget to the annual ideal.

Relation of Goals to End Products   To accomplish his charter or job, the manager has resources comprised of people with various abilities, space allotment for them, and capital equipment. His purpose is to use his resources integratively so that the power of their combination will be zeroed in on the accomplishment of his charter *and* the realization of his short-term goals. This means, for instance, that he maintains the current level of efficiency and effectiveness with which the ideal end products numbered 1, 3, and 4 are being produced while he concentrates the effort of his subordinates on achieving short-term goals 2, 5, and 6. The short-term goals will change with time if they are achieved, and the gains made must be held while attention is directed to other goals which have become critical.

In order to bring his resources to bear upon these goals and end products, the manager must carry out with skill the functions of planning, organizing, staffing, directing, and controlling. This he does by adhering to the principles of management and by applying them with the skill he has developed through experience. The manager is the key to this whole

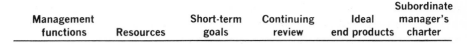

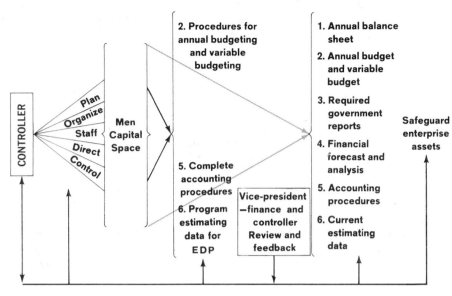

Fig. 22.3   Controller's Management System

operation. He needs conceptual skill to visualize his charter in its relationship to all other elements of the enterprise; he needs analytical skill to discern the critical discrepancies between his ideal and current end products; and he needs experience and knowledge to discern the most effective combination of resources and to execute the managerial functions so essential in their utilization.

Diagnosis of Performance   At the time when short-term goals are reviewed, the superior manager has available several diagnostic tools. The first one is the direct comparison of goal and performance. If these are equivalent, no further analytical steps are necessary. A new goal is selected to replace the old. If the goal is exceeded, it is important to examine the effect on other parts of the enterprise activity. If when the goal is exceeded it means that procedures are revised and made operable before the specified time, they can have a disrupting effect on other managers. This situation gives the superior manager an opportunity to coach his subordinate on the importance of activity integration. Overreaching a goal is not always good.

   If the degree of accomplishment of a goal is less than intended, the next step in analysis needs to be taken. It is necessary to find out why. One first looks to external and noncontrollable events which may have interfered. In this case, the goal is retained for achievement by a future date and/or is modified to suit the prospective environment. If the lack of achievement is the responsibility of the subordinate manager, a review of the skill with which he carried out his managerial functions is in order. For easy reference, he may find Figure 22.4 useful. It may be that the planning was incompetent, that there was a lack of skill in manning the project, that the control system failed to report deficiencies on time, or that there was a failure in communication. Once the deficiency is isolated, the superior can set in motion corrective action that he deems effective. This may be a session in coaching his subordinate. The result may be a review of his planning process, a change in the control system, better use of support departments, or agreement on communication techniques. The subordinate is reminded of the relevant management principles involved and shown how they should be applied in the instant case.

This diagnostic examination may point up the fact that the knowledge and skill in executing management functions are hindered by certain personality defects. The superior will inquire into the basic desire of his subordinate to manage. Without this quality, he can be only an indifferent manager. He may look into the educational record of his subordinate for deficiencies. It may lead him to inquire into the integrity of his subordinate. Thus, the assorted personality factors deemed essential in a manager become a third diagnostic tool in the search for the real cause of the deficiency in goal achievement.

It may be seen from the foregoing description that, while the purpose of diagnosis is to isolate the cause of failure, it provides the simultaneous opportunity for the superior to take corrective action through some type of training if the cause is correctable in time, or through a change in assignment which better fits the subordinate's capabilities. The possibility of nonachievement of goals is so important that the superior manager wants to follow the operation through the execution period. This practice will give him the time to take corrective action—an action that will be no surprise to the subordinate. The whole process envisions a close cooperation between superior and subordinate wherein the former provides effective leadership, sees that achievable-though-stretch goals are selected, makes certain that environmental conditions are as positive as possible, and coaches the subordinate as he goes along, while the latter practices with growing skill the application of his resources to goal accomplishment. The whole process may be conceived as a system, as reflected in Figure 20.1 (page 442), containing its own feedback, which ensures a gradual improvement in the manager's skill.

Both the goals and the results of the review process should be reduced to writing. This need not require a standardized form. If one is used, it should approximate Figure 22.5, which provides for agreed-upon goals, the results of the review (including causes and remedies), and the newly selected follow-on goals. In this way, a record will be created that is very useful for reference purposes where differences about past agreements can be resolved. It also becomes the best evidence for the superior manager to

Fig. 22.4 Manager's Functional Evaluation

Elements	Unsatis-factory	Fair	Good	Superior	Excep-tional
1. Organizing ability:					
Adherence to organization principles					
Proper use of staff, service groups, and committees					
Clarity of authority delegations					
2. Planning ability:					
Clarity of objectives, policies, and premises					
Consideration of alternative plans					
Implementation of plans					
Availability of plans					
3. Controlling ability:					
Selection of critical points for control					
Standards for measurement for completed plans					
Ability to pin-point responsibility					
Ability to take corrective action promptly					
4. Staffing ability:					
Skill in identifying managerial potential and selecting effective subordinate managers					
Skill in training subordinates					
Adequate provision for management succession					
5. Directing ability:					
Skill in orienting, motivating, and guiding subordinates					
Communication skill					
Skill in decentralizing authority					
Response of subordinates to direction					
6. Over-all ability:					
Quantity, quality, and timeliness of output of group supervised					

use when he has the occasion to justify his recommendations for merit increases, salary adjustments, or the selection of candidates for promotion or other change in position. Thus, the subordinate manager is being continuously and objectively appraised by the best of evidence—the effectiveness and efficiency with which he proceeds to the realization of his charter.

Conclusion Perhaps the most important advantage in looking upon the appraisal of managers in the manner described here is that the total process is now in perspective. The manager knows what is his job, he has some mature concept of what end products will make certain that his charter is accomplished in the interests of the enterprise, and he uses his resources in the manner that will make progress toward these end products realizable. Another advantage is that the manager's personality factors and his skills in executing his functions come into proper focus. No man is employed because he has certain personality characteristics, or because he is skilled in

Fig. 22.5 Manager Performance Record
sections one and four: completed by supervisor
sections two and three: completed by subordinate

Section one

Employee number	Employee name	Division/ location	Position code	Position title

Date of hire	Years in present job	Date to complete		

Section two

Objectives agreed to:	Results report	Evaluation (What did you do to affect results?)

Supervisor's comments:

Section three: future potential   Supervisor's comments

1. Could you make a more significant contribution in another department?
   Yes.... No.... Explain.

2. What is your occupational goal?

3. What do you consider your major development needs?

4. Outline a specific plan for your development during the next five years.

Section four: manpower planning

1. Outline near-term development plan for subordinate.

2. Rank promotional alternatives, ready date, and replacement, ready date.

3. Comments

planning, in directing, or in other managerial functions. These are simply the *means* by which the manager proceeds to accomplish his job. It is the job that is important, and for doing it he is paid. Therefore, a manager should be appraised not on the basis of personality factors or even on mere skill in applying management principles, but primarily with respect to the degree and quality of his job accomplishment.

Continuing Problems in Managerial Appraisal   It is both logical and desirable to appraise managers in terms of their end products, but this presents varying degrees of difficulty. For one thing, the existence and reliability of standards vary with the several functional activities. A balance sheet can be evaluated in terms of timeliness and accuracy, but what should it cost and what should it portray? The end products of an industrial relations department may include industrial peace, but what are the standards of cost and quality? If these really cannot be determined, how can the responsible managers be appraised?

Another difficulty arises in the area of comparative appraisals. In terms of the end products of a factory manager, standards do exist and a high degree of reliability can be assigned to an appraisal of him. But similar accurate standards may not exist against which the end products of a chief engineer can be compared; hence, his appraisal may have a much lower validity quotient. Many occasions arise which require the comparison of managerial peers. Among these are the division of moneys for merit, salary adjustments, bonus distributions, and candidacy for promotion to higher management levels. It becomes clear that while the logic of appraising managers on the basis of charter accomplishment is unassailable, it does leave difficult operational problems unsolved.

Even if these difficulties can be somehow overcome, there remains a difficulty caused by the very nature of man himself. He responds best to short-term goals or deadlines, and very poorly to long-term goals. His *modus operandi* is to delay action to achieve long-term goals until, through the passage of time, they become short-term. Only then does he bring his resources to bear on a crash basis, often at great cost, and certainly with the effect of uneven performance through time.

To this point, the implication for appraisal of managers is that if a man achieves his charter with passing time, he therefore should be considered excellent and be so rated. This conclusion is not accurate. Two further factors need to be considered. On the one hand, the manager should not woodenly identify his charter, look upon it as a kind of black box, and operate within the letter of its expression. We want managers who think in terms of charter enlargement, not by means of impinging upon the charters of other managers, but rather by an interpretation that will enhance the contribution of the manager's organizational unit to the welfare of the enterprise. On the other hand, the manager must be able to operate effectively with other managers at all levels. It is entirely conceivable that a satisfactory accomplishment of a charter can be made while, at the same time, a manager exhibits important shortcomings in knowledge of the state of an art, in negotiations with other managers, in achieving a leadership position with other managers, in integrity, or, indeed, in the very desire to dominate others that every manager must feel. Thus it is that personal qualities are very important in the relationships of managers. Since these may not be adequately reflected by the mere accomplishment of a charter, it is necessary to add this dimension to the problems of appraisal.

It is not too much to say that these problems will continue to impede the whole process of evaluating managers for some time to come. Managers simply must wrestle with them and follow a pragmatic solution until such times as new knowledge comes to their aid.

THE MANAGER INVENTORY

Annual evaluations of the over-all efficiency of subordinate managers are important in addition to their use as a basis for appraisal or merit review. They provide the data for the development of a manager inventory which reflects specific information about every subordinate manager in terms of his promotability. Viewed from this point, both superior and subordinate are in a position to understand the implications of the evaluations. The superior can review the need of the firm for managers and the action he must take to safeguard its future in this regard; the subordinate can determine the status of his career in management.

Inventory Chart Every responsible manager needs to know where he stands with respect to the capability of present subordinates and their potential for promotion. This knowledge is necessary to his staffing function. The periodic appraisal of subordinates provides information on their age, efficiency, and readiness for promotion. For an over-all perspective of where he stands, an inventory chart is recommended. This is simply an organization chart of his unit with all managerial positions indicated and keyed as to the promotability of each incumbent.

Figure 22.6 is a typical inventory chart. At a glance the controller can see where he stands with respect to his staffing function. His own successor is the manager of general accounting, and this man in turn has a successor ready for promotion. Supporting him in turn is a subordinate who will be ready for promotion in one year, but below him is one man who does not have potential, and two new hires.

The cost accounting manager represents the all-too-frequent case of a man who is acceptable but not promotable. He stands in the way of one subordinate who is promotable now. The remaining men in this department represent extremes of nonpromotability and good potential. Over-all, the staffing pattern in this department is not satisfactory.

The manager of budget and analysis has considerable development to

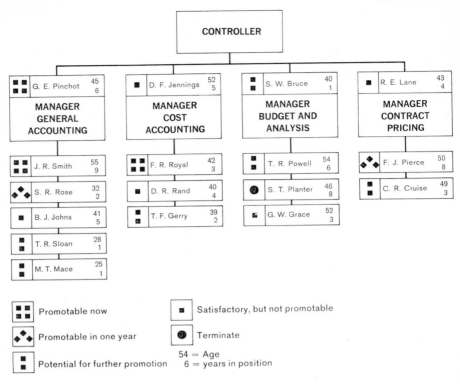

Fig. 22.6 Manager Inventory Chart

accomplish before he is ready for promotion. He does not have an available successor. And to complicate matters, no further potential exists among the remaining subordinates.

Contract pricing portends some problems. Its manager is not promotable but he has good potential in his subordinates.

Actions to Be Taken On the basis of the inventory chart, a plan of action can be developed, geared to both the short term and the long run. For the short term, action may be taken to replace an unsatisfactory manager, to begin the training of a successor for the next higher level, to transfer a manager in order to broaden his experience specifically for his next promotion, or to transfer surplus men, now ready for promotion, to other departments where managerial vacancies exist.

For the long run, age may play as important a part as efficiency.[6] If it is true, as is sometimes asserted, that a manager's most productive age is from forty to sixty years, then it is important to the future welfare of a firm that

---

[6] J. F. Garde, Jr., "The Insidious Management Cycle," *Dun's Review*, vol. 79, no. 4 (April, 1962).

its managers—especially its top managers—be at varying ages above forty. If they are not scattered along the productive age range, it might happen that in ten years' time all top managers would be over sixty. Such a situation may be avoided by judicious promotion of persons in the right age group. The long-run plan of action for qualified managers needs to be integrated with short-run action. For instance, it is clearly inadvisable in the short run to identify a backup man (successor) who is the same age as his immediate superior, for they will both grow old together. It may be clearly advantageous to name as immediate successor a man ten years older than the incumbent and to begin to train as ultimate successor a third man ten years his junior. This arrangement will satisfy the short-run requirements for a trained successor in the person of the older man, and the long-run needs in the person of the trainee.

One question that the manager inventory chart does not answer is the question: Promotable to what? It is not enough to become aware that a man is promotable. Provision needs to be made for its actualization. One may take the position that, with respect to his area of specialization, the promotable person in the controller's division or in the manufacturing division simply remains there in abeyance until an opening occurs vertically above him. Is he really promotable if he happens to be listed in this way by the production control manager and an opening occurs for a manager of industrial engineering or general superintendent? In the case of Figure 22.6, is J. R. Smith in general accounting promotable to manager of budget and analysis? If his departmental training is narrow, one cannot say that he is promotable horizontally. Nor is this problem solved if a manager inventory is comprehensive to the point where all managers in all subordinate organizations are included. The question remains unanswered: Promotable to what?

This common difficulty of the promotion process can scarcely ever be solved in the short run. It is essential for the top managers of every enterprise to insist that young men with managerial potential be identified in the very early years of their employment and be given real opportunities to broaden their experience through lateral assignments. Breadth of experience is essential during the years *prior to* succession to most managerial positions. From a practical point of view, at lower levels of management such experience should be provided on an intradivisional, but not interdivisional, basis. This practice will maintain the integrity of the divisional staffing plan and permit the promotable manager to be an active candidate for interdepartmental openings. Interdivisional training for promotable candidates for upper-level management positions is considered in the following chapter.

Another difficulty encountered in large enterprises is the hoarding of promotable men by their immediate superiors. Quite naturally, these managers are averse to depriving themselves of able subordinates, but the interests of the enterprise are paramount. Therefore, vigorous surveillance of the manager inventory must be maintained by the division manager. Only he can make the basic staffing strategy of top managers work.

Importance in Staffing By systematically examining his staffing needs, a manager will give adequate attention to this often-neglected function. He will be alert to the requirements for potential managers to be at specific levels of preparation at a given time, and he will funnel off to other departments excess subordinates *before* they become disenchanted with their prospects and leave the firm.

This manager will also be serving the best interests of his subordinates, who want to know their prospects so that they can determine whether *their* needs may best be served by remaining with the firm or by leaving to take advantage of other opportunities. They can now be answered with confidence by their superior. He has a moral responsibility to be honest in his answer, even though this may mean that the subordinate will resign. This situation is not seen fairly by superior managers who think only of what the resignation will mean to themselves. They should realize that the highest good for the company may arise from recognition of the career interests of the individual.

FOR DISCUSSION

1. Do you think managers should be appraised regularly? If so, how?
2. What problems may arise from the fact that different managers, on the same level, appraise differently, some being generally higher than others?
3. Many firms still evaluate middle and top managers on such personality factors as aggressiveness, cooperation, leadership, and attitude. Do you think this makes any sense?
4. The argument has been made in this book for appraising managers on their ability to execute their functions. Should anything more be expected of them?
5. How do you feel about an appraisal system based upon results expected and realized? Would you prefer to be appraised on this basis? If not, why?

SELECTED REFERENCES

Crawford, C. M.: "Business Bigotry," *Michigan Business Review*, vol. 18, no. 5, pp. 23–29 (November, 1966).

Drucker, P. F.: *Managing for Results*, New York: Harper & Row, Publishers, Incorporated, 1964.

Ewing, D. W.: "The Knowledge of an Executive," *Guideposts to Executive Growth*, pp. 72–81 (Cambridge: Harvard University, 1956–1965).

Heyel, C.: *Appraising Executive Performance*, New York: American Management Association, 1958.

Hughes, C. L.: *Goal Setting: Key to Individual and Organizational Effectiveness*, New York: American Management Association, 1965.

Kellogg, M. S.: *What to Do about Performance Appraisal*, New York: American Management Association, 1965.

Maremont, A. H.: "A Plea for the Abrasive Personality," *Dun's Review*, vol. 88, no. 5, pp. 48–49ff. (November, 1966).

McConkey, D. D.: *How to Manage by Results*, New York: American Management Association, 1965.

Odiorne, G. S.: *Management by Objectives,* New York: Pitman Publishing Corporation, 1965.

Payne, B. L.: "An Appraisal of Managers and Management Development," *Management Record,* vol. 23, no. 3, pp. 8–17 (March, 1961).

Randle, C. W., and W. H. Monroe: "Better Ways to Measure Executive Performance," *Management Methods,* vol. 19, no. 4, pp. 64–66ff. (January, 1961).

Schlek, E. C.: *Management by Results,* New York: McGraw-Hill Book Company, 1961.

Valentine, R. F.: *Performance Objectives for Managers,* New York: American Management Association, 1966.

Weingarten, J.: "The 'Hard' Look in Employee Appraisal," *Dun's Review,* vol. 88, no. 3, pp. 41–42ff. (September, 1966).

Wikstrom, W. S.: "Management by Objectives or Appraisal by Results," *The Conference Board Record,* vol. 3, no. 7, pp. 27–31 (July, 1966).

development and training of managers

Good executives look to the future. Every firm has the responsibility of helping in the development of men who have the requisite potential to contribute their full measure to the welfare of the firm and to society.

In the days before World War II when management was less clearly understood, the generally accepted viewpoint was that somehow or other men acquired whatever it took to be a manager. Given sufficient exposure to practical experience, by starting from the humble jobs made so famous by Horatio Alger and by Sir Joseph Porter of *Pinafore*, the man destined to rise to high managerial position was thought to be marked in some fashion easily distinguished by his superiors, who saw to it that he was put through the fires of nasty jobs and fierce trials to be properly chastened for the welcome burdens of later positions of great trust.

This dream world of the business tycoon, based on an economy of Victorian vintage, was rudely shattered in the depression years of the 1930s. Executives lost their aura of omnipotence. Probably for the first time in industrial history they began to question their views about business success and, by the time World War II was upon them, decided they needed help fast. The first answer was training at the foreman level. At middle and higher levels, men were simply assigned responsible jobs with a prayer that nothing too disastrous would happen.

The lessons learned from these experiences were so valuable that the idea that managers possessed special skills which could be explained took firm hold. By 1950 training was at a critical stage. Although it was then making inroads into enterprises heretofore firm in their skepticism, it was also being reexamined with a critical eye by its early adherents. The conclusions seemed to be that it had value but had been marred by the barnacles of fad and ignorance.

MANAGER DEVELOPMENT VERSUS MANAGERIAL TRAINING

Terminology is ambiguous in this area, but it need not be. The authors of this book use "manager development" to refer to the progress a manager makes in learning how to manage, and "managerial training" to refer to the program devised by top management to facilitate this learning progress. Thus, the firm is seen as providing training; the manager, as developing efficiency by way of this training.

THE NATURE OF MANAGER DEVELOPMENT

The nature of manager development has been obscured by confusing it with training. A developed manager is a mature manager, successful because he has grown in wisdom. Managerial wisdom requires time and rests upon the ancient truth—first attributed to Homer—that a man may be taught but he does not necessarily learn. In current business literature, the proposition often takes the form of a warning that a firm cannot develop a manager; it can only provide the opportunity for a manager to develop. Accepting this proposition as fundamental, we made the point in Chapter 21 that a prime qualification for manager selection is his keen desire to manage. Only a person with such motivation, provided he has the essential intelligence, will take full advantage of opportunities to acquire the wisdom of a mature executive. In other words, he must learn what he is taught; he must be able, and anxious, to absorb knowledge.

The practice of management training encompasses formal schooling or on-the-job training or it may be as remote as theoretical psychology; it may cover all of the managerial functions, some of them, or only aspects of them; and it may be given to individuals or groups within or without the firm.

A man may also develop by learning from experience. In manager development, experience[1] is considered more important than formal training, partly because the time scale of varied experience cannot be telescoped; a man can be told what he should know in a few months, but it may take twenty-five years for him to acquire essential experience for a top-level position. Learning a skill requires practice and the development of generalizations about good practice on the basis of both theoretical and practical experience.

Manager development, then, is possible if the man has the intelligence and the desire to make the best use of his learning opportunities; if he is well trained in what he should be doing in each successive position; and if he practices management with insight and growing skill. Unless this comprehensive view of development is grasped, enterprise managers are likely to settle for unsatisfactory scraps of training—and continue to wonder why training doesn't pay.

---

[1] Opinions vary concerning the proportion of science and art in management practice. The educated guesses vary from 20 to 30 per cent science, at this time, with every prospect of increasing this proportion as research in management expands.

The ultimate objective of training is to encourage the development of men in whom others have confidence. Stockholders and directors want a president who can be relied upon to guide the firm in the best interests of the owners. Subordinates of the president want a superior they can trust. Confidence rests upon the security which men of judgment can provide. Manager training is an effort to bolster knowledge and experience in the interest of developing judgment. Indeed, knowledge and experience, whether acquired in school or by practical pursuits, are the whetstones upon which natural intelligence is sharpened.

CURRENT APPROACHES TO MANAGER TRAINING

Executives who have given thought to manager training have displayed considerable ingenuity in devising ways of achieving results. Some have relied exclusively on certain favored methods, while others have combined any promising approaches that appeared to fit their needs. The following analysis of the more prominent techniques describes their merits and shortcomings.

Planned Progression The technique of planned progression is concerned with blueprinting the path of promotion that lies before the manager in any given position. Sometimes the path is traced through the successive levels of the functional organization structure. Thus, the foreman may be told that his path will lead to general foreman, superintendent, works manager, and production manager. Or the supervisor in the sales department may be informed that his path of promotion lies through branch manager, district manager, and assistant general sales manager to sales manager. This, however, gives an overoptimistic picture to the subordinate; it encourages undue specialization; and it provides insufficient training.

There is, however, a concept of planned progression with proved merit. A committee, responsible for developing candidates for promotion, can settle in conference the alternate positions into which a man occupying a given post may be promoted. Thus, three or four positions at the next higher level in a number of different departments may be specified. If this progression *into the next higher level* is worked out for *each* candidate, the advantages are obvious. The superior who is asked about promotion opportunities will have a definite answer to give; the alternatives are broad enough to provide for needed diversity of experience; and the candidate can be informed with some exactitude about the requirements of the next alternative positions and the most appropriate means of achieving them. From the psychological point of view planned progression has the merit of being geared to immediate rather than distant opportunities.

Job Rotation Few terms are as common in management literature as "job rotation," and it is safe to say that few are as misunderstood. In general, job rotation refers to a technique according to which men receive diversified training. But the questions are: Who is to be trained? Why? At what levels?

Those concerned with the answers seem to have one or more of five potential situations in mind.

Rotation in nonsupervisory work Firms that confine job rotation to nonsupervisory work visualize the process as one in which selectees for training are assigned to predetermined jobs within several departments for a given period of time. At the end of each stage, the selectees are reshuffled among the same group of jobs until all have had diversified experience. The trainees may learn how to sell, receive and mark merchandise, recruit and interview applicants, read blueprints, and write bills of materials. There are long lists of such jobs to be selected for their experience value and in which trainees will quickly earn their way. The evident purpose is to acquaint trainees with the range of activities undertaken by the firm.

There are, however, several serious disadvantages to this type of job rotation. The trainee being groomed for supervisory work can learn the details of these work assignments in a short time, and keeping him on such jobs for weeks and months will add nothing to his progress. In fact, the actual selection of work for its experience value is extremely difficult. Furthermore, after the trainee has been rotated through the series of jobs, no one can guarantee him a supervisory position. If none is available, he is likely to leave the firm in discouragement. Or if a permanent opening occurs before he has completed the cycle, should he accept and thus miss the remainder of the program, or should he refuse and take his chances on a later opening? The first alternative fails to achieve the purpose of training; the second risks losing out entirely. Finally, the departments offering the training may object to bearing the allocated salary expense; and other employees, jealous of the opportunity provided trainees, may resent what they consider taking jobs away from the permanent help.

Rotation in observation assignments A second concept of job rotation allows trainees to observe a group of department managers on a rotating basis. Its purpose is to acquaint the trainee with the work of department heads. For the trainee, the advantages of this method include acquaintance with various techniques in handling diverse situations, the possibility of "selling" one's self to a given manager, and an opportunity to get a close-up of the work one thinks one wants to do. The firm, on the other hand, considers that it has developed a pool of potential managers.

There are disadvantages, however. Many department heads feel that the trainee does not know what to observe, that it is wasteful to watch the decision-making process in so many situations, and that the training expense should not be borne by the departments. As far as the trainee is concerned, there is a great gap between watching and doing, and there is a question whether he will be able to apply anything he has observed. This concept of job rotation, therefore, lacks the basic ingredient of practical experience.

Rotation among managerial training positions A third concept involves the designation of certain managerial positions, on the same level in the organization structure, as training stations, to be successively occupied by selectees. Although the positions are a regular part of the organization structure of the enterprise and, consequently, bona fide managerial posts, they are filled solely by successive trainees and not by promotion from lower-level jobs. The purpose of this type of job rotation is to give trainees actual supervisory experience in a variety of positions in several departments.

There are two evident advantages of this type of rotation. First, the trainees obtain actual experience in managing, an important matter since it is the only known means of discovering whether they have leadership ability and good judgment. Secondly, the trainees develop an appreciation of the viewpoints of various departmental personnel and acquire, as well, an understanding of interdepartmental relationships.

The disadvantages of any plan to rotate trainees among predetermined supervisory positions include the difficulty of identifying appropriate positions for this purpose; the resentment of subordinates because these jobs are reserved for management trainees; and the frequent delay in making permanent assignments to those who have completed their training.

In deciding which supervisory posts may be appropriately reserved for training purposes, the value of the experience to be obtained must be weighed in the various departments and some post found in which turnover would be rather unimportant. How long it will take a new man in these positions to become productive seems to depend upon the degree to which the department activities are standardized, the presence of experienced subordinates, and the stability of the operation. Posts that fit these requirements might include the supervision of accounts payable, personnel recruitment, production follow-up, and the requisitioning of raw materials.

No matter how much publicity is given the training program and the jobs reserved for training, it seems impossible to eliminate the resentment of qualified subordinates who are passed over when such positions are filled by trainees. The young and capable subordinate is almost certain to leave the firm in protest; the older subordinate, who would find openings elsewhere scarce, harbors a smoldering resentment against the trainees. Only the routine nature of the operation keeps it from disintegrating in hostility.

Finally, this type of rotation suffers from the disadvantage of all pool arrangements: those who complete their training are eager to be placed permanently; disillusion grows greater the longer the period of waiting.

Rotation in middle-level "assistant" positions There are firms that conceive of job rotation as the process of shuffling managerial trainees among positions as assistant managers in several departments. The advantage for the men involved is the broadening of their experience at a high level. The firm gains from the creation of a pool of trainees for later appointment to department managerships.

As with other types of rotation, this does not solve the difficulties of permanently locating a man whose training is complete. It also creates considerable resentment among subordinates in the several departments. The most serious disadvantage concerns the type of training received. There is a good deal of difference between being a high-grade messenger or observer and making analyses and decisions for department managers. Clearly, if the "assistant" position involves the latter kind of experience, it is valuable training.

Unspecified rotation in managerial positions By resorting to an unspecified, and often unplanned, rotation of managers, some companies have effectively used job rotation without encountering the difficulties enumerated in the alternative approaches outlined above. These companies make it a practice to move promising managers from one department or activity to another. These are often lateral rather than vertical moves and are made in the spirit of giving the manager a "permanent" job. Thus, a manager in the production department may be offered a position in sales and, later, one in finance or on an important staff. In each of these changes the manager is given no indication as to how long he will be in the job, and there is usually no specified time actually in the minds of those responsible for his training. The manager may be in the position for several years, and if he does not show promise of growth he may not be rotated further.

The purpose of this kind of program is to give managers responsible continuing experience in a variety of situations. It avoids the feeling, so prevalent in most kinds of job rotation, that the incumbent is on a visit. It likewise avoids making him look to his fellows like a "crown prince." And it eliminates the dangers and costs of reserving special managerial positions for training purposes. Indeed, this type of informal program appears to be the most effective kind of managerial job rotation.

Creation of "Assistant-to" Positions The "assistant-to" position, frequently used as a training device, permits the trainee to broaden his viewpoint by exposing him to many areas of managerial practice. This technique should be by no means routine. The position may have been specially carved out for training purposes and may be eliminated after it has served this purpose. However, many needed and permanent "assistant-to" positions exist and are valuable posts for training.

The advantage of "assistant-to" positions from the viewpoint of the superior is that he can most satisfactorily exercise his function as a teacher, tailoring the training period to the assistant's needs and making assignments to test his judgment. Facets of his experience that need buttressing can be filled out by carefully chosen tasks, and his decision-making and leadership ability can be tried in selected cases.

The disadvantage of this type of training procedure becomes apparent when the superior executive fails to teach properly. If he lacks understanding of the assistant's needs, if he is authoritarian, or if he feels that he is being pushed into this relationship, the training will certainly be poor and the trainee's position is likely to degenerate into a reviewing stand. Attention soon flags in repetitive exposure to activity in which the observer is charged with no duty. Able assistants, placed in such an environment, would soon be lost to the firm.[2]

Psychological Approaches to Training   During the past decade social scientists,[3] particularly psychologists, have been active in training experiments using two basic techniques, role playing and the unstructured discussion.

Role playing   This technique is commonly applied by clinical psychologists since they discovered that a patient appears to gain understanding of an emotionally disturbing situation when encouraged to act out roles involved in that situation. As applied in enterprises with (we hope) normal people the purpose of role playing is to aid trainees to understand certain business problems and enable observers to evaluate various reactions to them. Thus, for the problem of handling grievances, two individuals from a class would be selected to act out the parts of employee and supervisor. When this situation is enacted by various pairs among the class and the techniques and results are discussed, the auditors are presumed to reach conclusions about the most effective means of handling similar situations.

There are several obvious drawbacks to this technique. It is not possible to recreate the environment of the work situation. The roles played have no necessary relation to actual practice, and, consequently, the players feel no practical *responsibility* for handling their roles realistically. Also, the technique is not subject to validation. On the other hand, it is an interesting device that may have some value in broadening the viewpoints of the participants.

Unstructured discussion   This technique, with its variations, is based upon the experience of group psychotherapists that people with mild emotional disturbances can be helped through the device of group discussion. It has apparently been successful in the rehabilitation of war prisoners, delinquents, and alcoholics, and its practitioners believe that it can be successful in leadership and sensitivity training. The latter is well known in academic circles and some large enterprises. Subjected to it, individuals become involved in a cathartic group experience which presumably results in self-knowledge and insights into interpersonal relationships. Out of this strong emotional experience one is supposed to gain an awareness valuable to his future behavior.

Since psychologists deal with people, their training activities have piqued the interest of human beings, which probably accounts for the great popularity of their techniques. As for sensitivity training, a wide variety of

[2] See L. F. Urwick, *Profitably Using the General Staff Position in Business*, General Management Series No. 165 (New York: American Management Association, 1953), and C. O'Donnell, "The Role of the Assistant: A Modern Business Enigma," *California Management Review*, vol. 2, no. 3, pp. 65–69 (Spring, 1960).

[3] See I. L. Heckmann, Jr., and S. G. Huneryager, *Human Relations in Management* (Cincinnati: South-Western Publishing Company, 1960), pp. 748–753.

opinions of its value and place in management development may be found. Many participants claim tremendous benefits, particularly in understanding their impact on others. Other participants have reported virtually no benefit. And lasting benefits, especially if the participant returns to his pretraining environment, do not appear to be great. However, for those who understand, preferably in advance, what to expect and who can enter into this experience without too great a traumatic effect, it has often proved to be an interesting device. But still too little evidence exists to weigh it adequately as a management training tool.

Temporary Promotions   Although many firms may occasionally resort to temporary promotions, the use of this technique for training purposes entails difficult problems of organization. The large firm that desired to train a group of candidates by this method would need to make certain that a given number of departments or sections would be without a permanent head or that this position could be vacated on schedule, an arrangement obviously impossible. Nor would it be possible to assess personal responsibility for the conduct of departmental affairs.

On the other hand, the medium-sized and the small firm may find temporary promotion an ideal way to train a candidate. Since training in such firms is necessarily discontinuous, the man tapped for future greatness may very well be moved up to acting head when the permanent head is temporarily absent. The candidate would then presumably be responsible for departmental conduct during this period of service.

Certain drawbacks are inescapable. Is it possible to hold a man responsible for the conduct of a temporary position? Can the performance of a temporary appointee be evaluated? A large degree of drift or procrastination is permitted the occupant of any managerial position surrounded by well-known and tested policies and procedures. Furthermore, the attempt of a candidate to do something different, such as to reverse a previous decision or to introduce new working relationships, is quite unlikely to be productive of good results. If expectations are moderate in view of these limitations, temporary promotion can be useful, but it is much inferior to the real test of a permanent appointment.

Committees and Junior Boards   When used as a training technique, the committee and the "junior board" have come to be known as multiple management.[4] These committees are composed of a group of middle-level managers, selected on the basis of merit ratings, who meet regularly to consider any proposal affecting the firm's welfare. Decisions reached by these "idea men" are forwarded to the responsible general officer of the firm, who may adopt, reject, or table them, refer them back for further consideration, or send them

---

[4] The original idea is commonly credited to McCormick and Company, Inc., Baltimore. See Charles McCormick, *Multiple Management* (New York: Harper & Row, Publishers, Incorporated, 1938).

to the board of directors. The advantages claimed for this type of training are that the perspective of the committee members is broadened and a sense of responsibility for the welfare of the firm is developed.

Where this technique has been used there have been strong overtones of paternalism exercised by senior officers, despite loud protests of noninterference. One cannot afford not to interfere when he designates the persons receiving the training, evaluates their deliberations, and promotes from among them. Perhaps they can "afford" to devote an enormous number of man-hours to the solution of issues involving these skills, especially when the candidates are investing their own time.

There is, of course, universal recognition of the value a manager may gain from membership on a regularly established company committee. The new junior man is soon likely to be placed in one or more of these groups. Here he acquires a broader viewpoint, develops an understanding of enterprise needs and purposes, and gets experience in leadership. But this is in the ordinary course of employment; it is not in any sense extracurricular.

Conference Programs Another widely used training device is that of conference programs. This consists of group exposure to ideas developed by a leader or speaker. It is a direct and economical method of transmitting information that applies to all members of a group. Thus, a class of junior trainees or a new foreman group may be effectively instructed in the history of the firm, its purposes and policies, and its attitudes toward customers, employees, consumers, and other groups.

It is easy to overestimate the values derived from conference training. Its employment represents the adoption of time-honored teaching techniques and its failure often follows poor teaching methods and a lack of understanding of what can be taught by this means. It is as wrong to assume that any manager can teach in such conferences as to believe that any teacher can manage.

University Management Programs In recent years many universities have organized courses, institutes, conferences, and rounded formal programs for the training of managers. These efforts may be as simple as offering an evening course for management students and as complex as offering a full graduate curriculum. The purposes vary from a refresher course in new techniques to instruction in the nature and principles of management.

Such programs present opportunities for the exposition of management principles, a review of these principles in the light of practical experience, and explanation of new ideas with possible application to the firm. There is the added advantage of valuable group contacts. All these values can be important to the efficiency of individual managers.

The drawbacks of university management programs are related to the quality of the instructor and of the subject matter. Businessmen, in their eagerness to learn, are often misled by extravagant claims. Unless those who teach in these programs *really* know what managing is, the "training" is all too likely to degenerate into social clubs or the teaching of specialized skills in engineering, accounting, statistics, or other areas.

American Management Association's Workshop Program   The educational efforts of the American Management Association include workshop or seminar instruction in an unusually wide variety of subjects. In most instances, the particular subject is narrowly defined so that it can be handled effectively in one to three days. Classes are confined to a limited number of participants, and the discussion method is employed to facilitate interchange of varied experiences. The leader of each workshop is usually an operating business executive who, presumably, possesses both experience and teaching ability.

The advantages of such training are knowledgeable leadership, cooperative learning through the exchange of ideas with experienced managers, and concentration upon a limited subject. The program has certain disadvantages, however. Most of the sessions are held in a few large cities, and it is therefore difficult for many managers to attend. Another weakness arises from the concentrated attention to restricted problem areas presented from the viewpoint of "how to do it" and the failure to generalize on the basis of principles applicable to all enterprises.

In summary, let us reflect upon the wide variety of approaches and subject matter offered under a heading such as "management training." Do the "trainers" really know what they are doing, or are they simply taking advantage of the willingness of enterprises to pay for anything called "training"? The authors of this book are not the only ones who raise this question. After a decade of sending forth their managers to be "trained," top executives are beginning to ask for a demonstrable payoff from the training dollar. They have paid huge sums to get their men registered in anything called "training," and it is time to consider whether they are getting their money's worth.

It would appear, from nearly two decades' experience with training schemes, that there is a need for development of a philosophy of management. This philosophy should rest on principles from which there can be projected specific kinds of opportunities which should be made available to men wanting to be managers or wanting to improve their management skills. The satisfactory development of such principles is much to be desired.

MANAGEMENT TRAINING: SUGGESTED PROGRAM

In formulating a training program, there are certain elements of which we have some knowledge: purpose, general premises, the nature of positions at various levels, past experience in training, and the nature of man himself. Building upon these is precarious, because no theory of learning is generally accepted. Still, there is a pressing need to examine this matter as comprehensively as possible, for managers must manage even while theorists theorize.

Purpose   One reason for the dissatisfaction managers feel for training programs is that the *over-all* purpose is rarely clarified.

The major purpose of training should be the creation of opportunities to develop skills directly related to the execution of the managerial functions. They are acquired through study and through the practice of management—the application of learning to experience in solving problems of planning, organizing, staffing, directing, and controlling.

Premises   Clarity of training method is served by a specific exposition of the basic facts or assumptions on which a program rests. The validity of the training program which follows rests on seven premises.

Top managers must actively support the program   The support of top managers, such as presidents and executive vice-presidents, is essential if a program is to apply throughout the firm at all levels. Effective training in engineering, finance, or other single divisions can be provided, but the needs of the enterprise as a whole are not satisfied unless the program is generally available. Subordinates at all levels look to their superiors for signals as to what to support enthusiastically and what to ignore. If the superiors' signal indicates understanding and support of a training program, it will be actively embraced by subordinates.

Top managers must be trained first   In order for top managers to prove their interest in the program, demonstrate their willingness to learn, and know the content of the program, training should start at the top. Top managers who are opposed to this are in a poor position to encourage training. And yet it may be too optimistic to expect company presidents to submit to training; those who have reached their position without a comprehensive philosophy of management are almost sure to feel that training is probably unnecessary, especially for themselves. Thus, the best that can be expected is that their more or less immediate subordinates will take kindly to the exercise. When top managers reporting to the president have had theoretical training in management principles, there is no problem, for they are certain to support a feasible program. However, when they have not had such training, they should certainly be exposed to it prior to implementing the program at lower levels. Only then will their support be characterized by understanding and vigor. Awareness must precede action.

Learning is voluntary   Since there is no generally accepted theory of learning, this premise must be qualified. Some psychologists feel that learning occurs through emotional experience, as on the level of fear. For instance, many of us can remember our refusal to learn to swim, but, on being thrown into the water, we learned—involuntarily, as it were—because of our fear of drowning. Similarly we, as all animals, learn through instinct, unstudied observation, or chance.

However, these basic motivations have little to do with the learning processes of an enterprise manager. Even clarity and brilliance in teaching won't make a man learn; you can lead him to class, but you can't make him think.

Training needs vary with manager levels On an organization chart, managers are classified by levels. Top management usually includes the general managers and their immediate line and service subordinates. Thus, in a functionally organized firm, the top managers would include the president and the heads of functional divisions such as marketing, manufacturing, engineering, finance, and accounting. At the other extreme are front-line supervisors—managers on the lowest administrative level, who stand between their superiors and the technicians. Between these two clearly defined levels stand the inchoate middle managers who may occupy one or more levels of management.

The training needs of these three groups are somewhat different. The front-line supervisor must learn to carry out efficiently the programs allotted to his shop or section; the middle managers, having been supervisors, stand to benefit most by learning management theory; and the top managers, who are candidates for general management positions, need a broader and deeper understanding of the firm and its environment as well as the theory and techniques of management.

Training needs determine methods Training needs should be satisfied optimally, and the methods chosen should be most effective for the purpose. Therefore, the needs of the three levels of managers should be specifically identified and the most economical and precise method of fulfilling them selected.

Methods must work at all levels It will not do for training methods to be ineffective for front-line supervisors but effective for middle managers. Such spotty results would endanger not only the program but the firm and make impossible promotion from within. Managers should develop through effective training at each successive level to become prime candidates for promotion.

Theory and practice must go hand in hand Learning what a manager does, does not make a manager. It is one thing, in halls of learning, to suggest that managers should make subordinates happy, that authority relationships should be turned upside down, or that subordinates must sometimes revolt against the formal organization. Academicians can do this, because they have no responsibility for results. It is also one thing to demonstrate budget making and to lecture on a philosophy of management. It is quite another to demonstrate proficiency in management when theory is applied in actual environments calling for the attainment of business goals.

This takes meaningful practice, for which theoretical training is no substitute. Consequently, training is a coin, one side of which is the teaching of theory and the demonstration of techniques, the other, the actual practice of management.

THE PROGRAM ITSELF

Based upon the foregoing premises, a practical program can be constructed for providing learning opportunities for aspiring managers at the front-line, middle, and top-management levels and—within each of these categories— for individual managers to satisfy specific personal requirements.

Front-line Supervisory Training Candidates for front-line supervisory positions and incumbent supervisors who have not been trained need the same kind of training.

Objective Men must be trained to develop and carry out approved programs within a budget, to obtain and use service and staff help, and to meet the requirements of their superior managers. In each category they need special information about the firm, the division, the department, and the section.

Programs are needed wherever supervisors are found, whether it be in scheduling, engineering drawing, area sales and service, record keeping and financial reporting, servicing delinquent accounts, or operating a purchasing program. Every supervisor must accomplish certain activities such as recruiting, training, and motivating subordinates; providing for adequate space and equipment; integrating operation rates with the requirements of other departments; selecting and training a successor; reporting progress and anticipating trouble; carrying out the provisions of the labor contract; and keeping an eye on public relations.

Technique On-the-job training by the incumbent supervisor is best, if he has the interest and patience, because no one knows the job better.

From an organizational point of view, there is great merit in having a special training slot created and titled "assistant to the supervisor,"[5] and the trainee moved into this position. This has the advantages of cutting off his responsibility for technical assignments, permitting full attention to the learning process, and keeping him available for instruction.

The training technique recommended here is the time-honored and proved one of explanation, demonstration, practice, and critique. The supervisor explains why an activity is performed, demonstrates it, has the trainee practice it under supervision, and criticizes the performance until it is mastered. This works well with respect to the areas of procedures and poli-

---

[5] For more detail on this suggestion see C. O'Donnell, "The Role of the Assistant: A Modern Business Enigma," *California Management Review*, vol. 2, no. 3, pp. 65–69 (Spring, 1960).

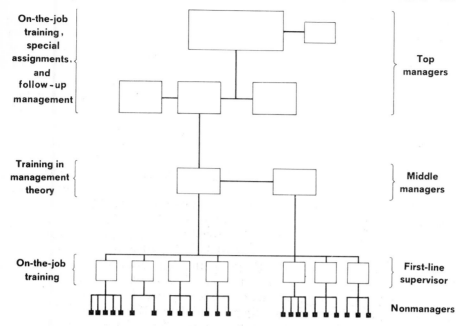

On-the-job training, special assignments, and follow-up management

Top managers

Training in management theory

Middle managers

On-the-job training

First-line supervisor

Nonmanagers

Fig. 23.1 Training Methods for Three Levels of Management . . . *Training for first-line supervision is most often done on the job by operating supervisors who can explain, demonstrate, and criticize. If possible, the trainee should experience all the activities and functions of his future job while in training. After some years of supervisory experience, the same man may be selected for a middle-management position. At this point he should receive thorough training in the theory of management. This can be done effectively in formal training sessions. But when a man at the middle-management level goes into training for a top-management position, the most appropriate training is again on-the-job training, although additional training and refresher work in management theory, principles, and techniques are also required. Such training can often be best accomplished through making the individual an assistant to executives in a wide variety of top-level positions or appointing him to a position in which he performs all varieties of top-level work, though not at the very highest level. The plant manager position, in a company having several plants, is often regarded as a good training ground for future top managers.*

cies, organizational interrelationships, budget formation and other planning activity, control processes, and to some extent the hiring of technicians (skilled nonmanagers). It is less effective in areas of interpersonal relationships, such as effective communication, instruction and motivation of subordinates, and cooperation and competition with peers. Here there is no science, no generally accepted guiding principle. In these areas the supervisor can but explain the techniques which work well for him; he cannot instruct the trainee to go and do likewise, because the techniques are personal, depending partly on character and personality, and may not work for others. The trainee knows that he must communicate, instruct and motivate, cooperate, compete, and perhaps oppose, but his learning will follow from trial and evaluation, followed by correction and more trial and evaluation, until workable techniques result. He will find that even empathy and the golden rule—the best and most generalized guides available for interpersonal relationships—need, at times, to be supplemented by discipline and by strategies of attack and retreat, in order to achieve department goals.

Specific problems Specific problems center on both instructor and trainees. In regard to the instructor, his effectiveness will depend on his ability to teach. If among professional educators teaching ability varies from poor to excellent, among supervisors there will be similar variation. The question is whether the poor teacher should be permitted to instruct. If there is no alternative, the answer must be affirmative and the instruction accomplished under the watchful eye of the supervisor's superior. But in many firms, and especially within divisions of firms where there is no technological barrier, it is a good practice to identify the able instructors among the supervisors and have them train all candidates. This is readily done, for it is almost as easy to train two or three men in "assistant-to" positions as it is to train one.

In regard to trainees, there will be some who fail to learn. These, of course, must be removed from their trainee position and permitted either to return to their former post, to transfer, or to resign. Those who satisfactorily complete training will be ready for assignment as supervisors, but if there are no openings they will be on a stand-by basis which may require them to return to their old jobs. This is far from satisfactory if it involves much waiting, because the men are likely to become restless and to terminate. As a consequence, enterprise managers try to keep the number of trainees at a minimum or to adopt an expansionist policy in order to absorb surplus managers produced by the training program.

Here again is a problem for enterprise managers. When the number of trainees is minimized, technicians who want to manage but have little prospect of being trained are very likely to terminate. This is why college men so often leave their first employer summarily. Again, there are other technicians who do not think they want a management career and who continue in nonmanagement positions until they can go no further. After perhaps ten years of this, they suddenly decide they want to manage. Engineers typically have this experience. The refusal of enterprise managers to train able subordinates is inexcusable. The manager has a moral responsibility to train, or to provide training opportunities, for every *qualified* subordinate, irrespective of number. Why? Because it is a national concern that every man be permitted to develop his socially approved capabilities whatever they may be. And only the enterprise can provide full opportunities for management development.

Practice of supervision At the point where a trainee is assigned to a supervisory position, the practice of management begins. Over a range of time of some several years, the new incumbent practices, with full responsibility for results, what he has learned about supervision and refines his peculiar techniques of interpersonal relationships. His further career depends upon his developed skills, for an unsuccessful supervisor must be removed, demoted, transferred, or terminated; the average performer will be acceptable at the front-line level but will have no promotability; and the outstanding men will become candidates for promotion to middle-management positions.

Middle-management Training The men training to enter the middle-management group are generally supervisors who have had several years of successful on-the-job practice. They will most likely have achieved specified goals in such major matters as production, expense control, budgeting, recruiting, training and directing subordinates, and dealing with peers and superiors. What further development is required of these men?

Objective These men stand most in need of a knowledge of management theory. True, they will have spent a great deal of time developing techniques of direction, achieving teamwork among subordinates, handling grievances, fitting specific skills to program requirements, planning budget proposals, and reporting progress. Thus, on the practical side, there is much about management that they know informally.

Now, when they are about to manage managers and not technicians, they will find themselves removed from close contact with the people who actually do the work. No longer can they rely on technical proficiency to get things done. To manage managers they particularly need an understanding of the functions of managers because these are the means they utilize to accomplish their charters or jobs.

Technique To teach the theory of management, it is best to borrow the effective technique employed for the same purpose in our universities. Basically, this consists of lectures, discussions of theory, and case studies relating to business functions and general management. It is best applicable to groups ranging from ten to forty, and its effectiveness depends on timing, location, and the instructors.

Timing relates to the relative net advantages of live-in courses, in which the participant devotes from a week to three months full time to his training, as opposed to part-time courses, in which instruction is given on an after-working-hours basis. Either type can fail or succeed, and there are variations of the two extremes. The amount of time required obviously depends on the scope of the curriculum, the efficiency of the instructor, and the aptitude of the students. It is probable that sharply diminishing returns will be encountered after three full weeks, even under optimum circumstances, because concentrated and continuous mental effort is fatiguing; there is a limit to what can be learned in a given period of time; and trainees long disassociated from the environment of their firms grow restless and anxious.

The relative quality of results from different course formats is still uncertain.[6] Full-time training permits a participant to concentrate on the intellectual fare, get to know his colleagues, and avoid the daily problems at the plant. On the other hand, material presented too fast to be absorbed is not learned. Weekly exposure to instruction in the same subject matter has the great advantage of permitting trainees the opportunity to think through and perhaps apply what is learned from week to week; it also permits training of men who could not be spared to attend a live-in course.

The location of training sites is largely a matter of convenience and economy. Full-time training, designed to keep trainees away from their employers, often takes place at university or country club locations. The weekly format, designed to keep trainees at their jobs, demands the use of in-plant or reasonably nearby classroom facilities.

The management of the training program may also be either external or internal to the firm. From an economic point of view, the enterprise seeking to train one or a few middle managers will necessarily apply for admission to university-, association-, or consultant-managed courses. There the trainees will mix with those from other enterprises. On the other hand, large firms with many men to be trained sometimes establish their own programs for their exclusive use, using owned or leased facilities and inside or outside instructors. The type of program management does not seem to be critical in terms of results achieved. There are failures as well as successes in both external and internal forms, depending on subject matter and the quality of instruction.

Again, who should teach? Echoes of this question have sounded throughout this discussion of training, because, assuming that proper objectives and subject matter have been selected, the success of any course depends largely on the instructor. Lack of appreciation of this simple point has permitted use of the ill-equipped, the charlatans, the men who simply can't teach, the actors with irrelevant gimmicks. For some reason, it is rare for the astute business managers who pay the tuition to see through these incompetents; they seem to prefer wondering why training is a failure. Surely, it should be obvious that the successful instructor knows his material and teaches it with confidence, skill, and insight, and thereby attracts the attention of his students and inspires them to learn, apply what they learn, and become themselves creative. Such instructors are rare, as every college student knows, but they should be deliberately sought, for they are much more effective in encouraging men to develop than are those chosen solely for books they have written, the school they represent, or convenience.

[6] See R. M. Powell, *The Role and Impact of the Part-time University Program in Executive Education: A Case Study* (Los Angeles: Division of Research, Graduate School of Business Administration, University of California, 1962).

Top-management Training The men to be trained at this level are normally plant and division managers who are candidates for general management positions designated by such titles as general manager, executive vice-president, or president. Assuming that they have had training comparable to that suggested for front-line and middle managers, plus enough years of practical management experience to create an emerging maturity, the problem becomes one of determining their needs for additional training and the best means of providing it.

Objective What additional knowledge should a successful division manager have in order to manage a whole enterprise? Functional managers who have stepped up the promotion ladder within their division—controllers coming up through accounting, sales managers through marketing, engineering directors through engineering—require training in the management of functions which are strange to them. Although a director of engineering may have learned something about accounting, he has no deep understanding of the controller's management problems. The manager of a plant organized on a product-line basis is in an entirely different position. He has functional subordinates reporting to him and thus is already proficient in the knowledge of various functions. However, all potential top managers have some need for training, whether it be in labor relations, in relations with the financial community, trade association work, governmental relations such as negotiation and perhaps lobbying, or foreign relations.

Although it is assumed here that top managers have a substantial grounding in the fundamentals and techniques of management, unfortunately this is not always the case. Moreover, the knowledge and technical aspects of managing are rapidly changing and the perceptive top manager will never assume that his education in management is complete. Consequently, one of the objectives of top-management training must be the review of management theory and principles and the updating of the manager's knowledge of the latest developments in the field. As any top manager knows, not only must he be aware of the changing and developing concepts and techniques in this field, but there is no stronger inducement to his subordinates to learn than the example of those at the top of the organization.

Technique The basic technique recommended is on-the-job training, supplemented by flexible variations depending upon training needs or special situations and upon continuing education in management theory, principles, and techniques through such devices as special seminars and guided reading.

In the case of the functional manager, he should be relieved of his job and should enter a deliberate program of learning the jobs of his peers. Thus, the head of manufacturing needs to understand in depth the operations of marketing, engineering, and accounting. Two alternatives are available: he may be slipped into "assistant-to" positions and receive direct instruction from the department head of each of the functions to be studied for as long as a year per function. Or, as some firms do, he may be placed in direct control of the function to be learned and, for a year, be responsible for its operation. The deficiencies of the latter alternative are that no instruction beyond the superior's normal direction is available, and that it is a rare function which can survive for a year while its head is training elsewhere or which can operate while its trainee-head is learning. Consequently, the first alternative is much the better in terms of quality of results and the continuing efficiency of the functional operation.

If the "assistant-to" device is used, there is the question whether to leave open the old position of the trainee, in anticipation of his temporary return, or to fill it with another and rely on the ability of the firm to absorb the newly trained man in a general management position. The second alternative is recommended, because it would be unwise to have the old position without an active head for the three or four years of the internal training period. And only a prosaic enterprise could live under a program which embodied the rotation of several functional heads.

Training in its external aspects can be most effectively accomplished through special assignments. The trainee may be required to participate in contract negotiation or renegotiation, in union bargaining, in trade association assignments, or he may be sent abroad to survey a market or run a foreign subsidiary. No training could be more effective than this exposure to actual responsibility for operations.

The number of trainees for general management positions would always be small, possibly limited to one or two, occasionally none at all. The actual number at a given time would depend on the needs of the enterprise for available successors or to fill vacant positions. There would be few of these unless a vigorous expansion program were being followed. As a consequence, the dangers of uncertainty and change due to the training program would always be minimal.

If the training program were looked upon as a necessary exercise grudgingly undertaken and happily concluded, its value would be largely lost. Such an attitude would reflect managerial disinterest, and nothing kills an activity faster than executive indifference. Training is a continuing process which lasts a lifetime.

FOLLOW-UP TRAINING

So many executives look upon a formal program as the end of training that it seems necessary to answer the question: After formal training, what should we do? Follow-up training is achieved by coaching, refresher courses, and personal reflection upon the meaning of practical experience.

Coaching As a training technique, coaching begins when a subordinate is promoted to a managerial position. It receives considerable attention at such a time but superiors need to understand that coaching is essential for all subordinates, whether they are titled supervisors, managers, or vice-presidents. Perhaps coaching is most effective when an individual has had other formal or informal training, and in this sense it may properly be looked upon as a follow-up training technique.

Coaching is face-to-face counseling. Its success depends upon the proper combination of personal qualities of superior and subordinate and upon the environment. The superior takes pride in grooming able managers, develops the ability and patience to teach, and delegates authority wisely. The subordinate should have confidence in his superior, be interested in his own work, and analytical in his approach to problems, and should possess the strength of character to use his authority. The environment for successful coaching requires easy access to the superior.

Coaching is a critical process. It involves the *continuous* analysis by both superior and subordinate, on a face-to-face basis, of the latter's performance. Rather than leaving to chance what is learned from experience, the coach makes certain that lessons are learned.

Such counseling is a good way for a subordinate to become oriented in his job. It helps him understand the way his superior looks at interdepartmental relationships and personalities. Analysis of a specific performance gives both superior and subordinate an opportunity to learn why the results were good or bad. The superior can then demonstrate the importance of considering alternative ways and give the trainee some idea of how to weigh intangibles. Particular managerial skills may come up for discussion, covering the gamut of interpersonal relations, leadership, getting things done, and follow-up. Eventually, the trainee will develop a variety of skills and judgment as to when to apply each.

Standardization of counseling techniques is obviously impossible. Blind imitation by one superior of an effective method employed by another gives no assurance of similar results. The superior must use a method effective for *him*, but even this must be varied to fit the different personalities of his subordinates.

Confidence and coaching The belief on the part of the subordinate that his superior has confidence in him is a strategic element in coaching. In such a climate the exchange of information can be extremely valuable. The trainee may even feel that no harm will come to him if he brings bad news. Indeed, the superior can, through expressions of encouragement and confidence, create in the subordinate a feeling that under no circumstances would he disappoint his boss. Many assignments that look too big are carried off by men who "couldn't let their superior down."

The edifice of confidence is very difficult to build up and can be easily impaired or destroyed. It requires immense patience and wisdom. The superior can, through carelessness, ambition, or pressure of other matters undermine this carefully constructed relationship with a frown, a slight, an impoliteness. Or sometimes a weak superior permits a subordinate to exhibit boldness, poor taste, boastfulness, and the appearance of special favor. The dignity of the superior's position is clearly assailed by such behavior.

Maintenance of the correct level of confidence is the responsibility of the superior. If he is an able man, he has two advantages over his subordinates: the authority and tradition of his office and the assurance that rests solidly upon a sense of superior ability.

The superior must act as a superior is supposed to act, according to the traditionally approved behavior patterns of a boss. He is supposed to have an air of success, be a decision maker and a leader, and obey with conscientiousness the mores of society. This means that the superior must be both a moral being, who does nothing to offend his subordinates, and an aggressive, effective manager, who decides issues positively and with wisdom.[7]

The personal dignity of the superior rests upon self-respect. He must earn the respect of his subordinates by his moral courage, his skill as a manager, and his personal attitudes. Whether he is gruff, amiable, or shy is really of no importance, but he must be fair.

Encouraging executives to coach The superior who is sure that training capable future managers is a major service enjoys coaching, but this attitude is difficult to retain because immediacy is given such high priority in business operations. The question is whether the present or the future is more important to the firm. If "there is nothing about an organization more important than its future,"[8] then superiors should be encouraged to adopt this viewpoint, in which case coaching may well be used as a training technique. Trainees who have been wisely chosen will exhibit unexpected talents in the hands of a superior who takes pride in training executives, who evaluates mistakes in terms of the lessons they teach, and who is content unobtrusively to watch a subordinate use delegated authority to carry out an exacting assignment.

Refresher Courses There is a general feeling that the time devoted to refresher courses should be short—from one day to a week—but there is no consensus about subject matter. The views on this phase of training vary from "more of the same" through "advanced training" to "group problem solving."

Those who favor the first approach base their case on two reasons. Because they were happy with the results of the original training and have no idea what else could be done, they would like to reactivate the spirit achieved by the original trainees. This position is questionable because diminishing returns might be accompanied by disappointment. Others argue that managers, engaged in pressing daily problems, forget much of what they learned and should have the opportunity, after two or three years, to repeat their training. This position is also ill-chosen, because after a few

---

[7] E. P. Learned, D. N. Ulrich, and D. R. Booz, *Executive Action* (Boston: Division of Research, Harvard Business School, 1951), pp. 53–58.

[8] P. E. Holden, L. S. Fish, and H. L. Smith, *Top-management Organization and Control* (New York: McGraw-Hill Book Company, 1951), p. 4.

years the original trainees are not the same people they were. If they have learned to manage, a repetition of the original training would be a waste of time; if they have not learned, they should be relieved of their position.

The advocates of "advanced training" are often confused. If they wish to extend their knowledge of management, they apparently need only will power to study independently; university libraries and publishers provide what should be read. However, since most people need the discipline of regular classes, this is the main thing this type of refresher course can provide. Sometimes advocates of advanced training are thinking of opportunities to acquire certain technical knowledge omitted from the original training, such as corporation finance, bank relationships, and labor relations. But this is not advanced training; it involves additional technical knowledge to be acquired through college or extension courses, reading, using available services, or employing a consultant.

The enterprise which views refresher courses in terms of group problem solving is usually one whose managers have had original training and which yet is faced with serious problems. Top management of such firms often retreats to a quiet environment for the purpose of reaching a consensus on how to solve their problems. On their return, announcements may be made of new or redefined policies or of other decisions, and the firm presumably starts off on a new tack. This technique is excellent if the decisions are within the responsibilities of the men present. Examples include decisions on pricing, recentralization, or the adoption of a budget.

The Vertical Slice For solving problems which adversely affect operating efficiency at all levels, the technique of the "vertical slice" may be effective. A group comprised of all managers—or representatives of all managers, in large firms—from front-line supervisor to division head or company president, meet to identify and solve management problems facing the division or firm, such as lack of cooperation, excessive decentralization, and poor communication. Variations in technique, such as introducing competition between subgroups and insisting on representation from all enterprise activities, may be adopted. But the essential feature of the vertical slice should always be maintained, because it provides all managerial levels with insights into problems and the way others see them that is difficult to acquire in other ways.

The disadvantages of the vertical slice include fear of repercussions caused by the presence of superiors and, especially, fear of group criticism, both of which may lead to innocuous discussion. Furthermore, managers at different levels view situations differently; and untenable positions may be taken too early as a result of limited knowledge of situations. On the other hand, the advantage of multilevel exchange of views can be marked. Communication can be facilitated. Once the whole problem is seen, effective solution is made easier. This advantage can outweigh the disadvantages if the members of the vertical slice consider problems and not personalities. Not that people can be overlooked, for the sessions will make clear who are the effective managers and who are merely part of the problem; action on the latter can be taken later by the appropriate superior. Nor is it possible to wave a wand and eliminate status, for admonitions to do so and adoption of the artifice of first names are childish and impractical measures. But the concerted determination to stick to issues is the mature way to reap the advantage of the vertical slice.

SPECIAL PROBLEMS IN TRAINING AND DEVELOPMENT

Undoubtedly there are several practical problems that are not easily solved through the device of three-level training as described above. They certainly would include time-in-position, integration of managers acquired through mergers and purchases, and improving the accountability of managers for the training and development of their subordinates.

Time-in-position Potential as well as operating managers are often concerned about this problem. It is typical that the person who wants to be a manager is first assigned to technical jobs that are quite unrelated to the managing process. They may wait a long time before they are promoted to supervisory positions because no openings occur. These same people know that if they do not get started up the promotional ladder before they are thirty, they probably will not make it at all.

Under these circumstances, it is essential for the top managers of the enterprise to assess their needs for new supervisors and to develop some tangible means of letting potential candidates know that they are important in the firm's future. The former problem was discussed in Chapter 20. A variety of approaches suggest themselves in communicating the need for managers. Certainly, it is important to carve out for these men a scope of work that is challenging and important. In these days, when future managers are most likely to be well-educated people, it is wasteful and humiliating to assign routine and menial work. The candidate with potential will not wait around to be claimed by the future. Neither will he respond positively, unless he is given a responsible job as soon as he is ready for it and is held accountable for its performance. Superior managers must not hold back because the candidate is young or make excuses about his unreadiness. On the other hand, it is really notorious that the restless want prompt promotion, while there still is much they need to learn about their present job. This issue is best joined through the coaching process: readiness is a vague concept and two-way communication about it is the best means of reaching an understanding.

Some business, government, and other enterprises are experimenting with the technique of positively identifying potential candidates and providing some distinct training opportunities prior to their selection for front-line training. For instance, a cadre of potentials may be developed through a careful recommendation and screening process. These men may be exposed to a two- or three-day orientation, at which time they are addressed by high-level managers who tell them the needs of the enterprise for managers, the philosophy of management adhered to, the details of the program, and the bases for their own selection. Special programs, task forces, and challenging assignments are created for training purposes, although most often these are entirely productive activities. Most of the time, the special work is simply added to the regular assignments of the candidates; sometimes they may expect to be sent away to carry out special assignments. From among those who profit by this training, and still want to become supervisors, all selections are made. Thus, the group is a select one about which a good deal is known; the risks of making a mistake in selecting front-line supervisors is considerably reduced. Certainly, the men in the group like this approach; and, equally certainly, the superior managers who want to promote a favorite employee are considerably restrained. It is quite probable that, in large enterprises where many appointments are annually made at the supervisory level, this technique will prove very rewarding.

Time-in-position is also a concern to middle and top managers. The able and ambitious man who works for a superior who, for one of many reasons, is not promotable is in a frustrating position. So also is the man who is ready for promotion but has no opening to aspire to. The time that these men spend in a particular position can be unreasonably long. The only real solution is for the top managers to promote an expansionary program that will absorb the energies and satisfy the ambitions of these able people.

Integration of Managers Inherited from Acquisitions This is a pressing problem for those firms that grow through mergers, purchases, and consolidations. In the case where the acquisition was a profitable one, the best practice is to leave in place the managers who brought the firm to this desirable state. However, if the firm has not been successful, or if it has been merged or consolidated, there are always difficult problems relating to the newly inherited managers. Sometimes they come as part of the package deal; sometimes jobs are created for them. Over all, the experience of firms with this kind of problem is that most of these managers will be replaced sooner or later. The few who are retained have important potential, and these are not difficult to integrate. They catch up quickly in the training programs of their new employer; they absorb the new management philosophy without trouble.

Accountability for Training Superior managers *are* accountable for the training of their subordinates, though, in many institutions, one would not suspect it. Too often the practice is to assign training to someone else and ignore the whole event. One way to give encouragement for the training of subordinates is to hold managers strictly accountable and let their accomplishment be appraised as part of the regular program of measurement. Men readily attend to goal achievement if they know it will be appraised, and subordinates more easily identify with superiors if the latter take a personal interest in their development. Another, and more subtle, way is to involve middle and top managers in the in-plant training programs. These can be readily structured in such a way as to provide opportunities for operating managers to instruct through such devices as case histories, incidents, and illustrations of the applications they have made of management principles. This technique has a high payoff value. The manager takes great pride in doing well, he gets to know the group of subordinate managers in the conference, and they likewise get to know their superiors.

MEASUREMENT: THE TRAINING PAYOFF

As was mentioned earlier, there has risen a question among firms about the productivity of training programs. Specifically, executives want to know whether they are repaid for the expense of classroom training. And well they might, for the quality of training has not been high. Logically, a case can be made for the right kind of training; the question is, does it really pay off?

At this stage in our knowledge it must be confessed that no one knows. In fact, training is in somewhat the position of basic research. Does basic research really pay, and if so, how much? Over all, we may not be sure, but we are convinced that it must be undertaken. So with training. This area requires concentrated attention to creating a means of measurement. There are many instances where managers credit improvement in their skill to their training, but it is really not possible to generalize these views, for who can assign specific credit for a skill that may be an end product of personal aptitude, logic, imitation, and pressures in the environment, as well as of exposure to formal discussion?

SUMMARY OF MAJOR STAFFING PRINCIPLES

Although no generally accepted principles of staffing have, as yet, been codified, careful consideration leads to the following formulations underlying the purpose and means of staffing.

The Purpose of Staffing   The purpose of staffing can be summarized in the following principles:

Principle of staffing objective   The objective of managerial staffing is to assure that organization roles are filled by personnel able and willing to occupy them.

Principle of staffing   The better the clear definition of an organizational role and its translation into human requirements and the better candidates and incumbents are evaluated and trained, the more the quality of personnel can be assured.

The first principle stresses the fundamental importance of desire and ability to undertake the responsibilities of management. There is understandably a good deal of evidence that failure in managerial assignments results when these qualities are lacking. The second principle rests upon an important body of knowledge concerning management practices. Those firms which fail to establish the requirements for job definition and the appraisal and training of managers are forced to rely upon coincidence or outside sources for able managers. On the other hand, management succession is no problem for firms that implement the principle of staffing.

The Process of Staffing   A number of principles appear to explain the means by which staffing is most effectively accomplished.

Principle of job definition   Specifications for the job rest on the need for results from plans, the requirements of a clear structure of roles, and the provision for incentives to induce efficient and effective performance.

Principle of managerial appraisal   Complete appraisal of managers requires appraisal of performance in terms of verifiable objectives and in terms of the quality of managing.

Principle of open competition in promotion   If an enterprise is to assure maintenance of the best quality of management, it is necessary to open selection of candidates for promotion to those available both inside and outside the enterprise.

Principle of management development   The more programs of management development aim at improving the abilities of existing managers in their present positions, as well as making it possible for them to be promotable, and the more top managers give example and encouragement through participating actively in the leadership and operation of such programs, the more effective such programs will be.

Principle of universal development   Since management techniques and knowledge and the total environment of managing change constantly, the enterprise that would assure its managerial competence cannot tolerate managers who are not interested in their continuous development.

Since formal organization structure creates roles by establishment of objectives, grouping of activities, specification of authority delegations, and clarification of information relationships, it follows that accomplishment of these activities and exercise of authority should be assigned to department managers. Although this relationship seems obvious, it is often violated, much to the discomfort of the particular manager and of the enterprise itself. Hence, the first step in tailoring the process of staffing to its purposes is to make the organization roles of a department or division consistent with and supportive of objectives. Since organizational roles must be filled by people, it is obvious that built into these roles must be those many elements—such as pay, status, power, discretion, and possibility of accomplishment—that induce people to wish to perform.

The principle of managerial appraisal highlights the fact that an enterprise can hardly wish to have managers who apparently know management but who cannot perform. And, since performers are often "flashes in the pan" or perform well or poorly sometimes because of factors beyond their control, there is danger in having a performer who cannot manage. The best assurance for the future is a person who is both a good performer and a good manager. Therefore, appraisal methods should encompass both areas of a manager's role.

Violation of the principle of open competition in promotion has led many firms to appoint managers whose ability is inferior. Although the social pressures are strongly in favor of promoting men from within the firm, these should be resisted whenever better candidates can be brought in from the outside. Otherwise, it is not possible for the superior to discharge his responsibility to stockholders, employees, and society in general, for these interests cannot be served by mediocrity.

Since many diverse practices are undertaken in the name of management development, it is fair to assume that diverse objectives are sought. Management development means one thing: improving the ability of existing managers to perform their functions. As a consequence, it will always be a process of education directed toward overcoming the weaknesses of individual managers as these are identified through the appraisal program.

The principle of universal development may seem unduly harsh, yet the competitive demands upon an enterprise and its social responsibilities are such that it cannot afford to muddle through with managers who have no interest in overcoming their weaknesses and developing themselves. The authors have seen firms in which managers have lacked the desire for competitive effectiveness. Invariably, such enterprises are sluggish, they fall behind their competition, and they fail to measure up to their social responsibilities.

FOR DISCUSSION

1. It has been argued that firms have an obligation to train all employees with managerial potential. Would you agree?

2. What differences do you see in policies to train managers for promotion and to train them to perform better in their existing positions? Should a firm have both policies or choose one of them?

3. Who are the "middle managers" in enterprise? Would you advocate on-the-job training for them? Why?

4. Job rotation is sometimes used as a means of training managers. Does such rotation involve promotion? What gains may be expected from this practice? What difficulties do you see in actually carrying out this policy?

SELECTED REFERENCES

Andrews, K. R.: *The Effectiveness of University Management Development Programs,* Boston: Division of Research, Harvard Business School, 1966.

Bower, M.: *The Will to Manage,* chap. 6, New York: McGraw-Hill Book Company, 1966.

Craf, J. R.: *Junior Boards of Executives,* New York: Harper & Row, Publishers, Incorporated, 1958.

Huse, E. F.: "Putting in a Management Development Program That Works," *California Management Review,* vol. 9, no. 2, pp. 73–80 (Winter, 1966).

Levinson, H.: "A Psychologist Looks at Executive Development," *Guideposts to Executive Growth,* pp. 57–63 (Cambridge: Harvard University, 1956–1965).

Mace, M. L.: *The Growth and Development of Executives,* chaps. 5–8, Boston: Division of Research, Harvard Business School, 1950.

McGregor, D.: *The Professional Manager,* W. G. Bennis and C. McGregor (eds.), chap. 10, New York: McGraw-Hill Book Company, 1967.

Powell, R. M.: *The Role and Impact of the Part-time University Program in Executive Education—A Case Study,* Los Angeles: Division of Research, Graduate School of Business Administration, University of California, 1962.

Tosi, H. L., and R. J. House: "Management Development beyond the Classroom," *Business Horizons,* vol. 9, no. 2, pp. 91–101 (Summer, 1966).

Wilkerson, C. D.: "A Results-oriented Development Plan," *The Conference Board Record,* vol. 3, no. 3, pp. 40–45 (March, 1966).

part five

DIRECTING

To direct subordinates, a manager must motivate, communicate, and lead. Faulty directing can completely nullify all the work that has gone into organizing and staffing the enterprise, and it can make the attainment of objectives called for by plans impossible. The first chapter of this part gives the reader a view of the entire subject and relates directing to the other management functions. In the other three chapters, motivation, communication, and specific techniques of leadership are dealt with in more detail.

Motivation is a difficult subject to approach because the management theorist now is using ideas and discoveries of the sociologist and the psychologist. Chapter 25 gives the reader a useful orientation to the best modern techniques from disciplines primarily outside management. But the authors are of the "management process," or "operational," school and believe that work of any kind ought to be directed at attaining enterprise objectives.

Communication in management is a constant problem. Organized enterprises grow and move at a constantly increasing pace. It becomes more and more difficult simply to keep everybody in management informed of current developments. But communicating with superiors and subordinates so that they really understand can be done effectively. Chapter 26 develops some very useful techniques. To obtain the greatest benefit from them, the most important point to remember is that selectivity is essential. Clear, crisp, precise language is useless if the *content* of the message is not worth communicating.

The final chapter of this part deals with leadership techniques. A good leader evokes zeal and confidence in subordinates. Without this quality, the enterprise may be superbly organized and staffed and may have excellent plans but its performance may be mediocre. Leadership techniques are quite as difficult to grasp as are techniques of communication. They must be treated in abstract language, and their adaptation requires a great deal of native insight on the part of the practitioner.

$45,000 your Income
× .35 tax
———————
225 000
135 00
———————
15,750.00 To Feds

          45,000
        - 15,750
        ———————
        $29,250 what's left

nature of directing

Directing is a complex function that includes all those activities which are designed to encourage subordinates to work effectively and efficiently in both the short and the long run. This function of the executive is difficult. The reason for this is that the manager is dealing with a complex of forces about which little is known and over many of which he has no control.

The student who wishes to examine this function and try to understand it is at a considerable disadvantage. As he looks into the literature on the subject, he is appalled by its volume, the varied claims of truth, the diverse interpretations of the same research data, and the assurance of many writers that their specialty comprises the sum total of "management." The executive looks at the same materials and wonders just what use he can make of them. Perhaps the first step in understanding the nature of directing is to review the purpose of enterprise, the productive factors necessary for achievement, and the nature of the human factor.

THE OBJECTIVE OF ENTERPRISE

Economics is the most advanced of the social sciences and from it we can best understand enterprise. All organized effort is undertaken to produce wealth, a term that includes goods and services. This effort is by no means restricted to business activity; it is also applied to universities, hospitals, associations, and governments. The economist has long looked upon the process of turning out end products as a system (despite the current popularity of this term). The individual or group that conceived the enterprise applied capital, land, and manpower in judicious proportions to the essential activities required to produce a flow of goods or services. The income from the exchange of this flow was applied to the sustenance of the productive factors. This conception comprised a true system of interdependent parts whose proper interactions were essential for survival.

The student will note that the objective of every business is to survive. To do this, it cannot even stand still, let alone decline in vigor. It ordinarily must grow, especially if it is a competitive business. It must also produce goods or services that are in demand, that is, that others want, in a volume and quality and at a price that will keep the firm competitive. The degree to which the objective is attained is the measure of success. The productive factors are the means used to secure the objective. The manager selects them in terms of quantity and quality and maintains them to that degree which is most efficient. This means that the human factor in production must be managed in such a way as to promote its full contribution. Thus, the objective of enterprise is not to provide for the whole life of the employee; but the enterprise will establish an environment that caters to those needs whose fulfillment contributes to the achievement of its objective.

This viewpoint sometimes encourages critics to leap to the conclusion that the human factor is merely a purchased commodity. Nothing is further from the truth. The individual is much more than a productive factor: he is a consumer of the produced goods and services and, thus, he vitally influences demand. He is a member of such institutions as the family, school, business, church, and fraternal associations, and he is a citizen. In these several capacities, he exercises influence that establishes laws which govern managers, ethics which guide his behavior, and a vision of human dignity which is the special contribution of our society.

Nor should the student think of organized enterprise as being an arena for one big boss. Managers are human, too. They manage other managers as well as nonmanagers. It is true that they exercise power over others and that this sometimes leads to forms of exploitation. But this phenomenon is as typical of one institution as it is of another; exploiters are rather evenly dispersed in schools and universities, hospitals, trade associations, churches, and businesses. It is the special virtue of our society that it is concerned about improving man's humanity.

The human factor of production is much more than this phrase implies. He is a complex individual with a long series of needs that are often changing. He embodies productive power that is required in any enterprise. The manager's problem is to evoke this power. This is his function of directing. Thus, it simply is not true, as Schein states when he evaluates the implication of the classical school's view of man, that "Management's responsibility for the feelings and morale of people is secondary."[1] Quite the contrary; managers are very much concerned about human feelings and morale. Management is not a one-way street; all of us have superiors. It is human to be more concerned about one's own feelings than about others', but a manager cannot achieve his objectives if he treats his subordinates as

[1] Edgar H. Schein, *Organizational Psychology* (Englewood Cliffs, N.J.: Prentice-Hall, Inc., 1965), p. 49.

a commodity. The manager, in the interests of his job, cannot be held responsible for the total care of subordinates. He is held responsible, however, for exercising such care as will encourage subordinates to contribute fully to enterprise objectives.

THE HUMAN FACTOR

In applying the objective and inanimate land and capital factors of production, managers have developed a great deal of skill. Guided first by economists, and later by such specialists as industrial engineers, financiers, and technologists, they have learned much about the nature of these resources, and they have been able to estimate accurately the cost-output relationships. The human factor has remained largely an unknown element of production. It was utilized, nonetheless, because it was indispensable. Managers, as well as other men, held varying views of the nature of man, and these have changed as our knowledge has broadened. It is certain that the managers of all types of enterprises make implicit assumptions about man's nature when they employ the human factor. It is more than probable that, at any time in history, they generally made the same or still other assumptions. Thus, when the economic historians of the industrial revolution reported on the exploitation of labor that was so characteristic of that age, they were observing the end product of implicit assumptions concerning man's nature that were held by the employers of labor. The latter acted as though labor was a commodity. Ancient and modern slave states have always treated the labor factor as a commodity. As time passed, the employers in the great Western tradition have gradually changed their views; since they are a part of a larger society, they have adopted the changing viewpoints of that society. Of course, in any institution there will be different levels of aspiration, and this is true of our own. The creators and innovators are out front, always dissatisfied with "progress." This is as it should be, but one should not assume that the managers of enterprise are the typical laggards.

Managers are not the only people who exhibit implicit assumptions about man's nature. Up to a few years ago, practically everyone who wrote about management also made assumptions that they failed to identify. This was just as true of the philosophers, economists, psychologists, sociologists, and mathematicians as it was of writers who were specifically concerned with the management of organized effort. Indeed, this situation is still typical, although, in very recent years, attempts at clarification have been made.

One of the first to raise the question explicitly was Douglas McGregor. In his well-known *The Human Side of Enterprise*,[2] he set forth—at opposite extremes—two pairs of assumptions about human beings which he thought were implied by the actions of autocratic and permissive managers. It is important to note that these were intuitive deductions and were not based on

---

[2] (New York: McGraw-Hill Book Company, 1960).

any research whatsoever.[3] The autocratic, or "Theory X," manager is presumed to make the following assumptions about his employees:

1. The average human being has an inherent dislike of work and will avoid it if he can.
2. Because of this human characteristic of dislike of work, most people must be coerced, controlled, directed, threatened with punishment, to get them to put forth adequate effort toward the achievement of organizational objectives.
3. The average human being prefers to be directed, wishes to avoid responsibility, has relatively little ambition, wants security above all.

At the opposite extreme the permissive, or "Theory Y," manager assumes:

1. The expenditure of physical effort and mental effort in work is as natural as play or rest.
2. External control and the threat of punishment are not the only means for bringing about effort toward organizational objectives. Man will exercise self-direction and self-control in the service of objectives to which he is committed.
3. Commitment to objectives is a function of the rewards associated with their achievement.
4. The average human being learns, under proper conditions, not only to accept but to seek responsibility.
5. The capacity to exercise a relatively high degree of imagination, ingenuity, and creativity in the solution of organizational problems is widely, not narrowly, distributed in the population.
6. Under the conditions of modern industrial life, the intellectual potentialities of the average human being are only partially utilized.[4]

The experienced teacher will see at once an effective use of the device of comparing extremes. It is an excellent technique by which to make a point. The harm that it does is to leave the clear impression that managers *are* Theory X practitioners and that they *ought* to be Theory Y adherents. Actually, these are straw men set up to be attacked or approved. In the real world of institutional management, it would be most difficult to find a manager who was all one or the other. Managers do not hire "average" men: they employ individuals. The more definite their accountability, the more care they will exercise in utilizing the factors of production—human factors included. In fact, they employ all degrees of direction and control, depending upon the nature of the subordinate, for in the end they want the full effort of employees.

Following the McGregor lead, an increasing degree of attention has been given to the need for a more explicit statement of assumptions about man. Inevitably and properly, more detailed analyses have been made. For instance, Schein[5] sees four conceptions of man in the order of their historical

---

[3] *Ibid.*, Preface, p. vi.
[4] *Ibid.*, chaps. 3, 4.
[5] Schein, *op. cit.*, pp. 49–63.

appearance. The assumptions which are deduced from the concept of a rational economic man are:

1. Man is primarily motivated by economic incentives and will do that which gets him the greatest economic gain.
2. Since economic *incentives* are under the control of the organization, man is essentially a passive agent to be manipulated, motivated, and controlled by the organization.
3. Man's feelings are essentially irrational and must be prevented from interfering with his rational calculation of self-interest.
4. Organizations can and must be designed in such a way as to neutralize and control man's feelings and therefore his unpredictable traits.

To this list Schein adds the McGregor deductions about the assumptions of the Theory X manager.

Schein does not say who, specifically, held these ideas about man, or how he deduced the ideas, or when these ideas were prevalent. It must have been sometime before the Hawthorne studies, because these and others are cited as the basis for conceiving social man. The assumptions about human beings that are implicit in the reports of Elton Mayo and others are said to be:

1. Man is basically motivated by social needs and obtains his basic sense of identity through relationships with others.
2. As a result of the industrial revolution and the rationalization of work, much of the meaning has gone out of work itself and must therefore be sought in the social relationships on the job.
3. Man is more responsive to the social forces of the peer group than to the incentives and controls of management.
4. Man is responsive to management to the extent that a supervisor can meet a subordinate's social needs and needs for acceptance.

According to Schein, there are psychologists—among whom he includes Argyris, Maslow, and McGregor—who believe that the ". . . loss of meaning from work is not related so much to man's *social* needs . . . as to man's inherent need to use his capacities and skills in a mature and productive way."[6] The assumptions which these writers seem to make about self-actualizing man are:

1. Man's motives fall into classes which are arranged in a hierarchy: (*a*) simple needs for survival, safety, and security; (*b*) social and affiliative needs; (*c*) ego-satisfaction and self-esteem needs; (*d*) needs for autonomy and independence; and (*e*) self-actualization needs in the sense of maximum use of all his resources.
2. Man seeks to be mature on the job and is capable of being so.
3. Man is primarily self-motivated and self-controlled.
4. There is no inherent conflict between self-actualization and more effective organizational performance.

[6] *Op. cit.*, p. 56.

Schein's own views about man seem to be embodied in a set of assumptions which he makes about complex man:

1. Man is not only complex, but also highly variable.
2. Man is capable of learning new motives through his organizational experiences.
3. Man's motives in different organizations or different subparts of the same organization may be different.
4. Man can respond to many different kinds of managerial strategies.

Even though it is precarious to lean too heavily on a stage theory of the evolution of ideas about the nature of man, it is nonetheless refreshing to note that research has contributed a great deal to our knowledge. The student should feel that man is less a stranger, but only slightly less; the manager will feel that though he may know men better, they still must be managed.

Gibson[7] has looked at the same problem and reached an essentially similar classification of views about man. With rational-economic man, he equates the mechanistic view; with social man he associates the humanistic view; and with self-actualizing and complex man, he identifies the realistic synthesis. With each group he deduces essentially the same assumption regarding man as Schein. It is significant that both authors seem quite unwilling to build organization theory solely on any of the assumptions attributed to rational or humanistic approaches. The eclectic view, whether it is called rational synthesis or complex man, is preferred.

If one sets out to consider the nature of man, it is quite essential that the whole man come under review. This has not been done by the writers considered above. Man is indeed complex. That part of his nature that seems to be involved in organized effort cannot be studied apart from his own nature without producing a caricature. One cannot manage part of a man; all aspects of his nature are "hired" when he becomes an employee. Not only do all aspects interact, their priorities change quickly and, as yet, largely unpredictably.

In facing up to the problem of describing the nature of man, the authors of this book continue to look for the answer to the musical line: "How do you hold a moonbeam in your hand?" We are not at all sure that the question can be fully or adequately answered; neither are we certain that the best approach has been taken. The concept of man's nature is achieved through the research and observations of many writers. They have seen many aspects, but have they seen all of them? When the aspects that have impressed various scholars are considered, there arises the problem of classification. For our purposes, it has seemed best to describe man's nature as a complex comprised of his animal inheritance, his individualistic-social tendencies, and his spiritual endowment.

---

[7] J. L. Gibson, "Organizational Theory and the Nature of Man," *Academy of Management Journal*, vol. 9, no. 3 pp. 233–245 (September, 1966).

The fact that man has evolved from primitive life forms is of over-whelming significance.[8] Man retains all of the aspects of his animal nature. He has a recurring need for food. He considers his safety—the keeping-alive aspect—of first-rate importance. He has a recurring need for sex and group associations. Man is curious and, from this trait, he has occasionally become inventive. Man can be calculating and cunning. In earlier times, he ex-ercised dominance over others whenever he could, but he readily saw that, before the greater power of others, the safest strategy was retreat and/or submission. These may not be considered admirable qualities by the present generation, but they certainly enabled man to survive. The student can readily illustrate each of these aspects with examples from the animal kingdom.

In some ways the dichotomy of individual-social aspects of man's nature may appear to be an unhappy basis for classification. We propose this basis because the difficulties in treating these aspects separately are even more formidable, and because we prefer to look at man as an individual in a social environment. The individual is the paramount factor. He created the social environment and, while he is certainly affected by it, he still remains the prime mover, as he can change it to suit his collective desires.

By the time he became Homo sapiens, man's nature had grown in com-plexity. He still has his inherited rational-emotional structure although the relative importance of the former has risen. But who would doubt, as he looks about him, that we are still largely creatures of emotion? The enlarg-ing role of rationality has made it possible for man to see and to practice the virtues of order which are achieved through discipline. The greatest change in man's nature, as compared with his natural inheritance, lies in his social behavior. As an individual, he yearns for liberty; in his appearance before others he may exhibit pride, dignity, and sometimes character; he is acquisitive in an environment of future risks and if this activity is socially approved; he may be compassionate toward others. Conflicts in loyalties do not bother him and neither does competition; he has learned to live with these contradictions. He has sometimes invented complex forms of com-petition simply to enjoy them, forms which have a strong survival factor in the sense that ever-greater efficiencies may be achieved.

While we may agree with the oft-repeated remark that man is a social animal, we think it is important to inquire into the relationship of group size to personal satisfaction and into the need for solitary retreat. Even be-fore he became "man," he lived in small groups and frequently alone. The eons of time during which he existed in this fashion have left an important imprint on his nature. While man has been able to build large societies and large institutions, he is not always well prepared to live in them or to be a part of them. The stresses and strains of a life lived in close proximity to

---

[8] For the best summary of the implications of evolution to man, see *Scientific American*, vol. 203, no. 3 (September, 1960).

large numbers of people are all too evident in our own times. There is a real question whether man will ever be able to cope with this type of environment.

The spiritual aspects of man's nature seem to be wholly free from his animal inheritance. When he became Homo sapiens, he seemed not able to abide with the thought of mortality. He seemed to draw upon his imagination to provide a solution for his ego-satisfaction. He invented immortality. Often frightened by unknown forces, he invented explanations for them and took to propitiative practices to "bribe" his gods. The tremendous strides that he has been able to make in expanding his knowledge of things and life has certainly reduced his needs for anthropomorphic explanations. But man still has a need for the concept of immortality. It contributes to his sense of well-being not only because he has overcome death itself, but also because he has created a world in which the disagreeable features of this life are overcome. This is powerful medicine for those who suffer from the inequities of this mortal world. Without it, there is reason to believe that many people could not abide in the world about us.

Mankind has superimposed an intelligence upon his animal nature and has succeeded in modifying that nature. His mind and conceptual ability have enabled him to create an imaginative world, to realize a degree of foresight, and to acquire the conviction that the demands of his basic nature can be modified and channeled to such a degree that their satisfaction can indeed lead to his perfection. This view of the nature of man makes it possible to deduce certain conclusions that are of utmost importance to the manager. These may be listed as follows:

1. The individual is the primary concern of man.

   Man looks after himself both in the extremities of life or death and in the modern affluent society. It is he who wants preferment, who wants to win. He may very well enjoy the success of others *after he has achieved,* although his jealous and skeptical nature shows through. True, we do have our unselfish heroes, men who willingly have laid down their lives for others, the wholly unselfish mother, the man who will step aside for the benefit of others. The rarity of these people makes them subject to comment and to award.

2. The individual will work to satisfy the demands of his basic nature if the benefits exceed the costs.

   It is often said that man enjoys work. This is certainly true if the the effort is directed toward satisfying the demands of his complex nature. He is doing this even when he tinkers. As he approaches the point of marginal satisfaction, he scarcely has the will and verve to apply himself to the specific labor *for the same reason.* For instance, he may work at his bench with unusual productivity in order to save time at the end of the day to experiment with a new tool or a new method he has invented. In this view, the objective of work may change for the worker several times a day.

3. The individual can be led.

    Man responds to leadership. He can be persuaded through many devices to take the desired road, but the devices themselves must be selected, tuned, and timed to the individual's need to satisfy his basic nature. Appeals to pride, status, greed, and many other aspects of man's nature are sometimes successful. Ancient armies were led with promises of booty; modern armies would have none of this. The leader must be intuitive in identifying the persuasive device to which another, at a given time, will respond positively.

4. The individual wants to live and work in a social environment.

    This seems to be true most of the time. There is a definite need for solitude, however; sometimes people cannot bear people; many scientists still work best alone. In general, these periods of time are much shorter than those when man desires group associations. Both aspects rest squarely upon man's basic nature. Man may be largely a social animal, but he is not entirely so.

5. The individual helps to create institutions to serve the needs of their memberships.

    There are many needs that man alone cannot satisfy. He can achieve them only through cooperative effort. If they promise a surplus of benefits over costs, he is likely to accept the implied limitations upon his individuality. For these reasons man creates government, educational, religious, health, and many other institutions. His chief problem in large-scale society is to retain his mastery of the institutions he has created and not become their slave.

6. There is no average man.

    Attempts to take the square root of mankind, on the assumption that people are all alike, are bound to fail. People are not all alike. Natures are different and, for the individual, his nature may differ from time to time. Man does not, even as an individual, proceed to accommodate all aspects of his basic nature in the same degree at a given time. He exhibits priorities and these are kaleidoscopic.

7. The individual rises to the challenge of his full capabilities.

    Man is impatient to use his abilities to their fullest extent. He resents the lack of opportunities to apply his knowledge and skills and to shoulder the responsibility for results. He becomes bored working at half speed, with routine. He is curious to learn the maximum level of his capabilities and he wants to operate at this level.

The implications of this concept of the nature of man are especially critical in the management of enterprise. Man is an important factor of production, but he cannot be treated as if he were inanimate. Neither can he be treated solely as rational-economic, or social, or self-actualizing. He is all of these in varying degrees and at varying times. The instability of this complex creature makes it quite impossible to measure his capabilities and apply them on the basis of an exact input-output calculation. The manager is probably better able to approximate such an equation than is most anyone else, as he has more experience in directing the efforts of men. Nevertheless, he would be the first to acknowledge how poorly the job is done. This is why his directing function is often ineffectively executed.

MANAGING THE HUMAN FACTOR

In turning to a more detailed examination of the implications of this view of the nature of man to the management process, it is important to stress that the manager himself possesses as variable and complex a nature as does any of his subordinates. He is part of the problem; he cannot deal as objectively with the human factor of production as he can with land or capital. His spirits rise as he views excellent results; they are depressed by troubles. He brings to work attitudes that are allowed to influence his reactions to events. He is responsible for results and often feels helpless to achieve them. Indeed, the interactions between superior and subordinates are endless, but they must be managed.

It is also important to recall that the aspects of human nature set forth above are those with which the manager is directly concerned. The human being is far more complicated than he appears to be if viewed as a totality described according to the foregoing aspects of his nature. He is a total man, interested in himself, and therefore conscious of the inputs he receives from external factors, such as family, neighbors, schools, churches, unions or trade associations, political associations, and fraternal groups. He cannot divest himself of the impact of these forces as he presents himself before the firm that employs him. He brings within the gate, and within the work situation, a whole man that is only partially motivated by the need to work. What he cannot do is to leave outside the gate the influences, the ambitions aroused, and the means of satisfaction of many of his natural demands that no firm can satisfy. He may be intent upon family formation, the education of his children, the purchase of a house, his candidacy for political office, or his religious life. None of these concerns can be sloughed off as the worker passes through the gate of the employer's premises, even though he enters this gate solely because he needs an income and has contracted to exchange services for that income. Man is a whole man; he is not political man, or social man, or union man, or religious man, or working man. His capability for work is hired by the enterprise, but he brings with him his total nature. His manager must recognize this fact and be prepared to deal with it.

How to deal with this problem has been the subject of considerable discussion during the last ten years. Some psychologists have been so concerned about the problem that they have tended to take the position that the enterprise has an obligation to satisfy the needs of the whole man. This is, of course, untenable on its face. No business firm could live under these requirements. None, especially those who criticize business managers, would accept the manager's decision as to how to provide for family life, political associations, religious ties, and other social necessities of employees. And the firm itself could not maintain its competitive position vis-à-vis those enterprises that are operated on the assumption that the business of business is business.

On the other hand, the manager who thinks and acts as if he is hiring *only* the working man is bound to be inefficient and ineffective. The employee's nature is an indivisible whole. It is also something else: it is a whole within which the establishment of priorities is a viable process. When a man reports for work, he has clearly established an income priority. For the time established by the employer, effort will be exchanged for progress toward achieving the employer's objectives. True, it will not be undiluted effort. It will be affected by the impact of noneconomic influences, but these can be modified to a greater or lesser extent by the leadership ability of the manager.

The Manager Must Act His Part   Exactly because he *is* the manager and thus exercises a superior power position, it is important that the manager first be in command of himself. He should see himself as objectively as possible and act his expected part.[9] In the first edition of this book, the authors expressed this view as follows:

> The superior must act as a superior is supposed to act. Society has traditions of approved behavioral patterns, and the particular role expected of the boss is no exception. He is viewed as an isolated individual who has an air of success, is a decision maker, is an inspired leader, and obeys with unusual conscientiousness the mores of society.[10]

Nothing has occurred to modify this concept in the intervening time. What has occurred is that managers seem to be more conscious of the impact of their behavior on others, and their activities are now undertaken with more circumspection.

Individual arrangements   In view of those aspects of man's nature which bear upon his role as a factor of production, the manager should attempt to create an internal environment that will induce subordinates to work at the

---

[9] Many years ago, D. N. Ulrich, E. P. Learned, and D. R. Booz wrote with deep insight on this aspect of the manager's behavior. See their *Executive Action* (Boston: Division of Research, Harvard Business School, 1951), pp. 53–58.

[10] H. Koontz and C. O'Donnell, *Principles of Management*, 1st ed. (New York: McGraw-Hill Book Company, 1955), p. 379.

level of their full capabilities. Since it is known that the individual is primarily concerned with what happens to him in the work situation, it is important that procedures be established that will cater to him. The selection, appraisal, and promotion processes should be tied in with individual competence. The training should be directed to personal needs. The work assignment should challenge the capabilities of the individual. When personal trust is established, authority to make decisions should be decentralized. Those who want responsibility should have it; those who do not want it should not have it. Salary and perquisites should be related to job responsibility on a personal basis and not on a manager-level basis. The environment that is constructed along these lines will resolve preferment on a competitive basis and will enable the individual to take care of himself along lines that redound to the achievement of group purpose.

Why Men Work Work is effort directed to the accomplishment of some objective. Work is certainly accomplished outside organized enterprise, not only as a requirement for making a living but also as tinkering with no economic end in view. In unorganized activity, a great deal of freedom is often permissible, since the individual can choose not to tinker, not to go to his law office, or not to go to the clinic. The individual is much more restricted when he works for organized enterprise. To make them viable at all, it is necessary to establish rules concerning attendance, hours, place of work, behavior on the job, and what comprises the job itself. Inevitably, the employee feels a loss of freedom. Why, then, do men work in organized enterprises? It must be because this is their best opportunity to make a living. The need for income to purchase scarce, and therefore costly, goods and services requires men to work. Taking stock of their existing knowledge and skills, men will choose—in the United States—to secure income in ways which will achieve their best input-output ratio. This is why doctors may desert a clinic for private practice, scientists will work in industry, and engineers will shift jobs "for ten cents an hour." Since men must work, they will hope to find an environment in which nonmonetary income is also received. They prefer pleasant to unpleasant surroundings, pleasant to unpleasant co-workers, interesting to uninteresting work, recognition to nonrecognition. The essential point is that all of these are in the nature of fringe benefits; all of these could be obtained if they did not work at all. Thus, they do not work *for* these benefits. If they had to, they would work without them, because they need a job that will yield income.

As a manager looks at this aspect of man's nature, he will attempt to satisfy it by paying the value of the employee's contribution (insofar as this can be measured) and by doing his best to provide the fringe benefits in terms of work environment, group size and personality, freedom and encouragement in innovation, and personal recognition, to the extent that these contribute positively to achieving enterprise objectives efficiently and effectively.

The Individual Can Be Led There is abundant evidence that this is true. The reasons why men follow a leader may not be fully understood. They include safety, income, power, and admiration. The leader is followed if it is believed that he can best provide, within the limits of time, place, and ability of the subordinates, the satisfactions for which men strive. On the other hand, the leader has no followers if he misjudges their needs and moods and the way they see to best accomplish these ends. The zeal of followers correlates positively with the quality of leadership.

Managers should surely take advantage of this aspect of human nature in the work situation. Subordinates want to be led, and led effectively. They will work just hard enough to get by if there is little or no leadership; with effective leadership they will work with zeal and confidence toward the peak of their capabilities.

The implication of this aspect of human nature for the enterprise is that managers should develop and apply their leadership abilities. This is not something that can be taught; one may be guided by the techniques of other leaders, but these procedures and those he himself develops need to be tried out in the work situation. Only in this way, through trial and evaluation of effects, can managers improve this elusive skill. The payoff for effective leadership can be immense. As a consequence, the need to develop leadership skill in all managers, at all levels, is pressing. It should ever be in the minds of managers everywhere.

Social Nature of Man It is sometimes difficult to arrange for subordinates to work in association with other people to the degree to which they want, but managers should, at least, recognize the need. For those who want to be alone, it is often possible to arrange the work and the place of work satisfactorily. The position requirement can be tailored to minimize personal contacts, and, the more these are lessened, the easier it is to locate space and equipment in isolation. Of course, these concessions will not be a major item for the enterprise. They can be effected by positioning the work place, providing partitions, etc. Indeed, the factor of a preference for isolation has been given little attention. It may be because its incidence is small, or it may be because the costs of catering to it are inconvenient.

On the other hand, the propensity for people to enjoy a social environment is probably much more pertinent for managers to consider. The need for company, for conversation, for companionship, is very real for most people. Insofar as these needs can be satisfied without interfering with production, they should be catered to; indeed, productivity may well be much greater if this is done. On a broader scale, the informal organization is a reflection of the individual's social needs. It should not be interfered with unless its objectives are a deterrent to the accomplishment of enterprise goals.

While recognizing the social needs of subordinates, the manager has a rather difficult time deciding just what size the social group should be. At the extreme, the large bull pen with hundreds of employees is clearly inefficient because of the noise level, the encouragement to visiting, and even the fear that some have of being in crowds. Despite the lack of behavioral guides, managers have tended to cut down on group size in order to minimize its disadvantages. But they can go too far in this regard.

An executive, following the customary practice of isolating his secretary in an enclosed office, was complaining about her work habits. He observed that she was encouraging visitors in rather large numbers, thus disrupting their work as well as her own. He recognized her need for human contact but was not sure how to handle the situation.

A production manager had just finished tearing down the offices of his foremen. "These men like their offices so well, they never get out on the floor. They enjoy the status symbol. Production has dropped off because they are not on the line keeping things moving, answering questions, and showing a new employee how to do things."

The president of a firm was concerned about the isolation of the members of his management team. Many did not know each other, and the quality of their cooperation dwindled. At noon everyone took off for restaurants far and near. To remedy at least part of the problem, the president had an excellent executive dining room installed. His view was that managers should be encouraged to use it through an attractive price schedule and, incidentally, thereby get to know each other better. Use, of course, was voluntary.

"You won't see me in there," said one executive. "The company does not own my lunch hour, and I will eat with whom and wherever I choose."

Managers are often on the horns of a dilemma in trying to accommodate the social needs of subordinates. They do not want to be accused of paternalism in this regard; they do not want to be put in the position of requiring social contacts; they do not want to deprive subordinates of this aspect of need satisfaction. Without scientific guides, they can only experiment by modifying the variables with a view to maximizing output.

Men in general, and Americans in particular, seem to be "joiners." They quickly recognize their inability to achieve many objectives as individuals and characteristically turn to group effort. Of course, there may be a strong admixture here of satisfying a social need for companionship while realizing a personal need for achieving an end that is out of their reach through individual effort. The discipline enforced by the created institution may well be restrictive, and the lack of personal influence in controlling the created "monster" may be terrifying, but these drawbacks do not impede the tendency to create specialized groups.

This tendency reveals itself within the enterprise. Employees join together, in part or in whole, to organize a credit union, a charitable group, a trade union, a professional union, or numerous recreation groups. The number of such groups is astonishing: look at the bulletin boards!

The manager must cope with this phenomenon. He is torn between noninterference in the personal freedom of subordinates and the potential for this desire to interfere with productivity and with the achievement of enterprise objectives. Productivity may well be affected adversely where company time is used for group activities and where the purpose of the activity is to restrict output. In the former case, a compromise is ordinarily reached wherein the group may use company time either wholly or partially, or not at all. Such a decision may not adversely affect output because encouragement of voluntary group activities can have a favorable impact on zeal. In the latter case, managers are especially concerned. Output restrictions are often an end result of inept management. Managers need to be trained to understand and to anticipate the potentialities so that they can take remedial action, if necessary, or so that they can prepare a position of strength.

No Average Man   That there is no average man the manager would be the first to acknowledge. Yet the exigencies of organized enterprise require that the assumption be made. Order and discipline are prime requisites for organizational success. To this end, rules and procedures are developed; concerted hours of work are essential, safety is imperative, division of labor is often paramount in achieving maximum productivity, wage and salary levels must be harmonious, and equality of opportunity must be preserved. In all of these fields, individuals must be treated alike.

Despite these standardized techniques designed to treat the undifferentiated, managers do have considerable opportunity to make personal adjustments within the established environment. The needs of the enterprise for order and discipline do not wholly preclude their devising adjustments for the differentiated individual. Opportunities for marginal differential treatment should be vigorously sought. Work can be rearranged and various degrees of job enlargement can be achieved. Merit, promotions, and other symbols of success can be individually treated. Hours of labor can sometimes be modified, or a choice of shifts can be provided.

The tendency of managers to treat individuals in a standardized and routine way is very strong because such a practice greatly simplifies the manager's job. However, this attitude should be resisted consistently, for individuals want individualistic—but fair—treatment. Standardization is contrary to the nature of human beings, and it should be avoided within the enterprise so far as is possible. It is perfectly obvious not only that the needs of individuals vary at a given moment of time, but that they vary within the working day for the individual himself. These little-understood characteristics of human nature are important nonetheless as far as output is concerned; therefore, it behooves the manager to respond constructively to them, as far as it is economical to do so.

The Desire for Responsibility   Of course, it would be a mistake to assume that all employees will rise to a challenge of their full capabilities. One need only to walk through a plant, a hospital, or the premises of any organized enterprise to see that many employees work at a level much below their potential, even after they are invited and exhorted to earn the rewards of higher effort. They simply do not rise to a challenge—for reasons that may include work restrictions by unions, work definition spelled out in the union contract, job security protected by law, ineffective discipline, tolerance by managers, lack of belief in the importance of their work, or acceptance of the propaganda that they are somehow being exploited. These attitudes and beliefs are exhibited not only in the shop, but by work gangs outside the premises, engineers, stenographers, nurses, and clerical employees, whether in business or in universities, libraries, and government agencies. Indeed, they are observable wherever men are employed.

The proportion of employees who refuse to accept the challenge of greater responsibilities is unknown. Those whose biases are with the employee seem to ignore the question or to minimize it; those whose biases are with the employer are concerned with the problem and may exaggerate it. There is a need to know. However, the employer, insofar as he is permitted by law or union contract, should recruit with a view toward selecting those employees who will respond to the challenge of responsibility, *and he should provide the challenge.* The authors of this book are not strangers to the frustrations of able employees that arise from a lack of job challenge.

Jim, a college graduate just returned from a tour of duty as a naval officer, set out to find a firm that would provide him with a challenging career. He was attracted by the advertisement of a bank which offered an exciting career, broad job challenges, management training, and promotional opportunities. These factors were also stressed by the bank's recruiting officer. Jim took the job, only to resign after nine months because the bank failed to live up to its promises. It insisted on college graduates spending the same time on routine duties as was required for the training of clerks assigned permanently to the job, and it defined jobs in ways which did not require college-trained men.

A middle manager in a prosperous business phoned the professor for an appointment. "I would like to confer with you about my career," he said. A time was arranged and the manager was prompt for the meeting.

"I am a middle manager. Although only thirty-two years old, I feel that there may be nothing further for me in the way of job challenge or promotion. As far as I know, I am appraised as a man with good potential. I am paid a good salary. However, I find time hanging on my hands. I willingly perform certain staff assignments in my spare time. In addition, I am now rather far along in my doctoral studies at a neighboring university. I am really at the point where I am uncertain whether to change my career objectives."

Recently, a consultant was heard to remark upon the large number of engineers who attended management development conferences. "These men seem to have reached the top of their salary scales and have no place to go. All of them cluster around the age range of thirty-five to forty."

The provision of challenging opportunities, especially for able managers, requires a radical change in the attitudes and practices of superior managers in all organized enterprises. Of course, it is very human to want to standardize, routinize, and specialize procedures. This course, however, minimizes the discriminatory attention that should be paid to individuals. It may contribute to over-all productivity and provide an environment of "equal" treatment for employees, but it also creates just those conditions that are so frustrating to subordinate managers who long to feel the bit of responsibility. The steady hand of the superior is needed to make certain that these men understand that they need time to assimilate their experience. Just when a subordinate is ready for a promotion is something of a "no man's land," but surely the best way to find out is to challenge his ingenuity to expand his contribution to the enterprise and to keep the rein of accountability taut.

The implications of the many-faceted aspects of human nature bear heavily upon the executive function of directing. Although a manager applies resources of men, capital, and space, he directs only men. The human factor is employed because it has the potentiality for productive effort and, in terms of relative cost and indispensability, it competes effectively with nonhuman factors. In greater or lesser degree, it will always be a required factor of production. Under these circumstances, the skill with which managers direct human effort becomes a critical factor in the efficiency of organized enterprise.

THE DIRECTING FUNCTION

As a manager concerns himself with the directing function, he begins to grasp something of its complexity. First of all, he is dealing with people, but not on an entirely objective basis, for he is a person himself and often becomes part of the problem. He is in direct contact with people, both as individuals and as groups. He soon discovers that, as a productive factor, people are not singly interested in enterprise objectives; they have objectives of their own. In order to direct human effort toward enterprise objectives, the manager soon realizes that he should think in terms of the issues related to orientation, communication, motivation, and leadership. A consideration of the more general aspects of directing is provided in the following sections. Separate chapters will be devoted to the major directing activities of managers.

THE MANAGER'S RELATION TO SUBORDINATES

Although the manager is part of the group, it is convenient for many reasons to look upon him as apart from his subordinates. Resources—human and otherwise—for achieving enterprise objectives are assigned to him, and he must integrate them. Easy when it comes to capital, buildings, and land, this is difficult when it comes to people, for they require skilled directing.

It is also convenient to think of the manager apart from the group because he is its leader. As leader he is not so much one of the group as he is the one to persuade the group to do his will. Leadership involves wise use of a motivational system plus a personality which engenders zeal in others.

The manager is also perceived by his employees as one apart for other reasons. He knows more than they do about company goals, policies, new programs, and expected changes; he is considered to have good judgment because of his varied experience.

On the other hand, his foibles had better be socially acceptable, else he will lose the respect of his subordinates. The image of what a superior manager should be like is usually quite different from what is observed in our peers.

Finally, the superior is ever apart from the group, because he holds in his hands the careers of his subordinates. His opinion is important above all others, because he decides who will be promoted, transferred, or terminated, and who will be given merit and salary increases.

The behavior of a group largely depends on the kind of manager it has. His leadership style, the quality of his communications, the respect of his peers, his general character, the degree to which he can be trusted, his human attitudes—all these influence the morale of subordinates, which, in turn, reflects his skill in directing them.

TWO IMPORTANT PRINCIPLES

The first of these principles applies to the purpose of directing; the second, to the directing process.

The Principle of Harmony of Objective   Confusion has accompanied the many efforts to describe the harmony that must exist between subordinates' objectives and those of the firm. Different viewpoints reflect different ways of visualizing social cooperation. Preoccupation with labor-management issues, military organization, or the question of the individual's place in society has led to biased views.

Fayol,[11] writing a half century ago, pointed out that the manager who retained his authority in a high degree could direct employees with few counterinfluences and, consequently, could maintain a unity of view among them with respect to enterprise objective. On the other hand, when orders were filtered down through several echelons of intermediaries, they became altered, even unintentionally, permitting the growth of divergent views of the firm's objectives among personnel. Fayol's sixth principle states that the business interest must prevail over the interest of employees.[12] He also sug-

[11] Henri Fayol, *General and Industrial Management* (New York: Pitman Publishing Corporation, 1949), p. 33.
[12] *Ibid.*, p. 26.

gests that ignorance, ambition, selfishness, laziness, and other human weakness are forever at war with the best interests of the firm.

As Barnard[13] has pointed out, "the preponderance of persons in a modern society always lies on the negative side with reference to a particular existing or potential organization." In other words, usually only a very small minority of persons in an enterprise, or in a department of it, actually identify their objectives with those of the organization. Nor should a manager expect the goals of his subordinates and the goals of the group to be identical. But in directing subordinates, he must take advantage of individual motives to gain group goals; in interpreting plans and job assignments, he must harmonize individual and group objectives. A "company" man may make the manager's job easier, but the manager must never assume that selfless devotion exists in many, if any, of his subordinates.

Although employees work to satisfy some needs not related to the firm's objectives, these needs must be in harmony with and complementary to the interests of the firm, and not contrary. A good motivation system must encourage the fulfillment of those human needs which employees will work to satisfy while at the same time contributing to the achievement of enterprise objectives.

The Principle of Unity of Command The principle of unity of command is a directing, as well as an organizing, principle. As described in Chapter 4 it reflected the desirability of subordinates being responsible to only one superior. It is well known that employees work better this way, which avoids division of loyalties, problems of priorities, and conflicting orders. The importance of such a restriction was not realized by F. W. Taylor[14] when he experimented with an organization structure that permitted eight functional foremen to give orders to the individual workmen.

In military organizations, unity of command is followed "so that its [organizational element] responsible head can be held solely accountable for results to higher authority."[15] The emphasis is placed upon protection of the superior, through the personal obligation of a subordinate to see that assigned activities are properly performed. Little thought is given, apparently, to the improved efficiency of the subordinate as a result of this unity of command.

The complex of personal forces that every manager must manipulate to accomplish a task through other people, permits no outside interference in supervision of subordinates. Directing can be most efficiently carried on by one person. He knows, better than others, the nature of the subordinate,

---

[13] Chester I. Barnard, *The Functions of the Executive* (Cambridge, Mass.: Harvard University Press, 1938), p. 84.

[14] F. W. Taylor, *Scientific Management* (New York: Harper & Row, Publishers, Incorporated, 1947).

[15] J. R. Beishline, *Military Management for National Defense* (Englewood Cliffs, N.J.: Prentice-Hall, Inc., 1950), pp. 89–90.

to which motivation he best responds, and his technical proficiency. Consequently, the immediate superior is in the best position to select whichever directing techniques maximize productivity, not of the individual employee particularly, but of the group of subordinates.

ORIENTATION

Orientation is used here in the sense of providing information necessary for intelligent action. Starting with the introduction of each new employee to his physical and human environment, it more importantly includes the briefing of all employees on both immediate and continuing enterprise activities. Obviously, the more one knows about one's work and its environment the more intelligently he can work. It is up to the superior manager to determine what information is essential for good performance and how and by whom it will be transmitted.

Orienting New Employees   Managers too often leave the orientation of new employees to the personnel department, which is skilled in providing both general and specific information about the nature of the firm and its history and about details of employment, such as pay, hours, and fringe benefits. But much more information is required from a new employee's immediate superior.

Every manager is responsible for the specific orientation of a new subordinate. It is part of his directing function to take the time and to exercise the patience required to give the employee information essential to his assignment.

The employee's job and its relationship to other activities require detailed explanation. The job itself, its scope, purpose, and authority delegation, must be clearly described. The subordinate should be informed about how to report and how his performance will be evaluated. To portray organization relationships, an organization chart is helpful, showing how activities are divided and related to each other.

The subordinate's relationships with other employees need careful explanation. He should be introduced personally to managers with whom he will have considerable contact, so that information and transactions will flow smoothly and help will be readily available. For instance, the new head of a contract administration group will have continuous contact with the heads of production control, engineering, pricing, administration, purchasing, and finance and with the armed services' representative. Subordinates who have to establish rapport with complete strangers may be slow to develop their jobs.

The new subordinate must also know how to get things done and how to utilize support services. He needs to know what services are available, where they are, what they can do for him, and what procedures to follow in requesting them. Failure here often results in the subordinate establishing his own service that duplicates an existing activity, with attendant high cost.

Continuing Orientation Orientation is not to end with new employees but should continue as long as there are subordinates to supervise. There is a constant need for orientation to new assignments, changes in company activities—as related to products, policy, organization, and customers—and changes in managerial personnel. For continuing orientation, managers use techniques including written communication—memoranda, bulletins, control reports, duty assignments—and oral information at staff meetings, conferences, committee meetings, and daily coaching sessions.

The difficulty in continuing orientation is that human beings grow indifferent to activity that must be repeated indefinitely. People don't mind doing what they can finish. The orientation of a new employee can be readily and definitely accomplished, but managers need tenacious will power to provide continuing orientation. There is, for example, the continual problem of getting subordinates to coordinate their activities. Their original orientation convinced employees of the need for this, yet they often fail. It is so much easier to act alone than to bother about checking with others who will be affected.

Strange to say, an important source of failure in continuing orientation is the neglect of superiors who know what should be done but may fall victim to their busy routines, to the fear of reporting reverses, lost contracts, and layoffs, or—stranger yet—to the fear of reporting their successes.

Orientation of Superiors Poor as the orientation of subordinates often is, it is at least a recognized aspect of directing. But the orientation of superiors is a blank; it is not even a recognized necessity. True, superiors try to keep themselves informed through control reports and group meetings, but this is inadequate.

Every subordinate should keep his superior informed. The subordinate is in command of operational detail, and some of this is reported periodically in control reports. But daily the nagging question arises, What should be reported to the boss? The subordinate will try to protect his superior from the burden of too much information and, therefore, he will select what to report. What is to be the basis for this discrimination? Basically, it should be to convey only information that the superior needs to keep out of trouble. This vague rule is difficult to follow, for it opens wide the discretionary door; the subordinate must correctly apprehend his superior's needs and overcome a strong temptation to censor information adversely affecting himself. The proper discharge of this responsibility requires men of character.

ISSUING ORDERS

Orders are important in directing subordinates. An order initiates, modifies, or stops an activity; it is the impetus by which an organization is activated or disbanded. Managers must thoroughly understand its meaning, uses, and limitations.

In American enterprises, the right to command proceeds from a legally enforceable contract involving the personnel services of subordinates. The superior alone possesses this right. He employs the subordinate to perform certain duties and undertakes to explain what is needed and to pay for the service as or after it is accomplished; the employee undertakes the specified activities and receives his remuneration. Which party initiated the agreement is immaterial; the contract still provides that the employer give the orders and the employee obey them.

Definition of an Order The term "order" has many connotations, as any standard dictionary will confirm. As a directional technique, an order is understood to be a command by a superior requiring a subordinate to act or refrain from acting in a given circumstance. Several elements in this definition require clarification. A personal relationship in direct line of command from superior to subordinate is implied. The relationship is not reversible. Two managers of equal rank cannot qualify in this relationship. And, except for functional authority, the relationship cannot exist between a superior in one department and a person of lower rank in another.

Another implication of this definition is that the content of an order be germane to the achievement of the enterprise objective. Just what this includes is not always clear. On the one hand, there is no question that a production manager may have his foremen work a nine-hour shift. On the other hand, there may be a real question whether foremen can be ordered not to fraternize with their employees, or whether a sales manager can require his advertising head to misrepresent a product. Orders of this type are frequently given and almost as frequently obeyed, despite the fact that repercussions can be most unfortunate for everyone concerned.

Finally, the definition of an order implies that it is enforceable. The manager's position would be untenable if, as a last resort, he could not employ sanctions against a subordinate who either refuses to carry out an order or who does so in an inappropriate manner. The ultimate sanction is the loss of a job. But before this stage is reached, intermediate steps may be taken, such as holding hearings, coaching, and possible transfer to other departments.

Techniques The techniques of issuing orders have received very little consideration in management literature, although military establishments have given the problem considerable attention.[16] The relevant questions to be considered here are whether an order should be general or specific, written or oral, and what its degree of formality should be.

General or specific Whether an order should be specific or general seems to depend upon the preference of the manager, his ability to foresee attendant circumstances, and the response made by the subordinate. Managers who have a rigid view of delegation of authority seem predisposed to

---

[16] *Ibid.,* chap. 14.

phrase orders in specific terms. Such managers prefer to direct their subordinates very closely. They feel that they have clearly in mind just what is to be done and the best way to accomplish it, and they want the subordinate to carry out the order in this particular way.

In situations where it is not possible to foresee all the circumstances attendant upon carrying out the order, it is more likely to take a general form. When it must be carried out far from the personal supervision of the superior, no effort should be made to give specific orders. For instance, district sales managers, regional plant managers, and representatives located at a distance from the home office are, perforce, likely to operate under general orders, because local influences, unforeseen factors in a negotiation, and other questions may affect the way in which the orders are carried out.

The response of a subordinate to the type of order received is important in determining its nature because some employees prefer close supervision and, consequently, do best under specific orders. On the other hand, many subordinates chafe under this treatment. They prefer to exercise initiative and are quite willing to be judged by the results. This type of person does not work well under close direction and may resent specific orders.

Written or oral   In deciding between written or oral orders, consideration is given such questions as the permanency of the relationship between superior and subordinate; the quality of trust that exists between them; and the necessity of some device—especially in large firms—for avoiding overlapping orders and acquainting all personnel concerned with the fact that an order has been issued. If it were safe to assume that the superior-subordinate relationship would continue between the same two persons, it would often be unnecessary to write orders. If the rate of job turnover is high, it is unsafe for a firm to operate without written general orders, especially those which will require considerable time to carry out.

The quality of trust existing between superior and subordinate affects the desirability of writing orders, since in this relationship the major risk is carried by the subordinate, who may prefer written orders for several reasons. He may be averse to accepting responsibility and, when this is forced upon him, may want to be covered by a written, specific order. Or he may have been accused of exceeding his authority in the past and now seeks the protection of a written order. Or he may have had bitter experience with a superior who fails to remember giving an order, who changes an order and forgets that he has done so, or who blames the subordinate for poor results attendant upon carrying out his orders.

The written order is often used for preventing overlapping instructions and preventing jurisdictional disputes. If, perchance, confusion does develop, it is considerably easier to straighten matters out if the original orders were in writing.

In addition, it is often convenient to announce a particular assignment to all interested personnel by a written order. The need to do this arises particularly when the order involves a somewhat unusual assignment. A president may instruct his personnel director to make a study of accidents, their causes and incidence, and develop a program for minimizing them. Should no public notice be given and no public request for the cooperation of all division, department, and section heads, such an assignment might meet with resistance, sabotage, and other forms of noncooperation.

Formality and Informality   In most enterprises—exclusive of the military—such terms as "command" or "order" are rarely used. The manager is accustomed to command by informally suggesting, "Let's do this," "Suppose you go ahead with this thing," or "Why not confer with Production on this?" The outsider might not recognize these as orders, but the subordinate seldom mistakes them. Sometimes, however, a formal written or spoken order, phrased exactly as a military officer would give it, is salutary. Some employees require this sort of formal direction at all times, while others would instantly quit their jobs if anyone gave them such orders. There is a subtle skill in selecting precisely the right degree of formality to use with each subordinate, and doing this well often spells the difference between good and bad motivation.

Timing   Contrary to military practice, the informality and spontaneity with which businessmen reach decisions and give orders often result in little apparent attention to timing. This can be deceptive. If decisions are customarily reached after permitting broad participation by subordinates, relatively little explanation is needed, and timing of implementing action is often implied. In businesses operated on the basis of opportunism and immediacy, action is probably simultaneous with the decision. On the other hand, firms engaging in considerable planning necessarily follow the planned steps quite rigidly and the timing of orders is given careful attention.

DELEGATION AS A MEANS OF DIRECTING

Delegation of authority is a more general form of directing than issuance of orders. In delegation, the superior customarily gives a subordinate authority to command or to act in a large area of affairs by means of a general statement. As the previous section pointed out, orders are issued when a superior knows (or thinks he knows) exactly what the result of the specific order will be. In many circumstances, the result cannot be anticipated or known in detail. When this is the case, more general delegation is appropriate.

Although delegation was discussed in Chapter 4, the subject deserves further attention as a specific technique of directing.

Difficulties in Assignment   It might appear that to assign duties one has only to specify which man is in charge of purchasing, production control, maintenance, or some other task. Upon a closer look, however, what is involved in these assignments? Breakdowns are attempted in job descriptions, but it is difficult to make these clear and definite, on the one hand, or distinguishable from similar assignments on the other. For example, one firm assigns to the purchasing agent the following duties: (1) to advise his superior on the formulation of procedures relating to procurement; (2) to make the necessary contacts with vendors and to study the commodity market constantly; (3) in accordance with authorized requisitions, to purchase materials and supplies; (4) to negotiate with vendors claims arising from inspection rejections; (5) to administer personnel and financial policies as they apply to his operation; and (6) to accumulate information for the preparation of his budget.

At first glance, the assignment may appear clear and exact. But let one place himself in the position of the purchasing agent. Just what, when, and how much effort is called for? Does "advising his superior" about procedures mean constructive written suggestions, based upon an analysis by an industrial engineer? What are "necessary" contacts with vendors? What does one do to study the commodity market "constantly"? Does claims negotiation mean exclusive power to conclude an agreement? Raising these questions illustrates the common inexactitude of work assignments. The man who undertakes a job described in this fashion will have to play it by ear. In fact, perhaps most managers do!

Overlapping of work assignments made to two or more subordinate managers is another common difficulty. So long as assignments are made in general terms, this is certain to happen. For instance, in negotiating sales contracts or claims on vendors, the legal department will be involved as well as the sales and buying departments. Just where the duty of one manager leaves off and that of the other begins can scarcely ever be made clear. Managers learn to live with these uncertainties, to interpret them in the light of the facts in any given situation, and to voluntarily coordinate their activities in the best interests of the enterprise.

Difficulties in Delegation   Delegation of authority is even less exact, often stating merely that the subordinate is authorized to carry out the assigned duties. Since the duties themselves are not clear, the subordinate will have difficulty in interpreting his authority to do anything. For instance, in the case of the aforementioned purchasing agent, just how free is he to negotiate claims with vendors? Can he settle for any percentage of the claim? Can he cut off the vendor if there is not full satisfaction? Can he require or recommend prosecution? Even though he asks his superior for clarification, he may not get it.

Detailed versus Broad Authority   This is often not a matter of choice. It involves the question, how detailed should a grant of authority be? The answer depends upon how detailed the work assignment is. In an assignment to discipline subordinates, the delegation of authority will be broad. On the other hand, if the assignment specifies that disciplinary action is limited to a referral to the grievance committee or a request that the employee be transferred, authority to discipline is strictly spelled out. Generally, (1) detailed authority is associated with detailed work assignments; (2) delegation of authority is broad at the top of the organization structure and becomes increasingly narrow as lower echelons are reached.

Implied Authority Purely from the point of view of efficiency, the implication of authority adheres to all managers. The importance of acting in the best interests of the firm overrides any nice delegation of limited authority. Probably there is no manager of any experience who has not exceeded his delegated authority. An unforeseen bargain tempts many buyers to exceed their contractual powers; a sale that rests upon a relaxation of price or terms is often confirmed by superiors, notwithstanding strict orders forbidding such practices; violations of company rules are sometimes condoned; and the firm is often committed financially by a manager who is believed to have the authority but who does not. The pattern emerging from these examples shows that trusted managers are presumed to act in the best interests of the firm, whether they occasionally override their authority or not. In this way an enterprise can benefit from unforeseen opportunities and avoid stultification.

Rigidly Delegated Authority As was indicated in Chapter 4, some managers view authority delegation with untoward rigidity. They dislike to delegate and, when forced to do so, endeavor to circumscribe the grant with a neat exactitude. They feel that delegations can be made accurately and that the results which they personally anticipate will be achieved. Disappointments are likely to be followed by harsh judgments on the ability of their subordinates. When everything seems neat and clear to these managers, they feel frustration when their plans fail.

The effects of this attitude upon the firm are serious. In the first place, such a manager is incapable of developing a successor. Many types of subordinates refuse to work for him, and the quality of those willing to work in this environment is subject to question. Then, subordinates learn to manage by managing. Deprived of opportunities to make their own decisions, to exercise their own judgment, and to act on their own volition, they will neither make errors for which they are personally responsible nor learn much about managing.

In the second place, a rigid concept of delegation limits the size of the enterprise and stultifies its growth. This follows naturally from the principles of departmentation. A manager who makes little use of his subordinate managers must, of necessity, make the decisions himself. The span of management places limits on what one person can do. Even if the regular workday is supplemented by long hours of nightwork, this restriction still holds. Beyond a certain point nothing can get done. This span binds the firm in iron and prevents its growth.

Positively Delegated Authority Executives with a positive attitude toward delegating authority view their directing function entirely differently. Personal security is not a consideration, and—with the confidence resulting from intelligent selection and an appraisal program—they willingly trust their subordinates. Such executives consider their greatest service to the firm to be one of developing future managers.

This does not imply neglect of daily tasks, but errors made in them are turned into object lessons for subordinates and not looked upon simply as catastrophes. Errors are, of course, minimized by appropriate safeguards, a point that will be developed later. Proper analysis of the issue and the way it was attempted is valuable in developing judgment. Such attention to training subordinates reflects the belief that nothing is more important to a firm than its future.

Also according to the positive attitude, subordinates are encouraged to accept responsibility. Their superiors want them to become self-starters and grow in the exercise of authority. For this, the superior must study each subordinate, give him gradually expanding authority, and hold before him the challenge of unusual accomplishment.

With the positive attitude, it is necessary to keep open the channels of communication between superior and subordinate. The superior must be *available,* although unobtrusive, and must permit the subordinate to "pick his brains," because this is a short cut to experience. At the same time, the temptation to tell the subordinate what to do and how to do it must be firmly resisted. Yielding at this point will undo all the advantages of delegating authority, discourage the subordinate's self-starting proclivities, and limit his personal experience. In fact, "telling" is an actual revocation of delegated authority.

Finally, the positive attitude implies immense patience. It takes a long time to acquire good judgment and develop leadership ability. The temptations of short-run opportunism are often overwhelming. The experienced superior can see what must be done, but he must not order it done, for this would deprive the subordinate of a chance to figure it out for himself. It takes patience to put up with mistakes, fumbling, and the slow acquisition of good business sense. The supervisor can only obtain his satisfaction from success in developing capable men.

Degrees of Delegation It is clearly unwise to carve out a group of duties and the authority to undertake them and hand this bundle to an inexperienced supervisor. He needs time to grow. Consequently, his authority should be gradually expanded, as the superior oversees, instructs, and tests the subordinate through successive assignments. Thus, the group of duties is completed under relatively close supervision, and, as the capacities of the subordinate increase, his superior will relax the overt overseeing and expand authority, allowing the employee to devise ways to accomplish assignments.

Since the degree of delegation is highly correlated with proved capacity, in delegating authority to several subordinates in different stages of development the extent of delegation to individuals will vary. Several subordinates will ordinarily be at various stages of development at any given time. Those who have shown ability will be tested by having their authority expanded; those who have not handled authority well will lose it.[17]

In a program of this type, there will be subordinates who overestimate their capacities and who will resent relatively limited authority; and there may be subordinates capable of further development. In dealing with the first category, the superior must try to demonstrate his impartiality and his sincerity. Failure to prove these will ordinarily result in dissatisfied subordinates and the probable loss of some with real potential. Dealing with subordinates of limited capacities can be more clear-cut.

Such individuals should not, of course, have been made supervisors in the first place. There is no alternative but to remove them from supervisory work. This can be done by talking to the supervisor (taking the blame for the appointment in the first place) and trying to find an assignment better suited to his capacities—a nonsupervisory position in the department or another department—or else separating him from the firm. The superior who by nature and training possesses a positive attitude toward delegation simply cannot permit subordinates without a potential for managing to act as supervisors. If he does, frustration and unhappiness will be the lot of all.

FOR DISCUSSION

1. It is in the directing function that managers "get things done by, with, and through people." Is this also true of the organizing and planning functions?

2. Do you believe managers must have authority to command their subordinates? If not, what would you suggest?

3. Do you, as a student, work at your top capacity? Do you believe employees in enterprise do?

4. Do you believe "continuing" orientation of subordinates is desirable? Why? How should it be accomplished?

SELECTED REFERENCES

Argyris, C.: *Integrating the Individual and the Organization,* New York: John Wiley & Sons, Inc., 1964.

Bernthal, W. F.: "Integrating the Behavioral Sciences and Management," *Journal of the Academy of Management,* vol. 3, no. 3, pp. 161–166 (December, 1960).

Blough, R. M.: "Business Can Satisfy the Young Intellectual," *Harvard Business Review,* vol. 44, no. 1, pp. 49–57 (January–February, 1966).

Bower, M.: *The Will to Manage,* chap. 8, New York: McGraw-Hill Book Company, 1966.

Brooks, T. R.: "Can Employees 'Manage' Themselves?" *Dun's Review,* vol. 86, no. 5, pp. 59–60; 135–136 (November, 1965).

[17] For the necessity of establishing controls simultaneously with delegating authority, see p. 72.

England, G. W.: "Organizational Goals and Expected Behavior of American Managers," *Academy of Management Journal,* vol. 10, no. 2, pp. 107–118 (June, 1967).

Gibson, J. L.: "Organizational Theory and the Nature of Man," *Academy of Management Journal,* vol. 9, no. 3, pp. 233–245 (September, 1966).

Knowles, H. P., and B. O. Saxberg: "Human Relations and the Nature of Man," *Harvard Business Review,* vol. 45, no. 2, pp. 22–48 (March–April, 1967).

McGregor, D.: *The Human Side of Enterprise,* New York: McGraw-Hill Book Company, 1960.

Schein, E. H.: *Organizational Psychology,* chap. 4, Englewood Cliffs, N.J.: Prentice-Hall, Inc., 1965.

Scott, W. E.: "The Creative Individual," *Academy of Management Journal,* vol. 8, no. 3, pp. 211–219 (September, 1965).

CHAPTER TWENTY-FIVE

motivation

THE NECESSITY

It has been taught for many decades that men cooperate in an enterprise in order to accomplish a desired goal that they cannot attain individually. This explanation seems to fit well the building "bees" of Western farmers, the stone removal illustration, the creation of the United States, the establishment of a university—events, large and small, wherein *equal* participators combine effort to produce a result that is shared with approximate *equality*. The anticipated satisfaction of sharing the results seems to be individually articulated, and, therefore, contributed effort seems to be largely self-motivated. This apparent lack of a need for someone to motivate others seems to be particularly characteristic of those ventures which can be shortly achieved. The distant goal, or the result that seems far distant, does not receive the same degree of self-motivated effort from cooperators. Many of these abandon the goal, many become laggards, and some even become "traitors."

The equal-cooperation theory must also seem a poor explanation of why a person applies for a position in a church, a university, or a business. He surely does not feel like an equal cooperator; he often sees these organizations as monolithic enterprises, vigorous (at least in their outward appearance), and little in the need of the services of *the* applicant. His motivation is seldom to share in the group goal; he usually wants a job with a salary that will pay his bills. If his motivation were not economic, he would usually find some other way to fulfill his noneconomic needs. For this reason, enterprise managers have a pronounced need to understand the motivational process and to develop their skills in its application.

How Much Responsibility? The responsibility for motivation is always limited by the delegated authority of the subordinate manager and the philosophy of top management. A department head is obviously limited by company policy on wages and salaries, fringe benefits, promotion, and centralization of authority. Company presidents, though less restricted, are limited by policies of the board of directors, the legal system, and competition. Thus, managers at each organization level have limited authority to do those things that motivate subordinates, and the restrictions become more severe the lower down the manager stands.

Every manager is responsible, within his authority, for motivating his immediate subordinates *and* for motivating all subordinates down to the bottom of the relevant organization structure. A president should feel responsible for motivating, primarily, those reporting directly to him and, secondarily, *all* the enterprise employees; an army corps commander and a plant manager should view their responsibilities for motivation in the same primary and secondary light.

Understanding Human Needs It is important to realize that motivation (providing with a motive—or, in this usage, a motive to act in a desired manner) has no meaning outside the needs of subordinates. Efforts to provide a motive not related to needs would have zero results. Therefore, it is essential to understand the needs of subordinates. Motivation can then be supplied through satisfying or withholding satisfaction of these needs—high and low values of the same variable[1]—with the purpose of achieving the desired kind of work.

Although we do not have a complete understanding of human needs, social scientists have suggested numerous lists of them. Sociologists recognize broad groups of physical (health and safety) and social (emotional and educational) needs. Man is truly a "wanting" animal, and he wants progressively different things rather than merely more of the same. As one trio of authors put it:[2]

> Once his basic needs for food, clothing, and shelter are satisfied, he wants friends and to get folksy and groupy. Once these needs for belonging are satisfied, he wants recognition and respect from his fellow men and he wants to achieve independence and competence for himself. And once these needs for status and self-esteem are satisfied, he seeks for self-fulfillment, for freedom, and for higher and higher modes of adjustment and adaptation.

One theory is that the priority of man's needs changes from the physical to the "higher" social needs as the former become comparatively satisfied. Being complex, man does not first satisfy his basic needs and then turn to means of satisfying his higher needs but rather shifts his emphasis while

[1] G. C. Homans, *Social Behavior* (New York: Harcourt, Brace & World, Inc., 1961), p. 19.

[2] A. Zaleznik, C. R. Christensen, and F. J. Roethlisberger, *The Motivation, Productivity, and Satisfaction of Workers* (Boston: Division of Research, Harvard Business School, 1958), p. 399.

proceeding to satisfy both categories simultaneously. The theory is vague about just when the priority changes and about how the change takes place in different kinds of people. It does not explain the retrogressive process of "lowering" priorities from one specific need to another; the periodic return to basic-need satisfaction; and the contradictions found in men who don't act in line with the theory at all. Accordingly, managers should be wary of any motivational system based on unproved theories of social behavior.

What Kind of Motivation?   Developing a sound motivational system is very difficult. Traditionally, managers have provided work opportunities to employees and motivated them merely by a wage scale generally related to productivity and by penalties for violating company rules. Largely on this system, American workers have achieved the world's highest living standard—an immense accomplishment. With this in view, some behavioralists argue[3] that motivation aimed at the satisfaction of basic needs is no longer necessary because satisfied needs are not motivators. Errors of two kinds are contained in this view. Although we do have an affluent society, practically everyone in it must continue to work to satisfy basic needs. True, some could live off their savings and capital for some time before being forced to again seek work. It is also true that most Americans could not afford to be without work for very long before feeling an urgent need to earn an income that would pay for basic needs. The airy statements of some academic types of persons about the affluent society relieving us of the need to work may be applicable in Utopia, but they do not appear to be applicable in this world. Earning one's living is still essential even though it is not always billed as respectable.

A second error occurs when the recurrency of the need to satisfy physiological requirements is overlooked. Even academic types of people return to the table three times a day, they renew their clothing and housing, they buy a new-model car occasionally, and they probably have a recurrent need for love. These needs simply have to be fulfilled and, in our day, they can be largely satisfied through the power of a paycheck. Recognizing that people must work, managers compete for the best of them in ways that include money, hours, location, and fringe benefits. All these elements are critical motivators aimed at the individual's attempts to satisfy his basic needs.

For those who are employed, and who thus have a salary that takes care of basic needs, the enterprise managers should obviously provide additional motivators that relate to self-actualizing needs. These are the "higher" needs to which one turns *after* making as certain as is individually possible that the recurring, basic needs will be satisfied. To a greater or lesser extent, these needs are really not satisfiable, but this, if true, does not subtract from their potential as a means for motivation. Indeed, the *striving*

[3] W. G. Scott, *Organization Theory* (Homewood, Ill.: Richard D. Irwin, Inc., 1967), p. 77.

for self-actualization is probably more important to the human being than its *realization*.

Which Subordinates? Many writers are typically vague in identifying the levels and functions of the people they study, and their work in motivation is somewhat blighted by this deficiency. However, it is probably correct to say that their experimental data have been concerned with the motivation of nonmanagers. The managers seem to remain in the background, appearing as autocratic "ghosts." This is not to deny the importance of motivational studies. We do need to learn much more about this aspect of employees, particularly in its relationship to union membership, the dichotomy of power sources as seen by the membership, and the management of intrusions from external sources which affect employee attitudes.[4]

The manager is a person and he is the prime focus of this book. It is the motivation of such men which concerns us at this point. In addition to being human, and thus affected by the same forces as nonmanagers, these men occupy positions that clothe them with attributes that are uniquely associated with managers. Both aspects of the "enlarged" personality will need attention in the sections that follow.

WHAT WORK IS

The word "work"[5] as used here means the exertion of effort to accomplish something. The effort may be mental or physical, voluntary or forced; the acomplishment may be complete or limited. A farmer visualizes the result of work in terms of specific agricultural products in certain volume and quality; a corporation director, in terms of profit dollars. It is the latter who needs the cooperation of many people, each contributing effort to produce the effect envisioned.

We make a distinction here between effort directed to recreation (which also accomplishes something) and effort directed toward working for a living. The latter must contribute, either directly or indirectly, to the living standard of the worker.

Why Men Work Work must be undertaken, primarily, to satisfy basic human needs. If these needs could be satisfied without work, comparatively little work would be done. Adam had no requirement to work before he was expelled from the Garden of Eden. In the world as we know it, work is the only way (excluding crime, past savings, lucrative investments, and inherited riches) to satisfy the basic needs.

If man were simple enough or sophisticated enough to value freedom

---

[4] The difficulty of even identifying all the variables relating to motivation comes through clearly as J. G. March and H. A. Simon struggle with classification problems in *Organizations* (New York: John Wiley & Sons, Inc., 1958).

[5] For an excellent analysis of this subject, see Wilfred Brown, "What Is Work?" *Harvard Business Review*, vol. 40, no. 5, pp. 121–129 (September–October, 1962).

and leisure to develop himself more than this world's goods, he would work just enough to satisfy his basic needs and only when they required satisfaction. If this were the nature of man (and it seems to be in some societies), a simple system of rewards would suffice to motivate employees, but manhours of work would be very low.

In the United States, people probably could satisfy basic minimum needs by working an hour or two per day. But Americans don't act this way, because they want a considerably more complex level of satisfaction and are willing to work longer for it. The exact level differs for everyone, but the cooperative system now calls for standard workdays of seven or eight hours. Rising personal productivity levels may permit a shortening of the future work week, although people have a way of increasing their material demands even as their income rises. Otherwise, people might elect to cut down on material wants in favor of increased leisure. This obviously entails many complex social riddles.

In Primitive Societies   Work in primitive societies is largely associated with effort to meet biological needs. The amount of effort required varies from a short workday in areas blessed with mild climate, abundant food resources, and low population, such as much of Melanesia, to a long day in such areas as northern Australia. The work—carried on by the entire population—is closely interwoven with aesthetics, religion, and social life.

The direct relationship of effort to end product to the satisfaction of concrete needs is interesting to us. People experience their own accomplishments fully and are intensely motivated, because results of effort are immediately applicable to satisfying their needs and are rewarded by the esteem of others.

The Industrial Revolution   The industrial revolution changed the work of much of the world. Factory labor became specialized and required an insistent routine of physical action. To refer to these workers as cooperators is technically correct, but they were often really economic slaves with no alternative way to make a living. They were motivated by biological needs, social pressure, and employer coercion. In every respect, the quality of this motivation was much inferior to that of the aborigine. Not only was what Herzberg[6] calls "hygiene" bad—and this includes supervision, interpersonal relations, working conditions, wages, policies and practices, and job security—but the relation of effort to the finished product, including its quality, was totally obscured. There was no place for pride of accomplishment or opportunity to innovate.

In Highly Organized Societies   Not only have businesses grown in size but so have city, state, and, especially, the Federal government, also hospitals, schools, churches, and organized labor. Today, the last refuge of the small-

---

[6] F. Herzberg, B. Mausner, and B. B. Snyderman, *The Motivation to Work* (New York: John Wiley & Sons, Inc., 1959), p. 113.

scale operation is in certain sectors of agriculture, retailing, and craftsmanship.

Characteristic of highly organized societies is their affluence. Living standards considerably exceed minimum requirements. Conditions of work conform more generally to civilized standards.

Better Motivation Needed Along with affluence has come a need for added incentives to work, particularly in large organizations. The search of social scientists for the motivating spark has been focused mainly on business—a restriction never explained. A broader view is necessary to solve this universal problem of large-scale cooperative endeavor.

To explain the purpose and techniques of cooperative enterprise, social scientists often choose simple examples of the joyful bygone neighborliness of agricultural people in joining hands to build a house or harvest a crop. These examples are of little help in understanding the nature of modern cooperative effort. Except at home, modern life is lived as part of several huge endeavors. People "belong" to a fraternal association, trade union, public school system, church, or business enterprise. These huge enterprises are all cooperative undertakings, yet the member does not consider himself a cooperator. When a man accepts a job, he sees himself as someone agreeing to an employment contract. A salary is the only way left for most people to make a living—by selling their efforts for purchasing power with which to acquire goods and services they want.

The results of the job itself are often unrecognizable as part of the goods or services produced by the enterprise. Supervising a clerical pool, a drafting group, an in-plant travel facility, or the assembly of circuits bears no obvious relation to the production of electronic medical equipment, a missile, or a pair of shoes. For those being thus supervised, these end products are even more unreal. The worker is one of thousands, the supervisor one of hundreds, and the middle manager one of dozens. The only way we have learned to operate large-scale enterprises—whether the Internal Revenue Service, an air force, or an electronics firm—is to divide the total job into its elements, in pieces that one person can master. Because individual contributions must mesh, procedures leave small scope for personal initiative.

A job is usually equated with a paycheck. To follow simple rules and procedures is to be secure in one's job. Work can often be done at very slow speed. Union members sometimes deliberately restrict output, and salaried people often work six desultory hours of the eight-hour day. In short, motivation to work conscientiously and with some zest is notably absent.

Nor is this a phenomenon of nonmanagers only. Supervisors are often oriented toward their subordinates, not their superiors; many middle managers merely carry out assigned duties and keep out of trouble. And even high-level managers may lose their jobs, not because of inefficiency but because they may lack good fellowship.[7]

[7] See V. Packard, *The Hidden Persuaders* (New York: David McKay Company, Inc., 1957), and K. McFarland, "Why Men and Women Get Fired," *Personnel Journal*, vol. 35, no. 8, pp. 307–308 (January, 1957).

AS THE PSYCHOLOGIST SEES IT

Worried as managers were about lack of motivation, they did little or nothing beyond preaching about an honest day's work. But both amateur and professional psychologists—sometimes lightly referred to as "happiness boys" and human relations scientists, but now preferring to be called behavioral scientists—became interested. Indeed, since the well-known work of Elton Mayo, there have been many studies[8] devoted to motivation, stressing among other things work satisfaction, participation, leadership, supervisory techniques, communication, group dynamics, and behavioral environment.

Although many of the reports seem unrelated to the furtherance of enterprise purposes, all have tried to find ways to improve motivation. Managers have been overwhelmed with isolated prescriptions: understand others, practice empathy, improve the working environment, improve communication, practice leadership, and avoid injuring a subordinate's psyche. Studies indicated that employees like to participate in decision making, that they respond better to employee-centered supervisors, and that their self-esteem should be cultivated, not damaged. However, in the firms that tried some or all of these techniques, although the work environment improved, motivation to do better work has not been clearly and universally generated.

The explanation for failures has been the assumption that people are inefficient because their work environment is negative. Contrary to Herzberg's view[9] that the hygienic factors may have a negative motivation, many instances of high productivity in adverse circumstances might be cited: the Seabees of World War II, a struggle to build a new university, keeping enterprises solvent during a depression. No, it is not the general work environment that necessarily correlates with motivation, but the nature of man himself. This must be understood before motivation can be practiced successfully. To further this purpose, it is useful to review some of the approaches to motivation studies selected by familiar pioneers.

Maslow   Perhaps the best-known classification of human needs was proposed

---

[8] Carried on mainly at Harvard, Ohio State, and Michigan Universities, and supported by schools such as Carnegie, Massachusetts Institute of Technology, Yale, and UCLA. The reports are too numerous to cite here, but the pioneer works include: E. Mayo, *The Human Problems of an Industrial Civilization* (New York: The Macmillan Company, 1933); A. H. Maslow, "A Theory of Motivation," *Psychological Review* (1943); F. S. Roethlisberger and W. J. Dickson, *Management and the Worker* (Cambridge, Mass.: Harvard University Press, 1939); W. F. Whyte, *Leadership and Group Participation*, Bulletin No. 24 (Ithaca, N.Y.: State School of Industrial and Labor Relations, Cornell University, May, 1953); A. Zaleznik, *Worker Satisfaction and Development: A Case Study of Work and Social Behavior in a Factory Group* (Boston: Division of Research, Harvard Business School, 1956); D. Katz, "Morale and Motivation in Industry," in W. Dennis (ed.), *Current Trends in Industrial Psychology* (Pittsburgh: University of Pittsburgh Press, 1949); K. Lewin, *Resolving Social Conflict* (New York: Harper & Row, Publishers, Incorporated, 1950) and R. Tannenbaum, I. R. Weschler, and F. Massarik, *Leadership and Organization* (New York: McGraw-Hill Book Company, 1961).

[9] Herzberg et al., *op. cit.*, p. 127.

by A. H. Maslow nearly fifteen years ago.[10] He thought of human beings as having needs that ranged from those that are physiological through safety, love, and esteem to self-actualization. The former were classified as "lowest" and the latter as "highest." His system also included the concept of regression from the higher- to the lower-level needs.

From many points of view, this is a useful theory. Man is thought of as being first concerned about satisfying his needs for food and shelter. Once these are attained, they lose top priority and are succeeded by the need for safety from external forces that endanger life itself. These forces include such threats as assault, murder, expropriation, and natural cataclysms. Once a sense of comparative safety has been achieved, the individual finds that love, or the desire for more or less affectionate relationships with family, friends, and groups, assumes top priority. This need is then succeeded by esteem, the good opinion of others and of one's self, and finally by self-actualization, which the author explains (page 92) as ". . . the desire to become more and more what one is, to become everything that one is capable of becoming."

This classification is an aid in thinking of man's needs, but it does carry the implication of successive saturation. This aspect is not essential. Human beings certainly move from satisfying one need to satisfying another before much more than the "edge" is taken off the requirement having top priority. Also, the need satisfactions are not mutually exclusive. Perhaps the most curious terminology is used in reference to "low"- and "high"-need satisfaction. Intrusion of this value system is wholly unnecessary and, indeed, pernicious. The dignity of the human being is *equally* served through the process of satisfying each of his needs.

March and Simon   These authors[11] were concerned not so much with the needs of men as with the influences which their value systems, the needs of the organization, and the extraorganizational factors as a totality have upon a particular organization. The operation of enterprise certainly has to take cognizance of the individual's value system if it hopes to attract employees and to keep them. It also will be affected by external forces. The summary of research data reported by March and Simon which relates to these influences is a useful reference for managers.

As far as motivation is concerned, the authors concentrate upon the unanticipated consequences which may result from organizational stimulation, and upon the decision of the individual to participate in the organization. In the former case, it is suggested that:

1. A stimulus may evoke a larger set of possible responses than is expected, or the set is different than expected. This reminder underlines the importance of being aware of the very complex nature of human beings and that narrow anticipations of rational reactions

---

[10] *Motivation and Personality* (New York: Harper & Row, Publishers, Incorporated, 1954).

[11] J. G. March and H. A. Simon, *Organizations* (New York: John Wiley & Sons, Inc., 1958).

that some managers demonstrate often lead to confused disbelief. For instance, efforts to improve job satisfaction do not result in higher productivity—a point made in all editions of this book.

2. The stimulus itself may include unintended elements. The manager may decide that overtime should be offered in terms of equal opportunity for group members. He views this arrangement as an elemental practice in equal treatment, but the group membership may have an informal organization that provides for unequal overtime opportunities based upon seniority, or as a reward for the informal leader.

3. The responding subordinate may mistake one stimulus for another. This proposition reminds managers that subordinates may not possess the faculty for close distinctions. In this situation, it is readily understood why response can often be widely at variance with what was intended.

The decision of a prospective employee to participate in the enterprise, or that of a current employee to continue participating, is analyzed in terms of utility functions. These are extraordinarily complex and equally impossible of prediction because they are really unmeasurable. Of course, it goes without saying that all the elements in a utility function cannot be provided by management: a favorable response may occur because a friend is employed, or an unfavorable response if he is terminated. The manager knows that the balance of utility is in his favor only *after the event* by observing the response to his motivation system. But he rarely knows where the margin is. He makes very good motivational decisions, however, because shortage of employees usually reflects a generalized condition of the market and not a unique enterprise phenomenon.

While it was not the purpose of these authors to provide managers with some clues about the relative degree of the influences they enumerate, or what response managers might take in view of these influences, these aspects are vital to any operating executive. Perhaps the task is impossible of accomplishment because too many influences are cited, without any attempt to suggest an operational classification. The book is marred by unfounded disparagement of the classical and/or management process approach to organization theory. The former writers are reproved for not taking account of present-day knowledge when they wrote sixty years ago. This is much like accusing Lister of not using present-day medical knowledge. Also, it is simply not true as March and Simon state that the classicists regarded the human being as an inert instrument.

Argyris   The motivational theories of this author center around the dynamic aspects of human psychological development.[12] He is not so much concerned with systems of classifying human needs as he is with the personality char-

---

[12] C. Argyris, *Personality and Organization* (New York: Harper & Row, Publishers, Incorporated, 1957).

acteristics of individuals as they grow from childhood to maturity. He postulates that individuals move from being passive and dependent as children to being active and independent as adults. In addition, he thinks that the adult's emotional responses are more varied as his attention is differentiated, thus permitting the complex classification of phenomena, that adults tend to develop lasting interests, and that adults become aware of their independence and develop a control system over their actions.

Managers are not surprised by this theory of motivation. They feel that Argyris is making sense of what they have always known or suspected about the individual's psychological development. While they are not so much interested in child psychology, they do feel a real need to understand the adult so that the motivational system which is created will complement the individual employee's psychological drives. In particular, this means that organizational design should facilitate the adult need for self-actualization, and that the capabilities of the adult should be identified and utilized.

Momsen, Saxberg, and Sutermeister This trio of writers approaches the theory of motivation by identifying the sources of pressures on human beings and deducing the implications in terms of response.[13] The pressures are classified as the achievement drive in human personality and as environmental forces exerted by small and large groups.

The human desire for achievement is viewed as a motive in its own right which is consciously or unconsciously internalized. The strength of this motive varies widely among people and appears to be present in its greatest degree among those who are raised amid the Protestant Ethic, brought up to be self-reliant and independent, are identified with the professions or business, and have an above-average education.[14] The cultural environment is seen as governing the level of aspiration, wherein even the fear of nonachievement may be high or low.

The measure of achievement is found in man's desire to maximize his total income. Dollars, profits, power, and status are not motives in themselves; rather, they are the measures of achievement. This is why profit is seen as the ultimate test of achievement in business. McClelland, whose views are summarized by Momsen and his co-authors, is not merely rationalizing the success of the American middle class. He has also engaged in a research program to determine whether the achievement factor cannot be built up in a sample of Indians.[15] The possibility of evoking this motive, especially among the low-income peoples of the world, is fascinating.

If men feel a pressure to achieve, and this is clearly seen among busi-

---

[13] R. J. Momsen, B. O. Saxberg, and R. A. Sutermeister, "The Modern Manager: What Makes Him Run?" *Business Horizons,* vol. 9, no. 3, pp. 23–34 (Fall, 1966).

[14] At this point, the authors are reviewing the research data of D. C. McClelland. His most noted work is *The Achieving Society* (Princeton, N.J.: D. Van Nostrand Company, Inc., 1961).

[15] D. C. McClelland, "Achievement Motivation Can Be Developed," *Harvard Business Review,* vol. 43, no. 6, pp. 6–25 (November–December, 1965).

ness managers, it is important that those who construct a motivation system take cognizance of the fact. This must be done through identifying the variant measures of the degree of achievement which our culture has sanctioned and which, therefore, have become appropriate goals for achievers. Thus, status and power are not needs of the human being in and of themselves but are socially sanctioned measures of success in the satisfaction of the need to achieve.

The external pressures to which human beings respond are thought of as emanating from small and large groups. Managers are members of many small groups, and these associations affect their motivations. The authors cite examples: (1) the manager who is a member of his industry's managerial group, if he becomes aware of rising competition among them, may be motivated to improve his own competence. (2) The manager who wants to develop satisfactory peer-group relationships will strive for recognition, status, and prestige among his peers. (3) The manager who is subordinate-oriented may be concerned about his actions, interactions, and his prestige within this group. (4) The manager who is interested in subordinates as individuals may be motivated to help them develop their own individual abilities.

The pressures to react to the influences of large, external groups also motivate managers. A manager may see that his promotion, with its rewards, rests upon a reputation for maintaining good relations with relevant trade unions, upon skill in conciliation, upon the making of decisions which are not attacked, and upon speed in the settlement of disputes. His behavior may be affected by government through taxes and regulations; he may dislike government actions that he views as negative and approve those actions that aid him. If he is in large-scale industry, he may view his competitors as peers and adopt their mores and rules of conduct. He may see the educational process as the transmitter of approved cultural values and norms which raise the aspiration level of the community, thereby contributing to achievement needs. The manager who is upwardly mobile may see the bureaucracy as a useful tool for himself, as well as a discriminating device that leaves behind the indifferent, the frustrated creators, and the mediocre—certain other-directed organization men. He may, as well, feel a strong pressure for accepting vague concepts of his social responsibility voiced by others.

To the above motivational pressures the manager will respond by seeking short-term goals in order to maximize both his monetary and his nonmonetary income. Money may be an indicator of power, status, prestige, and competence. Affiliative interaction, a source of psychic income, may be achieved through the development of supportive relationships with subordinates and through insightful support of the informal organization. Indeed, psychic income may even be derived from a strong personal devotion to the enterprise itself. Assuming the same motivations for his subordinate managers, he will see that his reward system amply fulfills their aspirations.

Conclusions   The many and diverse viewpoints about motivation which have been considered in this section should have the effect of cautioning the student that the present state of knowledge of this subject is far from adequate. Michael Beer, who has recently completed research in this area, concludes:[16]

> The accepted notions about leadership and motivation have not been confirmed. The results cast serious doubts on McGregor's theory and other theories which employ the Maslow need hierarchy as means of explaining the dynamics of leadership and human motivation at work. In fact, the usefulness of the Maslow theory as a framework for an industrial theory of motivation is open to question. . . .

Beer sees the problem of motivation as extremely complex, and he cautions against global theories and oversimplified models. With him, managers would agree; they have always known that they were dealing with complex forces. They have been troubled, however, because they have not been able to understand the unexpected behavior of subordinates, and they have received little help from the simple explanations offered by some academicians.

WHAT GOOD MOTIVATION DOES

In order to induce subordinate managers to work efficiently, the superior manager will take advantage of their personal and environmental reasons for cooperating and *add to these* certain other inducements. There cannot be a single source of motivation: a *system* of motivation is required—a coordinated set of inducements, positive and negative, available for selective application to elicit the best effort of individual managers. The system is not designed solely for across-the-board application but permits the use of any one or group of inducements which will fulfill the desires of subordinate managers to satisfy their top-priority needs within the framework permitted by the enterprise.

A sound motivational system is based on sociological principles, the practices of enterprise, and convictions concerning the ends of man. The bases discussed below apply to all motivational systems and should be integrated into the development of systems designed for a particular enterprise.

Satisfies Needs   Managers must attempt to understand their subordinates in order to select intelligently effective elements of a motivational system to be applied to individual subordinates. This is difficult, because needs are so numerous and expansible, their priority shifts, and they vary greatly from person to person. Thus, the best that the manager can do is to build a system

---

[16] M. Beer, *Leadership, Employee Needs and Motivation,* Bureau of Business Research Monograph No. 129 (Columbus, Ohio: The Ohio State University Press, 1966).

of motivation based on satisfying common needs, keep it consistent with his experience with men, and keep it flexible enough to respond to variations in individual reactions.

Every manager will select, from among an unknown number of needs, those whose promise of some degree of satisfaction will elicit productive effort on the part of subordinates. Every enterprise aims to satisfy its co-operators' basic needs at some level; the higher needs it aims to satisfy are selected on the basis of how much effort is expended to satisfy them.

Basic needs Irrespective of his living standard, a manager, like every-one else, is always concerned about satisfying his needs for food, clothing, and shelter. True, he may not be primarily concerned, if he holds a well-paying position and can give preference to the satisfaction of higher needs. But while he does this, he assumes no change in his basic need satisfactions.

In cooperative activities basic needs are satisfied through pay and through job continuity. The manager may be paid in one or more ways, depending on his firm and on competitive practices. Some firms can only pay a salary, while others develop sources of compensation including incentive pay and fringe benefits. The motivational system must offer a level of compensation which will attract and hold managers of the quality required by the firm.

Job security assures the fulfillment of basic needs in the long run. It normally means that the incumbent is secure in his job so long as his work is satisfactory, he reacts to the requirements of the work environment, and the job exists. He should be able to rest assured that he will not become unemployed through any unjustified action or complaint of others. This is the most job security any motivational system can provide; there is no such thing as a job guaranty.

Social needs Any enterprise can provide for the satisfaction of certain of a manager's social needs, chiefly the needs for status and for group relatedness. Status needs reflect the desire for distinction both within and without the enterprise, because most people crave social approval. Some of this can be partially satisfied by a motivational system that includes promo-tions and status symbols. Promotions—especially those carrying titles and perquisites—are common rewards for demonstrated ability. Status symbols include little things like reserved parking spaces, especially those labeled with names; closed offices and preferred office space; better office equipment and furnishings; and private secretaries. To be most effective, status symbols and perquisites should be carefully graduated by position in the organization structure, because distinction is highly correlated with scarcity.

The need to relate to other people also seeks fulfillment both within and without the enterprise. People form social groups on an informal basis, selecting congenial co-workers with whom to exchange news, ideas, or plans, to confide in, and to enjoy companionship. Because the same group or the same size group may not satisfy enough of the social needs, it is common practice to belong to more than one.

It is important to a motivational system that constructive groups be encouraged and destructive groups broken up. The former are maintained through the stability of the organization, and any changes in assignments should be made, if possible, so that these groups can remain intact. On the other hand, destructive groups should be rendered harmless or transformed by removing ringleaders or by scattering the members through transfers.

Ego In this classification are the needs for self-esteem and for self-fulfillment. The former, though vague in conception, are fulfilled by a combination of self-satisfaction as a result of conduct in accordance with one's own principles and by social approval. How can a motivational system take cognizance of the need for self-esteem? By encouraging conformance to acceptable standards of job performance, ethics, dress, and language and through evaluations for merit and for promotion.

The need for self-esteem is not strong in all subordinates, but for properly selected subordinate managers—the people of prime interest here—the need for self-esteem is strong and can be useful in the motivational system. By providing for delegating authority, encouraging subordinates to contribute recommendations, and rewarding creativity, the system can help fulfill this need.

Opportunity to participate in management may readily satisfy self-fulfillment needs. Subordinates always feel that they possess valuable information which, if used, would improve the quality of decisions of their superiors. Subordinates are close to the scenes of action and often have insight into operations which superiors cannot acquire. To evoke their views, experience, and recommendations is definitely part of a motivational system, but this technique must be considered carefully.

Contributing to a superior's decision making is an exercise of influence. Whether the contribution is important or not may not be apparent to a subordinate. He has had his chance to be heard. But the superior quite obviously cannot call for the views of subordinates on all decisions. He must select those decisions which promise the maximum payoff and which he should not make before fortifying himself with information possessed only by subordinates. Of course, subordinates may take this opportunity to sit back and second-guess the boss. As this attitude becomes known, the superior will invite only the really creative among subordinates to make recommendations. He is under no obligation to ask anyone's advice: he will do so with respect to those whose judgment and knowledge he trusts and to situations in which he might benefit.

On the other hand, participation should be confined to recommendations. No superior can long maintain his position if he abdicates his decision-making power in favor of a majority vote of his subordinates.

Participation varies widely as a motivational force from one subordinate to another. Many feel they are not paid for taking part and resent the invitations. Others—and good managers are represented here—are pleased to work hard to help an ambitious subordinate: the chance of influencing action fulfills ego needs.

For those with a strong need for self-fulfillment the encouragement of *creativity* [17] is included in the manager's motivational repertoire. In an organizational sense, to be creative means to produce new and practical ideas, to envision productive innovation. Unfortunately, creative subordinates are rare, because our social system tends to make conformists of people. On the job, as well as outside, employees are hedged in by the forces of conformity. They are required to follow precept, policy, and procedure; they work in a risky environment where conservatism—the voice of experience—reigns and where their supervisors feel there are no new ways to do things unless they thought of them first. Consequently, our society views creativity favorably in the abstract but tends to discourage it in practice.

Nevertheless, some subordinates overcome this barrier. They are the dissatisfied ones who are curious and imaginative about constructive change. They feel a glow of triumph in solving a knotty problem and particularly in seeing the solution put into operation, although over this they may have little control. A mature manager will motivate and encourage these people.

The motivational techniques vary from the generalized suggestion system or cost-saving system—where rewards, usually monetary, are given for accepted ideas—to personal rewards. Since managers do not ordinarily participate in suggestion or cost-saving systems, the personal rewards are pertinent here—including citations, public acknowledgements, conferring of distinguished-service buttons, salary improvements, registration of patents for their inventions, and promotions. Personal rewards invented by the immediate superior can be used to good advantage. Strange as it may seem, the social approval attached to membership in an exclusive group designated even by a tin button can be a stimulant to creativity as well as to other qualities. It remains only for the superior manager to develop a reward system for creativity, publicize it, and otherwise encourage the creative subordinate to try for the golden apple.

Saturates Basic Needs Since the satisfaction of higher needs will elicit more effort once basic needs are largely filled, greater rewards applicable mainly to the satisfaction of basic needs can be ineffective. Firms whose reward system is confined to remuneration find that more dollars sometimes fail to satisfy social and ego needs. For instance, the highly paid airline pilots may settle a strike by a deal for still higher salaries, which will add little, if any, more satisfaction of their basic needs. Though pilots search for a means of satisfying other needs—for instance, a keen desire to advise superiors concerning safety or cockpit design, or to be treated as a manager—they are not

[17] See R. Bellows, T. Q. Gilson, and G. S. Odiorne, *Executive Skills* (Englewood Cliffs, N.J.: Prentice-Hall, Inc., 1962), chap. 19.

invited. Frustrated here, they settle for more money, plus perhaps the side benefit of increased status that a higher salary provides.

Releases Work Capacity   Differences in productivity reflect the quality of motivation. There is abundant evidence that people have immense reservoirs of physical and mental capabilities largely untapped by employers. A good motivational system should release this resource.

Enhances the Firm's Image   Sometimes enterprise and its objectives will rivet the attention and spark enthusiasm in a subordinate. People prefer to work at a certain university or a certain firm because of glamor, a sympathetic outlook, congenial co-workers, opportunities to acquire and use research funds, or because others hold the organization in high esteem. Any such preference will stimulate employees to high productivity; hence, every advantage the firm can offer should be built into its motivational system.

Depends on Proper Selection and Orientation of Personnel   Obviously, the better qualified and trained the subordinate, the more productive his effort. This is in the nature of a prerequisite, because it reduces the need for and cost of motivation and makes possible a simpler system. No motivational system can explain itself or put itself into effect. The part played by leadership can be critical. Good leadership can often overcome the deficiencies of a poor motivational system; poor leadership can ruin a good motivational system.

WHAT A SOUND SYSTEM MUST BE

A sound motivational system, after squaring with the above description, must also be productive, competitive, comprehensive, and flexible.

Productive   Obviously, the motivational system must be productive in the sense of inducing subordinates to work efficiently and effectively and continue to do so. But a productive system has two more facets. First, productivity refers to output in excess of input but does not indicate *how much* excess is possible or probable. In many positions, productivity can be estimated as value of product compared with cost of input. To measure the productivity of a manager is more troublesome. With a manager, comparison may be attempted between cost to the enterprise and the value of the product of the group supervised. Sometimes close approximations can be made, especially where the supervised group is a profit center or produces a service upon which a profit can be calculated. If the group happens to be the personnel or accounting department, with no measurable value of product, its manager is only *presumed* to be motivated productively.

The problem of determining how much the excess over input should be remains unsolved. Where competition does not exist, one would compare the output of comparable units experimentally to measure response to various stimuli. For instance, the treasury department of a government might organize teams of bond salesmen, or even tax collectors, to work comparable areas and then measure relative productivity.

Competitive business has an advantage in expanding output over input, because success depends on it. Although the superior still has no bead on what maximum efficiency could be, he at least hopes that his managers can be as productive as his competitors'.

The second facet of a productive system concerns the fact that the system includes motivation from outside the enterprise, in the social environment, as referred to above. The enterprise should supplement these external factors in persuading subordinates to maximize their productivity.

Competitive   A carefree excursion into establishing a motivational system is a luxury that private enterprises cannot afford. In competitive business the cost of the motivational system, at the margin, can never exceed its productivity at that point without violating the economic principle that marginal revenue should equal marginal cost.

Clear though the principle may be, its application is difficult. The motivational system includes the totality of stimuli selected to produce a desired response. It includes more than wages and fringe benefits; it is also attitude and philosophy of operation. Thus, to measure its marginal cost appears beyond all possibility. To keep from being completely in the dark, managers proceed by innovation and imitation. Measurable aspects of motivational systems—such as salaries, insurance, and expense allowances—are carefully kept in a given relationship to competitive practice; so also—at least by method or name—are enterprise practices in training, decentralization, and opportunities for creativity. It is hoped that comparable input costs will yield comparable profitability. And always at the margin of opportunity, managers innovate to attempt to secure lower relative motivational costs. A firm may employ men at above-competitive wage levels or men with better-than-average education, or may provide better working conditions, on the chance that total productivity will rise above the average. Success is always imitated (and, often, so is failure, as evidenced by the popularity of costly "training"), which is why any lead in innovation is rapidly wiped out.

Comprehensive   Modern motivational systems must be comprehensive. Systems aiming only to provide for the satisfaction of basic needs arouse a flood of criticism, so managers endeavor to develop a system that reflects higher needs.

This has difficulties. In the first place, as explained above, the system cannot ignore the basic needs; they must be satisfied continuously, and managers recognize this in the heavy costs of wages, salaries, and fringe benefits.

In the second place, the system must be integrated with external sources of motivation, such as the needs of dependents, conspicuous consumption, and the desire for the respect or envy of neighbors and friends. The manager should identify and measure these needs of subordinates with a view to supplementing rather than substituting for them in his own motivational system.

In the third place, it must be decided which needs the system will incorporate. Inevitably, basic needs must be met through competitive levels of wages, salaries, and fringe benefits. But should the needs for "belonging," participation, and self-development also be met? This decision should be viewed in terms of cost and productivity. If efforts to satisfy these higher needs cost more than they are worth, they should be abandoned or omitted. No enterprise operates to satisfy the needs of employees if this conflicts with the achievement of group goals.

Flexible A motivational system needs to be flexible in time and with respect to individuals. Modifications based upon changes in the environment and in the light of new knowledge are obviously required. But often overlooked is the need to adapt the system's various stimuli to the individual. Differential application of motivational stimuli to account for differences between individuals should be built into the system. People differ, and they respond to stimuli in various degrees. Those who have a low level of basic-need satisfaction do not respond to higher pay or overtime pay with more work; many are those who prefer not to have the responsibility of participation; most persons are probably noncreative; and some certainly prefer isolation to belonging. Differential application of motivational stimuli to relative differences between individuals should be built into the system.

Use of a flexible motivational system to meet these differences requires a high order of discernment on the part of the manager. It obviously calls for ability to relate changes in productivity to opportunities for association or isolation, for participation or none, or for self-development or not.

Finally, this discernment implies the need for review. The flexible system must be kept in tune with the environment and employed with skill to produce the desired results. Considerable experimentation is also implied, because we are without standards for stimulating human production and for measuring its potential.

WHAT A SOUND SYSTEM PROVIDES

Although the following broad provisions for inclusion in a motivational system deal specifically with managers, applications also may be made, in many instances, to nonmanagers.

Financial Opportunities Men of managerial caliber are not primarily concerned about their basic needs: These could be met in many ways. But the manager is vitally interested in financial opportunities; financial independence equates with personal freedom. Attainment of this basic value in our society should be facilitated.

In meeting this provision, the motivational system will, first, offer a competitive basic salary. This also fulfills a status need. The manager is satisfied with the competitive rate, outraged to be offered less.

Second, low-cost insurance—especially catastrophe insurance—will conserve his cash outlays and defend him and his family from the high cost of sickness and accidents. And third, an opportunity should be provided for all managers to acquire an estate. Stock purchase and stock option plans are particularly suitable and, in addition, promote employment stability and a genuine interest in the profit position of the firm.

Growth in Stature and Responsibility Assuming that financial motivation has been provided for, there is no question but that managers yearn for stature and responsibility. This is, by all the evidence available,[18] the most important aspect of their motivation. It is a direct outgrowth of man's need for status and self-development and thus rests upon a firm sociological basis.

To satisfy this requirement, the motivational system depends upon the enterprise being organized so that each manager, together with his subordinates, is responsible for an identifiable end product. This is rather easy at top levels of an organization structure, where activity is grouped functionally or by customer, territory, or product. It is not as easy at middle- and front-line levels or for service and staff groups. For the former, a regrouping of activities should be considered. By careful planning, quantitative objectives can be developed for the latter.[19]

Opportunities should also be available for individual managers to be creative and innovative. Authority should be decentralized and assignments revised to encourage managers at all levels not to "play safe" but to use their ingenuity to develop new products and services and new business, improved efficiency in terms of cost reduction, and inspirational leadership. The exploration of such opportunities depends entirely upon the selection of trustworthy and talented managers.

To the two foregoing requirements, a third is a necessary corollary: The degree of success in producing the end product and the results of creativity and innovation must be measurable. General statements apparently approving of these requirements for successful motivation are virtually useless. The often-repeated declamation receives little attention and much ridicule if it stands alone. But a follow-up providing quantitative measures of accomplishment—targets, goals, or profit centers—defines success and failure.

A reward system may be based on such quantification. Rewards must be immediate and public in order to contribute to ego, status, and self-development needs and to satisfy the desire for recognition. Their form varies from letters of commendation to promotion in the management hierarchy.

Use of the Golden Rule Perhaps the very best guideline for a sound motivational system is the biblical admonishment to do unto others as you would have them do to you. If this were truly followed, any system of eliciting effort would be headed in the right direction.

---

[18] See Herzberg et al., *op. cit.*, p. 130.
[19] See, for instance, E. C. Schleh, "Make Your Staff Pay Its Way," *Harvard Business Review*, vol. 35, no. 2, pp. 115–122 (March–April, 1957).

DISCIPLINE AND MORALE

Every motivational system requires a provision for negative rewards; and morale is the subject of continual discussion by both theoreticians and practicing managers.

Discipline   In a broad view, discipline might be achieved through positive as well as negative motivation, by inducing desired behavior through rewards as well as punishments. But this view is not adopted here. Since subordinates are *expected* to conduct themselves properly and to work effectively, they are not to be rewarded for realizing these expectations. Rather, rewards are to be used to elicit superior performance, innovation, and creativity. Consequently, discipline is associated with negative motivation. Subordinates who do not conform to normal expectations are punished, in varying degrees depending upon the nature and circumstances of the lapse.

Discipline is necessary for managers because those who do not respond to rewards menace those who do. All enterprise activities must be closely coordinated, because they are interdependent. Thus, pace tends to be set by the least able manager, an obvious check on the potential of the other managers.

Inadmissible behavior on the part of incumbent managers includes dereliction of duty and lack or loss of integrity. Sometimes such behavior remains undetected for quite a while; and sometimes a manager, even after long and faithful service, will be tempted into dishonesty or conflicting interests. In either case, dismissal from his post should be prompt and complete.

Nature   Discipline, or orderly behavior, is necessary to the future welfare of the firm. The past is of no importance—beyond the possible provision of object lessons—because it is fruitless to punish a subordinate in a spirit of retribution or for the purpose of humiliating him. Disciplinary action, therefore, should contribute to improved behavior of subordinates in connection with various rules. For instance, it is important for employees to report on time, observe no-smoking and no-drinking rules, dress as required, follow official work procedures, behave in a socially approved manner with respect to other persons, and concentrate on doing acceptable work.

Subordinates need to know what behavior is expected of them and what quality and quantity of output, knowledge normally conveyed in the orientation process. They also need to know the negative motivations which will be applied and under exactly what circumstances each will be used.

Quality   The quality of discipline appears to be affected by two important factors. The first concerns "the strongest disciplinary force evidenced in human history, the power of faith." [20] Mooney relies upon the history of

[20] J. D. Mooney, *The Principles of Organization* (New York: Harper & Row, Publishers, Incorporated, 1947), p. 177.

church and military organizations for illustration of this point. His view is that faith depends upon the quality of understanding and that, "when the laborer and the boss are bound by the same common understanding of some common purpose, the discipline is on a plane that no other form can reach."[21] Our own army illustrated this idea in World War II, when the long-range purposes of a particular campaign were carefully explained to the troops destined to carry them out. There is abundant evidence that a lower quality of behavior results from the "tell them nothing" attitude of managers in all walks of life.

A second factor in the quality of discipline is leadership, a point mentioned by nearly all writers on the subject. Speaking of some conditions existing in the United States in the 1930s, Mooney[22] says that "the discipline was dependent entirely upon the disposition, mood, and character of the leader, variable in reason and justice, and temporary in value." Fayol[23] observes, "When a defect in discipline is apparent or when relations between superiors and subordinates leave much to be desired, responsibility for this must not be cast heedlessly, and without going further afield, on the poor state of the team, because the ill mostly results from the ineptitude of the leaders." A high quality of discipline is only one result of strong leadership, but it is "absolutely essential for the smooth running of business, and without discipline no enterprise could prosper."[24]

Evidences of poor discipline are many. Productivity may fall because of inattention to work, excessive visiting and talking, and slack work during straight-time hours in order to force overtime pay. The environment may also permit rule violation and disruptive attitudes toward the enterprise. The cause of poor discipline lies with the selection of poor managers. Managers are responsible for maintaining productivity, and this depends on discipline. They must know what to do and have the fortitude to do it.

Techniques Negative incentives can take the form of deferred or interrupted promotion, transfer to dead-end jobs or to less desirable jobs or shifts, deprivation of regular or special assignments, failure to earn merit wage increases, and even dismissal.

The immediate supervisor will select appropriate means of raising the quality of discipline to an acceptable level, as he is in a much better position to do so than is any other manager.

Formalities The standards of acceptable behavior derive from agreements between the firm and its employees. It makes no difference whether these agreements are formal or informal, written or unwritten, or whether

[21] *Ibid.*

[22] *Ibid.*

[23] Henri Fayol, *General and Industrial Management* (New York: Pitman Publishing Corporation, 1951), p. 23.

[24] *Ibid.*, p. 22.

they derive from rules and customs or from a union contract. The elements of acceptable behavior and the degree of freedom that the immediate supervisor has in enforcing discipline may be taken for granted or may be specified with great care and wide publicity. Enterprises that operate under union contracts undertake disciplinary action with considerable formality and presumed precision. There is also likelihood that those contracts severely restrict the prerogatives of managers, even to the extent of their being unable to separate the transgressor from the payroll and being forced to accept personnel against their own best judgment.

What subordinates expect   Employees know when they are out of line and expect to be disciplined. They also expect an inferior manager to be replaced. It is important to fulfill their expectations promptly and fairly. The manager who fails in these respects, because he is "soft" or fearsome or too sympathetic, sacrifices his subordinates' respect and forfeits his power to insist on an efficient operation. Procrastination disappoints subordinates.

Even more important is the quality of his judgments. Subordinates expect discipline to be administered evenly, without favoritism, excessive penalties, or arbitrary action.

Distasteful aspects   Few are the managers who do not have a strong distaste for administering discipline. They enjoy dispensing rewards, but this cannot always be done, human nature being what it is.

The manager often will delay action, find excuses for avoiding it, or entirely ignore the need for it. This behavior is irresponsible, discipline being part of the function of directing. Managers are employed and paid to maintain necessary discipline with their subordinates, among their other duties. If they fail in this duty, they fail as managers.

Morale   Napoleon[25] said, "In war, morale conditions make up three-quarters of the game: the relative balance of manpower accounts for the remaining quarter." It is dangerous to accept a quantifying statement without knowing the author's basic assumptions, but it is safe to say that morale is exceedingly important. It is the subject of great importance to both theoreticians and practicing managers.

Nature   Although variously defined, "prevailing mode and spirit conducive to willing and dependable performance and "whole-hearted cooperation in a common effort" describe its main elements. Morale will tend to exist when people see their personal needs and goals satisfied by their enterprise environment. Mooney[26] defines it as "the sum of several psychic quali-

---

[25] *Correspondence de Napoleon* (Paris: Imprimerie Imperiale, 1865), vol. 17, no. 14, 276, p. 549.

[26] Mooney, *op. cit.*

ties that include courage, fortitude, resolution, and above all, confidence."
Beishline[27] relates morale to "courage, confidence, and enthusiasm in the
performance of duty." And Urwick[28] suggests that tests of morale aim at the
elimination of sloppiness, the achievement of maximum performance, and
tenacity. Thus, it would appear that morale is a spiritual quality that reflects
zeal and confidence. Subordinates whose morale is high will work with vigor,
confident in their own ability and in the ability of their fellows to achieve a
given objective, as a team. Morale is a pervasive quality that subsumes good
discipline and unity of command. Consequently, it is a net result of effective
direction by individual superiors.

Achieving and maintaining good morale are essential to the manager
whose future is inevitably affected by the zeal and confidence with which
subordinates carry out their assignments. The morale of a subordinate group
is a fragile thing, and a motivational system, improperly devised and administered, can quickly destroy it. Its fundamental basis is personal faith; it can
be observed with sparkling clarity in times of adversity; its ultimate refuge
lies in the soul of mankind; it can be elicited but not forced.[29]

Variations Measures of morale remain most inexact, and symbols—
such as neatness, alacrity, promptness, genuine interest, and, especially, compliance with good grace—supply these measures. High morale does not depend upon favorable conditions and good news; indeed, such circumstances
can disguise its true quality. Morale is elusive and baffling in its variability,
and although the fact is well known, the causes are often not clear.

Relation to productivity Although a high correlation between morale
and productivity is generally assumed, research has turned up little to prove
this. This research has defined morale as job satisfaction, whereas, in the
opinion of the authors, its main characteristic is a spiritual quality reflecting
zeal and confidence. People perform with confidence if properly trained and
informed and with zeal if properly led. In this sense, there is evidence from
the long experience of many managers that morale does materially influence
productivity.

FOR DISCUSSION

1. What is work? What social, psychological, and physical pressures are
present to force men to work?
2. If there are external pressures which force men to work, why is it necessary to motivate them on the job?

[27] J. R. Beishline, *Military Management for National Defense* (Englewood Cliffs,
N.J.: Prentice-Hall, Inc., 1950), p. 229.
[28] From a seminar given at the University of California at Los Angeles (Apr. 14,
1953).
[29] See W. E. Hocking, *Morale and Its Enemies* (New Haven, Conn.: Yale University Press, 1918), for an exposition of morale that is thought by many still to be the
finest.

3. What means are available to managers who wish to motivate their subordinates? Is there some order in which they should be used?

4. How would you like to be motivated?

SELECTED REFERENCES

Bellows, R., T. Q. Gilson, and G. S. Odiorne: *Executive Skills,* chap. 10, Englewood Cliffs, N.J.: Prentice-Hall, Inc., 1962.

Bowles, W. J.: "Identifying and Challenging Management Potential," *Steel* (Jan. 3, 1966).

————: "The Management of Motivation," *Personnel,* vol. 43, no. 4, pp. 16–26 (July–August, 1966).

Brown, Wilfred: "What Is Work?" *Harvard Business Review,* vol. 40, no. 5, pp. 121–129 (September-October, 1962).

Herzberg, F., F. Mausner, and B. B. Snyderman: *The Motivation to Work,* New York: John Wiley & Sons, Inc., 1959.

Homans, G. C.: *Social Behavior,* New York: Harcourt, Brace & World, Inc., 1961.

Kast, F. E.: "Motivating the Organization Man," *Business Horizons,* vol. 4, no. 1, pp. 55–60 (Spring, 1961).

Lawrence, P. R.: *The Changing of Organizational Behavior Patterns,* chap. 10, Boston: Division of Research, Harvard Business School, 1958.

McDermid, C. D.: "How Money Motivates Men," *Business Horizons,* vol. 3, no. 4, pp. 93–100 (Winter, 1960).

McNair, W. P.: "What Price Human Relations?" *Harvard Business Review,* vol. 35, no. 2, pp. 15ff. (March–April, 1957).

Meyers, M. S.: "Conditions for Manager Motivation," *Harvard Business Review,* vol. 44, no. 1, pp. 58–71 (January–February, 1966).

Murray, T. J.: "How Do You Get Executives off Dead Center?" *Dun's Review,* vol. 89, no. 4, pp. 29–30; 103 (April, 1967).

Oxley, G. M., and G. B. Oxley: "Expectations of Excellence," *California Management Review,* vol. 6, no. 1, pp. 13–22 (Fall, 1963).

Patchen, M.: *Some Questionnaire Measures of Employee Motivation and Morale,* Ann Arbor, Michigan: Institute for Social Research Monograph No. 4, University of Michigan, 1965.

Zaleznik, A., C. R. Christensen, and F. J. Roethlisberger: *The Motivation, Productivity and Satisfaction of Workers,* chaps. 2, 11, Boston: Division of Research, Harvard Business School, 1958.

communication

Although communication has pervasive application to all phases of managership, it is particularly important in the function of direction. Good communication has been defined by The American Society of Training Directors as the interchange of thought or information to bring about mutual understanding and confidence or good human relations. Newman and Summer[1] define communication as an exchange of facts, ideas, opinions, or emotions by two or more persons. Communication is also defined as intercourse by words, letters, symbols, or messages; and as a way that one organization member shares meaning and understanding with another.[2]

In this book communication is viewed as the transfer of information from one person to another, whether or not it elicits confidence or becomes an exchange or interchange. But the information transferred *must* be understandable to the receiver.[3]

IMPORTANCE OF THE COMMUNICATION FUNCTION

It is no exaggeration to say that communication is the means by which organized activity is unified. Whether we are considering a church, a family, a scout troop, or a business enterprise, the transfer of information from one individual to another is absolutely essential. It is the means by which behavior is modified, change is effected, and goals are achieved. Communication as a topic of inquiry is of rather recent origin, not because the ancients

[1] W. H. Newman and C. E. Summer, Jr., *The Process of Management* (Englewood Cliffs, N.J.: Prentice-Hall, Inc., 1961), p. 59.

[2] R. Bellows, T. Q. Gilson, and G. S. Odiorne, *Executive Skills* (Englewood Cliffs, N.J.: Prentice-Hall, Inc., 1962), p. 59.

[3] See C. G. Browne, "Communications Means Understanding," *Personnel Administration*, vol. 31 (1958).

were ignorant of its critical function, but because "everybody knew" its essentiality and took part in it.

The topic of communication has emerged in management literature in rather recent times. It is fashionable today for writers to criticize the "classical" school for lack of attention to this matter,[4] but this attitude is just as inappropriate as asking where were today's behavioralists when Fayol wrote his book. The earlier writers largely assumed the need for communication and the importance of its understanding. However, when they mentioned the topic at all it was in the context of directions issued by officers or managers.

Barnard was one of the first and at least the best-known of authors who gave serious consideration to communication in large-scale enterprise.[5] He viewed it as the means by which people were linked together in an organization in order to achieve a central purpose. This is still the fundamental function of communication. Group activity is impossible without information transfer because, without it, coordination and change cannot be effected.

Several years later, when the psychologists became interested in the topic, the emphasis was placed on the human problems of transmission. Much of their research related to sending and receiving messages, and the barriers they found to "good" communication. Out of this work certain principles of communication have been developed; these are reported at a later point in this chapter.

The main stream of communication at the present time embodies the contributions of sociologists and psychologists but utilizes this information for the welfare of the enterprise. Purpose and goals are uppermost in the minds of those who manage enterprises. To achieve these ends, they seize upon the social principles and techniques of many contributors, including communication experts. It is the view of the authors of this book that the achievement of enterprise goals is of paramount importance and that communication is one of many tools available to the manager in seeking to attain these goals.

RESPONSIBILITY FOR COMMUNICATIONS

In all the attention given to communication during the past two decades, the subject of responsibility for information transfer has largely been ignored. It is a matter of some importance to understand that every person in organized enterprise shares the responsibility for good communications. It is not only a top manager who may initiate while all others receive, nor is it only the subordinate who originates while superiors listen. It is a fact that every-

---

[4] See, for instance, E. P. Learned and A. T. Sproat, *Organization Theory and Policy* (Homewood, Ill.: Richard D. Irwin, Inc., 1966), p. 77.

[5] C. I. Barnard, *The Functions of the Executive* (Cambridge, Mass.: Harvard University Press, 1938).

one is both an originator and a receiver of information, depending upon the authority relationships, functional relationships, and cooperative relationships which exist in any enterprise.

The real meaning of this set of arrangements is that everyone in the enterprise has a need to know when and what to communicate to whom, as well as to know the available means for information transfer, including the varieties of techniques and the use of both formal and informal avenues for transmitting messages. The enterprise requires skill in communication from every one of its employees, although it often has to cultivate this skill internally. The effort of educational institutions in this regard falls far short of the needs of all organized institutions.

PURPOSE

In its broadest sense, the purpose of communication in enterprise is to effect change—to influence action in the direction of corporate welfare. In a simple system in which the owner also supplies the labor, communication is totally external. The farmer, for instance, requires information flow from every external source that has knowledge which he can utilize for the prosperity of his operation. He needs the inward flow of knowledge about prices, competition, technology, and finance, as well as information about the business cycle, government activity, and the conditions of peace or war itself. This knowledge supplies the basis for decisions affecting product lines, production ratios, marketing strategy, quality, and the mix of productive factors.

The communication process of large-scale enterprise is largely the same, although the most important additional input concerns the internal information flow. The immediate absorption and action taken in response to inputs become impossible when the top manager has a large number of employees. The human factor of production requires special treatment, for it has to absorb and take action in turn; when several thousand subordinates are involved, the problem becomes monumental in scope and always something less than complete in solution. The more or less obvious principles of communication, cited later in this chapter, are important for their own sake but are applicable only after one considers what are the needs for information transfer.

The problem of classifying information needs for purposes of achieving clarity in understanding is important in itself. One simply cannot write about communication in general if he and the student do not want to lose their way. On the other hand, attempts to fractionate the subject into detail, such as memoranda, bulletin-board techniques, letter writing, or computer printing, would not contribute to the central idea of promoting a useful conception of the communication needs of a large enterprise. Neither would the written-oral dichotomy be helpful. To bridge these problems, it is hoped that the classification selected here will be helpful.

COMMUNICATION AND THE DECISION PROCESS

Of concern here is the information needed and what is done with it to enable managers to make operational decisions. The locus of most decisions is internal to the firm and much of the information required is generated by the firm itself. However, as we all know, even operational decisions rest partially upon external data.

The Manager's Need to Know If one were to observe the information, in all its variant forms, that flows to a manager in the typical American enterprise, he would have a word for it: chaos. Subordinates want to be helpful, or to promote themselves, or to reflect discredit somewhere, and they originate or serve as a transmission belt for information *they* think the manager should have. Furthermore, it is the nature of the business process that information is generated where it is most easily reflected and is very scarce in areas or phases where data are not readily available. If one could project a tape which showed "information" density through time, he would find areas of heavy concentration and areas of little or no cloudiness. This means two things: First, people seem to have an inner drive to report available information in many ways, many forms, and for many users. Note what an accountant or statistician can do with two figures—or a mathematician without any figures at all! Second, the lack of information in specific areas means only that it is not available; it does not mean that it is unnecessary. Indeed, the blind areas may be of the greatest importance for decision-making purposes.

The results of this state of affairs are not inconsequential. Duplications, overlaps, a mixture of the frivolous and the important, variant timing and rates of flow, and the irritations of nonavailability spell nothing but high cost and poor decisions. When one adds the immense cost of warehousing legal documents, engineering drawings, financial data, and other types of information—all often stored in quadruplicate—it is readily seen that enterprise and government have created a monster. While newer technologies are helpful in keeping pace with storage problems, little has been done to ensure discrimination in selecting information required for decision making.

Nothing can be done, in reality, until the manager himself poses and responds to the question, "What do I need to know?" Of course, it is a very difficult question to answer, which may be why it has not been asked. On the other hand, this is the proper place to start if one is seriously concerned about the communication of relevant information for making decisions. Furthermore, one should not assume that two successive managers of the same plant will answer the question in the same way. There will certainly be some common information, but there will also be unique data requirements. This fact is a serious reflection upon the success of efforts to create a uniform information system for any firm.

While it is not possible for the authors of this book to program what the manager should know for decision-making purposes, it is both possible and important to suggest a procedure. The manager will have to start with a clear conception of his job, that is, for what he is accountable. This topic was discussed in Chapter 20. This conception requires buttressing by the identification of those specific end products whose quality, timeliness, and scope will, in total, spell out the kind of performance the manager has achieved. Finally, the information inputs which are needed to produce the end products (including documents) can then be identified. Every manager in the enterprise should follow this procedure—but the process *must* start at the very top. It is a job for the president first; he sets the parameters and eases the job of his vice-presidents. They no longer will have to guess, be intuitive, or visualize what may be needed. Likewise, the second level of managers then establishes the parameters of the problem for their subordinate managers. Sources and systems are for information specialists to determine and provide, but now, for the first time, they will know what is needed.

An Information System   The considerable discussion about the possibilities of an information *system* in recent years reflects a concern for improved communications in enterprise. Theorists see a real possibility of conceptualizing information flow as a system. They have not succeeded because there has been an absence of a definition of manager needs, because they have not understood the problem of hierarchical information needs, and because of the unique factor in managerial information requirements. Nevertheless, the demand for an information system is of increasing importance as a communication technique.

The information system which is normally conceptualized is an open loop providing for a manager to specify, or have specified for him, certain inputs flowing from subordinates who tap internal and external sources. The received information is evaluated and decisions are set forth for the consideration and action of subordinates. This is a one-loop system; in modern enterprises, the loops are interrelated at each successive level of management. This concept provides for the flow of required information from bottom to top, and from top to bottom, in the organization structure *on the assumption that* the top executive has defined his needs.

Besides the lack of the pivotal assumption above, the development of an information system suffers from other unsolved problems. There is the problem of how long the existing system will suffice for the needs of the enterprise. Conceivably, the system should be changed with every change in the personnel occupying management positions. This, of course, can readily be arranged—but at what cost? There is a *constant* turnover of managers in large-scale enterprises and a *constant* change in the nature of required information. Second, the system will have to provide for the acceptance of certain types of new information (not in the programmed system) at almost every level of the organization. This is not an insurmountable problem, but it is a considerable accommodation problem. Third, the system will require centralized direction. He who heads it will be a service manager, but of a type not currently existing in enterprise.

Despite these difficulties, there is no longer any doubt that a large-scale enterprise will develop a centralized information system for the purpose of communicating information relating to decision issues. These may be largely of a technical nature in the near future, but there is little reason to assume that this will eventually be their sole scope.

Upward Flow of Information Summaries One conception of the information flow for decision purposes is closely related to organization levels. Information moves upward from the supervisory level and is summarized for the consumption of department managers, who take action within the scope of their authority. They, in turn, move this information upward one level, say to the division managers' level, at which point it is summarized for their action and for transmittal to the general officer, where it is summarized and serves him for decision purposes. This conception fits the thinking of systems- and computer-oriented people, but it is not realistic. First, every manager has other sources of information that he brings to bear on his decisions; he is not solely dependent upon data flow. For instance, at the lower levels, enterprise procedures and policies are notably important in this regard. Second, the conception is essentially static. New factors enter the picture continuously, such as internal and external changes in price, quality, markets, competition, technology, etc. Finally, changing managers weigh information differently, and much of the summarized information may not be needed for varying time periods.

The manager of the quality assurance department is concerned about the quality and delivery performance of a subcontractor. His internal data summaries spell out per cent unacceptable, days delay, and cost of unavailable components. External data include alternative sources, cost of putting them in business to produce the component, and government requirements to subcontract a given percentage of the contract.

The chief executive of a company is considering the question of adding a new product line through acquisition of another company. In view is a product family of items new to the present operation. From internal sources he has information that his existing channel of distribution cannot handle sales, newly developed financial data essential for a decision to acquire a firm which produces the new product line, and an estimate of the drain on managerial strength. Externally, he has information concerning the operation of the firm he is considering acquiring, an opinion from counsel concerning the probable position of the U.S. Department of Justice on the move, and an analysis of his future competitive position should the target firm be acquired. He wonders whether he is adequately informed to make the decision.

Downward Information Flow Timing, scope, and means are all involved in the flow of information downward in the decision process. Selecting the correct time and communicating a decision is the prerogative of the manager. Most decisions flow through the organization structure level by level. Time is involved in the process, and communication is ordinarily quick in getting decisions to the execution level. Of course, managers can—and sometimes do—procrastinate where an unsatisfactory basis has been laid for the decision, or where there is a history of check-orders. These, however, must be considered quite unusual in a well-run enterprise.

The scope of the communication is a highly variant matter. It is considered good practice to explain the reason for the decision to all those affected by it—not to get their approval, but to improve the quality of their response. Staff meetings are the usual technique chosen for this purpose.

MOTIVATION OF EMPLOYEES

The human factor of production is a special case so far as the purpose of communication is concerned. From an internal point of view, one does not have a communication problem with land or capital; externally, of course, communication relating to these factors occurs at the time of sale or lease negotiations with the owners. In all aspects of dealing with the human factor, however, from recruitment to retirement, the need for effective communication is paramount.

Recruiting The purpose of communication in this process is to persuade potential employees of the merits of working for the enterprise. It is essential to inform prospective recruits about the firm in general—its location, size, product lines, competition, and financial standing—so that a favorable image will be generated. The recruits also need information about internal policies and practices, organization structure, where they will fit in, and their alternative careers. Drawbacks are not overlooked but they are not stressed. They are dealt with in a manner that provides a favorable comparison with the conditions that are generally known to prevail in other enterprises.

Orientation The purpose of communication in this area is to provide the employee with a sense of familiarity and security in his job. Believing that people are more productive and more inclined to remain on the payroll if they are emotionally comfortable, considerable effort is directed toward making them acquainted with peers, superiors, and subordinates, toward familiarizing them with social and business groups, explaining procedures, policies, and practices, acquainting them with staff and service facilities, and making certain that they understand the operating philosophy of the enterprise.

Operational Information In order to execute his functions effectively, every employee stands in need of considerable information. The literate and responsible employee does not respond well to detailed directions and close supervision. He looks upon himself as accountable for a total job and, to do this well, he needs to know its relationship and importance to the over-all operation. Based on this information, he can take more intelligent action— he can better judge the importance of time and quality factors. Furthermore, some degree of zeal and confidence will creep into his work if he has more information about its nature.

Individual Appraisal   The need for the superior manager to communicate to his subordinates his evaluation of their contribution to enterprise activity is critical. This is their best means of knowing how they stand, what he considers their major attributes with respect to accomplishing their assignments, how their contributions can be improved, and what the future holds for them in terms of a career. The employee is entitled to know about his career prospects with the enterprise so that he may decide whether to change his employment. This evaluation contributes greatly to employee morale, provided it is intelligently done, a matter discussed above in Chapter 22.

Personal Safety   Enterprises go to great lengths today to provide information about employee safety on the job. From the employer's viewpoint, this is an essential activity because it keeps down the human cost of accidents, lowers the compensation insurance premiums and legal costs of defense, decreases recruitment and training costs for replacements, and contributes to the productivity of employees. From the employee's point of view, the communication of safety information and the enforcement of safety standards can only be morale builders. His life and welfare are, naturally, of primary importance to him.

Discipline   Everyone, and especially employees, recognize the need for discipline in organized activities. The purpose of communication on this subject is to acquaint employees with the rules and regulations of the enterprise in the first instance so that they can accommodate themselves to them. Such things as hours of work, parking, special clothing to be worn, care of equipment, and peaceful interpersonal relations come into focus here. Discipline on the job is equally important. Regulations relating to work output and work flow, maintenance and safety of work place, visiting, proper handling of complaints, and reward distribution are all subjects requiring clear and accurate communication with employees.

THE ENTERPRISE IMAGE

The image which an enterprise projects externally is a matter of vital concern. The very existence of the enterprise may be the measure of success in this regard. The recognition of this fact by universities, hospitals, governments, and businesses accounts for the extent and cost of "public relations" activities. The importance of broadcasting information about what an enterprise is doing, what it hopes to do, and why it is especially designed to accomplish these things, is rather obvious. It may romanticize the firm, it may stress efficiency, need, power, convenience, opportunities, or safety. These appeals are notably important in improving the capability of the enterprise to attract employees, customers, and stockholders, to excite students and scholars, to soothe the trepidations of the sick and forlorn, and to project what so often is not. To do these things, resort can be had only to communication. The ideas must be conveyed with skill if the desired change in attitudes is to be accomplished.

MAJOR PROBLEMS IN COMMUNICATION

It is important that the practical needs for communication be fully understood, and it is equally important that the issues involved in achieving good communication be clarified. These issues include getting ready to communicate, recognition of the barriers to communication, the principles of communication, the choice of techniques, crosswise communication, and the special problem of oral versus written communication.

GETTING READY TO COMMUNICATE

A review of the purposes of communication, similar to that of the foregoing section, leaves the impression that there exists a ready-made package of information which needs to be directed toward the decision makers, the motivation of subordinates, and the establishment of the enterprise image. Of course, this package is a result of getting ready to communicate. This is an interesting process if only because we carry it out so poorly. The evidence is everywhere that people start talking and writing without thinking. Getting ready to communicate is a very serious matter; it requires the time and the logic suggested in the previous discussion of the planning process. The objective must be clear, the premises known, the alternatives weighed, and the message selected. Thereafter the choice of communication techniques, and who is to execute the message, become critical. Treating the communication issue as a matter important enough to carry the cost and time of good planning techniques is most unusual, but it is essential if the change sought by a message is to be fully achieved.

BARRIERS

How can large enterprises such as the Federal government, a stock exchange, an airline, and a steel corporation operate with inadequate communications? Yet, if one inquires into the degree of understanding of necessary information at any given moment, one will be taken aback by its poor quality. This is possible because, even while successful in the long run, enterprises respond by fits and starts, and the flow of understanding among the cooperators tends to be discontinuous.

Notable improvement in efficiency could be made if communication barriers were torn down. Perhaps the following review will encourage the improvement of information transfer, for "improvement" is all that can be realistically expected. There is no such thing as perfect communication.

Badly Expressed Messages   Irrespective of how a communication is delivered, vagueness and murkiness are all too common. Such faults as poorly chosen and empty words and phrases, careless omission, lack of coherence, bad organization of ideas, awkward sentence structure, inadequate vocabulary, platitudes, numbing repetition, jargon, and failure to clarify implications occur everywhere and are attributable to carelessness or to poor instruction in our schools and colleges. This lack of clarity and precision leads to costly errors, costly corrections, and the need for otherwise unnecessary clarifications.

Faulty Translations   Managers sit at the communication centers of enterprise and function as receivers and transmitters of messages. They receive many types of communications from superiors, peers, and subordinates and, in turn, must translate information destined for subordinates, peers, and superiors into language suitable to each. It is often not enough to pass on a communication word for word; either it must be put into words appropriate to the framework in which the receiver operates, or it must be accompanied by an interpretation which will be understood by the receiver. This process calls for skill which is often nonexistent. Since enterprise members operate generally with only approximate understanding, efficiency continuously suffers, with attendant heavy cost.

Loss by Transmission and Poor Retention   Successive transmissions of the same message are decreasingly accurate: In oral communication something in the order of 30 per cent of the information is lost *in each transmission.* Therefore, in large-scale enterprise, it is quite impossible to rely on oral communication from one level to another. Even written communications accompanied by interpretations are subject to some loss of meaning in transmission.

Equally serious is poor retention of information. When studies show that employees retain but 50 per cent of communicated information, and supervisors but 60 per cent,[6] is it any wonder that enterprise operates under a cloud of ignorance? The necessity for repetition is obvious.

Inattention   The simple failure to read bulletins, notices, minutes, and reports is common. In regard to failure to listen to oral communications, psychologists and educators have noted that the nonlistener's "earphones" are often turned off while he is preoccupied with his golf score, with his family problems, or with what he can hardly wait to say—which, incidentally, may have nothing to do with the "message being sent." Unfortunately, nonlisten-

---

[6] Bellows et al., *op. cit.,* pp. 60–61.

ing seems to be a chronic human failing. This is illustrated by the common practice of arguing about an *agreed* matter. The reasons vary from impressing the speaker with one's virtuosity and self-centeredness to anxiety or plain contempt for another's viewpoint. In any case, effort to communicate with someone not listening will fail.

Unclarified Assumptions Often overlooked but critically important are the uncommunicated assumptions which underlie practically all messages. For instance, an authority delegation may appear specific, but how should a subordinate interpret it when he knows he should make a decision not specifically covered, but which he assumes to be implied? He can assume either that his superior meant only exactly what was specified, or he can assume implication of freedom to make unforeseeable decisions in the interest of the firm. The seeming clarity of the original delegation leads to this uncertainty—and, perhaps, to delayed action or costly lack of action—because of an unclear assumption.

Or, a customer sends a message that he will visit a vendor's plant at a particular time. Then he may assume that the vendor will meet his plane, reserve hotel accommodations, make transportation available, and set up a full-scale review of his programs at the plant. But the vendor is not clairvoyant, and he may assume that the customer is arriving mainly to attend a wedding and will make a routine call at the plant. These are unclarified assumptions in both instances, with possible loss of good will.

Insufficient Adjustment Period Sometimes communication announces change which seriously affects employees: shifts in the time, place, type, and order of work, shifts in group arrangements or skills to be used. Some communications point to the need for further training, career adjustment, or status arrangements. Changes affect people in different ways, and it may take time to think through the full meaning of a message. Consequently, it is important to efficiency not to force change before people can adjust to its implications.

Distrust of Communicator Some superiors are noted for the number of countermanding or modifying messages that follow an original communication. These naturally result from ill-considered judgments or nonlogical decisions. Repeated experience with these messages gradually conditions subordinates to delay action or to act unenthusiastically.

Premature Evaluation For some time Rogers and Roethlisberger's famous article[7] on barriers to communication has made the rounds of management literature. The barrier they stressed was the tendency prematurely to evaluate communications, rather than to keep an uncompromised position

---

[7] C. R. Rogers and F. J. Roethlisberger, "Barriers and Gateways to Communication," *Harvard Business Review,* vol. 30, no. 4, pp. 46–52 (July–August, 1952).

during the interchange. They felt that such evaluation stops the transfer of information, leaving the message sender with a sense of futility. In their thesis, those who would communicate should be listened to in noncommittal, unprejudiced fashion and thus be encouraged to state their full position before any response is generated. In this environment the complete message may be transmitted and received. Sagacious decision and action can follow.

Fear Experienced managers recognize that they must depend on their subordinates for information; but no foolproof classification of subject matter or of urgency has yet been developed to guide a subordinate in exactly what he should communicate upward. The timing and accuracy of control reports, problem reports, and special reports normally do not provide the superior with a sense of security.

Here the door is open to poor selection, partial truths, or entire omissions. Why do subordinates behave this way? Either because they truly believe the information is not important enough to communicate—this is a matter of judgment; or, too often, fearing the consequences of a full disclosure, they deliberately mislead a superior. Like the failure of a superior to communicate, this barrier may be considered "mechanical."

Failure to Communicate To the uninitiated, this "barrier" seems both astonishing and unforgivable, and yet it is a fact that managers fail to transmit needed messages. The reasons are found in well-known human tendencies to be lazy, to assume that "everybody knows," to procrastinate, to "hog" information, or deliberately to embarrass. Since one cannot communicate everything, it is obviously necessary to select. This leaves the door wide open to selecting nothing, of which all managers are sometimes guilty.

PRINCIPLES OF COMMUNICATION

The following principles are useful guides for establishing good communications because they direct attention to four critical areas: message quality, conditions for reception, maintenance of integrity of organized effort, and taking advantage of informal organization.

Principle of clarity Communicate in commonly understood language. It is the responsibility of the sender to formulate the communication and express it understandably, in writing or speech. This requires a literate approach to language and familiarity with language patterns of subordinates, peers, and superiors. Adherence to this principle will overcome several barriers to communication: badly expressed messages, faulty translations and transmissions, unclarified assumptions, and the need for follow-up clarifications.

Principle of attention Give full attention to receiving communications. Even though the principle of clarity is observed, no communication is completed unless the message is understood, and this requires attention. Getting full attention for even well-composed messages is no easy matter, because of both the quantity of messages competing for attention and the brevity of our human attention span. The receiver cannot listen or read with understanding unless he concentrates. Listening in a discontinuous and desultory fashion, behaving listlessly, or ignoring or skimming over written words ensures lack of understanding, to say nothing of being extremely discourteous to the communicator.

Adherence to the principle of attention will gradually overcome certain barriers to communication: inattention, loss in transmission, and poor retention. It will also improve the quality of listening and reading, and the communicator will most certainly feel encouragement for his efforts.

Principle of integrity Make communications support organizational objectives. The principle of integrity relates to the purpose of communications. To a manager, a communication is always a means, never an end. It is one of his tools for securing and maintaining cooperation in reaching enterprise objectives.

One aspect of this principle needs particular attention. The integrity of the enterprise depends in part on supporting the position of subordinate managers. Since they occupy centers of communication, they should be encouraged to use their positions for this purpose. Superiors often forget this and send messages bypassing subordinates in an effort to contact the ultimate employees directly. This can be approved only in those circumstances where simultaneous communication is essential: orders for evacuating a burning building or for taking cover from attack, information of a crisis nature such as a general wage cut or cutback in employment or the need for special effort to complete a contract, or news of equal concern to superiors and subordinates. Only special circumstances justify direct contact. It is very important for the immediate supervisor to transmit and interpret all other information. Only in this way will his subordinates recognize his superior status and feel properly dependent on him for official information, thus enhancing his authority.

Principle of strategic use of informal organization Use informal organization constructively as a means of communication. Informal organization arises from the need for transmission of information and thrives on information. Existing outside the formal structure, it endures with or without the approval of managers and can have destructive or constructive effects on the enterprise. Since it cannot be stamped out, it should not be ignored but should be mobilized to transmit and receive information supplementary to that provided by the formal organization in the coordination of enterprise effort.

Messages do flow, and sometimes are required to flow, formally from superior to subordinate and from subordinate to superior, but this channel is inadequate and unreliable for handling all messages expeditiously and with understanding. Therefore, managers often informally approach sub-ordinates—personally or through others—to establish contact with situations which would evade them otherwise. So long as no orders are given or im-plied, the intelligent use of this practice is highly recommended.

Implementation Putting the foregoing principles to work requires voluntary application by all members of an enterprise. This calls for a special provision in the motivational system. No one can point to dollar savings, for the cost of poor communication cannot be calculated; but that there will be cost improvements from better communication no one doubts.

Managers may send subordinates to classes in communications; they should coach them constantly; and they should overlook no opportunity to point out evidences of poor communication.

TECHNIQUES

The sheer mass of communication in the typical enterprise is overwhelming. Everybody initiates and receives messages in some form or other. Man is truly a loquacious animal! He is almost constantly either talking, writing, listening, or reading. He usually becomes more addicted to loquacity as the size of the organization to which he belongs increases. Indeed, the volume of communication may increase in geometric progression as the enterprise grows. In an attempt to determine the time spent in communicating, one investigator[8] reported that 232 technical employees of a research organiza-tion spent 61 per cent of their eight-hour workday in this activity: speaking and listening 35 per cent, writing 16 per cent, and reading 10 per cent. A manager's whole day may be occupied in reading, writing, speaking, and listening. Thus, from 60 to 100 per cent of working time may be spent sending and receiving messages.

Under these circumstances, unnecessary messages are all too common. Yet differentiating between necessary and unnecessary communication is complex, because there is no pat answer to the question, What does each individual in an enterprise need to know? Everyone has requirements of which he alone is aware, although sometimes even he is not aware of need-ing certain information. This situation makes communication largely a matter for personal decisions, for which no standards exist.

That repetitious, overlapping, and irrelevant messages are expensive is borne out by the number of persons, both inside and outside the firm, em-ployed to review, revise, consolidate, and simplify written messages. People like to be on distribution lists whether they use the information or not; they do not want to miss anything. They even insist on slightly different forms or arrangements of data, losing sight of the cost. All these practices burden communication techniques.

[8] *Ibid.*, pp. 61–63.

Choice of Presentation   Managers must often choose between presenting information in narrative, statistical, or graphic form. Trend data are easiest to understand in a graphic presentation; some items are more easily grasped in statistical form; and the unusual or complicated may be clearer in a narrative.

Recently, executives in business and government have become concerned about the ineffectiveness of voluminous and complicated communications which use all these types of presentation without being understandable. Seriously studying this problem, John Calvert[9] has developed a technique for presenting complicated information in simple form. Its success is chiefly due to the configuration of the data and to the fact that the totality of relationships can be grasped visually.

Integrated Data Processing   In speeding up the transfer of information, managers have studied and gradually adopted improved techniques for processing and reproducing data. The ultimate in these is integrated data processing. Electronic equipment has made it possible to communicate immense quantities of data on a regular schedule and to secure hitherto unavailable information for enterprise use.

The economy of providing computerized data is in serious question. Protagonists of integrated data processing make many unprovable claims for its use. Equipment and programming costs are very large; individual reports are costly, even on a continuing basis; the demand for computer time often forces priority scheduling; and the equipment is so interesting that its reports acquire status even though they may not be as useful, timely, or economical as an old-fashioned pencil jotting. On the other hand, a computer is indispensable for reducing large masses of data quickly and for producing new information from these data.

A manager must evaluate integrated data processing carefully. He will discover that many data transmissions are more economical and faster with simpler methods and that as much as three-quarters of the gain from employing high-speed computers could be obtained by better planning, a prior requirement for computer programming. He will become aware of outside service centers for handling his data. And he will keep posted on new developments, particularly in smaller, cheaper, and more versatile equipment.

CROSSWISE COMMUNICATIONS

All enterprises not only permit but insist on voluntary crosswise[10] or horizontal channels of communications at all levels, to speed information and improve understanding. Crosswise relationships exist between personnel in one division and personnel of equal, lower, or superior status in other divi-

---

[9] Manager, Commercial Sales Development, Garrett Corporation, Los Angeles, Calif. Full description and illustrated use of this technique are given in his *The Power to Convince* (unpublished manuscript, 1967).

[10] For a good discussion of this subject, see M. C. Niles, *Middle Management* (New York: Harper & Row, Publishers, Incorporated, 1949), chap. 4.

sions. Direct communication between them substitutes for making a message follow the chain of command upward through one or more superiors, horizontally across a level of organization, and thence downward to the particular recipient. Enterprises simply could not operate in such stilted fashion because the communication time would be excessively long and the quality of understanding would be inferior.

The proper safeguards to crosswise communication rest in an understanding between superiors that (1) crosswise relationships will be encouraged, 2) subordinates will refrain from making policy commitments beyond their authority, and (3) subordinates will keep their superiors informed of their interdepartmental activities.

Every manager should guide his subordinates in their conduct of crosswise relationships. In addition to their objectives of getting the work done and developing potential managers, division heads are conscious of the impact that crosswise relationships may have on themselves: Every time a subordinate communicates horizontally, his superior is evaluated by others as to his general efficiency as a manager, the quality of his directive skill, his choice of subordinates, and his planning and organizing ability. In such circumstances, the superior may feel quite as helpless as a parent who wants his child to make a good impression on friends but cannot control the situation.

Overcoming Barriers Departmentation automatically creates barriers to free communication between personnel and provides numerous points of friction. Proliferation of subdivisions based on geographic, product-line, or customer classifications, on the one hand, and the multiplication of staff and service groups, on the other, create further barriers to direct communication. People do not have time to become acquainted with the organization structure or with one another, and, as a consequence, they develop group loyalties that breed intolerance and untoward rivalry. But since organization is necessary, managers ameliorate these adverse results through directing subordinates' crosswise relationships.

In guiding and supervising subordinates in their crosswise relationships, managers attempt to anticipate points of friction. These usually involve lack of knowledge about the enterprise, personality clashes, and unsuitable grouping of activities.

Orientation Getting acquainted with the objectives, structure, and authority relationships of a large-scale enterprise is formidable, especially for new employees. The superior will try to orient the subordinate (see Chapter 24) and see that he masters organizational relationships. The superior will acquaint him, first, with the goals, plans, programs, and procedures of other divisions and, secondly, with the staff and service departments. The former present an integrated picture of the whole enterprise; knowledge of the latter may prevent the subordinate from duplicating such specialized functions within his department.

Several techniques are employed to orient subordinates in these areas.

Most common are general tours and classes of instruction for new employees. The new employees are given organization charts and manuals to study, are taken on tours through the firm or some of its divisions, and are lectured to by major department heads and perhaps general officers. A second technique is to give subordinates rotating assignments throughout the firm. Indeed, this technique is sometimes used in the training of middle- and senior-level managers. Its obvious objective is to familiarize the individual with the purposes, procedures, and problems of the various departments. Such familiarity helps prevent the growth of suspicion and intolerance.

Interpersonal relations Getting along with people is important in organized activity, particularly where democratic traditions are strong. This point is always stressed by managers because most work is accomplished by getting others to do it. In directing, managers should maintain respect for the authority and personal dignity of their subordinates. Such qualities as kindness, thoughtfulness, and an eagerness to understand others may seem too obvious to mention, yet lack of these are the cause of many poor personal relationships. Managers also need to caution subordinates to clear everything with everyone involved, not only as a matter of courtesy, but also to avoid presenting others with an unwelcome *fait accompli* which may or may not be workable.

An effective control on the quality of interpersonal relationships in crosswise communications is the requirement that subordinates keep their superior informed about their dealings with other departments. Periodic reports are often sufficient to take care of this, but on especially touchy matters or on subjects that require new policy formation immediate communication with the superior is essential.

Reorganization Sometimes crosswise relationships are unnecessarily time-consuming and perhaps even unnecessary, and it may be possible for the manager to have departmental processes or groups modified accordingly. For example, if the geographic factor is not carefully analyzed, it can occasion much loss of time, but it is often possible to change the location of an activity. Sometimes reorganization of an activity along product lines will bring related functions into close physical proximity. Of course, in such cases, other division heads will be involved. The single manager will not be able to accomplish this change himself, but he may accomplish it with other managers.

WRITTEN VERSUS ORAL MESSAGES

It is traditional in the literature that consideration be given to formal and informal communication. The authors of this book feel that such a classification creates more problems than it solves. It is often impossible to distinguish formal from informal communication. The objective of communication is change, whether or not it is achieved formally. It makes more sense, therefore, to retain the common purpose of communication, that is, achieve change, and inquire into the merits of written and oral information transfer.

Written Written communications have certain advantages: They can be retained as legal records and as reference sources; they are often more carefully formulated than oral communications; and they can sometimes save time and money. They are used for the mountainous paper work concerning transactions, proposals, and agreements; organization charts and rule sheets; corporate charters and other legal documents; bulletins, memoranda, contracts, and claims; advertising and public relations announcements and press releases; policy statements and procedure; manuals, authority delegations, and job descriptions; and many other things. Often their use is a matter of the communicator's preference and prudence.

There are also disadvantages to written communications. Although the writer has the opportunity to be carefully accurate in composing his message, he often fails in this and dictates so hastily that the message is couched in language not understandable to the reader. Such poorly written messages, followed by numerous written and oral "clarifications," make the ultimate message expensive as well as confused.

A second disadvantage of the written message also involves expense but for a different reason. Because—particularly in large enterprises—there exist opportunities for shifting blame to others and also for taking undeserved credit, people respond by keeping voluminous written documentation as a means of defense or attack. Unfortunate as this situation may be, it is a fact of cooperative life, and expensive. Since it may cost an enterprise from $12 to $15 to write a letter or issue a check and millions of dollars to write a proposal for a government contract, grossly unnecessary paper work may even bankrupt a firm.

Retention for legal purposes Every enterprise is required to retain particular information for various periods of time. It also elects to retain certain data to protect itself against charges, claims, and lawsuits that normally burden every concern. Examples include property titles, contracts, financial records, charters, and the minutes of boards of directors' meetings. The advantage of retention is often obvious, but there are numerous occasions in which retention for legal purposes is unnecessary and is duplicative. For instance, a firm doing business with the United States Defense Department may be required to retain a particular document, but several individuals are likely to save their personal copies to meet the over-all requirement. Furthermore, the uncertainty of eventual need for legal purposes results in squirreling information. However, managers can develop sensible standard practices in regard to retention if they put their mind to it.

Oral The chief advantage of oral communication is its potentiality for speedy and complete interchange. Questions can be asked and answered at once. The speaker is forced into direct contact with the listener and challenged to make himself understood. Unfortunately, for one reason or another, many listeners fail to ask the right questions and are left with inadequate or garbled information which can result in costly error.

Furthermore, oral communication does not always save time, as anyone who has observed the lavish expenditure of conference time knows. And when each committee member may be costing from $25 to $50 per hour, face-to-face group communication is hardly economical either.

Communication by Implication   Often neglected or unnoticed, communication may include implications conveyed by how something is said or what is left unsaid, and the important devices of nonverbal communication. Subordinates watch their superior intently for signs indicating what he thinks is important and signs which affect their own self-image. For example, if it is official policy to balance civilian and military business but a division superior prefers the latter, his subordinates will certainly neglect the former; and if by frown or continued unavailability the superior communicates to a subordinate a lack of respect, the chance of contented cooperation is lost.

Expediter or Liaison Man   In the foregoing discussion of written and oral communications it was assumed that the message was aimed at a willing recipient. This may not be the case at all. The recipient may have prejudged the message and decided he has no interest; he may distrust or be hostile to the sender; he may not listen and he may not read. Then there may be conflicting messages from the same or from different sources. The receiver may either do nothing or choose the message he prefers. And finally, multiple messages may require action involving time and resources far beyond those of the receiver and, therefore, the need arises to establish priorities in handling conflicting or excessive requirements.

To take care of these frequent situations, managers sometimes resort to the expediter and the liaison man. The former is chiefly used to help the receiver of the message assign the "proper" priority to work. If this is an internal arrangement, it can be a crutch to poor communication; if it is external and results in the expediters of customers storming the facilities of a vendor, it can be not only ridiculous but an open invitation to waste.

The function of the liaison person is quite different. He is a middleman communicator who carries messages between sender and receiver in the interests of saving time and interprets the message in the interests of better understanding. But he, too, is a crutch to poor communication. His mere availability encourages careless communication, delay of reorganization, or procrastination in adopting more efficient communication techniques.

CONTROL OVER THE COMMUNICATION PROCESS

In every enterprise, the practical difficulty of exercising control over communications is apparent to all managers. It does little good merely to describe the variety and techniques of communication; information explosion and concealment practices must be controlled in the interests of strong, progressive management. One suggestion has considerable merit.[11] Recognizing that there is a need for communicating upward information that is not reported in established channels, it has been suggested that, starting with front-line supervisors, subordinate managers should submit monthly a brief narrative statement of any item deemed important for the consideration of his superior manager. Shortly thereafter the line subordinates meet with their superior and discuss these issues, with the result that some may disappear, some may be resolved at once, some may be postponed, and some may become the subject for submission to the next higher level of management. This process is recommended sequentially for all management levels until it reaches the office of the president.

Several advantages of this technique appear at once. It forces every manager to think about his problems or potential problems. It requires each manager to select the issues he thinks should be reported. In the follow-up discussion, the relative maturity of subordinate managers becomes very clear. The technique also assures that both subordinates and superior will be prepared for the meeting. It makes certain that issues of importance, that would ordinarily be reported not at all or only too late for action, will be given appropriate attention. It gives operational purpose to staff meetings by bringing authority to bear on significant issues and thus eliminates the need for many meetings on the occasional problem, as well as meetings called to solve crises.

There is but one important disadvantage. Narrative reporting on a regular basis is a dangerous thing to require. This type of report easily gets out of hand in terms of irrelevancy, redundancy, scope, extent, mixing of the serious with the frivolous, and poor quality of writing. Managers on the same level compete with each other in the length, content, and appearance of their reports. And, of course, sheer volume practically guarantees that few, if any, of them will be read. It is perhaps much better to follow the practice of having the problem merely cited and defined, allowing the person who submits the item to bring with him any substantiating information he needs.

There may also be a need to caution managers that the information contained in their regularly scheduled reporting system should not be allowed to intrude into this monthly conference. Those reports should be examined for exceptions to planned performance, corrective action should be taken at once, and only those rare instances wherein the manager has need for his superior's help should be referred upward for person-to-person attention.

A second suggestion is that each manager should make a list of the written reports he submits to his superior, and also a list of regularly scheduled meetings held with him. The frequency of these reports and

[11] H. Saxenian, "Prescription for Old-Fashioned Leadership," *Business Horizons*, vol. 8, no. 3, pp. 45–53 (Fall, 1965).

meetings should be identified at the same time. Likewise, the manager should require that each of his subordinate managers do the same thing. This technique will cause everyone to evaluate the need and frequency of both reports and meetings—a first step in assessing the need for the reports and meetings.

"Why," the consultant wanted to know, "do you have that conference room filled with people every morning?" "Well," the factory manager replied, "the men in there, some 22 of them, represent assembly, production control, purchasing, liaison personnel, quality control, shipping, and accounting. They meet each day for three hours. They iron out the problems we have in coordinating effort around here. It is effective as a means of maintaining our billings schedule."

"I'm bushed," the contracts manager sighed. "We just completed the usual Tuesday meeting of managers relating to their departmental performance. I had an easy time today, but the boss certainly took care of engineering."

"Are not those problems of a general, rather than a departmental nature?" his friend inquired.

"Not a bit of it! Each of us has his turn on the carpet."

There is every reason to believe that communication will continue to be numbered among the unsolved problems of every enterprise. The only hope of keeping it within manageable proportions is to hold each executive responsible for the information he transmits. Such an accounting would cause him to think seriously about the problem, to take action to see that what should be communicated is identified, and to see that the most efficient technique is used for its transmission.

FOR DISCUSSION

1. Business managers spend much of their time in communicating. Can you suggest a good classification?

2. What should a manager do to make certain his communications are understood? Cite the principles involved.

3. Develop a plan to transmit decision-making data to the officer charged with buying the assets of another company.

4. From your own experience in the past week, list the barriers to communication you detected. Why did they occur?

SELECTED REFERENCES

Bellows, R., T. Q. Gilson, and G. S. Odiorne: *Executive Skills,* chap. 5, Englewood Cliffs, N.J.: Prentice-Hall, Inc., 1962.

Cohen, A. M.: "Changing Small-group Communication Networks," *Administrative Science Quarterly,* vol. 6, no. 4, pp. 443–462 (March, 1962).

Geneen, H. S.: "The Human Element in Communication," *California Management Review*, vol. 9, no. 2, pp. 3–8 (Winter, 1966).

Maier, N. R. F., et al.: *Superior-Subordinate Communication in Management*, Research Study No. 52, New York: American Management Association, 1961.

Melcher, A. J., and R. Beller: "Toward a Theory of Organization Communication: Consideration in Channel Selection," *Academy of Management Journal*, vol. 10, no. 1, pp. 39–52 (March, 1967).

Nirenberg, J. S.: *Getting Through to People*, Englewood Cliffs, N. J.: Prentice-Hall, Inc., 1965.

Rogers, C. R., and F. J. Roethlisberger, "Barriers and Gateways to Communication," *Harvard Business Review*, vol. 30, no. 4, pp. 46–52 (July–August, 1952).

Simpson, R. L.: "Vertical and Horizontal Communication in Organizations," *Administrative Science Quarterly*, vol. 4, no. 2, pp. 188–196 (September, 1959).

leadership

Along with motivation and communication, leadership is a means of directing. In the dictionary, synonyms for the verb "to lead" are "to guide, conduct, direct, and precede." This choice identifies the leader as part of the group and yet distinct from it. The leader acts to help a group attain objectives but never loses his own identity. The case of the orchestra leader is pertinent: his function is to produce coordinated sound and correct tempo through the integrated effort of the instrumentalists. But more than this is needed. The orchestra can respond in a desultory fashion or with wit and *élan,* depending upon its rapport with the conductor. This quality may be called interpersonal influence.[1]

Carter[2] identifies five approaches to leadership definition: (1) polarization of members of a group around some central person; (2) the person able to direct a group toward its goals; (3) the person selected by group members to lead them; (4) the person able to move a group along a specific dimension, such as sociability or integration; and (5) the person possessing certain behavior.

Managers should be leaders, but leaders need not be managers. In numerous studies during the past decade, it was assumed that leadership was merely a synonym for managership. While this is not true, it is apparent that the part of the manager's job which involves getting things done through people is undoubtedly made easier when the manager is a skillful leader. Although managers typically have the power to hire, fire, promote, and otherwise affect the ability of subordinates to realize personal goals, for

[1] After G. C. Homans, *Social Behavior* (New York: Harcourt, Brace & World, Inc., 1961), p. 283.
[2] L. F. Carter, "On Defining Leadership," in C. G. Browne and T. S. Cohn (eds.), *The Study of Leadership* (Danville, Ill.: Interstate Printers and Publishers, Inc., 1955).

maximum results men need to be voluntarily led, not driven. But the manager who creates and maintains an environment conducive to the effective and efficient performance of those individuals for whom he is responsible will be doing much to assure his leadership position.

THE NECESSITY

Let's say a manager has established plans and controls, grouped activities, and specified authority relationships, selected, trained, and oriented subordinates, established a motivation system, and then absented himself for a considerable time. What happens? There would be activity: Subordinate managers would try to carry out their assignments. But demoralization of group effort would gradually set in, even though the subordinates began with much enthusiasm. Why is this so? Why do subordinates *need* leadership? Although the views expressed here are tentative, it would seem that one reason is that no one but the manager has the authority to guide, and without guidance each subordinate is apt to go his own way, unless one subordinate assumes authority and actively performs the superior's function. As one authority remarks:[3]

> Having a common position with reference to the source of originations or direction, subordinates develop cooperative patterns toward one another that facilitate the work process. These would be much more difficult to develop were there not a common source of authority acting on them; witness the difficulties inherent in cooperative endeavors among individuals who have not had this experience.

Even more emphatically, the need for a "common sense of authority" is recognized by the distinguished anthropologist, Bronislaw Malinowski:[4]

> Authority means the privilege and the duty of making decisions, of pronouncing in cases of dispute or disagreement, and also the power of enforcing such decisions. Authority is the very essence of social organization.

It is believed also that a second and very complex reason accounts for the need of leadership. People seem to require frequent reminders of group goals to overcome forgetfulness and indifference, the presence of the superior as a shield from anxiety and insecurity, and his long view and foresight to overcome boredom and limited vision. In other words, humans may at times be shortsighted and apprehensive, opportunistic and selfish; although the manager may be so, too, he is not supposed to show it. These deadly foes of efficiency are the special targets of leaders.

[3] Leonard Sayles, *Managerial Behavior* (New York: McGraw-Hill Book Company, 1964), p. 145.

[4] *A Scientific Theory of Culture* (Fair Lawn, N.J.: Oxford University Press, 1960), p. 61.

Capability
utilization

Contribution induced by leadership ability of the manager	40%
Normal expectancy of capability utilization induced by social pressure, need for a job, authority of superior, and division of labor	60%

Fig. 27.1   Impact of Leadership on Employee Utilization of Capability . . .
Leadership is the ability of a manager to induce subordinates (followers) to work with confidence and zeal. Zeal reflects ardor, earnestness, and intensity in the execution of assignments; confidence reflects experience and technical ability. In the normal work situation, the manager exerts very little leadership. Subordinates are driven by the need for a job and income as well as by social pressure. If they are guided only by rules and requirements enforced by managerial authority, they tend to work at about 60 or 65 per cent of capacity—just enough to satisfy the requirements for holding their jobs. To raise output toward total capacity, the manager must induce zealous response on the part of efficient subordinates by exercising leadership. He does this through numerous means, all solidly based on the needs of subordinates, especially their ego and self-development needs.

THE FUNCTIONS OF LEADERSHIP

Singling out just what is the function of leadership from among the skills of a manager can be highly controversial. Practically all writers avoid much of the problem by identifying leadership and managership as synonyms. This practice grossly obscures the leadership skill itself and makes it very difficult to understand. Indeed, a definition of the term is far from generally accepted. It is probable that most social scientists would view leadership as essential to the gaining of cooperative effort at any level of action. This, however, is not the view of the authors of this book. Rather, leadership is understood to be that skill of a manager which enables him to persuade subordinates to apply themselves with zeal and confidence. Only at this level of activity will they realize their full capabilities. Leadership is, as Field Marshal Montgomery is reputed to have said, "the capacity and will to rally men and women to a common purpose."

Zeal reflects ardor, earnestness, and intensity in the execution of assignments; confidence reflects experience and technical ability. In many work situations, the manager exerts very little leadership. Subordinates are motivated by the need for a job and for income, as well as by social pressures to be employed. They are guided by rules and requirements defined by managerial authority. They may work at anywhere from 10 to 80 per cent of capacity—just enough to satisfy the requirements for holding their jobs. It is literally true that when a new employee reports for work, he is first concerned with determining how hard he must work to achieve minimum performance, that is, that level at which he will not jeopardize his employment and which is acceptable to his superior. In order to raise the productivity of the employee toward his total capability, the manager must induce zealous response on the part of the subordinate. This he does through his leadership skill. *How* is this accomplished?

The Psychological View   One widely accepted view is to place reliance on the stimulus-response relationship. Following the work of Maslow,[5] much emphasis is placed upon the requirement that enterprises must satisfy the needs of employees. The argument runs that people, since they have basic, social, and ego needs, will best respond in terms of output if the firm provides opportunities for them to realize these needs. Therefore, managers establish a motivation system that enables employees to meet their basic needs through adequate wage and fringe arrangements, their social needs through group efforts in the work situation, and their ego needs through rewards for innovation and creativity. This argument is basically sound from the viewpoint of motivation, but it does not establish the full scope for the exercise of leadership on the part of the manager.

The Sociological View   Sociologists, such as Selznick, see other functions of the leadership role.[6] They see the special function of leadership in setting goals, creating and molding organization, and reconciling internal and environmental forces. The leadership function gives character to the organization in the first instance by setting goals and defining the policies to attain them. The leader takes into account what the enterprise has accomplished to date, evaluates the future environment, and prescribes near and long-term goals. This is a creative function that must precede all efforts to persuade subordinates to work with zeal and confidence.

Second, the leader has the task of building goals and policies into the social structure of the enterprise. Likewise creative, it ". . . means shaping the 'character' of the organization, sensitizing it to ways of thinking and responding, so that increased reliability in the execution and elaboration of policy will be achieved according to its spirit as well as its letter."[7] Third, the leader must defend the integrity of the enterprise. Mere survival is looked upon as leadership failure; rather, survival requires that the values and the distinctive identity of the enterprise be maintained. From the point of view of the enterprise manager, this is probably an unrealistic position to take. Enterprises are often required to change direction, product line, and/or functions in order to survive at all. True, they will normally retain the same values through at least the short run, but their identity may be sacrificed in order to achieve other goals, such as competitive success, solve

[5] A. Maslow, *Motivation and Personality* (New York: Harper & Row, Publishers, Incorporated, 1964).

[6] P. Selznick, *Leadership in Administration* (New York: Harper & Row, Publishers, Incorporated, 1957), pp. 61–64.

[7] *Ibid.*, p. 63.

the problem of estate taxes, or change from private to public ownership in order to achieve a new position in their industry.

The fourth function of leadership is to manage internal conflict. Since large-scale organizations naturally degenerate into suborganizations, the struggle among competing interests requires the attention of the manager. Leadership must be exercised in order that new balances of power do not have the effect of changing the direction of the firm. The leadership function is to win the consent of the several groups in order to maximize their zeal and confidence. At the same time, however, what the groups propose must be consistent with the fulfillment of enterprise goals.

Directing Leadership functions may also be classified as directing, responding, and representing.[8] In the view of Leonard Sayles, directing is the essence of leadership. He points out that an organization cannot function on the basis of two-person or pair relationships. If two or more people shared the direction of an institution on an equalitarian basis, it would be formless and unable to act. This fact, recognized in organizational experience for several thousand years, is the basic reason for utilizing the superior-subordinate group concept. This permits the interlinking of groups through the scalar chain of managers and makes large-scale institutions feasible. It may also be remarked that the direction is provided by a manager who, hopefully, has leadership ability—a distinction not always made clear in the literature.

The effectiveness of the manager in initiating change in organized enterprise depends upon his behavioral skill in getting simultaneous action from his subordinates. The development of leadership skill requires practice. Members of an organization are conditioned to follow an initiated activity in well-understood areas. Employees readily respond to designated work hours, school children eagerly participate in song and recital, and members of Bible classes are placed in situations wherein they are conditioned to respond favorably to initiations by the leader. The person intent on refining his leadership techniques will begin with situations where reliable response may be anticipated and, from there, broaden the field gradually as his skills in leadership improve.

The leader may seek to legitimize his initiation function in several ways. He may take advantage of opportunities to be seen by his subordinates in the company of and in conference with already established leaders. Thus, a supervisor will want to be seen in a good relationship with his department manager. This sets him apart from his subordinates, as does his use of symbols, rank, office location, and so forth. What he is really doing is placing himself in a position wherein the aura of acceptance of established leaders reflects favorably upon himself.

The successful leader cannot permit initiations from other sources to intrude into his group. He must insulate his subordinates because such

---

[8] Sayles, *op. cit.*, chap. 9.

diffusion would destroy his own effectiveness. To accomplish this purpose, he isolates the group by stressing its peculiar virtues, competitiveness, appearance, success, and reputation to the disadvantage of rival initiations. The effective manager must be alert to and anticipate erosions from his leadership. He must ever be concerned about the responses of subordinates to his initiations; indeed, he trains them to respond in a positive manner.

Some managers endeavor to maintain effective leadership through direct contacts with subordinates one or more levels below them. So long as no command or suggestion is given to these people (which would violate the unity-of-command principle), it is good practice to make one's self known to subordinates once or more removed. It is not only a good communication technique, it is also evidence of applied leadership. It secures greater conviction about the enterprise goals, it associates reputation with personality, and it aids the building of zeal and confidence.

Finally, and very importantly, is the need for action. The leader *must* initiate; he cannot wait for others in this regard, and he especially cannot depend upon his subordinates to act in his place. This is a skill that needs much practice. It is perfectly clear that the manager who initiates too much and too often will only bewilder his subordinates and harm the achievement of goals. Time and attention are too limited to serve numerous ends simultaneously. Therefore, judgment is required if new actions are needed or new accomplishments undertaken. The action must not be routine; it relates to undertaking a *new* activity that will enhance the accomplishment of group goals but must always be at a rate that will enhance the zeal of subordinates.

Responding Responsiveness to the initiations of subordinates is an equally important aspect of leadership. Employees have a continuing need for many things. They often ask a superior for help in getting supplies or services that they are unable to obtain through their own efforts; they may require technical advice in design, assembly, procurement, or utilization of services that their superior can provide as a result of high technical knowledge and experience. They want to be assured that they stand well in the eyes of their superior. This is more than psychological assurance that is sought. The superior is the means of achieving rewards and promotions and of providing a buffer for the intrusions of others who have no legitimate claim on the services of the subordinate. Most of these aids will be forthcoming from the superior in the ordinary course of his management capacity. But the spirit and initiative with which they are accomplished go far to stamp a man with leadership skill.

The manager needs to be alert to the real reasons for these initiations of subordinates. They may, of course, be taken at their face value, but people may select any one of these types of initiations, not because there is a real or obvious need involved, but because there is a quite foreign need to be satisfied. A subordinate may raise questions about mundane problems while in reality he is trying to find out whether he is appreciated. This is the central issue for every subordinate: What he does, how he does it, the work challenge—in fact, all aspects of the working situation—are really subordinate to the need for assurance of self. In this respect it is very significant, as Sayles reports,[9] that during a twelve-day period on an engineering project, the numbers of initiated contacts between a superior and seven subordinates were 37, 26, 13, 12, 8, 6, and 0. In the first four cases, most of the contacts were initiated by the superior, probably because these were new employees who lacked training and experience. Nevertheless, it is certain that the number of contacts initiated by subordinates correlated highly with their sense of insecurity. The obvious conclusion is that superiors should make certain that their evaluation techniques, as recommended in Chapter 22, are both frequent and effective.

Representing This function of leadership is concerned with the relationship between a manager (and his group) and his superiors. Subordinates of a particular manager are quick to sense whether *their* boss effectively represents the interests of the total group among his peers and superiors. This is especially important where subordinates initiate action that can only be accomplished by superiors once or more removed from their own superiors. These subordinates not only want a chance to be heard—they want action. If their own superior is unable to get a positive response, or a salable reason for a negative response, he loses his effectiveness as a leader.

Of course, the problem can be very sticky. The relationship between the superiors at two or more vertical levels is of paramount importance. If their rapport is close and their goals mutually supportable, there is every reason for the subordinate to attain the initiation proposed by *his* subordinates. But this situation is often not the case. The superior once removed may have other fish to fry, he may be hostile to the activities of the group supervised by the subordinate manager, and he may be conscious of a personality clash. Situations of this kind often last for a long time, even though they are eventually resolved by the elimination of one or the other manager. In the meantime, the subordinates of the inferior manager may feel that he has little leadership ability.

Summary The approaches to the leadership function, as outlined in this section, can be conveniently categorized as psychological or sociological. Leaders must motivate people to work with zeal and confidence. If they approach this function from the point of view of enticing action as a reward for certain need satisfactions, they are inevitably bound to identify these needs and their incidence in each subordinate. This literally calls for successful psychoanalysis, an art that scarcely any manager has. The sociological approach to leadership is more direct, though not nearly as fundamental. It encompasses the reaction to felt and expressed needs of subordinates for direction, responsiveness to their needs, and effective representation of the

[9] *Ibid.,* p. 152.

group before superior levels of authority. In these categories, the call on superiors to exercise effective leadership is material, pertinent, and obvious.

DIFFICULTIES IN TEACHING LEADERSHIP

How do people come by leadership ability? Research on this is exceedingly limited. Numerous are the college classes and enterprise training activities dealing with leadership, but most of the work done boils down to descriptions of leadership acts and techniques, to theories about why leaders emerge, to understanding people, and to the dynamics of interpersonal relations. The implication that leadership ability can be taught is still open to question. Highly talented leadership ability is in evidence all around us—in formal groups ranging from kindergartens to universities, from social institutions to the underworld—and the untaught leaders often seem more successful than those who take formal training in leadership.

Perhaps the major problem in teaching leadership is that it is dynamic personal process—dynamic in the sense that techniques vary with circumstances and with the people involved—and personal in the sense that interpersonal influence is exercised. This does not always mean face-to-face contact, for, obviously, General MacArthur, Napoleon, Caesar, Churchill, De Gaulle, and Jefferson were personally known to few of their followers. Close interpersonal relations were felt to exist, nevertheless, and this is what counts. Devices for humanizing the distant leader rely on communications (Roosevelt's fireside chats) or on some dramatic display of heroism or of pomp and circumstances to create a feeling of close personal contact in the followers: the leader projects his personality and is viewed with favor and even with adulation.

In business, great leadership ability seems rare, partly because great ability is rare. Then again, employees may continue to work for an enterprise, though without zeal, for lack of alternatives or because they can't finance a change, are lazy, or are protected by a union. In these circumstances a manager does not have to employ much leadership and he is likely to rely upon his authority to command and on negative motivation. This is unfortunate for both superior and subordinates; it creates an attitude of defensiveness and unenlightened conformance to company procedures on the part of subordinates; initiative and self-development are stifled; and attention is focused upon merely pleasing the boss.

THE ENVIRONMENT

The environment in which interpersonal group relationships occur has a bearing on the quality of leadership. This environment is affected greatly by the leader's successes and failures, and these, in turn, result partly from the degree of managerial skill and partly from external factors. The hygienic factors—supervision, interpersonal relations, working conditions, wages, policies, and job security—come easy in times of prosperity. In times of adversity, when the hygienic factors may be gradually reduced in volume, scope, and quality—at least, when fringe benefits and even salary are reduced—human relations and supervision may even improve; certainly effort may be more productive, and more attention is given to leadership ability, because it may save the life of the firm. It can be decisive if the self-development and reward aspects of the motivational system are made prominent.

It thus appears that adversity fosters zeal and that some people prefer inefficiency when they can afford it. Take the great contrast between the zeal of the British worker during the 1930s and during World War II, or between that of American railroad employees before and after the intrusion of unions and of government regulation. In both cases the quality of leadership was decisive, but in the former case it shifted from desultory to brilliant, and in the latter case, from brilliant to desultory. In the thirties, when the British were pacifist-minded and bent on curious schemes for attaining security and sharing the wealth, they chose political leadership which promised these benefits. But when, through critical challenges, preservation of their freedom became more important than anything else, a leader was chosen who could satisfy this need. In the instance of the American railroads, employee morale was high in the dynamic years of construction, under the leadership of men like James Hill; but with the coming of the rail unions and with government regulation, the employees looked to others than managers for fulfillment of their needs, and managerial leadership suffered.

However, whatever the environment, leaders emerge to make decisions and take charge. The leader in a play group selects the game and settles disputes; at the scene of an accident a doctor may lead the rescue work.

Disappointed groups readily replace leaders who fail to satisfy their interests—when they have this prerogative—in the hope of experiencing greater satisfaction through the new leader's efforts. In formal organizations such as a school, a hospital, or a business, manager-leaders are ordinarily elected or appointed without subordinate participation. While subordinates may not be able to remove their business leaders, they can react negatively by slowdowns, by output restrictions, and even by quitting the job. This is why authority is insufficient to effect coordination, and why managers are forced to exercise influence beyond their authority.

CULTIVATED ATTITUDES OF LEADERS

In the discussion of leadership to this point, emphasis has been placed upon the interpersonal relationships of leader and followers. This relationship can be improved considerably as the leader cultivates certain attitudes. This is the area in which the more important contributions of psychologists aid us to understand the bases of influence. It becomes even more important than mere knowledge because these attitudes can be learned and used with skill. These are the more important elements which leaders use to create confidence and understanding.

Empathy Webster defines empathy as "the imaginative projection of one's own consciousness into another being." As commonly used, it is the ability to place one's self in the position of another, experiencing that person's feelings, prejudices, and values.

The manager without empathy has objectives, ambitions, values, and biases like any other man, and he often assumes that his subordinates have the same ones. It is not likely they would have. People widely differ from each other in every respect but one: They all are guided less by reason than by emotion, and the causes of emotion are deeply personal. Therefore, the leader could not be more wrong than to assume that his followers feel as he does. This wrong assumption underlies paternalism.[10] Many a manager provides subordinates with benefits he likes himself. The big difference is that *he* has freedom to choose, while his followers may value the freedom to choose more than they value any "given benefits." Then they are charged with a lack of appreciation.

In the international political field, Americans are guilty of the same error when they assume that because they like and practice democracy, other people should like and practice it, quite irrespective of their level of literacy, political training, economic and cultural development, variance in social values, and their desire for freedom to choose.

As the manager contemplates his subordinates with a view to understanding their feelings and attitudes, he is severely handicapped. Outside of their work, he knows very little about them—their personal relationships, economic and health conditions, ambitions, spiritual values, and loyalties. Each of us hardly knows himself that well, let alone our subordinates!

Placing one's self in the position of a subordinate—if you know that position—is but half the problem, because, even so, would you know his reaction to a business situation? Yet a forthright and conscientious effort to understand a subordinate is much better than none. The mere practice of asking, How would I react if I were he? is an attempt to learn, and with practice comes skill.

Objectivity With objectivity, managers may observe and trace the causes of events unemotionally. To see only results and to berate subordinates personally for stupidity or reward them for success—which they may not even have achieved—is not good leadership. Even though managers must depend heavily on subordinates and it is human to become emotional about them, it is important to evaluate from a distance, determine the actual causes of results, and take intelligent steps to correct poor ones and encourage good ones.

This is a tightrope to walk, particularly if empathy is overemphasized, because empathy requires an attitude opposite to remoteness and unemotional analysis. A neat balance between empathy and objectivity is difficult to achieve, but each has its place in effective leadership.

[10] For the effects of this policy on the firm, see S. Mahoney, "What Happened at Endicott Johnson after the Band Stopped Playing," *Fortune* (September, 1962).

To cultivate objectivity by schooling himself to analyze before taking action, the leader needs strong will power. With determination he can overcome a natural tendency toward snap judgment, anger, vituperation, or undue exuberance, even if he must follow the folk rule of counting to ten. Restraint and the habit of analysis are learned behavior.

Self-knowledge   The injunction of Socrates to "know thyself!" is used by psychologists in the context of making people aware of why they behave as they do and also what they do to draw forth certain response, lack of response, or even hostility from others. It is impossible to emphasize or to be objective without self-knowledge. The plain fact is that some people irritate others unwittingly by their habitual attitude, words, or actions. Of course, in other cases, this may be their intention! In some business situations this may be the correct technique to obtain a desired response. More usually friendliness, cooperation, and approval bring forth the desired response, whereas irritation will only negate it. Hence, it is well to know what one is doing.

The manager—like everyone else—should, therefore, learn the effects on others of his attitudes and habits so that he can correct those which elicit negative responses; that is, he should cultivate self-knowledge and put it to work intelligently by watching for favorable and unfavorable reactions to his behavior and trying to analyze their cause. He can make discreet inquiries, either direct or indirect, to learn the cause of an observed response. He can use the vertical slice technique (Chapter 23). For all this, he must not be touchy or let his false pride show.

One major point must be remembered here: People do not all respond in the same way to anything. People are different; not all are irritated by the same thing. Furthermore, people respond differently at different times to the same thing, depending on their immediate interior climate. Some personalities clash with few but please the many; some, conversely, seem badtempered but are amenable to certain personalities they find congenial. These variations in people explain, in part, why the much-publicized T training (sensitivity training) often demonstrates essentially that people respond differently to the same stimulus.

USE OF INFORMAL ORGANIZATION

"Informal organization"[11] applies to groups of two or more people who communicate more or less regularly for purposes of exchanging information, for pleasure, or for the development of a consensus with respect to future action. The term is really incongruous, because regularity of meeting and permanency of membership lend an aspect of formality to these groups, which have no organizational relationship to the employing firm but which do have structure in terms of the leader-follower relationship of their members.

[11] For a discussion of informal organization in relation to formal organization, see pp. 232–235.

Types There are several types of informal organizations, depending, in large part, upon their purposes.[12] Sociologists have classified them as kinship-friendship groups, cliques, and subcliques. The first, readily identified by its descriptive title, is most often confined to two persons between whom compatibility is of prime importance. Sociability is the chief objective, both at and away from work, but collateral purposes include the communication of information, whether fact or gossip, and mutual aid in achieving improved status through such means as promotion or transfer.

Cliques are composed of persons commonly in close working association: selected members of the payroll, personnel, engineering, or machine-shop "crowd," or persons representing different functional activities who feel the need for cooperation. Sometimes the group has certain standards to maintain or practices to retain, and members drift together for purposes of protection. Acceptance into such a group may require the approval of all the members. There is unlikely to be any democracy here.

Subcliques include one or a few persons identified with a clique. Other members of the subclique may be employed by another firm. Often, such a subclique can control the destinies of a clique or even of a professional or trade association by its insistence that standards or customs be adhered to by prospective members. The subclique may control a clique which, in turn, may control a whole formal group. In this way, a large number of people in an organized group may be controlled by a very few who have no formal authority.

Genesis The existence, variety, and virility of informal organizations leads to the conclusion that they satisfy human needs in a way that formal organizations do not. What are these needs? One of them is to perpetuate the culture of a group. For instance, a group may be unified in its desire to maintain a certain standard of education, discipline, or training. If a given department employs engineers exclusively, an informal group of them might oppose the use of technicians for some of the jobs. Or the insistence of an informal group upon the continuance of hazing new members of a department or of trade apprenticeship reflects the desire to perpetuate a highly prized cultural figment.

Need for information is a second reason for the existence of informal organizations—both the need for news and the need for *prompt* news. If information were communicated as soon as it was available, there would be no need for an informal organization to get information. In practice, enterprises often circulate news slowly, transmit it poorly, or even withhold it. Informal organizations provide the channels, or grapevine, for speedy com-

---

[12] C. I. Barnard, in *The Functions of the Executive* (Cambridge, Mass.: Harvard University Press, 1938), states on p. 114, in his pioneer chapter on informal organizations, that such groups have no ". . . specific conscious *joint* purpose. The contact may be accidental, or incidental to organized activities, or arise from personal desire or gregarious instinct; it may be friendly or hostile." Whatever the incident which originally throws people together, it appears that the continuing informal organization implies some kind of purpose, even though members may not be aware of it.

munication with their members. Management, however, cannot fully rely upon this method because persons not members of informal organizations cannot tap this grapevine.

A third need which informal organizations fulfill is to control social behavior. Members want to standardize the behavior of people with whom they are in contact, as a matter of personal pride or snobbery or as a badge of distinction or of assumed superiority. The desired conformity may relate to dress, behavior, ideas, or customs. The reality of the "grey flannel suit" attests to the power of informal organization, as do slowdowns and wildcat strikes.

Control Since informal organizations can either aid or interfere with enterprise interests, their activities should be directed into constructive channels. Once leaders of informal groups are identified and their cooperation gained, organizing and directing become markedly easier. The good will, energy, and initiative of informal organizations supplement the purposes of the formal organization, and each stands to gain from the satisfaction of the other's needs. Conversely, should the manager fail to win the cooperation of the informal group leaders, his leadership ability will be rated low and his performance will inevitably be harmed.

DYNAMICS OF CHANGE

Managers are continuously concerned with change. Two broad categories of change are common. Firms modify objectives and policies, location, organization structure, product lines, corporate structure, management philosophies, and methods of doing business. Sometimes these changes are voluntary; sometimes they are forced.

The other category of change involves human behavior. Managers are always faced with influencing subordinates to change. In all organization changes there is a corresponding need to change the activity of subordinates. Many subordinates do not want to change; they must be induced to do so in the interest of enterprise efficiency.

In his function of directing, a manager must overcome resistance to change—not only that of employees, but also that of customers, suppliers, and even government people to the extent that they may be involved. Without human resistance, achieving change would be a comparatively simple matter. People fear or welcome change depending on how it may affect them, how it may increase or decrease their well-being. The change may affect income, physical environment, status, the esteem of others, group relationships, power relationships, opportunity for self-development, or freedom of action. People need time, before committing themselves, to calculate the possible net advantage.

In the Material Environment Enterprises differ widely in the dynamics of operation. Some—like the electronics, chemical, and metallurgical firms—

must operate in an environment shifting with new knowledge and with changing competitive practices, political factors, and even power politics. Others—like financial and transportation institutions, or food producers and processors—are much less dynamic but still are affected by new competition, new markets, and even new institutions. The manager in any of these firms must continually lead subordinates in meeting and conquering the new circumstances. New plans, new money, new strategy, and even new jobs may be involved. Somehow, the manager must come up with a high enough order of leadership to convert the doubtful, the pessimistic, and the conservative to meet new challenges with zeal and confidence; since the environment continues to change, dramatically or imperceptibly, this job never is done—it is always in process.

In Subordinate Attitudes In addition to the dynamics of the material environment, the manager must deal with the dynamics of people's attitudes. As one looks at, or goes to work in, a firm, one gets the impression that the personnel is static in terms of number, relationships, and attitudes, and that one may depend on the stability of these factors. But before long one sees and senses changes. There are promotions and transfers, hirings and firings, labor union raids or contests or elections with attendant disputation, one side winning, one side losing. These changes, and many others, are disturbing to employees. They are also disturbed by changes in business volume, and their attitude toward the firm changes as their expectations change.

A manager must realize that attitudes do change, sometimes very quickly. He must feel the pulse of morale, assess the real cause of changed attitudes, and apply whatever leadership technique he judges appropriate. Since there is little science in this area, different managers will select different techniques in the same situation, some good, some poor.

Means of Implementing Change The means available for inducing changed behavior are based upon allaying fears and satisfying needs. Man has always feared the unknown, and change represents the unknown. He does not know how change in a business operation will affect him. He should be prepared in advance for this type of change, and this requires good communications, including an explanation of the purpose of the change, its timing, and the anticipated organizational effect on each individual. Then time must be allowed for the subordinate to get used to the idea and to assess the effect of the change on any informal organization to which he belongs, on personal relationships outside the firm, and on such situations as housing and transfer expenses. Numerous questions will demand answers by the superior, among them the question of the penalty for refusal to change.

Another kind of change must also be induced in the behavior of subordinates. How do you influence a subordinate manager to manage efficiently? To treat *his* subordinates with respect? To improve the efficiency of *his* subordinates? To induce *his* subordinates to act with dignity and respect? To take prompt action? To face reality? The available techniques here are communication and timing. The advantages of changing and the penalties of not changing are pointed out and perhaps demonstrated by means of the "horrible example." Formal and informal training may be used. The subordinate manager who does not understand what is being taught and the reasons for teaching it is well on the way to becoming an object lesson.

When group membership is important to the subordinate who needs to change, the group may induce the change. People will change to preserve their standing in groups to which they wish to belong.

Since the success attending a change depends partly on overcoming the resistance of affected people, managers must use leadership to motivate these people to accept change: Suppliers of capital, customers, and employees must be convinced that they stand to gain. Achieving change in circumstances involving two equal parties may be accomplished by direct negotiation, intrusion of third parties, or open warfare. Obviously, change can be imposed, though usually at great cost, and imposition is an inferior method.

The manager may give notice to all affected by a proposed change, evaluating the change as he sees it. This one-way communication usually produces poor results except under emergency conditions. Even the conference method, in which the affected persons may ask questions, is poor, because so many questions go unasked and there are so many possible interpretations of answers in this environment.[13]

One means of implementing change[14] has been found sometimes to be effective, given the necessary time for application. Here, the manager attempting change broaches the matter to his immediate subordinates. Small conferences—and there will be many—will achieve understanding of the reasons behind and expectations of the change. The subordinates will call conferences of their people to discuss the matter. This time-consuming method does inform people about how they will be affected, provides time for each person to evaluate his net position, and usually elicits suggestions for modifying the change to make it more effective, more acceptable, or both.

The behavioral scientists have given some insights into the relationships of group members and the nature of informal organization. Managers have also long taken into their confidence recognized leaders of affected informal groups in order to enlist their help in effecting change. This method is frequently successful, particularly when it is combined with the group discussion technique. But it may also be attended by rebellion of the group,

---

[13] W. Brown, *Exploration in Management* (New York: John Wiley & Sons, Inc., 1960).

[14] See D. Cartwright, "Achieving Change in People," *Human Relations*, vol. 4, no. 4, pp. 381–392 (1951); W. G. Bennis, K. D. Benne, and R. Chin, *The Planning of Change* (New York: Holt, Rinehart and Winston, Inc., 1961); R. H. Guest, *Organizational Change* (Homewood, Ill.: Richard D. Irwin, Inc., 1962); C. Argyris et al., *Social Science Approaches to Business Behavior* (Homewood, Ill.: Richard D. Irwin, Inc., 1962); and T. Burns, "Micropolitics: Mechanisms of Institutional Change," *Administrative Science Quarterly*, vol. 6, no. 3, pp. 257–281 (1961).

rejection of the group leader, and even character assassination. It may fail because the leader assesses the situation improperly or because he is induced to act against his better judgment.[15]

TECHNIQUES

It is currently fashionable to believe that a manager's leadership style may range from autocratic to laissez faire. For those holding this view, each manager can and should assume a predominantly autocratic, democratic, or laissez-faire attitude, depending on its appropriateness in a given situation. When selecting the autocratic technique, the manager relies on his authority to command subordinates. When choosing the democratic technique—in what is more accurately called participative management—he solicits advice and perhaps accepts majority decisions from subordinates. Choosing laissez faire or free rein, the manager goes so far as to practically abdicate his decision-making authority and becomes a mild consultant.

The historical position of most behavioral scientists has been anti-authoritarian and in favor of participative management.[16] Roethlisberger felt convinced enough of the righteousness of this position to comment in 1964 on how astonishing was the extent to which the findings of different investigators checked on the inadequacies of the traditional leadership style[17] and emphasized the need for more participative management, two-way communication, and permissive leadership. There is little question that the biases of these men show through. Now, however, it appears that their spokesmen are beginning to accept the position maintained by the authors of this book from the beginning, namely, that the manager will choose the most effective means *for him* to achieve enterprise objectives, quite irrespective of whether they are permissive, authoritarian, or in between.

Among those who have declared themselves in this regard are P. R. Lawrence and A. Zaleznik. The former is quoted by Learned and Sproat as saying:[18]

> There is now beginning to be some research evidence to support what many intuitive managers have known for a long time. And that is that the different departments, in which innovators and stabilizers work, function best when they are structured and run and led in quite different and distinct ways.

The innovators are found in research and development organizations. The scientist especially insists upon participating in goal-setting, once the general area of research is fixed for him. For instance, a firm may decide to build a

[15] See, for example, A. Zaleznik, C. R. Christensen, and F. J. Roethlisberger, *The Motivation, Productivity and Satisfaction of Workers* (Boston: Division of Research, Harvard Business School, 1958).

[16] E. P. Learned and A. T. Sproat, *Organization Theory and Policy* (Homewood, Ill.: Richard D. Irwin, Inc., 1966), p. 61.

[17] H. Koontz (ed.), *Toward a Unified Theory of Management* (New York: McGraw-Hill Book Company, 1964, pp. 41–67.

[18] *Op. cit.*, p. 62.

plutonium laboratory for the purpose of engaging in research and development work in this product. Just what will be undertaken will almost certainly depend upon the interests of the scientist, and such a person will want to have freedom of communication even though he may use it very little.[19] On the other hand, the stabilizers whom Lawrence finds in the typical functionalized organizations, where procedures and policies are well established and where the educational level is not so high, are likely to perform best under more authoritarian leadership.

Even more emphatic is Abraham Zaleznik in his rejection of participation when he writes:[20]

> I view with considerable pessimism the attempts . . . to develop a social movement around theories of permissive leadership, participation, and sensitivity training. . . . The research setting creates the condition for the redistribution of emotional investments that affect the levels of productivity and morale. When the researchers leave the setting, another redistribution takes effect that may result in, at best, a return to the prior situation, or, at worst, eynical and disillusioned individuals.

The manager who tries to use the results of behavioral research runs into difficulties. According to Zaleznik, he cannot act with the confidence and purpose which come from the utilization of his personal capacities because confidence is not built from without. Unless normative principles are really a part of the personality of the manager, a slavish adherence to them will develop a guilt-ridden and compulsive personality. The manager is a whole man. He must act consistently with his total personality, however it is developed, and whether this causes him to be cited as authoritarian or as permissive.

This view of human nature questions the opinion that a manager can and does readily shift his leadership style from one extreme to another, depending upon the situation with which he is confronted.[21] The authors of this book view this concept with some skepticism. Managers who are permissive by nature tend to choose a permissive style; an authoritarian manager tends to follow an authoritarian style. As a manager matures, he adopts a style that suits his personality and he is not likely to deviate much from it throughout his active employment.

The usually undefined terms "participative" and "permissive" applied to management have caused a great deal of unproductive discussion. The one thing that no manager should do is to abdicate his decision-making prerogative. If he needs information that one or more subordinates have in order to make a decision, he surely should obtain it from them. If he is uncertain how a decision will affect some of his people, he should find out *before* he makes the decision. Productive participation can be achieved

---

[19] C. O'Donnell, *The Productivity of Scientists* (unpublished manuscript, 1967).

[20] Quoted by Learned and Sproat, *op. cit.*, p. 64.

[21] See, for example, R. Tannenbaum and W. H. Schmidt, "How to Choose a Leadership Pattern," *Harvard Business Review*, vol. 36, no. 2, pp. 95–101 (March–April, 1958).

through work assignments, as is the case in planning. He should not assume that his subordinates want to or like to or can participate in the decision making entrusted to him. Where a manager has the responsibility for making a particular decision, he should not pretend that he is not deciding. Quite on the contrary, subordinates want clear, purposeful, and effective leadership. They are the first to detect in their manager incompetence, indecision, or yearning to be popular; and they complain about these qualities because they are adversely affected by them in terms of production, cost saving, ability to accomplish, growth, and pride.

On the basis of believing that the leader *must* lead, the United States Army and the United States Marines have what appears to be a sound approach. In demonstrating leadership one day the late General Patton called for a plate, a very wet noodle, and a fork. Tipping the plate, he tried to get the noodle from the bottom edge of the plate to the top edge by pushing the noodle with the fork. The futility of this became apparent. But when he pulled with the fork, the noodle readily rose to the top edge. A leader must be out in front to lead, but not so far that he loses contact with his subordinates.

Before discussing specific techniques, let us heed a warning about a pitfall dangerous to all managers: misinterpretation by subordinates of their boss's attitudes. This may be avoided only by managerial alertness and insight.

A manager's every word and action are interpreted by his subordinates, who watch him closely for signs of his opinion of them and of other matters. Subordinates usually try to please their superiors by acting in approved ways and attending to whatever seems to command the boss's attention. When the superior scowls, complains, or smiles, the over-self-conscious subordinate may assume that these signals are meant for him, although, of course, they may not be. A second kind of misinterpretation is even more undesirable. Managers must concentrate on matters that need correct accomplishment, although in so doing they do not lose interest in matters that are going well. The subordinate is then apt to misread signals and—concentrating on whatever the manager is looking at—neglect specific duties. Then, because no one thinks of assigning the neglected duties to another, trouble generates.

The alert leader not only halts this development by correcting false impressions but develops and maintains morale by evoking confidence and zeal—the elements of morale.

Confidence Building   The confidence exhibited by a subordinate manager as he carries out his functions rests upon the quality of his knowledge and his sense of security. Techniques of building confidence can be taught; they may be communicated by the immediate superior or through observation of the managerial skill of top managers. The development of a subordinate's confidence in his ability to manage depends on his orientation, his follow-up supervision, and a feeling of security in his position.

Orientation   Orientation comes first. The depth of this process is largely dictated by the knowledge of his position which a new manager brings with him. Providing him with the required information about his function and its relationships with other functions and their managers was described in some detail in Chapter 24.

Follow-up supervision   The superior must see to it that his subordinate actually has the opportunities for developing his management skill, in accordance with the suggestions set forth in Chapter 23. The quality of his skill can be evaluated in terms described in Chapter 22. It is the responsibility of the superior to guide his men into training situations wherever they may be, and, if none are provided within or without the firm, he must train the subordinate himself. While these procedures are currently receiving some attention, continued teaching is often ignored in business. This aspect of directing is not as enjoyable as conference attendance; in fact, it can be very time consuming and difficult.

Job security   Providing a subordinate manager—assuming he is efficient—with job security depends on the success of the enterprise; few department managers can take this responsibility. It is distinctly up to top managers to increase the scope and profitability of the enterprise, which results in wider spans of management, enlarged organization structure, more jobs to be managed—more management jobs both horizontally and vertically. This is the only way in which the manager can possess a really secure and promising position.

Zeal Building   The leader's function is to bring forth zealous effort on the part of subordinate managers. Yet the elusive nature of zeal permits it to escape scientific analysis. For what, after all, inspires enthusiasm or ardor resulting in effort beyond the merely acceptable? Sometimes a subordinate takes this path because he stands in great need of a superior's approval; on the other hand, his zeal may win only the disapproval of his competitive or envious peers. Sometimes a subordinate takes this road to secure promotion, to become eligible to join an elite group, or to achieve power; on the other hand, the costs in effort, tension, frustration, and hostile colleagues are great. Sometimes the subordinate greatly admires his superior and determines not to let him down; on the other hand, he may only be proving his boss wrong by effectively executing an order he is certain is faulty.

Inspiration   Since inspirational techniques to build zeal are so personal, they can only be described as observed. *This aspect of leadership probably cannot be taught.* Within the confines of enterprise policies, procedures, and rules, each manager must develop his own inspirational techniques.

The power of words and actions to inspire zeal is proverbial. The leader—standing between his group and the goals of all—beckons subordinates on with words and his own actions. It sounds old-fashioned when put into words, but old tactics and old knowledge are not necessarily obsolete. People want to be led and will work hard to satisfy the goals of an admired superior.

Then, to inspire his subordinates, a manager must be a success. Subordinates lose confidence in unsuccessful superiors and leave them as quickly as possible; if they cannot leave, as in the armed forces, they become dispirited.

Success may result from many factors, but its outward sign is the accomplishment of managerial objectives. In business, success may be measured in sales or profit, by expanding activities, or by rising stature within and without the enterprise. People enjoy the secondhand glory, the implied security, the prestige, and—sometimes—the profits of working for a success, whether the area is politics, religion, education, business, or war. And for superlative superiors they will work beyond the call of duty.

Strengthening personal qualities Creating enthusiasm in subordinates seems also to be largely a matter of the superior's personal attributes and of his judgment in making use of occasions. Probably most important in terms of the durability of inspiration is the quality of character or moral vigor with which the leader lives up to the social code and, by example, induces subordinates to do likewise.

Another quality essential to leadership is that the manager act his role. Subordinates want to work for a manager who really acts like one. People develop stereotypes which they do not want altered—an image of how someone should behave—and are disappointed if this vision is not made real. In the managerial stereotype, managers bask in the aura of success and competence, possess superior knowledge, are conservative in their habits, stand somewhat aloof from subordinates, are examples of justice, and strongly defend subordinates while raising their efficiency. Needless to say, such paragons may be largely imaginary, but subordinates want their managers to play this part believably. It is the way to earn respect, and zealous effort of subordinates correlates highly with the respect of subordinates for their leader.

A manager must be conscious of his effect on subordinates and wear a mask or adopt a demeanor which will direct subordinates as he intends, without altering the scope of positions or subtly changing the organization structure. It is hard to be an actor for eight hours a day, yet this is exactly what much business leadership requires.

From this review of zeal-building techniques, it can be seen that the power to inspire zeal is a personal quality. There are few principles or rules for all to follow. The inspirational aspect of leadership apparently cannot be taught. The masters cannot easily be imitated successfully.

What, then, is a manager to do? Lead he must, whether he occupies a high or a low step on the organization ladder. His leadership responsibility cannot be delegated. There are a few things he can do. He should remember to develop confidence in subordinates by making them technically proficient. He must develop his own zeal-building techniques by trial and error, weeding out unsuccessful techniques and cultivating successful ones. He need not be hasty, and many elements in the environment will work for him. A sound motivational system alone will go far to produce acceptable performance, and his delegated powers and organizational position place him in a strategic position. So he presumably has time to grow into being a good leader.[22]

SUMMARY OF MAJOR PRINCIPLES OF DIRECTING

Reflection upon the foregoing chapters on the managerial function of directing indicates that a tentative statement of some general truths can be developed. As in other areas of management, they seem to fall into primary classification of those principles that may be grouped around the purpose of directing and those that have to do with the process of directing.

The Purpose of Directing   The purpose of directing is achieved through adherence to:

Principle of harmony of objectives   Effective directing depends on the extent to which individual objectives in cooperative activity are harmonized with group objectives.

It is recognized that the individuals who are employed in enterprise have objectives to accomplish which are not only different from each other but are also different from those of the firm. It is of paramount importance that the latter be accomplished, for this is the sole reason for the organized activity. As a consequence, there must be complementarity between individual and enterprise goals—achieving certain individual goals can and does further the best interests of the firm and it is these for which subordinates are rewarded. Furthermore, it is vital that each individual make an effective contribution to enterprise goals because this is the basis of over-all efficiency.

The Process of Directing   The process of directing concerns the manner by which its purpose is executed. The principles upon which the execution of directing rests are:

Principle of unity of command   The more completely an individual has a reporting relationship to a single superior, the less the problem of conflict in instructions and the greater the feeling of personal responsibility for results.

Unity of command is a principle of both organization and direction. People respond best when they are directed by a single superior. They then have no divided loyalties and are thus in a position to give single-minded attention to the requirements of their superior. Of course, it is true that

---

[22] Even as there are few who are eager to lead at all. See Zaleznik et al., *op. cit.,* p. 396.

sometimes the net efficiency of an enterprise is improved by the introduction of functional authority over certain activities of the line subordinates of another manager. Since such situations lead to frustrations on the part of both managers and subordinates, multiple subordination should be used only when the gains clearly outweigh the costs.

Principle of direct supervision   Effective direction requires that managers supplement objective methods of supervision with direct personal contact.

While it is possible that a manager may be able to utilize objective devices to evaluate and correct activities of subordinates to assure accomplishment of plans, there can be no complete substitute for an appropriate amount of face-to-face contact with subordinates. Not only do people like to feel that their superior is personally interested in them and their work, but objective nonpersonal information is never adequate to give the manager all he needs to undertake his job effectively. Also, through face-to-face contact he is often better able to teach, to communicate, and, above all, to receive suggestions, a feeling for problems, and other information that he could not obtain otherwise.

Principle of supervisory techniques   Since people, tasks, and organizational environment vary, techniques of supervision will be most effective if appropriately varied.

Superiors have at hand many alternative techniques of directing. It is important that actual selections be made in terms of effectiveness. Because subordinates differ widely in their responsiveness to various need satisfactions, it is of utmost importance for superiors to select the most efficient means of evoking superior performance. Also, there are situations—such as when the superior is the only person who has information or when very quick action is required—where the superior must be authoritative and could not be participative. Consequently, not only must people be considered, but situations as well.

The Efficiency of Communication   Since communication is the means by which people in organized enterprise exchange information concerning the environment, operational requirements of superiors, program status, and ideas for improving operational efficiency, managers have a special need for excellence in communication. The following guidelines are pertinent to this subject:

Clarity   A communication possesses clarity only when it is expressed in language understandable to the receiver.

Integrity   All communications must be framed and transmitted in such ways as to support the integrity of the formal organization.

Strategic use of informal organization Managers should employ the informal organization to supplement and make operative the communication channels of the formal organization.

Research in the efficiency of communication highlights the fact that every message must be expressed in a language understandable to the auditor or recipient and that unless full attention is paid to the transmission little of it can be understood. The superior needs to make certain that he personally is a good sender and receiver of communications, and he should train his subordinates in the same facility.

The guidelines of integrity and the strategic use of informal organization concern the transmission of communications within an organized group. Since it is important to maintain the integrity of the formal organization, all communications must support its objectives.

Informal organization is a phenomenon which managers must accept. It operates on entirely different bases than formal organizations but is always a part of them. Information, true or not, flows quickly through informal organizations. As a consequence, managers should take advantage of this device to correct misinformation and to provide for transmission of information not appropriate for formal communication.

FOR DISCUSSION

1. There is a marked tendency in management literature to confuse managing and leading. How do you feel about this semantic problem?

2. Ability to lead is an important quality for the manager. What other abilities does he need?

3. Cite various definitions of leadership. Which appeals to you, keeping in mind the importance of semantic clarification?

4. If leadership is the ability to induce zeal and confidence in subordinates or followers (as in a political party), just what effect would it have in a business firm?

5. How is leadership related to motivation?

SELECTED REFERENCES

Beer, M.: *Leadership, Employee Needs and Motivation,* Bureau of Business Research Monograph No. 129, Columbus, Ohio: The Ohio State University Press, 1966.

Bennis, W. G.: "Revisionist Theory of Leadership," *Harvard Business Review,* vol. 39, no. 1, pp. 26–40 (January–February, 1961).

————, K. D. Benne, and R. Chin (eds.): *The Planning of Change,* chaps. 4, 5, 8, 9, New York: Holt, Rinehart and Winston, Inc., 1961.

Brown, W.: *Exploration in Management,* New York: John Wiley & Sons, Inc., 1962.

Browne, C. G., and T. S. Cohn (eds.): *The Study of Leadership,* Danville, Ill.: The Interstate Printers and Publishers, Inc., 1958.

Burns, T.: "Micropolitics: Mechanisms of Institutional Change," *Administrative Science Quarterly*, vol. 6, no. 3, pp. 257–281 (December, 1961).

Guest, R. H.: *Organizational Change*, Homewood, Ill.: Richard D. Irwin, Inc., 1962.

Lawrence, P. R.: *The Changing of Organizational Behavior Patterns*, Boston: Division of Research, Harvard Business School, 1958.

Sayles, L.: *Managerial Behavior*, New York: McGraw-Hill Book Company, 1964.

Selznick, P.: *Leadership in Administration*, New York: Harper & Row, Publishers, Incorporated, 1957.

Tannenbaum, R., I. R. Weschler, and F. Massarik: *Leadership and Organization*, New York: McGraw-Hill Book Company, 1961.

Yuzuk, R. P.: *The Assessment of Employee Morale*, Research Monograph No. 99, Columbus, Ohio: Bureau of Business Research, The Ohio State University, 1961.

part six

CONTROLLING

Controlling implies measurement of accomplishment of events against plans and the correction of deviations to assure attainment of objectives according to plans. Once a plan becomes operational, control is necessary to measure progress, to uncover deviations from plans, and to indicate corrective action. Corrective action may involve simple measures such as minor changes in directing. In other cases, adequate control may result in setting new goals, formulating new plans, changing the organization structure, improving staffing, and making major changes in techniques of directing. In reading the chapters on the control function, it is important to bear in mind that it involves much more than mere measurement of deviations from plans. True control indicates that corrective action can and will be taken to get wayward operations back on course.

The process of control is discussed in Chapter 28. Simple definition of the control function makes it apparent that it remains essentially the same no matter what activity is under consideration. The essential of control is some sort of feedback—the operating principle of a thermostat or a steam governor. When temperature or speed becomes too great, a thermostat or a governor corrects the condition automatically. When temperature or speed deviates from what is required by becoming too low, the control device makes the opposite correction through feedback. Although the cycle in management is of longer duration, good managerial control should function in the same manner. Because of the problem of time lags, this chapter emphasizes the importance of forward-looking control. "Ready-made" control techniques, currently popular in the literature, do exist and can be of use. But Chapter 28 makes the point that really good control involves the tailoring of control devices to suit the individual plan, the organization, the specific needs of the enterprise, and the personal requirements of the manager.

Chapter 29 considers some of the newer control techniques in current use. Many of these are actually improved planning techniques which enable the manager to check on performance more accurately than was possible in the past. If any of these techniques appear difficult to understand, a brief review of Part 2 of this book may make them clear, since planning and control techniques must be considered together. Other control techniques discussed in the chapter are mainly a matter of improved information gathering, storage, and manipulation through electronic data machines. Also, the quantitative devices of the physical sciences are coming into increased use largely because of this greater facility in using large amounts of quantitative data. Furthermore, control techniques utilize devices from psychology, such as the measurement of human attitudes. In reading this chapter, the reader should familiarize himself with the latest devices, such as PERT (Program Evaluation and Review Technique), but the primary import is still the basic method which is used in all control devices—measurement of achievement against plan and correction of negative deviation through feedback. It should not be forgotten that older forms of control devices fit this pattern, too. The more modern techniques have not yet replaced accounting, budgeting, and auditing.

Most controls are partial; they concentrate on one facet of operations— quality of product, cash flow, costs, or some other rather narrow aspect. In many enterprises, a difficult problem is the development of over-all control so that managers may have a check on the progress of the entire organization or of an integrated product or territorial division. Chapter 30 discusses the most widely used solutions. As one might expect, these over-all controls tend to be financial. The reader should recognize that financial or money measurement is a natural basis for control since inputs and outputs of a business are most easily expressed in the common denominator of money. Over-all financial controls are particularly appropriate for business enterprises, but some financial controls are also very useful in nonbusiness organizations. Their expenditures for personnel, material, and facilities are always an important factor against which to weigh results, and these are usually reflected in expenditures of money. The most valuable over-all control devices are budget summaries, profit and loss statements, rate of return on investment, and the enterprise self-audit.

In spite of traditional emphasis on financial controls, Chapter 31 demonstrates that the most direct form of control is assurance of the quality of managers. The chapter, of course, does not advocate scrapping other controls, but it does make the point that many deviations from plans will not occur if the enterprise is well managed. A major point made in this book is that almost all the devices traditionally thought of as control tools are indirect. They are based on the fact that human beings make mistakes. Controlling performance through control of the quality of managers is direct in that it is based on the belief that qualified managers make the fewest mistakes and therefore do not require as much "indirect" control. The authors believe that this direct control is more satisfactory to all the groups interested in the fate of the enterprise—investors, employees, customers, vendors, its managers, and society as a whole.

the process of control

The managerial function of control is the measurement and correction of the performance of subordinates in order to make sure that enterprise objectives and the plans devised to attain them are accomplished. It is thus the function whereby every manager, from president to foreman, makes sure that what is done is what is intended. As Fayol so clearly recognized decades ago,[1] "In an undertaking, control consists in verifying whether everything occurs in conformity with the plan adopted, the instructions issued and principles established. It has for object to point out weaknesses and errors in order to rectify them and prevent recurrence. It operates on everything, things, people, actions." Or, as Goetz put it,[2] "Managerial planning seeks consistent, integrated and articulated programs," while "management control seeks to compel events to conform to plans."

Since control implies the existence of goals and plans, no manager can control without them. He cannot measure whether his subordinates are operating in the desired way unless he has a plan, however vague or for however brief a period. Naturally, the more clear, complete, and coordinated plans are and the longer the period they cover, the more complete controlling can be.

A manager may study past plans to see where and how they missed fire, to ascertain what happened and why, and—on the assumption that history repeats itself—to take steps to avoid recurrence of mistakes. However, the best control prevents deviations from occurring by anticipating that they will occur unless action is taken *now*. This is what is referred to as "forward-

[1] Henri Fayol, *General and Industrial ·Management* (New York: Pitman Publishing Corporation, 1949), p. 107.
[2] Billy E. Goetz, *Management Planning and Control* (New York: McGraw-Hill Book Company, 1949), p. 229.

looking" control. The next best control detects them as they occur. As the navigator continually takes readings to ascertain where he is relative to a planned course, so should the manager take readings to see whether his enterprise or department is on course, and if it is not, should make corrections accordingly. In fact, it is the function of controlling to make the intended occur.

Occasionally, in view of the authority of upper managers and their resultant responsibility, top-management control is so emphasized that the impression is given that little controlling is needed at lower levels. Although control varies among managers, it is an essential managerial function at every level.

BASIC CONTROL PROCESS

Control techniques and systems are essentially the same for cash, office procedures, morale, product quality, or anything else. And they always assume that both plans and organization structure are clear, complete, and integrated to the extent that managers are sure of their course and that authority delegations and relationships are definite. If a manager is unsure of his assignment or if a subordinate does not have the power or does not know he has the power to carry out plans, it is unreasonable and difficult to hold anyone responsible.

The basic control process, wherever it is found and whatever it controls, involves three steps: (1) establishing standards, (2) measuring performance against these standards, and (3) correcting deviations from standards and plans.

Establishment of Standards   Standards are established criteria against which actual results can be measured. They represent the expression of planning goals of the enterprise or the department in such terms that the actual accomplishment of assigned duties can be measured against them. They may be physical and represent quantities of products, units of service, man-hours, speed, volume of rejections, etc.; or they may be stated in monetary terms, such as costs, revenues, or investments; or they may be expressed in any other terms which measure performance.

Standards are usually stated in specific units, but this need not be the case. A company may, for example, have for a goal a high level of foreman loyalty and morale, or it may develop a public relations program to gain acceptance as a constructive community force. Such goals can seldom be stated in numerical terms, but there are means of determining whether action is toward or away from them with new techniques of measuring such intangibles as customer, employee, and public opinion.

Measurement of Performance   Although it is not often practicable to do so, the measurement of performance against standard should ideally be on a future basis, so that deviations may be detected in advance of their actual occurrence and avoided by appropriate remedies. The alert, forward-looking manager can sometimes predict probable departures from standard. In the absence of such ability, deviations should be disclosed as early as possible.

If the standard is appropriately drawn and if means are available for determining exactly what subordinates are doing, appraisal of actual or expected performance is fairly easy. But there are many activities in which it is extremely difficult to develop sound standards, and there are many that are hard to measure. It may be quite simple, especially with present techniques of time and motion study, to establish man-hour standards for the production of a mass-produced item, and it may be equally simple to measure performance against these standards, but if the item is custom-made, the appraisal of performance may be a formidable task.

Furthermore, in the less technical kinds of work, not only may standards be difficult to develop but appraisal may also be exceedingly hard. For example, to control the performance of the finance vice-president or the industrial relations director is not easy, because definite standards cannot easily be developed or performance accurately measured. The superior of these managers often relies on vague standards, such as the financial health of the business, the attitude of labor unions, the absence of strikes, the enthusiasm and loyalty of subordinates, the expressed admiration of business associates, and the over-all success of the department (often measured in a negative way by lack of evidence of failure). His measurements are often equally vague. At the same time, if the department seems to be making the contribution expected of it at a reasonable cost, without too many serious errors, and if the measurable accomplishments give evidence of sound management, the unavoidably general appraisal may be adequate. The point is that, as jobs move away from the assembly line, the shop, or the accounting machine, controlling them becomes more complex and often more important.

Nevertheless, as managers at all levels develop verifiable objectives, stated in either quantitative or qualitative terms (see Chapter 22), these become standards against which all position performance in the organization hierarchy can be measured. Also, as new techniques are developed to measure, with a reasonable degree of objectivity, the quality of managing itself in upper, as well as lower, positions, these will become useful standards of performance.

Correction of Deviations If standards are drawn to reflect organization structure and if performance is measured in these terms, the correction of deviations is expedited, since the manager then knows exactly where, in the assignment of individual or group duties, the corrective measures must be applied.

Correction of deviations in performance is the point at which control coalesces with the other managerial functions: The manager may correct by redrawing his plans or by modifying his goal. (This is an exercise of the principle of navigational change referred to in Chapter 5.) Or he may correct deviation by exercising his organizing function, through reassignment or clarification of duties. He may correct, also, by additional staffing, by better selection and training of subordinates, or by that ultimate of restaffing —firing. Or, again, he may correct through better directing—fuller explanation of the job or stronger leadership.

It can even be argued that correcting deviations is no step in the process of control at all but merely the point where the other managerial functions come into play. Surely, control is not confined to measuring performance against standards without doing anything when performance falls short. This overlap of the control function with the others merely demonstrates the unity of the manager's job. It shows the managing process to be an integrated system. As has been previously emphasized in this book, separating control from the other managerial functions, particularly planning, has been done because (1) it is a useful, operational way to organize knowledge, and (2) practicing managers have long understood their functions this way.[3]

Control as a Cybernetic System Managerial control is essentially the same basic process as is found in physical, biological, and social systems. As pointed out by Norbert Wiener,[4] communication, or information transfer, and control occur in the functioning of many systems. Wiener used "information" in the general sense to include a mechanical transfer of energy, an electric impulse, a chemical reaction, a written or oral message, or any other means by which a "message" might be transmitted. In the science he called cybernetics, Wiener shows that all types of systems control themselves by a feedback of information disclosing error in accomplishing goals and initiating corrective action. In other words, systems use some of their energy to feed back information that compares performance with a standard. Simple feedback is charted in Figure 28.1.

The steam engine governor is a simple mechanical cybernetic system. In order to control an engine's speed under different load conditions, weights (balls) are whirled. As the speed increases, centrifugal force makes these weights exercise an outward thrust which, in turn, transmits a force (a message) to cut down the input of steam and thereby reduce the speed. As speed is reduced, the reverse occurs. Likewise, in the human body, a number of cybernetic systems control temperature, blood pressure, motor reactions, and others. In electrical systems such as a voltage regulator, the principle of feedback is used. And in social systems, even other than the managed formal organizations, one also finds feedback. For example, in the social system of baseball, there are such standards as three strikes and out

---

[3] But there are those who believe that the functions of planning and control should be combined in one—control. See, for example, R. N. Anthony, *Planning and Control Systems: A Framework for Analysis* (Boston: Division of Research, Harvard Business School, 1965), pp. 10–15.

[4] *Cybernetics: Control and Communication in the Animal and the Machine* (New York: John Wiley & Sons, Inc., 1948).

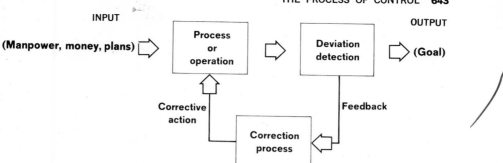

Fig. 28.1 Simple Feedback

and the seventh-inning stretch which are accomplished, essentially, by the feedback of information which corrects those who would deviate.

TEN REQUIREMENTS OF ADEQUATE CONTROLS

It is understandable that every alert manager should want to have an effective and adequate control system to assist him in making sure that events conform to plans. Much of the time and effort of accounting, statistics, and other information departments in the typical enterprise is spent on furnishing information for control. It is sometimes not realized that the control system used by managers, like any other control system, must be designed for the task it is intended to perform. While the principles of control are universal, the actual system requires special design. In this tailoring of control systems or techniques, there are certain requirements that the manager should keep in mind whether he is a top executive, checking whether new products are developed as planned, or a supervisor, checking only the operations of his work force.

1. *Controls must reflect the nature and needs of the activity.* All control systems should reflect the job they are to perform. A system useful for the vice-president in charge of manufacturing will almost certainly be different in scope and nature from that of a shop foreman. Controls of the sales department will differ from those of the finance department and these from the controls of the purchasing department. And a small business will need different controls from a large business.

   Certain techniques, such as budgets, break-even points, standard hours or costs, and various financial ratios have general application in many business situations. However, it should never be assumed that any of these widely used techniques is applicable in a given situation. The manager must be aware of the strategic factors in his plans and operations calling for control and use techniques suited to them.

2. *Controls should report deviations promptly.* As will be noted below, the ideal control system detects possible deviations before they actually occur. In any case, the information must reach the manager as soon as possible so that he can head off failures.

Because failures are not reported expeditiously, typical business accounting is often weak in furnishing control information. Accounting, having for its purpose the recording of transactions, naturally looks backward. Moreover, in the attempt to make accounting data comprehensive and accurate, it often reaches the manager weeks or months after the event. It does a manager little good to find in October that he lost money in July for what he did in May, though, if no better data are available, this information may be worth having. Even though new electronic data-processing machines are greatly speeding the flow of accounting data, most managers find that normally available accounting data must be supplemented with an accounting estimate of the present and future.

3. *Controls should be forward looking.* Although ideal control is instantaneous, as in certain electronic controls, the facts of managerial life include a time lag between the deviation and corrected action. Therefore, the manager should strive for a control technique which will forecast deviations in time for him to make corrections before the problem occurs. He would surely prefer a forecast of what will probably happen next week or next month—even though this contains a margin of error—to a report—accurate to several decimal points—of the past about which he can do nothing.

That this is possible is illustrated by such forward-looking devices as cash control. A company manager cannot very well find out in April that he ran out of cash in March. Properly, he forecasts his cash requirements to handle his payroll and other cash needs as they arise. This approach to control can surely be applied on a much broader front than is now the case.

4. *Controls should point up exceptions at critical points.* The time-honored exception principle, that the manager should only watch for and deal with exceptions, is not enough for effective control. Some deviations from standards have little meaning and others have a great deal. Small exceptions in certain areas have greater significance than larger deviations in other areas. A manager, for example, might be concerned if the cost of office labor deviated from standard by 5 per cent, but unworried if the cost of postage stamps deviated from budget by 20 per cent.

Therefore, controls should not only point up deviations but should pinpoint them where they are important or critical to his operations. This is a matter of critical standard selection, which will be dealt with presently.

5. *Controls should be objective.* Management necessarily has many subjective elements in it, but whether a subordinate is doing a good job should ideally not be a matter for subjective determination. Where controls are subjective, a manager's or a subordinate's personality may influence judgments of performance inaccurately; but people have difficulty in explaining away objective control of their performance, particularly if the standards and measurements are kept up-to-date through periodic review.

Objective control should be definite and determinable in a clear and positive way. Objective standards can be quantitative, such as costs or man-hours per unit, or date of job completion; they can also be qualitative, such as a better training program with specific characteristics or accomplishing a specific kind of upgrading of the quality of personnel. The point is that, in either case, the standard is determinable and verifiable.

In addition, subordinates react more favorably to objective standards. It is frustrating for a subordinate to be told in indefinite terms that he is not doing a good job. Faced with objective standards and measurements—particularly those he understood and agreed to—he may still try to explain away a failure, but he must see that failure occurred.

6. *Controls should be flexible.* Controls must remain workable in the face of changed plans, unforeseen circumstances, or outright failures. As Goetz has remarked:[5] "A complex program of managerial plans may fail in some particulars. The control system should report such failures, and should contain sufficient elements of flexibility to maintain managerial control of operations despite such failures."

The need for flexible control can be illustrated by the following instances. A budget system may project a certain level of expenses and grant authority to managers to hire labor and purchase materials and services at this level. If, as is usually the case, this budget is based on a forecast of a certain level of sales, it may become meaningless as a system of control if the actual sales volume is considerably above or below the forecast. Budget systems have been brought into ill repute among some companies because of inflexibility in such circumstances. What is needed, of course, is a system that will reflect sales variations as well as other deviations from plans. This has been provided, as will be noted presently, by the flexible budget.

In production scheduling, the production manager must be prepared for failures occasioned by the breakdown of a machine or the illness of a key worker. If his control system is too inflexible to

[5] Goetz, *op. cit.*, p. 229.

account for such hitches, the slowdown, even though temporary, may impair his control. Much flexibility in control can be provided by having alternative plans for various probable situations. In fact, flexible control is best achieved through flexible plans.

7. *Controls should reflect the organization pattern.* Organization, being the principal vehicle for coordinating the work of people with assigned duties and delegated authority, is also the means for maintaining control; and the manager is the focal point of control, just as he is the focal point for the assignment of tasks and the delegation of authority. This is well illustrated in cost accounting. Product cost accumulation is used to control unit cost in production. Yet unless costs are accumulated so as to fit the organization pattern of the production department, and unless each factory superintendent and foreman is shown cost accumulation in *his* department, actual costs may be out of line without the manager's knowing whether the cause was within his control. Fortunately, in recent years, cost accountants have recognized the importance of relating cost data to organized structure, and the cost centers now typically used in industry provide usable data for each manager concerned.

8. *Controls should be economical.* Controls must be worth their cost. Although this requirement is simple, its practice is often complex, for a manager may find it difficult to know what a particular control system is worth, or to know what it costs. Economy is relative, since the benefits vary with the importance of the activity, the size of the business, the expense that might be incurred in the absence of control, and the contribution the system can make.

A small company cannot afford the extensive control system of a large company. The elaborate charts and detailed analyses used by the top management of the Monsanto Chemical Company or the du Pont Company doubtless represent hundreds of thousands of dollars in investment of time and many more thousands each year for their maintenance. Expensive preparation, approval, and administration of complex budgetary control programs may be well worth their cost to the large enterprise but uneconomical for the small. Likewise, a finance vice-president may feel that many thousands of dollars have been well spent for historical and forecast data on cash flow or capital investment, but in the same company a much smaller expenditure for tracing the handling of scrap inventories might be too costly.

Since a limiting factor of control systems is relative economy, this, in turn, will depend a great deal on the manager's selecting for control only critical factors in areas important to him. If tailored to the job and to the size of the enterprise, control will probably be economical. On the other hand, one of the economies of large-scale enterprise results from being able to afford expensive and elaborate control systems. Often, however, the magnitude of the problems, the wider area of planning, the difficulty of coordinating plans, and poor management communication in a large business require such expensive controls that their over-all efficiency suffers in comparison to controls in a small business.

9. *Controls should be understandable.* Some control systems, especially those based upon mathematical formulas, complex break-even charts, detailed analyses, and statistical summaries, are not understandable to the managers who must use them. Sometimes the manager could understand them if he would take the time to learn the techniques, but whether his lack of understanding results from complex techniques or impatience in learning them, the effect is the same: The control system will not function well.

Many so-called experts in graphs, charts, advanced statistical methods, or exhaustive analyses fail to communicate the meaning of their control data to the manager who should use it. "Control" staffs and departments in business often develop needed information that cannot or will not be used by managers because it is not simple enough or adapted to the manager's understanding. What may be valuable and comprehensible to one manager may not be so to another, and it is up to the manager (or his staff assistant) to make sure that he has an adequate control system that he understands.

10. *Controls should indicate corrective action.* A control system that detects deviations from plans will be little more than an interesting exercise if it does not show the way to corrective action. An adequate system should disclose where failures are occurring, who is responsible for them, and what should be done about them.

THE KEY IMPORTANCE OF FORWARD-LOOKING CONTROLS

Perhaps there is no more important element of an adequate and effective control system or technique than the need for forward-looking controls. As is indicated in Figure 28.2, the actual feedback loop involved in usual man-

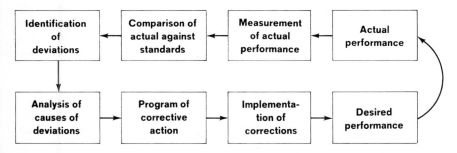

Fig. 28.2   Feedback Loop of Management Control

agement controls is comprised, as a minimum, of a number of very separate and identifiable steps. Mere observation of the steps in this loop will show that many of them can be very time-consuming. With the faster flow of information now available, even if it were possible (as it is now, but it is not often economically practicable) to measure actual performance quickly and to get a fast comparison of actual against standards, and even if it were possible (as it is in some, but not all, information systems) to get quick identification of deviations, there are still unavoidable time delays in the other steps. The analysis of causes of deviation in many instances requires considerable time. In nearly every case, the development of a program of correction and implementation of correction take time, varying from a few days to many months.

Thus, mere inspection of the actual feedback loop involved in management control will underline the fact that fast information itself will not solve the problems of such control. Even the fastest data collection, known as "real time" information (that is, information immediately available at the time events are occurring), will not meet the requirements of quick control. To be sure, saving time in collecting information on actual performance or comparing it against standards, or even identifying deviations, will shorten the loop. But the time interval of the other steps shows clearly that this will not result in automatic correction of deviations from plans.

This means that the intelligent manager, while encouraged by new systems of data collection and processing, will not be carried away with an exaggerated notion of their potentialities. He will, instead, recognize that what he needs is a system which will give him indication of deviations *before* they occur. This has been done, as noted, with cash planning and control. It is being done by such new devices as the networks approach (as in PERT, which is discussed in the next chapter) to planning and control. And the authors predict that, with the clear need recognized and new techniques developing, other devices will be invented in the near future to help in establishing an effective form of quick control.

CRITICAL CONTROL POINTS

The establishment of standards furnishes the basis against which actual or expected performance is measured. In a simple operation, a manager might control through over-all observation. However, as operations become more complex or a manager's authority broader, this becomes impracticable. The manager must then choose points for special attention and, by watching them, assure himself that his whole operation is proceeding as planned.

The points selected for control should be critical, in the sense either of being limiting factors in the operation or of showing better than other factors whether plans are working out. With such standards a manager can handle a larger group of subordinates and thereby increase his span of management, with resulting cost savings and improvement of communication.

There are, however, no specific guides to the selection of control points because of the peculiarities of enterprise and department functions, the variety of products and services to be measured, and the innumerable policies and plans. An almost unbelievable number of standards can be used to measure performance. The dimensions and contents of a product can be spelled out in great detail. Production can be gauged in rate per minute, hour, day, shift, month, or year. Cost can be measured in terms of its components, per unit or per varying lots. Business income can be measured by such widely different standards as profits before and after taxes and profits as a percentage of sales or return on investment. Standards for measuring financial soundness include desired inventory levels, cash availability, working capital, depreciation reserves, and the many ratios useful in analyzing balance sheets, such as the ratio of current assets to current liabilities or net worth to debt or net quick assets to short-term liabilities. Likewise, in personnel selection and training, supervision, purchasing, traffic, public relations, and all the many activities of business varying measurements of performance exist.

The ability to select critical points of control is one of the arts of management, since sound control depends on them. In this connection the manager must ask himself such questions as: What will best reflect the goals of *my* department? What will best show *me* when these goals are not being met? What will best measure any deviations? What will inform *me* as to who is responsible for any failure? What standards will cost the least? For what standards is information economically available?

Types of Critical Standards   As was noted above, every broad planning objective, every goal of the many planning programs, every activity of these programs, every policy, and every procedure become standards against which actual or expected performance might be measured. In practice, however, standards tend to be of the following types: (1) physical standards, (2) cost standards, (3) capital standards, (4) revenue standards, (5) program standards, and (6) intangible standards.

Physical standards   These deal with nonmonetary measurements and are common at the operating level where materials are used, labor employed, services rendered, and goods produced. They may reflect quantitative performance, such as man-hours per unit of output, pounds of fuel per horsepower produced, ton-miles of freight traffic carried, units of production per machine-hour, or feet of wire per ton of copper. Physical standards may also reflect quality, such as hardness of bearings, closeness of tolerances, rate of climb of an airplane, durability of a fabric, or fastness of a color. As Goetz has said,[6] these standards are the "building blocks of planning," since "whether management must choose between alternate policies, organizational configuration, procedures, or resources, it must always analyze the rival programs in terms of their physical elements, determine the financial

[6] *Ibid.,* p. 93.

implications of these elements, integrate or synthesize the elements into programs, and select the best program it can devise." As physical standards are the building blocks of planning, they are also the fundamental standards for control.

Cost standards   These deal with monetary measurement and, like physical standards, are common at the operating level. They attach monetary values to the costs of operations. Illustrative of cost standards are such widely used measures as direct and indirect cost per unit produced, labor cost per unit or per hour, material cost per unit, machine-hour costs, costs per plane reservation, selling costs per dollar or unit of sales, and costs per foot of well drilled.

Capital standards   These are a variety of cost standards, arising from the application of monetary measurements to physical items. But they have to do with the capital invested in the firm rather than with operating costs and are therefore related to the balance sheet rather than the income statement. Perhaps the most widely used standard for new investment, as well as for over-all control, is the ratio of net profits to investment, or return on investment. The typical balance sheet will disclose other capital standards, such as ratios of current assets to current liabilities, debt to net worth, fixed investment to total investment, cash and receivables to payables, notes or bonds to stock, and the size and turnover of inventories.

Revenue standards   These arise from attaching monetary values to sales. They may vary from such standards as revenue per bus passenger-mile and dollars per ton of steel shapes sold, to average sale per customer and sales per capita in a given market area.

Program standards   A manager may be assigned to install a variable budget program, a program for formally following the development of new products, or a program for improving the quality of a sales force. While some subjective judgment may have to be applied in appraising program performance, timing and other factors can be used as objective standards.

Intangible standards   More difficult to set are standards not expressed in either specific physical or monetary measurements. What standard can a manager use for determining the competence of the divisional purchasing agent or personnel director? What can he use for determining whether the advertising program meets both short- and long-term objectives? Or whether the public relations program is fully successful? Are foremen loyal to the company's objectives? Is the office boy alert enough? Such questions show how difficult it is to establish standards for goals that cannot be given clear quantitative or qualitative measurement.

Many intangible standards exist in business because thorough research into what constitutes desired performance has not been done above the level of the shop, the district sales office, the shipping room, or the accounting department. Perhaps a more important reason is that where human relationships count in performance, as they do above the basic operating levels, it is very hard to measure what is "good," "effective," or "efficient." Tests, surveys, and sampling techniques developed by psychologists and sociometrists have made it possible to probe human attitudes and drives, but many managerial controls over interpersonal relationships must continue to be based upon intangible standards, considered judgment, trial and error, and even, on occasion, sheer hunch.

However, with the present tendency for better-managed companies to establish an entire network of verifiable qualitative or quantitative goals at every level of management, the use of intangible standards, while still important, is diminishing. In complex program operations as well as in the performance of managers themselves, modern managers are finding that through research and thinking it is possible to define goals that can be used as performance standards. While the quantitative goals are likely to take the form of the standards outlined above, definition of qualitative goals represents a new development in the area of standards. For example, if the program of a district sales office is spelled out to include such elements as training salesmen in accordance with a plan with specific characteristics, the very fact of the plan and its characteristics furnish standards which tend to become objective and, therefore, "tangible."

THE BUDGET AS A CONTROL DEVICE

A widely used device for managerial control is the budget. Indeed, it has sometimes been assumed that budgeting is *the* device for accomplishing control. As will be noted, however, many nonbudgetary devices are also essential. In fact, many companies attain a high degree of control without formal budgets, although budgeting principles are usually necessary. In a number of companies, primarily because of the negative implications of budgeting in the past, the more positive phrase "profit planning" is used and the budget is known as the "profit plan."

Concept of Budgeting Budgeting is the formulation of plans for a given future period in numerical terms. As such, budgets are statements of anticipated results, in financial terms—as in revenue and expense and capital budgets—or in nonfinancial terms—as in budgets of direct-labor-hours, materials, physical sales volume, or units of production. It has sometimes been said, for example, that financial budgets represent the "dollarizing" of plans.

Purpose of Budgeting Through numerical statement of plans and breaking of these plans into components consistent with the organization structure, budgets correlate planning and allow authority to be delegated without loss of control. In other words, reduction of plans to definite numbers forces a kind of orderliness that permits the manager to see clearly what capital will be spent by whom and where, and what expenses, revenue, or units of physical input or output his plans will involve. Having ascertained this, he can more freely delegate authority to effectuate the plan within the limits of the budget.

Budgets sometimes serve purposes beyond that of control. A budget not only requires planning but is an instrument of planning. Moreover, a budget, to be useful to a manager at any level, must reflect the organizational pattern. Only when plans are complete, coordinated, and developed enough to be fitted into departmental operations can a useful departmental budget be prepared as an instrument of control.

Types of Budgets   Since budgets express plans and since the typical enterprise has a large variety of plans, there are many types of budgets. One author finds that the average manufacturing company requires thirty major types of budgets to have "complete" budgetary control.[7] These include the following types of budgets: sales order, sales shipment, inventory, production requirements, direct labor, material, direct manufacturing expense, prorated manufacturing expense, administrative, distributive expense, executive division expense, industrial relations, accounts receivable, purchasing division expense, distribution or sales expense, advertising, permanent plant expense, perishable plant expense, cost of sales, cost of goods manufactured, prepaid expense, purchase, accounting division expense, accounts payable, payroll, profit and loss, cash, balance sheet, and master budgets. These may be classified into five basic types of budgets, with a budget summary portraying the total planning picture of all the budgets: (1) revenue and expense budgets, (2) time, space, material, and product budgets, (3) capital expenditure budgets, (4) cash budgets, and (5) balance sheet budgets.

Revenue and expense budgets   By far the most common business budgets spell out plans for revenues and operating expenses in dollar terms. The most basic of these is the sales budget, the formal and detailed expression of the sales forecast. As the sales forecast is the cornerstone of planning, the sales budget is the foundation of budgetary control. Although a company may budget other revenues, such as expected income from rentals, royalties, or miscellaneous sources, the revenue from sales of products or services furnishes the principal income to support operating expenses and yield profits.

Operating expense budgets of the typical business can be as numerous as the expense classifications in its chart of accounts and the units of organization in its structure. These budgets may deal with individual items of expense, such as direct labor, materials, supervision, clerical, rent, heat, power, travel, entertainment, office supplies, shop supplies, and many others.

---

[7] J. K. Lasser et al., "How to Use Budgets for Control of a Business," in *J. K. Lasser's Executive Course in Profitable Business Management* (New York: McGraw-Hill Book Company, 1952), sec. 16, p. 553.

Sometimes the department head will budget only major items and lump together other items in one control summary. For example, if the manager of a small department is expected to take one business trip a year at a cost of $96, budgeting this cost each month at $8 would mean little for monthly planning or control.

Time, space, material, and product budgets   Many business budgets are better expressed in physical than in monetary terms. Although such budgets are usually translated into monetary quantities, they are much more significant at a certain stage in planning and control if dealt with in physical quantities. Among the more common of these are the budgets for direct-labor-hours, machine-hours, units of materials, square feet allocated, and units produced. Most firms budget product output, and most production departments budget their share of the output of components of the final product. In addition, it is common to budget manpower, either in labor-hours or man-days, by types of manpower required. Obviously, such budgets cannot be well expressed in monetary terms, since the dollar cost would not accurately measure the resources used or the results intended.

Capital expenditure budgets   The capital expenditure budget outlines specifically capital expenditure for plant, machinery, equipment, inventories, and other items. Whether for a short or a long term, these budgets require care in giving definite form to plans for spending the funds of the enterprise. Since capital resources are generally one of the most limiting factors of the business, and since investment in plant and equipment usually requires a long period for recovery of its cost from operations, thereby leading to a high degree of inflexibility, capital expenditure budgets must be diligently tied in with long-range planning.

Cash budgets   The cash budget is simply a forecast of cash receipts and disbursements against which actual cash experience is measured. Whether called a budget or not, this is perhaps the most important single control of a business. As was pointed out earlier, the availability of cash to meet obligations as they fall due is the first requirement of business existence, and handsome profits do little good when tied up in inventory, machinery, or other noncash assets. Cash budgeting also shows availability of excess cash, thereby making possible planning for profit-making investment of this cash.

Balance sheet budgets   The balance sheet budget forecasts the status of assets, liabilities, and capital account as of particular times in the future. Since the sources of change in balance sheet items are the various other budgets, this budget proves the accuracy of all other budgets.

In addition to the balance sheet budget, which forecasts the status of the business as a whole, many items of the balance sheet may be budgeted in various degrees of detail. The more common, in addition to cash and capital investments, are special budgets of accounts receivable, inventories, and accounts payable.

Budget summaries   Complete balance sheet budgets are a form of budget summary. In addition, a master budget gathers together all the budgets for the several departments of a business and summarizes them, first in a forecast income statement, and then in a forecast balance sheet. The former may be in detail, or it may be in a summary form showing only the principal items of revenue, expense, loss, and profit (for example, net sales, cost of sales, gross profit, administrative and selling expenses, net operating profit, other income and charges, income taxes, and net profit). The latter reflects the principal items of the balance sheet.

Dangers in Budgeting   Budgets should be used only as a tool of major planning and control. Some budgetary control programs are so complete and detailed that they become cumbersome, meaningless, and unduly expensive. There is danger in overbudgeting, through spelling out minor expenses in detail and depriving the manager of needed freedom in operating his department. For example, a department head was thwarted in important sales promotion because expenditures for office supplies exceeded budgeted estimates; new expenditures had to be limited even though his total departmental expenses were well within the budget and he had funds to pay personnel for writing sales promotion letters. In another department, expenses were budgeted in such useless detail that the cost of budgeting of many items exceeded the expenses controlled.

Another danger lies in allowing budgetary goals to supersede enterprise goals. In his zest to keep within budget limits, a manager may forget that he owes primary allegiance to the enterprise objectives. The authors recall a company with a thorough budgetary control program in which the sales department could not obtain information needed from the engineering department on the grounds that the latter's budget would not stand such expense! This conflict between partial and over-all control objectives, the excessive departmental independence sometimes engendered, and the consequent lack of coordination are symptoms of inadequate management, since no budget system can be so perfect or omniscient as to replace common sense and every budget should support enterprise objectives.

A latent danger sometimes found in budgeting is that of hiding inefficiencies. Budgets have a way of growing from precedent, and the fact that a certain expenditure was made in the past becomes evidence of its reasonableness in the present; if a department once spent a given amount for supplies, this becomes a floor for future budgets. Also, managers learn that budget requests are likely to be pared down in the course of final approval and therefore ask for much more than they need. Unless budget making is accomplished by constant reexamination of standards and conversion factors by which planning is translated into numerical terms, the budget may become an umbrella under which slovenly and inefficient management can hide.

Perhaps the greatest danger in controlling through budgets lies in inflexibility. Even if budgeting is limited to major items and is not used to supplant management, the reduction of plans to numerical terms gives them a kind of illusive definiteness. It is entirely possible that events will prove that a larger amount should be spent for this kind of labor or that kind of material and a smaller amount for another, or that sales will exceed or fall materially below the amount forecast. Such differences may make a budget obsolete almost as soon as it is made; and if the manager must stay within the strait jacket of his budget in the face of such events, the usefulness of the budget is reduced or negated. This is especially true where budgets are made for long periods in advance.

One of the primary problems of budgeting in government, for example, is that plans for expenditures must be made, and budgets thereby created, sometimes two or three years ahead of actual expenditures, to give ample time for appropriations to be presented to and approved by the legislature. It is not easy for the dean of a state college to foresee exactly his needs (for stationery, supplies, and travel expense, as well as instruction) or for the head of the research department of a state or Federal regulatory agency to foresee his needs for manpower and other expense allowances for years ahead.

In business the danger of inflexibility can be extremely important. With the dynamics created by change and competition, the manager must be ready to change his plans materially at short notice. Since budgetary rigidities may make it difficult or impossible for him to do so, many top managers shy away from such programs.

Variable Budgets　Because of the dangers arising from inflexibility in budgets and because maximum flexibility consistent with efficiency underlies good planning, attention has been increasingly given to variable or flexible budgets. These are designed to vary usually as the volume of sales or production varies and so are largely limited in application to expense budgets. The variable budget is based upon an analysis of expense items to determine how individual costs *should* vary with volume of output. Some costs do not vary with volume, particularly in so short a period as a month, six months, or a year. Among these are depreciation, property taxes and insurance, maintenance of plant and equipment, and the costs of maintaining a minimum staff of supervisory and other key personnel on a readiness-to-serve basis. Some of these standby costs—such as for maintaining a minimum number of key or trained personnel for advertising or sales promotion, and for research—depend upon managerial policy.

Costs that vary with volume of output range from those that are perfectly variable to those that are only slightly variable. The task of variable budgeting is to select some unit of measure that reflects volume, to inspect the various categories of costs (usually by reference to the company's chart of accounts), and, by statistical studies, methods-engineering analyses, and other means, to determine how these costs should vary with volume. At this stage, each category of cost is related to volume, sometimes with recognition of "steps" as volume increases and sometimes with a factor allowing increases in expenses with rising volume. Each department is given these variable items of cost, along with definite dollar amounts for its fixed costs. Periodically—usually each month—department heads are then given the volume forecast for the immediate future, from which is calculated the dollar amounts of variable costs that make up the budget. In this way, a basic budget can be established for six months or a year in advance but be made variable with shorter-term changes in sales and output.

This type of budget may be illustrated by Figure 28.3, which depicts the fixed and variable portions of business cost. A chart of a departmental budget would have essentially the same appearance, with suitable cost components. Although this chart uses units of monthly output as the base for volume, and direct labor and materials are included, many variable budgets assume that volume will automatically control direct labor and materials and are consequently used only to control indirect and general expense.

A difficulty in all kinds of variable budgets is that the department manager must still make future plans. It may be easy to tell a foreman that during the month of May he can have twelve trained electronic assemblers,

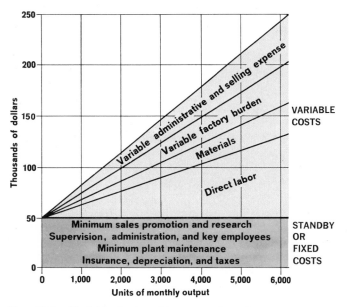

Fig. 28.3 Variable Budget Chart . . . As volume increases, certain costs remain fixed; others vary accordingly.

then, several weeks later, that he may have fifteen in June, and a month later that his budget for July will permit hiring only ten. But the problems of hiring and training competent personnel make accomplishing these variations more costly than their advantages—keeping expenses flexible and completely variable with volume—are worth. In other words, efficiency may demand that the department manager not vary certain of his expenses with short-term variations in volume. In the quest for flexibility in budgets, as with other tools of management, the intelligent manager will not lose sight of basic objectives and efficiencies by blindly following any system.

Observation of many variable budgets in practice leads to the conclusion that these work best when sales or other measures of volume can be reasonably well forecast and reasonably long-range plans made, so that the level of expenses will not have to be changed so often and on such short notice as to make the job of supervisors intolerable. Under these circumstances, one might well ask what the advantages of variable budgeting are. Although a fixed budget will work as well with good plans and sales forecasts, a variable budget *forces* study of and preoccupation with factors which translate work load into manpower or expense needs. Carefully worked out conversion factors are necessary for any good budgeting. This, rather than flexibility itself, appears to be the principal advantage of variable budgeting.

Alternative and Supplementary Budgets Another method of obtaining variable budgeting is to establish alternative budgets for alternative eventualities. Sometimes a company will establish budgets for a high level of operation, a medium level, and a low level, and the three budgets will be approved for the company as a whole and for each organizational segment for six months or a year in advance. Then, at stated times, managers will be informed as to which budget to use in their planning and control. Alternative budgets are a modification of variable budgets, the latter being virtually infinitely variable instead of limited to a few alternatives.

Budget flexibility is also obtained via a plan referred to as the "supplemental monthly budget." Under this plan, a six-month or one-year budget is prepared for the primary purpose of outlining the framework of the company's plans, coordinating them among departments, and establishing department objectives. This is a basic or minimum budget. Then a supplementary budget is prepared each month on the basis of the volume of business forecast for that month. This budget gives each manager authority for scheduling output and spending funds above the basic budget, if and to the extent that the shorter-term plans so justify. It also gives top managers the advantages of close control, at the same time giving department managers a minimum level of operations for long-term planning. Besides, it avoids some of the detailed calculations necessary under the typical variable budget. But these budget approaches do not usually have the advantage of forcing complete analysis of all costs and relating them to volume.

Making Budgetary Control Work   If budgetary controls are to work well, managers must remember that they are designed only as tools and not to replace management, that they have limitations and must be tailored to each job. Moreover, they are the tools of all managers and not alone of the budget administrator or the controller. The only persons who can administer budgets, since they are plans, are the managers responsible for the programs budgeted. No successful budget program can be truly "directed" or "administered" by a budget director. This staff officer can assist in the preparation and use of budgets by the responsible managers, but, unless the entire company management is to be turned over to the budget officer, he should not be given the job of making budget-commitment or expenditure decisions.

To be most effective, budget making and administration must receive the wholehearted support of top management. To establish an office of budget administrator by decree and then forget about him leads to haphazard budget making and to saddling subordinate managers with another procedure or set of papers to prepare. On the other hand, if top management actively supports budget making and grounds the company budget firmly on company plans, encourages divisions and departments to make and defend their budgets, and participates in this review, budgets encourage alert management throughout the organization.

Related to the participation of top management, another means of making budgets work is to make sure that all managers expected to administer and live under budgets have a part in their preparation. Just as wide participation is advisable for developing understanding and loyal acceptance of plans, so is it advisable for department managers to have a part in preparing their own budgets. Although these managers must often be overruled and some of their budget requests cannot be honored, managers should be told why and how the approved budget better serves the objectives of the enterprise. Real participation in budget making, rather than pseudoparticipation, is necessary. As one student of the subject found, most budget administrators and controllers recognize that participation is crucial to budget success, but too often in practice this amounts to pressured "acceptance."[8]

Important, too, for successful budgeting is taking care that budgets are not overdone to the extent of seriously compromising the authority of managers. Although budgets do furnish a means of delegating authority without loss of control, there is danger that they will be so detailed and inflexible that little real authority is, in fact, delegated. Some executives even believe that the best budget to give a manager is one that lumps all his allowable expenditures for a period of time into a single amount and then provides for him complete freedom as to how these funds are to be spent in pursuance of the company's goals. This kind of decentralization has much to commend it, although better planning and control might be forthcoming, without centralizing authority unduly, by allowing the department manager

---

[8] Chris Argyris, "Human Problems with Budgets," *Harvard Business Review,* vol. 31, no. 1, p. 108 (January, 1953).

real participation in budget making. It may also be well to allow the department manager a reasonable degree of latitude in changing his budget and in shifting funds, so long as he meets his *total* budget.

One of the keys to making budgeting work is to develop and make available standards by which the manager's work can be translated into needs for manpower, operating expenses, capital expenditures, space, and other resources. Many budgets fail for lack of such standards, and many upper-level managers hesitate to allow subordinates to submit budget plans for fear that there may be no logical basis for reviewing budget requests. With conversion factors available, the superior manager can review such requests and justify his approval or disapproval of them. Moreover, by concentrating on the resources required to do a planned job, a manager can base his request on what he needs to have for meeting output goals and improving performance. He no longer must cope with arbitrary across-the-board budget cuts—a technique more frustrating to the superior than to the subordinate who, on the occasion of the next request, has the foresight to pad for the inevitable slice. In fact, it can be said that across-the-board cuts are the surest evidence of poor planning and loss of control.

Lastly, if budgetary control is to work, the manager needs ready information as to actual and forecast performance under budgets by *his* department. This must be designed to show him how well *he* is doing, preferably before the fact, but it is usually not available until too late for him to avoid budget deviations.

TRADITIONAL NONBUDGETARY CONTROLS

There are, of course, many traditional control devices not connected with budgets, although some may be related to and used with budgetary controls. Among the more important of these are statistical data, special reports and analyses, analysis of break-even points, internal audit, and personal observation.

Statistical Data Statistical analysis of the innumerable aspects of a business operation and the clear presentation of statistical data, whether of a historical or forecast nature, are, of course, important to control. Some managers can readily interpret tabular statistical data, but most managers prefer presentation of the data on charts. Comprehensible presentation of statistical data, whether in tabular or chart form, is an art that requires imagination.

An increasing number of companies are making control data available to managers through the preparation of charts. One of the oldest and best-known chart systems is that of the du Pont Company. With its many divisions and subsidiary interests, the complexity of its operations, and the diversity of its product lines, its top management has found that it can best watch over the company, its plans, and results through charts. The executive committee, which is the top management of du Pont, meets one day a week.

During these meetings some 350 charts are reviewed and studied by small groups, so that in a year's time all the charts have been gone over several times. The primary control standard of the du Pont Company is return on investment, and the central theme around which each chart is developed for each division is profit on sales and sales turnover (sales divided by investment). Thus, the management is able to see, in terms of their primary control standard, how each division is performing.[9]

Special Reports and Analyses   For control purposes, special reports and analyses help in particular problem areas. While routine accounting and statistical reports furnish a good share of necessary information, there are often areas in which they are inadequate. One successful manager of a complicated operation hired a small staff of trained analysts and gave them no assignment other than investigating and analyzing operations under his control. This group developed a surprising sense for detecting situations where things did not seem just right. Almost invariably, their investigation disclosed opportunities for cost improvement or better utilization of capital that no statistical chart would have disclosed.

It may be that some of the funds being spent for elaborate budgetary control and information programs could be more profitably spent for special analyses. Their very nonroutine nature can highlight the unusual and, in so doing, reveal places for material improvement in efficiency. In routine search for pennies and accounting for them, opportunities for saving dollars may be overlooked. Good management requires constant searching out of exceptions, critical points, and limiting factors.

Break-even Point Analysis   An interesting control device is the break-even chart. This chart merely depicts the relationship of sales and expenses in such a way as to show at what volume revenues exactly cover expenses. At any lesser volume, the company would suffer a loss, and at a greater volume it would enjoy a profit.

Figure 28.4, a simple form of such a chart, shows the level of revenues and expenses for each volume of sales and indicates that at $17 million of sales the company would break even. (The break-even point can be expressed as well in units of goods sold, per cent of plant utilized, or similar terms.) It will be noted that the chart is similar to the variable budget chart (Figure 28.3), and break-even analysis is often confused with variable budgets. Although both use much the same kind of basic input data, the variable budget has as its purpose the control of cost, while the break-even chart has as its purpose the prediction of profit and, consequently, must incorporate revenue data. Moreover, utilized for budgetary control, the

[9] For a description of the du Pont chart system, see *How the du Pont Organization Appraises Its Performance*, Financial Management Series No. 94 (New York: American Management Association, 1950). See discussion of this system of control in chap. 30 of this book.

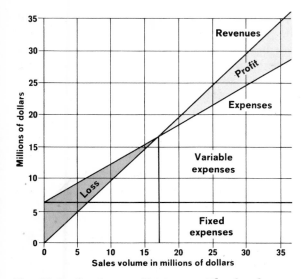

Fig. 28.4 Break-even Chart . . . *The break-even point is reached when revenues equal expenditures.*

variable budget must reflect organizational units, while the break-even chart is ordinarily used to determine profitability of a given course of action as compared with alternatives.

Break-even analysis is especially useful in planning and control because it emphasizes the marginal concept. Ratios, such as that of percentage of profits to sales, tend to overlook the impact of fixed costs, while the use of break-even points emphasizes the effects of additional sales or costs on profits. Likewise, in dramatizing the effect of additional expenses or incremental changes in volume, it brings to the manager's attention the marginal results of his decisions.

Internal Audit Another effective tool of managerial control is the internal audit. Internal auditing, in its broadest sense, is the regular and independent appraisal, by a staff of internal auditors, of the accounting, financial, and other operations of a business. Although more often limited to the auditing of accounts, in its most useful aspect internal auditing involves the appraisal of operations generally, weighing actual results in the light of planned results. Thus, the internal auditors, in addition to assuring themselves that accounts properly reflect the facts, might also appraise policies, procedures, use of authority, quality of management, effectiveness of methods, and other phases of operations. While most internal auditors limit themselves to the matter of the integrity of accounts and the corporate assets, there is no reason why the concept of internal auditing should not be broadened in practice. Perhaps the only limiting factors are the ability of a company to afford so broad an audit, the difficulty of obtaining men who can do a broad type of audit, and the very practical consideration that no one likes to be reported or spied upon. While persons responsible for accounts and for the safeguarding of company assets have learned to accept audit, those who are responsible for far more valuable things—the execution of the plans, policies, and procedures of a company—have not so readily learned to accept the idea of being audited. But where the broad form of internal audit has been employed constructively and where the auditors operate as a group of internal management consultants with a view to helping the operating managers, their acceptance has understandably been very high.

Personal Observation   In any preoccupation with the devices of managerial control, one should never overlook the importance of control through personal observation. Budgets, charts, reports, ratios, auditors' recommendations, and other devices of control can be helpful, if not essential to control. But the manager who relies on these devices and sits, so to speak, in a soundproof control room reading dials and manipulating levers can hardly expect to do a thorough job of control. Management, after all, has the task of seeing that the enterprise objectives are accomplished by *people,* and, although many scientific devices aid in making sure that people are doing that which the manager has hoped and planned for them, the problem of control is still one of measuring activities of human beings.

FOR DISCUSSION

1. Planning and control are often thought of as a system; control is also often referred to as a system. What is meant by this? Can both statements be true?

2. If you were asked to institute a system of "tailored" controls in a company, exactly what steps would you take to do so?

3. "Variable budgets are flexible budgets." Discuss.

4. It is often claimed that an operating expense budget must be set at levels lower than expected in order to assure the attainment of goals. Do you agree?

5. To what extent, and how, can budgeting be approached on a "grass roots" basis, that is, from the bottom of the organization upward?

SELECTED REFERENCES

American Management Association: *A Program of Financial Planning and Controls: The Monsanto Chemical Company,* Financial Management Series No. 103, New York: American Management Association, 1953.

———: *How the du Pont Organization Appraises Its Performance,* Financial Management Series No. 94, New York: American Management Association, 1950.

———: *Practical Uses of Break-even and Budget Controls,* Production Series No. 186, New York: American Management Association, 1949.

Anderson, D. R.: *Practical Controllership,* Homewood, Ill.: Richard D. Irwin, Inc., 1961.

Beyer, R.: *Profitability Accounting for Planning and Control,* New York: The Ronald Press Company, 1963.

Dean, J.: "Methods and Potentialities of Break-even Analysis," *The Australian Accountant*, vol. 21, nos. 10 and 11 (October and November, 1951).

Emch, A. F.: "Control Means Action," *Harvard Business Review*, vol. 32, no. 4, pp. 92–98 (July, 1954).

Gardner, F. V.: *Profit Management and Control*, New York: McGraw-Hill Book Company, 1955.

Goetz, B. E.: *Management Planning and Control*, chaps. 5, 10, 11, New York: McGraw-Hill Book Company, 1949.

Heckert, J. B., and J. D. Willson: *Business Budgeting and Control*, 2d ed., New York: The Ronald Press Company, 1955.

Heiser, H. C.: *Budgeting Principles and Practices*, New York: The Ronald Press Company, 1959.

Jerome, W. T., III: *Executive Control: The Catalyst*, chaps. 1–5, 10, 11, New York: John Wiley & Sons, Inc., 1961.

Jones, R. L., and H. G. Trentin: *Budgeting: Key to Planning and Control*, New York: American Management Association, 1966.

Knight, W. D., and E. H. Weinwurm: *Managerial Budgeting*, New York: The Macmillan Company, 1964.

Lamperti, F. A., and J. B. Thurston: *Internal Auditing for Management*, Englewood Cliffs, N.J.: Prentice-Hall, Inc., 1951.

Lasser, J. K., et al.: *J. K. Lasser's Executive Course in Profitable Business Management*, part 16, "How to Use Budgets for Control of a Business," and part 17, "How to Design Systems for Internal Control of a Business," New York: McGraw-Hill Book Company, 1952.

Pierce, J. L.: "The Budget Comes of Age," *Harvard Business Review*, vol. 32, no. 3, pp. 58–66 (May, 1954).

Rucker, A. W.: "Clocks for Management Control," *Harvard Business Review*, vol. 33, no. 5, pp. 68–80 (October, 1955).

Sord, B. H., and G. A. Welsch: *Business Budgeting*, New York: Controllership Foundation, Inc., 1958.

Welsch, G. A.: *Budgeting: Profit Planning and Control*, Englewood Cliffs, N.J.: Prentice-Hall, Inc., 1957.

———: "Controller's Function in Top Level Management," *Journal of Accountancy*, vol. 98, pp. 66–71 (July, 1954).

Wickenden, W. C.: "Flexible Budgets for Cost Control," *NACA Bulletin*, vol. 30, pp. 771–782 (March, 1949).

CHAPTER TWENTY-NINE

newer control techniques

Although the basic nature and purpose of management control do not change, new tools have brought it into sharper focus and promise increasingly to improve the quality of control. These tools, closely related to recent advances in planning techniques, have brought the scientific approach to problems of control—a recognition that better planning is of no avail without better control.

Perhaps the greatest challenge to managers in the period ahead is to develop an ability to meet problems of change in an environment of vigorous economic, political, and social rivalry. The modern firm must be able to take advantage of change, to develop flexibility in the management process, and to institute the kind of planning and control in which plans can be changed rapidly and results can be known quickly.

Even though these newer techniques cannot relieve the manager of responsibility for developing his own controls or making his own decisions, they can show the way to their improvement. They take advantage of the basic techniques of the physical sciences emphasized so strongly in this book: treating business operations as systems with information feedback control; the application of mathematical methods to express these system relationships in terms of goal optimization; the use of electronic machines to store and process data; and the use of time-event network analyses. In addition to techniques of the physical sciences, there are control techniques based upon the sociopsychological needs of human beings.

Only a superficial analysis of the most significant of these newer techniques can be given here; but some appreciation of them is needed by every manager at every level in modern enterprise.

IMPROVED INFORMATION TECHNOLOGY [1]

Electronic equipment permits fast and economical processing of huge amounts of data. While the machine cannot design relationships of data or originate basic information, it can, with proper programming, process data toward logical conclusions, classify them, and make them readily available for the manager's use. In fact, data do not become information until they are processed into a usable form.

As an astute business manager has observed, "The reach of an executive is determined by the information system at his command." [2] Note that the information must be at a manager's command; he must be able to use it. A good information system must furnish knowledge that is material to the manager's job, that can be weighed against goals; it must be designed to determine how and where goals are being missed. It must furnish intelligible data. Above all, its success depends on managers who will listen and act accordingly.

Expanding Basic Data The focus of attention on management information, coupled with its improved processing, has led to the reduction of long-known limitations. Managers for years have recognized that accounting information, aimed at the calculation of profits, has understandably been limited. Yet in many companies this has been virtually the only regularly collected and analyzed type of data. Managers have known that they need all kinds of nonaccounting information, including information on the social, economic, political, and technical climate in which plans must operate, as well as information on competitors and nonfinancial information on internal operations. [3] And such information should include both qualitative and quantitative data.

While not nearly enough progress has been made in meeting these requirements, the computer, plus operations research, has led to enormous expansion of available managerial information. Problems in developing information inputs to fill existing gaps still exist, but now the gaps are apparent, and company after company is beginning to undertake research to make basic data available. One sees this especially in relation to data on marketing, competition, production and distribution, product costs, technological change and development, labor productivity, and qualitative goal accomplishment. The expansion of such information—primarily required for planning but also necessary for control—is indicated for the marketing department of an oil company in Figure 29.1.

[1] Although many writers use this term to apply to the entire field of information handling, including operations research and simulation techniques, it is used here in the sense of providing information most suitable to the manager for plannng and control.

[2] Stahrl Edmunds, "The Reach of an Executive," *Harvard Business Review*, vol. 37, no. 1, pp. 87–96 (January–February, 1959).

[3] For an analysis of the problem, see D. R. Daniel, "Management Information Crisis," *Harvard Business Review*, vol. 39, no. 5, pp. 111–121 (September–October, 1961).

REPORTS FORMERLY USED FOR PLANNING

REPORTS USED AFTER THE MANAGEMENT INFORMATION STUDY

	Defects	Environment	Competition	Internal
Division and district expenses	No information on the total market for gasoline and other automotive products—its size, its location, its rate of growth, etc. No information on competitors—what they are doing, where, and how well	• 10-year industry sales by product, by marketing division, and where possible, by trading area • 10-year car registration records by state and trading area (where possible)	• 10-year share-of-market reports by product, by division, and where possible, by trading area • Special price reports intended to show (a) competitor's price strategy and (b) areas of the country classified by the nature of price conditions—stable, volatile, strong, weak, etc.	• 5-year sales and realizations by product, by division, by class of trade • Division and district expenses per gallon (without allocations of headquarters' expenses)
Sales volume by product for divisions and districts	Marketing "profit and loss" concept encouraged faulty planning because of arbitrary transfer prices No information that discloses the company's marketing strengths and weaknesses by class of trade, for example, company-owned stations, independent dealers, distributors, etc.	• 10-year population records by trading area • 10-year record of new road-mile construction by state and trading area (where possible) Purpose: to provide an over-all picture of the market, its composition, its size, its location, significant trends affecting any of these factors, etc.	• 5-year record of new station construction by competition, by division and trading area • 5-year summary of new refinery, terminal, and bulk plant construction by competition Purpose: to identify who competitors are, how well they've been doing, and the likely direction of their future efforts	• Marketing "net back" statements by product by division, by district, and by bulk plant (realizations less expenses) • "Laid-down" costs by product, by terminal and bulk plant Purpose: to assess the company strengths and weaknesses, thus permitting a correlation between the company's capabilities and the opportunities of the market place
Marketing department profit and loss	Marketing expense information misleading because of allocations of headquarters' overhead Inadequate data on size "mix" of stations, for example, number and percentage of stations selling different volumes of gasoline	• 5-year projection of 100 fastest growing trading areas in country—by percentage and absolute numbers • 5-year projection of car registration by state and trading area (where possible) • Report on Federal road-building program	• Analysis of 100 largest and 100 fastest growing markets (trading areas) showing leading competitors in terms of volume, market share, laid-down costs, facilities, construction or acquisition activity, etc.	• Frequency distribution studies of gasoline sales by size or retail station, by division and district • Share of company's total sales by product for each state
Capital budgets by division for five years	Inadequate data on the sales performance of newly built or acquired stations	• 5-year report (and 5-year projection) on composition of country's automobile population by size, weight, horsepower, etc. for each division	• Special reports on key market developments, for example, rebrander activity, additional qualities of gasoline, multiple octane pumps, etc.	• 5-year report of number of stations by type (owned, leased, etc.) by division and district • 5-year report of capital budgets by division and district (amounts authorized and spent)

Fig. 29.1 Comparative Analysis of Marketing Planning Information Needed by an Oil Company

SOURCE: D. R. Daniel, "Management Information Crisis," Harvard Business Review, vol. 39, no. 5, p. 118 (September–October, 1961).

Sharpening Accounting Data by Direct Costing The expansion of basic data is occurring not only in nonaccounting areas; accountants themselves have made great strides in developing more useful data. The technique of direct costing gives promise of revolutionizing managerial accounting.

Direct costing is simply recognition by accountants of certain basic economic principles. It is grounded on the fact that many costs, whether formerly classified as direct or indirect, vary in whole or in part with volume of output, while other costs (such as depreciation, advertising, general management salaries and expenses, and building rentals) are related to time. Thus, some costs are "direct" in the sense that they are based on producing as compared to not producing, or on selling as compared to not selling. Other costs are "period" costs in that they are committed to provide capacity which expires with time.

In traditional, or absorption, accounting, direct costs include only the direct material used in a product and the factory or engineering labor directly working on the manufacture or engineering of a product. All indirect costs are then allocated to the product in accordance with some formula, utilizing as a base direct-labor-hours or costs, or sales dollars, or some other measure. Also, in accounting for inventory, it has been customary to accumulate in inventory a pro-rata allocation of factory burden, thus inventorying many costs really related to time rather than to volume of production. This practice can distort product costs and profits when inventories are rising or falling. When inventories of goods in process or finished goods are rising, for example, burden costs are absorbed—that is, carried into inventory—and cost performance and profits tend to be better than when those burden costs not related to volume are charged off in the period incurred.

Direct costing gives the manager better information visibility in two major respects. From the standpoint of inventory and profit calculation, he knows that period costs have been written off as incurred, that an inventory does not include the "air" of costs not related to product volume, and that profits are more real when they reflect the write-off of costs related to time. From the standpoint of cost analysis of individual products or projects, a manager can now look at costs in more nearly marginal terms. If direct costing is thoroughly done, the manager can see whether the product is covering the costs ascribable to volume and how much remains as a contribution to period costs and profits. Thus, a product might show a loss by the customary formula of taking direct labor and material and allocating burden plus selling and administrative costs; but the same product may very well show a handsome contribution to period costs and profits by the direct-costing method.

Even though direct costing is difficult to put into effect and faces resistance, particularly from traditional accountants and tax authorities, it offers managers a number of advantages.[4] Direct costing was first suggested in

[4] For an excellent analysis of the advantages and disadvantages of direct costing, see Wilmer Wright and Felix P. Kollaritsch, "Direct Costing; Pro and Con," *The Controller*, vol. 30, no. 7, pp. 322ff. (July, 1962).

1936.[5] It was not until 1947 that a major company, the Pittsburgh Plate Glass Company, started using it. Even as late as 1953 only seventeen companies using it could be found by the National Association of Accountants, but by 1962, *Business Week* estimated, some 250 companies had adopted direct costing and more were converting to it. Experience with companies using direct costing has convinced the authors that this trend has continued rapidly and will accelerate in the future. In fact, there is a real possibility that direct costing will become the standard accounting in the future.

Information Indigestion versus Information Design Managers who have experienced the impact of better and faster data processing are justly concerned with the danger of information indigestion. Their appetite for figures whetted, the data originators and processors are turning out material at an almost frightening rate. Managers are complaining of being buried under reports, facts, projections, and forecasts which they either do not have time to read or cannot understand, or which do not fill their particular needs.

As was pointed out in the previous chapter, control techniques or information not properly aimed at the man and his job, or of a kind a manager cannot or will not understand, will not work. As one experienced executive declared:[6]

> If a little learning is a dangerous thing, too much—that is, knowledge not put to good use—can be a costly waste. Too many undigested facts can turn a man of action into a Hamlet, paralyzed by indecision. Like the raw materials of industry, information must be *converted* into something. What is required is a discriminating selection which can deliver relevant data in a form usable at the echelon of decision. The research study that collects dust on shelves may well have merit; the fault is failure to relate its data to the problem it was designed to solve.
>
> Information may involve anything from the most minute and finite to the universal. Processing information today calls not only for distinguishing the forest from the trees, but distinguishing leaves and chlorophyll—while still not losing sight of the forest.

To combat information indigestion, there arises the need to design information suited for special use at all levels and in all functions of management. Special design of information may seem to be in opposition to the mass-production techniques and economies of the electronic computer, but computer experts claim this is not so. They insist that, within reasonable limits, data can be designed for individual managers by proper programming and all the more modern machines permit easy change of programs by inserting appropriate cards or tape. They further insist that it is up to man-

---

[5] These and the following data are from "Direct Costing to the Rescue," *Business Week*, pp. 45–48 (Mar. 24, 1962).

[6] Marion Harper, Jr., "A New Profession to Aid Management," Charles Coolidge Parlin Memorial Lecture, p. 13 (Philadelphia: Philadelphia Chapter, American Marketing Association, 1960).

agers to know and ask for what they need in order to carry on planning and control effectively.

Intelligence Services   Attempts are being made to solve the dilemma posed by managers needing special digested and digestible information and by information processors who do not know what managers require. One such attempt consists of establishing in a company an intelligence service and developing a new profession of intelligence experts.[7] The service would be manned by experts in many fields and presided over by another group of experts who would know (or find out) what information managers need and who would know how to digest and interpret such information for management use.

This approach to making the new mass of information more usable has much to commend it, and a number of companies have already adopted it. However, few have gone so far as to design information for individual managers down the line of organization as well as at the top. Under such names as "administrative services" or "management analyses and services," many companies are recognizing that some sort of information digestion service is necessary if the expansion of basic data is to result in useful information. Some companies feel that this service should be centralized, and, in many cases, it can be. However, despite the efficiencies of a central department, doubt exists as to whether in medium-large and large companies centralization can satisfactorily cater to *all* managers or whether a number of such departments might understandably serve best those to whom they immediately report. Thus, it appears that the future will see multiple intelligence services located throughout an organization so that they can be more responsive to various information needs.

Information Systems   With the increasing use of the computer in recent years, a great deal of attention has been given to the development of information systems. This is a recognition of the fact that many items of input data may be useful for a number of different outputs. Thus, input data on inventory are useful for different kinds of reports, including those to accounting for asset recording, to purchasing for reorder action, to production for planning assembly operations, and to sales for availability of product. Payroll data, likewise, are useful for accounting, labor cost control and production, labor turnover, and other concerns of managers.

It is consequently obvious that data should not be independently gathered in many instances for special purposes, but rather the same basic input data should be made available for multiple end uses. Moreover, some data are developed in large part as a kind of by-product from the operation of procedures designed to get something done, such as material flow in production or computation of labor payroll. Likewise, many procedures are designed primarily to furnish data to guide managers in their decisions,

---

[7] Suggested by Marion Harper, Jr. (*ibid.*, p. 17), among others.

such as inventory procedures so useful to accurate accounting and financial planning and for procurement decisions.

As a consequence of these multiple uses of data and the demands of economy in data development and processing, it is understandable that specialists in this area, as well as managers, should hope to view and utilize data processing and information flow as a complete system. This becomes particularly urgent if the almost incredible conclusion of one information specialist is even somewhat true: that "at least 50 per cent of the cost of running our economy is information cost."[8]

When one looks on the one hand at the tremendous information requirements of managerial and nonmanagerial personnel in a typical enterprise for their innumerable decisions and evaluations of operations, and, on the other hand, at the tremendous mass of input data necessary to produce this information, he is appalled at the possibility of tying all this into a single system. Perhaps the best approach is that recommended by Dearden: to recognize that we are dealing, in the typical company, with three major information systems and many minor systems.[9]

Dearden points out that the three major information systems typically found are financial, personnel, and logistics. The basis of the financial system is the flow of money through a company. The personnel information system has to do with the flow of data concerning people. The logistics system applies to those data reflecting the physical flow of goods through an enterprise. Other information systems identified by Dearden are those dealing with marketing information, research and development, strategic planning, and executive compensation. While there are definitely interrelationships between all three, the interfaces are particularly noteworthy between financial, personnel, and logistics information systems.

Since most companies have traditionally kept information on financial and personnel matters, and a number have considerable logistics information, Dearden's suggestion has the merit of building on a practicable base. Also, by so classifying information into several systems, the approach recommended has the advantage of breaking the almost incomprehensibly complex total enterprise information system into more manageable parts. With the amount of hopeful talk aimed at using the computer as a catalytic agent to set up an entire system, and the relatively small real advances toward this goal thus far observed in practice, this appears to be an excellent way of approaching the problem of information systematization.

But in the understandable anxiety of alert managers to perfect information and utilize the computer for the improvement of managing, no one should overlook the fundamental problem of information as the authors of this book see it. Unless managers actively embrace the approach of tailored

[8] A. M. McDonough, *Information Economics and Management Systems* (New York: McGraw-Hill Book Company, 1963), p. 5.

[9] J. Dearden, "How to Organize Information Systems," *Harvard Business Review*, vol. 43, no. 2, pp. 65–73 (March–April, 1965).

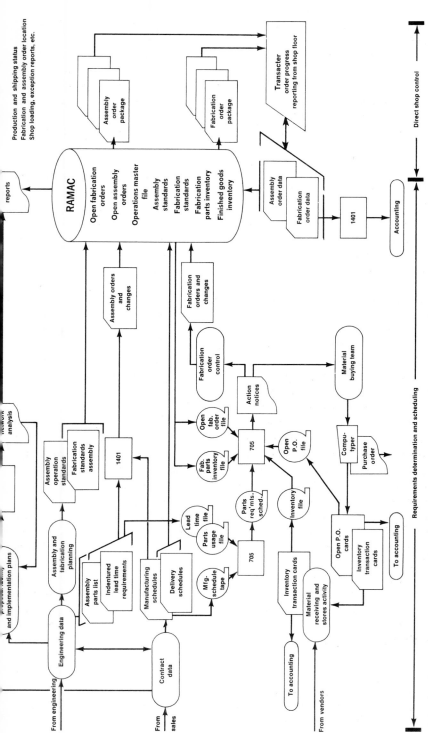

Fig. 29.2 Integrated Data-processing and Manufacturing Control Information Flow . . . *This chart shows how basic information from engineering, customers (sales), and vendors is combined with internal manufacturing standards and operational requirements to develop a complete and integrated system of manufacturing control information. This not only furnishes information required for buying, fabricating, assembling, inventorying, and accounting, but also provides needed management reports from the same source.*
SOURCE: J. B. Friauf, *Advanced Techniques for Manufacturing Control, Instrument Society of America, Conference Reprint 187–LA61 (1961).*

controls by deciding what end product they need for effective management, no information system can be successful. In the computer, systems analysis, and programming of data conversion, we have what has been referred to as an automated factory. And what has been often done is to pick up such raw materials as may be left lying around in the form of available data, put them in this automated factory, and then wonder why the end product is unsatisfactory. No manager would follow this process in manufacturing a product for sale. Instead, he would design the end product and work back through the production system to determine what raw materials were required. Unless this approach is more thoroughly and rigorously followed with management information, all the systems and hardware that experts can design will never solve the problem.

PROCEDURES PLANNING AND CONTROL

Procedures are also closely related to information, because they apply not only to operating tasks—such as purchasing or selling—but also, outstandingly, to accumulating information for planning and control.

Procedures present a rewarding area of planning and control to which a systems approach can be applied. The extraordinary complexity of procedures and their inflexible channeling of action were discussed under types of plans in Chapter 5. While desirable tools for efficiently getting things done in a given way or for control when it is necessary not to deviate from this way, procedures can make for departmental rigidity that thwarts creativity and response to change. Although they *should* be designed to implement plans and to respond to change, they too often do not.

In addition, procedures can be expensive. Modern enterprise has created a sensational increase in the number of people doing paper work. As was pointed out by Neuschel,[10] since 1870 clerical personnel in the nation has increased a hundred times, while the total number of gainfully employed increased five times; and it was estimated that, when the nation's employed work force numbered 65 million, more than 9 million were clerical workers.

Effective planning and control of procedures depend on recognizing that they are inherently systems. Procedures normally extend into various departments, and it is a rare procedure which does not concern itself with more than two. Therefore, procedures should be considered systems that reach into various parts of the enterprise. This is important to their control.

Accounting departments, for example, tend to regard procedures as purely concerned with their accounting function, yet a simple payroll or expense account procedure reaches into every nook and cranny of the company and affects nonaccounting activities. Personnel, purchasing, and other functional departmental procedures do likewise.

---

[10] R. F. Neuschel, *Management by System* (New York: McGraw-Hill Book Company, 1960), p. 3. It should be pointed out, of course, that not all this increase in clerical work force can be ascribed to procedures.

How Procedures Get out of Control Because of the specialized approach of each organization function in setting up procedures for its particular operation, procedures often get out of control. Accounting procedures may conflict with or overlap purchasing procedures, differ but slightly from personnel procedures, and somewhat duplicate sales department procedures. Duplication, overlapping, and conflict are usually elusive and partial; there is rarely either complete duplication or clear disagreement. Commonly, different forms and records are called for though they use the same subject matter.

Procedures also get out of control when managers try to use them to solve problems instead of solving the problems through better policies, clearer delegations, or improved direction. Then again, many procedures are instituted to correct a mistake which might never be made again. In one case, a division head ordered development of a complete system of procedures to prevent overlooking one serious customer complaint. This had only happened once. Instead of complex procedures that would burden his organization, a clear policy statement, simple routing of complaints, and assigning the handling of complaints to the service manager would have taken care of the situation.

Procedures also evade control by becoming obsolete, either because they are not kept up-to-date or because failure to police them permits deviations in practice. Moreover, procedures have a way of becoming customs, ingrained in departments and individuals and accompanied by stubborn resistance to change. Then managers find it expedient to impose new procedures on the old, a haphazard practice.

Finally, a major way that procedures get out of control is through managers not being clear as to what procedures should do, how much they cost, when they are duplicated, how to overhaul them, and how to control them. And to top all this, managers often fail to obtain the interest and support of top management in the tedious and unromantic planning and control of procedures.

Guidelines In planning and control of procedures, managers should follow these guidelines.

✓ *Minimize procedures* The first and perhaps most important guideline for the manager is to limit procedures to those which are clearly called for. The costs of procedures in paper handling, stifled thinking, delay, and lack of responsiveness to change are such as to make a manager think twice before initiating them. In other words, he must weigh the potential gain in money or necessary control against the disadvantages and costs.

✓ *Make sure they are plans* Since procedures are plans, they must be designed to reflect and help accomplish company (not just departmental) objectives and policies. Have they been planned? If they are necessary, are they designed effectively and efficiently to accomplish plans? For example, in a procedure to handle orders for spare parts or repair defective parts, the procedure must ordinarily expedite the job so as to meet customer service standards without undue delay.

‹ *Analyze them* Procedures should be carefully analyzed to assure a minimum of duplication, overlapping, and conflict. To do this, the procedures must be visualized. This, in turn, necessitates mapping them in a visual presentation, with their various steps identified and interrelated. That this is not always easy is exemplified by a defense company material procurement procedure which, when charted, took a piece of paper 27 feet long and involved over 250 definite related required actions!

‹ *Recognize procedures as systems* One of the failures of procedure design is to neglect to regard procedures as systems. Any given procedure, whether one specifying the handling of payroll, procurement, inventory planning and control, or other of many uses, is in itself a system of interrelated activities normally in a network rather than a pure linear form. Likewise, various procedures with special purposes are usually closely interrelated. As was pointed out above, accounting procedures, for example, tend to be intertwined with personnel, purchasing, and other procedures. Therefore, groups of procedures are usually interrelated systems.

The problem of procedures planning and control is not likely to be solved unless their complex systemic structure is recognized. And, when their structure is recognized, it would be natural to expect that their design and improvement would call for the same kind of analytical talent so readily applied to the design of a complex instrument or machine. But seldom do companies give procedures planning and control this kind of treatment or bring to bear on them the same high level of engineering and design talent they give to products. That this should be done, particularly when one considers the cost in money, time, and organization friction losses caused by procedures, is obvious.

‹ *Estimate their cost* The analysis of a procedure should be accompanied by an estimate of what its operation will cost. While some costs cannot be ascertained, such as the cost of possible frustration to those involved, an estimate may bring into sharper focus the answer to the question: Is this procedure worthwhile?

‹ *Police their operation* Procedures are merely plans until they are executed. Execution involves three steps: First, knowledge of procedures must be made available in manual or other form to those who must follow them. Second, employees must be taught how to operate under them and, ideally, why the procedures are necessary and what purpose they are designed to serve. Third, there must be machinery to assure that people do understand procedures, that they are employing up-to-date procedures, and that the procedures are doing the job intended. This step involves keeping manuals up-to-date and requires a kind of constructive auditing of how procedures are operating.

Procedures Analysis and Electronic Data Processing An encouraging consequence of present systems and procedures planning and the analysis of procedures as systems is that procedures can now be programmed on electronic data-processing (EDP) equipment. There remains the danger that the systems and procedures expert will become so enamored of programming as to forget that electronically processed procedures must represent good procedures without the machine.

Despite this danger, EDP has made possible broad analysis and improvement of procedures. It is so frightening and expensive for top management to put a personnel, accounting, or purchasing procedure on a machine that a strong effort is normally made to assure a workable and clear procedure before it is automated. Moreover, the orderly systems approach of the programmer forces an orderly approach to procedure analysis. Since, at the very least, a procedure cannot be put on a machine without having been mapped, the very process of mapping often shows up the existence of overlapping and the need for simplification, as well as the means of achieving it.

So far, analyzing and rationalizing procedures for EDP have mainly brought the subject to the surface and have unearthed the need for experts in this kind of planning and control. Nor are the universities doing much about training such experts. One wonders whether, if some of the intelligence and effort now applied to deriving exotic mathematics of programming were applied to the more mundane problems of procedures analysis, the improvement of enterprise efficiency would not be vastly accelerated. The need is great for experts who understand the nature of procedures as a management tool and their importance in accomplishing enterprise objectives. Systems and procedures analysis—like improved information technology—is high-level, difficult, and challenging work.

LOGISTICS SYSTEMS

As was made clear from the discussion of operations research in Chapter 8, research methodology is a study of logical relationships. It is thus a study of systems so conceptualized as to show the way to manipulating variables in order to optimize some desired goal. It was also pointed out that the best use of operations research occurs when inputs are quantifiable, but that the method can be useful even when variables are little more than broad approximations. Operations research, therefore, has shown its greatest promise in logistics systems, because in areas involving labor input and the flow of materials, the variables can be credibly quantified. Consequently, operations research has proceeded from subsystem areas, such as production and inventory, and by linking these subsystems has gone on to planning and control of the broader field of production and distribution combined.

Operations Research for Inventory Control   Although space does not permit a discussion of the application of operations research to all types of production or distribution subsystems, its early application to inventory control is selected as an example. For one thing, perhaps in the history of operations research more attention has been directed to inventory control than to any other area in business and industry.[11] For another thing, the path from inventory control has led to utilization of broader forms of systems control.

If one wished to see the essential systems relationships as a little "black box" without going into detailed mathematics, he could depict it as is done in Figure 29.3.

Or, if these conceptual relationships were placed into one of the simpler mathematical forms covering approximately the system in Figure 29.3, it might look something like this:[12]

$$Q = \sqrt{\frac{2R[S + E(s)]}{I}}$$

where
Q = Reorder quantity
R = Sales requirement per year
S = Setup cost (per order)
I = Interest and carrying cost, including storage, all expressed per piece, per year
$E(s)$ = Expected cost of stockouts per order cycle

and where $E(s)$ is defined by this equation:

$$E(s) = \pi \sum_{u=r+1}^{u_{max}} (u - r)p(u)$$

where
u = Usage during any lead time
$p(u)$ = Probability of usage greater than u
r = Reorder point in units
u = Expected usage during lead time
π = Stockout cost per unit demanded but not available

As can be seen, even the simple "black box" representation of a subsystem of control can be very complex. Each of the inputs can be variable or constant. Each can be discrete or continuous, and the rate of distribution over time can be variable or constant. Moreover, as this is a planning model, feedback of information—to make sure the model attains the goals desired—should be added to make it a planning and control system.

With all its complexities, the model illustrates several things. It forces consideration of the goals desired and of the need for placing definite values

[11] C. W. Churchman, R. L. Ackoff, and E. L. Arnoff, *Introduction to Operations Research*, p. 195 (New York: John Wiley & Sons, Inc., 1957).

[12] E. H. Bowman and R. B. Fetter, *Analysis for Production Management* (Homewood, Ill.: Richard D. Irwin, Inc., 1961), pp. 330–332.

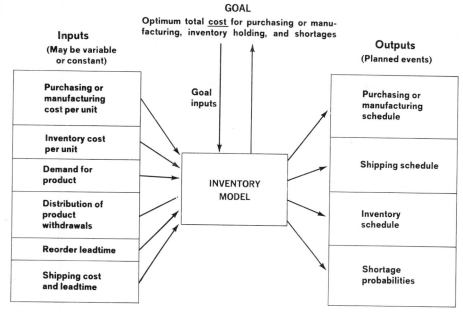

GOAL

Optimum total <u>cost</u> for purchasing or manufacturing, inventory holding, and shortages

Inputs

(May be variable
or constant)

Goal
inputs

Outputs

(Planned events)

Inputs
Purchasing or manufacturing cost per unit
Inventory cost per unit
Demand for product
Distribution of product withdrawals
Reorder leadtime
Shipping cost and leadtime

INVENTORY
MODEL

Outputs
Purchasing or manufacturing schedule
Shipping schedule
Inventory schedule
Shortage probabilities

Fig. 29.3   Inventory Control Model

on outputs and inputs. It also furnishes a manager with the basis for plans and with standards by which to measure performance. However, with all its advantages, this is a subsystem and does not incorporate other subsystems, such as production planning, distribution planning, and sales planning.

Distribution Logistics   One of the more exciting and profit-promising ways of using systems logistics in planning and control is in the expansion of inventory control to include other factors, referred to here as distribution logistics.[13] In its most advanced form currently in operation in a few companies, this treats the entire logistics of a business—from sales forecast through purchase and processing of material and inventorying to shipping finished goods—as a single system. The goals are usually to optimize the *total* costs of the system in operation, while furnishing a desired level of customer service and meeting certain constraints, such as financially limited inventory

[13] Often referred to as "distribution management," or "physical distribution management," and called by some specialists "rhochrematics," the science of materials flow. See S. H. Brewer and J. Rosensweig, "Rhochrematics and Organization Adjustments," *California Management Review*, vol. 3, no. 3, pp. 52–71 (Spring, 1961). Another excellent study is John F. Magee, "The Logistics of Distribution," *Harvard Business Review*, vol. 38, no. 4, pp. 89–101 (July–August, 1960). See also E. W. Smykay (ed.), *Essays on Physical Distribution Management* (Washington: The Traffic Service Corporation, 1961), and J. A. Constantin, *Principles of Logistics Management* (New York: Appleton-Century-Crofts, Inc., 1966).

levels. This gathers into one system a large mass of relationships and information, so as to optimize the whole. In doing so, it is entirely possible that transportation, manufacturing, or any other *single* area of cost will not be optimized, but the total cost of materials management will be.

Schematically, a distribution logistics system might appear as shown in Figure 29.4. This model, represented by a "black box," would be expressed in mathematics in an operating system.

This figure shows the relationships between the goal desired, the input variables and limits, and the expected outputs. The company represented by this model is a consumer goods company with a fairly broad line of products, a number of plants (some producing the whole line, others producing only part of the line), a number of finished-goods warehouses, and national distribution to grocery chains and wholesalers. It will be noted that customer service standards (that is, maximum time permitted between receipt and shipment of an order) are here inserted as a constraining input.

That the mathematics of this model would be exceedingly complex can be appreciated when it is assumed that the company had a line of 200

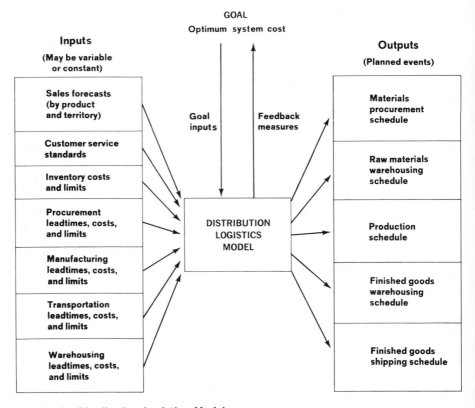

Fig. 29.4 Distribution Logistics Model

products (including sizes), 16 plants, 60 warehouses, and 70 sales districts. Also, this system would require fast feedback for control, adequate inventories to meet unforeseen contingencies, good sales forecasting, and territorial distribution managers able to override the system by quick change of local plans if schedules got out of control.

A fully developed distribution logistics system is a fine instrument of planning and control. By optimizing *total* costs in a broad area of operation, even though certain costs might not be optimized if looked upon separately, the system might show it would be cheaper to use more expensive transportation on occasion rather than to carry high inventories. Or it might show that production at less than economic order quantities would be justified in order to get better transportation or warehousing utilization or to meet customer service standards with limited inventories.

Moreover, such a system gives a manager a means of control which a disparate system of isolated, unconnected plans could not. By seeing how activities interlock and by setting up a system of interrelated plans, control of the entire production and distribution system can be obtained. That this could not be done on such a scale without mathematics and electronics computation is beyond question. But what is interesting, in the experience of one of the authors, is that where distribution logistics has been undertaken intelligently and patiently, its costs of operation have not been really high, while the benefits, although difficult accurately to assess, have been extraordinary.

To be sure, even such a broad distribution logistics system is not a total system of a business enterprise, but it does apply to a considerable part of the total business operation. And it applies to those parts where the inputs can be quantified with a reasonable degree of accuracy.

Industrial Dynamics Another systems approach to planning and control is called "industrial dynamics" by Prof. J. W. Forrester, of the Massachusetts Institute of Technology.[14] This approach is based on the idea that a company is "not a collection of separate functions" but a system in which the *flows* of information, materials, manpower, capital equipment, and money set up forces that determine the basic tendencies toward growth, fluctuation, and decline.[15] In other words, industrial dynamics anticipates adding to a distribution logistics system many factors of change, with their influence on each other, and many inputs currently not quantifiable enough to satisfy managers, such as consumer response to advertising, policies regarding work-force reduction, and the likelihood of results from research expenditures.

Industrial dynamics also takes into account fluctuations caused primarily by delays in the system. For example, if a sudden increase of sales

[14] "Industrial Dynamics," *Harvard Business Review*, vol. 36, no. 4, pp. 37–66 (July–August, 1958). See also by the same author *Industrial Dynamics* (New York: John Wiley & Sons, Inc., 1961).

[15] "Industrial Dynamics," p. 52.

should occur in January, delays in decision making and information flow (such as those in mailing, accounting, purchasing, and production schedule changes) may cause a cyclical effect. Thus, because of delays, sales may increase 10 per cent at the retail level but might peak at 16 per cent at the distributors' level, at 28 per cent at the factory warehouse level, and at 40 per cent at the factory production level. This fluctuation, brought on by accumulated lags, can be further amplified by random fluctuations in the consumers', retailers', or distributors' behavior.

Forrester's concept of industrial dynamics thus brings into the planning and control model the very important input of cyclical business behavior under conditions of change. He also includes more variables in his model than have been included in models so far suggested. However, being grounded on delay factors and lack of adequate sales forecasts, one might ask whether many dynamic lags would be solved by control of delays and of poor information inputs that lead to exaggerated fluctuations. In fact, Forrester recognizes that better sales data, faster order handling, and better inventory planning are needed to improve control. However, introduction of the concept of flow of manpower, money, technology, and equipment to flow of materials does promise improvement in planning and control. And what is perhaps most exciting about Forrester's work is that he is undertaking to include in the system of a business the larger system of its business environment.

Operations Control Systems Another interesting type of planning and control system is one designed to integrate information on virtually an instantaneous basis, thereby cutting down considerably the delays that Forrester finds cause inefficient fluctuations. With development of the necessary hardware and software, it is now possible for virtually any measurable data to be reported as events occur. Systems are available to provide for fast and systematic collection of data bearing on a total operation, for keeping these data readily available, and for reporting without delay the status of any of thousands of projects at any instant. They are thus primarily information systems designed to improve planning and control.

In establishing a system, its developers aim to meet three requirements: (1) to produce reports ideally suited to give each level of management the tools needed for purposeful decision making; (2) to utilize as inputs only basic data necessary to accomplish the reporting (developers have found that much data believed necessary were, on critical evaluation, not required); and (3) to design a dynamic system that would feed information into a computer simultaneously as events occur and make it immediately available for control purposes. Interesting, too, is the attempt to feed data immediately into a central part of the system to avoid manual preparation of the same data for use in many different reports.

Such systems, now fairly frequently used and specially useful for a business making many items, can nonetheless be useful in any complicated operation. Applied widely only to the complex of purchasing, storing, manufacturing, and shipping, they operate through dispatch stations, widely dispersed in the plant, and input centers, also located throughout the plant. At the dispatch centers, events are recorded as they occur and the information dispatched immediately to a computer. For example, when a foreman finishes his assigned task on the assembly of a product, the work-order time-card is put into a transactor which electrically transmits to a computer the information that item x has passed through a certain process, has accumulated y hours of labor, and other pertinent data. The input centers are equipped automatically to originate, from programmed instructions, purchase orders, shop orders, and other authorizations. These data are likewise fed into the computer to be used as standards against which the actual operations, transmitted from the dispatch stations, may be compared.

In addition to fast entry, comparison, and retrieval of information, such an integrated operations control system furnishes needed information for planning programs in such areas as purchasing, production, and inventory control. Moreover, it permits almost instantaneous comparison of results with plans, pinpointing where they differ, and provides a regular (daily or more often, if needed) system of reports on items behind schedule or costs running above budget.

This and the other systems sketched here—as well as many more which use the technology of science and fast computation—clearly promise to hasten the day when planning can be more precise and control more effective. The main drawback is not the cost but, rather, the failure of managers to appreciate the potential. Therefore, they are often unwilling to put in the mental effort to conceptualize the system and its relationships or to see that someone in the company does so.

TIME-EVENT NETWORK ANALYSES

One highly publicized planning and control technique is a time-event network analysis called Program Evaluation and Review Technique (PERT). There have also been other techniques designed to watch how the parts of a program fit together during the passage of time and events.

The first of these were the chart systems developed by Henry L. Gantt early in the twentieth century and culminating in the bar chart bearing his name. Although simple in concept, this chart showing time relationships between "events" of a production program has been regarded as revolutionary in business management. What Gantt recognized was that total program goals should be regarded as a series of interrelated derivative plans (or events) that people can comprehend and follow. The most important developments of such control reflect this simple principle and also such basic principles of control as picking out the more critical or strategic elements of a plan to watch carefully.

As the result of developing further techniques from the principles of the Gantt chart, and with better appreciation of the network nature of programs, "milepost" or "milestone" budgeting and PERT have been devised in recent years, contributing much to better control of research and development.

Milestone Budgeting   Used by an increasing number of companies in recent years in controlling engineering and development, milepost or milestone budgeting breaks a project down into controllable pieces and then carefully follows them. As was pointed out in the discussion of planning, even relatively simple projects contain a network of subsidiary plans or projects. In this approach to control, milestones are defined as segments. When physical accomplishment of a given segment occurs, cost or other results can be determined.

Engineering control was long hampered because few people have known how much progress was being made on a project. The common device of estimating completion time, with planned inputs of manpower and materials, runs into the difficulty that, although accurate records of personnel and material costs can be kept, estimates of percentage of completion tend to reach 85 or 90 per cent and stay there, while time and costs continue.

The best way to plan and control an engineering project is to break it down into a number of determinable events, for example, completion of preliminary drawings, a "breadboard" model, a package design, a packaged prototype, and production design. Or a project might be broken down vertically into subprojects—for example, the design of a circuit, a motor, a driving mechanism, a sensing device, a signal feedback device, and similar components—that can be designed, individually, in a time sequence, to be ready when needed. Milestone budgeting allows a manager to see a complex program in its simpler parts, thereby giving him some control through knowing whether it is succeeding or failing.

Program Evaluation and Review Technique   Developed by the Special Projects Office of the United States Navy,[16] PERT was first formally applied to the planning and control of the Polaris Weapon System in 1958 and worked well in expediting the successful completion of that program. It has since been so enthusiastically received by the armed services that it is virtually a required tool for major contractors and subcontractors in the armament and space programs and is also gaining acceptance in private industry. Construction and other companies with special engineering or product development projects find it an excellent tool.

Major features   In a sense, PERT is a variation of milestone budgeting. It uses a time-event network analysis, as shown below in Figure 29.6. This very simple example illustrates the basic nature of PERT. Each circle

---

[16] But also separately developed as the Critical Path Method by engineers at the du Pont Company at virtually the same time. Only PERT is discussed here because the Critical Path Method, although different in some respects, utilizes the same basic principles.

I. GANTT CHART

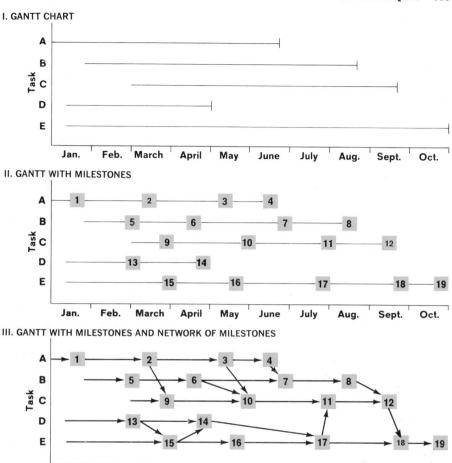

Fig. 29.5 Transition from a Gantt Chart to PERT . . . *The Gantt Chart in I above shows the scheduled time of accomplishing a task, such as procurement (Task A), and the related schedules of doing other tasks, such as manufacture of parts (Task B). When each of these tasks is broken down into milestones, such as the preparation of purchase specifications (Task A–1), and then network relationships between the milestones of each task to those of other tasks are worked out, the result is the basic elements of a PERT chart.*

represents an event—a subsidiary plan whose completion can be measured at a given time. Each arrow represents an activity—the time-consuming element of a program, the effort that must be made between events; "activity time" is the elapsed time required to accomplish an event.

In this example only a single time is shown, but in the original PERT program there were three time estimates: "optimistic" time, an estimate of time required if everything goes exceptionally well; "most likely" time, an estimate of what the project engineer really believes necessary to do the job; and "pessimistic" time, an estimate based on the assumption that any logically conceivable bad luck—other than a major disaster—will be encountered. These estimates are often included in PERT because it is very difficult, in many engineering and development projects, to estimate time accurately and partly, it is believed, because engineers will be willing to make a variety of estimates and will do their level best to beat the pessimistic estimate. When several estimates are made, they are usually averaged, with due weight given to probabilities, and a single estimate then used.

The next step is to compute the "critical path," that sequence of events which takes the longest time and which involves, therefore, the least slack time. In Figure 29.6, the critical path is indicated as from events 1-3-4-8-9-13. Over this path, the activity time for the entire sequence of events is 131.6 weeks; if promised delivery is in 135 weeks, even this critical path would have a slack of 3.4 weeks. Some of the other paths are almost as long as the critical path. For example, the path 1-2-9-13 is 129.4 weeks. This is not unusual in PERT charts, and it is customary to identify several critical paths in order of importance. Although the critical path has a way of changing, as key events are delayed in other parts of the program, identifying it at the start makes possible close watching of this particular sequence of events to assure the total program being on schedule.

Typical PERT analyses run into hundreds or thousands of events. Even though smaller PERT analyses—including the input of event accomplishment and the frequent calculation of critical path—can be done manually, it is estimated that when upward of approximately 700 events are involved, it is virtually impossible to handle the calculations without an electronic computer.[17]

It is customary to summarize very large and complex time-event networks by subnetworks and to prepare the summarized network for top-management consideration. Thus, the top-management network might include some forty or fifty major events, each a summary of a number of subsidiary events. In fact, it is possible to group, or to break down, events so as to have a PERT network appropriate to every level of management.

Strengths and weaknesses   There are five strong advantages of PERT. First, it forces managers to plan, because it is impossible to make a time-event analysis without planning and seeing how the pieces fit together. Second, it forces planning all down the line, because each subordinate manager must plan the event for which he is responsible. Third, it concentrates attention on critical elements that may need correction. Fourth, it makes possible a kind of forward-looking control; a delay will affect succeeding

---

[17] As estimated by Ivars Avots, "The Management Side of PERT," *California Management Review*, vol. 4, no. 2, pp. 16–27 (Winter, 1962). Most experts would estimate far fewer than 700 events.

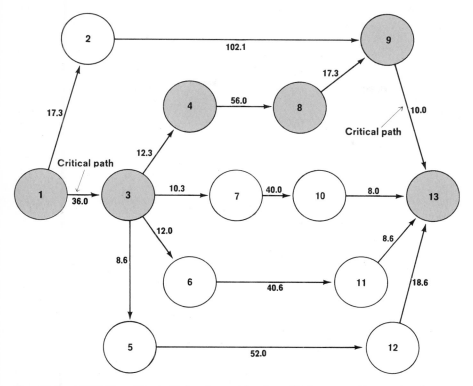

Fig. 29.6 PERT Flow Chart: Major Assembly of an Airplane . . . *Events (each major milestone of progress) are: 1—program go-ahead; 2—initiate engine procurement; 3—complete plans and specifications; 4—complete fuselage drawings; 5—submit GFAE requirements; 6—award tail assembly subcontract; 7—award wings subcontract; 8—complete manufacture of fuselage; 9—complete assembly of fuselage-engine; 10—receive wings from subcontractors; 11 receive tail assembly from subcontractor; 12—receive GFAE; 13—complete aircraft. (Note GFAE is government furnished airplane equipment.)*

SOURCE: *P. J. Klass, "PERT/PEP Management Tool Use Grows," Aviation Week and Space Technology (Nov. 28, 1960). Reproduced by permission.*

events, and possibly the whole project, unless the manager can somehow make up the time by shortening that of some action in the future. Fifth, the network system with its subsystems makes possible aiming of reports and pressure for action at the right spot and level in the organization structure at the right time.

PERT also has certain limitations. Because of the importance of activity time to its operation, it cannot be useful when a program is nebulous and no reasonable "guesstimates" of schedule can be made; even here, however, insurance can be "bought" by such devices as putting two or more teams to work on an event when costs permit. PERT is also not practicable for routine planning of recurring events, such as mass production; while it could be used here, once a repetitive sequence of events is clearly worked out so elaborate a continuing control is not required. A major disadvantage of PERT has been its emphasis on time only, not costs. While this is suitable for programs where time is of the essence or where, as so often is the case, time and costs have a close direct relationship, the tool is more useful when considerations other than time are introduced.

PERT/COST The above description of PERT is called PERT/TIME and has led logically to the development of PERT/COST with the application of costs to activities in the PERT network. While this would appear to be an easy transition, a number of complications exist. In the first place, the PERT network must be complete enough to reflect any activity which incurs cost. In the second place, in any complex project, the number of events is so great that it becomes difficult and expensive to establish job center cost accounts for each activity. As a result, in practice, the events are grouped in what are known as work packages for purposes of accumulating costs. A third complication is one of working into the cost structure a number of overhead costs not directly related to an activity or even a work package. For example, the cost of over-all project management would be one extending over the entire network while the cost of project direction for a portion of the network would be spread over that series of events. Likewise, the progress of a program against the time budget is not likely to be the same as against a cost budget.

There is no question that PERT/COST has added considerably to the managerial effectiveness of the PERT approach to planning and control. But it is also true, particularly in many large programs such as those contracted for by the Department of Defense, that the complexity of the PERT system has been greatly increased.

PERT is not a cure-all. It will not *do* the planning, although it *forces* planning. It will not make control automatic, although it establishes an environment where sound control principles may be appreciated and used. And it apparently involves rather less expense that might be thought. Setting up the network, its analysis, its interpretation, and reporting from it probably requires little, if any, more expense than most other planning and control techniques, unless, of course, these are made unduly complicated.

FORMALIZED PRODUCT DEVELOPMENT

Organizational devices may also furnish an important kind of control technique. Among the best of these is one in which the responsible manager establishes the environment for a job and keeps informed as to whether it is being done. A good example of this exists in connection with the practice of formalizing new product development.

The Need Because new products mean future sales, because their development uses up scarce resources and time, and because new products may

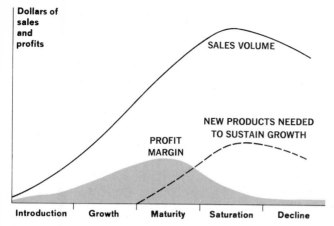

Dollars of sales and profits

SALES VOLUME

NEW PRODUCTS NEEDED
TO SUSTAIN GROWTH

PROFIT
MARGIN

Introduction | Growth | Maturity | Saturation | Decline

Fig. 29.7   The Basic Life Cycle of Products . . . *Profit margin tends to rise until maturity while sales volume increases until saturation is reached. But profit margin tends to fall as the market is saturated because of increased expenses and competing products. The curves demonstrate that most companies must introduce new products if they are to survive. A new product (dotted line), introduced during the maturity of the first, can sustain the company's income. It, in turn, must be followed by another new product. Product life cycles differ. Fashion goods and novelties have cycles, from introduction to saturation, of only a few months; most products have much longer lives.*

make existing products obsolete, companies are now emphasizing product planning. It has been estimated that, in the immediate future, some 75 per cent of the nation's growth in sales volume will come from new products, that most new-product ventures fail, and that unsuccessful products take about four out of five hours of scientific and engineering time.[18] Companies traditionally have had difficulty in developing products efficiently, fitting them to the company's strengths, and making them profitable.

The Steps   Formalization of product development may be undertaken in several ways: Some companies establish a special department reporting high in the organization structure; some create a special committee; and many set up special implementing procedures. In any case, the program normally establishes the following steps with built-in control machinery:

Encouraging of ideas   It is usual to open up all possible channels for ideas both inside and outside the company. A company executive may ordinarily be assigned to search out product ideas by studying markets and technology, soliciting ideas from sales and research departments, or

[18] Booz, Allen & Hamilton, Inc., *Management of New Products* (Chicago: Booz, Allen & Hamilton, Inc., 1966), p. 2.

developing idea-generating groups to be guided by company strengths and weaknesses.

Screening Because the objective of most formalized programs is to get maximum exposure to new-product ideas and spend money and time only on the most promising, preliminary screening is important. First, an idea's potential is given quick, inexpensive analysis, being weighed against company product policy and its marketing or technical strength in the light of immediately available cost, market, and technical information. Screening by a committee of varied specialists readily eliminates product ideas of little promise.

Evaluating Product ideas surviving the screening may be subjected to a preliminary evaluation involving expenditure of some money and manpower in market, technical, or other investigations and in an estimate of the cost of a complete study of the feasibility of going ahead with the new product. At this step—because important money may be spent—the question of whether to make the expenditure for a feasibility study may be submitted to the new-product committee and even to higher company authority.

The feasibility study If the feasibility study is undertaken and if it indicates favorable prospects for the product, the findings are usually submitted for approval to the president or the firm's top-management committee. The study ordinarily includes analyses of design, development, and manufacturing costs; selling costs; and marketing and profit potentials. It also includes the nature of development assignments to the technical, marketing, and other company organizational areas.

Development of the product If the recommendations of the feasibility study are positive and if they are approved, technical development of the product—usually a prototype or "first article"—is accomplished. Also, at the same time, preliminary marketing (including packaging) and manufacturing plans are made. This is, of course, the step in product planning where fairly large sums of money are likely to be spent.

Testing After the product has been technically developed and manufacturing and marketing (including packaging) plans made, the product may be subjected to technical and market tests to see if it meets specifications and is acceptable or whether it needs any change in design or marketing approach. If the product passes the tests, the company is ready to move into the final phases of the program.

Final design and operational plans When product design and marketing approach are found satisfactory, the next step is to make a final product design, detailed production plans, and complete plans for putting the product on the market.

Commercializing The final step is to "commercialize" the product, making it an actuality by releasing it to manufacturing and marketing.

The Advantages The above eight steps in formalized product development point to a number of advantages. This procedure—when reflected in the organization structure, with specific delegations of authority, and subject to upper-level management review—develops new products in accordance with company product policy and in the light of company strengths and weaknesses. Its milestone approach allows managers to see a complex program in its parts and to control and evaluate it at each step.

It is interesting that a study made in depth of some 200 companies disclosed that management problems, rather than the difficulty of getting new ideas or of creativity or personnel qualifications, were the major ones that counted in effective new-product development.[19] Of all the problems reported by these companies as interfering with their opportunities for new-product development, 55 per cent were organizational (definition of responsibilities, working and reporting relationships, communications, organization structure, etc.), 12 per cent were in management control, and 9 per cent were in definition of objectives. Thus, in what is normally regarded as a technical or marketing area, 76 per cent of the problems reported were purely managerial. There is probably no more convincing proof of the need for managers to establish and maintain an environment for performance.

While product development is the example used here, a formalized program, with adequate review, can be used in any significant area of control. The important thing is to chart the area, establish an organizational environment for doing the job, and see that the process has the attention of responsible management as its proceeds and money is spent. Proper organization can always be used as a means for focusing and channeling special effort.

MEASUREMENT OF HUMAN VARIABLES

A control area being increasingly emphasized is that of human resources in an enterprise. An expert in this area points out that measurement of profits, costs, and other such concrete factors may mislead by not taking into account a manager "milking the human franchise."[20] In other words, even though numerical measurements are important, varying human factors may jeopardize enterprise goals.

No sound management control can overlook the quality of the human factor. What is needed is not simply a knowledge of employee attitudes, but a measurement of human variables that can assure achievement of group goals.

[19] *Ibid.*, pp. 16–17.
[20] Rensis Likert, "Measuring Organizational Performance," *Harvard Business Review*, vol. 36, no. 2, pp. 41–50 (March–April, 1958). See also *New Patterns of Management*, chaps. 3, 5, 13 (New York: McGraw-Hill Book Company, 1961); and Chris Argyris, "The Organization: What Makes It Healthy?" *Harvard Business Review*, vol. 36, no. 6, pp. 107–116 (November–December, 1958).

The Variables   Students of human behavior believe that progress in the social sciences has made it possible to measure a wide area of variables affecting the quality and capacity of human organization. According to Likert, techniques are available—or can be developed by existing methodology—to measure the following: [21]

The extent of member loyalty to an organization and identification with it and its objectives.

The extent to which members of the organization at all hierarchical levels feel that the organization's objectives are consistent with their own needs and goals and that the achievement of company objectives will help them achieve their own.

The extent to which the goals of units and of individuals are of a character to facilitate the organization's achievement of its objectives.

The level of motivation among members of the organization with respect to such activities as:

Performance, including both quality and quantity of work done.

Elimination of wastes and reduction of costs.

Improving technological processes.

Improving the organization and its procedures.

The extent to which members of the organization feel that the atmosphere of the organization is supportive and helps maintain each individual's sense of personal worth.

The degree of confidence and trust among peers, between the different hierarchical levels, and between the different organizational units. . . .

The amount and quality of co-operation within each unit of the organization, between units, and between line and staff.

The amount of stress and anxiety felt by members of the organization and the source of stress. . . .

The character of the organizational structure: what it is supposed to be and what it is in actual fact. . . .

The character of the decision-making process. . . .

The level of competence and skill of the different groups in the organization to interact effectively in solving problems and doing other tasks. . . .

The efficiency and adequacy of the communication process upward, downward, sideward. . . .

The efficiency of the influence process in each unit and throughout the organization. . . .

The extent to which the roles of each of the members of the organization are clear, unambiguous, and functionally appropriate. . . .

The level of leadership skills and abilities of supervisors and managers, including their basic philosophy of management and orientation toward the processes of leadership, and their sensitivities and skills in using group methods of supervision.

The actual behavior of managers and subordinates as revealed through focused observations of them at work during samples of time. . . .

The native ability and personality traits of members of the organization.

[21] Likert, *New Patterns of Management*, pp. 192–194.

If aptitude scores are obtained as people join the organization, then trends in these scores will show whether the current management is improving the basic quality of the personnel through its hiring practices or is letting the quality deteriorate through unfavorable turnover.

The Measurements Every one of the above behavioral variables is important to every department and to the enterprise as a whole, and to the extent that they can be measured, this can be a valuable area of control. While the authors agree to the importance of measuring the human assets of an enterprise, and certainly the areas outlined above are appropriate to this measurement, they have yet to see systems which effectively measure them. To be sure, a number of these areas can be credibly measured by technically competent people. But no manager should expect the amateur psychologist or questionnaire interpreter to make such appraisals, any more than it is expected that managers would entrust the measurement of costs or product quality to the inexpert.

Also, one of the difficulties with this technique lies in the lack of generally accepted standards. In undertaking to measure the level of leadership skills, for example, we might ask, compared to what? Or in measuring the efficiency of the influence process—again, compared to what?

Likert and others do show some progress toward the development of standards. In a study published in 1967,[22] Likert presented limited but impressive evidence of measuring prevailing management systems against four models: exploitative-authoritative, benevolent-authoritative, consultative, and participative-group. In each model, analysis was made of operating characteristics of companies, including within these such classifications of items, with appropriate underlying variables, as character of motivational forces, communication processes, interaction-influence processes, decision-making processes, goal setting and ordering, control processes, and performance characteristics. Although the extent of his empirical data is not clear, Likert found that the most productive enterprises in terms of such basics as sales volume and profit were those approaching in nature the highly participative management system.

What is interesting in Likert's approach and in his findings is that in almost every one of the underlying operating variables that he analyzes, the higher performance systems are close to that which effective management, as perceived by the authors of this book, would accomplish. If managers realize that their essential task is to create and maintain an environment for the performance of people, and if they do this through exercising the managerial functions and underlying techniques as outlined in this book, the results which Likert finds and predicts should follow. His research, in general, appears in essence, and with few differences, to reflect the practice of management as perceived and recommended here.

---

[22] R. Likert, *The Human Organization: Its Management and Value* (New York: McGraw-Hill Book Company, 1967).

FOR DISCUSSION

1. The newer techniques of control appear to be as much techniques of planning as they are of control. In what ways is this true? Why would you expect it to be so?

2. PERT is a management invention that takes basic principles and knowledge and, through design to get a desired result, comes up with a useful technique of planning and control. Analyze PERT with this in mind.

3. Why would one call distribution logistics a complex system of operations research? Can this system be conceptualized without mathematics and the computer? Can it be operated in the typical multiproduct, multiplant, multicustomer firm without mathematics and the computer?

4. How would you set out to solve the problem of "information indigestion" that faces many managers today?

5. Product planning, performance and planning review, and other techniques of assuring planning and control are increasingly being formalized. Why is this? Do you agree that this should be done?

SELECTED REFERENCES

American Management Association: *Advances in EDP and Information Systems,* Management Report No. 62, New York: American Management Association, 1961.

Argyris, Chris: "The Organization: What Makes It Healthy?" *Harvard Business Review,* vol. 36, no. 6, pp. 107–116 (November–December, 1958).

Avots, Ivars: "The Management Side of PERT," *California Management Review,* vol. 4, no. 2, pp. 16–27 (Winter, 1962).

Baumes, C. G.: *Administration of Electronic Data Processing,* New York: National Industrial Conference Board, Inc., 1961.

Brewer, S. H., and J. Rosenzweig: "Rhochrematics and Organization," *California Management Review,* vol. 3, no. 3, pp. 52–31 (Spring, 1961).

Burlingame, J. F.: "Information Technology and Decentralization," *Harvard Business Review,* vol. 39, no. 6, pp. 121–126 (November–December, 1961).

Constantin, J. A.: *Principles of Logistics Management,* New York: Appleton-Century-Crofts, Inc., 1966.

Daniel, D. R.: "Management Information Crisis," *Harvard Business Review,* vol. 39, no. 5, pp. 111–121 (September–October, 1961).

Dearden, J.: "Can Management Information Be Automated?" *Harvard Business Review,* vol. 42, no. 2, pp. 128–135 (March–April, 1964).

————: "How to Organize Information Systems," *Harvard Business Review,* vol. 43, no. 2, pp. 65–73 (March–April, 1965).

Edmunds, Stahrl: "The Reach of an Executive," *Harvard Business Review,* vol. 37, no. 1, pp. 87–96 (January–February, 1959).

Falcon, W. D. (ed.): *Reporting Financial Data to Management,* New York: American Management Association, 1965.

Forrester, J. W.: "Industrial Dynamics," *Harvard Business Review,* vol. 36, no. 4, pp. 37–66 (July–August, 1958).

————: *Industrial Dynamics,* New York: John Wiley & Sons, Inc., 1961.

Gallagher, J. D.: *Management Information Systems and the Computer,* New York: American Management Association, 1961.

Girouard, W. F.: "Dynamic Control of an Organizational Complex," *California Management Review*, vol. 4, no. 4, pp. 44–56 (Summer, 1962).

Hansen, B. J.: *Practical PERT*, Washington, D.C.: America House, 1964.

Johnson, S. C., and C. Jones: "How to Organize for New Products," *Harvard Business Review*, vol. 35, no. 3, pp. 49–62 (October, 1955).

Levin, R. I., and C. A. Kirkpatrick: *Planning and Control with PERT/CPM*, New York: McGraw-Hill Book Company, 1966.

Likert, Rensis: "Measuring Organizational Performance," *Harvard Business Review*, vol. 36, no. 2, pp. 41–50 (March–April, 1958).

————: *New Patterns of Management*, New York: McGraw-Hill Book Company, 1961.

————: *The Human Organization: Its Management and Value*, New York: McGraw-Hill Book Company, 1967.

Magee, J. F.: "Guides to Inventory Policy," *Harvard Business Review*, vol. 34, no. 1, pp. 49–69; no. 2, pp. 103–116; no. 3, pp. 57–70 (January–February, March–April, May–June, 1956).

————: "The Logistics of Distribution," *Harvard Business Review*, vol. 38, no. 4, pp. 89–101 (July–August, 1960).

Malcolm, D. G., and A. J. Rowe: "Computer-based Control Systems," *California Management Review*, vol. 3, no. 3, pp. 4–15 (Spring, 1961).

McDonough, A. M.: *Information Economics and Management Systems*, New York: McGraw-Hill Book Company, 1963.

Miller, R. W.: "How to Plan and Control with PERT," *Harvard Business Review*, vol. 40, no. 2, pp. 93–104 (March–April, 1962).

————: *Schedule, Cost and Profit Control with PERT*, New York: McGraw-Hill Book Company, 1963.

National Association of Accountants: *Current Application of Direct Costing*, Research Report No. 37, New York: National Association of Accountants, 1961.

Neuschel, R. F.: "How to Make Physical Distribution Pay Off," *Harvard Business Review*, vol. 45, no. 2, pp. 125–134 (March–April, 1967).

————: *Management by System*, New York: McGraw-Hill Book Company, 1960.

Smykay, E. W.: *Essays on Physical Distribution Management*, Washington: Traffic Service Corporation, 1961.

control of
over-all performance

Control techniques and systems must be tailored to the areas they are designed to measure and correct. Most controls are designed for specific things: policies, wages and salaries, employee selection and training, research and development, product quality, costs, pricing, capital expenditures, cash, and other areas where performance should conform to plans. Such controls are partial in the sense that they apply to a part of an enterprise and do not measure total accomplishments against total goals.

There is not space in this book to discuss in detail the entire subject of control. However, to the extent that any control technique is sound, it will reflect the basic nature of control and its prerequisites as outlined in Chapter 28. Moreover, it is not possible to be precise about practical details of partial control without, at the very least, reference to a given plan, to the personality of the manager involved, and to specific enterprise goals.

As was shown in the previous chapter on newer techniques of control, planning and control are being increasingly treated as an interrelated system. Along with these newer techniques, and preceding many of them, control devices have been developed to measure the over-all performance of an enterprise—or an integrated[1] division or project within it—against total goals.

There are many reasons for control of over-all performance. In the first

---

[1] "Integrated" here is used as meaning that an operation includes the functions necessary to gain an over-all objective. Thus, a product division of a company would normally include engineering, manufacturing, and marketing, and this represents enough of a total operation for the division manager—even though subject to some direction and control from headquarters—to be held basically responsible for a profit. To a lesser degree, but nonetheless important, an engineering design operation might be regarded as integrated: if the head of an engineering project has under him all the engineering functions and specialties necessary for complete product design, he can then be held responsible for the efficient accomplishment of the project.

place, as over-all planning must apply to enterprise or major division goals, so must over-all controls be applied. In the second place, decentralization of authority—especially in product or territorial divisions—creates semiautonomous units, and these must be subjected at least to over-all controls to avoid the chaos of complete autonomy. In the third place, over-all controls permit measuring an integrated area manager's *total* effort, rather than parts of it.

To a great extent, over-all controls in business are, as one might expect, financial. Business owes its continued existence to profit making; its capital resources are a scarce, life-giving element; and, in the environment in which it operates, the best gauge of effectiveness is the dollar. Since finance is the binding force of business, financial controls are the most important single objective gauge of the success of plans.

Financial measurements also summarize, through a common denominator, the operation of a number of plans. Further, they accurately indicate total expenditures of resources in reaching goals. This is true in a business enterprise and it is also true in other forms of enterprise. Although the purpose of an educational or government enterprise is not to make monetary profits, any responsible manager must have some way of knowing what his goal achievement has cost in terms of resources. Therefore, in all forms of enterprise, control of over-all performance is likely to be financial. Moreover, financial analyses furnish an excellent "window" through which accomplishment in nonfinancial areas can be seen. A deviation from planned costs, for example, may lead a manager to find the causes in nonfinancial factors.

BUDGET SUMMARIES AND REPORTS

A widely used control of over-all performance takes the form of a summary of budgets. A budget summary, being a résumé of all the individual budgets of the company, reflects company plans so that sales volume, costs, profits, utilization of capital, and return on investment may be seen in their proper relationship. In these terms, it shows top management how the company as a whole is succeeding in its objectives.

The comprehensive nature of this final budget may be readily grasped if consideration is given to the preliminary steps required. These involve the sales forecast and its translation into expenditure budgets with statements of costs, output, and attendant requirements. As these are summarized, the budget maker is in a position to develop a pro forma balance sheet and statement of profit and loss to accompany the final budget. These three documents permit top management to weigh the effect of departmental activities on the business as a whole or on an integrated division.

Need for Reports A budget summary is of limited use for control without reports comparing performance with plans. If a budget summary is properly drawn, with responsibility for performance easily ascertainable, these reports need only list the data, calculate the variances, and explain major differences.

Explanation of variances is often overlooked in budget reports, but if the reports—whether in summary for the whole enterprise or for a department or function—are not supplemented with reasons for any significant differences between budget and actual costs, the manager may be frustrated in using them for control. Although the manager of a minor department may know, from intimate acquaintance with his operations, why his performance has diverged from plans, the higher in the organization structure the budget summary is prepared and presented, the less likely a manager will know the reasons for budget deviations.

Especially important in making budgets operate for control purposes is the promptness of issuance of reports. Historical data, such as normally found in budget reports, are useful only when (as is often the case) what has happened will continue to happen. Obviously, the more promptly a report is issued, the more useful it is for purposes of control.

Uses   For the best control through a budget summary, a manager must first be satisfied that total budgets are an accurate and reasonably complete portrayal of the company's plans. The budget reports and any material accompanying them should be scrutinized to determine whether the comparison of budget and actual costs shows the real nature of any deviations. As an example of where this was not done, a company head criticized his factory manager for being considerably over his labor budget in a month when the labor force had been materially reduced and the temporary increase in expenses was due to severance pay.

Minor discrepancies should receive appropriately little attention. The purpose of a control system is to draw attention to important variations, and both the budget reports and the attention paid to them should reflect this. Above all, the manager should never forget that a budget summary is no substitute for profitable operation. There is danger in manipulating budget figures and forcing revenues and expenses to conform. Moreover, budgeting is never more perfect than the planning behind it, and plans—especially long-range plans—are subject to the imperfections wrought by change and uncertainty. There may even be times when the manager must forget his budget and take special action to meet unexpected events. Budgets are meant to be tools, and not masters, of managers.

On the other hand, the value of budget summaries, in providing an effective means for over-all control in the face of decentralization of authority, should not be underestimated. They furnish a means whereby enterprise objectives can be clearly and specifically defined, and departmental plans can be made to contribute toward such objectives. Should the budget summary and the reports of actual events indicate that the enterprise as a whole is not tending toward its objectives, the top managers have a convenient and positive means of finding out where the deviations are occurring. The summaries thus furnish a useful guide for corrective action.

PROFIT AND LOSS CONTROL

The profit and loss statement for an enterprise as a whole serves important control purposes, largely because it shows the constituent parts of a profit or a loss for a given period and, therefore, is useful for determining the immediate revenue or cost factors that have accounted for success or failure. Obviously, in the form of a pro forma forecast, it is even a better control device, in that it gives a manager a chance, before the event, to influence revenues, expenses, and, consequently, profits.

Since enterprise survival usually depends on profits and they are a definite standard against which to measure business success, many companies use the profit and loss statement for divisional or departmental control. Because this is a statement of all revenues and expenses for a given time, it is a true summary of the results of business operations. Profit and loss control is usually applied to divisions or departments, based on the premise that if it is the purpose of the entire business to make a profit, each part of the enterprise should contribute to this purpose. Thus, the ability of a part to make an expected profit becomes a standard for measuring its performance.

In profit and loss control, each major department or division details its revenues and expenses—normally with a pro-rata share of the company overhead—and calculates periodically a statement of its profit or loss. Some units have their own accounting group, while in others the statement is prepared by the central accounting department. In either case, the organizational unit, in being expected to turn in a separate record of profitable operation, is considered by the enterprise in much the same way that a holding company considers its subsidiary companies.

Profit and loss control usually is practicable only in major segments of the company, since the paper work in building up profit and loss statements for smaller departments tends to be too heavy. Also, profit and loss control usually implies that the manager of the division or department has a fairly wide authority to run his part of the business as he sees fit, with profit the primary standard of success. However, many companies that do not so decentralize authority have nonetheless found profit and loss control valuable. The focus on profit and the sensitiveness of the organizational unit to it are worthwhile even when the manager has limited independence to seek profit as he wishes.

The more integrated and complete the organization unit, the more accurate a measuring stick profit and loss control can be. For this reason, it works best in product or territorial divisions, where both sales and production functions for a product or service are under one jurisdiction. For example, it is much easier to use the standard of profit for measuring the operations of the general manager of the Buick division of General Motors than it would be to use it in the motor-block boring section of the manufacturing department of this division.

At the same time, companies organized on a functional basis do occasionally employ profit and loss control. The heat-treating department may produce and "sell" its service to the machining department, which in turn "sells" its product to the assembly department, which in turn "sells" a complete product to the sales department. This can be done, although the paper work required is often not worth the effort, and the problem of determining the right transfer price may occasion much negotiation or difficult executive decision. If the transfer is made at cost, clearly only the sales department would show a profit. If it is made at a figure above cost, the question becomes one of what price to charge.

In most instances, profit and loss control is not applied to central staff and service departments. Although these departments could "sell" their services, the most satisfactory practice is to place them under some other form of control such as a straight expense budget.

Limitations Profit and loss control suffers its greatest limitations from the accounting expense and paper intracompany transfers. The duplication of accounting records, the effort involved in allocating the many burden and overhead costs, and the time and effort required to calculate intracompany sales can make this control too costly when its application is carried too far.

Profit and loss control also may be inadequate for complete over-all performance. Top managers may not wish to yield so much authority to division managers and may at least desire the additional assurances of good budgetary control. In addition, profit and loss control in and of itself does not provide a standard of desirable profits or policy controls in the areas of product line, development, or other matters of long-term over-all company concern.

Another limitation of profit and loss control, especially if carried very far in the organization, is that departments may come to compete, with an aggressive detachment not conducive to enterprise coordination. On the other hand, in many companies there is not enough feeling of departmental responsibility for company profit, and departments may develop the smugness of a monopolist with an assured market. The fabrication department that knows its products must be "bought" by the assembly department, the manufacturing or service department that can force its output on the sales department, and the engineering group that has a monopolistic hold on both production and sales are dangerous monopolists indeed. Profit and loss control can break down these islands of monopoly. So, in spite of limitations—and especially if accompanied by an intracompany pricing policy requiring departments to meet outside competitive prices rather than being based on cost—profit and loss control can give top managers an extraordinary measure of over-all control.

CONTROL THROUGH RETURN ON INVESTMENT

One of the most successfully used control techniques is that of measuring both the absolute and relative success of a company or a company unit by the ratio of earnings to investment of capital. This approach has been the core of the control system of the du Pont Company since 1919 and has received much attention in recent years. A large number of companies have adopted it as their key measure of over-all performance.

This yardstick is the rate of return that a company or a division can earn on the capital allocated to it. This tool, therefore, does not look at profit as an absolute, but as a return on capital employed in the business. The goal of a business is, accordingly, not to optimize profits but to optimize returns from capital devoted to business purposes. This standard recognizes the fundamental fact that capital is a critical factor in almost any business enterprise and through its scarcity limits progress.

Some Examples   As the system has been used by the du Pont Company,[2] return on investment involves consideration of several factors. Return is computed on the basis of capital turnover multiplied by earnings as a percentage of sales. This calculation recognizes that one division, with a high capital turnover and a low percentage of earnings to sales, may be more profitable in terms of return on investment than another with a high percentage of profits to sales but with a low capital turnover. Turnover is computed on the basis of total sales divided by total investment, and investment includes not only the permanent investment in plant facilities but also the working capital of the unit. In the du Pont system, investment and working capital represent amounts invested without reduction for liabilities or reserves, on the grounds that such a reduction would result in a fluctuation in operating investments, as reserves or liabilities change, which would distort the rate of return and render it meaningless. Earnings are, however, calculated after normal depreciation charges, on the basis that true profits are not earned until allowance is made for the write-off of a depreciable asset.

Return-on-investment control is perhaps best summarized in chart form, as in Figure 30.1. Here, an analysis of variations in rate of return leads into every financial facet of the business. Rate of return is the common denominator used in comparing divisions, and with its differences can easily be traced to their causes.

The Monsanto Chemical Company, like du Pont, in using rate of return as its primary control, has employed gross asset values as the basis of investment, on the grounds that, until an asset is retired from use, it produces net income.[3] Monsanto also eliminates from the investment figure excess cash

[2] This system is well explained in *How the du Pont Organization Appraises Its Performance*, Financial Management Series No. 94 (New York: American Management Association, 1950). See also *Executive Committee Control Charts* (Wilmington, Del.: E. I. du Pont de Nemours and Company, 1959).

[3] For a summary of financial controls in this company, including return on investment, see *A Program of Financial Planning and Controls: The Monsanto Chemical Company*, Financial Management Series No. 103 (New York: American Management Association, 1953). Note especially pp. 6–10 and pp. 38–43.

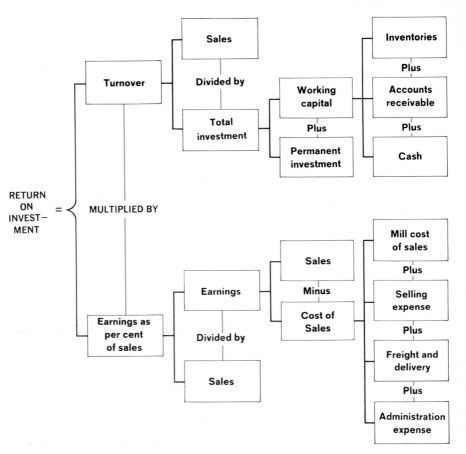

Fig. 30.1 The Relationship of Factors Affecting Return on Investment

and securities balances over normal requirements and uncompleted investments in fixed assets not in operation.

However, other companies, such as the H. J. Heinz Company,[4] have taken the position that the return on investment should be calculated on fixed assets less depreciation. Such companies hold that the depreciation reserve represents a write-off of the initial investment and that funds made available through such charges are reinvested in other fixed assets or used as working capital. Such a treatment appears more realistic to operating people, partly because it places a heavier rate-of-return burden on new fixed assets than on worn or obsolete ones.

In any control through return on investment, the number of ratios and

[4] See explanation by T. G. Mackensen in *How H. J. Heinz Manages Its Financial Planning and Controls*, Financial Management Series No. 106 (New York: American Management Association, 1953), p. 42.

comparisons behind the final yardstick figure cannot be overlooked. Although improvement in rate of return can come from a higher percentage of profit to sales, improvement could likewise come from increasing the rate of turnover by reducing return on sales. Moreover, the ratio of return on investment might be improved by getting more product (and sales) out of a given plant investment or by reducing the cost of sales for a given product.

Application to Product Lines The H. J. Heinz Company,[5] a typical functional-line organization without integrated product divisions, has applied return-on-investment control to its various product lines. By grouping its many products into a number of major classifications, this company follows through with the allocation of sales, costs, and investment in fixed assets and working capital to arrive at the same kind of rate-of-return analysis used by multidivision companies. A simplified example of these results is shown in Table 11.

To operate the rate-of-return yardstick for product lines, the Heinz Company has allocated certain expenses and assets, but these allocations apparently have not caused much difficulty. Most production costs are maintained by product, and common costs, such as sales branch expenses, are allocated by volume of sales. More difficulty is incurred in determining asset usage by product lines, but cash, accounts receivable, and administrative

[5] *Ibid.* See especially articles by F. B. Cliffe and T. G. Mackensen, pp. 3–8 and pp. 37–45.

TABLE 11   COMPARATIVE RATES OF RETURN: MULTIPRODUCT COMPANY (in thousands of dollars)

	Total sales		Assets employed		Operating income*		
	Amount	Per cent of total	Amount	Per dollar of sales	Amount	Per cent return on sales	Per cent return on assets
Base year:							
Product A	$ 39,300	40%	$ 20,700	52.9%	$ 4,800	12.2%	23.1%
Product B	29,500	30	16,900	57.3	2,800	9.4	16.4
Product C	19,600	20	8,900	45.1	2,100	10.8	23.9
Product D	9,800	10	2,700	27.5	500	5.1	18.5
Total	$ 98,200	100%	$ 49,200	50.1%	$10,200	10.4%	20.8%
Current year:							
Product A	$ 48,100	25	$ 28,400	59.0	$5,600	11.6	19.7
Product B	96,200	50	75,300	78.3	8,500	8.8	11.2
Product C	38,500	20	19,500	50.7	3,900	10.2	20.1
Product D	9,600	5	2,900	29.9	500	5.2	17.2
Total	$192,400	100%	$126,100	65.5%	$18,500	9.6%	14.6%

* Before interest on borrowed money and Federal income taxes.

and sales facilities are allocated in accordance with sales; inventories and factory and plant equipment are prorated to the various products on the basis of special analyses.

In addition to comparative rates of return as between products, as indicated in Table 11, the company compares actual experience with trends for the various products (identified for purposes of simplicity as the "base year" in the table). An advantage of these comparisons is that the company is able to maintain a sharp look at its product lines, with a view to determining where capital is being most efficiently employed and as a guide toward obtaining a balanced use of capital for maximum over-all profit. Thus, the company has been able to identify products that are either strong and established, new and improved, or past their peak in growth and profitability.

Advantages and Limitations One of the principal advantages of using return on investment to control over-all performance is that it, like profit and loss control, focuses managerial attention on the central objective of the business—to make the best profit possible on the capital available. It measures the efficiency of the company as a whole, its major divisions or departments, its products, and its planning. It takes attention away from mere increase in sales volume or asset size, or even from the level of costs, and draws attention to the combination of factors making for successful operation.

Another advantage of control by return on investment is that it is effective where authority is decentralized. It not only is an absolute guide to efficiency but offers the possibility of comparing efficiency in capital employment, both within the company and with other enterprises. By holding departmental managers responsible for performance in terms of the dollars invested in their segments of the business, it forces them to look at their operations from the point of view of top management. Managers often insist on heavy capital for new equipment or drive for lower prices to increase sales without taking into account the possible effect of their requests on the company as a whole. They also often feel isolated, particularly in large businesses, with respect to their performance. If they are furnished a guide to efficiency that reaches into so many facets of the business, managers develop a keener sense of responsibility for their department or division, and top managers can more easily hold subordinate managers responsible.

A further advantage of return-on-investment control, if it is complete and shows all the factors bearing upon the return, is that it enables managers to locate weaknesses. If inventories are rising, the effect will be shown on the rate of return, or if other factors camouflage inventory variations and leave the rate looking good, tracing back influences will disclose any weakness of the inventory situation and open the way for consideration of a remedy.

With all its advantages and with its increasing use by well-managed and successful companies, this method of control is not foolproof. Difficulties involve availability of information on sales, costs, and assets and proper allocation of investment and return for commonly sold or produced items. Does the present accounting system give the needed information? If not, how much will it cost to get it, through either changes in the system or special analyses? Where assets are jointly used or costs are common, what method of allocation between divisions or departments shall be used? Should the manager be charged with assets at their original costs, their replacement costs, or their depreciated values? Setting up a return-on-investment control system is no simple task.

Another question is, What constitutes a reasonable return? Comparisons of rates of return are hardly enough, because they do not tell the top manager what the optimum rate of return *should* be. Perhaps as good a standard as any is one that meets or surpasses the level of competition of other firms, since, in a practical sense, the optimum tends to be measured not by an absolute level but rather by the level of the competition for capital.

Perhaps the greatest danger in return-on-investment control, as with any system of control based on financial data, is that it can lead to excessive preoccupation with financial factors, either within a firm or within an industry. Undue attention to ratios and financial data can cause a firm to overlook environmental factors such as social and technical developments. It might also lead the company to overlook the fact that capital is not the only scarce resource from which a business can grow, prosper, and endure. Every bit as scarce are competent managers, good employee morale, and good customer and public relations. A well-managed company would never regard any financially based control as the sole gauge of over-all performance.

EXTERNAL AND INTERNAL AUDITING CONTROL

Many companies limit the work of their internal audit staffs to the primary task of verification of accounting and financial transactions, thus supplementing, for the purpose of internal management, the work of the outside auditing firm. In most auditing, external or internal, more would probably be gained by care taken to avoid errors and departures from goals, policies, and procedures than by detection of errors in accounts.

External Auditing   The outside auditing firm reviews the financial accounts of a business primarily to determine whether they portray, with reasonable accuracy, the financial condition in the light of accepted accounting principles. Outside auditing is limited to financial matters and is essentially a verification of balance sheet items. However, the ramifications of these items extend into all aspects of the business that bear in any financial way on assets, liabilities, and net worth.

Although the independent audit has a limited management-control function, so many measures of performance are based upon financial information that the integrity of the accounting system is a prerequisite to effective control. Moreover, through their interpretation and application of accepted accounting principles, the independent auditors exercise a degree of control over the operations of the business itself. Thus, a business might wish to charge capital investments to current operating expenses, or it might wish to overcost a product to show an inventory reduction or to understate profits. But the outside auditing firm, by refusing to certify accounts with such deviations from standard practice, can materially affect any such contemplated policy.

Internal Auditing   In Chapter 28 internal auditing was discussed in its broadest sense as being the appraisal of the accounting, financial, managerial, and other operations of the business by a staff of auditors employed by the company. Since 1950,[6] practically all large companies have had internal auditing programs.

In addition to the primary task of internal auditing mentioned above, an increasing number of companies are using this device to serve managers by checking on compliance with policies, plans, and procedures. On the basis of this check, the auditing staff recommends the correction of detected deviations.

Internal auditors are also active in the appraisal of procedures. Procedures have a way of being misunderstood or disregarded—even when they may be essential to the orderly flow of activities—and also a way of becoming obsolete. To guard against serious breakdowns in procedures, especially since they cut across departmental lines, careful observation by experts is helpful. Some companies find a similar advantage in using internal auditors to check on interdepartmental policies.

Many audit staffs also handle special assignments generally related to the subject matter of their audits. For example, in one company,[7] the staff assisted the controller in establishing procedures for meeting price and material regulations and for profit renegotiation, also procedures for auditing government contracts and for controlling construction projects.

The internal auditing staff contributes to the control of over-all performance by assuring that accounting and financial data accurately portray the facts. In a broad program of audit, it can also communicate facts to management about the operation of plans, by detecting deviations and informing managers where and what corrections are needed. Furthermore, the very fact of an internal audit program causes managers and their subordinates to hew to the line of company policy and procedure.

But there are several limitations to internal auditing. In the first place, a complete program is expensive, and many smaller companies cannot afford one. In the second place, appraisal by an internal auditor is ineffective without corrective action. Too often internal auditors fail to impress the respon-

---

[6] According to a survey reported in F. A. Lamperti and J. B. Thurston, *Internal Auditing for Management* (Englewood Cliffs, N.J.: Prentice-Hall, Inc., 1953), pp. 84–86, only 9 of the 132 large companies studied had internal auditing departments in 1920, and only 58 by 1940, but all had such departments by 1950.

[7] *A Program of Financial Planning and Control: The Monsanto Chemical Company*, p. 20.

sible manager, because they irritate him with undue detail, because they cannot convince him of the soundness of their analysis, or because their reports are too complex. An internal auditor bears a staff relationship to the manager and therefore he can only recommend and persuade.

Internal auditing makes its major contribution to the control and improvement of over-all performance in those relatively rare instances where the auditors are accepted, by managers at all levels, as a kind of management consulting corps. In one large company, in which the emphasis of internal auditing is less on "snooping" and more on the "outside" look of the consultant, and where the auditors are conversant with management principles and company policies and plans, the line managers welcome the auditors and use them to improve operations. As one of the manufacturing managers informed the authors, the audit staff had immeasurably assisted him and his superintendents by advising on company policies and plans; raising questions about operations which had never been raised because of preoccupation with the work; and suggesting solutions for vexing managerial problems. Thus, the success of this program depended largely upon the concept of the task, the leadership given by the head auditor, and the quality of his subordinates.

THE CONTROL UNIT

The control unit centralizes information necessary to the control function in a staff reporting to a manager, usually the president, although it might be to any manager.

The importance and nature of the control unit are indicated by the following rather optimistic statement from a book by two authorities on internal controls.[8]

> The control unit is new as a separate important top management tool. It is the latest step in the evolution of managerial controls. It is simply the gathering of all these activities into one co-ordinated unit under the supervision of a top executive. This places new emphasis on these functions, acknowledges their importance, and usually results in substantial economies in the costs of effecting proper control of the business. Duplication of effort, work at cross purposes, overemphasis on the importance of one function at the expense of another are eliminated. Erroneous interpretations or lack of unity of purpose, which can happen unintentionally when two people examine the same situation independently, are eliminated. The whole flow and channeling of control data from source to directive action is co-ordinated under uniform guidance and without extraneous motion.

The Koppers Company   The development of the centralized control unit has often been ascribed to B. B. Somervell, who reputedly used this technique as commanding general of the Army Service Forces during World War II.

---

[8] Lamperti and Thurston, *op. cit.*, p. 95.

After the war, Somervell became president of the Koppers Company, where he established a control unit that became a pattern for this technique.[9]

The Koppers control unit was conceived as an aid to the president, whose job was to determine company action by establishing company goals. The control unit was to determine how company action should be carried out and how well this was being done. Since the president could not possibly do his job alone, the control unit provided him with more eyes, more ears, and more hours per day. Whatever the control unit undertook, it was acting for the president.

More specifically, the Koppers control unit had five principal functions:

1. It determined and agreed upon programs, developing them with the assistance of the operating and staff departments concerned and reviewing objectives and programs in the light of their continued attainability and desirability.
2. It guided and coordinated performance of the division managers through constant review of the organization of the company, of policies affecting the company generally, and of procedures involving actions between operating divisions and staff departments.
3. It appraised results against the standard of the programs through monthly reports on operations and through audits of the financial and nonfinancial factors involved.
4. It assisted the president in the correction of unsatisfactory conditions by locating and analyzing troublesome conditions and by preparing recommendations of remedial action.
5. Subject to the prior demands of the president's job, it provided control service to other units of the company as requested, with respect to organization planning, policy development, procedure design, program development, information clearance, special reports, mediation, coordination, special studies, control installations, control training, and report design.

Koppers encouraged the development of control units at levels below the office of the president, provided that the size and importance of the division or department were sufficient to justify it. An attempt was also made to develop a functional liaison between control units at various levels to expedite and improve the quality of control.

Emphasis was placed on properly understanding the unit's organizational relationship. Although the top-level control unit assisted the president, it exercised no authority whatever. On this point, the company stated that

---

[9] T. J. McGinnis, *The Control Section as an Aid to Management* (Pittsburgh: Koppers Company, Inc., no date). This booklet describes in detail the organization and functions of the control unit at Koppers. The material in this section is drawn from it. Upon the reorganization of the company after General Somervell's death in 1958, the control unit was placed in the corporate finance department and ceased to operate as outlined here.

"should the attitude be taken . . . that it is a super-management agency with power to control and direct in itself, its value is lost and it will very likely become a liability rather than an asset."[10] However, the breadth of duties of the control unit, acting only in a staff capacity to the president, made this difficult to practice. The rather unusual extension at Koppers of the office of the president into the control unit gave the unit a position of great authority despite the disclaimers that were made. Indeed, the subordination of the control unit to a position in the corporate finance department after General Somervell's death is believed to have been due to this problem and to the resentment of operating managers.

Other Companies Although the Koppers Company control unit generally set the pattern for other companies that have gone far in this direction, some units vary markedly from this pattern and are little more than a centralized cost- and financial-data dispensing agency. In others, the unit combines accounting and statistical work, furnishing the various parts of the company with planning and control data. In still others, these functions are combined with special reporting.

A control unit organization differing materially from that at Koppers is a type that centralizes *activities* with respect to planning, budgeting methods and procedures engineering, statistics and reports, internal auditing, and organization and policy manuals.[11] Although the *breadth* of such a control department does not differ substantially from the Koppers pattern, the Koppers practice was designed to aid key executives at, perhaps, different levels, while with the centralized activities unit, the control department vertically integrates activities in the manner of a centralized service department. This kind of control unit is particularly dangerous because it tends to concentrate the tools of management in a place beyond the reach of lower managers.

The Control Unit and Modern Management The control unit is discussed here, not because it has been widely adopted as such in practice, since it has not, but because the basic concept is often used in other forms in practice. Sometimes it is the duty of the assistant to the president. More often it is the task pressed on the vice-president–finance or a controller. Its functions are also found in the position of assistant to the general manager or in the position of the division controller.

The advantages, problems, and dangers of the control unit exist wherever the *function* is located. One can understand the difficulties facing a chief executive officer, a division general manager, or, for that matter, a department director or section chief. He knows that he bears the responsibility for effective management of his enterprise or department of it. He

[10] *Ibid.*, p. 16.
[11] J. B. Thurston, *Co-ordinating and Controlling Operations* (New York: Funk & Wagnalls Company, 1948), p. 11.

normally does not have the time to discharge this responsibility without help. He, therefore, understandably needs staff assistance and this should be given to him. Analyzing planning proposals and control information is a difficult and time-consuming task, yet the results of such analyses and information are necessary for the effective manager.

So long as this assistance is actually regarded as staff, it is helpful and important for the modern manager. But when those charged with assisting a manager begin to take over the managerial responsibilities and functions of their superior, this is a different thing. It takes a wise and careful superior to be able to receive and use the information, analyses, and recommendations of a staff but to preserve for himself the real responsibility for actual planning and control that can be only his. Likewise, perhaps one of the major tasks of an effective staff assistant is his ability to resist the satisfaction and feeling the power of acting in place of his superior. But it cannot effectively be otherwise, unless, of course, the superior wishes to delegate functional authority to his staff assistant in certain areas and makes this crystal clear to the assistant and to the superior's line subordinates, or where the superior wishes to make his staff assistant a true line assistant with definite authority to act for his boss.

The Control Unit and the Controller   Many companies actually merge the activities of the control unit with those of the controller, historically the chief accounting officer of a company. Since statistical and financial data are of prime importance to control and usually originate in the controller's department, the tendency to expand his functions to include policy, procedural, and other planning and control matters is not unnatural.

The danger of expanding the controllership to include general planning and control is that the controller may tend to look at his task through the eyes of accounting or finance only. There is danger, too, of undermining responsible managers by removing from their jobs the functions of planning and control. Every top manager should be careful not to take the title of "controller" too literally or to set up a control department with too much concentration of activities.

CONTROL THROUGH KEY RESULT AREAS

Another approach to control of over-all performance was instituted by the General Electric Company (GE) some years ago.[12] Realizing the central importance of profit as a measure of over-all control but aware of the limitations involved, that company undertook a program of measurements aimed at eight key areas. This program contemplated establishment of indexes of

---

[12] See *Planning, Managing and Measuring the Business*, especially part 5, contributed by R. W. Lewis (New York: Controllership Foundation, 1955). See also W. T. Jerome, III, *Executive Control: The Catalyst* (New York: John Wiley & Sons, Inc., 1961), chap. 14.

performance that could be applied against goals in comparing one organization unit with another in a uniform and meaningful way.

The Areas The key areas in which it was attempted to measure results are profitability, market position, productivity, product leadership, personnel development, employee attitudes, public responsibility, and the balance between short- and long-range goals. Indexes developed for these were to be used to measure performance against established goals, modified from time to time and used as standards against which both objective and subjective measurements were to be applied. The content of each key area is briefly outlined below.

Profitability This area heads the list. GE felt that rate-of-return-on-investment or other profit indexes had certain shortcomings and that pure profit indexes encouraged concentration on percentages—rather than on total dollar profits—and might dampen the incentive to growth. In other words, the company believed that capital should be looked upon as a cost and that the manager should optimize profits after all costs, including the costs of capital, rather than concentrate on any percentage return on investment.

Market position The second key area for which GE attempted to develop measurements was the acceptance of the company's products and services by the market. This position reflected the company's intelligence in choosing the "right" markets as well as its ability to meet competition in quality and price, in distribution and promotion, and in technical advancements. Share of the market was, of course, an important index. In addition, attempts were made to measure customer satisfaction with GE and with its competitors, and to find out what the customer wanted but was not getting.

Productivity In measuring the area of productivity—the "ability of a business to utilize its human, capital, and material resources to the best advantage and to the best balance"[13]—GE concentrated on the physical aspects—goods and services produced and sold compared to the physical inputs required to provide or manufacture and sell them. In this index, the company sought to measure the productivity of the *company's* operations, as contrasted to those of a supplier, and to distinguish between productivity of labor and that attributable to capital and management.

Product leadership The area went beyond immediate considerations of market position and took in the ability of the company to meet customer needs at minimum costs for developing, manufacturing, and marketing new products. In it was measured the ability of the company—or an integrated segment of it—to exploit new scientific and technical knowledge (in manufacturing and marketing as well as engineering) and to lead competition in

---

[13] Lewis, *op. cit.*, p. 34.

aggressively applying such knowledge in the creation and marketing of new products.

In approaching its measurement of product leadership, GE took into account not only innovation, but also the ability to capitalize on new ideas at the right time and at cost—depending on quality desired—that would appeal to the customer and make a new product a success. Granting that much of this evaluation was subjective, the company periodically tested existing and new products for leadership.

Personnel development   In the fifth area, the company recognized that, because competent people at all levels are necessary for business growth, this must be planned systematically. GE objectives in personnel development required (1) all employees to perform on their current assignments to the limit of their capabilities; and (2) an adequate supply of promotable manpower for new and more complex job assignments as well as for filling vacancies as they occur.[14]

Perhaps the best index to good performance here was whether or not qualified people were available when needed. The basic index was supplemented by personnel inventories (particularly those emphasizing promotability), record of promotions from within, the extent of advancement traceable to development programs, and the adequacy of available manpower as compared to requirements.

Employee attitudes   GE claimed to use employee attitudes as a key area of control, because (1) they reflect the extent to which managers have acted responsibly in satisfying personnel needs and goals of employees; (2) they play a major part in the appraisal of the company in a plant community; and (3) an employee attitude of active and willing cooperation is of great importance to business success. Thus, this area included not only the employee in *his* job, but also the company in the community.

Employee attitudes toward the company could be measured by such generally accepted indicators as labor turnover, absenteeism, safety records, and the extent that employees make suggestions for improvement. Another means of measuring was to approach employees directly through surveys.

Public responsibility   The seventh area that the company aimed to measure was its conduct as a good citizen. The large industrial corporation is an institution responsible to the social, economic, and political environment in which it operates. A component of the larger complex, each integrated division, operating essentially as a smaller and separate business, must make its contribution. In this area GE did not imply that an economic enterprise should be transformed into a welfare institution, but rather that *one* measurement with long-run implication is how seriously the company regards its public responsibilities in conducting its business.

[14] See R. W. Lewis, "Is the Measurement of Net Profit Enough?" Address to Ohio Society of Certified Public Accountants (Sept. 16, 1958).

To get this index, a variety of approaches were aimed at employees, at vendors, and at the plant and business communities. With respect to employees, measurements included such factors as job and family security, wages and working conditions, and standard of living. With respect to vendors, there might be an attitude survey comparing vendor appraisals of the company with vendor appraisals of competitors. Plant community standing can be ascertained by surveys supplemented by quantitative data on comparison of community wage rates, number of applications for work, local purchases, charitable contributions, and participation of leading employees in non-company organizations in the community. Position in the business community was ascertained by studying how the company was regarded by retailers and competitors.

Integration of short- and long-range goals   The eighth key area aimed at ascertaining how well managers integrate their short-range planning with long-range plans and goals. Control through this area emphasized the extent and nature of each manager's long-range plans and goals, how well outlined and specific they were, and what accomplishments were expected at what costs. The company expected that, by merely making sure that long-range plans were made and reviewed, short-range plans would reflect longer-range goals. At least, in reviewing short-range plans, managers would be able to gauge whether this balance was being achieved.

A Comprehensive System   General Electric was not able to develop desired measurements for all these areas, whose breadth and importance, nevertheless, are significant and impressive. Even though a company might wish to use other areas in measuring over-all performance, measurements over so broad a territory as incorporated in these eight areas should give an excellent appraisal of the management of an entire company, a subsidiary, or a division.

There might be some concern that this wide-ranging control technique, in which seven of the eight key areas did not immediately deal with profits, could dull the sharpness of the profit motive. If, however, it is realized that each of these areas is closely related to a company's success in its unavoidable political, economic, and social environment, detraction from profit goals should not occur. In other words, only if employee attitudes and public responsibility become ends in themselves might they water down into other ends. But this need not happen. Those who measure over-all performance via key areas need enough insight and judgment to view the results as interrelated in their effect on the company's basic goals.

THE ENTERPRISE SELF-AUDIT

J. O. McKinsey, who achieved an outstanding position in the realm of management approximately four decades ago, came to the conclusion that a business enterprise should periodically make a "management audit," an appraisal of the enterprise in all its aspects, in the light of its present and probable future environment. This type of audit has been referred to by Goetz[15] as "much the most comprehensive and powerful of these problem-seeking techniques" because it seeks in an over-all way "to discover and correct errors of management." Although McKinsey called this a management audit, it is actually an audit of the entire enterprise.

The enterprise self-audit appraises the company's position to determine where it is, where it is heading under present programs, what its objectives should be, and whether revised plans are needed to meet those objectives. In most enterprises of all kinds, objectives and policies become obsolete. If the enterprise does not change course to suit the changing social, technical, and political environment, it loses markets, personnel, standing, and other requirements for continued existence. The enterprise self-audit is designed to force managers to meet this situation.

Procedure The self-audit may be made annually or, more likely, once every three or five years. The first step is to study the outlook of the firm's industry. What are recent trends and prospects? What is the outlook for the product? Where are the markets? What technical developments are affecting the industry? How may demand be changed? What political or social factors may affect the industry?

A second step in the self-audit is to appraise the position of the firm in the industry, both currently and in prospect. Has the company maintained its position? Has it expanded its influence and markets? Or has competition reduced its position? What is the competitive outlook? To answer such questions, the company may undertake studies on competitor standing, development of competition, customer reactions, and other factors bearing on its position within the industry.

On the basis of such studies, the next logical step for the company would be to reexamine its basic objectives and major policies to decide where the company wishes to be in, say, five or ten years. After this reexamination, the company may audit its organization, policies, procedures, programs, facilities, financial position, personnel, and management. This examination should show up any deviations from objectives and facilitate the revision of many major and minor plans.

Contribution Most top business managers do not think in terms of the company's future or evaluate over-all performance in relation to long-range objectives. The enterprise self-audit has the distinct advantage of forcing them to appraise over-all performance in terms not only of current goals but also of future ones. Top managers who expend mental effort for this kind of audit will almost certainly be well repaid and will be surprised at how many day-to-day decisions will be simplified by a clear picture of where the business is attempting to go.

[15] Billy E. Goetz, *Management Planning and Control* (New York: McGraw-Hill Book Company, 1949), p. 167. For a discussion of the management audit, see pp. 723–731 in the present book.

FOR DISCUSSION

1. Why do most controls of over-all performance tend to be financial in nature? Should they be? What else do you suggest?

2. Profit and loss control is defective in that it does not emphasize return on investment; the latter is defective in that it places too great an emphasis on present results with possible endangering of future results. Discuss.

3. What kind of internal audit program would you recommend for a company that wants to use it as a constructive force for improving the quality and effectiveness of management? How would you organize and staff it?

4. In applying rate of return on investment as a control tool, would you favor using an undepreciated or a depreciated asset base?

5. Do you believe that the centralized control unit can be made to work effectively?

6. J. O. McKinsey's enterprise self-audit has seldom been used in industry. Why do you feel this has happened? Do you believe this device would be worth its cost?

SELECTED REFERENCES

American Management Association: *A Program of Financial Planning and Control: The Monsanto Chemical Company,* Financial Management Series No. 103, New York: American Management Association, 1953.

————: *How H. J. Heinz Manages Its Financial Planning and Controls,* Financial Management Series No. 106, New York: American Management Association, 1953.

————: *How the du Pont Organization Appraises Its Performance,* Financial Management Series No. 94, New York: American Management Association, 1950.

————: "Return on Investment: Tool of Modern Management," in *Improved Tools of Financial Management,* Financial Management Series No. 111, pp. 3–30, New York: American Management Association, 1956.

Anderson, D. R., and L. A. Schmidt: *Practical Controllership,* Homewood, Ill.: Richard D. Irwin, Inc., 1961.

Brink, V. E.: *Internal Auditing,* New York: The Ronald Press Company, 1951.

————: "The Controller's Management Role," *The Controller,* vol. 28, pp. 403ff. (September, 1960).

Buchele, R. B.: *Business Policy in Growing Firms: A Manual for Evaluation,* San Francisco: Chandler Publishing Company, 1967.

————: "How to Evaluate a Firm," *California Management Review,* vol. 5, no. 1, pp. 5–16 (Fall, 1962).

Controllership Foundation: *Planning, Managing, and Measuring the Business: A Case Study of Planning and Control at General Electric,* New York: Controllership Foundation, 1955.

Executive Committee Control Charts, Wilmington, Del.: E. I. du Pont de Nemours and Company, 1959.

Goetz, B. E.: *Management Planning and Control,* pp. 167–175, New York: McGraw-Hill Book Company, 1949.

Heckert, J. B., and J. D. Willson: *Business Budgeting and Control,* 2d ed., New York: The Ronald Press Company, 1955.

Jerome, W. T., III: *Executive Control: The Catalyst,* chaps. 13–15, New York: John Wiley & Sons, Inc., 1961.

Lamperti, F. A., and J. B. Thurston: *Internal Auditing for Management,* Englewood Cliffs, N.J.: Prentice-Hall, Inc., 1953.

Miller, G. G.: "The Controller's Relationship to Planning," *The Controller,* vol. 27, no. 12, pp. 552–557 (December, 1959).

National Accounting Association: *Return on Capital as a Guide to Managerial Decisions,* Research Report No. 35, New York: National Accounting Association, 1959.

Plummer, G. F., and G. Moller: "The Financial Executive: His Role in Corporate Organization and in Overall Company Planning," *The Controller,* vol. 30, no. 1, pp. 16ff. (January, 1962).

Ravencroft, E. A., "Return on Investment," *Harvard Business Review,* vol. 38, no. 2, pp. 97–109 (March–April, 1960).

Shillinglaw, G.: "Divisional Performance Review: An Extension of Budgeting Control," in C. P. Bonini et al., *Management Controls,* pp. 149–163, New York: McGraw-Hill Book Company, 1964.

———: "Guides to Internal Profit Measurement," *Harvard Business Review,* vol. 35, no. 2, pp. 82–94 (March–April, 1957).

Walsh, F. J.: *Internal Auditing,* New York: National Industrial Conference Board, Inc., 1964.

control of management quality

The preceding analysis of control stresses the variety of approaches that managers follow to make results conform to plans. If managers believed plans would be automatically accomplished, control would be unnecessary.

At the base of control is the fact that the outcome of plans is influenced by people. For instance, a poor educational system cannot be controlled by criticizing its product, the unfortunate graduate; a factory turning out inferior products cannot be controlled by their consignment to the scrap heap, or a firm plagued with customer complaints cannot be controlled by ignoring the complainers. Responsibility for controllable deviations lies with whoever has made unfortunate decisions. Any hope of abolishing unsatisfactory results lies in changing the *future* actions of the responsible person, through additional training, modification of procedures, or new policy. This is the crux of controlling the quality of management.

There are two ways of seeing that the responsible person modifies future action. The normal procedure is to trace the cause of an unsatisfactory result back to the person responsible for it and get him to correct his practices. This may be called "indirect control." The alternative is to develop better managers who will skillfully apply principles and thus eliminate undesirable results caused by poor management. This is called "direct control."

INDIRECT CONTROL

In every enterprise hundreds, and even thousands, of standards are developed to compare the actual output of goods or services—in terms of quantity, quality, time, and cost—with plans. Excessive deviation from standards may necessitate indirect control, as defined above. A negative deviation indicates—in terms of cost, price, personnel, man-hours, or machine-hours—that performance is less than good or normal or standard, and that results are not conforming to plans.

Causes of Negative Deviations from Standards The causes of negative deviations will often determine whether control measures are possible. Although an incorrect standard may cause deviation, if the standard is correct, plans may fail because of (1) uncertainty, and (2) lack of knowledge, experience, or judgment.

Uncertainty Elements affecting a given plan may be grouped into facts, risks, and uncertainty. Facts are known, such as number of employees, costs, or machine capacity. Considerably less is known about the element of risk. Insurable risks are readily converted to factual status through the payment of a known premium. Noninsurable risks are included in a business decision on the basis of probability. The total of facts and risks is small, compared to the element of uncertainty, which includes everything about which nothing is certain. For instance, the success of a plan to manufacture aluminum pistons will depend not only on known facts and risks but on such uncertainties as future world conditions, competition of known and yet unknown metals, and power technology that may eliminate all piston prime movers. Not even probability can be estimated for the uncertain factors, yet they can wreck a plan.

Managerial errors caused by unforeseeable events cannot be corrected. The fixing of personal responsibility by indirect control techniques is of no avail in such situations.

Lack of knowledge, experience, or judgment Plans may misfire and negative deviations occur when men appointed to managerial posts lack the necessary background. The higher in the organizational structure a manager is placed, the broader the knowledge and experience he needs. Long years as an engineer, a sales manager, a production executive, or a controller may be inadequate in qualifying a man to be a general officer.

Good judgment marks the mature man who intelligently applies his educational and business experience and is known for his common sense. Unfortunately, some top managers who have gone through the motions of formal education and practical experience seem incapable of sound decisions and display poor judgment about such matters as product lines, expansion policy, innovation, and decentralization. At the top level, the chance of correction through separation from the firm is very small. On the other hand, continuing errors of judgment at middle and lower levels are often followed by demotion, transfer, or separation.

If the cause of error is poor judgment, whether due to inadequate education or experience or to failure to use appropriate information in decision making, correction can be made. The manager may improve his education, be transferred to acquire broader experience, or be cautioned to take better stock of the situation before making decisions.

From this discussion, an interesting question arises. How often can negative deviations from standard be corrected? At present, little is known about this. But it is vital. If, for instance, only 40 per cent of errors in decision making are subject to correction, then the effort made to place responsibility is of no avail 60 per cent of the time. Such a ratio is likely to place on indirect controls an insuperable burden of expense.

Questionable Assumptions In addition to its cost, the shortcomings of indirect control rest on certain questionable assumptions: (1) that performance can be measured; (2) that personal responsibility for performance exists; (3) that the time expenditure is warranted; (4) that mistakes can be discovered in time; and (5) that the person responsible will take corrective steps.

That performance can be measured At first glance, almost any enterprise appears to be a jungle of controls. Input, output, cost, price, time, complaints, and quality are subject to numerous standards; and the standards may be expressed in terms of time, weight, tolerances, averages, ratios, dollars, and indexes. In terms of usefulness, the standards may be correct, acceptable, or merely better than nothing. Close analysis will often reveal shortcomings of two types. In the first place, the ability of a manager to develop potential managers, the effectiveness of research, the amount of creativity, foresight, and judgment in decision making can hardly be measured accurately.

The second shortcoming concerns the location of the control. Managers know that critical stages exist in acquiring input factors, manipulating them to produce a finished product, and selling and delivering the product. In a factory operation, for example, critical stages would include receiving inspection, inspection for each assembly process, shipping, and billing. These are critical because effective control here will minimize costs. No amount of control at other points can make up for lack of control at these stages and yet these points are often missed.

That personal responsibility exists Sometimes no manager is responsible for poor results. For example, government restrictions imposed in 1950 on the use of copper resulted in many poor-quality products, such as automobile bumpers. Scarcity of a particular fuel may necessitate use of less economical sources of power. And markets may shrink for reasons unconnected with the firm.

That the time expenditure is warranted Whether a manager undertakes the inquiry himself or assigns it to others, executive time must be spent in ferreting out causes of poor results. Large scrap losses, for example, may call for meetings attended by men representing quality control, production planning, engineering, purchasing, and manufacturing. Besides, passage of time may make the recall of facts quite difficult. These drawbacks may convince the manager that the cost of investigation exceeds any benefit he may derive. This often precludes investigation of clear violations of standards.

That mistakes can be discovered in time   Discovery of deviations from plans often comes too late for effective action. Although true control can be applied only to future action, most controls depend on historical data—all that a manager has available. The manager should interpret such data in terms of their implications for the future.

The costs of errors in major areas—such as cash or inventories—have led to the use of forecasts as the basis for control. Since forecasts are difficult to make and subject to error, the natural tendency to rely on historical reports seriously blocks adequate controls. No manager really has control unless he can correct mistakes. And the best way to correct mistakes is to avoid them.

That the person responsible will take corrective steps   Fixing the responsibility may not lead to correction. High production costs, for example, might be traced back to a sales manager who insists that "slight" product modifications will make selling easier and that this involves "really" no change in a production run. If the sales manager is a member of top management, a subordinate investigator may be intimidated; the president may attempt to mediate between sales and production executives; and the sales manager will remain unreconstructed. Although great effort may be made to correct subordinate managers, it is sometimes very difficult to correct superior executives.

THE PRINCIPLE OF DIRECT CONTROL

The principle of direct control embraces the idea that personal responsibility for negative deviations from standards can be fixed by applying principles of management. It draws a sharp distinction between performance reports, essential in any case, and determining whether managers act in accordance with established principles in carrying out their functions.

It is possible that the principle of direct control was vaguely perceived by Fayol, who possessed a mature and practical understanding of management. In a 1925 interview with the editors of *Chronique Social de France*, Fayol said that the best method of looking at an organization and determining the necessary improvements was "to study the administrative apparatus. . . . One can ascertain immediately that forecasting and planning, organization, command, co-ordination, and control are properly provided for, that is to say, that the undertaking is well administered."[1]

The extensive adoption of direct control must await a wider understanding of managerial principles and functions of managers and also of management philosophy. While such an understanding is not achieved easily, it can be gained in universities, through on-the-job experience, through coaching by the superior, and by means of constant self-education.

---

[1] Quoted by L. Urwick in his foreword to *General and Industrial Management* (New York: Pitman Publishing Corporation, 1949), p. x.

Assumptions of the Principle of Direct Control   The desirability of direct control rests upon four valid assumptions: (1) that qualified managers make a minimum of errors, (2) that managerial performance can be measured, (3) that management principles are useful diagnostic tools in measuring management performance, and (4) that the application of management principles can be evaluated.

That qualified managers make a minimum of errors   J. P. Morgan has been often quoted as saying that the decisions of good managers are right two-thirds of the time. However, an accurate analysis of the quality of decision making should not rely upon quantity of errors but be concerned with the nature of the error. As J. Paul Getty once told one of the authors, his concern in his world-wide empire was not percentage of time an executive was right or wrong; he could be wrong only 2 per cent of the time and seriously endanger a company by these errors if they were critical to the company's success. Managers can logically be held strictly accountable for the performance of their functions, because these functions should be undertaken in conformance with the principles of management. However, accountability cannot be exacted for errors attributable to factors beyond the manager's authority or his ability reasonably to forecast the future.

That management quality can be measured   An approach to a proper evaluation of managerial performance was set forth in Chapter 22. Management assignments contain built-in controls which superiors may use to evaluate the ability of subordinate managers. The performance of his group is an over-all measure of the total efficiency of a subordinate manager. The authors know of many business firms and some government agencies that have applied this procedure successfully.

That management principles may be used to measure performance   The chief purpose of this book has been to draw together principles of management and relate them to management functions. As was stated in previous chapters, the completeness and certitude of management principles vary considerably, depending largely upon the state of knowledge concerning the managerial functions. There is, for instance, greater general acceptance of some of the principles of organizing than there is of the principles relating to other functions. Nevertheless, the authors are convinced that the principles set forth here are useful in measuring managerial performance even though their statement will undoubtedly be refined and better verified by future experts.

That the application of management principles can be evaluated   Evaluation can provide for periodic measurement of the skill with which the manager applies management principles to his five functions. This can be done not only by judgment of performance against the principles as stated but by casting the principles into a series of fairly objective questions.

Advantages Directly controlling the quality of managers and thus minimizing errors has several advantages. In the first place, greater accuracy is achieved in assigning personal responsibility. The periodic evaluation of managers is practically certain to uncover deficiencies and should provide for specific training to eliminate them.

In the second place, direct control hastens corrective action and makes it more effective. Knowing that errors will be uncovered in a periodic evaluation, managers will try to determine their responsibility and make voluntary corrections. For example, a report of excessive scrap will cause the department foreman to determine quickly whether the excess was due to poor direction of subordinates or to other factors. The same report will cause the chief inspector to look into whether his men acted properly, the purchasing agent to check the material purchased with engineering specifications, and the engineers to determine whether appropriate material was specified. All this action is immediate and voluntary. Any manager who concludes privately that he was in error will do his best to prevent a recurrence, for his future is in jeopardy.

The third advantage of direct control is its potentiality for lightening the burden now caused by indirect control, largely of determining personal responsibility. This is a net gain, since the periodic evaluation of managers is already part of staffing. The amount of potential savings is as yet unknown, although it must be considerable.

Last, the psychological advantage of direct control is impressive. The feeling of subordinates that superiors do not rate fairly, rely on hunch and personality, and use improper measuring standards is almost universal, but direct control removes this feeling. Subordinate managers know what is expected of them, understand the nature of managerial functions, and feel a close relationship between performance and measurement. The intelligent superior manager will reciprocate this feeling, because he will know what he is expected to evaluate in subordinates and will have a technique for doing so.

Direct Control Applied to Managerial Functions The principles outlined in each section of this book may be used as standards in objective quality control of managers. By framing these principles in the form of objective questions, even though most of the answers will have qualitative elements, much subjective evaluation can be removed, and the questioner can establish whether managers are operating essentially in accordance with principles.

Planning A high degree of exactitude can be reached by a superior who wishes to determine the planning ability of a subordinate manager, because planning is a logical process, calling for clear definition of objectives, thorough understanding of planning premises, and careful analysis of alternatives. Evidence as to whether the subordinate has carried out this process is easy to get. The existence of alternative plans also will reflect the care and scientific attitude with which a plan was chosen. The superior can check whether harmony exists between plans, whether attention has been given to building flexibility into operating plans, and whether they are reviewed periodically. Estimates based upon these specific points can be highly valuable in measuring knowledge of planning principles and ability to use them.

Organizing To determine the organizing skill of subordinates, a superior will methodically check grouping of activities and authority delegations to see how much they contribute to departmental goals. The departmental chart will reveal information on the first point. Grouping can be checked against the guides for associating activities, and the reasons for any nonconformance can be evaluated. Authority delegations can be compared with assigned duties to determine whether they jibe. At the same time, the clarity, completeness, and timeliness of the authority and the duties can be determined. Finally, the superior will evaluate the organization balance, its ability to facilitate leadership, and the span of management. These are important for measuring the subordinate's understanding of the relationships of those who report to him; here will be shown any propensity to create so little organization as to be ineffective or so much as to delay action and limit initiative. The superior may wish to develop scales for reporting on these points.

Examples of appropriate questions to be raised here are: Does the manager look at an organization unit as being independent, or does he consider how it contributes to company or division goals? Does he analyze whether the unit is set up in a way to minimize costs, or even whether the unit is necessary at all? Is this span of management too large, or too small? Why? What is he doing to make his span more efficient? Does he delegate authority in accordance with results expected? Do his subordinates understand their authority delegations? Does he make decisions that should be made by his subordinates? Does he hold people responsible for more than their authority covers, or less? Do any of his subordinates report to more than one superior, and, if so, are the reasons good enough to offset the disadvantages?

Staffing The authority of a manager to select his subordinates is affected by the degree to which the staffing function of the firm is formalized. In large-scale enterprises, recruitment, selection and training, and minimum qualifications are usually predetermined. In small and middle-sized firms, each manager may have to invent and implement staffing procedures.

The superior wishing to assess the staffing ability of his subordinates will first examine the job profile or description for each person reporting to the subordinate to see whether it is up-to-date and its specifications clear and pertinent. If selection is not formally predetermined by company policy, the superior will inquire carefully into the subordinate's operations to see whether they are logical, practical, and in line with accepted practice.

Another point for evaluation is whether the subordinate temporizes in filling positions. Procrastination and temporary assignments can be fatal to an operation. The alternative is not a hasty decision. Rather, it involves the weighing of relevant factors and making a prompt decision. A show of firmness at this point is vital to morale.

In looking for a balanced staff, the superior must proceed with special care. Balance is difficult to define. It results from such personal characteristics of a group as their age distribution, varied experience, and relative promotability. A balanced staff of managers was described by L. C. Sorrell in an early class lecture as composed of "those who will achieve, those who are achieving, and those who have achieved." The dangers of lack of balance are obvious. A group of sexagenarians may possess wisdom but little drive or imagination. A group in their prime may be exceedingly good in the short run but dangerous to the long-run welfare of the firm by failing to provide for future managerial needs. And a group of young men tends to lack the wisdom that tempers undue risk taking.

The superior will assess his subordinate in developing promotable personnel. Enterprises of varying size will weigh this factor differently. Large firms can place qualified men, but small firms can rarely satisfy the legitimate demand for promotion. Consequently, the superior in the large firm will expect subordinates to develop a planned program for training their successors. No matter that such people may be promoted to managerial posts in other departments. The important thing is that the firm's future is tied to its success in developing promotable people, and every manager must carry his share of the training.

Appropriate questions to be raised in controlling quality of the staffing function are: Do the positions a manager fills reflect definite plans and objectives? Are job descriptions clear, the authority for performance clearly in the position description and in the manager's mind? Does the manager appraise a subordinate's performance by definite standards? Does he coach, and, if so, how well? Does he develop promotable subordinates? Does he promote on the basis of the best available man to fill the position? Does he have means of recognizing the best available man?

Directing Determining the manager's ability to direct requires extreme caution, because there are many ways to guide and supervise. Indeed, choice of method often depends on the personalities of all involved, including the superior manager.

One point of inquiry concerns the skill with which a manager guides his subordinates. A second point concerns the extent of communication both inside and outside the department. The manager who insists that his subordinates know the relationship between their activities and those of others throughout the enterprise, who insists that these be coordinated and superiors kept informed, will find his ability to direct rated highly.

In evaluating directing ability, the appraiser also looks to see whether a motivation system—which meets the ego and self-development needs of subordinates and provides both positive and negative incentives—is influencing subordinates to work zealously. The manager as leader may stress respect for unusual abilities, opportunities to feed self-esteem, chances to do special work, or pride in belonging to a successful operation. Thus, successful leadership must exhibit skill in using a motivational system.

Finally, the quality of direction can be rated on such matters as the manager's intelligent use of the grapevine, his insistence upon a high standard of business ethics, and his ability to develop loyalty and integrity in subordinates.

The following are examples of questions which involve principles of direction: Does the manager, in guiding and supervising, make plans and goals clear to subordinates? Does he teach rather than just tell? Does he inspire such confidence that his subordinates feel that their own interests are served by following his guidance? Does he communicate freely and clearly with his subordinates? Does he make sure that they truly comprehend his instructions and other communications? Is he aware that interests unrelated to their jobs are important to subordinates? Does he use different direction techniques for different situations and different people?

Controlling Since controlling is related to the determination of success in planning, the superior, in judging a subordinate manager's ability to control, can check the standards used to measure results of planned activity. Significant standards, properly located, which avoid overlapping and obsolescence, will reflect good judgment.

The superior will examine his subordinate's attention to the review and revision of standards typically based upon performance, in terms of cost, output, man-hours, or profitability. The relativity of standards tends to be forgotten by engineer, accountant, and statistician who may view them as absolutes. A good manager must demonstrate his understanding of the nature of standards by being continually on the alert for evidence of their questionable applicability.

Examples of the principles of control framed as questions follow: Do the manager's control techniques detect deviations from plans clearly enough for corrective action to be possible? Are they pointed toward the more important, or critical, areas of control? Are the controls tailored to the manager's position, plans, and needs? Do they cost more than they should or interfere unduly with the work of subordinates? Are steps being taken to minimize the necessity for indirect control by improving the quality of subordinates? Are objective standards, quantitative or qualitative, being developed as much as possible? Is attention being given primarily to exceptions at strategic points? Will the controls remain effective in the face of unplanned events? Does the manager recognize that control techniques must be dynamic, and does he review them periodically?

MANAGEMENT AUDITS

The application of the principle of direct control leads fundamentally in two similar directions. One has been stimulated by the improved programs in recent years to appraise individual managers on the basis of performance against verifiable goals; these programs have been discussed above in

Chapter 22. But, as was pointed out earlier, these measure performance in the setting and accomplishment of enterprise and department objectives and, through their certain weaknesses, is showing the importance of supplementing these techniques by additionally appraising managers *as managers*. While little progress has yet been made in this direction, a few companies are experimenting with tools of this kind, and one of the authors is undertaking such an experimental program in a business corporation.

Another direction in which the principle of direct control has led is in the developing interest in management audits. This approach in general aims at evaluating the entire management system of an enterprise or a division. While little progress has actually been made in such management audits, some pioneering programs have been undertaken, certain specialists in the field are working in this direction, and the Department of Defense has approached the concept of internal audit in appraising companies for the receipt of major contracts.

American Institute of Management Program   One of the earliest programs of management audit was that developed by the American Institute of Management. This institute, founded and operated by Jackson Martindell and active in management investigation, developed some years ago a procedure for direct control. This includes an extensive questionnaire based on Martindell's management principles and designed to test the extent to which a firm follows these principles.[2]

Martindell's original program   In his original book, published in 1950, Martindell writes of the fundamental of management as "unflinching control."[3] He thus saw control as the essence of what a management auditor must search out, and its achievement as depending on the following principles:[4]

1. Thorough knowledge of a company's officers is indispensable for appraisal purposes.
2. An outside board of directors is to be preferred.
3. Where authority is concentrated and who exercises it are questions of paramount importance.
4. The product-division type of organization is a true expression of large-scale business.
5. Teamwork is of the essence in the modern corporation.
6. Financial management should always lean toward conservation.
7. Efficiency and production may determine the whole future of the enterprise.

[2] Jackson Martindell, *The Scientific Appraisal of Management* (New York: Harper & Row, Publishers, Incorporated, 1950).

[3] *Ibid.,* p. 267.

[4] This formulation of principles is deduced from *The Scientific Appraisal of Management,* where they are described without exact formulation; it is believed to be a fair reflection of Martindell's thinking.

8. Management gains by giving others the main fruits of improved technology.
9. Management must foresee changes in its market.
10. Management should strive to minimize distribution costs.
11. Profit may be the corporate objective, but service is the means of achieving it.

The questionnaire   From his principles of management, Martindell constructed 301 questions[5] to be employed in analyzing a firm. The questions are put to corporate officers and to other inside, as well as outside, sources; inside information is compared with outside information in making judgments. In order to achieve the Institute's designation, "excellent management," a firm's score must fall within a high range of points.

The questionnaire has ten classifications: economic function, corporate structure, health of earnings, fairness to stockholders, research and development, directorate analysis, fiscal policies, production efficiency, sales vigor, and executive evaluation. The number of questions under each class varies from twelve in the section "health of earnings" to fifty-nine in "production efficiency." They vary from one extreme to another in terms of objectivity, generality, and the possibility of developing measurable information, so it is difficult to report an adequate sample, but the following give some idea:[6]

Has the company ever engaged a registered lobbyist? In what legislatures? Has there ever been a contest for stock control? What were the circumstances and the outcome?
What per cent of the department's work is basic or fundamental research (not focused on solution of specific problems)? What per cent is engineering (process) research? What per cent is analysis and/or testing?
What studies have been initiated by the board?
What per cent of profit on merchandise is considered desirable? What overhead is allocated in arriving at this? Has this changed over the past ten years? Is there a profit-sharing plan? Please describe it.
Does the company engage in co-operative advertising? If so, please describe policy. What proportion of advertising budget is allocated to co-operative advertising?
How many hours a week, on the average, has the president devoted to business in the past month? Each vice-president?

The apparent objectivity of this method of evaluating management can be misleading. Not only is the assignment of "points" to categories and questions arbitrary, but the evaluation of answers tends to be subjective. Furthermore, practice between industries and even between firms in an industry varies widely. A public utility uses a capital and debt structure entirely different from that of other industries; some merchandising firms find that

[5] *Manual of Excellent Managements* (New York: American Institute of Management, 1957).
[6] *Ibid.*, pp. 253–265.

cooperative advertising works well for them, while others do not; some firms find that formalized management development programs improve the quality of their managers, while others find nothing but disappointment in such programs. In this situation, any attempt to measure on the basis of the evaluator's bias is bound to give nothing but a personal view of the efficiency of the enterprise.

The revised program Many of the critical questions and comments aimed at Martindell's original attempt at scientific appraisal of management have been answered in a revision of his program,[7] which is nevertheless still heavily investment-oriented. Out of a total of 10,000 points, he allows only 2,200 for executive evaluation, 500 for corporate structure, and 800 for directorate analysis, for a total of 3,500 points, in contrast to a total of 4,100 points for economic function, health of earnings, service to stockholders, research and development, and fiscal policies. The remaining 2,400 points are assigned to sales vigor and production efficiency.

However, in his revised program, Martindell is far less dogmatic about some of his basic guidelines for excellent management. For example, he properly makes the key standard for organization structure the extent to which it meets a company's needs, and he recognizes that closely knit functional organization may be as suitable to one company as organization along product lines is to another. Likewise, in setting standards for corporate fiscal policies, Martindell recognizes that various sources of capital may be employed if they fit the company's needs for sound and healthy growth. On the other hand, he has not moved from his original standard that more than half of the board of directors should be outside directors, not salaried executives.

In executive evaluation, Martindell emphasizes three basic qualities.[8] The manager must have ability—"specialized knowledge and skills, intelligence, and creative talent, according to the field, on the one hand, and insight and skill to work with and through people, on the other." In the second place, he must have industry—"the desire to apply his abilities." And, finally, he must have integrity—"honesty to himself, his employer, and his associates." In addition to these qualities, Martindell emphasizes management development and objective executive selection as important to the well-managed firm.

While Martindell's American Institute of Management program leaves much to be desired, its pioneering nature deserves praise. It has focused attention on control of over-all management and on the results that can be expected from "excellent management."

Moreover, Martindell's position that those investment-oriented areas he weights so heavily are evidences of an intelligently managed company is not

---

[7] Jackson Martindell, *The Appraisal of Management* (New York: Harper & Row, Publishers, Incorporated, 1962).

[8] *Ibid.,* p. 123.

unreasonable. Although true in many instances, however, this is not always true. There have been many examples of poorly managed companies with high earnings in a growing industry, companies that have prospered despite the inferior quality of management, although perhaps not for long. Management quality almost invariably has an eventual impact on the earnings statement.

It appears to the authors that it is better to appraise management purely on the excellence of its managers, excluding, to the extent possible, fortuitous circumstances where profits are made despite poor management. Even for the investor, this preference provides a better means of prophesying future potentials.

Questionnaire Check Lists   Occasionally questionnaires have appeared in print that managers are encouraged to answer in order to determine their personal effectiveness.[9] The valuations of the answers usually run from poor to outstanding or on a numbered scale. The former method makes no provision for weighting, while the latter method weights each question by assigning a value to each item.

Since these check lists vary in quality, the best that can be said of some is that they do no harm and may conceivably do good. If the check list reflects the fundamentals of good management practice, if the manager estimates honestly, analyzes his poor performance, plans to correct faults and generally improve, and carries out his plan, self-appraisal can be advantageous.

The shortcomings of relying upon the disclosures of the completed check list arise from the subject matter covered, the way questions are worded, and the difficulty of designing adequate forms. Assumptions made by the author of a check list about the subject matter are decisive in their effect on the questionnaire. For example, someone who feels that management is mainly concerned with human relations will emphasize these at the expense of other factors. The necessity to cover the several managerial functions evenly is of primary importance.

Again, the question-and-answer form encounters difficulties of semantics and complex functioning. Words like "responsibility," "delegation," or "centralization" are variously understood. The author of the questionnaire frames his questions on the basis that his understanding is generally acceptable. Without a glossary of terms, there seems little possibility of achieving a common understanding. Or the questionnaire may employ single or multiple-choice answers on the assumption that there is one correct response, when such may not be the case. The correct action in a given situation may involve several steps not mutually exclusive. College professors who have

---

[9] See, for example, "How Good an Executive Are You?" *Modern Industry,* vol. 23, no. 5, pp. 48–49 (May, 1952). See also Metropolitan Life Insurance Company, *Outline for a Management Audit* (New York: Policy Holders' Service Bureau, Metropolitan Life Insurance Company, 1947).

wrestled with objective tests know only too well the numerous pitfalls encountered in devising appropriate questions.

Other Approaches to Management Audit   A comprehensive study of the management audit is one made by William P. Leonard and published in 1962.[10] Although this study deals more with methods of organizing, initiating, interpreting, and presenting a management audit than with the content of the audit itself, and it is valuable from this point of view, it does indicate what a management audit should cover.[11] Leonard's check list deals with a number of searching questions on the subjects of (1) plans and objectives (for example, "Have definite plans and objectives been established?"); (2) organization structure (for example, "Is there any overlapping or duplication of functions?"); (3) policies, systems, and procedures (for example, "Are the policies positive, clear, and understandable?"); (4) department personnel (for example, "What is the rate of turnover?"); (5) layout and physical equipment (for example, "Is the office laid out in a manner to get maximum utilization of space and efficient work areas?"); and (6) operations and methods of control (for example, "What consideration has been given to the adequacy, clarity, and promptness of management reports?"). While the suggested check list and audit approach made by Leonard does not distinguish carefully between operating-performance factors and management factors, and while many significant management factors are overlooked or are not gone into in any depth, it is an interesting starting point for anyone wishing to study the possibilities of a management audit.

One of the more interesting approaches toward developing a technique of management audit is that suggested by William T. Greenwood.[12] Although his approach is really a mixture of an enterprise performance audit and a management audit, he does attempt systematically to evaluate management performance in the framework of such operating areas as long-range planning, marketing, and production. Thus, in his audit of the area of marketing, he includes in his check list questions for information on goals, strategies, policies, and marketing functions (selling, salesmen, advertising and sales promotion, marketing research, transportation, and storage) with emphasis on the what, how, and how well in these areas. But he also has questions delving into organizing, planning, and control, with some very perceptive and pointed inquiries on how these functions are performed in the marketing area and how their effectiveness is evaluated.

Another interesting development approaching the nature of a management audit is the activity of the Department of Defense in evaluating companies bidding on major defense contracts. Not only is the Department

---

[10] *The Management Audit* (Englewood Cliffs, N.J.: Prentice-Hall, Inc., 1962).

[11] *Ibid.*, pp. 120–126.

[12] *A Management Audit System* (Athens, Ohio: Ohio University, 1964). See excerpts from this work in W. T. Greenwood, *Management and Organizational Behavioral Theories: An Interdisciplinary Approach* (Cincinnati: South-Western Publishing Company, 1965), pp. 868–880.

interested in engineering concepts and capabilities, probable price, and delivery promises, but it has delved deeply into the kind of organization and management the company has and, particularly, the company's plans to manage the defense contract should it be the successful bidder. The authors have seen cases where this investigation was very penetrating and information was required from the bidder, and audited by the buyer, in virtually every function of managing. Among other things, the bidder was required to submit his proposed organization structure, his precise staffing in key positions, and his approach to and methods of planning and control.

That this makes sense from the standpoint of the Department of Defense is clear. After all, in a major program there is almost certainly no single factor more important to economical and dependable performance than the quality of the company's management. Also, an interesting and beneficial result of this evaluation by the Department of Defense, particularly after word is circulated that a certain company lost a contract because of management deficiencies, is that a number of defense contractors have overhauled their complete management system to remove these weaknesses.

The Certified Management Audit An interesting possibility for the future is the development of a certified management audit, an independent appraisal of a company's management by an outside firm. For years investors and others have relied on an independent certified accounting audit designed to make certain that the company's records and reports reflect sound accounting principles. From the standpoint of the investors and even from that of the managers and those desiring to work for the company, an independent audit of management quality would be extremely important. It is probably not too much to say that an investor would get more value from a certified management audit than from a certified accounting audit, since the future of a company is likely to depend more on the quality of its management than on any other single factor.

To assure objectivity, the certified management audit should be the responsibility of a recognized outside firm, staffed with individuals qualified to appraise a company's managerial philosophy and the quality of its managers. Although this would require considerable study from the inside and a set of reasonably objective standards, it probably would require little more time than that required for a thorough accounting audit. Moreover, except for final responsibility, the audit of top-level managers, and the seeing of a company's entire management as a total system, much work on the management audit could be done, as in the case of accounting audits, with the help of suitable inside managerial and staff personnel. Furthermore, as with the accounting audit, when a group of special auditors once becomes familiar with a company, subsequent audits take less time than the first. In order to assure real objectivity, a management audit should be made by a recognized and qualified group of management appraisers with a reporting responsibility, like that of most accounting auditors, to the board of directors.

As standards for appraising, principles of management as outlined in this book would be appropriate. Since the managerial job is essentially the same everywhere, even though its environment and specific techniques may differ widely, the fundamentals—handled by persons experienced in recognizing them—should provide investors, boards of directors, and line management with knowledge of a company's strengths and weaknesses. There is reason to believe that the certified management audit will be a future step toward management competence. It would certainly fill a need, particularly in companies whose future has been placed in the hands of professional managers.

The foregoing analysis points to several rather clear conclusions about current and prospective trends in the control of management quality. The attempt to appraise the quality of managers is not new, although it has often been crude. Political leaders have been toppled from power; heads of religious and educational institutions have suffered favorable or unfavorable reactions to their stewardship; and business managers also have experienced punishment for failure and reward for success. But evaluations of top-level managers frequently take considerable time, and a long tenure is frequently undeserved.

The historical method of control has been indirect, with evaluations starting from reports of unfortunate occurrences and responsibility being assigned, either by hunch or by careful detective work, on a personal basis. The indirection of this, its chance of error, and its great cost have resulted in the identification of personal responsibility in only the more flagrant cases. Much of the time, knowledge of an error does not lead to identification of the responsible person. Consequently, indirect control of management quality alone is unsatisfactory.

Theoretically, direct control has long been very attractive. Its important advantages include the direct, purposeful, and regular evaluations of all managers and the confidence engendered by appraisers who know what they are doing. It has been impossible to implement this method until quite recently, because it rests upon the existence of management principles and their understanding by managers. It is now possible to take the first steps toward direct control, and its extended use may be expected in the relatively near future.

In supplementing indirect with direct control there will still be need for control records, always essential for determining where the enterprise is and where it is going. The difficulties of strategic controls and reporting will remain, but they should be dealt with as issues entirely separately from the evaluation of the quality of management.

Finally, the theoretical advantages of direct, as opposed to indirect, control are so pronounced that executives should bear them in mind in planning the future course of management. The gaps in present-day knowledge have been pointed out at every opportunity in this book. The inadequate education of managers in their functions has likewise been highlighted. Cooperation between management associations, universities, executives, and others interested in management research and education will yield rich dividends in making more efficient and more effective the task of joint human endeavor.

SUMMARY OF MAJOR CONTROL PRINCIPLES

The basic principles of control[13] can be grouped into three categories, reflecting their purpose and nature, structure, and process. In view of the unity of management and the tendency for functions to coalesce in practice, certain of these principles are similar to those of other managerial functions.

The Purpose and Nature of Control   The purpose and nature of control are reflected in the following principles:

Principle of assurance of objective   The task of control is to assure accomplishment of objectives by detecting potential or actual deviation from plans early enough to permit effective corrective action.

As with the other functions of management, the purpose of control is the attainment of objectives. This it can accomplish by detection of failures in plans that are, in turn, designed to attain objectives.

Principle of efficiency of controls   The more control approaches and techniques detect and illuminate the causes of potential or actual deviations from plans with the minimum of costs or other unsought consequences, the more efficient these controls are.

The principle of efficiency is particularly important in control, because techniques have a way of becoming costly, complex, and burdensome. A manager may become so engrossed in control that he spends more than it is worth to detect a deviation. Also, should a control technique be employed by a manager with such vigor and thoroughness as to negate the authority delegation to his subordinate, or should it seriously interfere with the morale of those who must execute plans, it can easily result in costs beyond any possible value. Detailed budget controls that hamstring a subordinate, complex engineering controls that thwart creativeness, and purchasing controls that delay deliveries and cost more than the item purchased are instances of inefficient controls.

Principle of control responsibility   The primary responsibility for the exercise of control rests in the manager charged with the execution of plans.

---

[13] This section follows the analysis made by Harold Koontz in "Management Control: A Suggested Formulation of Principles," *California Management Review*, vol. 1, no. 2, pp. 47–55 (Winter, 1959).

Since delegation of authority and assignment of tasks make a manager responsible for certain work, it follows that control over this work should be exercised by him. His responsibility cannot be waived or rescinded without changing the organization structure. This simple principle clarifies the often-misinterpreted role of controllers and control units. These agencies may act in a staff or service capacity to furnish control information to managers, but they cannot exercise control without assuming the managerial responsibility and managerial authority for the things controlled.

Control, like planning, must be forward-looking. This principle is often disregarded, largely because control has been dependent upon accounting and statistical data instead of upon forecasts and projections, and managers have been preoccupied with decimal accuracy, only to be attained—if at all—from past events. To regard planning as looking ahead and control as looking back is fallacious. Lacking means of looking forward, reference to history, on the assumption that "what is past is prologue," is better than not looking at all. But no manager attempting control should be satisfied with using historical records, adequate as they are for tax collection and for the determination of stockholders' earnings.

Ideally, a system of control should operate with instantaneous feedback, like the servo system of an automated machine tool, so that tendencies to stray from desired performance are corrected before the straying goes too far. In the absence of servomechanisms for most managerial tasks, control can be based on forecasts carried far enough into the future to foresee deviation tendencies in time to act. Even though forecasts are subject to inaccuracy, they are likely to be more satisfactory for control than reliance on history. Many firms rely on cash forecasts, and many owe their solvency to foreseeing cash shortages and preventing them. Such new techniques as PERT also make possible control that is forward-looking.

Principle of direct control The higher the quality of managers and their subordinates, the less will be the need for indirect controls.

Most controls used today are grounded on the fact that human beings make mistakes. They are usually used as simple indirect controls aimed at catching errors, often after the fact. Wherever possible, direct controls—aimed at preventing errors—should be used. Unquestionably, the best means of assuring that plans work out is to secure the best possible quality of managers at all levels. Such managers make the fewest mistakes and carry out all their functions to the best advantage.

The Structure of Control These principles that follow, dealing primarily with making control devices and practices fit in with plans and with organization structure, cast light on the structure of the controls themselves.

Principle of reflection of plans The more controls are designed to deal with and reflect the specific nature and structure of plans, the more effectively they will serve the interests of the enterprise and its managers.

This principle recognizes the fundamental truth that, plans being a prerequisite of control and control the task of making sure that plans are accomplished, control devices or techniques must reflect plans. In cost control, for example, the control must be based on planned costs of a definite and specific type; in control of application of policy, the nature of the policies and where they are to apply should be clear; and so on in all enterprise areas.

Principle of organizational suitability The more controls are designed to reflect the place in the organization structure where responsibility for action lies, the more they will facilitate correction of deviation of events from plans.

Since plans are carried out by managers and their subordinates, controls must fit a manager's authority area and therefore be designed to reflect organization structure. Consequently, any device of control must be tailored to the organization structure, and information to appraise performance against plans must be suitable to the position of the manager who is to use it. Urwick expresses this idea as the principle of uniformity and emphasizes that "all figures and reports used for purposes of control must be in terms of the organization structure."[14]

Principle of individuality of controls Since it is the task of controls to inform people who are expected to act to avoid or correct deviations from plans, effective controls require that they be consistent with the position, operational responsibility, competence, and needs of the individual concerned.

Although some control information and techniques can be utilized in the same form by various companies and managers, as a general rule control should meet the individual needs of each manager. The scope and detail of information requirements vary with managerial level and function. Furthermore, managers differ widely in their preferences for various methods of presenting information and in the type of units selected for reporting. Certainly, the corporate president, the controller, the vice-president in charge of manufacturing, the plant superintendent, and the foreman would not use the same type of control. The authors have seen both company presidents and factory foremen throw up their hands in dismay (for quite different reasons) at the unintelligibility and inappropriate form of control informa-

[14] L. Urwick, *The Elements of Administration* (New York: Harper & Row, Publishers, Incorporated, 1943), p. 107.

tion that was a delight to the figure- and table-minded controller. Control information which a manager cannot or will not use has little value.

The Process of Control Control, being largely a matter of technique, rests heavily on the art of management, on "know-how" in a given instance. However, these principles, arising from experience with control, have wide applicability.

Principle of standards Effective control requires objective, accurate, and suitable standards.

There should be a simple, specific, and verifiable way to measure whether a planning program is being accomplished. Control is accomplished through people. Even the best manager cannot help being influenced by personal factors, and actual performance is sometimes camouflaged by a dull or a sparkling personality or by a subordinate's ability to "sell" a deficient performance. By the same token, good standards of performance, objectively applied, will more likely be accepted by a subordinate as fair and reasonable.

Principle of critical-point control Effective control requires attention to those factors critical to appraising performance against an individual plan.

It would ordinarily be wasteful and unnecessary for a manager to follow every detail of planning execution. What he must know is that plans are being executed. Therefore, he concentrates his attention on salient factors of performance that will indicate, without watching everything, any important deviations from plans. There are no easy guidelines to determine the critical points he should watch, since their selection is predominantly a matter of managerial art. Perhaps the manager can ask himself what things in *his* operations will best show *him* whether the plans for which he is responsible are being accomplished.

The exception principle The more a manager concentrates his control efforts on exceptions, the more efficient will be the results of this control.

This principle, first formulated by Taylor,[15] holds that the manager should concern himself only with significant deviations, the especially good or the especially bad situations. It is often confused with the principle of critical-point control, and they do have some kinship. However, critical-point control has to do with recognizing the points to be watched, while the exception principle has to do with watching the size of deviations, logically at these points.

[15] Frederick W. Taylor, *Shop Management* (New York: Harper & Brothers, 1919), pp. 126–127.

The exception principle makes for managerial efficiency, and if the points at which the manager watches for exceptions are also critical points, efficiency can be further improved. The number of critical points at which to apply standards will vary with the importance of the plan, the significance of deviations, and the extent to which these points indicate quality of performance. Thus, one would expect more critical points to be applied and exceptions to be watched more carefully in cash planning and control than in the planning and control of plant maintenance.

Principle of flexibility of controls   If controls are to remain effective despite failure or unforeseen changes of plans, flexibility is required in the design of controls.

According to this principle, formulated by Goetz,[16] controls must not be so inflexibly tied in with a plan as to be useless if the entire plan fails or is suddenly changed. Note that this principle applies to failure of plans, not failure of people operating under plans, although the latter is the primary subject of control. The principle is best explained by the reasons given for the variable budget. Variable budgeting arose because of the fear that inadequate or inaccurate sales forecasting would, under fixed budgets, authorize continued expenditures at a level not justified by sales and that variability in budgeting would give the needed flexibility.

Principle of action   Control is justified only if indicated or experienced deviations from plans are corrected through appropriate planning, organizing, staffing, and directing.

There are instances in practice where this simple truth is forgotten. Control is a wasteful use of managerial and staff time unless it is followed by action. If deviations are found in experienced or projected performance, action is indicated, either in the form of redrawing plans or in making additional plans to get back on course. It may call for reorganization. It may require replacement of a subordinate or training him to do the task desired. Or there may be no other fault than a lack of direction in getting the subordinate to understand the plans or to be motivated to accomplish them. But, in any case, action is implied.

Because this action must necessarily be that of the manager in whose department the deviation occurs, this principle underscores the importance of responsible managers' being given the means not only of controlling their operations, but of undertaking the other managerial functions. It affirms the essential unity of management, the fact that no one can effectively manage who cannot undertake the functions of planning, organizing, staffing, directing, and controlling.

[16] Billy E. Goetz, *Management Planning and Control* (New York: McGraw-Hill Book Company, 1949), p. 229.

FOR DISCUSSION

1. If direct control were completely effective, would a company need any indirect controls?

2. What distinction would you draw between management appraisal, as dealt with in Chapter 22, and the control over the general quality of management dealt with in this chapter?

3. How would you proceed to make a management audit? Are there any similarities between it and an accounting audit?

4. Looking at the major management principles highlighted in this book, do you believe that their application in practice could improve effectiveness and efficiency of group operation by establishing an environment for performance, while still leaving flexibility to meet change and take into account individual differences? By reference to any of the principles, explain the extent to which these things are so.

SELECTED REFERENCES

Allen, G. H. (ed.): *Individual Initiative in Business,* part 2, sec. 4, Cambridge, Mass.: Harvard University Press, 1950.

Dimock, M. E.: *The Executive in Action,* chap. 21, New York: Harper & Row, Publishers, Incorporated, 1945.

Dooher, M. J., and V. Marquis (eds.): *The Development of Executive Talent,* chaps. 29, 30, New York: American Management Association, 1952.

Greenwood, W. T.: *A Management Audit System,* Athens, Ohio: Ohio University, 1964.

Hooper, F. C.: *Management Survey,* chap. 6, London: Sir Isaac Pitman & Sons, Ltd., 1948.

Leonard, W. P.: *The Management Audit,* Englewood Cliffs, N.J.: Prentice-Hall, Inc., 1962.

Martindell, J.: *The Appraisal of Management,* New York: Harper & Row, Publishers, Incorporated, 1962.

————: *The Scientific Appraisal of Management,* New York: Harper & Row, Publishers, Incorporated, 1950.

Metropolitan Life Insurance Company: *Outline for a Management Audit,* New York: Policy Holders' Service Bureau, Metropolitan Life Insurance Company, 1947.

Rose, T. G.: *The Management Audit,* 3d ed., London: Gee & Company, Ltd., 1961.

Wilson, A. P.: "The Management Audit Comes of Age," *The Controller,* vol. 18, pp. 411ff. (September, 1950).

part seven

MANAGERS AND THE CHANGING ENVIRONMENT

Although the primary focus of this book has been on the principles and techniques underlying development of an internal enterprise environment conducive to the effective and efficient operation of individuals working together in groups, other environmental factors affecting a manager can never be overlooked.

This point has been made on numerous occasions. For example, much of the task of establishing consistent planning premises involves identifying those economic, technological, social, political, and ethical factors which influence the selection of goals and the plans made to meet them. Likewise, among many other examples that could be mentioned, there are the many influences of the external environment that are recognized when taking into account human factors in organizing, staffing, and directing.

There are also many environmental elements which affect the management process itself. New techniques, new hardware such as the computer, and new knowledge or knowledge transferred from other sciences have had a tremendous influence on management.

Moreover, all the various factors so affecting the manager's role are not static. On the contrary, they change, some rapidly and some slowly. But the fact is that virtually nothing in the environment in which we live remains unchanged. Furthermore, as managers become more aware of the demands of their tasks and as competitive forces induce this awareness, the effective manager must emerge from undue preoccupation with his internal problems and overcome his limitations of experience to take these changes into account.

Unfortunately space does not permit treatment of all the forces of a changing environment which bear on the managerial position. But a few areas are so important that they are given special attention here.

The managerial role is viewed in its total social setting in Chapter 32.

This chapter outlines and discusses the moral and ethical elements of the external environment that bear on practicing managers. While primary emphasis is placed on the manager in business enterprises, much of what is discussed applies to nonbusiness undertakings as well.

Chapter 33 on "Comparative Management" outlines the problem of management operations in various cultural environments. One of the difficulties many scholars and observers have in considering the concept of universality of management theory and basic knowledge is their failure to separate fundamentals of managing from the practical application of these in different environments. Clearly, a manager must manage something and operate in a given environment. He does not manage in a vacuum. This is most obvious in considering the differences in managing production and managing sales. Both managers manage, but the subject matter they deal with, the goals they pursue, the plans they follow, and the people with whom they deal will vary.

This fact is even more apparent in operating as a manager in widely varying social cultures. Consequently, the authors have selected in their analysis of comparative management the area of international cultural differences and their impact on actual managing. Two of the leading models useful for separating managing from cultural variables are studied. Also, such comparative studies as have been made are noted. Even though the available evidence is sketchy, it does indicate that cultural differences, while often influencing management practice, do not appear to disprove in any way the universality of management fundamentals.

In the final chapter, the authors have undertaken to summarize a number of major factors which are changing the role of the manager and to outline problem areas believed to be of great importance for managers of tomorrow to deal with if they are to do their jobs effectively. Also, this chapter serves to underscore the fact that managing is an intellectually demanding occupation which can challenge the highest talents that can be brought to bear on it. The chapter concludes with some suggestions for needed action if the socially important task of optimizing group effort in accomplishing desired objectives is to be attained.

the enterprise manager in his social setting

Enterprises, like men, do not live unto themselves alone. They are inter-locking institutions that man has found it beneficial to organize to serve his needs. This may not have always been so. In the dim past, even the family, man's first and continuing institution, may have existed in the short and happenstance fashion of our animal forebears. But at the dawn of history, this institution was well established, as was the tribe. Increasing population and the agricultural revolution were new forces with which men had to deal. These could not be managed by the individual alone, and he gradually created institutions, such as the town, government, army, education, and religion, to help him. The proliferation of institutions and enterprises has proceeded down to our own day, where they often exist in bewildering confusion.

It is commonplace to observe that while the primacy of the individual is paramount, man has created his institutions to perform functions for the group which the individual members of the group cannot perform for them-selves alone. True, the individual is the most important character in the social setting, his interests must be served, and the institutions which he creates must serve these ends. In an ideal society, populated by a people who seized opportunities to make themselves equal in all respects, the individuals would in concert determine when and which institutions and enterprises they would create to better serve themselves. But, in fact, no ideal situation exists. As always, people vary from the stupid to the genius, from the passive to the aggressive, from the kind to the cruel, from the slothful to the energetic, from the cunning to the artless, from the humble to the proud. The institutions and enterprises which have been created to serve them are the products of aggressive leaders—the few who care for the many—and not always merely because they "care"; probably more often for reasons of self-aggrandizement than for reasons of social welfare.

However institutions and enterprises are created, they securely enfold the individual beyond any possibility of escape. As Gotshalk sees it:[1]

> Every human being is born into a social order. This order begins with the family, or at least with the parent-child relation, but it is actually as extensive as the human race. This complex order with its many interior orders provides the setting and chief condition of the individual's existence. . . . Romantics have dreamed of escaping it. Not only is there no place one can go, on earth or elsewhere, independent of society, but for a good segment of the individual's life . . . he is incompetent to go.

Our own experience confirms this view. The one great and overriding social institution is the state. It was created as the most desirable means of maintaining peace and justice for citizens and residents alike. Subservient to the state are uncounted institutions and enterprises of varying scope and purpose. They include educational, subgovernmental, religious, and business institutions, health and recreation organizations, trade unions, professional societies, farm unions, war veterans' associations, political parties, charter parties, and bridge clubs. No individual is a member of every group, but each is a member of many. His membership often shifts with age and time, but his whole life is spent as an active or passive member of several groups simultaneously. From this fact of our lives there emerges a number of major problems.

Membership in several groups is bound to create a conflict in loyalties for the individual. As a member of a union, one may support the leadership in striving for higher wages, but his family may suffer from a strike; he may have to weigh the advantages of a higher living standard against pressures to make religious or charitable contributions; he may want a "welfare state" but dislike paying the taxes to support it. These and many other sets of circumstances pose difficult psychological problems. Some individuals respond by being consumed with frustration; most seem able to cope with diverse purposes, seeking refuge in compromise and in their lack of discernment.

The tyranny of the majority is a major trial. In the United States, our tradition is to strive vigorously for what one thinks is right but to submit to the majority if one loses. In small matters, this is a convenient formula; but in large matters, especially those wherein principles are at stake, the very life of the institutional group may be risked by an undiscerning majority. Resigning from a group may not solve the problem—nonmembership may be even worse—and at the very highest level, one cannot resign his citizenship without becoming an expatriot. For those who find themselves in a hopeless minority in vital matters, only a life of difficulty awaits them.

The egotistical position taken by those at the institutional power center is hard to bear. They may take the position that they alone know what is good for the membership. This contempt for the collective good sense is

[1] D. W. Gotshalk, *Patterns of Good and Evil* (Urbana, Ill.: University of Illinois Press, 1963), p. 128.

often illustrated among the professional managers of charities, of political parties, and, indeed, of most other enterprises. They take advantage of the multitudinous interests of the membership, its lack of active participation, and its lack of attention. A tiny minority at the power center of the majority usually suffices to manage affairs to *their* personal satisfaction.

Finally, man being man, there is always a sense of lost freedom of action among members of institutional groups. It is not merely because man is romantic or nostalgic about the past days of freedom. His very nature rebels at constraints. He wants to make his own decisions, act as he feels he ought, be free of social pressures—follow his own rational and emotional drives. Mistakes he will undoubtedly make; but who in our society does not similarly make them? He wants to self-actualize in his own way. Is the way that is marked out for him by our institutions and social pressures a better way? Of course, one must be realistic even while sympathizing with man's struggle to be a man. There are few places on this earth where real freedom can be found. Our society has been organized to the point that one cannot longer satisfy his basic needs by his own means. Americans cannot hope to achieve these satisfactions without working for somebody else. This means that man will be forever responding to social pressures to live in the "right" way, to work at certain hours—in short, to conform. Men can learn to do a certain amount of this; they will have to learn to do more. As they do so, their bright light of freedom will continue to fade away.

The foregoing problems stress the issues which men face as institutional members. This view of interpersonal relationships is often contested by those who see no difference between the interrelationships of institutions and of their members.[2] This position is difficult to accept, however, since no institution can act unless the men who occupy its power center act. It has no personality, no conscience of its own. Although it is convenient to personify the state, the corporation, the church, or the university, it is readily understood that these organizations are lifeless without the actions of the men who make decisions in their name. Thus, the actions of groups are, in reality, the actions of the men who manage them, and these actions emanate from the principles and convictions of those who exercise power within them. The degree of power has no bearing on the matter. It is the men who manage with whom we have to deal.

Although the remainder of this chapter is primarily concerned with the business enterprise in its social setting, the point should not be forgotten that the behavior of the men who manage other enterprises is of equal concern. The finger of reproach is so often pointed at businessmen that the student may forget that the rules of social behavior apply equally to professional men, educators, churchmen, and politicians, and the need for men in these realms is equally great. Moreover, as was pointed out in the

[2] Cf. B. W. Dempsey, "The Roots of Business Responsibility," in E. C. Bursk (ed.), *Business and Religion* (New York: Harper & Row, Publishers, Incorporated, 1959), p. 111.

introductory chapter of this book, the goal of all managers in all enterprises must be the effective accomplishment of purpose (whatever it is) with the most efficient utilization of resources—human and material—at their disposal. It happens that the objectives of the business enterprise are the production and distribution of economic products and services, while that of the city police department is the protection of lives and property. But these different enterprise purposes should never obscure the fact that the managers in each type of enterprise have the same goals of effectiveness and efficiency in attaining various purposes.

THE HISTORICAL FUNCTION OF BUSINESS

When a business enterprise is the subject of discussion, it is probable that most people conjure up visions of a manufacturing firm, a department store, a railroad, or a brokerage house. These and similar enterprises are rather clearly defined, but their listing does not convey the extent and variety of business. It is necessary to turn to the economist for a comprehensive definition. He conceives a business to be any activity that is concerned with the production (or purchase) for sale of scarce goods and services. Such an enterprise may be conducted by one person or thousands, and may be owned and operated in many different ways.

The purpose of economic activity is always the same: it is to employ human and natural resources, and the capital that is accumulated through savings, in the production of goods and services which the ultimate consumers want. So far as we know, the wants of consumers are infinitely expansible, even while particular wants for any individual may well become satiated. Because resources are not free but are scarce, a decision has to be made concerning how they are to be employed, that is, what will actually be produced. What we know as high living standards result from the skillful use of relatively opulent capital and skilled human as well as natural resources to produce large volumes and wide varieties of goods and services relative to the number of consumers. Thus, the purpose of business is to satisfy the economic wants of people, and, since resources are scarce, their efficient use is a moral requirement.

Economic Organization There are a variety of ways in which economic activity may be organized. The typical classifications include free enterprise, socialism, communism, and the welfare state. If enterprise is really free, it permits individuals to establish and operate a business as they see opportunities to profit from the exchange of goods or services. Strictly speaking, such freedom would be complete; the assumption would be that consumer wants would be identified by entrepreneurs who would see profit-making opportunities in satisfying them. Of course, totally free enterprise has never existed. Even Adam Smith reserved to government such functions as protection of the people from foreign and domestic aggression, the administration of justice, and the production of services or goods that private business was unable to accomplish.

This conception of how enterprise should be organized did not work very well in England largely because of the unequal bargaining power of the owners of the factors of production. In the United States, the coincidence of the appearance of Smith's work and the Declaration of Independence, both in 1776, was truly providential. America began with a free enterprise organization of the economy, and it worked well because of the relative equality of bargaining power among the owners of resources and between producers and consumers of economic goods.

A fundamental assumption of a free enterprise system is the existence of effective and responsible competition. Thus, the "invisible hand" of competition will lead sellers to produce those things desired by buyers—as expressed by their purchasing choices—at the lowest possible prices. If any seller either makes too much profit or produces goods inefficiently, it is postulated that competitive forces will bring other sellers into the market. The result is that competition plus desires for goods at lowest prices and desires for profits will give rise to a total system where those products and services most desired will be made available at the lowest possible costs.

The British socialists advocated an economic organization wherein the state would own and operate the basic means of production, by which they meant enterprises concerned with transportation, power, steel, and textiles. These were typically large enterprises (although not by American standards) whose power the socialists feared. Free enterprise would be permitted elsewhere in the economy, however. Communist theory, on the other hand, requires that the state own and operate all types of enterprises. Thus, communists would go further down the road to state ownership and simply prohibit any and all kinds of private economic activity. But this does not mean that business does not exist in a purely communistic country. It means, rather, that the state owns and operates business enterprises. Thus, economic goods and services are produced, as they always must be, but this is accomplished through a system of public ownership.

None of the foregoing types of economic organization really describes accurately the relationships that currently exist in the United States. Beginning with almost totally free enterprise, restrictions upon the freedom of businessmen to make decisions have been gradually introduced. These limitations relate to such restrictions as those involved in central banking, regulation of monopolies, control of price-fixing, and prevention of certain advertising and fraudulent practices. On the positive side, legislation now requires bargaining with trade unions under certain conditions, collecting taxes without recompense, fair employment practices, etc. In addition, the state provides a wide variety of services, such as social security and medicare. Fortunately, the state has not seen fit to own and operate many businesses. The special genius of Americans is to modify free enterprise through regulation rather than through public ownership and operation.

This suits the American temperament, is more in line with our economic traditions, and can be made workable *provided* that the following principles are adhered to:[3]

1. Primacy of Free Enterprise: Government interference in free enterprise is permissible only after a clear public advantage has been demonstrated.
2. Democratic Action: Every instrument designed to limit, channel, or coerce private economic activity must be instituted by the democratic process.
3. Clarity and Unity of Purpose: The purpose of government interference in private economic activity should be clearly stated, be integrated, and be periodically reviewed.
4. Provision for Authority: Administrative authority should be adequate for the purpose and be indirectly applied.

The Business of Business   There is no doubt whatever that the function of business is to make economic goods and services available for consumption. Neither is there any question about the magnitude and complexity of this work. It is one of the historical trio of major functions of society, the others being government and religion. But it is not enough to produce economic goods; the first duty of business is to produce them efficiently. As Donald K. David remarked:[4]

> I feel strongly that operating a successful business is the first responsibility of a business leader. The simple fact is that in our society the businessman is primarily responsible for organizing the production and distribution of the nation's goods and services. He can meet that responsibility only through the competent management of business enterprise and through the creation and development of healthy business concerns. To me it is unrealistic to presume that the business leader can discharge any other responsibility if he fails in this, his foremost job.

Since businessmen obtain control of scarce resources by the purchase or lease of land and capital and hire human services, they have a moral responsibility for using them efficiently in the production and distribution of consumer goods. Only in this way can every person in the society obtain access to its resources, and this is their right.

Quite irrespective of the type of economic organization, the moral responsibility remains with those who own and operate or regulate business enterprise. It is the business of society to prescribe which type of economic organization best discharges the responsibility for use of resources. Efficiency in resource employment is undoubtedly best achieved through free enterprise. It is the business of the state to make sure through legislation and regulation that the private economy does not fail in its function to efficiently utilize resources to maximize the satisfaction of consumer wants

---

[3] C. O'Donnell, "Coordination des Plans des Entreprises et des Objectifs Economiques de la Nation," *Economie Appliquée*, Tome XVIX, I, II, pp. 209–233 (1965).
[4] Quoted by Dempsey, *op. cit.*, p. 110.

for economic goods and services. The state is not equipped to accomplish this result by means of a monolithic bureaucracy.

CRITICISMS OF THE PROFIT MOTIVE

The accomplishments of the free enterprise system, with appropriate regulation in the United States, are tremendously impressive. The volume and quality of goods and services which it has produced were inconceivable in even the recent past and there is little question that these will continue to be expanded into the future. This enjoyable circumstance would seem to convince us that the function of business has been truly executed with very great skill. And yet, in this plethora of wealth that surrounds us, there are many individuals who take serious exception to our accomplishments, who are dissatisfied with the economic organization which produced these results, and who would have us so modify the system, through changing the ground rules, as to make it more like the social systems found in Europe. These critics are willing to give up an efficient system they know for a system that has not worked efficiently and with which they have had no experience.

The Critical Positions   Central to the criticisms directed toward the economic organization of this society is the attack upon the profit motive. It matters little whether these people are regurgitating the views of Marx, Lenin, or Sydney Webb; whether, as Levin thinks,[5] they are ignorant of economics and are victims of self-pity; or whether they desire power and have an immense envy of success. The profit motive is attacked because, allegedly, it is responsible for materialism and because, as Galbraith[6] asserts, it provides the motivation for producing goods that consumers should not want to want.

Materialism   If the charge of materialism proceeds from those who are envious, it does not merit a reply. But if it is made by those who are seriously concerned about the direction of man's efforts, it is important to inquire into the bases for their position and into what they think men "ought" to do. These critics of our materialism rest their case upon personal conviction; they have no authority of position or of uncontestable source. They have suggested, at one time or another, that men should be devoted to the spiritual life, to humanitarianism, to aestheticism, to stoicism. To these people, these ends seem superior to an asserted devotion to materialism. Their views are based upon various assumptions about man's nature and his purposes. They are selective in stressing certain facets of man's nature, such

---

[5] R. I. Levin, "Profits and Responsibility," *Mississippi Valley Journal of Business and Economics*, vol. 1, no. 1, p. 92 (Fall, 1965).

[6] J. K. Galbraith, *The Affluent Society* (Boston: Houghton, Mifflin Co., 1958), chap. 22.

as his wish for immortality, his tolerance and compassion, his striving for beauty, and his pride in emotional repression, each of which is considered admirable.

This manner of extrapolating from man's nature seems very unrealistic. Man is not divisible. He is a whole being and has inherited much from his animal forebears. No one can make him what he is not. Man looks first to his material well-being, but in doing so, he has time and attention for his spiritual life, humanitarianism, and aesthetics. In America, we pursue material well-being with a *joie de vivre* that is unique. We combine our resources with technology and management to turn out a prodigious volume of goods and services and we actually make a game of it. The huge surpluses we produce are devoted to the support of religions, the arts, and the poor because we *are* indeed religious and do have a spiritual life, we *are* humanitarians and support the poor, and we *are* devotees of beauty. The achievement of the modern-day American is the high degree to which he has perfected his nature.

Poor Choice of Goods   Galbraith's view that people cannot be trusted to determine what they want because they do not want what they should, proceeds from a monolithic egotism. The point at issue here is: Who is to judge? In our society, we do have certain laws that restrict or prohibit the production and consumption of goods that are dangerous to our personal well-being. This is a proper test to apply. Beyond this, it is important to remember that man is a wanting animal and that none of us is endowed with either the right or the prescience to restrict these desires in others.

Dislike of the Economic System   Perhaps the positions taken by the critics of profit making are not real. It may well be that they are shadow-boxing; they really want to destroy the profit objective of business. If this is true, the question merely becomes one of economic organization. Students already know what are the alternatives. The free enterprise, regulated in fairness to all, utilizes scarce resources most effectively. This is what an economic system is supposed to do. Those who receive profits are the men and women who successfully risk their capital by investing in small business or in the stock of large businesses; all others concerned with these enterprises are employees who receive their income from wages and salaries. No one has ever calculated the return on total investment in any country, but it must be very small, considering the large number of failures that must also be included. It is the individual opportunity which attracts investment. The profit motive may be condemned not because we are a nation of exploiters, but because those who dislike the concept want to replace our economic organization with some form (always unspecified) of socialism or communism. If the question is to be decided on the basis of efficiency of the function and not on political or imperialistic grounds, there is no question of the superiority of the responsibly competitive free enterprise system.

Fear of Power   There are other critics who are impressed with the great power of large-scale corporations and assert that if they are to retain this power, they should be held responsible for supporting other commendable institutions, such as the community, government, and education. The power[7] of large corporations is expressed in their ability to command resources and to control access to them by employees through the hiring process, by consumers through the price structure, and by their competitive ability to attract able personnel and to acquire property. Looking internally at any large business enterprise, one is bound to be impressed with the scope of these powers. But the large firm finds itself considerably restricted in their use. First, there is the competitive structure of enterprise. In this environment any one firm must be aware of the competition of thousands of other firms for land, capital, and personnel. As it acquires resources, it must compete with many others who are in the market for them. As it sells its products, it must compete for the buyers' dollars. In this situation, no firm can be arbitrary.

Second, there are important legal safeguards. There are laws against collusion, monopolies, and various forms of unfair competition. The right of eminent domain gives governmental bodies access to the land they need. And there is always the threat that antisocial activity will result in further limiting their freedom of action.

Third, there is the force of voluntary restraint. For instance, the pension and investment funds do have power to vote the shares they own in corporations. In this way, they, being few but potent, could easily control numerous businesses. To date they have not chosen to exercise this right, perhaps because they fear potential regulation by government, or perhaps they realize that they may be expert in fund management but not in the management of other enterprises. In the opinion of Berle,[8] there is no present danger that the funds will further centralize the control of business. But, even should he be wrong, the regulatory power of government is always available as a last resource.

Social Irresponsibility   There are other critics of business who stoutly maintain that these enterprises do not discharge their social responsibilities. All of the critics are extremely vague and the terms used are rarely defined. It seems that business is supposed to be a better citizen by taking better care of employees, consumers, and the community; by contributing more to religious institutions, charity, and education; and by helping government carry the social load.

---

[7] See A. A. Berle, Jr., *Power without Property* (New York: Harcourt, Brace & World, Inc., 1959), p. 79. See also K. Davis, "Can Business Afford to Ignore Social Responsibilities?" *California Management Review*, vol. 2, no. 3, pp. 70–76 (Spring, 1960).

[8] *Ibid.*, pp. 54–56.

It is the large-scale business that tends to be regarded as most suspect. Somehow, farmers, organized labor, educators and other professional men, churchmen, and small business firms either do not have these responsibilities or they are assumed to be discharging them adequately. These critics are careful not to say what is owed to whom and how much. They avoid specifications for operating the business. Most of them simply seem to look at the large number of employees or plants or total dollars of profit, or some other measure of size, and conclude that these firms can afford to support the myriad social institutions and individuals who want help. Several of them fear the power of the large-scale business firm over employees, consumers, government, and the community, and propose that it be curbed by somehow requiring the firm to care for more social projects. The vagueness of the positions and programs of these critics is frustrating, but nevertheless there is an important point that is being made. The concept of social responsibility is sound.

William was a bank teller. One of his regular customers was Mrs. Brand. She always had two checks, one made out to her husband and one made out to Mrs. Sikorski.

"Who is Mrs. Sikorski?" asked William.

"That was my name before I remarried. The check with that name on it is my widow's pension. The other is my husband's."

William checked out the obvious violation of the law with the operations manager. "Oh, that's all right," he responded. "We're just glad she does her business with us."

RATIONAL VIEW OF SOCIAL RESPONSIBILITY

A clear understanding of the terminology selected to describe a concept is very difficult to attain. The phrase "social responsibility" is widely used in the literature of sociology, anthropology, economics, politics, and business management. One writer defines the concept as the ". . . obligation [of businessmen] to pursue those policies, to make those decisions, or to follow those lines of action which are desirable in terms of the objectives and values of our society."[9] Despite the seeming clarity of this definition, it still contains vague phrases and assumes everyone knows those to whom an obligation is owed and the meaning of social values. Presumably, businessmen are obliged to make decisions that are within the framework of the nation's social values, about which there is no consensus, and whatever they do, they must support all values whether they approve of them or not. Clearly, there is much to be desired that is not present in this "definition."

Since an obligation can only be owed by one person to another, social responsibility is an interpersonal relationship that exists when people are continuously or discontinuously dependent upon one another in both an

[9] H. R. Bowen, *Social Responsibilities of the Businessman* (New York: Harper & Row, Publishers, Incorporated, 1953), p. 6.

organized and an unorganized way. As a working definition, social responsibility, as used in this book, is the personal obligation of everyone, as he acts in his own interests, to assure that the rights and legitimate interests of all others are not impinged. It is perhaps unfortunate that this concept is stated negatively, but social responsibility has to be conceived in this way. The individual certainly has a right to act and speak in his own interests, but he must always have due regard that this freedom does not restrict others from doing the same thing.

Thus, the socially responsible will obey the laws of the land because the rights of others are at stake. He is free to support the institutions and individuals of his choice, or he may take a neutral stand, neither supporting nor interfering with the well-being of institutions and individuals. But he may not by word or deed attempt to destroy institutions or impinge upon the rights and interests of individuals except through legal processes.

The implications of this view of social responsibility are several. First, the neutral and negative aspects of personal behavior are as important as the positive. For instance, an individual nonmember is not obliged to support a trade union. He may be quite neutral, but he may not set forth to destroy it except through the legislative or judicial process. Similarly, a person is not obliged to support a church, a charity, a university, or a community, so long as there is no legal requirement for membership or for the payment of taxes in their behalf.

The same view is held on interpersonal relationships. Except for unlawful discrimination on the basis of race, sex, or religion, one person may well give preference to another in terms of a job (other than those covered in a union contract), a promotion, or an advance in status, because none of these acts, and similar marks of interest, restricts the rights of others. On the other hand, while one may not be required to prefer anyone, he may not slander or disparage the reputation of another.

A second implication is that the social obligation is owed by individuals and not by institutions. A club, a church, a university, or a corporation does not discharge a responsibility; it can act only by means of the persons who invoke its name. Social responsibility is a personal attribute; there is no action without personal action. To be sure, this viewpoint is frequently obscured by our habit of personifying enterprises and by the legal fiction that clothes a corporation with personality. But this is no reason why students should not make the appropriate distinction. When a state university uses its funds to engage in politics, a church burns a heretic, a club blackballs a candidate for membership, a business corporation violates antitrust legislation, or a charity supports the indigent, some individual or a group of individuals made each decision. No individual can escape his social responsibility by the artifice of the fictional person; neither can the totality of social responsibility be increased by adding thereto the obligation of the fictional person. As will be seen later, this concept is absolutely essential if we are to make sense of ethical responsibilities.

A third implication is that not only businessmen but every person in society has a social responsibility to discharge. The same rules apply to professors, churchmen, lawyers, and doctors as apply to the men who act for and in the name of corporations, governments, and other organized enterprises. Unfortunately, the literature generally tends to pillory only the businessmen for their lack of social responsibility. It does not include the professors who do not distinguish between academic freedom and propaganda, the judges who use the legal processes to reflect personal biases, the ministers who substitute social action for preaching the word of God, and the union members who resort to autocratic pressures.

Businessmen have shortcomings indeed, but in that respect they are surely not unique in our society. If they can be distinguished in any way, it is by their haste in using resources in ways that will placate their critics. Businessmen find themselves accused of social irresponsibility by those who fear their power, who beg for contributions, and who want to change the economic order. Still, they do have social obligations to discharge. Let us see what *is* the social responsibility of business.

The Business of Business Is Business   The people of societies create many institutions to accomplish their purposes. Governmental institutions have many purposes, among them protection from foreign intrusion, the administration of justice, the amelioration of gross inequities, and aid for the unfortunate, all designed to protect and encourage the people of the society in their pursuit of happiness. Religious institutions are designed to care for the spiritual needs of their memberships. Educational institutions are a society's great teaching and research arm. Labor and farm unions look to material benefits for their memberships.

Economic enterprises are designed to produce goods and services to satisfy the material wants of man. Their managers' first responsibility is efficiency in the use of resources to produce economic wealth. Their second responsibility is to accomplish this purpose in such a way that no restriction is placed upon the legitimate rights and interests of any person. Their third responsibility is to observe, by word and deed, the ethical standards of society.

Those who want businessmen to accept a wider social responsibility than is suggested here insist that business enterprises discharge their "obligations" to employees for better-than-competitive wage and fringe benefits, those to consumers through uneconomical prices and quality of merchandise, those to educational endeavors through gifts, those to the community by donating services and maintaining uneconomic operations, those to the unemployed by placing them in jobs they cannot perform, those to government through free tax collections and donations of the services of gifted managers, and those to unions by sacrificing the right to manage.

These critics want businessmen to do more than operate efficiently; they want business to engage in activities which many other institutions are organized to achieve. For businessmen to do this would certainly blur responsibility for results and establish themselves as potential scapegoats. The proper way to make certain that each enterprise achieves the results it was designed to secure is to have it properly managed. If the results are unsatisfactory, perhaps subsidies are appropriate, or perhaps the enterprise should be abandoned.

There is another reason for keeping businessmen within their own function. They are not experts in everything. The choices they would make and the support they would choose to provide might fail to meet the expectations of those who manage other enterprises. The late Senator Robert Taft said several years ago that businessmen are not wanted in politics because they do not understand the political processes. It is equally certain that businessmen are not always wanted at decision-making levels in other enterprises for similar reasons. The critics want the financial support of businessmen but not their interference in policy or at decision levels. Such an arrangement would deprive businessmen of opportunities to do that which they are trained to do.

The appropriate way out of this dilemma is to distinguish between the business firm and the businessman. It is clearly the function of the firm to produce wealth efficiently because, as Levin[10] says, the maximization of profits and social benefits are interdependent. Furthermore, the managers of the modern firm are typically employees of the firm and not its owners. Thus, managers must act in a trustee relationship for those who risk their capital in the business venture.[11] Morally, they are not free to use corporate resources for any purpose which, in their prudent judgment, does not redound to the welfare of the owners. In practice, corporate managers go far beyond this standard. With the blessing of the Supreme Court, they can make donations out of profits to educational institutions;[12] they are under extreme pressure from Federal agencies to employ unemployables; they make large grants to charities.

Where a business manager engages in or supports nonbusiness enterprises at company expense, there is ever a danger, of course, that he may be using the property of owners in ways to which they would not consent. On the other hand, support of such nonbusiness enterprises as education and research may have a direct relationship to the future of a business by making more available better trained human resources or advanced knowledge which will be beneficial to the business. Also, if the support of such nonbusiness enterprises as charities is regarded as necessary evidence of responsiveness of the business enterprise to its social environment, such responsiveness may well be in the owners' long-range self-interest. No enterprise exists in isolation from its external environment whether social, economic, technological, political, or ethical.

[10] Levin, *op. cit.*, p. 88.

[11] See A. W. Lorig, "Corporate Responsibilities," *Business Horizons,* vol. 10, no. 1, pp. 51–54 (Spring, 1967).

[12] Probably first advocated and implemented by Frank W. Abrams. See A. H. Cole, *Business Enterprise in Its Social Setting* (Cambridge, Mass.: Harvard University Press, 1959), p. 241.

Businessmen are, of course, individuals, and as such they are members of many social groups. *In this capacity,* they can and should actively support and help to direct the causes in which they believe. They may wish to contribute out of their own pocket to various causes and to contribute their personal time to clubs, charities, school boards, and numerous committees of institutions. This is as it should be.

In rebuttal to this position is the claim that, after all, one cannot expect outsiders to distinguish between the businessman and the firm that employs him. The distinction can readily be made by the businessman when someone outside the firm solicits him for support; the businessman can tell him that the support must come from his personal resources and not from those of the firm. But there is an aspect of the argument which is valid. For publicity purposes, the institution receiving support from a businessman will identify him with his firm, especially if the latter is well-known, even though the individual makes clear that it is his personal support that he is giving and not the support of the firm. From the point of view of the business firm, superior managers and directors may not want to have the business associated with the outside institution through the name of its employee. It is their judgment that the individual cannot be disassociated from the firm. This is very likely to be true, and will lead to the individual dropping the outside association if he has a greater loyalty to the firm that employs him.

"Did you hear on the newscast last night that some professors and ministers of several churches joined the freedom marchers?" one manager asked.

"Well, what's the matter with that?" his companion replied.

"I just don't see that they have a social responsibility to do that," the first responded. "Of course, if they are doing it on their own time and are not representing their employers, it is probably all right."

Feasibility of the rational view   It is all very well to build a theoretical structure that compartmentalizes nicely the activities of man in his social environment. The view that the business firm should confine itself to the production of wealth, that individuals and not institutions have obligations of an interpersonal nature, and that the businessman acts in his personal capacity when he supports other institutions may be criticized as simplistic. The question is, Can a system of relationships which embodies these views be made to work?

In the present-day world they clearly are not working this way. Institutions overlap in purpose and activity, they support and harm each other, depending upon what is conceived to be their interests; the business enterprises that produce wealth and thereby have the resources are sometimes unreasonably taxed and pressured to support other causes, and the concept of trusteeship is fading. In some cases this situation was produced because there has been no clear set of principles to guide action; in others, the principles were simply smothered and ignored.

Despite these circumstances which, in the short run, seem to overwhelm us, pessimism is not in order. The future decades will be devoted to research and teaching by scholars who are trying to learn something about the nature of man. These efforts are directed toward the development of a science wherein principles will provide standards for governing the conduct of interpersonal affairs. Even more important is the realization that perhaps man does not take too kindly to rational governance. He will need persuading that rationality, in separating out his social responsibilities, can lead to a rational integration of them with his emotional life.[13]

BUSINESS ETHICS

It was pointed out above that the practice of ethics is one of the social responsibilities of businessmen. This is a problem of universal concern. Unethical conduct is highly publicized wherever it is found, but most of the "sharp" practices remain hidden within the organizational structures.[14] Also, it is a problem very difficult to get hold of because there is no science of ethics resting, as one should, upon principles having general acceptance.

The Causes of Confusion   There are several factors that have led us into the present state of uncertainty about ethical standards. In the first place, the successive waves of immigration have brought to the United States masses of people with widely varying practices of ethical behavior. Their cultures have not yet been wholly integrated into a national culture and, until this occurs, there is very little reason to anticipate any *national* ethical standards. In the second place, there is no recognized source of ethical standards. In nations that have a state religion, there does exist a central source of authority to teach ethical practices. In the United States, with its myriad cultures and religions, no one can look to church, government, educational institution, or private association as the center of ethical teaching. And, in the third place, there is no concerted effort on the part of teachers of ethics to develop a science.

Definition   In the consideration of this subject, the student is first beset with terminological problems. Such words as "ethics" and "morals" seem to be used interchangeably, but neither is consistently employed. Indeed, in our own day, "ethics" seems to be a term chiefly referring to high standards of business and professional conduct. This narrow application is unfortunate, for it leaves us without a similar word with which to characterize high standards of conduct in other affairs. For the purposes of this analysis, it is

[13] Perhaps this statement needs clarification. It is believed that much of man's actions are explainable in rational and emotional terms. The direction of our civilization is to stress the former. Thus, a manager will operate rationally and will include in his calculus an attempt to manage as rationally as possible his own and others' emotions.

[14] See, for instance, "Wall Street's Own Watch Dogs," *Business Week*, pp. 90–96 (July 29, 1967).

perhaps best to define ethics as the collective term for principles of personal conduct. Being principles, they should be universally applicable and they should also provide the standards with which the conduct of all persons, including businessmen, may be compared. Being principles, they can also be taught and, in this way, help to establish general standards of personal conduct throughout the land.

Morals are often quite a different matter. While ethics are grounded on moral standards, "morals" can refer to any generally accepted customs of conduct and right living in a society. There are many societies and there are many changes in these societies. Furthermore, within a society numerous local customs emerge. Therefore, what is moral in one society may be immoral in another; and what is moral in one sector or province may be immoral in another area within the same society. For our purposes, then, there can be no prescriptive *science* of morals; there are merely customs of a high degree of social acceptance. There is every reason to suspect that the moral practices of a given society are probably more closely adhered to than are any universal principles of ethics. Furthermore, what is considered moral in certain groups or societies may well be contrary to some more universally held ethical principle. For instance, in some countries it is a moral practice to bribe an official to secure a favor, but surely an ethical principle is fractured in the process.

The material that follows is concerned with ethics. Consideration is given to the need for a science of ethics, the sources of ethical teaching, the relation of ethics to laws and codes governing personal conduct, and some thoughts on the development of a science of ethics.

Need for a science of ethics   The need for a set of generally accepted and practiced standards of personal conduct is evident in all parts of the world. Nothing but confusion best describes the current situation. The need is plainly evident in the conduct of heads of state, politicians, judges, professors, churchmen, lawyers, accountants, and just plain workers. We live at a time when it is easier to describe personal conduct as "a-ethical." The single advantage of such a situation is that everyone can proceed on the assumption that there is no such thing as principles of right conduct. Of course, things are really not that bad, but the lack of universal ethical practices forces everyone onto a middle ground where none can be sure just what ethical standards guide each interpersonal contact.

This situation is especially distressing because one really does not know what ethical standards will guide the conduct of the man he votes for, of his lawyer, of the judge who tries his case, of the teacher of his children, of the minister of his church, of the labor union leader, of the businessman he deals with, or even of his neighbor and his neighbor's wife. In the United States, the assumption is chiefly made that others will abide by the same principles as one's self. To a considerable extent, this is all to the good because it assumes a certain degree of commonality of ethical standards.

But care must be taken. For instance, the *now* is a point in history. What has been the trend of ethical experience? Since the seventeenth century it has probably declined, but in the last fifty years it may have improved. Again, the uncertainty concerning another's ethical standards establishes a situation in which we learn of them through trial and error. This hazard would be of small concern if interpersonal relationships were localized and continuous.

But in the world as it stands today, these relationships are world-wide in scope. We make treaties with unknown heads of state and commercial agreements with distant and often foreign strangers; we send our children to distant colleges to be instructed by unknown professors. In these and many similiar situations, trial-and-error methodology is, perhaps, often disastrous.

The professor concluded his lecture on business ethics by remarking that the Golden Rule seemed to be about the only general guide that was available.

"I don't see how that can be a general guide in a dynamic environment in which morals change," observed an alert student.

"It seems to me that a businessman is taking a big risk in assuming that others will treat him in the same way," remarked another.

If ethical standards could be incorporated in statutes, there would be much less reason to feel the vacuum created by the lack of a science. But even here it is simply not possible to establish such needed standards by law. By their very nature, laws tend to deal with specific acts, and these must be in the billions. No legislature could hope to deal with them all. Perhaps only a theocratic state would undertake the codification of a set of ethical principles.

The lack of a science of ethics is a cause of suffering by every person in a society except those at the no-ethics end of the scale. The pressing populations of our times, the small world constricted by communications networks and fast travel time, the pressing interpersonal relationships, all are forces that demand the development of ethical principles. Fortunately, these same forces will provide the pressure on individuals to practice right conduct once this is taught. A world packed with people will force the standardization of ethical practices—but this state of affairs will be a long time coming.

Variant sources of ethical teaching The search for the sources of ethical teaching in the United States leads us back to the major religious contributions.[15] It is not that this is necessarily true, because it is conceivable that lay scholars could develop a science of ethics. This they have not done.

[15] For an excellent summary see J. W. Clark, *Religion and the Moral Standards of American Businessmen* (Cincinnati: South-Western Publishing Company, 1966), part I, pp. 1–75.

Even lay writers on this subject return to the prominent religions for guidance, for they, like most everyone else in this country, have been touched by an admonishing finger in their youth.

Protestant contributions to the teaching of ethics have had an outstanding influence upon the American people. The religion of most early colonists was a strong force in molding the behavior of the people. With the passage of time, these original immigrants achieved and maintained positions of wealth and power in all walks of life. From pre-Revolutionary times to the present, the impact of the Protestant Ethic has been of first-rate importance. Men were taught to perform good works, to practice the virtues of austerity, frugality, and industry, and to act as stewards in the management and disposition of wealth. Even in recent times these virtues have been practiced by businessmen who may not even know their origins. In the opinion of Kenneth E. Boulding, "Looking at a perspective of three or four hundred years, the Protestant economic gospel has been a fantastic success."[16]

Clark[17] believes that the contribution of the Jewish faith has been more than proportional to the population of those who profess it. In attempting to identify a set of values that can be attributed to these people, an important problem presents itself: there is no single set of universally accepted values. The Jewish community is divided on the scope of Judaism—whether it should be viewed as a whole way of life, or whether it should be viewed as wholly religious. Illustrative, but assuredly not comprehensively, the religious teaching of the Jews seems to include an appreciation for the love of life and the importance of social consciousness. These values have been modified in the American environment to the point where there is positive acceptance of wealth as a value in itself, even though, to be sure, the literature of the Old Testament emphasizes the importance of charity and stewardship. Social consciousness has been the chief reason for an emphasis upon the value of social responsibility. As we have noted in an earlier section, this is a viable position so long as the individual businessman and not the business firm is viewed as having a social consciousness.

According to Clark,[18] much of Catholic social theory is derived from a basic concept of man that regards him as possessing both individual and social aspects. The dignity of the individual is given its just due, but the point is made that it may not be achievable outside the social organization established by man. These values are expressed in Catholic social doctrine in rather specific ways. The concept of justice guides human beings on the interpersonal level and on the social level. The first is concerned with giving to another what is his due; the second involves the individual's duties to society and vice versa. For instance, private property is strongly sup-

---

[16] "Our Lost Economic Gospel," *Christian Century*, vol. 67, no. 33, p. 972 (Aug. 16, 1950).

[17] *Op. cit.*, p. 28.

[18] *Op. cit.*, p. 58.

ported because it is not only natural to the individual but it also contributes effectively to his development and to his dignity. At the same time, it must be used in ways that advance the social good. Thus, the element of steward-ship, common also to the Protestant Ethic and to Jewish doctrine, is strongly stressed. Similarly, the concept of fair price guides the interrelationships of individuals in such a way as to make certain the mutual advantage from exchange and its potential contribution to society as a whole.

Ethical standards and the law The absence of a set of ethical prin-ciples has not impeded the effort of government to regulate interpersonal standards of conduct. Since the state has the obligation to administer justice, it must proceed on whatever principles seem to be at hand to protect indi-viduals from the effects of unethical behavior. Most people have some con-cept of what is ethical, at least in particular cases, and on many of these there is considerable agreement. Our legislative representatives assess this consensus and act to establish statute and administrative laws in critical areas of interpersonal conduct where the safety and personal welfare of the people can be vitally affected by unethical practices. Government cannot, by any means, cover all cases in point because, by its very nature, a law is aimed at specific unethical acts and not at the establishment of a principle. This accounts for the long list of criminal and civil laws aimed at practices that seriously affect the rights of individuals to life and liberty.

The effect of the just administration of such laws is important for the development of a future science of ethics. The mere fact that a people is required to obey this legislation develops in them a strong agreement about the relevant ethical standards. Mistakes, of course, are bound to develop, but the remedy is to change the law through the processes provided. In this way agreement is achieved about a large body of ethical practices, and from these a start can be made to deduce the principles upon which they rest.

"Can you give me some examples of conflict of interest?" the professor asked the members of his class.

"Yes," one answered. "I know of a director of a manufacturing company who is also a director of a financial institution. The manufacturer desperately needed capital and the director arranged for the loan to be made by the financial firm."

"I thought that would be unlawful under the antitrust legislation," remarked another.

"Is this a question of ethics?" the professor wanted to know.

Business and professional codes Another phenomenon that has some potential in the area of furthering ethical practices is the rather widespread tendency of business groups, professional people, and even politicians to adopt or to consider the adoption of codes of conduct.[19] Examples abound

---

[19] For a good summary of these codes, see B. Y. Landis (ed.), "Ethical Standards and Professional Conduct," *The Annals of the Academy of Political and Social Science*, vol. 297, pp. 1–124 (January, 1955).

in the codes adhered to by the medical, legal, and accounting professions and the many business codes usually developed by trade associations and in various proposals for codes to govern the conduct of professors and politicians.

Purpose The usual reasons for the development of these codes are two. In the first place, it is considered that the publication of a code of ethics will improve the confidence of the customer, client, patient, or voter in the quality of service he may expect. A reason of this type must assume that past practices of the group membership have undermined the trust of the very people whose custom is essential for the support of the group. This is why education, which is presumed to be the best safeguard against quackery, is stressed. So also are truth-in-advertising, something more than *caveat emptor,* conflicts of interest, and similar matters covered in the codes.

A second reason for the development of this practice concerns the inter-relationships of the members themselves. Business simply cannot be carried on in its present complexity without trust in the ethical standards of vendors and suppliers, of financial houses, and of government agencies. It is believed that their business risks will be somewhat minimized if the competitors within the group, and between groups, can rely upon at least some expectation of a given standard practice.

McGuire[20] believes that there are two additional reasons for codes. They can be used as a crutch for the weak, who, if approached to undertake some unethical act, can point to the code to underwrite their refusal. And then there is the practical result that codes simplify the detection of unethical behavior in competitors and employees.

The apparent need for codes is a sad commentary upon the absence of the teaching and practice of ethical principles. Those who feel strongly about the need for codes are really crying out to the academic and religious communities for progress in the development of a science of ethics. In the meantime, they try this means of placing a floor under the practices of individuals so that some positive element of security will prevail. The strong pull of personal advantage that works to the detriment of others is truly a widespread phenomenon.

Voluntary nature of codes Since there is no legal requirement that anyone subscribe to an ethical code, reliance must be placed on the voluntary action of the group membership. People are notoriously slow to volunteer, not usually because they are indeed unethical, but because they feel codes to be a restriction upon their freedom and that such subscribing to them would imply a reflection upon their practices. In the face of these problems, means are sought to "require" voluntary adherence. Penalties are sought in the legislatures against the nonconformist; preferences are granted

[20] J. W. McGuire, *Business and Society* (New York: McGraw-Hill Book Company, 1963), p. 285.

for those who do sign the code by way of according the legal right to make audits, in the administration of legislation affecting the group, and in protecting the fundamental right to practice a profession. Members are protected through limitation upon the number of men admitted to the profession and through bringing pressure on hospitals, for example, to admit only members to their staff positions. And if the group feels strongly enough about it, it may terminate the membership of defectors.

Provisions of ethical codes McGuire is of the opinion that the provisions of codes of ethics are either dogmatic or meaningless.[21] He feels that dogmatic provisions do not permit adjustment to change in a dynamic and complex world. To avoid this dilemma, many groups resort to a meaningless statement of generalities that could be interpreted in ways to suit the convenience of the individual.

Even more important is the question: Are ethical codes really codes of ethics? In general, they are not. They are concerned with local custom in respect to particular circumstances. For instance, the chief provisions of the code for professional accountants include:[22]

A. Professional conduct.
  1. An appropriate firm name, style, and description.
  2. Practice as a corporation is forbidden.
  3. Occupations incompatible with public accounting are prohibited.
  4. If engaged in another business, the same rules of conduct apply.
  5. Advertising and solicitation of business are prohibited.
  6. Members of the American Institute of Accountants must observe the rules of State societies, where they exist, on competitive bidding.
  7. Offers of employment to employees of other accountants are forbidden.

B. Confidence of clients.
  1. Confidential relationship must not be violated.
  2. Splitting fees with, or paying commission to, the laity is forbidden.
  3. Excepting partners and employees, members may not permit others to use their names on financial documents.
  4. Members may not sign the work of others, excepting their own associates or other accredited accountants.

C. Confidence of third parties.
  1. Members must conform to generally accepted accounting and auditing standards in certifying statements.
  2. Contingent fees relating to audits are prohibited.
  3. Members must not vouch for the accuracy of earnings forecasts.
  4. Members may not express an opinion on financial statements of an enterprise financed by public issues of securities if they, or their immediate relatives, have a substantial financial interest. With private financing, their interests must be exposed.

[21] *Ibid.*, p. 286.
[22] Landis, *op. cit.*, p. 2.

What is called professional conduct should more properly be called competitive conduct. The requirements and proscriptions relate to inter-member competition, and they have the effect of reducing the area of competition between accounting firms. None of these rules is to be disparaged, but it is equally clear that few ethical principles are involved. The same may be said of fee-splitting and contingent audit fees. The remainder of the items are chiefly concerned with potential fraud and, therefore, are concerned with an ethical principle.

In this example the purpose of the code comes through very clearly. The accountants want somewhat to reduce competition by regulating business practices among themselves, and they want to keep their present and potential clients by improving their image. In other words, the membership look upon as good that behavior which is good for business. They are not unique. An examination of other codes yields the same conclusion. In none of them is there much concern for a science of ethics.

Enforcement of ethical codes The student will infer from the foregoing discussion that the difficulties of enforcing ethical codes are monumental. Some kind of board, elected by the membership, would have the problem of trying to determine what is really the standard and assessing the occurrence of an actual offense against it. Words, terms, and lack of principles would work against them. Loyalty to members, even when accused, may be found to have a higher value than enforcement of the code. Sanctions against a member may well result in the disintegration of the group. For all of these reasons, the ethical codes are often pointed to with pride but are ignored in practice.

Conclusion The so-called ethical codes are, at best, a stopgap and, at worst, deceptions. As a stopgap, they are employed as a means of trying to provide some assurance of ethical conduct on the part of a membership. In this sense they may be making a contribution if only in pointing up the critical need for the development and teaching of a science of ethics. As a deception, they easily give the appearance of restricting the behavior of members to some recognized standard, but in fact they are incapable of so doing. In this sense they are notoriously misleading, especially to the customer, patient, consumer, and voter.

"This emphasis on the ethics of businessmen seems to me to be unfair," observed a student. "I think they are no more unethical than anyone else."

"I believe you are right," replied the professor. "All of us live in the same environment. We all have temptations of a similar nature. Even those of us who preach most about it," he slyly remarked, "are in the same category with everyone else in our society."

This state of affairs does not mean that businessmen are helpless. Even though they recognize that virtue does not always triumph, that kindness may not be its own reward, and that ethical practices are not necessarily profitable, the manager who is really convinced that he must and will operate ethically can do many things. For instance, he can establish clear policies and enforce them; he can exert strong pressures on his subordinates and his superior; he can take a position of leadership among his peers in persuading them to follow ethical standards; and, above all, he can think through to his own position and resolve to cultivate the character needed to adhere to his principles. Indeed, in the real world, there are many businessmen who are doing just this. As McGuire states:[23]

> Like other men, businessmen sometimes succumb to [these] temptations. This should not surprise us. What should surprise us is that so many businessmen withstand the temptations and that they have an ethical code of values which would do justice to men in any occupation.

TOWARD THE GOOD SOCIETY

This is not good enough. Businessmen have an obligation to all others in society to use scarce resources efficiently and, in so doing, to make certain that every decision stands firmly upon the applicable moral customs and any generally accepted ethical principles. It is urgent that our scholars set out now to develop a science of ethics, for this can offer the standard for the teaching and practice of the desired quality of interpersonal conduct. Scholars do not have to start from zero. They may proceed inductively by synthesizing such evidences of ethical standards as are found in the Golden Rule, the Ten Commandments, legal standards, and codes of associations. Others, if they prefer, may proceed deductively and develop a system of ethical principles based upon their conceptions of the end of man. Through research, teaching, and in interchange of ideas, it is not too much to hope that there will some day emerge a science of ethics.

Such a science is urgently needed, not only by businessmen, but by all men as they carry out their proper roles in a complex world. Only in this way can a good society be developed, one ". . . whose aim is an inwardly well-developed people in a world as mechanically secure as possible."[24]

FOR DISCUSSION

1. Some people fear the power of large corporations. How do such organizations exercise power? Are people safe in a world of big business?

2. Can an enterprise act responsibly, as distinguished from the behavior of its managers?

3. In what sense are social responsibilities a product of interpersonal relationships?

4. Do you think there is really a good way to distinguish ethics and morals?

5. What problems do congressmen face in developing and applying a code of ethics to themselves?

[23] *Op. cit.*, p. 280.
[24] Gotshalk, *op. cit.*, p. 130.

SELECTED REFERENCES

Barr, S.: *The Three Worlds of Man*, Columbia, Mo.: University of Missouri Press, 1963.

Bartels, R. (ed.): *Ethics in Business*, Columbus, Ohio: Bureau of Business Research, The Ohio State University, 1963.

Berle, A. J., Jr.: *Power without Property*, New York: Harcourt, Brace & World, Inc., 1959.

Bowen, H. R.: *Social Responsibilities of Businessmen*, New York: Harper & Row, Publishers, Incorporated, 1953.

Bursk, E. C. (ed.): *Business and Religion*, New York: Harper & Row, Publishers, Incorporated, 1959.

Clark, J. W.: *Religion and the Moral Standards of American Businessmen*, Cincinnati, Ohio: South-Western Publishing Co., 1966.

Clausen, E. A.: "Marketing Ethics and the Consumer," *Harvard Business Review*, vol. 45, no. 1, pp. 78–86 (January–February, 1967).

Cleveland, H., and H. D. Lasswell (eds.): *Ethics and Bigness*, New York: Harper & Row, Publishers, Incorporated, 1962.

Clough, S. B.: *Basic Values of Western Civilization*, New York: Columbia University Press, 1960.

Cole, A. H.: *Business Enterprise in Its Social Setting*, Cambridge, Mass.: Harvard University Press, 1959.

Davis, K., and R. L. Blomstrom: *Business and Its Environment*, chap. 6, New York: McGraw-Hill Book Company, 1966.

Gotshalk, D. W.: *Patterns of Good and Evil*, Urbana, Ill.: University of Illinois Press, 1963.

Levin, R. I.: "Profits and Responsibility," *Mississippi Valley Journal of Business and Economics*, vol. 1, no. 1, pp. 87–93 (Fall, 1965).

Leys, W. A. R.: *Ethics for Policy Decisions*, Englewood Cliffs, N.J.: Prentice-Hall, Inc., 1952.

Lorig, A. W.: "Corporate Responsibilities," *Business Horizons*, vol. 10, no. 1, pp. 51–54 (Spring, 1967).

McGuire, J. W.: *Business and Society*, New York: McGraw-Hill Book Company, 1963.

O'Donnell, C.: "Coordination des Plans des Entreprises et des Objectifs Economiques de la Nation," *Economie Appliquée*, Tome XVIX, I, II, pp. 209–233, 1965.

Olafson, F. A. (ed.): *Society, Law, and Morality*, Englewood Cliffs, N.J.: Prentice-Hall, Inc., 1961.

Schneider, H. W.: *Morals for Mankind*, Columbia, Mo.: University of Missouri Press, 1960.

comparative management

In the study of management theory and principles, the authors have emphasized the operation of managers in molding the internal environment of an enterprise. Indeed, the definition of managing used has been that it involves the design and maintenance of an internal environment for the effective and efficient operation of individuals working together in groups. It has, however, been recognized throughout this book that the effective manager must also be responsive to his external environment if the enterprise is to thrive.

The authors have also taken the position that management fundamentals—theory and principles—have universal application in every kind of enterprise and at every level of an enterprise. Yet they have constantly acknowledged that the specific problems with which a manager deals, the individuals and groups with which he interacts, and the elements of the external environment will differ. One would expect, therefore, that given techniques and approaches, even though based upon the same fundamentals, would vary because of these differences, just as engineering design would vary if a mechanical engineer were planning a bridge rather than a precise pressure measuring instrument, even though many underlying physical principles would be the same.

It is true that most studies of management fundamentals have been made without regard to specific external cultural environments. It is likewise true that most have been made against the backdrop of culturally well-developed and predominantly private enterprise societies. However, in approaching the study of comparative management, two basic questions may be posed: (1) Do management fundamentals, in contrast to specific management techniques and approaches, vary with external cultural—social, economic, political, technological, or ethical—differences? (2) To what extent should we expect managerial practice—the art of managing—to differ with variations in the external environment? These questions have not yet been answered conclusively, but recent studies have cast some interesting light on them.

MANAGEMENT AS A CRITICAL ELEMENT IN ECONOMIC GROWTH

In the increasing concern with what makes for economic growth in a country, it is natural for social scientists to look for underlying causes of growth. Why is it that one country has a higher per capita national income than another? Why is it that only 18 countries of the world were found in 1966 to have a Gross National Product per capita of more than $1,000 per year, while 33 had GNP per capita of $201–$1,000 per year, and 66 had GNP per capita of less than $200 per year?[1]

Because of the disparity of national incomes and the problems caused in much of the world by incomes which do not allow for adequate subsistence, let alone the raising of cultural standards, attention of world leaders and development economists has naturally turned to the need for increasing productivity and production. Indeed, one author has described this widespread movement as "one of the great world crusades of our time."[2] Until recent years, the necessities for development were thought to be the transfer of technology, education, and capital. But as important as these are, it has come to be recognized that advanced managerial know-how[3] is probably the most critical of all elements responsible for growth. As one Chilean executive has put it:[4]

> Perhaps it is time to alter our concept of underdevelopment and think in terms of management. This would focus our attention on helping mismanaged areas to improve their organizations and knowledge. No amount of capital investment will succeed in furthering human progress if such wealth producing resources are mishandled or undermined through lack of fundamental concepts. This lack of knowledge exists and the modern tools of finance, marketing, etc. are not common knowledge in underdeveloped areas and their absence prevents the rapid and successful expansion of areas. Capital alone will not replace this information, but likewise the lack of such capital will make it impossible to bring about the looked for development.

This opinion is buttressed by other findings. Rostow recognized the importance of entrepreneurial skills in management and economic growth

[1] R. N. Farmer and B. M. Richman, *International Business: An Operational Theory* (Homewood, Ill.: Richard D. Irwin, Inc., 1966), p. 39.

[2] M. D. Bryce, *Industrial Development* (New York: McGraw-Hill Book Company, 1960), p. 3.

[3] "Know-how" is used differently by various authors. Here it is used to connote the ability to apply knowledge effectively in practice; it therefore includes both knowledge of underlying science and the artful ability to apply it to reality.

[4] J. Ross, "The Profit Motive and Its Potential for New Economies," *Proceedings, International Management Congress, CIOS XIII* (New York: Council for International Progress in Management (USA), Inc., 1963).

when he pointed out that "A small professional elite (of entrepreneurs and executives) can go a long way toward initiating economic growth."[5] Sayles expresses the same viewpoint even more strongly when he concludes that "In the world race for economic growth and for the allegiance and stability of lesser-developed sections of the globe, United States management 'know-how' is a crucial factor."[6]

These conclusions are not difficult for a person knowledgeable in management to understand. The goal of managing is making it possible for people to operate in groups in such a way as to gain the most, in terms of objectives sought by an enterprise or a part of it, with the human and material resources available. Clearly, ineffectual managership leads to inefficient use of these resources. And whether the goal of an enterprise is economic, political, or other, it is not difficult to see that waste of resources will occur with poor managing.

Although one must grant that technical knowledge is necessary for economic growth, this is fairly readily transferable between countries and no nation long holds a monopoly on it. Even so sophisticated a technology as the atomic bomb, whose secrecy was actively protected by the United States, became known in Russia, France, China, and elsewhere in less than two decades. Most advances in technology are neither as complex nor as well-guarded, so that their transfer is not likely to be difficult, particularly when one realizes that in any country few people need to have this knowledge to make it available for adequate use.

On the other hand, such cultural factors as the level of education, particularly knowledge of skills, has an important impact on economic progress. Also, such cultural variables as desire for more of the products and services that a country *can* provide can likewise be significant. Similarly, constraining on economic progress are a large number of political factors, such as fiscal policy, labor regulations, business restrictions, and foreign policy. But even with these and other constraints, which may limit managerial effectiveness, qualified managers can do much to bring economic progress to a society by identifying them and by designing a managerial approach or technique to take them into account.

Two prominent scholars of comparative management have said in this connection:[7]

> We view management as the single most critical social activity in connection with economic progress. Physical, financial, and manpower resources are by themselves but passive agents; they must be effectively combined and co-ordinated through sound, active management if a country is to experience a substantial level of economic growth and development. A country can have

---

[5] W. W. Rostow, *The Stages of Economic Growth* (Cambridge, Mass.: Harvard University Press, 1962), p. 52.

[6] L. R. Sayles, *Managerial Behavior* (New York: McGraw-Hill Book Company, 1964), p. 17.

[7] R. N. Farmer and B. M. Richman, *Comparative Management and Economic Progress* (Homewood, Ill.: Richard D. Irwin, Inc., 1965), p. 1.

sizeable natural and manpower resources including plentiful skilled labor and substantial capital but still be relatively poor because very few competent managers are available to put these resources efficiently together in the production and distribution of useful goods and services.

The United States leads the world in per capita Gross National Product and is generally credited as being the world leader in the development of management know-how. It is, therefore, not surprising that American management is regarded widely as the standard of the world and that most scholars regard the problem of comparative management as one of transferring American management knowledge and practice to less developed countries.

This may be a justifiable point of view. But the authors of this book do not base any of their position on management universality on such a premise. After all, the earliest and most perceptive managerial insights were those of a Frenchman, Henri Fayol. Many early and present management pioneers were British, and many other management scholars have come from a host of other countries and cultures. It is rather the authors' position that effective management knowledge and art are not uniquely American. In their writing on management and in their experience in leading seminars for managers and scholars throughout the world, it has never been the position of the authors that their task was to export American management, but rather to identify and discuss management fundamentals.

IS MANAGEMENT CULTURE-BOUND?

A few scholars of management have concluded that management is culture-bound. In other words, since management practices differ and people and their environment vary, there is believed by some to be persuasive evidence that management theory and principles—the framework of management knowledge—are applicable only in developed societies similar to that existing in the United States. Also, there are some who believe that not only are the structure and content of management science not so transferable but, also, that the application of these to specific enterprise situations in the same national culture is not necessarily possible.

The Differing Views The findings of Gonzalez and McMillan are among those that are often quoted to show that management is culture-bound. These scholars, on the basis of a two-year study in Brazil, concluded that "American management experience abroad provides evidence that our uniquely American philosophy of management is not universally applicable but is a rather special case."[8] Note that these authors refer to "philosophy" and not to "science" or "theory" or "principles," and have emphasized that "that aspect of management which lacks universality has to do with inter-

---

[8] R. F. Gonzalez and C. McMillan, Jr., "The University of American Management Philosophy," *Journal of the Academy of Management*, vol. 4, no. 1, pp. 33–41 (April, 1961), at p. 41.

personal relationships, including those between management and workers, management and suppliers, management and the customer, the community, competition and government."[9]

On the basis of similar research, Oberg appears to agree with Gonzalez and McMillan and expresses doubt that the "game" of management in Brazil, being so different from that played in the United States, would permit application of management principles, useful in the United States, to Brazil.[10] It is Oberg's belief that the applicability of management principles may be limited to a particular culture or situation and that it may be fruitless to search for a common set of "principles," "absolutes," or "determinate solutions." It is even argued that since management principles appear not to be adaptable between cultures, they may not even be applicable between subcultures such as those of a rural businessman versus the manager of a large corporation within the United States.[11]

On the other hand, even those who question the transfer of managerial knowledge have admitted that it has often been successfully applied. For example, Gonzalez and McMillan, in their article indicating belief that the American philosophy of management is culture-bound, stated that:[12]

> The science of management has reached its highest state of development in the U.S., and it is for this knowledge, this know-how, that American management is most highly respected abroad. Transferred abroad, this know-how is first viewed with skepticism. Foreign national employees and partners are slow to respond and understand the American scientific approach to management problems. However, once fully indoctrinated, they accept and support this way of doing things. The superiority of this more objective, systematic, orderly and controlled approach to problems is seen and appreciated. For the host country, for American international relations, and for the American parent firm itself the export of American managerial know-how as well as technological know-how has yielded great dividends.

Also, Harbison and Myers, in their study of management in a number of countries of the world, have concluded that there is a "logic of industrialization." They moreover indicated that "organization building has its logic, too, which rests upon the development of management. And this brings us to the fundamental premise of our study: there is a general logic of management development which has applicability both to advanced and industrializing countries in the modern world."[13] While offered as a premise, their study of management in twelve foreign countries supports it. As will be pointed out below, other studies, particularly those carried on by the

---

[9] *Ibid.*, p. 39.

[10] W. Oberg, "Cross-cultural Perspectives on Management Principles," *Academy of Management Journal*, vol. 6, no. 2, pp. 129–143 (June, 1963), at p. 120.

[11] *Ibid.*, pp. 142–143.

[12] Gonzalez and McMillan, *op. cit.*, p. 39.

[13] F. Harbison and C. A. Myers, *Management in the Industrial World* (New York: McGraw-Hill Book Company, 1959), p. 117.

Comparative Management Program of the University of California, Los Angeles, also support this view.

The Problem of Semantics in Assessing Transfer of Management In looking over the altogether too scant evidence on the transferability of management knowledge between countries and cultures, one is struck by the fact that differences of opinion seem to arise largely from semantics. The concepts of "management philosophy," "management know-how," "management theory," "management principles," and "management knowledge" are often left undefined. The authors of this book have attempted to give the concepts of management theory, principles, and science careful definition. In essence, science is organized knowledge, theory is a structure of fundamental concepts and principles around which knowledge in a field is organized, and principles are regarded as fundamental truths which can be used to describe and predict the results of certain variables in a given situation.

On the other hand, it is the authors' belief that management "philosophy" has such a variable meaning as almost to defy definition. Strictly speaking, philosophy is the love, study, or pursuit of knowledge and is sometimes used, but certainly not always, as equivalent to science. On the other hand, in looking at the studies of comparative management, one finds "management philosophy" sometimes used to indicate attitudes of managers toward such groups as consumers, stockholders, suppliers, unions, and government.[14]

One of the pioneering scholars in the management field has referred to philosophy as "a body of related knowledges that supplies a logic for effective thinking for the solution of certain kinds of problems" and includes within it philosophies of private property, free market, competition, profit as a reward, leadership, organizational morale, the right of collective bargaining, and various beliefs in managerial approaches to enterprise.[15]

As can be seen, if a concept of management science includes underlying basic knowledge of management and, in addition, the application of this knowledge in given situations and cultures, the difference in interpretation of what a researcher finds in comparative societies would naturally be wide. Likewise, if a concept of management philosophy includes not only basic management theory and principles, but also beliefs as to such societal matters as ownership of property and attitudes toward individuals, one would expect that the resultant concept would vary between cultures as attitudes on fundamental social matters differ. In this context, it is easy to understand how Gonzalez and McMillan could come to the conclusion that American business philosophy is culture-bound, while they admit that the export of American managerial know-how has yielded great dividends.

---

[14] A. R. Negandhi and B. D. Estafen, "A Research Model to Determine the Applicability of American Management Know-how in Differing Cultures and/or Environments," *Academy of Management Journal*, vol. 8, no. 4, pp. 309–318 (December, 1965), at p. 312.

[15] R. C. Davis, "A Philosophy of Management," *Journal of the Academy of Management*, vol. 1, no. 3, pp. 37–40 (December, 1958).

The essential point is simply this: No one can argue that cultural differences exist between various countries and societies, sometimes to a marked degree. There are even subcultural variations of an important nature in the same country or society. It is therefore important in any study of the transferability of knowledge to separate the fundamentals of management from their application to given situations. For example, one might well expect, as these authors do, that basic management theory and principles would have universal applicability, and yet equally expect that management approaches and techniques would vary in different cultures. In other words, the only approach toward comparative management believed to be valid is to distinguish carefully between management fundamentals, or the science of management, and management practice.

When the distinction is made between management fundamentals, as expressed in basic concepts, theory, and principles, and management practice—the application of management fundamentals to a given situation—progress can be made in determining the extent of management universality and the transferability of managerial fundamentals. With the common knowledge of variations in cultures, one would not expect that *application* of management fundamentals to these varied cultures would always be the same.

The importance of this distinction cannot be overlooked, particularly if basic knowledge of management in one culture is to be transferred to another. In view of the critical importance of management to economic development, and the desire to improve management practice, this distinction is important. However, this does not mean that a management technique or approach successful in one society may not work with few, if any, changes in another. It simply means that the manager who would design a technique or application in a different culture should ascertain the extent of change required to meet any existing differences. The same is true in any field of science. One would not necessarily expect a house to be designed the same way in Central Africa as it would be in Midwestern America. Nor would one necessarily expect an automobile designed for use in unpaved deserts or jungles to be the same as one planned for high-speed superhighways.

INTRODUCING THE EXTERNAL ENVIRONMENT: THE FARMER-RICHMAN MODEL

In order to fill the gaps which exist in the usual discussions of management theory, including that in this book, a few scholars have attempted to establish models for the analysis of management, taking into account the influence of external environments. In doing so, they have recognized that external cultural environments do affect the practice of management, whether an environment is a subculture such as that of a public utility versus that of a soap and detergent company within the United States, or whether one is considering environments in different countries.

Two promising approaches have been made to the subject. One of these is the model developed by Professors Farmer and Richman. Another is that developed by Professors Negandhi and Estafen. While similar in many particulars, both models attempt to identify and weigh the effect of cultural factors on the functional elements of the management process. As such, they furnish tools for assessing the operation of management theory and principles in varying cultural environments.

In the model offered by Professors Farmer and Richman,[16] their approach is, first, to identify the critical elements in the management process, on the one hand, and attempt to evaluate their operation in individual firms in different cultures. Second, they have attempted to identify the various environmental factors which are believed to have a significant impact on the management process and management effectiveness, classifying these constraints as (1) educational variables, (2) sociological-cultural variables, (3) political and legal variables, and (4) economic variables.

The Concept of Managerial Effectiveness Operating on the hypothesis that management of productive enterprises is directly related to the external environment in which a manager operates and that managers may, at times, affect this environment, Farmer and Richman believe that actual management practice and managerial effectiveness will depend to a major extent upon external environmental characteristics.

Assuming that one of the major goals of any society is productivity (even though this appears sometimes to be unrealistic), managerial effectiveness is defined as simply how well and efficiently the managers of an enterprise in a given environment accomplish enterprise objectives. If we can assume that the objective is productivity, then efficiency is given by $E = O/I$, where E is efficiency, O is output, and I is input. While this concept is clear, Farmer and Richman realize that, in measuring the efficiency of management, an analyst will encounter extremely difficult problems in measuring inputs and outputs. These include: (1) the problem of uncertainty, since management decisions and customs ever deal with the future; (2) the problem of clearly defining goals, since, if not so defined, outputs cannot be accurately measured and a knowledge of efficiency becomes impossible; (3) the problem of subsystem optimization, since the conceptual ability and measuring techniques are seldom available to measure adequately the enterprise as a total system over time; and (4) the problem of resource mobility, since inputs, such as labor and capital, cannot be easily shifted from less profitable opportunities to more profitable ones.

Although difficulties of measuring and other deficiencies exist, there are a number of means by which efficiency of a country or a firm's operation can be assessed. From the standpoint of a country, they include: (1) the level of real per capita Gross National Product; (2) the rate of growth of real per capita Gross National Product; (3) the rate of utilization of inputs (how well are labor, capital, and land utilized?); (4) the usability of out-

---

[16] *Comparative Management and Economic Progress.* The authors have drawn extensively from this interesting book in this section.

puts (are they needed, and how usable are they?); (5) the level of competition (how much rivalry is there to force entrepreneurs to be efficient?); and (6) how adequate and accurate is planning (are outputs available to avoid unwanted and unneeded items in some sections of the economy while shortages exist in others?).

From the standpoint of individual firm efficiency, this may be ascertained by looking at a number of factors. One of these is profitability as measured either by the return-on-net-worth or assets employed. Another is how well the firm competes in export markets with similar items. A third is the output per employee, such as tons of steel per employee. A fourth measure, as seen by Farmer and Richman, is the extent to which a firm utilizes its plant capacity. A fifth factor, where applicable, is the level of cost and prices and their relationship to those of another firm. A final type of measurement involves the matter of long-run innovation and whether policy and actions are optimizing short-range performance at the expense of long-range, or vice versa.

It does seem that these measures of management effectiveness, both in a nation and within a firm, are appropriate. Fairly accurate data exist for some. Data subject to various degrees of inaccuracy exist for others. And, for still others, credible data may not currently be available. Also, there is the danger that different statistical and accounting treatments between countries and firms may be such as to make comparisons difficult or invalid.

Managerial Elements   In order to separate the elements of the management process from the external constraints of the environment, Farmer and Richman use the framework of management and most of the fundamentals outlined in this book. Thus they pick the critical elements of the management process as follows:[17]

Critical Elements of the Management Process

Planning and innovation
1.1   Basic organizational objectives pursued and the form of their operational expression.
1.2   Types of plans utilized.
1.3   Time horizon of plans and planning.
1.4   Degree and extent to which enterprise operations are spelled out in plans (i.e., preprogrammed).
1.5   Flexibility of plans.
1.6   Methodologies, techniques and tools used in planning and decision making.
1.7   Extent and effectiveness of employee participation in planning.
1.8   Managerial behavior in the planning process.
1.9   Degree and extent of information distortion in planning.
1.10 Degree and extent to which scientific method is effectively applied by

[17] *Ibid.*, pp. 347–348.

enterprise personnel—both managers and non-managers—in dealing with causation and futurity problems.

1.11 Nature, extent, and rate of innovation and risk taking in enterprise operations over a given period of time.

1.12 Ease or difficulty of introducing changes and innovation in enterprise operations.

Control

2.1 Types of strategic performance and control standards used in different areas; e.g., production, marketing, finance, personnel.

2.2 Types of control techniques used.

2.3 Nature and structure of information feedback systems used for control purposes.

2.4 Timing and procedures for corrective action.

2.5 Degree of looseness or tightness of control over personnel.

2.6 Extent and nature of unintended effects resulting from the over-all control system employed.

2.7 Effectiveness of the control system in compelling events to conform to plans.

Organization

3.1 Size of representative enterprise and its major subunits.

3.2 Degree of centralization or decentralization of authority.

3.3 Degree of work specialization (division of labor).

3.4 Spans of control.

3.5 Basic departmentation and grouping of activities. Extent and uses of service departments.

3.6 Extent and uses of staff generalists and specialists.

3.7 Extent and uses of functional authority.

3.8 Extent and degree of organizational confusion and friction regarding authority and responsibility relationships.

3.9 Extent and uses of committee and group decision making.

3.10 Nature, extent, and uses of the informal organization.

3.11 Degree and extent to which the organization structure (i.e., the formal organization) is mechanical or flexible with regard to causing and/or adapting to changing conditions.

Staffing

4.1 Methods used in recruiting personnel.

4.2 Criteria used in selecting and promoting personnel.

4.3 Techniques and criteria used in appraising personnel.

4.4 Nature and uses of job descriptions.

4.5 Levels of compensation.

4.6 Nature, extent, and time absorbed in enterprise training programs and activities.

4.7 Extent of informal individual development.

4.8 Policies and procedures regarding the layoff and dismissal of personnel.

4.9 Ease or difficulty in dismissing personnel no longer required or desired.

4.10 Ease or difficulty of obtaining and maintaining personnel of all types with desired skills and abilities.

Direction, leadership, and motivation

5.1 Degree and extent of authoritarian vs. participative management. (This relates to autocrats vs. consultative direction.)

5.2 Techniques and methods used for motivating managerial personnel.

5.3 Techniques and methods used for motivating nonmanagerial personnel.

5.4 Supervisory techniques used.

5.5 Communication structure and techniques.

5.6 Degree and extent to which communication is ineffective among personnel of all types.

5.7 Ease or difficulty of motivating personnel to perform efficiently, and to improve their performance and abilities over time (irrespective of the types of incentives that may be utilized for this purpose).

5.8 Degree and extent of identification that exists between the interests and objectives of individuals, work groups, departments, and the enterprise as a whole.

5.9 Degree and extent of trust and cooperation or conflict and distrust among personnel of all types.

5.10 Degree and extent of frustration, absenteeism, and turnover among personnel.

5.11 Degree and extent of wasteful time and effort, resulting from restrictive work practices, unproductive bargaining, conflicts, etc.

In addition to the management process areas and elements, Farmer and Richman expand their listing of critical elements of the management process to include major policy areas of management planning in order to obtain a view of the policies followed by various companies. These policies are classified as those related to marketing, production and procurement, research and development, finance, and external relations. Each of these in turn is broken down into a number of elements. In the area of marketing policy, for example, channels of distribution and types and location of customers are listed. In the area of production and procurement, policy with respect to making or buying items is one of those listed, and in the area of finance, policy with respect to distribution of earnings is an example.[18]

External Environmental Constraints Farmer and Richman, as noted, divide external and environmental constraints into four classes: educational, sociological-cultural, legal-political, and economic.

Educational constraints Among the major educational constraints noted are literacy level, the availability of specialized vocational and technical training and secondary education, higher education, management development programs, the prevailing attitude toward education, and the extent to which education matches requirements for skills and abilities. Mere reference to these educational factors indicates how they may support

[18] For a full listing of these policy areas, the reader is referred to *ibid.*, pp. 348–349.

or limit effective management. Moreover, where education is inadequate, not only will economic enterprises themselves tend to suffer thereby, but political and legal systems are likely to be poor. Even in advanced societies, where education appears to be more closely matched with requirements, there is always the phenomenon of a shortage of educational brain power, since it is a characteristic of all societies that the more that is available, the more is needed.

Sociological-cultural constraints In the sociological-cultural area, Farmer and Richman identify a large number of factors. They name such factors as (1) the general attitude of the society toward managers (for example, is a career in the profession of medicine or law, or in government, regarded as of higher status than in business management?); (2) the dominant views of authority and subordinates (for example, are subordinates expected to follow the all-knowing, paternalistic decisions of the top manager, or is participation of subordinates accepted and encouraged?); (3) the extent to which cooperation between various groups is a way of life (for example, are class structures rigid or are the means for advancement open to a person who is capable regardless of his class affiliation?); (4) the extent of union-management cooperation; (5) the view of achievement and work (for example, does the society value economic achievement through hard work as a desirable personal trait, or is achievement in the arts or preparation for life-after-death regarded as paramount?); (6) the extent of inflexible class structure and individual mobility (for example, are individuals moved to positions on the basis of their abilities, or are they restricted by caste systems or other forms of discrimination not related to ability?); (7) the dominant view of wealth and material gain, such as attitudes toward saving and the desire for material wealth versus religious satisfaction, the "good life," or other nonmaterial stimuli; (8) the view of scientific method (for example, is the society interested in preserving traditional cultures and patterns or in following a given ideology regardless of the logic involved or the empirical evidence and new discoveries available, or does the society understand the basic relationships between such economic factors as demand, price, wages, training, absenteeism and turnover, etc.?); (9) the view of risk taking (for example, are nations, enterprises, and individuals willing to take reasonable risks?); and (10) the view of change (for example, do the people in a society maintain their basic faith in traditions—old ways of doing things—or do they embrace change which promises to improve productivity?).

Legal-political constraints The major legal-political constraints in an external environment have been identified by Farmer and Richman as falling into six categories: (1) relevant rules of the game; (2) defense policy and national security; (3) foreign policy; (4) political stability; (5) political organization; and (6) flexibility of law and legal changes.

There are, as one might expect, a number of legal rules in any business game. One is the general business law which provides a framework within which the firm must work. Important factors in this framework are codes of fair and effective competition, the law of contracts, and laws pertaining to trademarks, copyrights, and patents. Likewise, general laws governing society, such as those affecting health, welfare, and safety, have their effect, as automobile and pharmaceutical manufacturers, among others, in the United States are well aware.

Another legal area constraining the manager is that dealing with prices and competition. The United States has been the leader in the work of framing and enforcing laws to require a responsible level of competition, and these have had both a constraining and a constructive effect on a manager's environment. But elsewhere in the world these laws differ, ranging from those coming somewhat close to American legislation in enforcing competition to laws which permit and encourage monopoly or monopolistic practices.

Still another area of law which has a far-reaching effect on management is labor law. In most countries these laws are extremely complex. They usually apply to hours and conditions of work, use of women and minors, tenure and job security, employer responsibility for health and welfare, use of nationals, and unemployment compensation. But differences in requirements may be considerable. In the United States, for example, a company manager is normally permitted to discharge or lay off an employee with little or no difficulty or cost. But in many other countries he may find it virtually impossible to do so, especially if the employee has fairly long tenure. Furthermore, in one country the cost of social benefits may be virtually nonexistent while in another it may amount to nearly half of the payroll costs.

Tax law variations are also significant. Tax regulations and the impact of taxes are different in various jurisdictions. Some may even materially affect whether a business operates as a proprietorship, partnership, or corporation. Possibilities of evasion differ considerably. It is customary for businesses in many countries to evade taxes to a great extent. This is epitomized by the statement of a Latin American business owner to one of the authors that he kept three sets of books: one for the tax collector, one for the person who might wish to buy his business, and one for himself. Also, the extent of tax benefits or penalties to encourage or discourage a business obviously has a significant effect on management policy.

Another political factor affecting management is the country's policy toward defense and national security. Where huge sums are spent toward this end, as in the United States, the effect is obvious. Defense policy often has considerable impact on the allocation of manpower and resources. Draft of manpower and allocation and rationing of materials are cases in point.

Foreign policy also has its influence on the management of enterprises. Tariffs and quotas, economic aid, protection of local businesses by restricting foreign ownership, monetary exchange controls, and control of imports or exports are conspicuous and widespread examples. Managers always have to contend with these influences, and companies domiciled in one country and doing business in another, either through export or through license, joint venture, or wholly owned subsidiary, have special problems in dealing with them.

Still another environmental factor is the extent of political stability which a country enjoys. Where political systems and leadership are highly unstable, as has been the case in many Latin American and African nations, the manager faces an area of uncertainty which cannot help but materially affect his planning. Even moderate political uncertainties can have consequences. The changing policy in Great Britain with respect to nationalizing the steel industry, as Labor and Conservative elements come into and lose power, cannot help but have a detrimental effect on planning in this industry—planning which in many respects unavoidably involves commitments of a long-range and inflexible nature.

Likewise, the type of political organization has an important influence on managers. If a country is operated under a federal system, as are the United States and Australia, the environment is different from one operated under a highly centralized political organization, such as France. The more government levels with power to affect a manager's operation, the more complicated his task may be in meeting legal requirements. But it is also likely that he will receive more local understanding of his problems than under a highly centralized government.

Farmer and Richman further identify as an important factor in the political environment the flexibility of law—the ease with which legal changes are brought about in a society. Law is notably conservative, largely because it is designed to correct past abuses and conditions. But as conditions change, if the law itself is not flexible or cannot be changed readily, the manager may have a critical problem on his hands. Thus, many German companies find themselves hampered in their economic growth by a law—which many people agree should be changed but has not been—that a company, now organized as a proprietorship or partnership, cannot convert to the corporate form without suffering a tax to the owners for any appreciation in his equity. This has, of course, caused many family-owned companies to continue as proprietorships or partnerships rather than to gain the advantage of corporate form and additional capital through public sale of stock ownership.

Economic constraints   Farmer and Richman likewise identify a number of economic constraints which differ between countries and affect the practice of managing. Among these are the basic economic system, whether predominantly private or public in ownership, whether competitive, whether exchange is based on sound money, and the extent to which the government controls economic activities.

There are economic differences in whether the central banking system and national monetary policy work to help or to thwart managers. Does the banking system provide needed money and credit expansion as businesses grow? Does it control monetary supply to avoid unsettling inflation? Does it operate to stabilize the economy, or does it contribute to excess booms? Does it support or hinder export business? These questions are closely tied in with fiscal policy in the extent to which the public sector of an economy creates price stability, tax fluctuations, booms, and recessions. Obviously, this element of a manager's environment greatly influences his managerial policies.

Economic stability is a significant economic variable in societies. A degree of price stability is highly desirable, since a manager is required to make many fairly long-range commitments and is almost forced to rely very largely upon financial data for much of his planning and control. Utilization of production factors is an environmental matter of importance; cycles in employment of capital and land can understandably have a disturbing effect on enterprises that must use, and plan to utilize for some time, these resources. While no manager would expect perfect stability in either prices or the economy and would normally prefer a growing economy, and while he is usually able to live with moderate price changes, uncertainty in these economic elements cannot help but hinder planning effectiveness and compel shortening the time span of decision commitment.

Since capital is the lifeblood of any business enterprise, organization of capital markets is an important environmental factor. The manager operating in an environment where capital is fairly readily available at reasonable cost has, of course, a tremendous advantage over one who operates in an environment where capital is scarce and expensive. Even in completely government-planned and controlled economies, this problem exists. Capital needs may be furnished as a government service, but with all the problems of restriction and bureaucratic friction which exist.

In addition to the above economic controls, Farmer and Richman identify three all-pervasive economic constraints. One they refer to as factor endowment—the extent to which a country has available natural resources, adequate and useful labor, and capital which can be employed for efficient production. Another is the size of markets. Obviously, to take advantage of many of the economies of large-scale production, the size of a market open to a firm is important. Closely related are the extent to which competition exists and whether there are legal or other limitations on a manager reaching a market.

A third major pervasive economic constraint outlined by Farmer and Richman is the extent to which social-overhead capital is available, that is, the supply and quality of public utility-type services. These refer to a host of services necessary to support production, distribution, and consumption. They include transportation, communication, energy production and transmission, warehousing, and sewer and water facilities.

The Farmer-Richman Model From their identification of the various elements of the management process and of a manager's external environment which affect the way he manages, Farmer and Richman have constructed a model.

While new and probably subject to revision in the future, this model none-theless distinguishes the management process from the environment of managing. In doing so, it appears to be a useful tool for evaluating management as management and for understanding what may make effective management practice differ as between varying cultures.

The model may be depicted as in Figure 33.1.

The Farmer-Richman Model and Principles of Management   Farmer and Richman express the belief that external conditions of the type outlined above will affect both managerial effectiveness and the elements of the management process. Managerial effectiveness will, in turn, determine a firm's efficiency and consequently the efficiency of a given country or society (a "system").

They put it in this way. If a country has a negative attitude toward education, it presents a manager with staffing difficulties if a level of un-available education is important to his operations. If a population has a negative attitude toward scientific method, staffing with people having abilities to analyze and act rationally will be difficult. Or if a law against pollution of streams exists in a country, this will, in turn, affect production policies and activities. A lack of an established communications system will also have an effect on the efficiency of many firms. While they may furnish their own system, this is likely to be less efficient.

Other factors may only affect the operation of the management process.

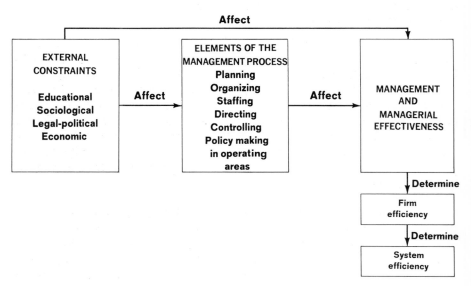

Fig. 33.1   Farmer-Richman Model for Analyzing Comparative Management
SOURCE: *Adapted from R. N. Farmer and B. M. Richman,* Comparative Management and Economic Progress *(Homewood, Ill.: Richard D. Irwin, Inc., 1965), p. 35.*

The planning time horizon may be limited by political instability or rapid inflation. A paternalistic attitude toward people may influence organizational patterns by restricting delegation. Or an accounting system based on tax evasion may so contort financial data as to make managerial control information misleading. Likewise, management development and promotion may be thwarted by a caste system or racial or religious discrimination. As can be seen, these and many other cultural variables may materially influence management functions and the way a manager undertakes them.

But there is no evidence in the Farmer-Richman model or in their study of comparative management that the *fundamentals* of managing are changed by these environmental constraints. For example, the limitation of the planning horizon caused by rapid inflation does not invalidate the principle of commitment. It only means, as many Brazilian businessmen have found, that the period and means of obtaining recovery of costs plus return-on-investment are shortened. Nor does a level of education affect the principle of job definition, although its application in terms of a given structure of roles and provisions for incentives will vary. Also, even though a caste system or an attitude of racial or religious discrimination may not permit operation of the principle of open competition and promotion, this does not mean that the principle is untrue. It means, rather, that managerial efficiency is hampered by these external constraints, since a manager is not able to apply the principles completely.

INTRODUCING THE EXTERNAL ENVIRONMENT: THE NEGANDHI-ESTAFEN MODEL

Another model for separating the influence of the external environment from the analysis of management fundamentals has been formulated by Professors A. R. Negandhi and B. D. Estafen. First offered in 1965,[19] it has been more recently refined by Professor Negandhi.[20] The Negandhi-Estafen model differs somewhat from the Farmer-Richman model although it still includes as a major independent variable external cultural factors affecting managerial action. However, Negandhi and Estafen believe that the Farmer-Richman model does not go far enough in indicating major influences on managerial practice and that another independent variable, that of management philosophy, should be given weight.

Introduction of Management Philosophy Negandhi and Estafen believe that it is a mistake to regard management philosophy as only a product of the cultural environment. In their paper, the opinion was expressed that certain elements of management philosophy can be and have been successfully imported from one culture to another. In this paper, management philosophy

---

[19] Negandhi and Estafen, *op. cit.*

[20] To be published in A. R. Negandhi and S. B. Prasad, *Management Philosophy and Management Practices* (New York: Appleton-Century-Crofts, Inc., 1968).

was defined as "the expressed and implied attitude or relationships of a firm with some of its external and internal agents" such as consumers, stockholders, suppliers, distributors, employee unions, community, and local, state, and federal governments.[21] To support that position, Negandhi and Estafen have given as an example the finding of two researchers with respect to two textile mills in India.[22] One mill had a philosophy of "quick profit," which is hardly a culturally limited attitude, while the other had a similarly culturally widespread philosophy in being "product conscious" and embracing "long-range profit." These two philosophies had a considerable and different impact on employee morale, productivity, organization structure, delegation of authority, span of management, and communication patterns.

Thus, it is Negandhi and Estafen's position that certain areas of management philosophy should be introduced as a variable which may or may not be influenced by cultural differences. These are the expressed and implied attitudes toward such agents as: (1) the consumer (does the company regard consumer loyalty as important?); (2) the company's involvement in community welfare activities and educational institutions; (3) the company's relationship with local, state, and national governments; (4) the company's attitude toward and relationship with unions and union leaders; (5) the company's relationship with employees; and (6) the company's relationship with suppliers and distributors.

The Negandhi-Estafen Model Consequently, the Negandhi-Estafen model may be essentially depicted as in Figure 33.2 on page 781.

The Two Models It is interesting that so little difference exists between the Farmer-Richman model and the Negandhi-Estafen model. Both recognize, and do so properly, the fact that the external cultural environment does have an effect on the operation of the management process. Such a way of managing will then affect management effectiveness. As has been pointed out, the only difference in the Negandhi-Estafen position is that managerial attitudes ("philosophy") are believed to be important enough to identify separately as independent variables. Farmer and Richman, on the other hand, place policy making in operating areas as elements of the management process, and thereby they imply that the benefits or attitudes which lead managers to follow one policy rather than another are affected by the same external constraints as affect the functions of managers.

There is much to be said for both types of models. There can be little doubt that policies are influenced by external cultural factors. On the other hand, many of these policies do not appear to be culture-bound. One finds,

---

[21] Negandhi and Estafen, *op. cit.*, p. 313.

[22] K. Chowdhry and A. K. Pal, "Production Planning and Organization Morale," in A. H. Rubenstein and C. J. Haberstroh (eds.), *Some Theories of Organization* (Homewood, Ill.: The Dorsey Press, Inc., and Richard D. Irwin, Inc., 1960), pp. 185–196.

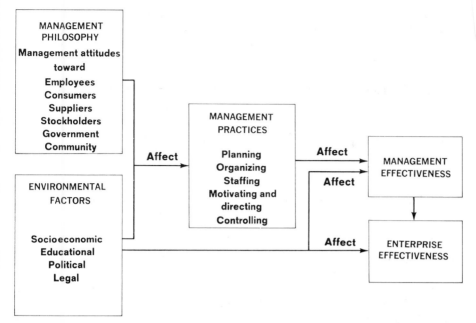

Fig. 33.2 Negandhi-Estafen Model for Analyzing Comparative Management

SOURCE: *Adapted from A. R. Negandhi and B. D. Estafen, "A Research Model to Determine the Applicability of American Management Know-how in Differing Cultures and/or Environments,"* Academy of Management Journal, *vol. 8, no. 4, pp. 309–318 (December, 1965), and from materials obtained from Professor Negandhi to be published in A. R. Negandhi and S. B. Prasad,* Management Philosophy and Management Practices *(New York: Appleton-Century-Crofts, Inc., 1968).*

for example, both the "quick profit" and the "long-range profit" attitude in many cultures. Likewise, the same attitudes toward such things as product quality, community relations, and fair dealing tend to exist in various cultures. It may be, however, and probably is, that where these similar attitudes exist, they are simply reflections of like characteristics found in different cultures. Thus, as every businessman dealing in international business knows, the attitude toward accepting business bribes (as we understand this term by standards applied in the United States) as a way of life has been found in otherwise widely varied cultures.

What concerns the authors of this book regarding the Farmer-Richman model in this connection is that its inclusion in the management process of policies with respect to operational matters (marketing, production and procurement, research and development, finance, and public and external relations) tends to detract from the more meaningful focus on the management process itself. To be sure, policy making as a *function* is a part of management planning. But the type of policy pursued in given instances will probably be strongly influenced by factors external to managing itself. Consequently, for purposes of determining the transferability of fundamentals of the management process between nations or cultures, it would be preferable to separate as a variable the types of policies pursued. But the process of policy making itself and the fundamentals underlying it are proper elements of planning and should be included in the management process.

INTRODUCING THE EXTERNAL ENVIRONMENT: SIGNIFICANCE

Both the Farmer-Richman and the Negandhi-Estafen models go far toward removing much of the confusion that has attended early study of comparative management. By narrowing the concept of management to the process of management and separating from it consideration of external environmental factors which can influence actual practice in given instances, these models make it possible to test the area of universality of management theory and principles. They even give a basis for testing whether certain management techniques have more universal application than is often believed. For example, techniques of delegation, of using rate of return on investment for over-all control, or of applying operations research or networks analyses are probably not as culture-bound as is often believed. There may also be good reason for many other techniques to be fairly broadly applicable. After all, we should not forget that the best techniques are simply ways of doing things that are based on applying principles to a given situation.

Also, one of the advantages of the model approach to comparative management is that it can be a useful practical device for companies operating businesses in varying environments. By outlining areas of external constraints which can exist and giving an orderly means for identifying the elements in each, these models offer multinational companies tools for being better able to select and train managers, understand and devise differences in managerial techniques and approaches, and succeed in varying environments.

COMPARATIVE MANAGEMENT: SOME CONCLUSIONS

It is believed now that some progress can be made in accepting universality of management theory and principles and in exporting at least the structure of this science to less scientifically oriented managers in various societies. The latter advantage is particularly important if, as appears clearly to be true, economic development depends critically on effective management. If the fundamentals of managing can be increasingly identified and more generally understood, and if their application to varying cultures can be studied, there is reason to believe that improved management practice, tailored to a given society, can result. It may be found also that many managerial attitudes, techniques, and approaches, applied scientifically in one society, may be applicable with a minimum of basic change to another.

As a matter of fact, the limited research which has already been done indicates this. With a better understanding of the basics of comparative management, more studies of business management in various countries, and growing interest in multinational companies, increasing light should be shed on this problem. There are already significant findings available. The work of Harbison and Myers in a number of nations, that of Richman on Soviet Russia,[23] of Fayweather on Mexico,[24] the various publications of the National Planning Association,[25] of Abegglen in Japan,[26] to mention only a few of the more noteworthy studies, are cases in point.

Also, in recent years such programs for the orderly study of comparative management as that at the University of California, Los Angeles, have indicated that there is much universality in the application of management principles. Those that have been completed to date do indicate fairly persuasively that well-managed American-owned companies, operating in less developed countries, have in general shown superiority in management and economic effectiveness.[27]

Now that the study of comparative management has been aided by sharper definition of concepts and the construction of useful operational models, one can expect continued progress in this area. It may even be possible, as Farmer and Richman believe,[28] to give usefully credible quantitative measures to the many independent variables in these models and thereby obtain a gauge of managerial effectiveness in different cultures. At least, to date, the study of comparative management has not offered evidence to shake the belief of the authors of this book in the universality of the fundamentals of management, particularly so long as we separate theory, principles, and the fundamental scientific content of management from the art of their application. And we must ever separate science from art if science itself is to have any meaning.

[23] B. M. Richman, *Soviet Management* (Englewood Cliffs, N.J.: Prentice-Hall, Inc., 1965).

[24] J. Fayweather, *The Executive Overseas* (Syracuse: Syracuse University Press, 1959).

[25] See, for example, F. Brandenburg, *The Development of Latin American Private Enterprise* (1964); T. Geiger, *The General Electric Company in Brazil* (1961); T. Geiger and W. Armstrong, *The Development of African Private Enterprise* (1961); and S. Kannappan and E. Burgess, *Aluminum Ltd. in India* (1961).

[26] *The Japanese Factory* (New York: The Free Press of Glencoe, 1958).

[27] Research completed as doctoral dissertations include B. D. Estafen, *An Empirical Experiment in Comparative Management: A Study of the Transferability of American Management Policies and Practices into Firms Operating in Chile* (1967); A. J. Papageorge, *Transferability of Management: A Case Study of the United States and Greece* (1967); F. C. Flores, Jr., *Applicability of American Management Know-how to Developing Countries: Case Studies of U.S. Firms Operating Both in the United States and the Philippines in Comparison with Domestic Firms in the Philippines* (1967); John Jaeger, *A Comparative Management Study: Organization Patterns and Processes of Hotels in Four Countries* (1965).

[28] Farmer and Richman, *Comparative Management and Economic Progress*, chaps. 12–13.

FOR DISCUSSION

1. Why is management quality a crucial factor in economic growth? Can a country thrive economically with poor or average management?

2. From your knowledge of any foreign country, outline the major elements of its culture that would in your judgment influence the kind of management you would expect in a typical firm.

3. Take any selected management technique or approach (such as budgeting, a training program, participative management, an executive committee operation, or engineering project management) and divide it into management fundamentals and those aspects which might be affected by cultural variables.

4. Compare and contrast the Farmer-Richman and Negandhi-Estafen comparative management models. Which do you prefer? What are the advantages and disadvantages of each? Would you construct a different model?

5. In accepting or rejecting the concept of universality of management, do you agree that separation of fundamental management knowledge from application to practice is a useful and logical approach to comparative management?

SELECTED REFERENCES

Brandenburg, F.: *The Development of Latin American Private Enterprise* (Washington: National Planning Association, 1964).

Chorafas, D. N.: *Developing the International Executive,* AMA Research Study No. 83 (New York: American Management Association, 1967).

Chowdhry, K., and A. K. Pal: "Production Planning and Organization Morale," in A. H. Rubenstein and C. J. Haverstroh (eds.), *Some Theories of Organization* (Homewood, Ill.: The Dorsey Press, Inc., and Richard D. Irwin, Inc., 1960).

Farmer, R. N., and B. M. Richman: "A Model for Research in Comparative Management," *California Management Review,* vol. 7, no. 2, pp. 55–68 (Winter, 1964).

————: *Comparative Management and Economic Progress* (Homewood, Ill.: Richard D. Irwin, Inc., 1965).

————: *International Business: An Operational Theory* (Homewood, Ill.: Richard D. Irwin, Inc., 1966).

Fayweather, J.: *The Executive Overseas* (Syracuse: Syracuse University Press, 1959).

————: *Management of International Operations* (New York: McGraw-Hill Book Company, 1960).

Geiger, T.: *The General Electric Company in Brazil* (Washington: National Planning Association, 1961).

Geiger, T., and W. Armstrong: *The Development of African Private Enterprise* (Washington: National Planning Association, 1961).

Gonzalez, R. F., and C. McMillan, Jr.: "The Universality of American Management Philosophy," *Journal of the Academy of Management,* vol. 4, no. 1, pp. 33–41 (April, 1961).

Harbison, F., and C. A. Myers: *Management in the Industrial World* (New York: McGraw-Hill Book Company, 1959).

Hartmann, H.: *Authority and Organization in German Management* (Princeton, N.J.: Princeton University Press, 1959).

Jacoby, N. H., and J. E. Howell: *European Economics: East and West* (Cleveland, Ohio: The World Publishing Company, 1967).

Kannappan, S., and E. Burgess: *Aluminum Ltd. in India* (Washington: National Planning Association, 1961).

Martyn, H.: *International Business* (New York: The Free Press of Glencoe, 1964).

Negandhi, A. R., and B. D. Estafen: "A Research Model to Determine the Applicability of American Management Know-how in Differing Cultures and/or Environments," *Academy of Management Journal,* vol. 8, no. 4, pp. 309–318 (December, 1965).

Oberg, W.: "Cross-cultural Perspectives on Management Principles," *Academy of Management Journal,* vol. 6, no. 2, pp. 129–143 (June, 1963).

Prasad, S. B. (ed.): *Management in International Perspective* (New York: Appleton-Century-Crofts, Inc., 1967).

Richman, B. M.: *Soviet Management* (Englewood Cliffs, N.J.: Prentice-Hall, Inc., 1965).

Rostow, W. W.: *The Stages of Economic Growth* (Cambridge, Mass.: Harvard University Press, 1962).

management and the future

Despite recognized deficiencies and crudities in the state of organized knowledge underlying the managerial job, the fact is that a science of management is developing. Likewise, managerial techniques and tools are evolving rapidly, borrowing, as so many other fields have, from the systems approach long applied with benefit in the physical sciences. As the science improves, so should the art of managing, for it is the working basis of any art.

But the rapid growth of management knowledge is not the only factor involved. The pace of change in all fields of human activity—technological, economic, and social, as well as managerial—has been extremely great. Change always progresses geometrically. But in the past half-century it has been accelerated by such major events as two world wars, a long cold war, and a space age.

Also, as was noted in the early part of this book, human activity and motivation have been quickened by a growing world-wide era of super-competition—an era of the opening of markets, sharing of technological ability, greater complexity and higher capital investment in enterprise, and a competition on virtually a world-wide basis for men, materials, markets, and ideas. The effect of these competitive pressures are seen not only in business but also in nonbusiness enterprises. In government, for example, we see the pressures for effectiveness and efficiency in the rivalry between the needs of society which only government can serve and the patience and resources of the taxpayer.

There can be no question that the manager's role—in every kind of enterprise and at every level—is expanding materially. And, as new knowledge and techniques become better known and applied, and as these lead to the creation of environments in which people can perform with greater effectiveness and efficiency, the varied demands of society will force managers to take increasing advantage of this science and its resulting tools. Indeed, those managers who do not will be at the mercy of those who do. Thus, virtually every manager will be faced with opportunities and requirements for improvement and his need for a more intellectual approach to managing will be increasingly perceived.

All this means for those who manage that the danger of becoming obsolete for the task will be continually greater. So long as managing was a task only learned from experience, obsolescence was unimportant. But now experience has been distilled into meaningful and useful principles and theory, inadequate as they may be. These are furnishing structures on which both distilled experience and new findings in management and related sciences can be arranged and made meaningful for the practitioner. Now there is no time for individuals to reach the state of managerial excellence necessary to meet the demands of the task by means of trial and error.

MANAGING MUST BE FOR REALITY

Despite the growth of science in the area of managing, there is ever the danger that management knowledge will not be used to obtain results in practice. It has been one of the major purposes of this book to present fundamental knowledge regarding managing in an operational way so that it can be made useful. Such knowledge must be operational. It must be for reality, since managing, as an art, requires using knowledge to solve real problems, to develop operating systems or environments in which people can perform. This means several things. In the first place, knowledge of management is not enough. There is always the danger, in any field, of developing a science aimed at elegance or polish rather than results. Every science has its "educated derelicts" who know a field but cannot apply it to gain useful results.

Moreover, the reality with which a manager must deal is always tomorrow. As it has been well said, reality is a moving target. In looking at management for tomorrow, it may be well to identify a few of the major challenges which managers face, as well as what this future means to managers, and to call specific attention to the urgency of intellectual leadership in management.

THE NEED TO MEET CHANGE WITH FLEXIBILITY

The most effective management is flexible management. Since the environment in which an enterprise operates is certain to change, and since the attitudes and motivations of people likewise vary, it can be no exaggeration to emphasize the importance of flexibility in managing. Not only must an effective manager be able to recognize change but, preferably, so that he will have time to meet it, he should be able to anticipate change. Likewise, the internal environment of the enterprise which he creates, if it is to remain consistent with and responsive to the external environment, must be flexible.

The problem of managerial flexibility is made even more challenging and difficult by a number of inflexibilities which tend to be built into the operation of any enterprise. One finds too often enterprises regarding their policies as something written on stone rather than as guides to thinking for future decision making. Likewise, almost all enterprises find themselves enmeshed in procedures which have usually grown up without plan and which tie up action and stultify thinking. In addition, inflexibilities are likely to be imposed upon an enterprise by stubbornly resistant government regulations and labor rules and by customs frozen into union contracts and thinking. But perhaps the greatest element of inflexibility is the natural human resistance to change. The nuclear scientist Edward Teller once declared that, in all of his scientific explorations, the most inert material he had ever encountered was the human mind, with one exception, a group of human minds. And these are what managers must make flexible.

To say that this challenge of the future exists is not to imply that the art and science of management have found adequate ways to deal with areas of inflexibility. However, merely recognizing their existence is a step in the direction of solving the problems involved.

A BALANCED ENVIRONMENT FOR CREATIVITY AND CONFORMITY

One of the major problems facing every manager is that of designing and maintaining a balanced environment for creativity and conformity. Perhaps there is, as William Whyte pictured in his *The Organization Man*,[1] too much conformity, too much belongingness, too much togetherness, and too little individual responsibility. Perhaps there is too much reliance on group operations and committees. Perhaps there is some foundation to the charge of the many psychologists who decry tendencies toward conformity and toward stultification of individuality and creativity.

However, one can grant the underlying thesis of Whyte and many other management critics that people rarely think or create as groups but rather as individuals. One can agree that the want satisfactions of people go far beyond the paycheck, without casting any necessarily damaging criticisms on formalized management, particularly as exercised by intelligent practitioners in many of our outstanding enterprises. The question is not conformity, but the degree; no one can operate as a member of a group without some conformity. Any effective group activity implies some structure of roles.

This is not a question of looking upon all formalized management as one wherein an authoritarian hand suppresses the needs and wants of intelligent human beings. It is not a question of dividing practitioners into a category of "Theory X" or "Theory Y,"[2] but rather one of whether a manager is

[1] (New York: Simon and Schuster, Inc., 1956).

[2] Made famous by Douglas McGregor in *The Human Side of Enterprise* (New York: McGraw-Hill Book Company, 1960), pp. 33–57. Theory X managers, defined as "traditional," are seen as those who regard people as disliking work and who need there-

utilizing his formal organizational structure, formal plans, or formal controls as environmental devices that make desired performance possible.

What is needed, of course, is balanced design. The creation of a role or the establishment of goals or plans does not, by any stretch, imply a detailed, narrow role or objectives which cannot stretch the imagination and creativity in anyone. In other words, the total environment should provide for a role that allows and encourages creativity and imagination where it is wanted. There are also many cases where complete conformity is required. There are times, for example, when basic accounting records must be prepared in a precise way in order to assure accurate financial statements, or where billing on a government contract must follow in strict conformity the requirements of the contract if the company is to be paid. Likewise, there are many areas in a typical company where chemicals create an explosive atmosphere and when a rule against smoking means exactly that. What is often forgotten is that the conformity necessary for people to live and work together may be unbending in one area of activity and yet there can be provided ample opportunity for innovation and creativity in another.

In fact, it is the sign of an effective manager when he recognizes the necessity of designing these various environments. The challenge involved is to comprehend what managing is, to be aware that managers who follow the principles of operational management theory do not thereby stifle individuality and creativity, where it is desirable, but rather establish an environment for performance. Understanding of these principles, appreciation of the contributions of behavioralists and the physical scientists, and orderly rearranging of the jungle of management theory would go far toward meeting this challenge.

PRESERVING THE CARROT AND THE STICK

One of the major problems facing the manager of the future is that of balancing for best results the carrot and the stick. Some two decades ago, the British *Economist* pointed out that "The human donkey requires either a carrot in front or a stick behind to goad it into activity." Perhaps, in modern society, there has been a tendency to overemphasize the carrot and forget the stick. Perhaps, what is even worse, we have tended to whittle away both the carrot and the stick. The passion for equality may have removed much of the stick. Such practices as promotion by seniority, level pay, automatic merit increases, executive bonuses not based on individual performance,

---

fore to be coerced, controlled, and threatened, and who prefer to be led. Theory Y managers are seen as those who regard expenditure of human effort in work to be as natural as play or rest, who see that man will exercise self-direction and self-control in the service of objectives to which he is committed, who see the human being as one who seeks responsibility, who recognizes that imagination and creativity are widely, not narrowly, distributed in the population, and who see that under modern industrial life the intellectual potentialities of the average human being are only partially utilized.

and guaranteed wages, while having a desirable sound, may have, in many instances, removed much of the stick.

Perhaps, also, much of the carrot has been taken away. Progressive income taxation, increased government regulation which may dull enterprise, and ever growing social insurance, may have removed much of the carrot. This is nowhere more evident than in the action of a misguided United States Congress which, in 1964, apparently misunderstanding the motivating factors involved in executive stock options, shortened the option period from ten years to five and increased the period an executive must hold options to qualify for capital gains from six months to three years. As any informed corporate shareholder knows, a fair and well-administered stock option plan which gives executives in a publicly held company the same motivation as owners has long proved to be in the interest of those who own a company. It is overlooking the fact that, not only do executives, like other people, react to a carrot but, in this case, the carrot can also be sweet for the other shareholders.

There are questions in this area of great importance to the manager. How can he maintain incentive, either through the carrot or the stick, without abandoning the aims of equality of economic opportunity? How can a society have the worthwhile goals of social security and still maintain motivation for accomplishment? As the famous editorial said, "How can the carrot and the stick be combined with a pleasant life for the donkey?" That this requires managerial ingenuity for finding means of sharpening the appropriate sticks or sweetening the right carrots is both obvious and challenging.

COPING WITH INCREASED SOPHISTICATION

One of the major problems facing the manager of the future is that of coping with increased sophistication in all aspects of managing. Of particular importance has been the introduction of newer techniques in the areas of management planning and control. These, based upon the systems approaches brought over from the physical sciences, include applications of such important techniques as operations research, network analysis, and the new information technologies. Likewise, there have been the many findings of the behavioral sciences, which, if they can be intelligently applied to managing, can improve personal efficiency.

But evidence exists that practice has been slow to adopt many of these new techniques and findings. There appears to be far too much talk and too little action. In most cases, it is the authors' opinion that practicing managers have not adopted them simply because they do not understand them. What individuals in a responsible position do not understand, they are not likely to trust or to use. Much of this has arisen from the fact that experts in these fields seem to thrive on a kind of mysticism and jargon which protects their image as experts but which becomes unintelligible to most managers. For example, in the area of operations research, there has appeared to be too much emphasis on the mathematics of models and too little recognition that the model is, as was pointed out earlier in this book, a "little black box" the internal workings of which a manager need not understand. The need, of course, is for emphasizing the key importance of conceptualizing problem relationships and leaving the model to the specialist. Likewise, experts in the field should realize that, if their findings are to be useful, they must engage in fewer gymnastics, less self-gratification from complexity, and more realization that there are practical problems which need to be solved.

The challenge in the new areas of sophistication is for better and more useful end-product development. While it is still important to expand the frontiers of knowledge in the new techniques, it is even more important for creative minds to develop better ways of making this knowledge operational.

There are still many relatively unsophisticated management techniques that are too little used or too ineptly applied. When one looks at such "cloud one"-level techniques as authority delegation, variable budgeting, formalized product planning, market-oriented organization, and appraisal of managers by results one can see that these are not based upon highly sophisticated concepts. Likewise in the control area, the approach of tailoring control for plans and individuals, as well as organization structure, is another example where managing might be made far more effective. Even though these and other tools are relatively simple in concept, they may be admittedly difficult to apply in practice. But those managers who have earnestly tried to apply them have reaped tremendous benefits.

NEW INFORMATION VISTAS

Another challenge to the manager and one changing his role materially is that related to new vistas of information and new ways of systematizing it. As was pointed out in Chapter 29, the reach of an executive is determined by the information at his command. This, in turn, implies information, preferably of a forecast nature, material to a manager's task, weighed against goals and analyzed to determine why and where actions are missing goals.

What has not been as widely recognized as would be desirable is that the spectrum of information has been widening considerably. Financial data have been greatly widened through direct costing, a program of accounting which altogether too few companies have adopted and which is virtually unknown in nonbusiness enterprises. Likewise, the alert manager of today will insist upon considerable information inputs from social, economic, and technical sources to supplement the limitations of financial or physical input or output data.

Another problem emphasized in this book is the need for information design. Data are only a raw material until designed and produced to make information. What is often forgotten is that, despite the tremendous potentials of electronic data-processing equipment, no one can expect a useful end product unless he knows what product he wishes and develops and utilizes the raw materials to make the product. In fact, it can be well understood that the long-promised information revolution is still much further away than most people suspect. It can hardly be made a reality unless the highest order of intelligence and analysis are applied to the basic tools at hand.

ABSORBING NEW FINDINGS

As is indicated above, one of the most interesting challenges facing the manager of today and tomorrow is how to absorb the methods and findings of the physical and behavioral sciences into the fundamental scheme of management. Even though it may be unfairly argued that the outpouring of behavioral research has had limited practical value to managers, one can truly agree that this research has not been adequately integrated into operational management thought nor utilized to a material extent by practitioners.

Likewise, one of the most exciting phenomena of our times is the conscious attempt to utilize the methods of the physical sciences to solve managerial problems. One can certainly see the relevance and value to management of the methodologies of the physical sciences—such as simulation, the systems approach, symbols, models, approximation, and other tools of mathematical analysis, the logic of rationality and optimization, and the need for balance in design. But one may ask a question as to whether they have really been adequately absorbed in the operational science of management.

Perhaps the greatest challenge lies in finding methods of integrating these new findings and approaches into the basic theory of operational management science. Within the limitations of this book, the authors have made an attempt to do so. However, as was indicated in previous sections of this chapter, what is needed even more is for the specialists in these fields to undertake, more thoroughly than has yet been the case, to make their findings operational. One of the ways this can be done is for more of these specialists to understand the total of the manager's task and the theory underlying it. Another need is for some of these specialists to undertake *applied* research and development in their field. As one of the leading behavioral scientists said, "I think the thing we do not have is any meaningful applications from behavioral research at the basic level to practice."[3]

ASSURING MANAGERIAL QUALITY

Despite remarkable advances in the past quarter-century, the needs for assuring the quality of managers are greater than ever before. The position

---

[3] As stated by Professor Mason Haire in H. Koontz (ed.), *Toward a Unified Theory of Management* (New York: McGraw-Hill Book Company, 1964), p. 224.

advanced in this book is that the most direct of all control is to control the quality of managers. Even though tremendous progress has been made in management appraisal and training, needs tend to outdistance action. The rapid growth of management knowledge and technique, the pace of change, and competitive urgencies have been noted. Considerable headway has already been made in this field but appraisal is perhaps still the weakest link.

In the first place, many appraisal programs still do not aim at measuring what the manager does rather than what people think of him. Many appraisers do not know what to appraise or how. Too many appraisal systems are involved in a maze of forms, systems, records, and marks. While a huge step has been taken in the fast-growing programs of appraisal by verifiable results, as was pointed out in Chapter 22, these are still subject to inadequacies. It is hoped by the authors that, in the near future, appraisal by results may not only be widespread but may also be supplemented by appraisal of the quality of managing itself. The need is for performers, to be sure. But long-term results are best assured by managers who are both good managers and good performers.

Once adequate appraisal systems are developed and utilized, the next step is logically to gear programs of management development to alleviate the gaps disclosed and to satisfy the need for individual managers to acquire new knowledge and techniques.

WHAT THE FUTURE MEANS

There has been considerable speculation on what future developments mean to the manager.

1. Structure of Organization and Automation of Management   One of the early forecasts indicated that new information technology would change materially the entire structure of management. In their article in 1958, Professors Leavitt and Whisler forecast that the new information technology would: (1) move the boundary between planning and performance upward in the organization structure; (2) result in considerable recentralization so that top managers would take on an even larger proportion of the innovating, planning, and other creative functions than they have now; (3) move certain classes of middle management downward in status and compensation while others would move upward into the top management group; and (4) result in a clear and more impenetrable line separating the top from the middle of the organization.[4] In summary, these authors anticipated that the organization structure of the future would resemble a football balanced on the top of a church bell. Another author has forecast that operations research techniques and the computer will result in automation through solving not only well-structured programs but also ill-structured programs,

[4] H. J. Leavitt and T. L. Whisler, "Management in the 1980's," *Harvard Business Review*, vol. 36, no. 6, pp. 41–48 (November–December, 1958).

and that the computer can be used even to simulate the thinking of managers themselves.[5] That these and other predictions have had a considerable effect on managers and their concerns for the future is understandable.

That new programming and problem-solving techniques, as well as new information technology, buttressed by the tremendous calculating speed of the computer, will affect managing there can be no doubt. However, predictions which indicate that these developments will change the fundamental structure of organization or automate management itself are not persuasive.

As for the forecast of the changing structure caused by new information technology, it appears that those who make such predictions overlook certain basic facts. If one could contemplate skipping ahead for twenty years and placing the technology then available in *one* company, these predictions would probably be correct. But it is hardly correct to assume that "other things" will remain constant. What is far more likely to happen is that the whole level of sophistication of management will increase and competitive forces, plus widely shared knowledge, will tend to make this improved level fairly widespread. It is perfectly true that the content of many managerial positions, particularly those at the middle level, will change as the manager needs to spend less of his time on the kinds of analyses and information seeking which he does now. It is also true that many of his tasks of decision making will be given over to the computer.

What is overlooked in such prophecies is that, in the first place, managing involves people, and so long as there are people, there will be limits of effective supervision and, therefore, hierarchies of organization structure similar in shape to those now existing. In the second place, forecasters overlook the fact that most managers now can accomplish only a small part of the potential of their jobs because of time spent in work currently necessary but which may be taken out of a manager's hands in the future. What the authors of this book would predict is simply that the managerial job can be done better and competitive forces will require that it be.

Much the same thing might be said concerning the automation of management decision making. To be sure, most structured decisions and, perhaps, some unstructured decisions may be made quickly through the help of analyses and information made available by the computer. But just as managing today is far more sophisticated than it was three decades ago and information is far more available than it was then, so would one expect in the future an increasing ability of managers to deal intelligently with far more complex problems and to push back the frontiers of information required for doing so.

In summary, then, there is certainly ample evidence that the nature of the managerial task will change greatly, that planning and innovation will

---

[5] H. A. Simon, "The Corporation: Will It Be Managed by Machines?" in M. Anshen and G. L. Bach (eds.), *Management and Corporations 1985* (New York: McGraw-Hill Book Company, 1960), pp. 17–55.

be more sophisticated, and that competition for success will be more sharp. But these do not imply the elimination of middle managers or the automation of management.

2. Importance of Planning for Innovation As competition becomes sharper, problem solving more advanced, and knowledge expands, one would expect that the manager of the future would have to place greater importance on planning for innovation. Even now it is widely recognized that a business enterprise, at least, must "innovate or die," that new products just do not happen, and that new marketing ideas do not often occur by luck. The manager of the future must place more emphasis than ever before on developing an environment for effective planning. This means, even more than at present, planning goals which call for stretch, creating policy guidelines to channel thinking toward them without stifling imagination, designing roles where people can be creative, keeping abreast of the entire external environment which affects a business, and recognizing the urgency of channeling research toward desired ends.

To develop these and other environmental elements for effective planning requires the highest order of intelligence and skill. Reference to those principles, techniques, and requirements for effective planning outlined in this book underline the difficulties the manager of the future might expect. Moreover, as the future unfolds, the manager concerned may be certain that new and improved techniques and approaches will be discovered.

3. Removal of Inflexibility The problem of inflexibility which faces the manager was discussed above and some major inflexible elements outlined. To remove these inflexibilities so that an enterprise might move with change will require a high order of research to find out the basic causes of these inflexible elements. It will also require determination to exercise the utmost effort toward their removal. Even those inflexibilities apparently beyond the control of a manager, such as government regulations and labor union rules, may very well be modified or removed if those responsible for management will research the problems thoroughly, present their cases accurately and unemotionally, and take the time patiently to teach to the public and legislators their requirements for flexibility.

4. A Willingness to Learn If a manager is to avoid the stultifying effect of basing too much of his learning on experience, he must be aware of the dangers of experience. As was indicated earlier in this book, undistilled experience can lead an individual toward assuming that events or programs of the past will or will not work in a different future. But the manager needs more than this. He needs to be *willing* to learn and to take advantage of new knowledge and new techniques. This necessitates a humble approach to his successes and limitations. It demands a recognition that there is no finishing school or terminal degree for management education.

5. Acceleration of Management Development The above discussion under-lines the urgent importance of an accelerated program of management development. This implies not only more pertinent management seminars and conferences, but other means of transmitting to practicing managers in as simple and useful a way as possible the new knowledge and tools in the field of management.

One of the major challenges in this connection is one of compressing and transmitting that knowledge which is available. Every field of art based on a burgeoning science has the same problem. No field has completely solved it, although certain areas, such as specialized aspects of medicine and dentistry, have made considerable progress.

The authors have no adequate answer for this problem. It does appear that those on the management faculties of our universities have an obligation to practicing managers to do much of the task of compressing and transmitting this knowledge as easily and quickly as possible. There is still inadequate evidence that many university professors see the social importance of this role. Also, one might expect a greater contribution from various management associations, as well as from the management consultants, who can certainly greatly improve their value to clients by doing this. Perhaps something can be done through intelligent digesting of articles and books, although this does not appear too hopeful, since those who probably know what is significant to managers and how to transmit it to them are not likely to be in the position of digesters. Also, it is entirely possible that there might be regularly established a series of special management clinics in which managers at all levels in alert companies would spend a day every few weeks being brought up-to-date on a specific area of new knowledge and technique. But more and better techniques must be found if the widening gap between knowledge and practice is to be narrowed.

6. Controlling Information Another important area for the manager of the future is to obtain the right information in the right form and at the right time. Tailoring information, as outlined in this book, requires a high order of intelligence and design. Until managers realize that very little of their operation can be planned and controlled through "handbook" approaches, and until they recognize that they themselves must become involved in tailoring the information they require, little progress may be expected in this area. So long as information design is confused with the clerical work of information gathering and summarizing, managers will understandably continue to fret about the inadequacy of the data on which they are forced to act.

7. Measuring and Rewarding Management One of the significant areas of proper concern to the manager of the future is the importance of both objectively measuring managerial performance and rewarding good performance or of imposing sanctions on poor operation or providing corrective action where it is inadequate. Managers must be willing to work toward establishing objective measures of performance through both a verifiable results approach and the measurement of abilities of individuals as managers. Likewise, to sharpen the stick and sweeten the carrot for managers requires innovation of a very high order.

8. Need for Management Research and Development As can be seen from the above areas where the future should command managerial attention, perhaps one of the most challenging is that of obtaining more real research and development in management tools and techniques themselves. The level of research effort and support in the field of management is woefully low. It is also not particularly great in the disciplines underlying management and, for that matter, in the entire area of social science. Nevertheless, it is probable that research in underlying disciplines far outpaces that in the central area of management.

There are many reasons for this. General management research is a difficult field, exceedingly complex and dynamic. It is one where facts and proved relationships are hard to come by and where the controlled experiment of the laboratory is difficult to use without dangerous oversimplification. Likewise, management research is expensive and the funds that have gone into it are abysmally inadequate. It has been estimated that not more than 2 per cent of the total being spent annually for all research in this country, or approximately one-twentieth of one per cent of Gross National Product, goes into research in *all* social sciences. In turn, if funds spent on management and management-related research are more than one-tenth of this, or one-two-hundredth of one per cent of Gross National Product, the authors would be surprised.

Still another reason for the low state of management research is that there is a lack of clinical analyses, despite a considerable volume of clinical experience. Consulting efforts of both professional consultants and individual academics, extensive management case collections, and studies and analyses made internally in business, government, and other enterprise almost certainly encompass a huge mass of undigested, largely unsummarized, and relatively useless information. If this clinical experience could be given a kind of analytical and summarizing work so common in the health sciences, there might be now considerable evidence of what is workable in practice and where deficiencies exist.

In undertaking this research, patience and understanding are needed. Perfection of analysis to include all kinds of variables is a laudable goal for a researcher. But, particularly in the field of management, a little light can be a massive beam in a hitherto dark area of knowledge. We must often settle for small advances so that cumulatively, and over time, we may gain larger ones.

But research without development is insufficient. One of the major challenges for the manager of the future is the need for developing more managerial inventions. It is an interesting thing how so much creative talent has been channeled into the invention of physical designs and chemical compositions and how little into social inventions. The GANTT chart has sometimes been regarded as the most important social invention of the first half of the twentieth century. Other management inventions include the variable budget, rate-of-return-on-investment analysis, linear organizational charts, and PERT (Program Evaluation and Review Technique). Mere reference to these inventions underscores the fact that they are inventive tools developed from a base of principles on one hand and needs on the other. Reference to them indicates also that they are useful devices in improving the art of management.

Inventions tend to reflect the cultural level of an art. There are few of them in management. Surely even the present inadequate cultural level can be coupled with urgent management needs to give rise to many more management innovations, particularly if those concerned are willing to spend some time and money to direct their energies toward these inventions. It is very easy to see that one significant management invention, such as those mentioned in the previous paragraph, can make important contributions to management effectiveness and economy of operation. Applied research and development in this field surely justifies a considerable expenditure of time and money.

NEED FOR INTELLECTUAL LEADERSHIP

That intellectual leadership in management is urgently needed can hardly be denied. Managing can no longer be only a practical art requiring merely native intelligence and experience. The rapid growth of underlying knowledge and the obvious need for even more, particularly that knowledge which is organized and useful for improvement of practice, are requirements which have tremendous social significance. It is not difficult to anticipate a 10 per cent rise in productivity in the American economy due to improved management, or an effort, in sheer economic terms, worth to the United States alone some $80 billion per year. Even these dramatic data give no direct recognition to the rise in human satisfactions involved in such improvement.

This means that key elements in any society would do well to give the area of managerial scientific research and development a high priority. Our college and university administrators and scholars—leaders in what former President Clark Kerr of the University of California has called the "knowledge industry"—should take the lead by giving management research and teaching the support their social importance deserves. Private foundations have an obligation as instruments of social betterment to support meaningful research in this field. Likewise, there can hardly be a more important area of research for a government to support. Every part of society would do well to seize the opportunity to support management research and development with the same vigor they have pursued such goals as new products, improved physical health, defense, and public welfare. In short, what is needed is an awareness that the intellectual and practical requirements of management are urgent, manifold, and socially important.

The challenges for a better society through improved management practice in every type of enterprise and those involved in intellectual leadership in the field are impressive. History teaches us that when needs exist and are recognized and when the cultural level reaches the point of ability to meet these needs, leadership usually arises to inspire solutions. The challenging needs are here. The cultural level appears to be rising to the point where many answers are feasible. The question is simply where and how this leadership can be developed.

FOR DISCUSSION

1. Taking any major area of management theory and principles, how can they be applied to reality?

2. By reference to specific management problem areas, such as new-product development, organization structure, or budgets, what are the ways managers can introduce flexibility and what are the inflexibilities usually encountered in each?

3. How may a manager design an environment for imaginativeness and creativity?

4. How would you anticipate that the computer will affect the manager's role at the top-management level? The middle-management level? First-line supervision?

5. If you were asked to organize and operate an effective management research and development staff, how would you proceed?

SELECTED REFERENCES

Anshen, M., and G. L. Bach (eds.): *Management and Corporations 1985* (New York: McGraw-Hill Book Company, 1960).

Bennis, W. G.: *Changing Organizations* (New York: McGraw-Hill Book Company, 1966).

Koontz, H.: "Challenges for Intellectual Leadership in Management," *California Management Review*, vol. 8, no. 4, pp. 11–18 (Summer, 1965).

Leavitt, H. J., and T. L. Whisler: "Management in the 1980's," *Harvard Business Review*, vol. 36, no. 6, pp. 41–48 (November–December, 1958).

Mitchell, W. N.: *The Business Executive in a Changing World* (New York: American Management Association, 1965).

Simon, H. A.: *The New Science of Management Decision* (New York: Harper & Row, Publishers, Incorporated, 1960).

Suojanen, W. W.: *The Dynamics of Management*, chaps, 1, 14–17 (New York: Holt, Rinehart and Winston, Inc., 1966).

name and place index

subject index